Gender at the Crossroads of Knowledge

Gender at the Crossroads of Knowledge: Feminist Anthropology in the Postmodern Era

EDITED AND WITH AN INTRODUCTION BY
Micaela di Leonardo

UNIVERSITY OF CALIFORNIA PRESS
Berkeley   Los Angeles   Oxford

University of California Press
Berkeley and Los Angeles, California

University of California Press
Oxford, England

Copyright © 1991 by The Regents of the University of California

Library of Congress Cataloging-in-Publication Data

1. Anthropology—Philosophy.   2. Feminism.   3. Women.   4. Sex
Gender at the crossroads of knowledge : feminist anthropology in the
postmodern era / edited and with an introduction by Micaela di
Leonardo.
      p.   cm.
   Includes bibliographical references and index.
   ISBN 0-520-07092-5 (alk. paper).—ISBN 0-520-07093-3 (pbk.:
alk. paper)
      1. Anthropology—Philosophy.   2. Feminism.   3. Women.   4. Sex
   role.   I. di Leonardo, Micaela, 1949–   .
   GN33.G46   1991
   305.42—dc20   90-11297
                                                                  CIP

Printed in the United States of America
2   3   4   5   6   7   8   9

CONTENTS

v

FOREWORD

This collection of essays provides an exciting entrée into the current thinking and rethinking of feminist anthropology. Situated in a historical moment when a "crisis of representation" is said to pervade a number of disciplines within the social sciences and the humanities, the feminists represented here have been influenced by poststructuralist approaches to meaning and bring a critical stance to our traditional categories of analysis. Yet, influenced by Marxism, political economy, and other materialist perspectives, most of these papers are firmly rooted in an analysis of material realities that are theoretically separate from (though inextricably linked with) the construction of meaning and knowledge. This stance, best articulated in Micaela di Leonardo's introductory essay, has much to recommend it. It offers important insights to three audiences: feminist anthropologists, anthropologists of all theoretical persuasions, and feminists inside and outside the academy.

For feminist anthropologists, this collection demonstrates how far our thinking has evolved over the past fifteen years since the publication of *Woman, Culture and Society* (edited by Michelle Zimbalist Rosaldo and Louise Lamphere, Stanford University Press, 1974) and *Toward an Anthropology of Women* (edited by Rayna Rapp, Monthly Review Press, 1975). The central questions of feminist anthropology are no longer the universality of sexual asymmetry and the search for equality in gender relations in other cultures. The wealth of new research and theoretical analysis in a wide variety of societies, including our own, has produced a literature on gender in all four subfields of anthropology which is difficult to master, even for a specialist in feminist anthropology.

This collection, since it includes contributions from archaeology, physical anthropology, and linguistics as well as from sociocultural anthropology, provides an introduction to new debates within each subfield. These debates demonstrate that we have moved on to new and more complex problems that cannot be summarized by one or two issues. They also demonstrate our willingness to critique and to cast aside assumed categories of analysis whether feminist or nonfeminist. Here we see the influence of poststructuralist approaches to anthropology most clearly: in archaeology, for example, where feminist anthropology has had little impact, attention to the construction of texts demonstrates that this subfield is still preoccupied with "origin stories" that are deeply influenced by the construction of gender in our own society. Yet even within feminist anthropology the construction of the problem of "women and state" is also informed by these same origin issues and may have restricted the variability we have been able to see among different states as well as the kind of resistance women have mounted against state structures. To take another example from feminist analysis, accepted concepts like "the sexual division of labor" or "female farming systems" seem too simple and naive when actually applied to the change in Beti women's and men's agricultural activities during the colonial and contemporary period in Southern Cameroon. Such categories are not only stagnant but mask complex relationships between men and women and between local cropping techniques and larger systems of markets and capital as they affect the agricultural strategies of men and women.

For anthropologists who have not specialized in the study of gender, several contributions provide a particularly good overview of new approaches within particular subfields. They clarify ways in which bringing the issue of gender to the fore allows us to sharpen, refine, and reorient traditional anthropological problems. Attention to gendered practices and strategies in both everyday and public speech leads to new insights into the nature of silence and power in the use of language. Through an analysis of the history of primate studies which pays attention to male and female behavior in a variety of species, we can both understand the tenacity of functional explanations and the need for a biologically sophisticated feminist stance that would provide more complex models of differential male/female behaviors across primate species. In the field of development studies, positioning the cultural representation of gender at the center of our analyses helps to rethink the meaning of "technology" and "development," twin concepts rarely problematized in the current literature. Conversely, debates within kinship theory allow a critique of feminist thinking about the relationship between our analytical categories and constructions of gender and kinship. Even our accepted models of foraging societies can be challenged by more careful studies of gender relations among contemporary Australian Aborigines and Ituri Forest Efe (or Mbuti pygmies).

Finally, for feminists who feel unfamiliar with the developments within feminist anthropology this collection provides a wealth of examples, not only of the role of Western discourse in structuring our thinking about gender in other cultures but of potential ways to engage with important contemporary feminist issues. Close attention to the gender politics of colonial empires demonstrates that the casting of colonized peoples in categories of the "other" involved a number of complex processes, many of them centering around the control of sexual liaisons between colonial men and native women and the role of colonial women in "pasting over" class cleavages within the colonies themselves. Notions of racial supremacy were constructed in gendered terms; sexual ideologies and behavioral restrictions were historically variable and multilayered. Within our own societies, anthropologists have a great deal to contribute to the analysis of race, class, and gender. In examining the interaction of work and family among working-class Hispanics, feminist anthropologists are grappling with the way in which the different social locations of Chicana women in different jobs in contrasting local economies create variability in household gender politics. In the complex arena of reproductive technology, an anthropological approach that examines the cultural construction of a new language of pregnancy and birth arising in response to amniocentesis testing shows that there is no simple outcome from the cross-class and cross-cultural communications between genetic counselors and Hispanic, Haitian, Afro-American, and white families who hold very different views of reproductive processes than do medical experts.

In the 1990s gender is at the crossroads of knowledge. Anthropology has the potential of taking feminist thinking about gender differences out of a white, middle-class, and Western milieu, to expand our perspectives on past and present cultural constructions of gender and the material realities of women's situations and to provide multiple models for gender relations that go beyond our accepted Western dualisms.

Louise Lamphere

University of New Mexico

ACKNOWLEDGMENTS

Feminists are reputed to be particularly willing to acknowledge the wide-spread aid and comfort that brings most "one person" projects to culmination. In any event, I certainly wish to name those who have helped me with this volume. It began as a speaker series at the Yale University Department of Anthropology, and I thank the Department, the Wenner-Gren Foundation, the Women's Studies Program, the Yale College Dean's Office and the Yale Graduate School for funding the series. Any anthology editor knows the tempestuous waters in which such fragile vessels travel and sometimes founder. This project was uniquely arduous, in part for a gendered reason. Most of the contributors (and I) are women in "sandwich generation" positions: especially subject to medical and personal crises—and to those of kin and friends of both parents' and children's generations. My thanks to contributors who made valiant efforts in hard times, especially to those who wrote up to five drafts for the martinet figure Hal Scheffler denominated the Vampire Editor. Thanks also to my long-suffering friends, Brett Williams, Roberta Spalter-Roth, Mary Summers, Rogers Smith, Kathryn Oberdeck, and especially my husband, Adolph Reed, for their endurance as I passed on anxiety and ill temper in the process of nurturing the manuscript to fruition. Contributors and friends Susan Gal, Susan Sperling, and Patricia Zavella also offered key advice and comfort.

Many thanks to my anthropology of gender students, not only those over the years at George Washington University, Oberlin, and Yale but also the Yale class of Spring 1990, who field-tested the entire volume in typescript. These last students did not contribute to the book's shape or content (we were already in copyediting), but contributed to my peace of mind by voting *Gender at the Crossroads* their most valued course reading.

My association with University of California Press has been rewarding from the outset. The manuscript received excellent readings from Fitz John Porter Poole and Rena Lederman. Bruce Knox compiled an extensive index. Last, I wish to thank Liz Kyburg of the Department of Anthropology at Yale for skilled help, as always, far beyond the call of duty, on this and many other projects.

Introduction: Gender, Culture, and Political Economy
Feminist Anthropology in Historical Perspective

Micaela di Leonardo

The feminist project in anthropology has flown under several flags. It was at first termed the anthropology of women, as we focused on correcting male bias in the discipline. We have since written of the anthropology of gender to denote our concern with both sexes and their culturally and temporally varying relations. Sometimes we refer to feminist anthropology to acknowledge our interdisciplinary affinities with women's studies scholarship. Feminist-inspired anthropological research and writing on gender relations, after two decades of practice, has come of age.

Because anthropology stands at the crossroads of knowledge production, embracing scientific, social-scientific, and humanistic modes of interpretation, feminists in the discipline have worked in every part of the globe, in every specialized subfield, from primates to politics, from tropes to T-cells. Whether heralded by feminist sociologists for advanced theory (see Stacey and Thorne 1985) or ignored by some of our colleagues, feminist anthropologists have labored to develop a corpus of work in touch with developments in the field, in allied disciplines, and within feminism itself.[1]

But to describe the evolution of feminist anthropology in Whig-historical terms, to portray a linear progression from good to better, would be to paint over a nuanced, three-dimensional reality. Behind the facade of progress is a complex history of roads traveled and then abandoned, new starts, and alliances and fissures across disciplines and among anthropological subfields. Feminist anthropologists, like all scholars, have sharply disagreed among themselves and have revised their perspectives over time. As well, the feminist anthropological project has been influenced by shifts in the larger intellectual scene and in the global political economy in which we all live. This last point is crucial. Western feminist scholars twenty years ago had a sharp, taken-for-granted starting point: to expose sexism in public and private life,

1

to alter the male-biased presumptions of scholarly and popular culture. We now see both the adjective of location—we are *Western* feminists, and there are others—and the noun's contingent, historically determined existence. The political source of feminist scholarship, early 1970s feminism, was not the first but the second major wave of women's rights thought and activism. And there have been organized rebellions and individual protests among women in many cultures—even in the small-scale societies anthropologists have specialized in studying—and in numerous historical periods. We now see ourselves as part of global history.

In order to envision contemporary feminist anthropological work properly, then, we need to follow the project from its inception and to locate that changing body of thought within the kaleidoscopic crossroads of anthropological, feminist, intellectual, and political-economic history.

The early 1970s were years of closely linked scholarly and political ferment in the United States. The civil rights and antiwar movements of the 1960s had grown and given birth to theory and activism concerned with environmental issues, American foreign policy, gay, black, Latino, Asian, and Native American rights—and feminism.

All these movements were influenced by—and inspired—intellectual shifts of the 1960s. Foremost among these broad changes was the post-McCarthyite renascence of Marxist theory. Many others, however—such as the Kuhnian disrobing of "timeless" scientific authority, criticisms and radical revisions of Freudianism, and extensions of liberal pluralism to encompass new (ethnic, gay, female) claimant groups—were key to both scholarly and political movements of the era. Although each strand of 1970s radicalism had historical precedents, some predating the twentieth century, feminism's particular trajectory was unique. The late-nineteenth/early twentieth century woman movement in the United States and Western Europe (and, among anticolonialist nationalists, in many third-world societies) culminated in the achievement of suffrage in America and Britain, and subsequently entered a period of relative quiescence. Although one of the many victories of the period was the establishment of women's colleges and the entrance of women into the professions, most of these early feminists—as they began to be called in the first decade of the twentieth century—challenged neither domestic sexual divisions of labor nor the received wisdom of the contemporary scholarly and professional establishment.[2]

Late-twentieth-century feminists did precisely that. A relatively homogeneous cohort—at least in the first decade—these largely young, white, college-educated, middle-class women built a shared vision of the world turned upside down. In classic radical fashion, they questioned all received wisdom relating to their particular issue; and that issue, comprising the lives and statuses of all female humans, past and present, engaged every branch of

knowledge and labor.[3] This statue-toppling atmosphere bore parallels to the
French Revolution, when, as Wordsworth wrote,

> Bliss was it in that dawn to be alive,
> But to be young was very Heaven.

Both groups were convinced that politics and knowledge were innately intertwined, and for that reason set out to reconstruct knowledge. Each group
attempted to extirpate language deemed reflective of the political order to be
overthrown (French honorifics, women's married titles), and each coined
neologisms to substitute and to express new concepts and institutions
(*citoyenne/citoyen*, Ms.). And each group turned to ancient Greece and Rome
for models of prior political virtues—the Athenian republic, the myth of
matriarchal Amazonia.

Feminist anthropology reflected all these tendencies—absent the romance
with ancient Greece—in microcosm. Participants in early study groups and
seminars shared the vision of rethinking and reworking an entire discipline,
one that seemed vital to feminist thought. Because of American anthropology's historic, cross-cutting four-field emphasis, anthropology seemed to
cover women from soup to nuts—from female proto-humans and primates to
women in prehistoric societies to a survey of the lives of all contemporary
women, whether in the first, second, or third worlds. Feminist anthropologists had a strong sense, as well, that the results of their intellectual work were
of key importance to feminist political decision making. Only anthropology,
after all, occupied itself with the search for human universals and the documentation of cross-cultural variation. New interpretations of these phenomena seemed likely to aid us in discovering the key factors related to
women's secondary status, and thus to determine the Archimedean standpoint from which we could move the male-dominated globe. As Gayle Rubin
noted, somewhat tongue in cheek,

> if innate male aggression and dominance are at the root of female oppression,
> then the feminist program would logically require either the extermination of
> the offending sex, or else a eugenics program to modify its character. If sexism
> is a by-product of capitalism's relentless appetite for profit, then sexism would
> wither away in the advent of a successful socialist revolution. If the world-
> historical defeat of women occurred at the hands of armed patriarchal revolt,
> then it is time for Amazon guerrillas to start training in the Adirondacks. (1975:
> 158–159)

GENDER IN ANTHROPOLOGICAL HISTORY

This sense of anthropology's edificatory place in American life, of seeing
ourselves through seeing others, was in fact not an invention of 1970s feminists but was rooted in the history of American anthropology and, indeed, in

the discipline as a whole. The male Victorian British evolutionary theorists who would be labeled "anthropologists" only in the 1880s were concerned to taxonomize all known human groups, to place Hottentots, ancient Romans, and contemporary European bourgeoises on a stratified *scala naturae* according to their relatively savage, barbarous, or civilized characteristics. Although, as George Stocking (1987) demonstrates, much of the impetus behind Victorian anthropology lay in these men's efforts to establish and to make sense of a desacralized universe, moral anxieties in a newly Godless realm did not constitute the whole of their concern. Victorian Britain was the major world imperial power; it saw the growth of a vital, militant woman movement led by the daughters of its bourgeoisie. Victorian anthropology, then, was naturally engaged in attending to—legitimating but also protesting—the colonized status of third-world others. It also engaged, as Elizabeth Fee (1974) has shown, in a *dialogue in absentia* with the woman movement.

A central tension of mid-Victorian evolutionary debates was the problematized status of male rule over women. Had women once ruled and been deposed, as Bachofen asserted? Or were women now less exploited (especially sexually) than in the past and among primitives thought to be "living history"? Assertions of male lust, female purity or licentiousness, male anxieties over paternity, and female capacities for moral uplift were deeply woven into these accounts and found their way into the evolutionary schemata of those major late Victorians Marx and Freud.

In the years intervening between the Victorian evolutionists and the 1970s feminists, anthropology established itself, primarily in Britain and the United States, as a major academic field. Social anthropology in the United Kingdom and cultural anthropology in the United States jettisoned evolutionary thought and established the lengthy, intimate, daily living with and observing of people in another culture—fieldwork—as the constitutive practice of the discipline. British anthropologists, especially Radcliffe-Brown (1965), crafted structural-functionalism as a theoretical frame through which living societies could be seen to make sense. Societies were envisioned through an organic analogy: institutions such as kinship and marriage, politics, economics, and religion were demonstrated, again and again, to function in tandem with one another, like the individual organs in a body. Although Talal Asad (1973: 103–118) has noted that structural-functionalist assertions in British Africa functioned themselves as legitimations for indirect rule, the theoretical frame was also one strand of the growing hegemony of ethnographic liberalism. (James Clifford's useful term denotes a "set of roles and discursive possibilities" [1988: 78] through which ethnographers attempted to deal with their usually ambiguous roles both as advocates of particular groups and as citizens of colonizing states.)

American cultural anthropology focused largely on the Americas and the

Pacific until after World War II, and its primary early twentieth-century concern was the documentation of vanishing Native American cultures and languages. American extermination or forced relocation of Native American groups prevented the extensive use of the structuralist-functionalist frame. American anthropologists tended, instead, to practice "salvage ethnography"—the collection of any and all information with a heavy emphasis on vanishing languages. This American emphasis on culture (mental baggage)—rather than society (observable, patterned behavior)—was fueled also by contemporary American psychology's high status and conservative, especially racist presuppositions and applications. Liberal American anthropologists were, then, doubly inclined toward the psychological arena (Rosenberg 1982; Stocking 1982: 200 ff.)—thus the "culture and personality" theoretical leanings of the two best-known women anthropologists of the early twentieth century.

Margaret Mead and Ruth Benedict were students of Franz Boas, the notable German-born Columbia University anthropologist. Given their great fame and at least Mead's highly popular didactic writings on the cross-cultural malleability of "natural" sex roles, one would assume that women have been prominent in American anthropology and that anthropology has been a progressive force in providing empirical fodder for arguments in favor of gender equity. In fact, despite the admiration and envy of feminists in other fields, women have historically done poorly in anthropology departments: Mead never held an official departmental position, Benedict was passed over as chair for a man when Boas retired, and Elsie Clews Parsons achieved her influence through the use of an independent fortune to finance her own and others' field trips and publications.[4] In more recent years, studies have documented female anthropologists' significantly lower academic status (Sanjek 1982). Finally, not until the 1970s did some anthropologists begin to approach women's and men's differing experiences as topics on their own terms. Most of the notable theoretical movements of the 1920s through the 1960s—and particularly those bearing on topics of direct relevance to women's status, such as kinship and marriage or the sexual division of labor—ignored or naturalized sexual difference. Structural-functionalist work on kinship in Africa, for example, assumed natural male dominance in its considerations of kinship and marriage patterns, while the linguistics-inspired kinship analyses of the 1960s generally ignored sexual difference altogether. So great was prefeminist insensitivity that Ward Goodenough, a well-respected kinship theorist, could write approvingly of a Trukese man's beating of his daughter: "A good hard jolt was just what she deserved" (1965: 12). (Change has not come smoothly. As late as 1985, a former male colleague would assure me that the anthropology of gender was "just trivial me-tooism.")

Nevertheless, prefeminist anthropology was not like so many other branches of knowledge, such as literary criticism, which simply represented a largely male universe. Although one could—and many did—claim that few women had been important novelists or poets, it was much more difficult to represent functioning societies without female inhabitants. Similarly, ape and monkey populations are one-half female, as are prehistoric burials. It is for this reason that feminist anthropologists had little difficulty in switching early on from the anthropology of women to that of gender as their research focus. Prefeminist ethnographers often provided rich ethnographic information on gender. Oftentimes, the woman in husband-wife teams specialized in "women's affairs," and such information was woven, anonymously, into the ethnographic text. Other wives wrote independent, insightful analyses of female worlds in a variety of third-world contexts: Mary Smith on the life of Baba, a Hausa woman in Karo (1981); Elizabeth Fernea (1969) on village women in Iraq; Margery Wolf (1968) on peasant women in Taiwan; Marilyn Strathern (1972) on the Mount Hagen women of Papua New Guinea. In many cases, information in such work has been reinterpreted by subsequent generations of scholars. E. E. Evans-Pritchard, for example, whose 1940s work on the Nuer of then Anglo-Egyptian Sudan has the classic status of Malinowski's writings, overtly states that Nuer family life is characterized by the "unchallenged authority of the husband in the home" (1951: 133). But Evans-Pritchard also provides extraordinary vignettes of observed behavior which allow us to argue for modifications in that presumption:

> [S]hould she [a Nuer wife] in a quarrel with her husband disfigure him—knock a tooth out, for example—her father must pay him compensation. I have myself on two occasions seen a father pay a heifer to his son-in-law to atone for insults hurled at the husband's head by his wife when irritated by accusations of adultery. (1951: 104)

As I have observed elsewhere,

> [P]roprietary rights lose much of their powerful "ownership" connotation when we note that in this case, Nuer husband might say to his wife, "I have rights in you: if you insult me or knock my teeth out I can run to your father and make him pay me in cattle." (1979: 630)

Thus it was that feminist anthropologists, despite having been trained in a discipline literally saturated with gender, had the feeling of discovering the topic for the first time. They—we—strapped on the wide variety of theoretical oxygen tanks available, took deep breaths, and plunged in.

WRITING GENDER INTO ANTHROPOLOGY

These new feminist visions of anthropology's gendered seas were focused through both exogenous—popular cultural—and endogenous—professional—lenses. Two mid-1970s anthologies, Rayna Rapp Reiter's *Toward an Anthropology of Women* (1975) and Michelle Rosaldo and Louise Lamphere's *Women, Culture, and Society* (1974), responded to professional and public interest in bringing together much of this new work. These two volumes functioned as the "bibles" of feminist anthropology for the ensuing decade.[5]

As I have noted, American anthropology's edificatory tradition and second-wave feminism's penchant for fresh questioning led feminist anthropologists to problematize sexual relations to degrees unknown since the turn of the century. Physical anthropologists and zoologists challenged the dominant "Man the Hunter" model, which posited analogies between male-dominant African savanna baboons and the evolution of male-dominant human societies, and heralded cooperative male hunting as the key spur to human evolution. Thelma Rowell (1972), Sally Slocum (1975), and others pointed out, making use of already available information, that gendered primate social behavior varies greatly—and in any case, baboons are monkeys and are thus far more genetically distant from humans than are apes like chimpanzees, gorillas, and orangutans. Apes' social behavior, although various, evinces less visible male-female and intra-male stratification. Feminists also noted that in apotheosizing male hunting as the early human activity par excellence, "man-the-hunter" theorists ignored key evidence from contemporary hunting and gathering, or foraging, societies: women do some hunting, and female-gathered foods account for more than half and at times nearly all of what is eaten. (Unfortunately, these findings have had little effect on popular culture models of early human life, such as the still-ubiquitous caveman [sic] cartoons.)

Primatology and physical anthropology have been broadly influenced by the 1970s feminist critiques. Studies of gendered social behavior of primates in the wild, once the realm of projections of universal male rule, are now self-consciously careful to note variations between and within species. As well, primate studies have evolved to consider "primates in nature" (the title of Alison Richard's 1985 volume)—to see nonhuman primates less as Rorschach blots for human social and political concerns and more as animals existing and reproducing in a variety of floral and faunal environments.

The "woman-the-gatherer" challenge to the man-the-hunter model inspired Nancy Tanner and Adrienne Zihlman's (1976, 1978) female-focused model of human evolution. Turning man the hunter on its head, Tanner and Zihlman posited, for example, the key importance of gathered foodstuffs and thus the existence of "lost" female tools—fiber carrying nets and baskets which, unlike stone implements, would not fossilize. This model in turn stimulated consideration of food-sharing rather than hunting as a key spur to human evolution, and microwear studies on fossilized prehuman and human teeth to determine proportions of meat and plant foods in prehistoric diets.[6]

Feminists also attempted to review and reconsider gendered social relations in prehistoric state societies. Many made use of Engels's presumption that the "world-historic defeat of the female sex" coincided with the rise of private property and the state. Some, such as Eleanor Leacock (1981), used ethnohistorical evidence to argue for pre-Western contact and pre-state egalitarian societies. Others, such as Rayna Rapp (1977), concentrated on using theories of pre-state and state gender relations to rethink the meaning of kinship and its interrelations with differing economies and polities. In general, though, archeologists were slow to respond to the feminist challenge, and this lack of response stultified developments in both fields (see chaps. 2 and 3, this volume). At the same time, popular culture abhorring a vacuum, nonanthropologist feminist writers throughout the 1970s and 1980s were producing volume after volume of inferential histories of gendered humankind, many positing prior matriarchies. From Elizabeth Gould Davis's *The First Sex* (1971) to Elaine Morgan's *The Descent of Woman* (1972), these popular works merged with others recommending the "return" to Goddess worship or heralding the coming of a new "woman's era" of nurturance and nonviolence. At first, feminist anthropologists addressed this issue in popular feminist culture. Paula Webster (1975) explored the notion of matriarchy sympathetically, noting its millenarian appeal and development through Victorian kinship debates. Joan Bamberger (1974) analyzed South American Indian myths of prior matriarchy as legitimations of male rule. More recently, however, with both increasing specialization in feminist scholarship and the institutionalization of radical or cultural feminism as a counterculture, the gap between feminist anthropological knowledge and some popular feminist culture has grown. I will explore this issue, below.

Early social-cultural feminist anthropologists responded enthusiastically to the challenge of rewriting anthropology as if gender really mattered. One of their first and most important tasks was the reconsideration of entire subdisciplines in the light of feminist insights. Jane Collier's key 1974 piece on political anthropology, for example, redrew that discipline's map to include women's kinship struggles, which are concerned, after all, with the distribution of whatever domestic power is available to women and often also entail female influences on male public political actions. Louise Lamphere (1974) surveyed a wide variety of societies to consider the public political ramifications of women's cooperative and conflictual networks, and Sylvia Yanagisako (1979) wrote compellingly of the anthropological tradition of dichotomizing "male" public kinship and "female" domestic kinship—and, of course, of providing only "thin descriptions" of the latter. A number of feminist ethnographers, among them Pamela Constantinides (1979) considered women's strategic use of institutions and roles within organized religions in order to gain power, autonomy, or wealth.

Some feminist anthropologists of this period did restudies of populations well-known through earlier work. Annette Weiner (1976), for example, returned to Malinowski's Trobriand Islands to consider women's lives in great detail. Jane Goodale's 1980 ethnography of the Tiwi of Melville Island (Melanesia), earlier studied by C. W. M. Hart and Arnold Pilling (1960), was perhaps the most instructive of these works. Hart and Pilling had been fascinated by men's narratives of strategic acquisition of young wives as a form of property and had been uninterested in women's perspectives. Goodale discovered that Tiwi kinship was enormously complex, but that the key affinal relationship was *ambrinua*, the label by which son-in-law and mother-in-law referred to one another. These Tiwi mothers-in-law, however, usually contracted an ambrinua relationship as young adolescents. Each girl's ambrinua would then labor lifelong for her and eventually be allowed to marry her daughter. An older woman, far from being a "toothless old hag" (Hart and Pilling 1960: 14), held considerable power and prestige among the Tiwi.

Other feminist ethnographers studied third-world peasant populations, overturning in the process anthropological peasant studies' tendency to focus on the labor, perceptions, and decision making of only male householders and to assume that peasant women's activities and thoughts belonged to a "timeless" domestic realm. Anna Rubbo (1975) documented rural Colombian women's ability to manage small subsistence farms without the assistance of adult men. With capital penetration and development, however, and the state's introduction of Green Revolution seeds and pesticides, women lost their farming autonomy and were forced into urban migration as large landowners increased their holdings and turned to factory farming. Susan Brown (1975) considered poor women's and men's lives in the Dominican Republic and noted the political-economic realities behind the common, and commonly decried, pattern of female serial monogamy. Poor women strategically allied with and broke with poor men, from whom they could receive little financial support, while relying on female kin and older children to form networks of economic cooperation for survival.

In the process of rewriting subdisciplines and ethnographies, feminist anthropologists were also rewriting theory. Collier's and Lamphere's emphasis on the interpenetrating dynamic of kinship and politics is in part an improvement on Radcliffe-Brown. Yanagisako's focus on the symbolic realm in kinship is a feminist revision of the cultural approach to kinship elaborated by David Schneider. Rubbo and Brown, like many feminist anthropologists since, made use of a transformed Marxism. The influential essays of Michelle Rosaldo, Nancy Chodorow, and Sherry Ortner, as we shall see, reflected Weberian, Freudian, and Levi-Straussian frameworks, respectively. And the maverick Gayle Rubin (1975), whose coinage the "sex-gender system" has greatly influenced subsequent work on sexuality, employed a wild bricolage of reoriented Freud, Marx, Lévi-Strauss, and Lacan.

Whatever theoretical frame they worked within, however, feminist anthropologists were forced to deal with a key contradiction between their feminist conviction that male dominance over females, in any cultural setting, was fundamentally illegitimate, and the reigning notions of what would turn out to be the last gasp of ethnographic liberalism.

ETHNOGRAPHIC LIBERALISM AND THE FEMINIST CONUNDRUM

By and large, anthropologists in the mid-twentieth century heyday of ethnographic work tended to function as advocates for "their" groups, making sense (Western sense) of and justifying their "exotic" lifeways—right up to the boundaries of state power. Whether that authority was colonial (most often) or that of an independent capitalist or (rarely) communist state, it behooved the ethnographer who wished to be able to return to avoid criticism of government structures and policies. As well, anthropologists tended, in the great twentieth-century division of the pie of knowledge into lucrative disciplinary, professional, and departmental slices, to lay claim to social organization *beneath* state structures. Thus the liberal ideology of cultural relativism could decree that anthropologists justify cross-cousin marriage, ritual scarification, belief in witchcraft, or separate spheres of exchange but not protest against colonial domination, state-enforced economic and racial stratification, or the international economic pressures (such as austerity plans imposed by the International Monetary Fund) that may have been directly related to the continued operation of these customs. Thus the proliferation of liberal cultural relativist (and sexist) textbook titles in the 1960s and early 1970s: *Every Man His Way* (1968), *Man Makes Sense* (1970), *Man's Many Ways* (1973).

Feminist anthropologists in this period, then, were faced with a conundrum: how could we analyze critically instances of male domination and oppression in precisely those societies whose customs anthropology was traditionally pledged to advocate? I have discerned at least six separate modes of solving the conundrum, although of course many writers in practice combined two or more arguments. What follows, then, is a somewhat schematized typology of a complex two decades of feminist anthropological theorizing.

1. The first, and most traditional, response is to argue that women in a particular society actually enjoy a less onerous life or higher status—higher than one might have expected or higher than contemporary Western women. Margaret Mead, of course, is most well known for her 1928 argument that Samoan adolescent girls did not experience the anxieties and uncertainties of their American counterparts due to very different cultural constructions of sexuality, adulthood, and parenthood. Elizabeth Fernea, in her 1969 autobiographical ethnography *Guests of the Sheik*, argued that seclusion allowed village Iraqi women the opportunities to enjoy one another's company, offer genuine emotional support, and, most important, to attain status through specialization as religious or medical professionals, as men had to avoid intimate contact with unrelated secluded women. Susan Carol Rogers argued that women in peasant societies worldwide, "actually wield considerable amounts of power," while both sexes perpetrate "the myth of male dominance" (1975: 752). Annette Weiner, in her 1976 restudy of the Trobriand Islanders, argued that Trobriand women held high symbolic status as reproducers of social meaning. I discovered—in a 1979 review of the West African ethnographies cited by Ward Goodenough as underwriting a presumption of women's universal lower status—that the original (and all male but one) writers had documented extraordinary instances of female sexual autonomy, wives' rights to husbands' labor and sexual services, and women's economic parity (and sometimes superiority) to men.

Making the "native women better off" argument afforded feminist anthropologists a number of advantages. It fit well with the advocacy stance of ethnographic liberalism, thus neatly solving the feminist conundrum. It functioned to *epater* complacent Westerners, since one major legitimation of Western imperialism, after all, had been that "they are brutish to their women." There have been, as well, numerous third-world complaints about uninformed Western feminist deprecation of non-Western gendered practices. And finally, depending on our agreed-upon standards for cross-cultural comparison, to argue that women in a particular population experienced certain freedoms or status unavailable to specific groups of Western women was sometimes simply to tell the truth.

Other feminist anthropologists returned to the Marxist evolutionist model 2. Engels had put forward in *The Origin of the Family, Private Property, and the State* (1884). This work had key salience in the early 1970s for several reasons. First was the renascence of American Marxist thought after the period of McCarthyite censorship. Anthropologists such as Eric Wolf and Sidney Mintz were particularly active as writers and teachers in this era, and concern over the Vietnam War alerted many young anthropologists to the need for a radical rethinking of their theoretical premises. Returning to Marx led second-wave feminists to the text on which he and Engels worked together and that Engels had finished after Marx's death in 1883. Second, Marx and Engels relied on the extensive research and writing of a man who has been named the first American anthropologist, Lewis Henry Morgan. Morgan, a railroad lawyer in New York, became fascinated first by Seneca Indian life and then, more generally, by human kinship labeling systems around the world. Good Victorian that he was, Morgan linked differing terminology systems to evolutionary stages of humankind. Marx and Engels associated these kin terminology/social-level stages to particular modes of production, and to an originally egalitarian social structure that tipped to male dominance with the emergence of private property and institutionalized social stratification (see Trautman 1987: 252 ff.). Feminist anthropologists, who were living in the midst of revitalized debates in kinship theory, found provocative this systematic linkage of kinship and economy. Literally, the feminist slogan "the personal is political" came alive in theory.

Finally, Engels was a singularly attractive thinker to second-wave feminists, a modern-sounding advocate of women's rights who believed strongly in the arrival, with socialist revolution, not only of women's equal rights but of a new form of egalitarian romantic love:

> What we can now conjecture about the way in which sexual relations will be ordered after the impending overthrow of capitalist production is mainly of a negative character, limited for the most part to what will disappear. But what will there be new? That will be answered when a new generation has grown up: a generation of men who never in their lives have known what it is to buy a woman's surrender with money or any other social instrument of power; a generation of women who have never known what it is to give themselves to a man from any other considerations than real love or to refuse to give themselves to their lover from fear of the economic consequences. When these people are in the world, they will care precious little what anybody today thinks they ought to do; they will make their own practice and their corresponding public opinion about the practice of each individual—and that will be the end of it. (1972 [1884]: 145)

Several feminist anthropologists, most notably Karen Sacks (1975), returned to Engels's model to test and refine it. Sacks and Eleanor Leacock, who wrote the preface for a 1972 edition of *Origins*, made strong claims for sexually egalitarian foraging and early horticultural societies which then moved to male dominance with increasing societal stratification and the accompanying privatization of kinship. While this theoretical framework was explicitly used almost entirely by scholars concerned with ethnohistorical records of prehistoric state societies (see chap. 3, this volume), it had wide-ranging effects on feminist anthropologists in general, particularly those who were concerned with the impact of colonialism on third-world populations, which often involved the rapid imposition of state structures on nonstate societies. In contradiction to the reigning Western ideology that colonial rule had, without exception, extended theretofore unknown rights and privileges to women, these scholars asserted that, whether the colonizer-colonized relationship was the Spanish among the sixteenth-century Inca, the Quakers among the eighteenth-century Seneca, or the French among the twentieth-century Baule of the Ivory Coast, such rule had clearly worsened women's status and made their lives more onerous (see Etienne and Leacock 1980). Janet Siskind's powerfully evocative ethnography of the Sharanahua Indians of Peru tellingly contrasts the carefree and socially satisfying lives of Indian women in the forest both to *mestizas* in the pioneer town of Esperanza and to

Indian women who slept with Peruvian men and in so doing experienced the misogynous brutality of the colonizer for the first time (1973: 169–189).

Other feminist anthropologists, less influenced by Marxism and more interested in symbolic structures, took different tacks. Sherry Ortner, in a tour-de-force 1974 rereading of Lévi-Strauss's structural dichotomization of human thought into "raw" and "cooked" categories, asserted that, worldwide, females were thought to be natural—close to the earth, timeless, unthinking, inferior, untouched by human creativity—whereas males were cultural—transcending earthly bounds, living in history, intelligent and creative, superior and representing humanness. Ortner's formulation, which seemed to order and explain so much in contemporary sexist ideologies of women's inferiority, had widespread influence among feminists across many disciplines.

Michelle Rosaldo (1974) also posited a single key explanation for women's lower status, but, as would befit a scholar more influenced by Weber and British anthropologist Meyer Fortes than by Lévi-Strauss, hers was both symbolic and institutional, and varied across culture and across time. Thus, whereas for Ortner female:nature, male:culture was a human universal, Rosaldo assumed that her key, and thus women's lower status, would be more or less present in different societies. Rosaldo's focus was the relative separation of domestic and public domains, the world of household, reproduction, and maintenance of children and adults, and the world of extra-household labor, citizenship, public culture, and the state. Rosaldo argued that societies with very rigid public-domestic distinctions, such as Islamic societies that practice seclusion, or prerevolutionary China, or Victorian Europe and the United States, would devalue and disempower private spheres and thus the women with whom they were associated. Feminists concerned with the devalued, powerless, and yet crucially responsible role of the Western housewife found Rosaldo's formulation intriguing. Historical work on the relative divisions between household and public life in Western history, and women's roles in both realms, grew over the 1970s and 1980s.

Nancy Chodorow (1978) also offered a key explanation for women's lower status worldwide. Using a revised Freudian logic, she argued that female childrearing led to male resentment of female authority, weak female ego boundaries, and thus the tendency to male rule.

Finally, two groups of feminist anthropologists eschewed both Marxist evolutionism and the grand-theoretical search for key explanations of women's lower status. In the tradition of Weber's call for social-scientific *Verstehen*, the sympathetic entrance into the cultural worlds of others, some ethnographers wrote as closely as possible from inside the minds of their female informants—without, however, proffering larger theoretical points concerning women's status. Margery Wolf (1974) on village women in

Taiwan, Lois Paul (1974) on Guatemalan peasant women, and Liza Dalby (1983) on geisha represent this trend. Some feminist anthropologists, such as Penny Brown (1981) and Nicole-Claude Mathieu (1978), have argued that cross-cultural comparisons of women's status are impossible in any event, the arrogant imposition of philistine Western grids on deeply divergent cultural understandings.

The second group of ethnographers, many of whom were British or from commonwealth states, were strongly influenced by Marxist theory but did not use Marx and Engels for evolutionist grand theorizing. Instead, they focused closely on women's lives in particular groups and on seeing those lives in historical and political-economic context. Two edited collections, Patricia Caplan and Janet Bujra's *Women United, Women Divided* (1979) and Kate Young et al.'s *Of Marriage and the Market* (1981), among many other works, exemplify this trend in scholarship. The thread uniting the former collection is the examination of material conditions that may or may not lead to solidarity among particular populations of women in particular cultural contexts. The latter volume combined theoretical overview pieces, such as Diane Elson and Ruth Pearson's (1981) summation of first- and third-world women's intersection with the internationalization of factory production, with ethnographic articles linking, for example, the politics of domestic budgeting in Britain with larger political-economic shifts (Whitehead 1981). Both volumes actively speak to feminist scholarly concerns outside anthropology. The case study analyses of contingent women's solidarity parallel work among feminist labor historians and sociologists on women's resistance vs. women's consent in the workplace. *Of Marriage and the Market*'s contributors share the Marxist-theoretical frame of many other social scientists and historians in their efforts to describe women's varying household and extra-household roles in the evolving global economy.

Despite this interdisciplinary linkage, studies in this vein have not had as much influence on feminist thought as a whole as have others, for a number of reasons. First, although they narrate women's lives in other societies, they do so fundamentally in terms of economic and political contexts. That is, in order to understand Mathare Valley shantytown women's lives (Nelson 1979), one has to understand the political-economic process of the development of shantytowns in third-world states, prevalent kinship structures, and Kenyan state policies. Amassing this economic and institutional knowledge in preparation for the *Verstehen* moment is a far cry from plunging into Nisa's first-person narrative of her thoughts and emotions surrounding life passages (Shostak 1981). Second, Western feminist thought has moved progressively away from economic-historical considerations over the past decade and toward universalizing psychologies, a tendency compounded by Americans' historical penchant for psychologizing and related reluctance to think economically about social processes. Finally, these studies take a stance critical of all—not only male-female—stratification. Thus feminists uncomfortable with critiques of prior Western colonial or current postcolonial policies, of third-world state corruption, or even of class and race stratification in any state have difficulties with work in this vein. I once faced a minor student rebellion in a Yale anthropology seminar: the young women objected to two *Women United, Women Divided* ethnographers' critical analyses of the elite, class-maintaining activities of Brahmin women in Tamil Nadu (Caplan 1979) and of upper-status Creole women in Sierra Leone (Cohen 1979). In an interesting illustration of class interests *uber alles*, the students felt that women like their own mothers were being insulted.

Within the decade of the 1970s, many of these approaches to the feminist conundrum began to appear less satisfactory to anthropologists. Evolutionist Marxist explanations were hampered in two ways. First, they employed the hoary Victorian anthropological comparative method: considering contemporary cultures as though they were living history. Since all societies exist inside the same historical stream, have experienced the same number of years in which to alter, this perspective is both illogical and subtly deprecating to those considered less evolved, even when "less evolved" is interpreted as "better for women." Burgeoning interest in the arrogance of the West's representations of the rest, of the power dynamics of naming "others," enhanced this critical perspective. Second, the ethnographic record divulges too many counterexamples to the Marx-Engels model of sexually egalitarian small-scale societies. Some North American Native American populations such as the Seneca and the Pueblos seem to have been characterized historically by relatively high female status as evidenced by female political influence or autonomous marital decision-making (Brown 1975; Benedict 1934: 73–76). Others, such as the Plains Indians, who had less-complex, less-statelike social structures, were characterized by much lower status for women. Women in some South American horticultural groups (the Yanomama, the Mundurucu) experienced the threat of gang rape.[7] And women's lives in many Papua New Guinea societies involve much more arduous labor than do men's, while they are culturally characterized as distinctly inferior beings. Women among the Gainj, for example, even engage in ritualized revenge suicide to escape their onerous, unsatisfactory lives and to haunt abusive husbands—a custom with striking parallels to prerevolutionary China (Johnson 1981). Simply too many "primitive" women have been recorded as experiencing extreme exploitation and oppression at the hands of men in their own societies to lend credence to the argument that Western contact, colonialism, or capital penetration are alone responsible for all inegalitarian gender relations in foraging and horticultural societies. As Rapp points out, we now know that "changes brought about by colonialism, or, later, capitalist productive relations, are not automatically detrimental to women" (1979: 505).

Similarly, Ortner's compelling vision of women's universal symbolic association with inferior nature loses focus when we consider clear Western counterexamples: the Victorian "angel on the hearth" who enabled base men to transcend the contamination of their own brutish natures through contact with the "angel"'s spiritual, artistic capacities. Or there is the prevalent American myth of the cowboy civilized by the schoolmarm, classically embodied in a "primitive" third-world landscape in the film *African Queen* (Rogers 1978: 134). The contributors to Carol MacCormack and Marilyn Strathern's response to Ortner, *Nature, Culture and Gender* (1980), provided two other counterarguments. They noted first, in a number of separate ethnographic essays, that not only is the association nature:culture to female:male not universal, but that nature/culture and female/male are not even necessarily dichotomous pairs in non-Western cultures. Further, Maurice and Jean Bloch and L. Jordanova established the ambiguous, highly politically charged history of the concepts of nature, culture, and gender in the late eighteenth century. Far from being Western symbolic givens, these constructions were forged in the Enlightenment crucible as categories of challenge.[8]

Rosaldo's dichotimization of public and domestic spheres has also seemed less salient over time. Feminist historians have noted the ironies and ambiguities of separate spheres rhetoric in nineteenth-century Europe and the United States. Many woman movement activists, after all, made use of domestic, feminine, "moral motherhood" rhetoric to argue for women's rights to enter the public sphere. Jane Addams's coinage of "social housekeeping" is a case in point. As well, in class- and race-stratified societies, very separate spheres among one group may be quite permeable for others. Domesticated ladies coexisted with women miners and factory operatives— and street prostitutes. And of course for domestic servants, the largest group of employed women in Victorian Britain and the United States, household and workplace were profoundly interpenetrating institutions.[9]

Ruth Borker (1985) has also pointed out that the formulation domestic/public disguises a large number of separable phenomena—actual living spaces, specific social functions, personnel, linguistic categories. Rosaldo herself returned to her model in 1980 to interrogate her own assumptions and to link them to the heritage of dualistic nineteenth-century social science frameworks. Thus the domestic/public dichotomy has been demoted from a key explanatory factor to a research tool, a phenomenon that may exist in multiple forms with multiple meanings. Chodorow's dichotomizing Freudian model as well, although influential in feminist literary criticism, appeared to anthropologists similarly ahistorical and overly universalizing as the decade waned.

We are left, then, with the "native women better off," *Verstehen*, and historical Marxist perspectives as solutions to the feminist conundrum. Naomi Quinn, in a 1977 essay on anthropological studies of women's status, pointed

out that "status" is in actuality a portmanteau concept, encompassing at
different times relative share in productive activities, control over resources,
sexual autonomy, political power, and many other factors. Moreover, these
differing phenomena are noncomparable: how much weight do we attach to
absence of gang rape versus relative control over the food supply versus freedom to choose sexual and marital partners versus public political voice?
Thus the positive or negative evaluation of women's lives elsewhere will always be partial and selective. There are, of course, overarching grids of concrete, countable, material phenomena, such as the United Nations statistics
on women's versus men's caloric intakes and expenditures, the relative presence of forms of violence against women, specific state policies securing or
hindering women's rights, and so on. But such figures are necessarily crude,
subject to reporting bias and deliberate state obfuscation. Although aggregate figures can be used to brush large strokes—for example, worldwide,
women work harder than men for less reward—we can make only partial,
phenomenon-by-phenomenon comparisons among societies on this basis,
and these comparisons do not at all attend to the varying ways in which
women themselves perceive their situations.[10] The Strathern-Weiner debate
is a case in point. As well as making claims concerning Trobriand women's
high status, Weiner took Marilyn Strathern to task for not having attended
properly to Mount Hagen women's symbolic trading and its meanings for
women's (high) status (1976: 13). Strathern replied that although Mount
Hagen women, like Trobriand women, did have their own symbolic trading
networks, such trading simply did not bear the cultural meanings Weiner
claimed for the Trobriands: "What it means to be a woman in this or that
situation must rest to some extent on the cultural logic by which gender is
constructed" (Strathern 1981: 683). One cannot, in other words, simply read
out from institutions to their cultural constructions.

In the end (excluding the special problems of feminist physical anthropology and archeology), the careful attempt to discern the meanings of gender in
other cultural worlds and the bringing together of ethnographic, historical,
and political-economic knowledge of particular populations seem the most
fruitful modes of feminist anthropological practice. But we are now practicing anthropology in a strikingly changed political, social, and scholarly
climate. The era of ethnographic liberalism, and thus of the very raison
d'être of the feminist conundrum, has ended. It is to the shifts of the 1970s
and 1980s that I now turn.

FEMINIST ANTHROPOLOGY AND THE POSTMODERN ERA

The second-wave American feminist movement was almost immediately
challenged by backlash. No sooner were reproductive rights, entry into
formerly male jobs, rights to lesbian expression, male sharing of housework

and childcare, or protest against violence against women established as principles than they were attacked as unwarranted—even immoral—attempts at social engineering, even as improper tinkering with human nature. These attacks, and their institutionalized forms, such as Phyllis Schlafly's Eagle Forum and the Moral Majority, were directly connected to a larger "new conservatism" in the United States. New Right activism, incorporating anti-feminism, pro-United States imperialism, and anti–civil-rights and gay-rights stances, culminated in Ronald Reagan's 1980 presidential election and has had considerable influence on national political power throughout the decade.[11] Parallel developments took place across the Atlantic. Margaret Thatcher took power in the United Kingdom in 1979, and the governments of France, West Germany, Italy, and Spain (although some were nominally socialist) also took rightward turns.

The American rightward shift, coupled with demographic fluctuations and the Reagan administration's cutoff of many social programs, had immediate effects on American colleges and universities. Social science (excluding economics) and liberal arts programs lost student enrollments to business majors and to professional schools as undergraduates and graduates responded to economic insecurity and rightward shift through attempts to gain "practical" training. Anthropology departments in particular experienced the loss of questing students seeking to understand the lives of third-world populations and the effects of American and other imperialisms on those lives. At the same time, rightward shift and funding crises led anthropology departments to focus on staffing "traditional" fields and topics, and thus to neglect feminist, Marxist, and American-focused research.

Feminism (and Marxism, but that is another story)[12] nevertheless established itself in the American academy, having particular influence in literature and history departments but also through the maintenance of more than four hundred women's studies programs nationwide. Academic feminists, however, almost at once were forced to grapple with the question of "difference"—the multiple racial, ethnic, class, sexual, age, regional, and national identities of women—as they noted their own restricted demographic representation and research interests. Much feminist intellectual work of the two decades would attempt to redress this imbalance, whether through research focused on working-class, nonwhite, third-world, or lesbian women or through efforts to alter feminist academic personnel through affirmative-action hiring and the recruitment of minority and working-class (though not necessarily female) students.

These feminist academic efforts, however, took place in a rapidly altering intellectual environment, one we can only characterize as schizmogenetic—moving decisively in opposing directions. On the one hand, scholars of many sorts made renewed claims that the human world was characterized by order and regularities, and asserted the primacy of science—or the scientific status of non-hard-science disciplines. On the other hand, scholars of other stripes made revised arguments for attention to history rather than structure, for the recognition of short-term, nonrecurrent historical regularities or of sheer randomness in human affairs.[13] This historical frame was often tied to a dethroning of sciences' claims to superordinate status to which all other disciplines should be relativized. Critics instead viewed science as intrinsically socially constructed: as expressing, in differing historical eras, reigning notions of proper human social life in its representations of both human and nonhuman worlds.

Gathering in the "science and order" corner in the 1970s were a number of strange intellectual bedfellows. Lévi-Straussian structuralism had percolated outward across disciplines (Ehrmann 1970) and was taken up and fused with Marxism. As practiced particularly by Louis Althusser (1969, 1971), structuralist Marxism promised to set Marxist analysis once again upon a scientific footing, to allow the clear taxonomy of societies across time and space by mode of production, and to incorporate successfully theories of both state and ideological functioning within ongoing capitalist economies. Although structuralist Marxism was strongly represented in anthropology by scholars of Africa, such as Bloch (1984, 1985) and Meillassoux (1981), few feminist anthropologists (one exception was Brigid O'Laughlin's 1974 work on the Mbum) made use of its intellectual framework.

Structuralism had a very strong influence on anthropology, however, in terms of the study of symbolic systems. We have seen the feminist reflection of this trend in Sherry Ortner's work. As well, a different brand of structuralism entered anthropology via structuralist linguistics and stimulated anti-Lévi-Straussian, highly empirical work on the linguistic ordering of native conceptions of the natural world, of kinship, law, health, and disease. This school, labeled cognitive anthropology by its practitioners, claimed status as a "formal science" offering "complete, accurate descriptions of particular cognitive systems" (Tyler 1969: 14). More recently, anthropologists interested in cognition have taken a less scientistic and universalizing tack and have joined with cognitive psychologists to consider varying human constructions of "softer," more emotion-laden (from a Western perspective) institutions such as marriage. Not coincidentally, explicitly feminist work looking at the gendered character of cognition has come to the fore in this latter period (see Holland and Quinn 1987). And Catherine Lutz's pioneering work on emotion on Ifaluk provides a feminist meta-commentary in its edificatory concluding point: we in the West falsely universalize our related set of dichotomies, thought/emotion and male/female. Such divisions do not obtain on Ifaluk yet are a part of an overarching ideology that constrains both our research on gender and our efforts to bring about social change (Lutz 1988).

The assertion of widespread structural regularities across time and space also arose in biology and physical anthropology with the founding of "sociobiology." Entomologist E. O. Wilson, in the 1975 volume of that name, asserted that all living beings operate in some sense intentionally in order to maximize reproduction of their own genetic material. Thus all patterned behavior, Wilson argued, from beehives to Bauhaus, can be explained in terms of reproductive strategies.

Wilson's notorious chapter 27 applied sociobiological reasoning to human populations with results whose absurdity was quickly noted. Using already discredited "man-the-hunter" modeling and a clearly conservative political philosophy, Wilson asserted the genetic basis for racial or other IQ differences, for "natural" male dominance and "natural" class stratification.[14] Later sociobiologists would both make fewer claims about the functioning of human societies and would attempt to set the school up on a scientific basis. Some feminists became interested in revising sociobiology through attending to its neglect of the agency of female animals. These writers developed descriptions of female reproductive strategies and studied female primates with the presumption that they would display their own cooperative and competitive behavior (Hrdy 1981; and chap. 5, this volume).

During the same decades, the "history and critique of science" corner was also increasingly populated. There was a rediscovery of the refugee Marxists of the Frankfurt School, who had labored to use phenomenological insights on the social construction of knowledge to extend Marx's notions of culture and ideology (see Jay 1973). Previously, sociologists Erving Goffman (1959), Aaron Cicourel (1964, 1974), Harold Garfinkel (1967), and others also made use of phenomenology to found symbolic interactionism and ethnomethodology, schools of thought focusing on an antipositivist analysis of the effects of varying social contexts—intimidating questionnaires administered to poor people by middle-class people, for example—on the knowledge gathered within them. Work in anthropological sociolinguistics paralleled these schools in sociology through its emphasis on communicative contexts— courtroom, classroom, streetcorner—and the importance of individuals' race, class, and gender statuses in both constraining and enabling their speech strategies (see chap. 4, this volume).

Social scientists were also greatly influenced by historian of science Thomas Kuhn's *The Structure of Scientific Revolutions* (1970). Kuhn argued against official Whig histories of science, pointing out that in a series of key cases knowledge grew not through uncontroversial addition to accepted models, but through the clash of entirely opposed paradigms and the final triumph of one. Although Kuhn did not intend his work to apply to social science, his historical point—that received wisdom is the result of conflict among competing practitioners—was widely appreciated and extended the sociology-of-knowledge tradition begun in the work of Karl Mannheim (1936).

Critics of sociobiology and of other reductionists (such as the "IQ is genetic" school) used arguments from the sociology of knowledge, Marxism, and phenomenology to point out that these scholars were simply seeking to lay claim to the mantle of science for the legitimation of the status quo. Stephen Jay Gould and others documented the Western history of scientific "proof" of the inferiority of racial others, women, and the poor, and thus of the inherently ideological character of scientific practice.

Historian E. P. Thompson, whose 1963 volume *The Making of the English Working Class* had set the framework for the new "from the bottom up" cultural history, also joined the antistructuralist fray. Thompson (1978) and others argued that Althusserian structuralist Marxism allowed for neither the vagaries of historical change nor the role of human agency in effecting that change. Culture, in the structuralist vision, reduced to the "ideological state apparatus" and could not accommodate the contestation over meaning so evident in the history—particularly the labor history—of Western capitalist states and their colonies. Feminist historians found the cultural historical frame congenial, as it allowed (but had not been used for) the inclusion of differing and sometimes contesting women's perceptions of events and institutions. Historians of black Americans and other racial/ethnic populations, as well as those newly concerned with the histories of homosexual and heterosexual expression, also joined under the general cultural-history rubric.

Although structural Marxism had strongly affected anthropological work on Africa, other anthropological Marxist traditions continued throughout the 1970s and 1980s. The Latin American and Caribbean research of Eric Wolf and Sidney Mintz, in its concern with the perceptions and contestative actions of peasant populations experiencing colonialism and capitalist penetration, influenced a generation of anthropologists working in all areas of the globe. This trend, in conjunction with a renascent urban anthropology, encouraged radical studies of third world development. Feminist anthropologists, especially those working in Latin America, joined with feminist historians and other social scientists to create a massive and contentious field focused on "women and development" (see chaps. 7 and 8, this volume).

Radical and historical visions also influenced the framing of the discipline itself. Anthropologists began to look critically at the rise of anthropology as an auxiliary to British and other states' colonial ventures. Talal Asad's 1973 edited volume, *Anthropology and the Colonial Encounter*, offered case studies of such complicit ethnography. More important, though, Asad and his contributors documented the distortions of vision involved in ignoring the phenomenology of anthropological knowledge production. The colonial encounter itself, the interaction between the powerful and the powerless, was the seemingly neutral communicative context through which anthropologists historically had gained visions of other cultures. In the United States, the 1972 anthology *Reinventing Anthropology* represented this historical and self-reflexive trend. Contributors noted poor or absent work on Native Americans and black Americans, plumbed the history of American anthropology for positive and negative research traditions, and laid out radical research paths for the future.

Finally, Eric Wolf's monumental *Europe and the People Without History* (1982) attempts to set the specific histories of the peoples so often seen only in the timeless "ethnographic present"—the peasant and tribal peoples of the third and fourth worlds—in the context of European colonization, capital accumulation, the rise of global capitalism, and internationalization of labor. In focusing on the intimate historical interconnectedness of populations, on the fluctuating labels and self-identities of populations themselves, Wolf also argues strongly for anthropology's release from the "bounds of its own definitions" (1982: 18) into a Marxist perspective that reunites the sundered social sciences with history. None of the above works, however, really included gender analysis in its newly historical and self-reflexive considerations. A new generation of feminist scholars of empire (see chap. 1, this volume) has taken up this task.

Just as structuralism's sun was setting, however, a new set of intellectual tendencies, soon labeled poststructuralism, arose. Whereas structuralism originated in work in linguistics and folklore, spreading across disciplines via Lévi-Strauss's anthropology, poststructuralism was frankly literary from its inception. This was entirely appropriate, as poststructuralism's key claim was the supremacy not of social life, or even of language, but of texts. Poststructuralist writers (and here I am abridging mercilessly) tend to foreground textual art and to see all texts (narrative history, scientific reports, poems, novels, advertisements) fundamentally as more or less persuasive fictions. Many exciting insights have followed from this iconoclastic stance. Relations among differing texts are clearer to us, and this boundary-breaking function of poststructuralism has enabled feminists and antiracists, for example, to range widely across genres in redefining women's and minority writers' literature. They have also argued that "canonical texts"—those considered to be high art or key statements in Western civilization and thus most often taught—have been historically selected and reselected, in Foucauldian fashion, to enforce received wisdom and to legitimate the status quo. Thus "expanding the canon" to include texts by all women and racial minority and non-Western men challenges hegemonic ideas about which social groups have produced wisdom.

Outside literature per se, Hayden White's early (1978) *Tropics of Discourse*, which treated historical narratives as rhetorical art, had a major influence. Donald McClosky (1985) in economics and J. G. A. Pocock (1971) in political theory made analogous arguments about writing in their respective disciplines. And a similar school arose in anthropology, a group I label the ethnography-as-text school after a 1982 article of that title by George Marcus and Dick Cushman. Ethnography-as-text writers, particularly the prolific James Clifford, focus away from specific human populations, away from the ethnographic experience, onto an analysis of ethnographic texts them-selves.[15] Clifford (1983, 1988) and others were able to demonstrate the rhe-torical strategies used by ethnographers to lend authorial privilege to texts claiming to describe the lifeways and cultural worlds of other human groups. We inscribe "fables of rapport," narratives describing the process through which we become accepted in another culture—narratives intended to convince the reader of our hard-earned expertise. We select and describe "common denominator people," individuals who symbolize "normal" under-standings and actions among the "X." And we structure entire texts for specific effects—as allegories of lost paradise or of innately brutish human nature, for example.

Ethnography as text, then, has had a bracing, *epater l'ethnologiste* effect in anthropology, painting rude mustaches on some of our most sacred Mona Lisa texts. It is useful to remember that while we are attempting to convey with scientific accuracy the facts about a particular human group, we are also, if only behind our own backs, involved in constructing persuasive fictions for a particular, usually Western audience about some aspect of the meaning of human cultural difference. And ethnography-as-text writers tend to be very aware of anthropology's historic role in inscribing the lives of colonized or less-powerful others.

Clifford's work on the establishment of ethnographic liberalism and on the Western construction and exploitation of the notion of primitive art, the "restless power and desire of the modern West to collect the world" (1988: 196), attest to this concern. Ethnography-as-text writers, however, generally have had difficulties attending to gender in any context, whether as a cate-gory in the ethnographies they analyze or as a construct in the modern West. Indeed many ethnography-as-text writers find feminism itself problematic, deeming it, unlike their automatic anticolonialist perspective, to be a culture-bound ideology to be held at a distance and analyzed critically. Commentary on Margery Shostak's *Nisa* illustrates this point. Clifford asserts that "*Nisa* is a Western feminist allegory, part of the reinvention of the general category 'woman' in the 1970s and 1980s" (1986: 104). Marcus and Fischer allude to "Shostak's questions deriving from contemporary American feminism" (1986: 58), while Mary Pratt refers to "current Western conceptions of female solidarity and intimacy" in Shostak (1986: 45). Paul Rabinow, however, simply relies on synecdochic misidentification in his round declara-tion that "anthropological feminists work against an other cast as essentially different and violent" (1986: 257).

How can we understand the theoretical and political short-sightedness of these writers? Why do they insist on holding feminist perspectives at arm's length, insist on feminism's historical contingency, its status as a current intellectual and political movement, while experiencing no difficulty in strongly reprobating, for all time, colonialist, racist mentalities? Imagine Marcus and Fischer referring, in the 1960s, to "Martin Luther King, Jr.'s questions deriving from contemporary American antiracism." Certainly one interpretation would point to the antifeminist backlash so ubiquitous in politics and scholarship in the 1980s. But the full answer, I believe, is more complex and ultimately much more interesting. The full answer engages with the problematics of the logic of poststructuralism itself.[16]

Poststructuralist arguments, by their very nature, attempt to destabilize received conceptions of science, order, society, and the self. Poststructuralism is antiscience, antitheory; it levels our distinctions among truth and falsehood, science and myth. It denies the existence of social order or real human selves, declaring the death of the subject. Poststructuralism entails, then, what Peter Dews (1987) terms a "logic of disintegration": it cannot affirm any truth or claim any political stance. It can only deconstruct.

Clifford recognizes the poststructuralist conundrum, which we can see is structurally parallel to the feminist conundrum, in his analysis of Edward Said's *Orientalism*. He identifies with Said's dilemma:

> Should criticism work to counter sets of culturally produced images such as those of Orientalism with more "authentic" or more "human" representations? Or if criticism must struggle against the procedures of representation itself, how is it to begin? . . . These are fundamental issues—inseparably political and epistemological—raised by Said's work. (1988: 259)

In other words, there is no place for any morally evaluative or politically committed stance within the disintegrating logic of poststructuralism. It is fundamentally nihilist and gives permission to what Perry Anderson terms "a finally unbridled subjectivity" (1983: 54). Ironically, given its sometime association with radical political stances, poststructuralism does not challenge the status quo in an increasingly retrograde era.[17]

Ethnography-as-text writers simply fail to subject their own deeply held representations to the same operations they perform on feminism. Uninterrogated convictions inevitably come in the back door. What we need, then, is an acknowledgment of poststructuralisms' deficiencies. It is really only a research stance, a set of tools for ground-breaking, perspective-altering work. But the intellectual frame within which the research is oriented, whether admitted or not, will derive from outside poststructuralism's closed system, will involve some means of coming to terms with the (culturally constructed, but nevertheless) actually existing material world. Thus some feminist scholars' new tendency to define "feminist theory" as a totality in literary poststructuralist terms both ignores all of material, social life (and the feminists who attend to such) and leaves out of the equation any means for justifying a feminist-theoretical stance.

Feminist poststructuralism, indeed, is part of a larger academic turf war, in which literary critics and others jostle for ownership of (no longer social or political) "theory." Those outside literary criticism, such as former cognitive anthropologist Stephen Tyler, must declare the superiority of their topics: "Ethnography is . . . a superordinate discourse to which all other discourses are relativized and in which they find their meaning and justification" (1986: 122). But for poststructuralists in anthropology as in other disciplines, theory is now only discourse theory, so only discourses may be studied. The logic is this: since we culturally construct social and material realities, to study the "material world" in addition to or instead of discourse on material life is to consider a fiction. Seyla Benhabib notes that "contemporary feminism has shifted its attention from social analysis to discourse analysis, from power itself to the politics of its representation" (1989: 370).[18]

Thus while feminist kinship theorists Jane Collier and Sylvia Yanagisako perform a great service in their recent historical contextualization of anthropological kinship studies (1987), they also threaten to "tip over" into a radical idealism that would deny any connection between cultural constructions of kinship processes, human biology, and varying economic systems (see chap. 11, this volume). It is precisely the process of moving between contingent acceptance of current Western understandings of biology and economics and radically non-Western constructions of kinship that has produced feminist advances in understanding the mutual interpenetrations of gender, sexuality, kinship, and political economy at home and abroad (e.g., Young et al. 1981; Stack 1974; Rapp 1987; Lindenbaum 1987). Poststructuralism is also associated with the so-called "postfeminist" era, in which claims that women have already achieved equality jostle against continued job segregation, increasingly feminized poverty, little increase in male child care or housework, and high rates of male violence against women. All of these phenomena are intimately part of Euroamerican kinship processes, both as material realities and as ideological tropes. We cannot analyze them if we deny that intimate connection.

Poststructuralism in recent years has been seen in connection to another term, postmodernism. Postmodernism originally arose as a description of a specific architectural style, one that both deliberately eschewed the clean, monumental surfaces of modernist architecture and which also mixed stylistic elements of different historical eras (pastiche or bricolage). The term rapidly gained currency in the United States and Europe as it was applied, in ever-widening circles, first to all graphic art, then to all of literature, and finally to social life and politics in the West (see Jameson 1984). Each further application diluted meaning; and finally postmodernism and poststructuralism began to be used interchangeably to denote both our era, its art and politics, and poststructuralist interpretations themselves. Since postmodernism/poststructuralism has become an academic industry, it is

difficult to discern an arena of agreed-upon characterizations. But Perry
Anderson (1983, 1987), Edward Said (1987), Frederic Jameson (1984) and
Todd Gitlin (1989), at least, endorse the understanding that postmodernism
expresses the "cultural logic of late capital" (Jameson), a "moment in the
history of American empire" (Said). Anderson argues strongly that postmodernism entails an "embrace of commodification, a Nietzschean embrace of
the instant, a trivial and lighthearted rejection of politics."[19] Gitlin notes that
poststructuralism/postmodernism embroils adherents who wish to hold
political opinions in a fundamental contradiction:

> The impulse toward this sort of unmasking is certainly political: it stemmed
> from a desire to undo the hold of one system of knowledge/language/power
> over another. It followed from the 1960s revelation that various systems of
> knowledge were fundamentally implicated in injustice and violence—whether
> racist or sexist exclusions from literary canons, or the language and science of
> militarism and imperial justification. But the poststructuralist move in theory
> has flushed the Archimedean point away with the sewage of discourse. (1989:
> 357)

Said reminds us, however, that even the self-contradictory poststruc-
turalism/postmodernism stance is itself innately solipsistic. It expresses the
anxieties and obsessions, the political inaction and world-weary ennui, of a
narrow, privileged, class fraction of Westerners, ignoring the fact that the
present era has also seen the reemergence of notions of the "traditional, the
native, the authentic"—and the return of religion, especially in its seemingly
unpostmodern fundamentalist form. We should, then, disengage postmodernism, an intellectual approach, from the postmodern era, a descriptive
term for our contemporary period—which has apparently obliterated all
modernist conceptions of linear evolutionary change.

Just as the postmodern era has hosted the renascence of fundamentalist
religions at home and abroad, so it has witnessed the continuation and elaboration of cultural feminist essentialism. The proposition that women are,
across time and space, a single oppressed and virtuous class, and its entailed
refusal to recognize the transhistorical and cross-class existence of wealthy,
powerful, and evil women, has remained popular among many Western
feminists. The dichotomizing, essentializing threads in 1970s feminist evolutionary models today weigh, to paraphrase Marx, like a nightmare on the
brains of living feminists. Both feminist essentialists and conservative antifeminists have continued to draw on the nineteenth-century storehouse of
moral motherhood symbolism, stressing women's innate identity with and
nurturance of children and nature.[20] Popular volumes with both feminist and
antifeminist intent call on women to reclaim "the Goddess" in themselves
and to envision a new female and nurturing era to come. Rosalind Miles, for
example, offers up a potted combination of woman the gatherer, lunar cycles,
and goddess worship:

For woman, with her inexplicable moon rhythms and power of creating new life, *was* the most sacred mystery of the tribe. So miraculous, so powerful, she had to be more than man—more than human. As primitive man began to think symbolically, there was only one explanation. Woman *was* the primary symbol, the greatest entity of all—a goddess, no less. (Miles 1989: 17)

Even feminists with no interest in specious evolutionary reasoning have fallen victim to the vision of an innately nurturant, maternal womankind. Germaine Greer, whose prior literary and art-based scholarship was resolutely liberal feminist, recently (1984) converted to a pronatalist feminist essentialism. In the ultimate expression of privileged Western naiveté, Greer celebrated the lives of village women in India as the models for us all and singled out the close mother-in-law/daughter-in-law relationship for special approbation: all this in an era when Indian feminists are actively protesting ubiquitous, mother-in-law-sanctioned bride-burning.[21]

Both Anderson and Peter Dews call for the solution to the poststructuralist paradox in the recognition of its neglected antecedent, the critical-theory tradition in Marxism. Frankfurt School and other scholars recognized the need to develop much more realistic senses of the complex operations of culture and consciousness within particular political economies and were equally aware of the need to take language seriously as more than a transparent representational medium. At the same time, however, they did not take the "turn to language" so far as to envision it as "a system of floating signifiers pure and simple, with no determinable relation to any extralinguistic referents at all" (Anderson 1983: 46). They affirmed the existence of a real material world, of living beings, of humans living in varying social formations, of political struggle in history over the contours of power.

The solution to the poststructural paradox, then, is very like that to its feminist anthropological cousin. It was necessary to break out of the closed system of ethnographic liberalism, to recognize that no ethnography is ever entirely nonevaluative, that ethnography itself is a genre made possible by ongoing Western imperialism. Just so is it imperative that we see language and ideology as important in and of themselves and as part of the evolving material, social world. And indeed, "language and political economy" research in anthropology is growing rapidly (see Gal 1989).

FEMINISM, CULTURE, AND POLITICAL ECONOMY

Envisioning language and political economy as mutually constitutive exemplifies the larger "culture and political economy" tendency in anthropology. "Culture and political economy" is a phrase traceable to Peter and Jane Schneider's 1976 *Culture and Political Economy in Western Sicily*. It is now used to denote, loosely, new work in anthropology that attends both to economics and politics and to the ways in which they are culturally construed by differing social actors in history (see Roseberry 1988). Many anthropologists are now working in this general area, and a large subgroup of these foregrounds the issue of gender in research and theory. We can summarize the framework of feminist culture and political economy in five key points.

First is the radical rejection, for the second time in anthropological history, of social evolutionism. George Stocking has established that in Victorian anthropology "a pervasive evolutionary racism contributed to the dehumanization and objectification of anthropology's subject matter" (1987: 273). Although social and cultural anthropologists summarily rejected evolutionism in the early twentieth century, it remained as an organizing principle of "origins research" in archeology (see chap. 2, this volume) and as a subtext in synchronic ethnographic accounts. Thus Shostak portrays the !Kung as living as Paleolithic humans must have in order to use Nisa's oral history as an exemplar, not of one woman's life in a minute foraging group (a group with, in any event, a nonforaging past), but of Ur-woman, her life cycle and emotion (1981: 5–6). It is not Shostak's feminism, then, that is the problem: it is her evolutionary framework.[22]

We have seen how resurgent Marxism in the 1960s influenced feminist anthropologists of the 1970s to entertain evolutionary models, and the ways in which these models lost salience over the decade. Relatedly, many Marxist theorists abandoned stage-theory evolutionism and structuralism over this period in favor of the study of the unique histories of specific social formations. This is not to say that one should never claim the existence of structural regularities across time and space—of, for example, efforts by capitalists to drive down the cost of labor power, or of the likelihood of prevalent ideologies legitimizing the lower status of stigmatized social groups. But no human group on earth represents "living history": no matter how rudimentary its technological level, every human population has experienced as many thousands of years in which to alter its language, its religious ideologies, its social arrangements as has every other. Thus feminist anthropologists cannot locate the "key" to male dominance over women in small-scale societies. We can, however, assess the range of possible human gender arrangements and their connections to human biology through comparative ethnography (chap. 10, this volume). We can consider the many histories, in all types of societies, of changing gendered social life and its political-economic correlates, and join with other feminist social scientists, historians, and literary critics to research the mutually influencing histories of changing gender arrangements and ideologies in Western states and their colonized territories over the past centuries (see chap. 1, this volume).

Second, integrally connected to respect for history is the recognition that those institutionalized perceptions and patterns of behavior we may conceive as innately human or at least as well-established are most likely neither. The new historians of sexuality, for example, have charted the coming into being of the social labels "heterosexual" and "homosexual" in Europe and the United States over the nineteenth century, and the widely varying possibilities for female and male sexual expression across time and space. We now know that race and ethnicity are not immutable characteristics of individuals but emergent and shifting social categories, categories that can and do become the objects of intense politial struggle. Marx first established the historically contingent character of class divisions in developing capitalist states. Continuing Marxist debates over the empirical meanings of class in societies around the world indicate the continued evolution of varying class divisions. And, of course, how women and men are thought to be like and unlike one another as human beings, what they can and cannot do, are rarely givens, but historically and culturally contingent. Feminist anthropologists working in Melanesia in particular have elaborated on *Verstehen* in a series of careful studies of radically non-Western constructions of gender (Poole 1981; Strathern 1987; Errington and Gewertz 1987). These cultural logics vary widely but are linked in that they do not contain notions of individual, developing selves or of the male achievement of self-worth through the control of female others.

All of these understandings may be subsumed under the general rubric of social constructionism or antiessentialism. Social constructionism clearly implies a respect for historical difference and change, but it also entails an understanding of the human use of history—of constructions of the past—to legitimize or to contest the status quo. Thus antifeminists refer to "traditions" of male dominance and feminists counter with alternate traditions and with histories of women's struggles for equal rights. Recently, Marxist historians have paid particular attention to the histories of state and popular inventions of tradition (Hobsbawm and Ranger 1983). American anthropologists have followed with a series of investigations of social scientific constructions of imagined pasts in first and third world states—pasts which, even when they are conceived romantically to counter deprecatory images of the oppressed, misconceive their actual histories, perceptions, and actions (Roseberry and O'Brien 1991). Thus, for example, I follow the construction of the notions of American white ethnic community and white ethnic woman in the 1970s, note both their compensatory function in making up for decades of negative imagery and their reliance on black civil rights rhetoric, and demonstrate the ways in which the constructs were not only empirically false but were, and are, used in both racist and antifeminist political rhetoric (1991). As Rapp warned in 1979, "we must not allow our own need for models of strong female collectivities to blind us to the dialectic of tradition" (1979: 513).

Societal boundaries themselves, not just ethnic and racial categories, are historically contingent constructions as well. Benedict Anderson's 1983 study of the rise of European and then third world nationalisms compellingly por-

trays the repeated constructions of "imagined community" which attended
the creation and redrawing of national maps. Any assertion of unchanging
diachronic groupness, in effect, denies this complex historical process. Thus
some anthropologists' continued tendency to compare "cultures"—studied
at varying points in time—like so many checkers pieces cannot be justified.
To return to my discussion of comparative women's status: within the terms
of synchronic ethnographic liberalism, women in some small-scale societies
seem to have had a poor time of it. But the terms themselves must be interro-
gated. Not only are Quinn's disaggregated components, as she points out,
noncomparable apples and oranges; but each population must also be considered in terms of its place in regional, national, and global history.
"Women's status among the X" contains not one but three portmanteau
terms: status, women, and X. As populations (Xes) shift with changing
political-economic realities, so do their female components alter both demographically and in terms of their connections to those realities. And our
knowledge of past realities is dependent on past observers whose cultural
lenses may be unclear to us. As Lamphere notes: "In some sense, we really
will never know what it was like to be an Iroquois woman in the sixteenth
century or a Navajo woman in the eighteenth" (1987: 24).

Although social constructionism can shade into poststructuralism, it cannot, when it is located inside historical and social scientific analysis, degenerate into a nihilist stance holding either that there is no truth or that, in
Foucauldian logic, we are all trapped in the prisonhouse of language. Social
constructionism need not, as Stephen Horigan (1988) points out, stand
against the material world and the exigencies of biology. The very act of
taking such a stand perpetuates the false dichotomies that poststructuralism
tells us are ubiquitous and falsifying Western tropes. Although we recognize
that our Archimedean point may be historically contingent, it is nonetheless
real and we stand on it as we move the world.

The third and related insight is the embedded nature of gender, both as a
material, social institution and as a set of ideologies.[23] As we have seen, one
of the first developments of 1970s feminist scholarship, including feminist
anthropology, was the contention that women could not be studied ade-
quately in isolation. But recognizing the embedded nature of gender involves
as well an understanding that women must be seen not only in relation to
men but to one another. In any particular population, major social divisions—race/ethnicity, class, religion, age, sexual preference, nationality—
will crosscut and influence the meanings of gender division. "Embeddedness" determined my attention to the construction and political uses of
"white ethnic women" as it did Caplan's (1979) and Cohen's (1979) analyses
of Brahmin and upper-status Sierra Leonean women. Assuming embeddedness in all feminist analyses constructs "difference" inside the logic of analysis rather than appropriating it as an inorganic addition. Thus feminist schol-

ars can investigate both women's and men's differing economic activities
and cultural conceptions of gendered labor, both human sexual biology and
varying and changing cultural constructions thereof. Embeddedness follows
directly from social constructionism, but we could also have derived it from
anthropological tradition, from Frederick Barth's (1969) analysis of the
construction of ethnicity at its boundaries—or from Marx's epigram to *The
Critique of Political Economy*: "It is not the consciousness of men [*sic*] that
determines their existence, but their social existence that determines their
consciousness" (1970 [1859]: 21).

Gender embeddedness entails the fourth proposition that all forms of patterned inequality merit analysis. Stratification is visible in the realities of
individuals' and groups' unequal access to the material goods available in
particular societies. It is also materially present, as Raymond Williams
(1980) argues, in the ways in which social realities are expressed and contested in language. Thus the hoary anthropological shorthand, "the *X* say"
must be replaced with genuine attention to what varying populations among
the *X* say. Much work has been done in this area by historians, sociolinguists,
and anthropologists *tout court*. Brett Williams's (1988) ethnography of a gen-
trifying inner-city Washington, D.C. neighborhood, for example, contrasts
the actions and speech of black and Latin renters to the new white owners.
Differential visions of the uses of public space, community responsibilities—
even of favorite television programs—are linked to very different economic
and political resources and to the material and cultural realities of racial
difference in America. A large new group of studies of impoverished and
working-class women workers in first and third world states also examines
the intersection of class, culture, and gender in the ways women perceive and
respond to their situations. Whether they are Mexicana *maquila* workers getting
their own back on the male world by harassing a lone man on a bus, native
white and Portuguese garment workers in Providence maintaining labor solidarity through "female" celebrations of birthdays, marriages, and births, or
Malaysian factory operatives becoming hysterical and "possessed" and thus
disrupting the assembly line, women workers' actions cannot be analyzed
simply as "female," "working-class," or "cultural."[24] They occupy specific
locations in nexuses of multiple stratifications (see chap. 9, this volume).

Finally, and again relatedly, we need to attend to and to investigate
actively the multiple layers of context—or, in another formulation, social
location—through which we perceive particular cultural realities. The first
layer for ethnographers, one upon which much ink has been spilled, is the
power-laden encounter between researcher and researched. Feminists who
have claimed the existence of specifically feminist methodologies in social
research usually refer to this face-to-face level.[25] Such claims ignore the history of phenomenological work on precisely this issue, not to mention the
long-running "ethics" column in the American Anthropological Associa-

tion's *Newsletter* and the vast self-conscious literature on power dynamics in fieldwork. Although much of this work has not attended to gendered power dynamics, to do so is not to invent a new methdology but to extend an old.(26) Roger Keesing (1985), for example, has worked with the Melanesian Kwaio since 1969. His initial project was to contribute to cognitive anthropology's "grammar of culture," and to this end he elicited *kastom* (custom) from senior men. Over time, and particularly after he began working in the field with Shelly Schreiner, a female colleague, Keesing began to realize that "muted" Kwaio women were indeed capable of long, intricate, formal narratives reflecting on women's lives and their central roles in preserving kastom. The breakthrough came when senior men, in their efforts to "maintain control over the codification of women's rules and roles" (1985: 30) staged a recital for Keesing by a senior woman. She was agitated and nervous, and felt that a second, private session was necessary to make up for her poor showing. This session led to a series of "autobiographies" by Kwaio women of a wide age and status range, many of them with strong themes of women's unique cultural virtues and correctness in their opposition to kinsmen.

Less attended to are the more abstract and historical contextual forces, those of professional and larger intellectual location. The researcher's self exists not only in the "garrulous, overdetermined, cross-cultural encounter shot through with power relations and personal cross purposes" (Clifford 1983: 120), but also within networks of professional colleagues, and in historical *dialogue in absentia* with particular Western traditions. Sometimes it is the absence rather than presence of collegial networks, the clear social boundaries past which knowledge has not yet moved, that are most telling: witness the statements on feminism by ethnography-as-text scholars cited above. But in all cases we do intellectual work within particular collegial communicative frameworks, frameworks that are not immune to current political shifts. We need to be aware of the ways in which they tend to channel and shape our notions of what knowledge is and whom it should serve.

George Stocking, James Clifford, Donna Haraway, and others have labored to bring to light past and present intellectual frameworks in anthropology as a whole and to demonstrate the threads that tie them to material interests (or less directly, to sedimented structures of thought and feeling) connected first to British and continental European and later to American imperialism.[27] As Stocking summarizes, ". . . whether or not evolutionary writings provided specific guidelines for colonial administrators and missionaries, there can be no doubt that sociocultural thinking offered strong ideological support for the whole colonial enterprise in the late nineteenth century" (1987: 237). Clifford's dissection of the reign of ethnographic liberalism and Haraway's (1989) work in locating postwar primate studies within the political economy of African decolonization, shifting Western gender categorization and the hegemony of American imperialism, have also helped to extend this self-reflexive, sociology-of-knowledge history of the discipline itself.

Roger Keesing has made use of these new intellectual currents in his interpretation of Kwaio women's and men's talk. He now recognizes that in fieldwork "the genres and contexts we create together are alien and in some sense spurious" (1985: 32) and that,

> Our ethnographic encounters take place not only in contexts of the internal politics of the "society" we study but in wider historical and political contexts, in which we ourselves are inextricably situated. I have suggested that in the Kwaio case the ways in which women stepped into the role of ideologues in articulating accounts of their culture can only be understood in the historical context of colonial domination, the Kwaio struggle for autonomy, and the elevation of "culture" to the level of political symbol. . . . Perhaps we should go on to ask whether the cultural accounts *male* informants have constructed to ethnographers of tribal societies through the years must similarly be understood partly as artifacts of the historical context of colonial domination. (1985: 37)

The postmodern era, as Edward Said has noted, contains both social groups who seem to have lost political will and those who are just finding it. It is not really a period "beyond ideology" but one of very swift and confusing movements of capital and labor around the globe, and of equally rapid ideological shifts and rearrangements. Many feminist scholars are attempting to describe this moving stream, knowing all the while that we are moving with it, and knowing as well that our descriptions—and all descriptions—are profoundly ideological. The early feminist anthropologists saw no contradiction between their scholarship and anthropology's traditional edificatory role in the West. They felt that their work was directly relevant to American and European life and politics. Rayna Rapp declared both that her anthology had "its roots in the women's movement" and that the anthropology of women would "help feminists in the struggle against sexism in our own society" (1975: 11). Rosaldo and Lamphere linked their edited volume to the effort "to understand our position and to change it" (1974: 1). Even Naomi Quinn, in chiding other feminist anthropologists for faulty reasoning and in calling for more rigorous, less ideologically biased scholarship, celebrated "the social forces which inspired anthropological interest in women's status" (1977: 222). Most of us are now more chastened in our presumptions about the immediate utility of our work, while that work is worlds more sophisticated. But neither humility nor scholarly sophistication is a reason for ignoring Quinn's social forces, for withdrawing from anthropology's committed role. Our new knowledge should be broadly shared. It should affect the ways in which we see all women and men, including ourselves.

The dozen articles gathered here represent this recent sophistication in feminist anthropological work not only individually but collectively, not only in what they share but in the ways in which they differ. First, the writers themselves, though all anthropologists and all feminists, are not, as were the contributors to the two early bibles of feminist anthropology, all women and all white. As well, we represent an older center of gravity. We are no longer largely dissident graduate students and embattled young professors, with the addition of newly valued wives of well-known older male anthropologists. The bulk of us are solidly established in our fields.

Next, the contributors have self-consciously chosen a variety of genres through which to express their points: review essay (Gal, Warren and Bourque, Conkey), historical narrative (Stoler), straightforward ethnography (Povinelli, Rapp), single-issue critical essay (Scheffler, Sperling), and elegant genre combinations as well (Guyer, Peacock, Silverblatt). Then comes the matter of subdisciplinary specialization. Unlike so much recent scholarship, both feminist and nonfeminist, and in a return to the feminist pioneers, these writers stand squarely in their fields and yet speak to audiences far beyond a tiny group of specialists. Moreover, befitting the both/and stance of feminist culture and political economy, they acknowledge both material realities and cultural constructions. Archeologist Margaret Conkey "speaks" poststructuralism while remaining closely in touch with bones, stones, and shards. Sociolinguist Susan Gal articulates political-economic contexts for gendered language use around the globe. Cultural anthropologist Rayna Rapp helps us to perceive the material world of amniocentesis testing—the white rooms, the needles, the pregnant women's bodies—and the varying constructions of that experience expressed by New Yorkers across class, color, and gender lines.

The contributors also speak to one another. Although they may disagree (and disagree with me), they do not talk past one another, do not use disciplinary specialization to retreat from common intellectual projects. I originally organized the pieces in a classic linear Comtean fashion, starting with the physical anthropological "base" and ending with symbolic and linguistic studies. But while this structure has the virtues of convenience and familiarity—and also illustrates feminist anthropology's broad coverage of topics in all four fields—it tends to disguise connections among the studies and their fresh responses to the postmodern era.

One key connection is an emphasis on the politically constituted nature of knowledge production, and its historical embeddedness. In Part I, Gender in Colonial History and Anthropological Discourse, three scholars originally trained in economic anthropology (Stoler), Old World archeology (Conkey), and New World ethnohistory (Silverblatt) come together in tracing the histories of gendered meanings promulgated both by colonial powers and in anthropological subdisciplines. Recognition of the power and entailments of gendered representation also ties these pieces to one another. In Part II, Gender as Cultural Politics, a sociolinguist (Gal), biological anthropologist (Sperling), and cultural anthropologist (Povinelli) converge in analyzing histories of the representations of gendered worlds, whether in literary criticism and linguistic anthropology, in primatology, or among women and men on an aboriginal reserve. Each piece is simultaneously conscious of the cultural politics of representing gender in scholarly discourse and in popular culture. Serious attention to the ways in which women's lives intersect with larger economies constitutes a third point of convergence. In Part III, Representing Gendered Labor, Guyer, Warren and Bourque, and Zavella describe both women's and men's economic and kinship lives in particular social formations and locate our efforts to do so politically and historically. Thus they carry self-reflexive historical analysis into the too-often reductionist arena of economic studies. Each writer, as well, adds to our knowledge of varying Western representations of "Others," whether African female farmers, aggregated third-world women, or Chicanas in the western United States.

In the final section, Part IV, Contentious Kinship: Rethinking Gender and Reproduction, contributors rework old debates and break new ground. Peacock, trained in biological anthropology, uses her work with Efe in Zaire to rethink armchair feminist speculation on the biological channeling of sexual divisions of labor. Scheffler locates current problematic feminist tendencies in kinship studies within anthropological history. And Rapp, reversing popular cultural tendencies to focus on the American white, middle-class "norm," reports on her polyvocal, cross-class, multiracial study of amniocentesis testing in New York City.

The contributors speak to one another, as well, beyond these salient categories. Guyer, Silverblatt, and Stoler together engage new debates on historiography and gender. Gal, Warren and Bourque, and Scheffler unravel ragged arguments in contemporary feminist theory both inside and outside anthropology. Rapp, and Warren and Bourque, share a concern with the intersections of technology and women's lives, while Rapp and Peacock speak together on female biology and reproduction across major cultural divides. Silverblatt and Peacock write explicitly of the problematic heritage of early 1970s feminist anthropological models, while Conkey, Sperling, and Stoler converge in examining Western constructions of human sexuality wound into our interpretations of primates, prehistory, and the colonized third world. Zavella, Stoler, and Conkey all construct racial difference within, not as an addition to, their analyses. Peacock and Povinelli, at opposite ends of knowledge's Comtean scale, nevertheless both demonstrate for the reader the historically contingent, socially constructed nature of "gathering data."

Finally, all of these writers are self-consciously aware of their location in the mingling streams of anthropology, feminism, intellectual and political-economic history, and of the inevitable reflections of contemporary American concerns in their work. Rapp's and Zavella's pieces are the most obvious, as they are specifically about gender, race, economy, and family in the contemporary United States. But Conkey, Sperling, and Peacock also speak directly to the ideological uses of anthropological theory in constructing contemporary, politicized meanings of gender. All the work in this volume, in fact, stands on that bedrock of awareness. Even Jane Guyer's piece on changing gendered agricultural practice among the West African Beti, which would seem to be as exotically far as it could be from contemporary gender concerns in the advanced capitalist United States, leads us to an awareness of cross-cultural structural parallels and of their limits. In both the Beti case and in the last two decades of American life, changing political economies have led, on average, to an increasingly assymetric sexual division of labor and intensified female work effort. Beti women's double-cropping and added trade activities evoke American women's double day in the household and the paid workforce. And in each case, women's increased responsibilities and efforts to ameliorate them have led to court cases and to piecemeal legislation—and to the strategic political use, by all interested parties, of the language of "tradition." Nevertheless, as Guyer indicates, even intra-African historical comparisons can mislead. If such narrowly gauged analogies are faulty, even more should we tread carefully and use seemingly parallel cases to suggest possible insights, not to determine meanings.

Any collection of articles on a large topic suffers from gaps. Although this volume represents all four fields in anthropology, many subfields, and research in the United States, Europe, Africa, Southeast Asia, Latin America, and Melanesia, it cannot—fortunately—contain the richness of all contemporary feminist work in the field. Many important arenas, such as gendered religious practice, are touched on (by Povinelli, Silverblatt, Rapp, and Stoler) but not squarely addressed. Others, such as gender and artistic production, are entirely absent. Neither an atheoretical encyclopedia nor a narrow sample, this volume offers a broad and coherent representation of the current nexus of feminist culture and political economy in anthropology.

NOTES

Susan Gal, Bill Kelly, Fitz John Porter Poole, Susan Sperling, Judith Stacey, and especially Adolph Reed helped me to clarify the arguments in this piece.

1. Major bibliographic reviews of the field include Stack et al. (1975), Lamphere (1977), Quinn (1977), Rapp (1979), Rogers (1978), Atkinson (1982), Mukhopadhyay and Higgins (1988). See also Sandra Morgen's edited teaching module (1989). Moore's recent (1988) volume provides a narration of feminist shifts within British social anthropology alone. Her discussion of work on the interpenetration of kinship and economy, however, is very helpful. Although this piece focuses on all four fields of

American feminist anthropology, the discipline is genuinely transatlantic. Thus I include important British—and some French and third world—work as well.

2. On the American suffrage movement, see DuBois (1978), and Flexner (1974). On early twentieth-century third world feminism, see Jayawardena (1986). On continued American feminist activity in the "quiescent" period, see Cott (1987).

3. Two contemporary documents suffice to illustrate this revolutionary verve: Morgan (1970) and Gornick and Moran (1971). On the early history of the second wave, see Evans (1979).

4. See Howard (1984) on Margaret Mead; Modell (1983: esp. 256–258), on Ruth Benedict; and Rosenberg (1982) and Lamphere (1989) on Elsie Clews Parsons. See also Golde (1986) for women's first-person accounts of fieldwork experiences, and Gacs et al. (1989) for short biographies of selected women anthropologists.

5. See Lamphere (1987) for a first-person account of the making of *Women, Culture and Society* and for a history of American feminist anthropology with slightly different emphases.

6. See Potts and Shipman (1981), Shipman (1983), Isaac (1983).

7. See Shapiro (1976), Murphy (1985).

8. Ortner, with Harriet Whitehead, later altered her position to an assertion that "the cultural construction of sex and gender tends everywhere to be stamped by the prestige considerations of socially dominant male actors" (1981: 12). See Collier and Yanagisako for one set of criticisms of this formulation (1987: 27 ff.).

9. See Lerner (1969), Bloch (1978), Ryan (1979: 75–150), Hewitt, (1985).

10. See Seager and Olsen (1986: 108, 113) for statistical summaries.

11. See Crawford (1980), Piven and Cloward (1982), Phillips (1982).

12. See Jacoby (1987).

13. See also Vincent (1986) for an account of shifts from "system" to "process" analysis in legal, ecological, and symbolic anthropology.

14. See also Sahlin's (1976) extended critique of sociobiology.

15. Precursor to ethnography as text was Clifford Geertz's interpretive anthropology that envisioned cultures as texts. See Rabinow and Sullivan 1979.

16. See Mascia-Lees et al. (1989) for a spirited feminist critique of "the postmodernist turn in anthropology" from a very different set of presuppositions. See also work by two James Clifford students, Gordon (1988) and Visweswaren (1988), for attempts to read gender into the ethnography-as-text framework. Finally, see Strathern (1987, 1988) for interesting juxtapositions of anthropology and feminism from within the poststructuralist framework. Strathern, unlike the contributors to this volume, takes it as paradigmatic that feminism seeks to portray all males as Others. She is Rabinow's source for a similar assertion cited above.

17. See Polier and Roseberry (1989) for a somewhat separate set of critiques of the ethnography and text school. See also my review of James Clifford and Clifford Geertz.

18. Some examples are Flax (1987), Scott (1988). An interesting measure of American feminist theory's shift away from analysis of the actually existing world is the difference in content between the 1983 *Signs Reader* and that published in 1989. See Abel and Abel (1983), Malson et al. (1989). See Taussig 1989, for a poststructuralist anthropologist's criticism of Marxist historical anthropologists for choosing research

topics not amenable to discourse analysis; and see Mintz and Wolf (1989) for an embrace of culture and political economy research.

19. Unpaginated quotations from Anderson and Said are from talks given at "Postmodernism: Practice, Politics, Performance," Whitney Humanities Center, Yale University, February 21, 1987.

20. For critiques of feminist essentialism see Sayers (1982: 187–192), Echols (1983), Cocks (1984), di Leonardo (1985), forthcoming. Further examples of popular feminist essentialist writing include Eisler (1987), Andrews (1987), Cooey et al. (1987), Harris (1989).

21. See Shirley Lindenbaum's (1984) insightful review of Greer, Kishwar and Vanita (1984) for Indian feminists' protests against bride-burning.

22. *Contra* Shostak's assertion of the !Kung's "traditional value system" (1981: 6) see Schrire (1980) and Pratt (1986).

23. Naomi Quinn made this formulation, 1986.

24. See Lamphere (1985), Fernandez-Kelly (1984: 243), Ong (1983: 435–437).

25. See Oakley (1981), Bowles and Duelli-Klein (1983).

26. And, as Judith Stacey (1988) notes, even self-conscious feminist researchers find themselves complicit in the researcher's inevitable exploitation of subjects' friendship for privacy-invading information.

27. See also Kuper (1988) and Fabian (1983).

BIBLIOGRAPHY

Abel, Elizabeth, and Emily K. Abel eds. 1983. *The signs reader: Women, gender and scholarship*. Chicago: University of Chicago Press.

Althusser, Louis. 1969. *For Marx*. New York: Pantheon Books.

———. 1971. *Lenin and philosophy and other essays*. New York: Monthly Review Press.

Anderson, Benedict. 1983. *Imagined communities: Reflections on the origin and spread of nationalism*. London: Verso.

Anderson, Perry. 1983. *In the tracks of historical materialism*. London: Verso.

Andrews, Lynne V. 1987. *Crystal woman: The sisters of the dreamtime*. New York: Warner Books.

Asad, Talal, ed. 1973. *Anthropology and the colonial encounter*. London: Ithaca Press.

Atkinson, Jane. 1982. Anthropology: Review essay. *Signs* 8: 236–258.

Bamberger, Joan. 1974. *The myth of matriarchy: Why men rule in primitive society*. In *Women, culture and society*, Michelle Zimbalist Rosaldo and Louise Lamphere, eds. Stanford: Stanford University Press, pp. 263–280.

Barth, Frederick. 1969. *Ethnic groups and boundaries: The social organization of cultural difference*. Boston: Little, Brown.

Benedict, Ruth. 1934. *Patterns of culture*. Boston: Houghton Mifflin.

Benhabib, Seyla. 1989. On contemporary feminist theory. *Dissent* (Summer): 366–370.

Bloch, Maurice, ed. 1984. *Marxist analyses and social anthropology*. London: Tavistock.

———. 1985. *Marxism and anthropology*. Oxford: Oxford University Press.

Bloch, Maurice, and Jean Bloch. 1980. Women and the dialectics of nature in eighteenth-century French thought. In *Nature, culture and gender.* Carol MacCormack and Marilyn Strathern, eds. Cambridge: Cambridge University Press, pp. 25–41.

Bloch, Ruth. 1978. American feminine ideals in transition: The rise of the moral mother, 1785–1815. Feminist Studies 4 (2) (June 1878): 101–26.

Borker, Ruth. 1985. *Domestic/public: Concepts and confusions.* Paper presented at the American Anthropological Association Meetings. Washington, D.C.

Bowles, Gloria, and Renate Duelli-Klein, eds. 1983. *Theories of women's studies.* London: Routledge and Kegan Paul.

Brown, Judith K. 1975. Iroquois women: An ethnohistoric note. In *Toward an anthropology of women.* Rayna Rapp Reiter. ed. New York: Monthly Review Press, pp. 235–251.

Brown, Penelope. 1981. Universals and particulars in the position of women. In *Women in society: Interdisciplinary essays.* Cambridge Women's Studies Group. London: Virago Press.

Brown, Susan E. 1975. Love unites them and hunger separates them: Poor women in the Dominican Republic. In *Toward an anthropology of women.* Rayna Rapp Reiter, ed. New York: Monthly Review Press, pp. 322–332.

Caplan, Patricia. 1979. Women's organizations in Madras City, India. In *Women united, women divided: Comparative studies of ten contemporary cultures.* Patricia Caplan and Janet M. Bujra, eds. Bloomington: Indiana University Press, pp. 99–128.

Caplan, Patricia, and Janet M. Bujra, eds. 1979. *Women united, women divided: Comparative studies of ten contemporary cultures.* Bloomington: Indiana University Press.

Chodorow, Nancy. 1978. The reproduction of mothering: Psychoanalysis and the sociology of gender. Berkeley: University of California Press.

Cicourel, Aaron. 1964. *Method and measurement in sociology.* New York: Free Press.

———. 1974. *Theory and method in the study of Argentine fertility.* New York: Wiley.

Clifford, James. 1983. On ethnographic authority. *Representations* 2: 118–146.

———. 1986. On ethnographic allegory. In *Writing culture: The poetics and politics of ethnography.* James Clifford and George E. Marcus, eds. Berkeley: University of California Press, pp. 98–121.

———. 1988. *The predicament of culture: Twentieth-century ethnography, literature and art.* Cambridge: Harvard University Press.

Clifford, James, and George E. Marcus, eds. 1986. *Writing culture: The poetics and politics of ethnography.* Berkeley, Los Angeles, London: University of California Press.

Cocks, Joan. 1984. Wordless emotions: Some critical reflections on radical feminism. *Politics and Society* 13 (1): 27–58.

Cohen, Gaynor. 1979. Women's solidarity and the preservation of privilege. In *Women united, women divided: Comparative studies of ten contemporary cultures.* Patricia Caplan and Janet M. Bujra, eds. Bloomington: Indiana University Press, pp. 129–156.

Collier, Jane Fishburne. 1974. Women in politics. In *Women, culture and society.* Michelle Zimbalist Rosaldo and Louise Lamphere, eds. Stanford: Stanford University Press, pp. 89–96.

Constantinides, Pamela. 1979. Women's spirit possession and urban adaptation. In *Women united, women divided: Comparative studies of ten contemporary cultures.* Patricia Caplan and Janet M. Bujra, eds. Bloomington: Indiana University Press, pp. 185–205.

Cooey, Paula, Sharon Farmer, and Mary Ellen Ross, eds. 1987. *Embodied love: Sensuality and relationship as feminine values.* New York: Harper and Row.

Cott, Nancy. 1979. *The bonds of womanhood: Woman's sphere in New England, 1780–1835.* New Haven: Yale University Press.

———. 1987. *The grounding of modern feminism.* New Haven: Yale University Press.

Crawford, Alan. 1980. *Thunder on the right: The "new right" and the politics of resentment.* New York: Pantheon Books.

D'Emilio, John, and Estelle Freedman. 1988. *Intimate matters: A history of sexuality in America.* New York: Harper and Row.

Dalby, Liza Crihfield. 1983. *Geisha.* Berkeley, Los Angeles, Oxford: University of California Press.

Davis, Elizabeth Gould. 1971. *The first sex.* New York: G. P. Putnam.

Dews, Peter. 1987. *Logics of disintegration: Poststructuralist thought and the claims of critical theory.* London: Verso.

di Leonardo, Micaela. 1979. Methodology and the misinterpretation of women's status: A case study of Goodenough and the definition of marriage. *American Ethnologist* 6 (4): 627–637.

———. 1985. Morals, mothers, and militarism: Antimilitarism and feminist theory: Review essay. *Feminist Studies* 11 (3): 599–617.

———. 1989. Malinowski's nephews: Review of James Clifford's *The predicament of culture* and Clifford Geertz's *Works and lives. The Nation* (March 13).

———. 1991. Habits of the cumbered heart: Ethnic community and women's culture as invented traditions. In *Golden ages, dark ages: Imagining the past in anthropology and history.* William Roseberry and Jay O'Brien, eds. Berkeley, Los Angeles, Oxford: University of California Press.

———. Forthcoming. Women's culture and its discontents. In *The politics of culture.* Brett Williams, ed. Washington, D.C.: Smithsonian Press.

DuBois, Ellen Carol. 1978. *Feminism and suffrage: The emergence of an independent women's movement in America 1848–69.* Ithaca: Cornell University Press.

Dundes, Alan. 1968. *Every man his way: Readings in cultural anthropology.* Englewood Cliffs, N.J.: Prentice-Hall.

Echols, Alice. 1983. The new feminism of yin and yang. In *Powers of desire: The politics of sexuality.* Ann Snitow, Christine Stansell, Sharon Thompson, eds. New York: Monthly Review Press, pp. 439–459.

Ehrmann, Jacques, ed. 1970. *Structuralism.* New York: Doubleday.

Eisler, Riane. 1987. *The Chalice and the blade: Our history, our future.* San Francisco: Harper and Row.

Elson, Diane, and Ruth Pearson. 1981. The subordination of women and the internationalization of factory production. In *Of marriage and the market: Women's subordination internationally and its lessons.* Kate Young et al., eds. Cambridge: Cambridge University Press, pp. 18–40.

Engels, Frederick. 1972. (1884). *The origin of the family, private property and the state.* Edited by Eleanor Leacock. New York: International Publishers.

Errington, Frederick, and Deborah Gewertz. 1987. *Cultural alternatives and a feminist anthropology: An analysis of culturally constructed gender interests in Papua New Guinea.* Cambridge: Cambridge University Press.

Etienne, Mona, and Eleanor Leacock, eds. 1980. *Women and colonization: Anthropological perspectives*. New York: Praeger Publishers.

Evans, Sara. 1979. *Personal politics: The roots of women's liberation in the civil rights move-ment and the new left*. New York: Random House.

Evans-Pritchard, E. E. 1951. *Kinship and marriage among the Nuer*. Oxford: Oxford University Press.

Fabian, Johannes. 1983. *Time and the other: How anthropology makes its object*. New York: Columbia University Press.

Fee, Elizabeth. 1974. The sexual politics of Victorian social anthropology. In *Clio's consciousness raised: New perspectives on the history of women*. Mary Hartman and Lois W. Banner, eds. New York: Harper and Row.

Fernandez-Kelly, Maria Patricia. 1984. Maquiladoras: The view from the inside. In *My troubles are going to have trouble with me*. Karen Sacks, ed. New Brunswick: Rutgers University Press.

Fernea, Elizabeth. 1969. *Guests of the sheik: An ethnology of an Iraqi village*. New York: Doubleday.

Flax, Jane. 1987. Postmodernism and gender relations in feminist theory. *Signs* 12 (4): 621–643.

Flexner, Eleanor. 1974. *Century of struggle: The woman's rights movement in the United States*. New York: Atheneum.

Gacs, Ute, Aisha Khan, Jerrie McIntyre, and Ruth Weinberg, eds. 1989. *Women anthropologists: Selected biographies*. Urbana: University of Illinois Press.

Gal, Susan. 1989. Language and Political Economy. Annual Review of Anthropology, volume 18: 345–367.

Garfinkel, Harold. 1967. *Studies in ethnomethodology*. Englewood Cliffs, N.J.: Prentice-Hall.

Ginsburg, Faye. 1989. *Contested lives: The abortion debate in an American community*. Berkeley, Los Angeles, London: University of California Press.

Gitlin, Todd. 1989. Postmodernism: Roots and politics. In *Cultural politics in contemporary America*. Ian Angus and Sut Jhally, eds. London: Routledge & Kegan Paul, pp. 347–360.

Godelier, Maurice. 1977. *Perspectives in Marxist anthropology*. Cambridge: Cambridge University Press.

Goffman, Erving. 1959. *The presentation of self in everyday life*. New York: Doubleday.

Golde, Peggy, ed. 1986. *Women in the field*. 2d ed. Berkeley, Los Angeles, London: University of California Press.

Goodale, Jane. 1980. *Tiwi wives: A study of the women of Melville Island, North Australia*. Seattle: University of Washington Press.

Goodenough, Ward. 1965. Rethinking "status" and "role": Toward a general model of the cultural organization of social relationships. In *The relevance of models for social anthropology*. New York: Praeger, pp. 1–22.

Gordon, Deborah. 1988. Writing culture, writing feminism: The poetics and politics of experimental ethnography. *Inscriptions* 3/4: 7–26.

Gornick, Vivian, and Barbara K. Moran, eds. 1971. *Woman in sexist society: Studies in power and powerlessness*. New York: Basic Books.

Gould, Richard A. 1973. *Man's many ways: The natural history reader in anthropology*. Harper and Row.

Gould, Stephen Jay. 1977. Racism and recapitulation. In *Ever since Darwin: Reflections on natural history.* New York: Norton, pp. 214–221.

———. 1983. Science and Jewish immigration. In *Hens' teeth and horses' toes: Further reflections in natural history.* New York: Norton, pp. 291–309.

———. 1985. The Hottentot Venus. In *The flamingo's smile: Reflections in natural history.* New York: Norton, pp. 291–305.

Greer, Germaine. 1984. *Sex and destiny: The politics of human fertility.* London: Secker and Warburg.

Hammel, Eugene A., and William S. Simmons, eds. 1970. *Man makes sense: A reader in modern cultural anthropology.* Boston: Little, Brown.

Haraway, Donna. 1989. *Primate visions: Gender, race and nature in the world of modern science.* New York: Routledge.

Harris, Maria. 1989. *Dance of the spirit: The seven steps of women's spirituality.* New York: Bantam.

Hart, C. W. M., and Arnold R. Pilling. 1960. *The Tiwi of North Australia.* New York: Holt, Rinehart and Winston.

Hewitt, Nancy. 1985. Beyond the search for sisterhood: American women's history in the 1980s. *Social History* 10 (3): 299–321.

Hobsbawm, Eric, and Terence Ranger, eds. 1983. *The invention of tradition.* Cambridge: Cambridge University Press.

Holland, Dorothy, and Naomi Quinn, eds. 1987. *Cultural models in language and thought.* Cambridge: Cambridge University Press.

Horigan, Stephen. 1988. *Nature and culture in western discourses.* London: Routledge & Kegan Paul.

Howard, Jane. 1984. *Margaret Mead: A life.* New York: Simon and Shuster.

Hrdy, Sarah Blaffer. 1981. *The woman that never evolved.* Cambridge: Harvard University Press.

Hymes, Dell, ed. 1972. *Reinventing anthropology.* New York: Vintage Books.

Isaac, Glyn L. 1983. Bones in contention: Competing explanations for the juxtaposition of early Pleistocene artifacts and faunal remains. In *Animals and archeology 1: Hunters and their prey.* J. Clutton-Brock and C. Grigson, eds. Oxford: Oxford University Press, pp. 3–19.

———. 1983. The food-sharing behavior of protohuman hominids. In *Prehistoric times.* Brian Fagan, ed. New York: W. H. Freeman, pp. 56–69.

Jacoby, Russell. 1987. *The last intellectuals: American culture in the age of academe.* New York: Basic Books.

Jameson, Frederic. 1984. Postmodernism, or the cultural logic of late capitalism. *New Left Review* 146: 53–92.

Jay, Martin. 1973. *The dialectical imagination: A history of the Frankfurt school and the institute of social research, 1923–1950.* Boston: Little, Brown.

Jayawardena, Kumari. 1986. *Feminism and nationalism in the third world.* London: Zed Press.

Johnson, Patricia Lyons. 1981. When dying is better than living: Female suicide among the Gainj of Papua New Guinea. *Ethnology* 20 (4): 325–334.

Jordanova, L. J. 1980. Natural facts: A historical perspective on science and sexuality. In *Nature, culture and gender.* Carol MacCormack and Marilyn Strathern, eds. Cambridge: Cambridge University Press, pp. 42–69.

Keesing, Roger. 1985. Kwaio women speak: The micropolitics of autobiography in a

Solomon Island society. *American Anthropologist* 87 (1): 27–39.

Kishwar, Madhu, and Ruth Vanita, eds. 1984. *In search of answers: Indian women's voices from Manushi.* London: Zed Press.

Kuhn, Thomas. 1970. *The structure of scientific revolutions.* 2d ed. Chicago: University of Chicago Press.

Kuper, Adam. 1988. *The invention of primitive society: Transformations of an illusion.* London: Routledge & Kegan Paul.

Lamphere, Louise, 1974. Strategies, conflict and cooperation among women in domestic groups. In *Women, culture and society.* Michelle Zimbalist Rosaldo and Louise Lamphere, eds. Stanford: Stanford University Press.

———. 1977. Anthropology: Review essay. *Signs* 2 (3): 612–627.

———. 1985. Bringing the family to work: Women's culture on the shop floor. *Feminist Studies* 11 (3): 519–540.

———. 1987. Feminism and anthropology: The struggle to reshape our thinking about gender. In *The impact of feminist research in the academy.* Christie Farnham, ed. Bloomington: Indiana University Press, pp. 11–33.

———. 1989. *Feminist anthropology: The legacy of Elsie Clews Parsons.* Paper given at the annual meetings of the American Ethnological Society.

Leacock, Eleanor Burke. 1981. *Myths of male dominance: Collected articles.* New York: Monthly Review Press.

Lerner, Gerda. 1969. The lady and the mill girl: Changes in the status of women in the age of Jackson, 1800–1840. *American Studies* 10 (1).

Lindenbaum, Shirley. 1984. Getting the world in a family way. Review of Germaine Greer's *Sex and Destiny. New York Times Book Review* (April 29).

———. 1987. The mystification of female labors. In *Gender and kinship: Essays toward a unified analysis.* Jane Fishburne Collier and Sylvia Junko Yanagisako, eds. Stanford: Stanford University Press, pp. 221–243.

Lutz, Catherine. 1988. *Unnatural emotions: Everyday sentiments in a Micronesian atoll and their challenge to western theory.* Chicago: University of Chicago Press.

MacCormack, Carol, and Marilyn Strathern, eds. 1980. *Nature, culture and gender.* Cambridge: Cambridge University Press.

Malson, Micheline, Jean O'Barr, Sarah Westphal-Wihl, and Mary Wyer, eds. 1989. *Feminist theory in practice and process.* Chicago: University of Chicago Press.

Mannheim, Karl. 1936. *Ideology and utopia: An introduction to the sociology of knowledge.* New York: Harcourt Brace.

Marcus, George, and Dick Cushman. 1982. Ethnographies as texts. *Annual Review of Anthropology* 11: 25–69.

Marcus, George, and Michael J. Fischer. 1986. *Anthropology as cultural critique: An experimental moment in the human sciences.* Chicago: University of Chicago Press.

Martin, Emily. 1987. *The woman in the body: A cultural analysis of reproduction.* Boston: Beacon Press.

Mascia-Lees, Frances, Patricia Sharpe, and Colleen Ballerino Cohen. 1989. The postmodernist turn in anthropology: Cautions from a feminist perspective. *Signs: Journal of Women in Culture and Society* 15 (1) (Autumn): 7–33.

Marx, Karl. 1970 (1859). *A contribution to the critique of political economy.* Edited by Maurice Dobb. New York: International Publishers.

Mathieu, Nicole-Claude. 1978. Man-culture and woman-nature? *Women's Studies In-*

ternational Quarterly 1 (1).

McCloskey, Donald N. 1985. *The rhetoric of economics.* Madison: University of Wisconsin Press.

Mead, Margaret. 1928. *Coming of age in Samoa.* New York: American Museum of Natural History.

Meillassoux, Claude. 1981. *Maidens, meal and money: Capitalism and the domestic community.* Cambridge University Press.

Miles, Rosalind. 1989. *The women's history of the world.* Topsfield, Mass.: Salem House.

Mintz, Sidney. 1974. *Caribbean transformations.* Chicago: Aldine.

————. 1985. *Sweetness and power: The place of sugar in modern history.* New York: Viking.

Mintz, Sidney, and Eric Wolf. 1989 Reply to Michael Taussig. *Critique of Anthropology* 9 (1): 25–31.

Modell, Judith Schachter. 1983. *Ruth Benedict: Patterns of a life.* Philadelphia: University of Pennsylvania Press.

Moore, Henrietta L. 1988. *Feminism and anthropology.* Minneapolis: University of Minnesota Press.

Morgan, Elaine. 1972. *The descent of woman.* New York: Stein and Day.

Morgan, Robin, ed. 1970. *Sisterhood is powerful: An anthology of writings from the women's liberation movement.* New York: Vintage Books.

Morgen, Sandra. 1989. *Gender and anthropology: Critical reviews for reading and teaching.* Washington, D.C.: American Anthropological Association Press.

Mukhopadhyay, Carol C., and Patricia J. Higgins. 1988. Anthropological studies of women's status revisited: 1977–87. *Annual Review of Anthropology* 17: 461–495.

Murphy, Yolanda, and Robert. 1985. *Women of the forest.* 2d ed. New York: Columbia University Press.

Nelson, Nici. 1979. Women must help each other: The operation of personal networks among Buzaa beer brewers in Mathare Valley, Kenya. In *Women united, women divided: Comparative studies of ten contemporary cultures.* Patricia Caplan and Janet M. Bujra, eds. Bloomington: Indiana University Press, pp. 77–98.

O'Laughlin, Brigid. 1974. Mediation of contradiction: Why Mbum women do not eat chicken. In *Women, culture and society.* Michelle Zimbalist Rosaldo and Louise Lamphere, eds. Stanford: Stanford University Press, pp. 301–320.

Oakley, Ann. 1981. Interviewing women: A contradiction in terms. In *Doing feminist research.* Helen Roberts, ed. London: Routledge & Kegan Paul, pp. 30–61.

Ong, Aihwa. 1983. Global industries and Malay peasants in peninsular Malaysia. In *Women, men, and the international division of labor.* June Nash and Maria Patricia Fernandez-Kelly, eds. Albany: SUNY Press.

Ortner, Sherry. 1974. Is female to male as nature is to culture? In *Woman, culture and society.* Michelle Zimbalist Rosaldo and Louise Lamphere, eds. Stanford: Stanford University Press, pp. 67–88.

Ortner, Sherry, and Harriet Whitehead. 1981. Introduction: Accounting for sexual meanings. In *Sexual meanings: The cultural construction of gender and sexuality.* Sherry Ortner and Harriet Whitehead, eds. Cambridge: Cambridge University Press.

Paul, Lois. 1974. The mastery of work and the mystery of sex in a Guatemalan village. In *Women, culture and society.* Michelle Zimbalist Rosaldo and Louise Lamphere, eds. Stanford: Stanford University Press, pp. 281–300.

Phillips, Kevin. 1982. *Post-conservative America: People, politics and ideology in a time of crisis*. New York: Random House.

Piven, Frances Fox, and Richard A. Cloward. 1982. *The new class war: Reagan's attack on the welfare state and its consequences*. New York: Pantheon Books.

Pocock, J. G. A. 1971. *Politics, language and time: Essays in political thought and history*. New York: Atheneum.

Polier, Nicole, and William Roseberry. 1989. Tristes tropes: Post-modern anthropologists encounter the other and discover themselves. *Economy and Society* 18 (2): 245–264.

Poole, Fitz John Porter. 1981. Transforming "natural" woman: Female ritual leaders and gender ideology among Bimin-Kuskusmin. In *Sexual meanings: The cultural construction of gender and sexuality*. Sherry Ortner and Harriet Whitehead, eds. Cambridge: Cambridge University Press, pp. 80–115.

Potts, Richard, and Patricia Shipman. 1981. Cutmarks made by stone tools on bones from Olduvai Gorge, Tanzania. *Nature* 191: 577–580.

Pratt, Mary Louise. 1986. Fieldwork in common places. In *Writing culture: The poetics and politics of ethnography*. James Clifford and George E. Marcus, eds. Berkeley, Los Angeles, London: University of California Press, pp. 27–50. *[shostack]*

Quinn, Naomi. 1977. Anthropological studies on women's status. *Annual Review of Anthropology* 6: 181–225.

———. 1986. Comments, panel on "Speaking women: Representations of contemporary American femininity," Annual Meetings of the American Anthropological Association, Philadelphia, December 5. *Embeddeness*

Rabinow, Paul. 1986. Representations are social facts. In *Writing culture: The poetics and politics of ethnography*. James Clifford and George E. Marcus, eds. Berkeley: University of California Press, pp. 234–261.

Rabinow, Paul, and William M. Sullivan, eds. 1979. *Interpretive social science: A reader*. Berkeley, Los Angeles, London: University of California Press.

Rabuzzi, Kathryn Allen. 1988. *Motherself: A mythic analysis of motherhood*. Bloomington: Indiana University Press.

Radcliffe-Brown, A. R. 1965. *Structure and function in primitive society*. New York: Free Press.

Rapp, Rayna. 1977. The search for origins. *Critique of Anthropology* 9/10: 5–24.

———. 1979. Anthropology: Review essay. *Signs* 4 (3): 497–513. *R*

———. 1987. Toward a nuclear freeze? The gender politics of Euro-American kinship analysis. In *Gender and kinship: Essays toward a unified analysis*. Jane Fishburne Collier and Sylvia Junko Yanagisako, eds. Stanford: Stanford University Press, pp. 119–131.

Reiter, Rayna Rapp, ed. 1975. *Toward an anthropology of women*. New York: Monthly Review Press, pp. 11–19.

Richard, Alison F. 1985. *Primates in nature*. New York: W. H. Freeman.

Rogers, Susan Carol. 1975. Female forms of power and the myth of male dominance: A model of female-male interaction in peasant society. *American Ethnologist* 2: 727–756.

———. 1978. Woman's place: A critical review of anthropological theory. *Comparative Studies in Society and History*.

Rosaldo, Michelle Zimbalist. 1980. The use and abuse of anthropology: Reflections on cross-cultural understanding. *Signs* 5 (3): 389–417.

————. 1974. Women, culture and society: A theoretical overview. In *Women, culture and society*. Michelle Zimbalist Rosaldo and Louise Lamphere, eds. Stanford: Stanford University Press, pp. 67–88.

Rosaldo, Michelle, and Louise Lamphere, eds. 1974. *Women, culture and society*. Stanford: Stanford University Press.

Roseberry, William. 1988. Political economy. *Annual Review of Anthropology* 17: 161–185.

Roseberry, William, and Jay O'Brien, eds. 1991. *Golden ages, dark ages: Imagining the past in anthropology and history*. Berkeley, Los Angeles, Oxford: University of California Press.

Rosenberg, Rosalind. 1982. *Beyond separate spheres. Intellectual roots of modern feminism*. New Haven: Yale University Press.

Rowell, Thelma. 1972. *The social behavior of monkeys*. London: Penguin Books.

Rubbo, Anna. 1975. The spread of capitalism in rural Colombia: Effects on poor women. In *Toward an anthropology of women*. Rayna Rapp Reiter, ed. New York: Monthly Review Press, pp. 333–357.

Rubin, Gayle. 1975. The traffic in women: Notes on a "political economy" of sex. In *Toward an anthropology of women*. Rayna Rapp Reiter, ed. New York: Monthly Review Press, pp. 157–210.

Ryan, Mary. 1979. *Womanhood in America: From colonial times to the present*. 2d ed. New York: Franklin Watts.

Sacks, Karen. 1974. Engels revisited: Women, the organization of production, and private property. In *Women, culture and society*. Michelle Zimbalist Rosaldo and Louise Lamphere, eds. Stanford: Stanford University Press, pp. 207–222.

Sahlins, Marshall. 1976. *The use and abuse of biology: An anthropological critique of sociobiology*. Ann Arbor: University of Michigan Press.

Said, Edward W. 1978. *Orientalism*. New York: Random House.

Sanjek, Roger. 1982. The AAA resolution on the employment of women: Genesis, implementation, disavowal and resurrection. *Signs* 7 (4): 845–868.

Sayers, Janet. 1982. *Biological politics: Feminist and antifeminist perspectives*. New York: Tavistock.

Schneider, Jane, and Peter Schneider. 1976. *Culture and political economy in western Sicily*. New York: Academic Press.

Schrire, Carmel. 1980. An inquiry into the evolutionary status and apparent identity of San hunter-gatherers. *Human Ecology* 8 (1): 9–32.

Scott, Joan. 1988. *Gender and the politics of history*. New York: Columbia University Press.

Seager, Joni, and Ann Olsen. 1986. *Women in the world: An international atlas*. New York: Simon and Schuster.

Shapiro, Judith. 1976. Sexual hierarchy among the Yanomama. In *Sex and class in Latin America*. June Nash and Helen I. Safa, eds. New York: Praeger.

Shipman, Patricia. 1983. Early hominid lifestyle: Hunting and gathering or foraging and scavenging? In *Animals and archeology 1: Hunters and their prey*. J. Clutton-Brock and C. Grigson, eds. Oxford: Oxford University Press.

Shostak, Marjorie. 1981. *Nisa: The life and words of a !Kung woman*. Cambridge: Harvard University Press.

Siskind, Janet. 1973. *To hunt in the morning*. London: Oxford University Press.

Slocum Sally. 1975. Woman the gatherer: Male bias in anthropology. In *Toward an anthropology of women*. Rayna Rapp Reiter, ed. New York: Monthly Review Press, pp. 36–50.

Smith, Mary. 1981. *Baba of Karo: A woman of the Muslim Hausa*. New Haven: Yale University Press.

Stacey, Judith. 1988. Can there be a feminist ethnography? *Women's Studies International Forum* 11 (1): 21–27.

Stacey, Judith, and Barrie Thorne. 1985. The missing feminist revolution in sociology. *Social Problems* 34 (4): 301–316.

Stack, Carol. 1974. *All our kin: Strategies for survival in a black community*. New York: Harper and Row.

Stack, Carol, et al. 1975. Anthropology: Review essay. *Signs* 1 (1): 147–160.

Stocking, George. 1982. *Race, culture and evolution: Essays in the history of anthropology*. 2d ed. Chicago: University of Chicago Press.

———. 1987. *Victorian anthropology*. New York: The Free Press.

Strathern, Marilyn. 1972. *Women in between: Female roles in a male world: Mount Hagen, New Guinea*. London: Seminar Press.

———. 1981. Culture in a netbag: The manufacture of a subdiscipline in anthropology. *Man* 16: 665–688.

Strathern, Marilyn, ed. 1987. Dealing with inequality: Analysing gender relations in Melanesia and beyond. Cambridge: Cambridge University Press.

———. 1987. An awkward relationship: The case of feminism and anthropology. *Signs* 12 (2): 276–292.

———. 1988. The gender of the gift: Problems with women and problems with society in Melanesia. Berkeley, Los Angeles, London: University of California Press.

Tanner, Nancy, and Adrienne Zihlman. 1976. Women in evolution, part one: Innovation and selection in human origins. *Signs* 1 (3): 585–608.

Taussig, Michael. 1989. History as commodity in some recent American (anthropological) literature. *Critique of Anthropology* 9 (1): 7–23.

Thompson, E. P. 1963. The making of the English working class. New York: Random House.

———. 1978. The poverty of theory and other essays. New York: Monthly Review Press.

Trautmann, Thomas R. 1987. *Lewis Henry Morgan and the invention of kinship*. Berkeley, Los Angeles, London: University of California Press.

Tyler, Stephen A., ed. 1969. *Cognitive anthropology*. New York: W. H. Freeman.

———. 1986. Post-modern ethnography: From document of the occult to occult document. In *Writing culture: The poetics and politics of ethnography*. James Clifford and George E. Marcus, eds. Berkeley, Los Angeles, London: University of California Press, pp. 122–140.

Vincent, Joan. 1986. System and process, 1974–1985. *Annual Review of Anthropology* 15: 99–119.

Visweswaren, Kamala. 1988. Defining feminist ethnography. *Inscriptions* 3/4: 27–46.

Webster, Paula. 1975. Matriarchy: A vision of power. In *Toward an anthropology of women*. Rayna Rapp Reiter, ed. New York: Monthly Review Press, pp. 141–156.

Weiner, Annette. 1976. *Women of value, men of renown*. Austin: University of Texas Press.

White, Hayden. 1978. *Tropics of discourse: Essays in cultural criticism*. Baltimore: Johns Hopkins University Press.

Whitehead, Ann. 1981. "I'm hungry, mum": The politics of domestic budgeting. In *Of marriage and the market: Women's subordination internationally and its lessons*. Kate Young, et al., eds. London: Routledge & Kegan Paul, pp. 93–116.

Williams, Brett. 1988. *Upscaling downtown: Stalled gentrification in Washington, D.C.* Ithaca: Cornell University Press.

Williams, Raymond. 1980. Base and superstructure in Marxist cultural theory. In *Problems in materialism and culture*. London: Verso, pp. 31–49.

Wilson, E. O. 1975. *Sociobiology*. Cambridge: Harvard University Press.

Wolf, Eric. 1959. *Sons of the shaking earth*. Chicago: University of Chicago Press.

————. 1969. *Peasant wars of the twentieth century*. New York: Harper and Row.

————. 1982. *Europe and the people without history*. Berkeley, Los Angeles, London: University of California Press.

Wolf, Margery. 1968. *The house of Lim: A study of a Chinese farm family*. New York: Appleton-Century-Crofts.

————. 1974. Chinese women: Old skills in a new context. In *Women, culture, and society*. Michelle Rosaldo and Louise Lamphere, eds. Stanford: Stanford University Press, pp. 157–172.

Yanagisako, Sylvia Junko. 1979. Family and household: The analysis of domestic groups. *Annual Review of Anthropology* 8: 161–205.

Yanagisako, Sylvia, and Jane Fishburne Collier. 1987. Toward a unified analysis of gender and kinship. In *Gender and kinship: Essays toward a unified analysis*. Jane Fishburne Collier and Sylvia Junko Yanagisako, eds. Stanford: Stanford University Press, pp. 14–50.

Young, Kate, Carol Wolkowitz, and Roslyn McCullagh, eds. 1981. *Of marriage and the market: Women's subordination internationally and its lessons*. London: Routledge & Kegan Paul.

Zihlman, Adrienne. 1978. Women in evolution, part two: Subsistence and social organization among early hominids. *Signs* 4 (1): 4–20.

PART ONE

Gender in Colonial History and Anthropological Discourse

ONE

Carnal Knowledge and Imperial Power
Gender, Race, and Morality in Colonial Asia

Ann Laura Stoler

Over the last fifteen years the anthropology of women has fundamentally altered our understanding of colonial expansion and its consequences for the colonized. In identifying how European conquest affected valuations of women's work and redefined their proper domains, we have sought to explain how changes in household organization, the sexual division of labor, and the gender-specific control of resources within it have modified and shaped how colonial appropriations of land, labor, and resources were obtained.[1] Much of this research has focused on indigenous gendered patterns of economic activity, political participation, and social knowledge, on the agency of those confronted with European rule—but less on the distinct agency of those women and men who carried it out.

More recent attention to the structures of colonial authority has placed new emphasis on the quotidian assertion of European dominance in the colonies, on imperial interventions in domestic life, and thus on the cultural prescriptions by which European women and men lived (Callan and Ardener 1984; Knibiehler and Goutalier 1985, 1987; Callaway 1987; Strobel 1987). Having focused on how colonizers have viewed the indigenous Other, we are beginning to sort out how Europeans in the colonies imagined themselves and constructed communities built on asymmetries of race, class, and gender—entities significantly at odds with the European models on which they were drawn.

Feminist attempts to engage the gender politics of Dutch, French, and British imperial cultures converge on some strikingly similar observations; namely that European women in these colonies experienced the cleavages of racial dominance and internal social distinctions very differently than men precisely because of their ambiguous positions, as both subordinates in colonial hierarchies and as active agents of imperial culture in their own right

(Callan and Ardener 1984; Knibiehler and Goutalier 1985; Reijs et al. 1986; Callaway 1987). Concomitantly, the majority of European women who left for the colonies in the late nineteenth and early twentieth centuries confronted profoundly rigid restrictions on their domestic, economic, and political options, more limiting than those of metropolitan Europe at the time and sharply constrasting with the opportunities open to colonial men.[2]

In one form or another these studies raise a basic question: in what ways were gender inequalities essential to the structure of colonial racism and imperial authority? Was the strident misogyny of imperial thinkers and colonial agents a by-product of received metropolitan values ("they just brought it with them"), a reaction to contemporary feminist demands in Europe ("women need to be put back in their breeding place"), or a novel and pragmatic response to the conditions of conquest? Was the assertion of European supremacy in terms of patriotic manhood and racial virility an expression of imperial domination or a defining feature of it?

In this chapter I explore some of the ways in which imperial authority and racial distinctions were fundamentally structured in gendered terms. I look specifically at the administrative and medical discourse and management of European sexual activity, reproduction and marriage as it articulated with the politics of colonial rule. In this initial effort I focus primarily on the dominant male discourse (and less on women's perceptions of those constraints), on the evidence that it was the way in which women's needs were defined, not *by*, but *for* them which most directly accounted for specific policies.[3]

Focusing on French Indochina and the Dutch East Indies in the early twentieth century but drawing on other contexts, I suggest that the very categories of "colonizer" and "colonized" were secured through forms of sexual control that defined the domestic arrangements of Europeans and the cultural investments by which they identified themselves. In treating the sexual and conjugal tensions of colonial life as more than a political trope for the tensions of empire writ small, but as a part of the latter in socially profound and strategic ways, I examine how gender-specific sexual sanctions and prohibitions not only demarcated positions of power but prescribed the personal and public boundaries of race.

Colonial authority was constructed on two powerful but false premises. The first was the notion that Europeans in the colonies made up an easily identifiable and discrete biological and social entity; a "natural" community of common class interests, racial attributes, political affinities, and superior culture. The second was the related notion that the boundaries separating colonizer from colonized were thus self-evident and easily drawn (Stoler 1989). Neither premise reflected colonial realities. Settler colonies such as those in Rhodesia and Algeria excepted—where inter-European conflicts were violent and overt—tensions between bureaucrats and planters, settlers and transients, missionaries and metropolitan policy makers, *petits blancs* (lower-class whites), and monied entrepreneurs have always made Euro-colonial communities more socially fractious and politically fragile than many of their members professed (see, e.g. Cooper 1980; Drooglever 1980; Ridley 1981; Comaroff and Comaroff 1986; Kennedy 1987; Prochaska, 1989). Internal divisions developed out of competing economic and political agendas—conflicts over access to indigenous resources, frictions over appropriate methods for safeguarding European privilege and power, competing criteria for reproducing a colonial elite and for restricting its membership.

The shift away from viewing colonial elites as homogenous communities of common interest marks an important trajectory in the anthropology of empire, signaling a major rethinking of gender relations within it. The markers of European identity and the criteria for community membership no longer appear as fixed but emerge as a more obviously fluid, permeable, and historically disputed terrain. The colonial politics of exclusion was contingent on constructing categories. Colonial control was predicated on identifying who was "white," who was "native," and which children could become citizens rather than subjects, designating who were legitimate progeny and who were not.

What mattered was not only one's physical properties but who counted as "European" and by what measure.[4] Skin shade was too ambiguous; bank accounts were mercurial; religious belief and education were crucial but never completely sufficient. Social and legal standing derived from the cultural prism through which color was viewed, from the silences, acknowledgments, and denials of the social circumstances in which one's parents had sex. Sexual unions based on concubinage, prostitution, or church marriage derived from the hierarchies of rule; but in turn, they were negotiated relations, contested classifications, which altered individual fates and the very structure of colonial society (Martinez-Alier 1974; Ming 1983; Taylor 1983). Ultimately inclusion or exclusion required regulating the sexual, conjugal, and domestic life of *both* Europeans in the colonies and their colonized subjects.

POLITICAL MESSAGES AND SEXUAL METAPHORS

Colonial observers and participants in the imperial enterprise appear to have had unlimited interest in the sexual interface of the colonial encounter. Probably no subject is discussed more than sex in colonial literature and no subject more frequently invoked to foster the racist stereotypes of European society (Pujarniscle 1931: 106; Loutfi 1971: 36). The tropics provided a site of European pornographic fantasies long before conquest was underway with lurid descriptions of sexual license, promiscuity, gynecological aberrations, and general perversion marking the Otherness of the colonized for metropolitan consumption (Loutfi 1971; Gilman 1985: 79).[5] Given the rigid sexual protocols of nineteenth-century Europe some colonial historians have gone so far as to suggest that imperial expansion itself was derived from the export of male sexual energy (Hyam 1986b) or at the very least "a sublimation or alternative to sex [for European men]" (Gann and Duignan 1978: 240). The more important point, however, is that with the sustained presence of Europeans in the colonies, sexual prescriptions by class, race, and gender became increasingly central to the politics of empire and subject to new forms of scrutiny by colonial states.

The salience of sexual symbols as graphic representations of colonial dominance is relatively unambiguous and well-established. Edward Said, for example, argues that the sexual submission and possession of Oriental women by European men "fairly *stands for* the pattern of relative strength between East and West, and the discourse about the Orient that it enabled" (1978: 6, my emphasis). He describes Orientalism as a "male perception of the world," "a male power-fantasy," "an exclusively male province," in which the Orient is penetrated, silenced, and possessed (1978: 207). Sexuality, then, serves as a loaded metaphor for domination, but Said's critique is not (nor does it claim to be) about those relations between women and men. Sexual images illustrate the iconography of rule, not its pragmatics. Sexual asymmetries and visions convey what is "really" going on elsewhere, at another political epicenter. They are tropes to depict other centers of power.

If Asian women are centerfold to the imperial voyeur, European women often appear in male colonial writings only as a reverse image—insofar as they do not fulfill the power fantasies of European men.[6] Whether portrayed as paragons of morality or as parasitic and passive actors on the imperial stage, these women are rarely the object of European male desire (Loutfi 1971: 108–109). In assuming that European men and women participated equally in the prejudices and pleasures which colonial privilege bestowed upon them, such formulations obscure the fact that European women engaged in the construction and consequences of imperial power in ways that imposed fundamentally different restrictions on them.

Sexual domination has been carefully considered as a discursive symbol, instrumental in the conveyance of other meanings, but has been less often treated as the substance of imperial policy. Was sexual dominance, then, merely a graphic substantiation of who was, so to speak, on the bottom and who was on the top? Was the medium the message, or did sexual relations always "mean" something else, stand in for other relations, evoke the sense of *other* (pecuniary, political, or some possibly more subliminal) desires? This analytic slippage between the sexual symbols of power and the politics of sex runs throughout the colonial record—as well as through contemporary commentaries on it. Some of this may be due to the polyvalent quality of sexuality; symbolically rich and socially salient at the same time. But sexual control was more than a convenient metaphor for colonial domination; it was, as I argue here, a fundamental class and racial marker implicated in a wider set of relations of power.

Kenneth Ballhatchet's work on Victorian India points in a similar direction (1980). By showing that regulations on sexual access, prostitution, and venereal disease were central to segregationist policy, he links issues of sexual management to the internal structure of British rule. He convincingly argues that it was through the policing of sex that subordinate European military and civil servants were kept in line and that racial boundaries were thus maintained. This study then is about the relations of power between men and men; it has little to say about constraints on European colonial women since its emphasis is not on the relations of power between women and men.

As a critical interface of sexuality and the wider political order, the relationship between gender prescriptions and racial boundaries is a subject that still remains unevenly unexplored. Recent work on the oral history of colonial women, for example, shows clearly that European women of different classes experienced the colonial venture very differently from one another and from men, but we still know relatively little about the distinct investments they had in a racism they shared (Van Helten and Williams 1983; Knibiehler and Goutalier 1985; Callaway 1987; Strobel 1987).

In confronting some of these issues, feminists investigating colonial situations have taken a new turn, relating the real-life conditions of European and colonized women to imperial mentalities and to the cultural artifices of rule. Such efforts to sort out the distinct colonial experience of European women examine how they were incorporated into, resisted, and affected the politics of their men (Taylor 1983; Knibiehler and Goutalier 1985; Callan and Ardener 1984; Callaway 1987). Studies showing the intervention of state, business, and religious institutions in indigenous strategies of biological and social reproduction are now coupled with those that examine the work of European women in these programs, the influence of European welfare programs on colonial medicine, and the reproductive constraints on colonial women themselves (Knibiehler and Goutalier 1985; Hunt 1988).

Most of these contributions have attended to the broader issue of gender ideologies and colonial authority, not specifically to how sexual control has figured in the fixing of racial boundaries per se. Although feminist research across disciplines has increasingly explored the "social embeddedness of sexuality," and the contexts that "condition, constrain and socially define [sexual] acts" (Ross and Rapp 1980: 54), this emphasis has not been dominant in feminist studies of empire, nor has it refocused attention on the *racial* "embeddedness of sexuality" in colonial contexts as one might expect. Important exceptions include recent work on Southern Africa where changing restrictions on colonial prostitution and domestic service were explicitly class-specific and directly tied racial policy to sexual control (Gaitskell 1983; Van Heyningen 1984; Schmidt 1987; Hansen 1989; White 1990; also see Ming 1983 and Hesselink 1987 for the Indies, and Engels 1983 for India).

The linkage between sexual control and racial tensions is both obvious and elusive at the same time. Although we can accept Ronald Takaki's (1977) assertion that sexual fear in nineteenth-century America was at base a racial anxiety, we are still left to understand why it is through sexuality that such anxieties are expressed. Winthrop Jordan contends that in the nineteenth-century American South, "the sex act itself served as a ritualistic re-enactment of the daily pattern of social dominance" (1968: 141). More generally, Sander Gilman (1985) argues that sexuality is the most salient marker of Otherness and therefore figures in *any* racist ideology; like skin color, "sexual structures such as the shape of the genitalia, are always the antithesis of the idealized self's" (ibid., 25). If sexuality organically represents racial difference as Gilman claims, then we should not be surprised that colonial agents and colonized subjects expressed their contests—and vulnerabilities—in these terms.

This notion of sexuality as a core aspect of social identity has figured importantly in analyses of the psychological motivation and conseqences of colonial rule (Mannoni 1956; Fanon 1967; Nandy 1983). In this focus, sexual submission substantiates colonial racism, imposing essential limits on personal liberation. Notably, among colonized male authors, questions of virility and definitions of manliness are politically centerstage. The demasculinization of colonized men and the hypermasculinity of European males represent principal assertions of white supremacy. But these studies are about the psychological salience of women and sex in the subordination of men by men. They only incidentally deal with sex*ism* and racism as well as racism and sex.[7]

An overlapping set of discourses have provided the psychological and economic underpinnings for colonial distinctions of difference, linking fears of sexual contamination, physical danger, climatic incompatability, and moral breakdown to a European national identity with a racist and class-specific core. In colonial scientific reports and the popular press we repeatedly come across statements varying on a common theme: "native women bear contagions"; "white women become sterile in the colonies"; "colonial men are susceptible to physical, moral and mental degeneration when they remain in the tropics too long." To what degree are these statements medically or politically grounded? We need to unpack what is metaphor, what is perceived as dangerous (is it disease, culture, climate, or sex?), and what is not.

In the sections that follow I look at the relationship between the domestic arrangements of colonial communities and their wider political structures. Part I draws on colonization debates over a broad period (sixteenth–

twentieth c.) in an effort to identify the long-term intervention of colonial authorities in issues of "racial mixing," settlement schemes, and sexual control. In examining debates over European family formation, over the relationship between subversion and sex, I look at how evaluations of concubinage, and of morality more generally, changed with new forms of racism and new gender-specific expressions of them.

Part II treats the protection and policing of European women within the changing politics of empire. It traces how accusations of sexual assault related to new demands for political rights and restricted demarcations of social space in response to them. Part III examines what I call the "cultural hygiene" of colonialism. Taking the early twentieth century as a breakpoint, I take up the convergent metropolitan and colonial discourses on health hazards in the tropics, race-thinking, and social reform as they related to shifts in the rationalization of rule. In tracing how fears of "racial degeneracy" were grounded in class-specific sexual norms, I return to how and why racial difference was constituted and culturally coded in gendered terms.

PART I: SEX AND OTHER CATEGORIES OF COLONIAL CONTROL

> Though sex cannot of itself enable men to transcend racial barriers, it generates some admiration and affection across them, which is healthy, and which cannot always be dismissed as merely self-interested and prudential. On the whole, sexual interaction between Europeans and non-Europeans probably did more good than harm to race relations; at any rate, I cannot accept the feminist contention that it was fundamentally undesirable. (Hyam 1986a: 75)

The regulation of sexual relations was central to the development of particular kinds of colonial settlements and to the allocation of economic activity within them. Who bedded and wedded with whom in the colonies of France, England, Holland, and Iberia was never left to chance. Unions between Annamite women and French men, between Portuguese women and Dutch men, between Spanish men and Inca women produced offspring with claims to privilege, whose rights and status had to be determined and prescribed. From the early 1600s through the twentieth century the sexual sanctions and conjugal prohibitions of colonial agents were rigorously debated and carefully codified. It is in these debates over matrimony and morality that trading and plantation company officials, missionaries, investment bankers, military high commands, and agents of the colonial state confronted one another's visions of empire, and the settlement patterns on which it would rest.

In 1622 the Dutch East Indies Company (VOC) arranged for the transport of six poor but marriageable young Dutch women to Java, providing them with clothing, a dowry upon marriage, and a contract binding them to five years in the Indies (Taylor 1983: 12). Aside from this and one other short-lived experiment, immigration of European women to the East was consciously restricted for the next two hundred years. VOC shareholders argued against female emigration on several counts: the high cost of transporting married women and daughters (Blussé 1986: 161); the possibility that Dutch women (with stronger ties than men to the Netherlands?) might hinder permanent settlement by goading their burgher husbands to quickly lucrative but nefarious trade, and then repatriate to display their newfound wealth (Taylor 1983: 14); the fear that Dutch women would enrich themselves through private trade and encroach on the company's monopoly;[8] and the prediction that their children would be sickly and force families to repatriate, ultimately depleting the colony of permanent and loyal settlers (Taylor 1983: 14).

The Dutch East Indies Company enforced the sanction against female migration by selecting bachelors as their European recruits and by promoting both extramarital relations and legal unions between low-ranking employees and imported slave women (Taylor 1983: 16).[9] Although there were Euro-Asian marriages, government regulations made concubinage a more attractive option by prohibiting European men with native wives and children from returning to Holland (Ming 1983: 69; Taylor 1983: 16; Blussé 1986: 173). The VOC saw households based on Euro-Asian unions, by contrast, as having distinct advantages; individual employees would bear the costs of dependents; children of mixed unions were considered stronger and healthier; and Asian women made fewer demands. Finally, it was thought that men would be more likely to settle permanently by establishing families with local roots.

Concubinage served colonial interests in other ways. It permitted permanent settlement and rapid growth by a cheaper means than the importation of European women. Salaries of European recruits to the colonial armies, bureaucracies, plantation companies, and trading enterprises were kept artificially low. This was possible not only because the transport of European women and family support was thereby eliminated, as was often argued, but because local women provided domestic services for which new European recruits would otherwise have had to pay. In the mid-nineteenth century, such arrangements were de rigueur for young civil servants intent on setting up households on their own (Ritter 1856: 21). Despite clerical opposition (the church never attained a secure and independent foothold in the Indies), by the nineteenth century concubinage was the most prevalent living arrangement for European men (van Marle 1952: 485). Nearly half of the Indies' European male population in the 1880s was unmarried and living with Asian women (Ming 1983: 70). It was only in the early twentieth century that concubinage was politically condemned (van Marle 1952: 486).

The administrative arguments from the 1600s invoked to curb the immigration of European women, on the one hand, and to condone sexual access to indigenous women, on the other, bear striking resemblance to the sexual politics of colonial capitalism three centuries later. Referred to as *nyai* in Java and Sumatra, *congai* in Indochina, and *petite épouse* throughout the French empire, the colonized woman living as a concubine to a European man formed the dominant domestic arrangement in colonial cultures through the early twentieth century. Unlike prostitution, which could and often did result in a population of syphilitic and therefore nonproductive European men, concubinage was considered to have a stabilizing influence on political order and colonial health—a relationship that kept men in their barracks and bungalows, out of brothels and less inclined to "unnatural" liaisons with one another.[10]

In Asia and Africa corporate and government decision-makers invoked the social services that local women supplied as "useful guides to the language and other mysteries of the local societies" (Malleret 1934: 216; Cohen 1971: 122). The medical and cultural know-how of local women was credited with keeping many European men alive in their initial confrontation with tropical life (Braconier 1933). Handbooks for incoming plantation employees bound for Tonkin, Sumatra, and Malaya urged men to find a bed-servant as a prerequisite to quick acclimatization (Nieuwenhuys 1959: 19; Dixon 1913: 77). In Malaysia, commercial companies encouraged the procurement of local "companions" for psychological and physical well-being; to protect European staff from the ill-health that sexual abstention, isolation, and boredom were thought to bring (Butcher 1979: 200, 202).[11] Even in the British empire, where the colonial office officially banned concubinage in 1910, it was tacitly condoned and practiced long after (Hyam 1986b; Callaway 1987: 49; Kennedy 1987: 175). In the Indies a simultaneous sanction against concubinage among civil servants was only selectively enforced; it had little effect on domestic arrangements outside of Java and no perceptible impact on the European households in Sumatra's newly opened plantation belt where Javanese and Japanese *huishoudsters* (as Asian mistresses were sometimes called) remained the rule rather than the exception (Clerkx 1961: 87–93; Stoler 1985a: 31–34; Lucas 1986: 84).

Concubinage was a contemporary term which referred to the cohabitation outside of marriage between European men and Asian women. In fact, it glossed a wide range of arrangements that included sexual access to a non-European woman as well as demands on her labor and legal rights to the children she bore. Thus, to define concubinage as cohabitation perhaps suggests more social privileges than most women who were involved in such relations enjoyed.[12] Many colonized women combined sexual and domestic service within the abjectly subordinate contexts of slave or "coolie" and lived in separate quarters. On the plantations in East Sumatra, for example, where such arrangements were structured into company policies of labor control,

Javanese women picked from the coolie ranks often retained their original labor contracts for the duration of their sexual and domestic service (Lucas 1986: 186).

Although most of these Javanese women remained as servants, sharing only the beds of European staff, many *nyai* elsewhere in the Indies combined their service with some degree of limited authority. Working for wealthier men, these *huishoudsters* managed the businesses as well as the servants and household affairs of European men (Nieuwenhuys 1959: 17; Lucas 1986: 86; Taylor 1983).[13] Native women (like European-born women in a later period) were to keep men physically and psychologically fit for work, that is, marginally content without distracting them or urging them out of line (Chivas-Baron 1929: 103). Live-in companions, especially in remote districts and plantation areas, thus met the daily needs of low-ranking European employees without the emotional, temporal, and financial requirements that European family life were thought to demand.[14]

To say that concubinage reinforced the hierarchies on which colonial societies were based is not to say that it did not make those distinctions more problematic at the same time. In the first place, in such regions as North Sumatra grossly uneven sex ratios often made for intense competition among male workers and their European supervisors for indigenous women. *Vrouwen perkara* (disputes over women) resulted in assaults on whites, new labor tensions, and dangerous incursions into the standards deemed essential for white prestige (Stoler 1985a: 33; Lucas 1986: 90–91). In the Netherlands Indies, more generally, an unaccounted number of impoverished Indo-European women, moving between prostitution and concubinage, disturbed the racial sensibilities of the Dutch-born elite (Hesselink 1987: 216). Metropolitan critics were particularly disdainful of these liaisons on moral grounds—all the more so when these unions *were* sustained and emotionally significant relationships, thereby contradicting the racial premise of concubinage as an emotionally unfettered convenience.[15] But perhaps most important, the tension between concubinage as a confirmation and compromise of racial hierarchy was realized in the progeny that it produced, "mixed bloods," poor "Indos," and abandoned *métis* children who straddled the divisions of ruler and ruled and threatened to blur the colonial divide. These *voorkinderen* (literally, "children from a previous marriage/union," but in this colonial context usually marking illegitimate children from a previous union with a non-European woman) were economically disadvantaged by their ambiguous social status and often grew up to join the ranks of the impoverished whites (Nieuwenhuys 1959: 21).

Concubinage was a domestic arrangement based on sexual service and gender inequalities which "worked" as long as European identity and supremacy were clear. When either was thought to be vulnerable, in jeopardy, or less than convincing, at the turn of the century and increasingly through the 1920s, colonial elites responded by clarifying the cultural criteria of privilege and the moral premises of their unity. Structured sex in the politically safe context of prostitution, and where possible in the more desirable context of marriage between "full-blooded" Europeans, replaced concubinage (Taylor 1977: 29). As in other colonial contexts as we shall see, the ban on concubinage was not always expressed in boldly racist language; on the contrary, difference and distance were often coded to mark race in culturally clear but nuanced terms.[16]

RESTRICTIONS ON EUROPEAN WOMEN IN THE COLONIES

Colonial governments and private business not only tolerated concubinage but actively encouraged it—principally by restricting the emigration of European women to the colonies and by refusing employment to married male European recruits. Although most accounts of colonial conquest and settlement suggest that European women chose to avoid early pioneering ventures, the choice was rarely their own (cf. Fredrickson 1981: 109). In the Indies, a government ordinance of 1872 made it impossible for any soldier below the rank of sergeant major to be married; and even above that rank, conditions were very restrictive (Ming 1983: 70). In the Indies army, marriage was a privilege of the officer corps, whereas barrack-concubinage was instituted and regulated for the rank and file. In the twentieth century, formal and informal prohibitions set by banks, estates, and government services operating in Africa, India, and Southeast Asia restricted marriage during the first three to five years of service, while some simply prohibited it altogether. In Malaya, the major British banks required their employees to sign contracts agreeing to request prior permission to marry, with the understanding that it would not be granted in fewer than eight years (Butcher 1979: 138).

Many historians assume that these bans on employee marriage and on the emigration of European women lifted when specific colonies were politically stable, medically upgraded, and economically secure. In fact marriage restrictions lasted well into the twentieth century, long after rough living and a scarcity of amenities had become conditions of the past. In India as late as 1929, British employees in the political service were still recruited at the age of twenty-six and then prohibited from marriage during their first three probationary years (Moore-Gilbert 1986: 48). In the army, marriage allowances were also denied until the same age, while in the commercial houses restrictions were frequent but less overt (ibid.: 48; Woodcock 1969: 164). On the Ivory Coast, employment contracts in the 1920s also denied marriage with European women before the third tour, which meant a minimum of five years' service, so that many men remained unmarried past the age of thirty (Tirefort 1979: 134).[17]

European demographics in the colonies were shaped by these economic and political exigencies and thus were enormously skewed by sex. Among the laboring immigrant and native populations as well as among Europeans in the late-nineteenth and early twentieth centuries, the number of men was, at the very least, double that of women, and sometimes exceeded the latter by twenty-five times. Although in the Netherlands Indies, the overall ratio of European women to men rose from 47:100 to 88:100 between 1900 and 1930, representing an absolute increase from 4,000 to 26,000 Dutch women (Taylor 1983: 128), in outlying islands such as Sumatra the ratios were kept far more uneven. Thus on Sumatra's plantation belt in 1920 there were still only 61 European women per 100 men (*Koloniale Verslag* quoted in Lucas 1986: 82). On Africa's Ivory Coast, European sex ratios through 1921 were still 1:25 (Tirefort 1979: 31). In Tonkin, European men sharply outnumbered European women as late as 1931 when there were 14,085 European men (including military) to 3,083 European women (Gantes 1981: 138). While these imbalances are most frequently attributed to the physical hazards of life in the tropics, there are political explanations that are more compelling. In controlling the availability of European women and the sorts of sexual access allowed, colonial state and corporate authorities avoided salary increases as well as the proliferation of a lower-class European settler population. Such policies in no way muted the internal class distinctions within the European communities; they simply shaped the social geography of the colonies by fixing the conditions under which European privileges could be attained and reproduced.

SEX, SUBVERSION AND WHITE PRESTIGE: A CASE FROM NORTH SUMATRA

The marriage prohibition was both a political and economic issue, defining the social contours of colonial communities and the standards of living within them (Butcher 1979). But, as importantly, it revealed how deeply the conduct of private life and the sexual proclivities individuals expressed were tied to corporate profits and the security of the colonial state. Nowhere was the connection between sex and subversion more openly contested than in North Sumatra in the early 1900s. Irregular domestic arrangments were thought to encourage subversion as strongly as acceptable unions could avert it. Family stability and sexual "normalcy" were thus linked to political agitation or quiescence in very concrete ways.

Since the late nineteenth century, the major North Sumatran tobacco and rubber companies had neither accepted married applicants nor allowed them to take wives while in service (Schoevers 1913: 38; Clerkx 1961: 31–34). Company authorities argued that new employees with families in tow would be a financial burden, risking the emergence of a "European proletariat" and thus a major threat to white prestige (*Kroniek 1917*: 50; *Sumatra Post* 1913).

Low-ranking plantation employees protested against these company marriage restrictions, an issue that mobilized their ranks behind a broad set of demands (Stoler 1989a: 144). Under employee pressure, the prohibition was relaxed to a marriage ban for the first five years of service. This restriction, however, was never placed on everyone; it was pegged to salaries and dependent on the services of local women that kept the living costs and wages of subordinate and incoming staff artificially low.

Domestic arrangements thus varied as government officials and private businesses weighed the economic versus political costs of one arrangement over another, but such calculations were invariably meshed. Europeans in high office saw white prestige and profits as inextricably linked, and attitudes toward concubinage reflected that concern (Brownfoot 1984: 191). Thus in Malaya through the 1920s, concubinage was tolerated precisely because "poor whites" were not. Government and plantation administrators argued that white prestige would be imperiled if European men became impoverished in attempting to maintain middle-class life-styles and European wives. Colonial morality and the place of concubinage in it was relative, given the "particular anathema with which the British regarded 'poor whites'" (Butcher 1979: 26). In late-nineteenth-century Java, in contrast, concubinage itself was considered to be a major source of white pauperism; in the early 1900s it was vigorously condemned at precisely the same time that a new colonial morality passively condoned illegal brothels (Het Pauperisme Commissie 1901; Nieuwenhuys 1959: 20–23; Hesselink 1987: 208).

It was not only morality that vacillated but the very definition of white prestige—and what its defense should entail. No description of European colonial communities fails to note the obsession with white prestige as a basic feature of colonial mentality. White prestige and its protection loom as the primary cause of a long list of otherwise inexplicable colonial postures, prejudices, fears, and violences. As we have seen, what upheld that prestige was not a constant; concubinage was socially lauded at one time and seen as a political menace at another. White prestige was a gloss for different intensities of racist practice, gender-specific and culturally coded. Although many accounts contend that white women brought an end to concubinage, its decline came with a much wider shift in colonial relations along more racially segregated lines—in which the definitions of prestige shifted and in which Asian, creole, and European-born women were to play new roles.

Thus far I have treated colonial communities as a generic category despite the sharp demographic, social, and political distinctions among them. Colonies based on small administrative centers of Europeans (as on Africa's Gold Coast) differed from plantation colonies with sizable enclave European communities (as in Malaya and Sumatra), and still more from settler colonies (as in Algeria) with large and very heterogenous, permanent European populations. These "types," however, were far less fixed than some students of colonial history suggest. Winthrop Jordan, for example, has argued that the "bedrock demographics" of whites to blacks, and the sexual composition of the latter group, "powerfully influenced, perhaps even determined the kind of society which emerged in each colony" (Jordan 1968: 141).[18] North Sumatra's European-oriented, overwhelmingly male colonial population, for example, contrasted sharply with the more sexually balanced mestizo culture that emerged in the seventeenth and eighteenth centuries in colonial Java. As we have seen, however, these demographics were not the bedrock of social relations from which all else followed. Sex ratios themselves derived from the particular way in which administrative strategies of social engineering collided with and constrained people's personal choices and private lives. While recognizing that these demographic differences, and the social configurations to which they gave rise, still need to be explained, I have chosen here to trace some of the common politically charged issues that a range of colonial societies shared; that is, some of the similar—and counterintuitive—ways in which the construction of racial categories and the management of sexuality were inscribed in new efforts to modernize colonial control.[19]

PART II: EUROPEAN WOMEN AND RACIAL BOUNDARIES

Perhaps nothing is as striking in the sociological accounts of European colonial communities as the extraordinary changes that are said to accompany the entry of white women. These adjustments shifted in one direction; toward European life-styles accentuating the refinements of privilege and new etiquettes of racial difference. Most accounts agree that the presence of European women put new demands on the white communities to tighten their ranks, clarify their boundaries, and mark out their social space. The material culture of European settlements in Saigon, outposts in New Guinea, and estate complexes in Sumatra were retailored to accommodate the physical and moral requirements of a middle-class and respectable feminine contingent (Malleret 1934; Gordon and Meggitt 1985; Stoler 1989a). Housing structures in the Indies were partitioned, residential compounds in the Solomon Islands enclosed, servant relations in Hawaii formalized, dress codes in Java altered, food and social taboos in Rhodesia and the Ivory Coast codified. Taken together these changes encouraged new kinds of consumption and new social services catering to these new demands (Boutilier 1984; Spear 1963; Woodcock 1969; Cohen 1971).

The arrival of large numbers of European women thus coincided with an embourgeoisment of colonial communities and with a significant sharpening of racial categories. European women supposedly required more metropolitan amenities than men and more spacious surroundings to allow it; they had more delicate sensibilities and therefore needed suitable quarters—discrete and enclosed. Women's psychological and physical constitutions were considered more fragile, demanding more servants for the chores they should be spared. In short, white women needed to be maintained at elevated standards of living, in insulated social spaces cushioned with the cultural artifacts of "being European."

Thomas Beidelman, for example, writes for colonial Tanganyika that "European wives and children created a new and less flexible domestic colonialism exhibiting overconcern with the sexual accessibility or vulnerability of wives, with corresponding notions about the need for spatial and social segregation" (1982: 13). Whether women or men set these new standards and why they might have both done so for different reasons is left unclear. Who exhibited "overconcern" and a "need for" segregation? In Indochina, male doctors advised French women to have their homes built with separate domestic and kitchen quarters (Grall 1908: 74). Segregationist standards were what women "deserved," and more importantly what white male prestige required that they maintain.

RACIST BUT MORAL WOMEN, INNOCENT BUT IMMORAL MEN

Recent feminist scholarship has challenged the universally negative stereotype of the colonial wife in one of two ways: either by showing the structural reasons why European women were racially intolerant, socially vicious, abusive to servants, prone to illness and bored, or by demonstrating that they really were not (Gartrell 1984; Knibiehler and Goutalier 1985; Callaway 1987). Several recent works have attempted to confront what Margaret Strobel calls the "myth of the destructive female" to show that European women were not detriments to colonial relations but were in fact crucial to the bolstering of a failing empire, and charged with maintaining the social rituals of racial difference (Strobel 1987: 378–379).

Colonial rhetoric on white women was full of contradictions. At the same time that new female immigrants were chided for not respecting the racial distance of local convention, an equal number of colonial observers accused these women of being more avid racists in their own right (Spear 1963; Nora 1961). Allegedly insecure and jealous of the sexual liaisons of European men with native women, bound to their provincial visions and cultural norms, European women, it was and is argued, constructed the major cleavages on which colonial stratification rested. Thus Percival Spear, in commenting on the social life of the English in eighteenth-century India, asserted that women "widened the racial gulf" by holding to "their insular whims and prejudices" (1963: 140). Writing about French women in Algeria two hundred years later, the French historian Pierre Nora claimed that these "parasites of the colonial relationship in which they do not participate directly, are generally more racist than men and contribute strongly to prohibiting contact between the two societies" (1961: 174). Similarly, Octavio Mannoni noted "the astonishing fact" that European women in Madagascar were "far more racialist than the men" (1964 [1950]: 115). For the Indies "it was jealousy of the dusky sirens . . . but more likely some say . . . it was . . . plain feminine scandalization at free and easy sex relations" that caused a decline in miscegenation (Kennedy 1947: 164).

Such bald examples are easy to find in colonial histories of several decades ago. Recent scholarship is more subtle but not substantially different. In the European community on the French Ivory Coast, ethnographer Alain Tirefort contends that "the presence of the white woman separated husbands from indigenous life by creating around them a zone of European intimacy" (1979: 197). Gann and Duignan state simply that it was "the cheap steamship ticket for women that put an end to racial integration in British Africa" (1978: 242; also see O'Brien 1972: 59). Lest we assume that such conclusions are confined to metropolitan men, we should note the Indian pyschiatrist Ashis Nandy's observation—tying white women's racism to the homosexual cravings of their husbands—that "white women in India were generally more racist because they unconsciously saw themselves as the sexual competitors of Indian men" (1983: 9–10).

What is most startling here is that women, these otherwise marginal actors on the colonial stage, are charged with dramatically reshaping the face of colonial society, imposing their racial will on, as in the case of Africa, a colonial world where "relatively unrestrained social intermingling . . . had been prevalent in earlier years" (Cohen 1971: 122). Similarly, in Malaya the presence of European women put an end to "free and easy social intercourse with [Malayan] men as well," replacing "an iron curtain of ignorance . . . between the races" (Vere Allen 1970: 169). European women are not only the bearers of racist beliefs but hardline operatives who put them into practice. European women, it is claimed, destroyed the blurred divisions between colonizer and colonized, encouraging class distinctions among whites while fostering new racial antagonisms, formerly muted by sexual access (ibid.: 168).[20]

Are we to believe that sexual intimacy with European men yielded social mobility and political rights for colonized women? Or even less likely, that because British civil servants bedded with Indian women, somehow Indian men had more "in common" with British men and enjoyed more parity? Colonized women could sometimes parlay their positions into personal profit and small rewards, but these were *individual* negotiations with no social, legal, or cumulative claims. European male sexual access to native women was not a leveling mechanism for asymmetries in race, class, or gender (Strobel 1987: 378; Degler 1986: 189).

Male colonizers positioned European women as the bearers of a redefined colonial morality. But to suggest that women fashioned this racism out of whole cloth is to miss the political chronology in which new intensities of racist practice arose. In the African and Asian contexts already mentioned, the arrival of large numbers of European wives, and particularly the fear for their protection, followed from new terms and tensions in the colonial contract. The presence and protection of European women was repeatedly invoked to clarify racial lines. It coincided with perceived threats to European prestige (Brownfoot 1984: 191), increased racial conflict (Strobel 1987: 378), covert challenges to the colonial order, outright expressions of nationalist resistance, and internal dissension among whites themselves (Stoler 1989a: 147–149).

If white women were the primary force behind the decline of concubinage as is often claimed, they did so as participants in a much broader racial realignment and political plan (Knibiehler and Goutalier 1985: 76). This is not to suggest that European women were passive in this process, as the dominant themes in many of their novels attest (Taylor 1977: 27). Many European women did oppose concubinage—not because they were categorically jealous of, and threatened by, Asian women as often claimed (Clerkx 1961), but, more likely, because of the double standard it condoned for European men (Lucas 1986: 94–95). Although some Dutch women in fact championed the cause of the wronged *nyai*, urging improved protection for nonprovisioned women and children, they rarely went so far as to advocate for the legitimation of these unions in legal marriage (Taylor 1977: 31–32; Lucas 1986: 95). The voices of European women, however, had little resonance until their objections coincided with a realignment in racial and class politics in which they were strategic to both.

RACE AND THE POLITICS OF SEXUAL PERIL

The gender-specific requirements for colonial living, referred to above, were constructed on heavily racist evaluations, which pivoted on images of the heightened sexuality of colonized men (Tiffany and Adams 1985). Although, as we have noted, in novels and memoirs European women were categorically absent from the sexual fantasies of colonial men, the very same men deemed them to be desired and seductive figures to men of color. European women needed protection because men of color had "primitive" sexual urges and uncontrollable lust, aroused by the sight of white women (Strobel 1987: 379; Schmidt 1987: 411). In some colonies that sexual threat remained an unlabeled potential; in others it was given a specific name. The "Black Peril" referred throughout Africa and much of the British Empire to the professed dangers of sexual assault on white women by black men.

In Southern Rhodesia and Kenya in the 1920s and 1930s preoccupations with the "Black Peril" gave rise to the creation of citizens' militias, ladies' riflery clubs, and investigations as to whether African female domestic servants would not be safer to employ than men (Kirkwood 1984: 158; Schmidt

1987: 412; Kennedy 1987: 128–147; Hansen 1989). In New Guinea alleged attempted assaults on European women by Papuan men prompted the passage of the White Women's Protection Ordinance of 1926, which provided "the death penalty for any person convicted for the crime of rape or attempted rape upon a European woman or girl" (Inglis 1975: vi). And in the Solomon Islands authorities introduced public flogging in 1934 as punishment for "criminal assaults on [white] females" (Boutilier 1984: 197).

What do these cases have in common? First, the rhetoric of sexual assault and the measures used to prevent it had virtually no correlation with actual incidences of rape of European women by men of color. Just the contrary: there was often no ex post facto evidence, nor any at the time, that rapes were committed or that rape attempts were made (Schmidt 1987; Inglis 1975; Kirkwood 1984; Kennedy 1987; Boutilier 1984). This is not to suggest that sexual assaults never occurred, but that their incidence had little to do with the fluctuations in anxiety about them. Moreover, the rape laws were race-specific; sexual abuse of black women was not classified as rape and therefore was not legally actionable, nor did rapes committed by white men lead to prosecution (Mason 1958: 246–247). If these accusations of sexual threat were not prompted by the fact of rape, what did they signal and to what were they tied?

Allusions to political and sexual subversion of the colonial system went hand in hand. The term "Black Peril" referred to sexual threats, but it also connoted the fear of insurgence, of some perceived nonacquiescence to colonial control more generally (van Onselen 1982; Schmidt 1987; Inglis 1975; Strobel 1987; Kennedy 1987: 128–147). Concern over protection of white women intensified during real and perceived crises of control—provoked by threats to the internal cohesion of the European communities or by infringements on its borders. Thus colonial accounts of the Mutiny in India in 1857 are full of descriptions of the sexual mutilation of British women by Indian men despite the fact that no rapes were recorded (Metcalf 1964: 290). In Africa too, although the chronologies of the Black Peril differ—on the Rand in South Africa peaking a full twenty years earlier than elsewhere—we can still identify a patterned *sequence* of events (van Onselen 1982). In New Guinea, the White Women's Protection Ordinance followed a large influx of acculturated Papuans into Port Moresby in the 1920s. Resistant to the constraints imposed on their dress, movement, and education, whites perceived them as arrogant, "cheeky," and without respect (Inglis 1975: 8, 11). In post-World War I Algeria, the political unease of *pieds noirs* (local French settlers) in the face of "a whole new series of [Muslim] demands" manifested itself in a popular culture newly infused with strong images of sexually aggressive Algerian men (Sivan 1983: 178).

Second, rape charges against colonized men were often based on perceived transgressions of social space. "Attempted rapes" turned out to be "incidents" of a Papuan man "discovered" in the vicinity of a white residence, a Fijian man who entered a European patient's room, a male servant poised at the bedroom door of a European woman asleep or in half-dress (Boutilier 1984: 197; Inglis 1975: 11; Schmidt 1987: 413). With such a broad definition of danger in a culture of fear, all colonized men of color were threatening as sexual and political aggressors.

Third, accusations of sexual assault frequently followed upon heightened tensions within European communities—and renewed efforts to find consensus within them. Rape accusations in South Africa, for example, coincided with a rash of strikes between 1890–1914 by both African and white miners (van Onselen 1982: 51). As in Rhodesia after a strike by white railway employees in 1929, the threat of native rebellion brought together conflicting members of the European community in common cause where "solidarity found sustenance in the threat of racial destruction" (Kennedy 1987: 138).

During the late 1920s when labor protests by Indonesian workers and European employees were most intense, Sumatra's corporate elite expanded their vigilante organizations, intelligence networks, and demands for police protection to ensure their women were safe and their workers "in hand" (Stoler 1985a). White women arrived in large numbers during the most profitable years of the plantation economy but also at a time of mounting resistance to estate labor conditions and Dutch rule. In the context of a European community that had been blatantly divided between low-ranking plantation employees and the company elite, the community was stabilized and domestic situations were rearranged.

In Sumatra's plantation belt, subsidized sponsorship of married couples replaced the recruitment of single Indonesian workers and European staff, with new incentives provided for family housing and *gezinvorming* ("family formation") in both groups. This recomposed labor force of family men in "stable households" explicitly weeded out politically "undesirable elements" and the socially malcontent. With the marriage restriction finally lifted for European staff in the 1920s, young men sought wives among Dutch-born women while on leave in Holland or through marriage brokers by mail. Higher salaries, upgraded housing, elevated bonuses, and a more mediated chain of command between colonized fieldworker and colonial staff served to clarify both national and racial affinities and to differentiate the political interests of European from Asian workers more than ever before (Stoler 1985a). With this shift, the vocal opposition to corporate and government directives, sustained by the independent Union of European Estate Employees (*Vakvereeniging voor Assistenten in Deli*) for nearly two decades, was effectively dissolved (*Kroniek 1933*: 85).

The remedies sought to alleviate sexual danger embraced new prescriptions for securing white control; increased surveillance of native men, new laws stipulating severe corporeal punishment for the transgression of sexual and social boundaries, and the creation of areas made racially off-limits. These went with a moral rearmament of the European community and reassertions of its cultural identity. Charged with guarding cultural norms, European women were instrumental in promoting white solidarity. It was partly at their own expense, as they were to be nearly as closely policed as colonized men (Strobel 1987).

POLICING EUROPEAN WOMEN AND CONCESSIONS TO CHIVALRY

Although native men were the ones legally punished for alleged sexual assaults, European women were frequently blamed for provoking those desires. New arrivals from Europe were accused of being too familiar with their servants, lax in their commands, indecorous in their speech and in their dress (Vellut 1982: 100; Kennedy 1987: 141; Schmidt 1987: 413). In Papua New Guinea "everyone" in the Australian community agreed that rape assaults were caused by a "younger generation of white women" who simply did not know how to treat servants (Inglis 1975: 80). In Rhodesia as in Uganda, sexual anxieties persisted in the absence of any incidents and restricted women to activities within the European enclaves (Gartrell 1984: 169). The immorality act of 1916 "made it an offence for a white woman to make an indecent suggestion to a male native" (Mason 1958: 247). European women in Kenya in the 1920s were not only dissuaded from staying alone on their homesteads but strongly discouraged by rumors of rape from taking up farming on their own (Kennedy 1987: 141). As in the American South, "the etiquette of chivalry controlled white women's behavior even as [it] guarded caste lines" (Dowd Hall 1984: 64). A defense of community, morality, and white male power was achieved by increasing control over and consensus among Europeans, by reaffirming the vulnerability of white women, the sexual threat posed by native men, and by creating new sanctions to limit the liberties of both.

European colonial communities in the early twentieth century assiduously controlled the movements of European women and, where possible, imposed on them restricted and protected roles. This is not to say that European women did not work; French women in the settler communities of Algeria ran farms, rooming houses, and shops along with their men (Baroli 1967: 159; O'Brien 1972). On the Ivory Coast, married European women worked to "supplement" their husbands' incomes (Tirefort 1979: 112), while in Senegal the "supplementary" salary of French wives maintained the white standard (Mercier 1965: 292). Among women who were posted throughout the colonial empires as missionaries, nurses, and teachers, some openly questioned the sexist policies of their male superiors. However, by and large their tasks buttressed rather than contested the established racial order (Ralston 1977; Knibiehler and Goutalier 1985; Callaway 1987: 111; Ramuschack n.d.).

Particularly in the colonies with small European communities as opposed to those of large-scale settlement, there were few opportunities for women to be economically independent or to act politically on their own. The "revolt against chivalry"—the protest of American Southern white women to lynchings of black men for alleged rape attempts—had no counterpart among European women in Asia and Africa (Dowd Hall 1984). French feminists urged women with skills (and a desire for marriage) to settle in Indochina at the turn of the century, but colonial administrators were adamantly against their immigration. They not only complained of a surfeit of resourceless widows but argued that European seamstresses, florists, and children's outfitters could not possibly compete with the cheap and skilled labor provided by well-established Chinese firms (Lanessan 1889: 450; Corneau 1900: 12, 12). In Tonkin in the 1930s, "there was little room for single women, be they unmarried, widowed or divorced" (Gantes 1981: 45). Although some colonial widows, such as the editor of a major Saigon daily, succeeded in their own ambitions, most were shipped out of Indochina—regardless of skill—at the government's charge.[21]

Firmly rejecting expansion based on the "poor white" (petit blanc) Algerian model, French officials in Indochina dissuaded *colons* with insufficient capital from entry and promptly repatriated those who tried to remain.[22] Single women were seen as the quintessential petit blanc; with limited resources and shopkeeper aspirations, they presented the dangerous possibility that straitened circumstances would lead them to prostitution, thereby degrading European prestige at large. In the Solomon Islands lower-class white women were overtly scorned and limited from entry (Boutilier 1984: 179). Similarly, an Indies Army high commander complained in 1903 to the governor-general that lower-class European-born women were vastly more immodest than their Indies-born counterparts and thus posed a greater moral threat to European men (Ming 1983: 84–85). State officials themselves identified European widows as among the most economically vulnerable and impoverished segments of the Indies European community (Het Pauperisme onder de Europeanen 1901: 28).

Professional competence did not leave single European women immune from marginalization (Knibiehler and Goutalier 1985). Single professional women were held in contempt as were European prostitutes, with surprisingly similar objections.[23] White prostitutes threatened prestige, while professional women needed protection; both fell outside the social space to which European colonial women were assigned: namely, as custodians of family welfare and respectability, and as dedicated and willing subordinates to, and supporters of, colonial men. The rigor with which these norms were applied becomes more comprehensible when we see why a European family life and bourgeois respectability became increasingly tied to notions of racial survival, imperial patriotism, and the political strategies of the colonial state.

PART III: WHITE DEGENERACY, MOTHERHOOD, AND THE
EUGENICS OF EMPIRE

de-gen-er-ate (adj.) [L. *degeneratus*, pp. of *degenerare*, to become unlike one's
race, degenerate < *degener*, not genuine, base < *de-*, from + *genus*, race, kind: see
genus]. **1.** to lose former, normal, or higher qualities. **2.** having sunk below a
former or normal condition, character, etc.; deteriorated. **3.** morally corrupt;
depraved- (n.) a degenerate person, esp. one who is morally depraved or sexually perverted- (vi.) -*at'ed*, -*at'ing*. **1.** to decline or become debased morally,
culturally, etc. . . . **2.** Biol. to undergo degeneration; deteriorate. (*Webster's New
World Dictionary* 1972: 371)

European women were essential to the colonial enterprise and the solidi-
fication of racial boundaries in ways which repeatedly tied their supportive
and subordinate posture to community cohesion and colonial security. These
features of their positioning within imperial politics were powerfully reinforced at the turn of the century by a metropolitan bourgeois discourse (and
an eminently anthropological one) intensely concerned with notions of
"degeneracy" (Le Bras 1981: 77).[24] Middle-class morality, manliness, and
motherhood were seen as endangered by the intimately linked fears of
"degeneration" and miscegenation in scientifically construed racist beliefs
(Mosse 1978: 82).[25] Degeneration was defined as "departures from the normal human type . . . transmitted through inheritance and lead[ing] progressively to destruction" (Morel quoted in Mosse 1978: 83). Due to environmental, physical, and moral factors, degeneracy could be averted by positive
eugenic selection or, negatively, by eliminating the "unfit" and/or the environmental and more specifically cultural contagions that gave rise to them
(Mosse 1978: 87; Kevles 1985: 70–84).

Eugenic discourse has usually been associated with Social Darwinian
notions of "selection," with the strong influence of Lamarckian thinking
reserved for its French variant (Schneider 1982). However, the notion of
"cultural contamination" runs throughout the British, U.S., French, and
Dutch eugenic traditions (Rodenwaldt 1928). Eugenic arguments used to explain the social malaise of industrialization, immigration, and urbanization
in the early twentieth century derived from notions that acquired characteristics were inheritable and thus that poverty, vagrancy, and promiscuity
were class-linked biological traits, tied to genetic material as directly as
nightblindness and blonde hair. As we shall see, this Lamarckian feature of
eugenic thinking was central to colonial discourses that linked racial degeneracy to the sexual transmission of cultural contagions and to the political
instability of imperial rule.

Appealing to a broad political and scientific constituency at the turn of the
century, Euro-American eugenic societies included advocates of infant welfare programs, liberal intellectuals, conservative businessmen, Fabians, and

physicians with social concerns. By the 1920s, however, it contained an increasingly vocal number of those who called for and put into law, if not practice, the sterilization of what were considered the mentally, morally, or physically unfit members of the British, German, and American underclass (Mosse 1978: 87; Stepan 1982: 122).[26] Feminist attempts to appropriate this rhetoric for their own birth-control programs largely failed. Eugenics was essentially elitist, racist, and misogynist in principle and practice (Gordon 1976: 395; Davin 1978; Hammerton 1979). Its proponents advocated a pronatalist policy toward the white middle and upper classes, a rejection of work roles for women that might compete with motherhood, and "an assumption that reproduction was not just a function but the purpose . . . of women's life" (Gordon 1974: 134). In France, England, Germany, and the United States, eugenics placed European women of "good stock" as "the fountainhead of racial strength" (Ridley 1981: 91), exhalting the cult of motherhood while subjecting it to the scrutiny of this new scientific domain (Davin 1978: 12).

As part of metropolitan class politics, eugenics reverberated in the colonies in predictable as well as unexpected forms. The moral, biological, and sexual referents of the notion of degeneracy (distinct in the dictionary citation above), came together in the actual deployment of the concept. The "colonial branch" of eugenics embraced a theory and practice concerned with the vulnerabilities of white rule and new measures to safeguard European superiority. Designed to control the procreation of the "unfit" lower orders, eugenics targeted "the poor, the colonized, or unpopular strangers" (Hobsbawm 1987: 253). The discourse, however, reached further. It permeated how metropolitan observers viewed the "degenerate" life-style of colonials, and how colonial elites admonished the behavior of "degenerate" members among themselves (Koks 1931: 179–189). Whereas studies in Europe and the United States focused on the inherent propensity of the impoverished classes to criminality, in the Indies delinquency among "European" children was biologically linked to the amount of "native blood" children born of mixed marriages had inherited from their native mothers (Braconier 1918: 11). Eugenics provided not so much a new vocabulary as a new biological idiom in which to ground the medical and moral basis for anxiety over the security of European hegemony and white prestige. It reopened debates over segregated residence and education, new standards of morality, sexual vigilance, and the rights of *certain* Europeans to rule.

Eugenic influence manifested itself, not in the direct importation of metropolitan practices such as sterilization, but in a translation of the political *principles* and the social values that eugenics implied. In defining what was unacceptable, eugenics also identified what constituted a "valuable life": "a gender-specific work and productivity, described in social, medical and psychiatric terms" (Bock 1986: 274). Applied to European colonials, eugenic statements pronounced what kind of people should represent Dutch or

French rule, how they should bring up their children, and with whom they should socialize. Those concerned with issues of racial survival and racial purity invoked moral arguments about the national duty of French, Dutch, British, and Belgian colonial women to fulfill an alternative set of imperial imperatives: to "uplift" colonial subjects through educational and domestic management, to attend to the family environment of their colonial husbands, or sometimes to remain in the metropole and to stay at home. The point is that a common discourse was mapped onto different immediate exigencies of empire as variations on a gender-specific theme exalting motherhood and domesticity.

If in Britain racial deterioration was conceived to be a result of the moral turpitude and the ignorance of working-class mothers, in the colonies the dangers were more pervasive, the possibilities of contamination worse. Formulations to secure European rule pushed in two directions: on the one hand, away from ambiguous racial genres and open domestic arrangements, and on the other hand, toward an upgrading, homogenization, and a clearer delineation of European standards; away from miscegenation toward white endogamy; away from concubinage toward family formation and legal marriage; away from, as in the case of the Indies, mestizo customs and toward metropolitan norms (Taylor 1983; Van Doorn 1985). As stated in the bulletin of the Netherlands Indies' Eugenic Society, "eugenics is nothing other than belief in the possibility of preventing degenerative symptoms in the body of our beloved *moedervolken*, or in cases where they may already be present, of counteracting them" (Rodenwaldt 1928: 1).

Like the modernization of colonialism itself, with its scientific management and educated technocrats with limited local knowledge, colonial communities of the early twentieth century were rethinking the ways in which their authority should be expressed. This rethinking took the form of asserting a distinct colonial morality, explicit in its reorientation toward the racial and class markers of "Europeanness," emphasizing transnational racial commonalities despite national differences—distilling a *homo europeaus* for whom superior health, wealth, and education were tied to racial endowments and a White Man's norm. Thus Pujarniscle, a novelist and participant-observer in France's colonial venture, wrote: "one might be surprised that my pen always returns to the words *blanc* (white) or "European" and never to "Français". . . in effect colonial solidarity and the obligations that it entails allies all the peoples of the white races" (1931: 72; also see Delavignette 1946: 41).

Such sensibilities colored imperial policy in nearly all domains with fears of physical contamination, giving new credence to fears of political vulnerability. Whites had to guard their ranks—in qualitative and quantitative terms—to increase their numbers and to ensure that their members blurred neither the biological nor political boundaries on which their power rested.[27]

In the metropole the socially and physically "unfit," the poor, the indigent, and the insane, were either to be sterilized or prevented from marriage. In the colonies it was these very groups among Europeans who were either excluded from entry or institutionalized while they were there and eventually sent home (Arnold 1979; Vellut 1982: 97).

In sustaining a vision that good health, virility, and the ability to rule were inherent features of "Europeanness," whites in the colonies had to adhere to a politics of exclusion that policed their members as well as the colonized. Such concerns were not new to the 1920s (Taylor 1983; Sutherland 1982). In the 1750s the Dutch East Indies Company had already taken "draconian measures" to control pauperism among "Dutchmen of mixed blood" (*Encylopedie van Nederland-Indie 1919*: 367). In the same period, the British East Indies Company legally and administratively dissuaded lower-class European migration and settlement, with the argument that it might destroy Indian respect for "the superiority of the European character" (quoted in Arnold 1983: 139). Patriotic calls to populate Java in the mid-1800s with poor Dutch farmers were also condemned, but it was with new urgency that these proposals were rejected in the following century as successive challenges to European rule were more profoundly felt.

Measures were taken both to avoid poor white migration and to produce a colonial profile that highlighted the manliness, well-being, and productivity of European men. Within this equation, protection of manhood, national identity, and racial superiority were meshed (Loutfi 1971: 112–113; Ridley 1981: 104).[28] Thus British colonial administrators were retired by the age of fifty-five, ensuring that

> no Oriental was ever allowed to see a Westerner as he ages and degenerated, just as no Westerner needed ever to see himself, mirrored in the eyes of the subject race, as anything but a vigorous, rational, ever-alert young Raj. (Said 1978: 42)

In the twentieth century, these "men of class" and "men of character" embodied a modernized and renovated image of rule; they were to safeguard the colonies against physical weakness, moral decay, and the inevitable degeneration which long residence in the colonies encouraged, and against the temptations that interracial domestic situations had allowed.

Given this ideal, it is not surprising that colonial communities strongly discouraged the presence of nonproductive men. Colonial administrators expressed a constant concern with the dangers of unemployed or impoverished Europeans. During the succession of economic crises in the early twentieth century, relief agencies in Sumatra, for example, organized fundraisers, hillstation retreats, and small-scale agricultural schemes to keep "unfit" Europeans "from roaming around" (*Kroniek 1917*: 49). The colonies were neither open for retirement nor tolerant of the public presence of poor whites. During the 1930s depression, when tens of thousands of Europeans in the Indies found themselves without jobs, government and private resources were quickly mobilized to ensure that they were not "reduced" to native living standards (Cool 1938; Veerde 1931; Kantoor van Arbeid 1935). Subsidized health care, housing, and education complemented a rigorous affirmation of European cultural standards in which European womanhood played a central role in keeping men *civilisé*.

THE CULTURAL DYNAMICS OF DEGENERATION

The *colon* is, in a common and etymological sense, a barbarian. He is a non-civilized person, a "new-man,"... it is he who appears as a savage. (Dupuy 1955: 188)

The shift in imperial thinking that we can identify in the early twentieth century focuses not only on the Otherness of the colonized but on the Otherness of colonials themselves. In metropolitan France a profusion of medical and sociological tracts pinpointed the colonial as a distinct and degenerate social type, with specific pyschological and even physical characteristics (Maunier 1932; Pujarniscle 1931).[29] Some of that difference was attributed to the debilitating results of climate and social milieu, from staying in the colonies too long:

The climate affects him, his surroundings affect him, and after a certain time, he has become, both physically and morally, a completely different man. (Maunier 1932: 169)

People who stayed "too long" were in grave danger of overfatigue; of individual and racial degeneration (Le Roux 1898: 222); of physical breakdown (not just illness); of cultural contamination and neglect of the conventions of supremacy, and of *disagreement* about what those conventions were (Dupuy 1955: 184–185). What were identified as the degraded and unique characteristics of European colonials—"ostentation," "speculation," "inaction," and a general "demoralization"—were "faults" contracted from native culture, which now marked them as décivilisé (Maunier 1932: 174; Jaurequiberry 1924: 25).[30]

Colonial medicine reflected and affirmed this slippage between physical, moral, and cultural degeneracy in numerous ways. The climatic, social, and work conditions of colonial life gave rise to a specific set of psychotic disorders affecting *l'equilibre cerebral* and predisposing Europeans in the tropics to mental breakdown (Hartenberg 1910; Abatucci 1910). Neurasthenia was the most common manifestation, a mental disorder identified as a major problem in the French empire and accounting for more than half the Dutch repatriations from the Indies to Holland (Winckel 1938: 352). In Europe and America, it was "the phantom disease . . . the classic illness of the late 19th century," encompassing virtually all "psychopathological or neuropathological conditions," and intimately linked to sexual deviation and to the destruction of social order itself" (Gilman 1985: 199, 202).

Whereas in Europe neurasthenia was considered to be a consequence of "modern civilization" and its high-pitched pace (Showalter 1987: 135), in the colonies its etiology took the *reverse* form. Colonial neurasthenia was allegedly caused by a *distance* from civilization and European community, and by proximity to the colonized. The susceptibility of a colonial (man) was increased by an existence "outside of the social framework to which he was adapted in France, isolation in outposts, physical and moral fatigue, and modified food regimes" (Joyeux 1937: 335).[31]

The proliferation of hill-stations in the twentieth century reflected these political and physical concerns. Invented in the early nineteenth century as sites for military posts and sanatoria, hill-stations provided European-like environments in which colonials could recoup their physical and mental well-being by simulating the conditions "at home" (Spencer and Thomas 1948; King 1976: 165). Isolated at relatively high altitudes, they took on new importance with the colonial presence of increasing numbers of European women and children who were considered particularly susceptible to anemia, depression, and ill-health.[32] Vacation bungalows and schools built in these "naturally" segregated surroundings provided cultural refuge and regeneration (Price 1939).

Some doctors considered the only treatment to be *le retour en Europe* (Joyeux 1937: 335; Pujarniscle 1931: 28). Others prescribed a local set of remedies, advising adherence to a bourgeois ethic of morality and work. This included sexual moderation, a "regularity and regimentation" of work, abstemious diet, physical exercise, and *European* camaraderie, buttressed by a solid (and stolid) family life with European children and a European wife (Grall 1908: 51; Price 1939; also see Kennedy 1987: 123). Guides to colonial living in the 1920s and 1930s reveal this marked shift in outlook; Dutch, French, and British doctors now denounced the unhealthy, indolent lifestyles of "old colonials," extolling the energetic and engaged activities of the new breed of colonial husband and wife (Raptchinsky 1941: 46).[33] As women were considered most prone to neurasthenia, anemia, and depression, they were exhorted to actively participate in household management and childcare, and divert themselves with botanical collections and "good works" (Chivas-Baron 1929; Favre 1938).

CHILDREN ON THE COLONIAL DIVIDE: DEGENERACY AND THE DANGERS OF *MÉTISSAGE*

[Young colonial men] are often driven to seek a temporary companion among the women of color; this is the path by which, as I shall presently show, contagion travels back and forth, contagion in all senses of the word. (Maunier 1932: 171)

Racial degeneracy was thought to have social causes and political consequences, both tied to the domestic arrangements of colonialism in specific ways. *Métissage* (interracial unions) generally, and concubinage in particular, represented the paramount danger to racial purity and cultural identity in all its forms. Through sexual contact with women of color European men "contracted" not only disease but debased sentiments, immoral proclivities, and extreme susceptibility to decivilized states (Dupuy 1956: 198).

By the early twentieth century, concubinage was denounced for undermining precisely those things that it was charged with fortifying decades earlier. The weight of competing discourses on local women shifted emphasis. Although their inherently dangerous, passionate, and evil characters previously had been overshadowed by their role as protectrices of European men's health, in the new equation they became the primary bearers of ill health and sinister influences. Adaptation to local food, language, and dress, once prescribed as healthy signs of acclimatization, were now the sources of contagion and loss of (white) self. The benefits of local knowledge and sexual release gave way to the more pressing demands of respectability, the community's solidarity, and its mental health. Increasingly, French men in Indochina who kept native women were viewed as passing into "the enemy camp" (Pujarniscle 1931: 107). Concubinage became the source not only of individual breakdown and ill-health, but of the biological and social root of racial degeneration and political unrest. Children born of these unions were "the fruits of a regrettable weakness" (Mazet 1932: 8), physically marked and morally marred with "the defaults and mediocre qualities of their mothers" (Douchet 1928: 10).

Concubinage was not as economically tidy and politically neat as colonial policymakers had hoped. It was about more than sexual exploitation and unpaid domestic work; it was about children—many more than official statistics often revealed—and about who was to be acknowledged as a European and who was not. Concubine children posed a classificatory problem, impinging on political security and white prestige. The majority of such children were not recognized by their fathers, nor were they reabsorbed into local communities as authorities often claimed. Although some European men legally acknowledged their progeny, many repatriated to Holland, Britain, or France and cut off ties and support to mother and children (Nieuwenhuys 1959: 23; Brou 1907; Ming 1983: 75). Native women had responsibility for, but attenuated rights over, their own offspring.[34] Although the legal system favored a European upbringing, it made no demands on European men to provide it. The more socially asymmetric and perfunctory the relationship between man and woman, the more likely the children were to end up as wards of the state, subject to the scrutiny and imposed charity of the European-born community at large.

Concubine children invariably counted among the ranks of the European colonial poor, but European paupers in the late-nineteenth-century Netherlands Indies came from wider strata of colonial society than that of concubines alone (Het Pauperisme Commissie 1903). Many Indo-Europeans, including creole children born in the Indies of European parents, had become increasingly marginalized from strategic political and economic positions in the early twentieth century despite the fact that new educational facilities were supposed to have provided new opportunities for them. At the turn of the century, volumes of official reports were devoted to documenting and alleviating the proliferation on Java of a "rough" and "dangerous pauper element" among (Indo-)European clerks, low-level officials, and vagrants (*Encyclopedie van Nederland-Indie 1919*: 367). In the 1920s and 1930s Indies-born and educated youth were uncomfortably squeezed between an influx of new colonial recruits from Holland and the educated *inlander* (native) population with whom they were in direct competition for jobs (Mansvelt 1932: 295).[35]

European pauperism in the Indies reflected broad inequalities in colonial society, underscoring the social heterogeneity of the category "European" itself. Nonetheless, concubinage was still seen as its major cause and as the principal source of *blanken-haters* (white-haters) (Braconier 1917: 298). Concubinage became equated with a progeny of "malcontents," of "parasitic" whites, idle and therefore dangerous. The fear of concubinage was carried yet a step further and tied to the political fear that such Eurasians would demand economic access, political rights, and express their own interests through alliance with (and leadership of) organized opposition to Dutch rule (Mansvelt 1932; Blumberger 1939).

Racial prejudice against *métis* was often, as in the Belgian Congo, "camouflaged under protestations of 'pity' for their fate, as if they were '*malheureux*' [unhappy] beings by definition" (Vellut 1982: 103). The protection of *métis* children in Indochina was a cause célèbre of European women at home and abroad. The French assembly on feminism, organized for the colonial exposition of 1931, devoted a major part of its proceedings to the plight of *métis* children and their native mothers, echoing the campaigns for *la recherche de paternité* by French feminists a half-century earlier (Moses 1984: 208). The assembly called for "the establishment of centers [in the colonies] where abandoned young girls or those in moral danger could be made into worthy women" (Knibiehler and Goutalier 1987: 37). European colonial women were urged to oversee the "moral protection" of métis youths, to develop their "natural" inclination toward French society, to turn them into "collaborators and partisans of French ideas and influences" instead of revolutionaries (Chenet 1936: 8; Knibiehler and Goutalier 1987: 35; Sambuc 1931: 261). The gender breakdown was clear: moral instruction would avert sexual promiscuity among métisse girls and political precocity among métis boys who might otherwise become militant men.

Orphanages for abandoned European and Indo-European children were a prominent feature of Dutch, French, and British colonial cultures. In the Netherlands Indies by the mid-eighteenth century, state orphanages for Europeans were established to prevent "neglect and degeneracy of the many free-roaming poor bastards and orphans of Europeans" (quoted in Braconier 1917: 293). By the nineteenth century, church, state, and private organizations had become zealous backers of orphanages, providing some education and strong doses of moral instruction. In India the military orphanages of the late eighteenth century expanded into a nineteenth-century variant in which European and Anglo-Indian children were cared for in civil asylums and charity schools in "almost every town, cantonment and hill-station" (Arnold 1979: 108). In French Indochina in the 1930s virtually every colonial city had a home and society for the protection of abandoned métis youth (Chenet 1936; Sambuc 1931: 256–272; Malleret 1934: 220).[36]

Whether these children were in fact "abandoned" by their Asian mothers is difficult to establish; the fact that métis children living in native homes were sometimes *sought out* by state and private organizations and placed in these institutions suggests another interpretation (Taylor 1983). Public assistance in India, Indochina, and the Netherlands Indies was designed not only to keep fair-skinned children from running barefoot in native villages but to ensure that the proliferation of European pauper settlements was curtailed and controlled.[37] The need for specific kinds of religious and secular education and socialization of children was symptomatic of a more general fear; namely, that these children would grow into *Hollander-haters*, patricides, and anticolonial revolutionaries; that as adult women they would fall into prostitution; that as adult men with lasting ties to native women and indigenous society they would become enemies of the state, *verbasterd* (degenerate) and *décivilisé* (Braconier 1917: 293; Angoulvant 1926: 102; Pouvourville 1926; Sambuc 1931: 261; Malleret 1934).

EUROPEAN WOMEN, RACE AND MIDDLE-CLASS MORALITY

A man remains a man as long as he stays under the watch of a woman of his race. (George Hardy quoted in Chivas-Baron 1929: 103)

Rationalizations of imperial rule and safeguards against racial degeneracy in European colonies merged in the emphasis on particular moral themes. Both entailed a reassertion of European conventions, middle-class respectability, more frequent ties with the metropole, and a restatement of what was culturally distinct and superior about how colonials ruled and lived. For those women who came to join their spouses or to find husbands, the prescriptions were clear. Just as new plantation employees were taught to manage the natives, women were schooled in colonial propriety and domestic management. French manuals, such as those on colonial hygiene in Indochina, outlined the duties of colonial wives in no uncertain terms. As "auxiliary forces" in the imperial effort they were to "conserve the fitness and sometimes the life of all around them" by ensuring that "the home be happy and gay and that all take pleasure in clustering there" (Grall 1908: 66; Chailley-Bert 1897). The *Koloniale School voor Meisjes en Vrouwen*, established in The Hague in 1920, provided adolescent and adult women with ethnographic lectures and short childbearing courses to prepare them for their new lives in the Indies. Practical guides to life in the Belgian Congo instructed (and indeed warned) *la femme blanche* that she was to keep "order, peace, hygiene and economy" (Favre 1938: 217), "perpetuate a vigorous race," while preventing any "laxity in our administrative mores" (ibid.: 256; Travaux du Groupe d'Etudes coloniales 1910: 10).

This "division of labor" contained obvious asymmetries. Men were considered more susceptible to moral turpitude than women, who were thus held responsible for the immoral states of men. European women were to safeguard prestige, morality, and insulate their men from the cultural and sexual contamination of contact with the colonized (Travaux . . . Coloniales 1910: 7). Racial degeneracy would be curtailed by European women charged with regenerating the physical health, the metropolitan affinities, and the imperial purpose of their men (Hardy 1929: 78).

At its heart was a reassertion of racial difference that harnessed nationalist rhetoric and markers of middle-class morality to its cause (Delavignette 1946: 47; Loutfi 1971: 112; Ridley 1981; Mosse 1978: 86). George Mosse has characterized European racism as a "scavenger ideology," annexing nationalism and bourgeois respectability in such a way that control over sexuality was central to all three (1985: 10, 133–152). If the European middle-class sought respectability "to maintain their status and self-respect against the lower-classes, and the aristocracy," in the colonies respectability was a defense against the colonized, and a way of more clearly defining themselves (ibid. 1985: 5). Good colonial living now meant hard work, no sloth, and physical exercise rather than sexual release, which had been one rationale for condoning concubinage and prostitution in an earlier period. The debilitating influences of climate could be surmounted by regular diet and meticulous personal hygiene over which European women were to take full charge. British, French, and Dutch manuals on how to run a European household in the tropics provided detailed instructions in domestic science, moral upbringing, and employer-servant relations. Adherence to strict conventions of cleanliness and cooking occupied an inordinate amount of women's time, while cleanliness itself served as a "prop to a Europeanness that was less than assumed" (Ridley 1981: 77). Both activities entailed a

constant surveillance of native nursemaids, laundrymen, and live-in servants, while demanding a heightened domesticity for European women
themselves.

Leisure, good spirit, and creature comforts became the obligation of
women to provide, the racial duty of women to maintain. Sexual temptations
with women of color would be curtailed by a happy, *gezellig* (cozy) family life,
much as "extremist agitation" among Javanese plantation workers was to be
averted by selecting married recruits and providing family housing so that
men would feel *senang* (happy/content) and "at home" (Stoler 1985a: 42–44).
Moral laxity would be eliminated through the example and vigilance of
women whose status was defined by their sexual restraint and dedication to
their homes and their men.

IMPERIAL PRIORITIES: MOTHERHOOD VS. MALE MORALITY

The European woman [in Indochina] can only fulfill her duties to bear and
breast-feed her children with great hardship and damage to her health. (Grall
1908: 65)

The perceptions and practice that bound women's domesticity to national
welfare and racial purity were not confined to colonial women alone. Child-
rearing in late-nineteenth-century Britain was hailed as a national, imperial,
and racial duty, as it was in France, Holland, the United States, and Germany at the same time (Davin 1978: 13; Smith-Rosenberg 1973: 351; Bock
1984: 274; Stuurman 1985). In France, where declining birth rates were of
grave concern, fecundity itself had become "no longer something resting with
couples" but with "the nation, the state, the race . . ." (LeBras 1981: 90).
Popular colonial authors such as Pierre Mille pushed the production of children as women's "essential contribution to the imperial mission of France"
(Ridley 1981: 90). With motherhood at the center of empire-building, pronatalist policies in Europe forced some improvement in colonial medical facilities, the addition of maternity wards, and increased information and control
over the reproductive conditions of both European and colonized women.
Maternal and infant health programs instructed European women bound for
the tropics in the use of milk substitutes, wet nurses, and breastfeeding practices in an effort to encourage more women to stay in the colonies and in
response to the many more that came (Hunt 1988). But the belief that the
colonies were medically hazardous for white women meant that motherhood
in the tropics was not only a precarious but a conflicted endeavor.

Real and imagined concern over individual reproduction and racial survival contained and compromised white colonial women in a number of
ways. Tropical climates were said to cause low fertility, prolonged amenor-
rhea, and permanent sterility (Rodenwaldt 1928: 3).[38] Belgian doctors con-

firmed that "the woman who goes to live in a tropical climate is often lost for the reproduction of the race" (Knibiehler and Goutalier 1985: 92; Vellut 1982: 100). The climatic and medical conditions of colonial life were associated with high infant mortality, such that "the life of a European child was nearly condemned in advance" (Grall 1908: 65). A long list of colonial illnesses ranging from neurasthenia to anemia supposedly hit women and children hardest (Price 1939: 204).

These perceived medical perils called into question whether European-born women and thus the "white race" could actually reproduce if they remained in the tropics for an extended period of time. An international colonial medical community cross-referenced one another in citing evidence of racial sterility by the second or third generation (Harwood 1938: 132; Ripley quoted in Stocking 1968: 54; Cranworth quoted in Kennedy 1987: 115). Although such a dark view of climate was not prevalent in the Indies, psychological and physical adaptation were never givens. Dutch doctors repeatedly quoted German physicians, not to affirm the inevitable infertility among whites in the tropics, but to support their contention that European-born women and men (totoks) should never stay in the colonies too long (Hermans 1925: 123). French observers could flatly state that unions among creole Dutch in the Indies were sterile after two generations (Angoulvant 1926: 101). Medical studies in the 1930s, such as that supported by the Netherlands Indies Eugenic Society, were designed to test whether fertility rates differed by "racial type" between Indo-European and European-born women and whether "children of certain Europeans born in the Indies displayed different racial markers than their parents" (Rodenwaldt 1928: 4).

Like the discourse on degeneracy, the fear of sterility was less about the biological survival of whites than about their political viability and cultural reproduction. These concerns were evident in the early 1900s, coming to a crescendo in the 1930s when white unemployment hit the colonies and the metropole at the same time. The depression made repatriation of impoverished Dutch and French colonial agents unrealistic, prompting speculation as to whether European working-classes could be relocated in the tropics without causing further racial degeneration (Winckel 1938; Price 1939).[39] Although white migration to the tropics was reconsidered, poor white settlements were rejected on economic, medical, and psychological grounds. Whatever the solution, such issues hinged on the reproductive potential of European women, invasive questionnaires concerning their "acclimatization," and detailed descriptions of their conjugal histories and sexual lives.

Imperial perceptions and policies fixed European women in the colonies as "instruments of race-culture" in what proved to be personally difficult and contradictory ways (Hammerton 1979). Childrearing decisions faithfully followed the sorts of racist principles that constrained the activities of women charged with childcare (Grimshaw 1983: 507). Medical experts and women's organizations recommended strict surveillance of children's activities (Mac-kinnon 1920: 944) and careful attention to those with whom they played. Vir-tually every medical and household handbook in the Dutch, French, and British colonies warned against leaving small children in the unsupervised care of local servants. In the Netherlands Indies, it was the "duty" of the *hedendaagsche blanke moeder* (the modern white mother) to take the physical and spiritual upbringing of her offspring away from the *babu* (native nursemaid) and into her own hands (Wanderken 1943: 173).

Precautions had to be taken against "sexual danger," uncleanly habits of domestics, against a "stupid negress" who might leave a child exposed to the sun (Bauduin 1941; Bérenger-Féraud 1875: 491). Even in colonies where the climate was not considered unhealthy, European children supposedly thrived well "only up to the age of six" (Price 1939: 204) when native cul-tural influences came into stronger play. Thus in late-nineteenth-century Hawaii, for example, native nursemaids commonly looked after American children until the age of five at which point "prattlers" were confined to their mothers' supervision, prevented from learning the local language, and kept in a "walled yard adjacent to the bedrooms . . . forbidden to Hawaiians" (Grimshaw 1983: 507).

In the Netherlands Indies, where educational facilities for European chil-dren were considered excellent, it was still deemed imperative to send them back to Holland to avoid the "precocity" associated with the tropics and the "danger" of contact with *Indische* youths not from "full-blooded European elements" (Bauduin 1941: 63).

> We Dutch in the Indies live in a country which is not our own. . . . We feel instinctively that our blonde, white children belong to the blonde, white dunes, the forests, the moors, the lakes, the snow. . . . A Dutch child should grow up in Holland. There they will acquire the characteristics of their race, not only from mother's milk but also from the influence of the light, sun and water, of play-mates, of life, in a word, in the sphere of the fatherland. This is not racism. (Bauduin 1941: 63–64)

Such patriotic images culturally coded racial distinctions in powerful ways. Dutch identity was represented as a common (if contested) cultural sensibil-ity in which class convention, geography, climate, sexual proclivity, and so-cial contact played central roles.

In many colonial communities, school-age children were packed off to Europe for education and socialization, but this was rarely an unproblematic option. When children could not be left with family in the metropole, it meant leaving them for extended periods of time in boarding schools or, when they attended day-schools, in boarding houses catering to Indies youths. Married European women were confronted with a difficult set of choices that entailed separation either from their children or husbands (Angoulvant 1926: 101). Frequent trips between colony and metropole not only separated families but also broke up marriages and homes (Malleret 1934: 164; Grimshaw 1983: 507; Callaway 1987: 183–184).

Not surprisingly, how and where European children should be provided with a proper cultural literacy was a major theme addressed in women's organizations and magazines in the Indies and elsewhere right through decolonization. The rise of specific programs in home education (such as the *Clerkx-methode voor Huisonderwijs*) may have been a response to this new push for women to accommodate their multiple imperial duties; to surveil their husbands and servants while remaining in control of the cultural and moral upbringing of their children. The important point is that such conflicting responsibilities profoundly affected the social space European women (not only wives) occupied, the tasks for which they were valorized, and the economic activities in which they could feasibly engage.

THE STRATEGIES OF RULE AND SEXUAL MORALITY

The political etymology of colonizer and colonized was gender- and class-specific. The exclusionary politics of colonialism demarcated not just external boundaries but interior frontiers, specifying internal conformity and order among Europeans themselves. I have tried to show that the categories of colonizer and colonized were secured through notions of racial difference constructed in gender terms. Redefinitions of acceptable sexual behavior and morality emerged during crises of colonial control precisely because they called into question the tenuous artifices of rule *within* European communities and what marked their borders. Even from the limited cases we have reviewed, several patterns emerge. First and most obviously, colonial sexual prohibitions were racially asymmetric and gender-specific. Sexual relations might be forbidden between white women and men of color but not the other way around. On the contrary, interracial unions (as opposed to marriage) between European men and colonized women aided the long-term settlement of European men in the colonies while ensuring that colonial patrimony stayed in limited and selective hands. Second, interdictions against interracial unions were rarely a primary impulse in the strategies of rule. In India, Indochina, and South Africa in the early centuries—colonial contexts usually associated with sharp social sanctions against interracial unions— "mixing" has been systematically tolerated and even condoned.

I have focused on late colonialism in Asia, but colonial elite intervention in the sexual life of their agents and subjects was by no means confined to this place or period. In sixteenth-century Mexico mixed marriages between Spanish men and Christianized Indian women were encouraged by the crown until mid-century, when colonists felt that "the rising numbers of their own mestizo progeny threatened the prerogatives of a narrowing elite sector" (Nash 1980: 141). In eighteenth- and early nineteenth-century Cuba mild opposition to interracial marriage gave way to a "virtual prohibition" from 1864 to 1874 when "merchants, slave dealers and the colonial powers opposed [it] in order to preserve slavery" (Martinez-Alier 1974: 39).

Changes in sexual access and domestic arrangements have invariably accompanied major efforts to reassert the internal coherence of European communities and to redefine the boundaries of privilege between the colonizer and the colonized. Sexual union in itself, however, did not automatically produce a larger population legally classified as "European." On the contrary, even in early twentieth-century Brazil where miscegenation had made for a refined system of gradations, "most mixing . . . [took] place outside of marriage" (Degler 1971: 185). The important point is that miscegenation signaled neither the presence nor absence of racial discrimination; hierarchies of privilege and power were written into the *condoning* of interracial unions, as well as into their condemnation.

Although the chronologies vary from one colonial context to another, we can identify some parallel shifts in the strategies of rule and in sexual morality. Concubinage fell into moral disfavor at the same time that new emphasis was placed on the standardization of European administration. Although this occurred in some colonies by the early twentieth century and in others later on, the correspondence between rationalized rule, bourgeois respectability, and the custodial power of European women to protect their men seems strongest during the interwar years. Western scientific and technological achievements were then in question (Adas 1989); British, French, and Dutch policymakers had moved from an assimilationist to a more segregationist, separatist colonial stance. The reorganization of colonial investments along corporate and multinational lines brought with it a push for a restructured and more highly productive labor force; and with it more strident nationalist and labor movements resisting those demands.

An increasing rationalization of colonial management produced radical shifts in notions of how empires should be run, how agents of empire should rule, and where, how, and with whom they should live. Thus French debates concerning the need to systematize colonial management and dissolve the provincial and personalized satraps of "the old-time colon" invariably targeted and condemned the unseemly domestic arrangements in which they lived. British high officials in Africa imposed new "character" requirements on their subordinates, designating specific class attributes and conjugal ties that such a selection implied (Kuklick 1979). Critical to this restructuring was a new disdain for colonials *too* adapted to local custom, too removed from the local European community, and too encumbered with intimate native ties. As we have seen in Sumatra, this hands-off policy distanced Europeans in more than one sense: it forbade European staff both from personal confrontations with their Asian fieldhands and from the limited local knowledge they gained through sexual ties.

At the same time medical expertise confirmed the salubrious benefits of European camaraderie and frequent home leaves; of a *cordon sanitaire*, not only around European enclaves, but around each European man and his home. White prestige became redefined by the conventions that would safeguard the moral respectability, cultural identity, and physical well-being of its agents, with which European women were charged. Colonial politics locked European men and women into a routinized protection of their physical health and social space in ways that bound gender prescriptions to the racial cleavages between "us" and "them."

It may be, however, that we should not be searching for congruent colonial chronologies (attached to specific dates) but rather for similar shifts in the *rhythms* of rule and sexual management, for similar internal patterns within specific colonial histories themselves.[40] For example, we know that the Great Rebellion in India in 1857 set off an entire restructuring of colonial morality in which political subversion was tied to sexual impropriety and was met with calls for middle-class respectability, domesticity, and increased segregation—all focusing on European women—nearly a half-century earlier than in colonies elsewhere. Looking to a somewhat longer *durée* than the colonial crises of the early twentieth century, we might consider British responses to the Mutiny not as an exception but as a template, thereby emphasizing the modular quality of colonial perceptions and policies that were built on new international standards of empire, specific metropolitan priorities, and that were always responsive to the local challenges of those who contested European rule.

I have focused here on the multiple levels at which sexual control figured in the substance, as well as the iconography, of racial policy and imperial rule. But colonial politics was not just about sex; nor did sexual relations reduce to colonial politics. On the contrary, sex in the colonies was about sexual access and reproduction, class distinctions and racial demarcations, nationalism and European identity—in different measure and not all at the same time. These major shifts in the positioning of women were not, as we might expect, signaled by the penetration of capitalism per se but by more subtle changes in class politics, imperial morality, and as responses to the vulnerabilities of colonial control. As we attempt broader ethnographies of empire, we may begin to capture how European culture and class politics resonated in colonial settings, how class and gender discriminations were transposed into racial distinctions and reverberated in the metropole as they were fortified on colonial ground. Such investigations should help show that sexual control was both an instrumental image for the body politic, a salient part standing for the whole, and itself fundamental to how racial policies were secured and how colonial projects were carried out.

ACKNOWLEDGMENTS

The research for this paper was supported by an NSF Postdoctoral Fellowship for the International Exchange of Scientists (Grant #INT-8701561), by a NATO Postdoctoral Fellowship in Science (Grant #RCD-8751159), and by funding from the Centre National de la Recherche Scientifique in France. The Center for Asian Studies Amsterdam (CASA) and the Centre d'Etudes Africaines in Paris generously extended their facilities and collegial support. I owe particular thanks to the following people who have read various versions of this text and whose comments I have tried to take into special account here: Julia Adams, Etienne Balibar, Pierre Bourdieu, Robert Connell, Frederick Cooper, Linda Gordon, Lawrence Hirschfeld, Micaela di Leonardo, Gerda Lerner, George Mosse. A much shorter version of this paper has appeared under the title "Making Empire Respectable: The Politics of Race and Sexual Morality in 20th Century Colonial Cultures," *American Ethnologist* 16 (4): 634–660.

NOTES

1. See, for example, Etienne and Leacock (1980), Hafkin and Bay (1976), Robertson and Klein (1983), and Silverblatt (1987). For a review of some this literature in an African context see Bozzoli (1983), Robertson (1987), and White (1988).

2. This is not to suggest that there were not some women whose sojourns in the colonies allowed them to pursue career possibilities and independent life-styles barred to them in metropolitan Europe at the time. However, the experience of professional women in South Asia and Africa highlights how quickly they were shaped into "cultural missionaries" or, in resisting that impulse, were strongly marginalized in their work and social life (see Callaway 1987: 83–164; Ramuschack, n.d.).

3. In subsequent work, I focus explicitly on the contrasts and commonalities in how European women and men represented and experienced the social, psychological, and sexual tensions of colonial life.

4. See Verena Martinez-Alier's *Marriage, Class and Colour in Nineteenth-Century Cuba* (1974), which subtly analyzes the changing criteria by which color was perceived and assigned. For the Netherlands Indies, see Jean Taylor's (1983) exquisite study of the historical changes in the cultural markers of European membership from the seventeenth through the early twentieth centuries. Also see Van Marle's (1952) detailed description of racial classification, conjugal patterns, and sexual relations for the colonial Indies.

5. See Winthrop Jordan (1968: 32–40) on Elizabethan attitudes toward black African sexuality and Sander Gilman's analysis of the sexual iconography of Hottentot women in European art of the eighteenth and nineteenth centuries (1985: 76–

108). On colonial sexual imagery see Malleret (1934: 216–241), Tiffany and Adams (1985), and the bibliographic references therein. "The Romance of the Wild Woman," according to Tiffany and Adams, expressed critical distinctions drawn between civilization and the primitive, culture and nature, and the class differences between repressed middle-class women and "her regressively primitive antithesis, the working-class girl" (1985: 13).

6. Thus in Dutch and French colonial novels of the nineteenth century, for example, heightened sensuality is the recognized reserve of Asian and Indo-European mistresses, and only of those European women born in the colonies and loosened by its moral environment (Daum 1984; Loutfi 1971).

7. The relationship between sexual control, racial violence, and political power has been most directly addressed by students of American Southern social history: see Jordan (1968), Lerner (1972), Dowd Hall (1984), and the analyses by turn-of-the-century Afro-American women intellectuals discussed in Carby (1985). See Painter who argues that the treatment of rape as a symbol of male power was an interpretation held by both white and black male authors (1988: 59).

8. Fear of trade competition from European women is alluded to frequently in historical work on eighteenth-century colonies. In the French trading centers (factories) of the Middle East, for example, the Marseille Chamber of Commerce went to great lengths to ensure that no marriages would take place in their trading domain, fearing that European women and children would pose a threat to the French monopoly. In 1728 any French national married in a factory was prohibited from trading directly or indirectly with the royal government (Cordurie 1984: 42).

9. This exclusion of European-born women was also the case for much of the Portuguese empire from the sixteenth through eighteenth centuries (Boxer 1969: 129–130).

10. The references that Hyam (1986a) cites for homoerotic tendencies in British political biography are not, to my knowledge, paralleled for Dutch colonial officials in the Indies. Although the dangers of homosexuality are frequently invoked to justify prostitution among Chinese plantation workers and concubinage among common European soldiers, such arguments were rarely applied to higher-ranking European staff (Van den Brand 1904; Middendorp 1924: 51; Ming 1983: 69, 83).

11. The danger of sexual abstinence for young men was often invoked to license both concubinage and government-regulated prostitution at different times (Hesselink 1987: 208–209).

12. As Tessel Pollman suggests, the term *njai* glossed several functions: household manager, servant, housewife, wife, and prostitute (1986: 100). Which of these was most prominent depended on a complex equation that included the character of both partners, the prosperity of the European man, and the local conventions of the colonial community in which they lived.

13. Some women were able to use their positions to enhance their own economic and political standing. In Indochina and in the Indies a frequent complaint made by members of the European community was that local women provided employment to their own kin. There is far more evidence, however, that concubines exercised very few rights; they could be dismissed without reason or notice, were exchanged among European employers and, most significantly, as stipulated in the Indies Civil Code of 1848, "had no rights over children recognized by a white man" (Taylor 1983: 148).

14. Although prostitution served some of the colonies for some of the time, it was medically and socially problematic. It had little appeal for those administrations bent on promoting permanent settlement (Kohlbrugge 1901, Ballhatchet 1980; Ming 1983) and venereal disease was difficult to check even with the elaborate system of lock hospitals and contagious-disease acts developed in parts of the British empire. When concubinage was condemned in the 1920s in India, Malaysia, and Indonesia venereal disease spread rapidly, giving rise to new efforts to reorder the domestic arrangements of European men (Butcher 1979; Ming 1983; Taylor 1977; Ballhatchet 1980).

15. In the mid-nineteenth century these arrangements are described as a "necessary evil" with no emotional attachments to native women, for whom "the meaning of our word 'love' is entirely unknown" (Ritter 1856: 21). This portrayal of concubinage as a loveless practical union constrasted sharply with the image of the *nyai* in Chinese literature in the Indies. Bocquet-Siak argues that it was precisely the possibility of romantic love that made concubinage with Javanese or Sudanese women so attractive to Chinese men (1984: 8–9). Cf. Genovese's discussion of the categorical denial that love could enter into relations between slaveholder and slave in the American South: "the tragedy of miscegenation lay not in its collapse into lust and sexual exploitation, but in the terrible pressure to deny the delight, affection and love that so often grew from tawdry beginnings" (1976: 419).

16. In the case of the Indies, interracial marriages increased at the same time that concubinage fell into sharp decline (Van Marle 1952). This rise was undoubtedly restricted to *Indisch* Europeans (those born in the Indies) who may have been eager to legalize preexisting unions in response to the moral shifts accompanying a more European cultural climate of the 1920s (Van Doorn 1985). It undoubtedly should not be taken as an indication of less closure among the highly endogamous European-born (totok) population of that period (I owe this distinction in conjugal patterns to Wim Hendrik).

17. In British Africa "junior officers were not encouraged to marry, and wives' passages to Africa were not paid" (Gann and Duignan 1978: 240).

18. Degler makes a similar point, contrasting the shortage of European women in the Portuguese colonies to the family emigration policy of the British in North America; he argues that the former gave rise to widespread miscegenation and a vast population of mulattos, the "key" to contrasting race relations in the United States and Brazil (1986: 226–238).

19. Similarly, one might draw the conventional contrast between the different racial policies in French, British, and Dutch colonies. However, despite French assimilationist rhetoric, Dutch tolerance of intermarriage, and Britain's overtly segregationist stance, the similarities in the actual maintenance of racial distinctions through sexual control in these varied contexts are perhaps more striking than the differences. For the moment, it is these similarities with which I am concerned. See, for example, Simon (1981: 46–48) who argues that although French colonial rule was generally thought to be more racially tolerant than that of Britain, racial distinctions in French Indochina were *in practice* vigorously maintained. John Laffey also has argued that the cultural relativistic thinking tied to associationist rhetoric was used by Indochina's French *colon* to uphold inequalities in law and education (1977: 65–81).

20. Degler also attributes the tenor of race relations to the attitudes of European

women who, he argues, were not inherently more racist but able to exert more influence over the extramarital affairs of their men. Contrasting race relations in Brazil and the United States, he contends that British women in the English settlements had more social power than their Portuguese counterparts, and therefore slaveholding men could and did less readily acknowledge their mulatto offspring (1986 [1971]: 238).

21. Archive d'Outre Mer GG9903, 1893–1894; GG7663 "Emigration des femmes aux colonies 1897–1904."

22. See the Archive d'Outre Mer, Series S.65, "Free Passage Accorded to Europeans," including dossiers on "free passage for impoverished Europeans," GG 9925, 1897; GG 2269, 1899–1903.

23. European prostitutes and domestics-turned-prostitutes were not banned from South Africa, where at the turn of the century there were estimated to be more than 1,000. Van Onselen argues that their presence was secured by the presence of a large, white, working-class population and a highly unstable labor market for white working-class women (1982: 103–162). Also see Van Heyningen who traces the history of prostitution among continental women in the Cape Colony, arguing that its prohibition was led by white middle-class women "secure . . . in their respectability" and only came about with new notions of racial purity and the large-scale urbanization of blacks after the turn of the century (1984: 192–195).

24. On the intimate relationship between eugenics and anthropology see William Schneider on France (1982), H. Biervliet et al. on the Netherlands (1980), and Paul Rich on Britain (1984).

25. As George Mosse notes, the concept of racial degeneration had been tied to miscegenation by Gobineau and others by the mid-nineteenth century but gained common currency in the decades that followed, entering European medical and popular vocabulary at the turn of the century (1978: 82–88).

26. British eugenists petitioned to refuse marriage licenses to the mentally ill, vagrants, and the chronically unemployed (Davin 1978: 16; Stepan 1982: 123). In the United States a model eugenic sterilization law from 1922 targeted among others "the delinquent, the blind, orphans, homeless and paupers" (Bajema 1976: 138). In Germany during the same period "sterilization was widely and passionately recommended as a solution to shiftlessness, ignorance, laziness in the workforce, . . . prostitution . . . illegitimate birth, the increasing number of ill and insane, . . . poverty; and the rising costs of social services" (Bock 1984: 27). However, in pronatalist France, the sterilization of social deviants was never widely embraced (Leonard 1985).

27. The articles published in the bulletin of the Netherlands Indies Eugenics Society give some sense of the range of themes included in these concerns: these included discussions of "bio-genealogical" investigations, the complementarity between Christian thought and eugenic principles, ethnographic studies of mestizo populations, and the role of Indo-Europeans in the anti-Dutch rebellions (see *Ons Nageslacht* from the years 1928–1932).

28. See Mosse (1985) for an examination of the relationship between manliness, racism, and nationalism in a European context.

29. The linkage made between physical appearance and moral depravity was not confined to evaluations of European colonials alone. Eugenic studies abounded with speculations on the constellation of physical traits that signaled immorality in the

European lower orders, while detailed descriptions of African and Asian indigenous populations paired their physical attributes with immoral and debased tendencies. See, for example, Simon (1977: 29–54) on French descriptions of physical features among Annamites in colonial Indochina.

30. Historical analyses of earlier colonial ventures followed the same explanatory convention. Thus a 1939 publication of the American Geographical Society used the Portuguese colonies to "illustrate the factors that defeated the whites in the eastern hemisphere":

> The unbridled passions of the lower types of invaders, who included outlaws and prostitutes, brought scandal upon the Portuguese name. As few European women came out to India, miscegenation was common, and even the higher classes *degenerated*. . . . [L]ife in Goa became *orientalized*. The whites left all hard work to slaves and fell into luxury, vanity, and sloth . . . the whites adopted the enervating doctrines that trade disgraces a man and domestic work is beneath a woman's social status. These evils are still rampant in British India, as in most of the Eastern tropics where the Europeans hold sway. (Price 1939: 16)

31. Adherence to the idea that "tropical neurasthenia" was a specific malady was not shared by all medical practitioners. Those who suggested that the use of the term be discontinued maintained that tropical neurasthenia was a psychopathology caused by social, not physiological, maladjustment (Culpin [1926] cited in Price 1939: 211).

32. On the social geography of hill-stations in British India and on the predominance of women and children in them, see King (1976: 156–179).

33. Contrast this thinking on appropriate colonial life-styles to that of a Jamaican historian writing in 1793 on the physical characteristics of "tropical whites":

> The women lived calm and even lives, marked by habitual temperance and self-denial. They took no exercise . . . and had no amusement or avocation to compel them to much exertion of either mind or body. . . . Their mode of life and the hot oppressive atmosphere produced lax fiber and pale complexions. They seemed to have just risen from a bed of sickness. Their voices were soft and spiritless, and every step betrayed languor and lassitude. Eminently and deservedly applauded for heart and disposition, *no women on earth made better wives or better mothers.* (quoted in Price 1939: 31; my emphasis)

34. When children were recognized by a European father, a native mother could neither prevent them from being taken from her nor contest paternal suitability for custody.

35. The term *pauperism* was only applied in the Indies to those individuals legally classified as "European" (Ming 1983). At the turn of the century it referred primarily to a class of Indo-Europeans marginalized from the educated and "developed" elements in European society (Blumberger 1939: 19). However, pauperism was by no means synonymous with Eurasian status since 75 percent of the "Dutch" community were of mixed descent, some with powerful political and economic standing (Braconier 1917: 291). As Jacques van Doorn notes, "It was not the Eurasian as such, but the "kleine Indo" [poor Indo] who was the object of ridicule and scorn in European circles" (1983: 8). One could pursue the argument that the denigration of "poor Indos" coincided with a political bid for increased civil liberties among Eurasians at large; that it was as much the danger of Eurasian *empowerment* as pauperism that had to be checked.

36. Lest we assume that such support indicated a liberalization of colonial policy, it should be noted that such conservative colonial architects as van den Bosch (who

instituted the forced cultivation system on Java) were among those most concerned that the government take responsiblity for neglected European offspring (Mansvelt 1932: 292).

37. In colonial India, "orphanages were the starting-point for a lifetime's cycle of institutions" (Arnold 1979: 113). "Unseemly whites"—paupers, the sick, the aged, "fallen women," and the insane were protected, secluded from Asian sight, and placed under European control. In Indonesia, *Pro Juventate* branches supported and housed together "neglected and criminal" youth with special centers for Eurasian children. In French Indochina, colonial officials debated the advantages of providing segregrated education for *métis* youth "to protect" them from discrimination.

38. Not everyone agreed with this evaluation. Cf. the following medical report from 1875: "[I]f the white race does not perpetuate itself in Senegal, one need not attribute it to the weakened reproductive properties of the individuals, but to the thousands of other bad conditions against which they fight a desperate and incessant battle" (Bérenger-Féraud 1875: 491).

39. In search for some alleviation for metropolitan unemployment, a surge of scientific reports appeared reassessing the medical arguments against European settlement in the tropics (as in the proceedings of the 1938 International Congress of Geography).

40. I thank Barney Cohn for pressing me to engage this issue which I attend to more fully in subsequent work.

BIBLIOGRAPHY

Abatucci. 1910. Le milieu africain consideré au point de vue de ses effets sur le système nerveux de l'européen. *Annales d'Hygiène et de Médecine Coloniale* 13: 328–335.

Adas, M. 1989. *Machines as the measure of men.* Ithaca: Cornell University Press.

Angoulvant, Gabriel. 1926. *Les Indies Néelandaises.* Paris: Le Monde Nouveau.

Archive d'Outre–Mer. Aix-en-Marseille, France.

Arnold, David. 1979. European orphans and vagrants in India in the nineteenth century. *The Journal of Imperial and Commonwealth History* 7: 2, 104–127.

———. 1983. White colonization and labour in nineteenth-century India. *Journal of Imperial and Commonwealth History* 11: 2, 133–158.

Bajema, Carl, ed. 1976. *Eugenics then and now.* Stroudsburg, Pa.: Dowden, Hutchinson & Ross.

Ballhatchet, K. 1980. *Race, sex and class under the Raj: Imperial attitudes and policies and their critics, 1793–1905.* New York: St. Martin's Press.

Baroli, March. 1967. *La vie quotidienne des Français en Algérie.* Paris: Hachette.

Bauduin, D. C. M. 1941 (1927). *Het Indische Leven.* 'S-Gravenhage: H. P. Leopolds.

Beidelman, Thomas. 1982. *Colonial evangelism.* Bloomington: Indiana University Press.

Bérenger-Féraud, L. 1875. *Traité clinique des maladies des Européens au Sénégal.* Paris: Adrien Delahaye.

Biervliet, H., et al. 1980. Biologism, racism and eugenics in the anthropology and sociology of the 1930s. *The Netherlands Journal of Sociology* 16: 69–92.

Blumberger, J. Th. P. 1939. *De Indo-Europeesche Beweging in Nederlandsch-Indie.* Haarlem: Tjeenk Willink.

Blussé, Leonard. 1986. *Strange company: Chinese settlers, mestizo women and the Dutch in VOC Batavia*. Dordrecht: Foris.

Bock, Gisela. 1984. Racism and sexism in Nazi Germany: Motherhood, compulsory sterilization, and the state. In *When biology became destiny: Women in Weimar and Nazi Germany*. New York: Monthly Review Press. Pp. 271–296.

Bocquet-Siek, M. 1984. Some notes on the nyai theme in pre-war peranakan Chinese literature. Paper prepared for the Asian Studies Association of Australia, Adelaide University, May 13, 1984.

Boxer, C. R. 1969. *The Portuguese seaborne empire, 1415–1825*. New York: Knopf.

Bozzoli, Belinda. 1983. Marxism, feminism and South African studies. *Journal of Southern African Studies* 9: 2, 139–171.

Boutilier, James. 1984. European women in the Solomon Islands, 1900–1942. In *Rethinking women's roles: Perspectives from the Pacific*. Denise O'Brien and Sharon Tiffany, eds., 173–199. Berkeley, Los Angeles, London: University of California Press.

Braconier, A. de. 1913. Het Kazerne-Concubinaat in Ned-Indie. *Vragen van den Dag* 28: 974–995.

———. 1917. Het Pauperisme onder de in Ned. Oost-Indie levende Europeanen. *Nederlandsch-Indie* (1st yr.): 291–300.

———. 1918. *Kindercriminaliteit en de verzorging van misdadig aangelegde en verwaarloosde minderjarigen in Nederlandsche-Indie*. Baarn: Hollandia-Drukkerij.

———. 1933. Het Prostitutie-vraagstuk in Nederlandsch-Indie. *Indisch Gids* 55: 2, 906–928.

Brand, J. van den. 1904. *Nogeens: De Millionen uit Deli*. Amsterdam: Hoveker & Wormser.

Brink, K. B. M. Ten. 1920. *Indische Gezondheid*. Batavia: Nillmij.

Brou, A. M. N. 1907. Le Métis Franco-Annamite. *Revue Indochinois* (July 1907): 897–908.

Brownfoot, Janice N. 1984. Memsahibs in colonial Malaya: A study of European wives in a British colony and protectorate 1900–1940. In *The incorporated wife*. Hilary Callan and Shirley Ardener, eds. London: Croom Helm.

Butcher, John. 1979. *The British in Malaya, 1880–1941: The social history of a European community in colonial Southeast Asia*. Kuala Lumpur: Oxford University Press.

Callan, Hilary, and Ardener, Shirley. 1984. *The incorporated wife*. London: Croom Helm.

Callaway, Helen. 1987. *Gender, culture and empire: European women in colonial Nigeria*. London: Macmillan Press.

Carby, Hazel. 1985. On the threshold of woman's era: Lynching, empire and sexuality in black feminist theory. *Critical Inquiry* 12 (1): 262–277.

Chailley-Bert, M. J. 1897. *L'Emigration des femmes aux colonies*. Union Coloniale Française-conference, 12 January 1897. Paris: Armand Colin.

Chenet, Ch. 1936. Le role de la femme française aux Colonies: Protection des enfants métis abandonnés. *Le Devoir des Femmes* (15 February 1936): 8.

Chivas-Baron, C. 1929. *La Femme française aux colonies*. Paris: Larose.

Clerkx, Lily. 1961. *Mensen in Deli*. Amsterdam: Sociologisch-Historisch Seminarium for Zuidoost-Azie.

Cock, J. 1980. *Maids and madams.* Johannesburg: Ravan Press.

Cohen, William. 1971. *Rulers of empire: The French colonial service in Africa.* Stanford: Hoover Institution Press.

———. 1980. *The French encounter with Africans: White response to blacks, 1530–1880.* Bloomington: Indiana University Press.

Comaroff, John, and Jean Comaroff. 1986. Christianity and colonialism in South Africa. *American Ethnologist* 13: 1–22.

Cool, F. 1938. De Bestrijding der Werkloosheidsgevolgen in Nederlandsch-Indie gedurende 1930–1936. *De Economist* 87: 135–147, 217–243.

Cooper, Frederic. 1987. *On the African waterfront.* New Haven: Yale University Press.

Cordurie, M. 1984. Résidence des Françaises et Mariage des Français dan les Echelles du Levant au XVIIIe siècle. In *La Femme dan les Sociétés Coloniales.* Pp. 35–47. Aix-en-Provence: Institut d'Histoire des Pays d'Outre-Mer, Université de Provence.

Corneau, Grace. 1900. *La femme aux colonies.* Paris: Librairie Nilsson.

Courtois, E. 1900. Des Règles Hygiéniques que doit suivre l'Européen au Tonkin. *Revue Indo-chinoise* 83: 539–541, 564–566, 598–601.

Daum, P. A. 1984. *Ups and downs of life in the Indies.* Amherst: University of Massachusetts Press.

Davin, Anna. 1978. Imperialism and motherhood. *History workshop* 5: 9–57.

Degler, Carl. 1986. *Neither black nor white.* Madison: University of Wisconsin Press [1971].

Delavignette, Robert. 1946. *Service Africain.* Paris: Gallimard.

Dixon, C. J. 1913. *De Assistent in Deli.* Amsterdam: J. H. de Bussy.

Doorn, Jacques van. 1983. *A divided society: Segmentation and mediation in late-colonial Indonesia.* Rotterdam: CASPA.

———. 1985. Indie als Koloniale Maatschappy. In *De Nederlandse samenleving sinds 1815.* F. L. van Holthoon, ed. Assen: Maastricht.

Douchet. 1928. *Métis et congaies d'Indochine.* Hanoi.

Dowd Hall, Jacquelyn. 1984. "The mind that burns in each body": Women, rape, and racial violence. *Southern Exposure* 12: 6, 61–71.

Drooglever, P. J. 1980. *De Vaderlandse Club, 1929–42.* Franeker: T. Wever.

Dupuy, A. 1955. La personnalité du colon. *Revue d'Histoire Economique et Sociale* 33: 1, 77–103.

Encylopedie van Nederland-Indie. 1919. S'Gravenhage: Nijhoff and Brill.

Engels, Dagmar. 1983. "The age of consent act of 1891: Colonial ideology in Bengal. *South Asia Research* 3 (2): 107–134.

Etienne, Mona, and Eleanor Leacock, eds. 1980. *Women and colonization.* New York: Praeger.

Fanon, Franz. 1967 (1952). *Black skin, white masks.* New York: Grove Press.

Favre, J.-L. 1938. *La vie aux colonies.* Paris: Larose.

Feuilletau de Bruyn, Dr. W. K. H. 1938. Over de Economische Mogelijkheid van een Kolonisatie van Blanken op Nederlandsch Nieuw-Guinea. In *Comptes Rendus du Congrès International de Géographie, Amsterdam.* Brill: Leiden. Pp. 21–29.

Fredrickson, George. 1981. *White supremacy: A comparative study in American and South African history.* New York: Oxford University Press.

Gaitskell, Deborah. 1983. Houseswives, maids or mothers: Some contradictions of domesticity for Christian women in Johannesburg, 1903–39. *Journal of African History* 24: 241–256.

Gann, L. H., and Duignan, Peter. 1978. *The rulers of British Africa, 1870–1914*. Stanford: Stanford University Press.

Gantes, Gilles de. 1981. *La population française au Tonkin entre 1931 et 1938*. Mémoire de Maitrise, Aix-en-Provence: Université de Provence, Centre d'Aix: Institut d'Histoire des Pays d'Outre Mer.

Gartrell, Beverley. 1984. Colonial wives: Villains or victims? in *The Incorporated Wife*. Hillary Callan and Shirely Ardener, eds., 165–185. London: Croom Helm.

Genovese, Eugene. 1976. *Roll, Jordan, Roll: The World the Slaves Made*. New York: Vintage.

Gilman, Sander L. 1985. *Difference and pathology: Stereotypes of sexuality, race, and madness*. Ithaca: Cornell University Press.

Gordon, Linda. 1976. *Woman's body, woman's right: A social history of birth control in America*. New York: Grossman.

Gordon, Robert, and Meryvn Meggitt. 1985. The decline of the Kipas. In *Law and order in the New Guinea Highlands: Encounters with Enga*. R. Gordon and M. Meggit, eds., 39–70. Hanover: University Press of New England.

Grall, Ch. 1908. *Hygiène Coloniale appliquée: Hygiène de l'Indochine*. Paris: Baillière.

Grimshaw, P. 1983. "Christian woman, pious wife, faithful mother, devoted missionary": Conflicts in roles of American missionary women in nineteenth-century Hawaii. *Feminist Studies* 9: 3, 489–521.

Hafkin, Nancy, and Edna Bay, eds. 1976. *Women in Africa: Studies in social and economic change*. Stanford: Stanford University Press.

Hammerton, James. 1979. *Emigrant gentlewomen: Genteel poverty and female emigration 1830–1914*. London: Croom Helm.

Hansen, Karen Tranberg. 1984. Negotiating sex and gender in urban Zambia. *Journal of Southern African Studies* 10: 2, 218–238.

———. 1989. *Distant companions: Servants and employers in Zambia, 1900–1985*. Ithaca: Cornell University Press.

Hardy, George. 1929. *Ergaste ou la Vocation Coloniale*. Paris: Armand Colin.

Hartenberg. 1910. Les Troubles Nerveux et Mentaux chez les coloniaux. Paris.

Harwood, Dorothy. 1938. The possibility of white colonization in the tropics. In *Comptes Rendu du Congrès International de Géographie*. Leiden: Brill. Pp. 131–140.

Hermans, E. H. 1925. *Gezondscheidsleer voor Nederlandsche-Indie*. Amsterdam: Meulenhoff.

Hesselink, Liesbeth. 1987. Prostitution: A necessary evil, particularly in the colonies: Views on prostitution in the Netherlands Indies. In *Indonesian Women in Focus*. E. Locher-Scholten and A. Niehof, eds., 205–224. Dordrecht: Foris.

Het Pauperisme Commissie. 1901. *Het Pauperisme onder de Europeanen*. Batavia: Landsdrukkerij.

———. 1903. *Rapport der Pauperisme-Commissie*. Batavia: Landsdrukkerij.

Heyningen, Elizabeth Van B. 1984. The social evil in the Cape Colony 1868–1902: Prostitution and the contagious disease acts. *Journal of Southern African Studies* 10 (2): 170–197.

Hobsbawm, Eric. 1987. *The Age of Empire, 1875–1914.* London: Weidenfeld and Nicholson.

Hunt, Nancy. 1988. Le bébé en brousse: European women, African birth spacing and colonial intervention in breast feeding in the Belgian Congo. *International Journal of African Historical Studies* 21: 3.

Hyam, Ronald. 1986a. Empire and sexual opportunity. *The Journal of Imperial and Commonwealth History* 14: 2, 34–90.

———. 1986b. Concubinage and the colonial service: The Crewe circular (1909). *The Journal of Imperial and Commonwealth History* 14: 3, 170–186.

Inglis, Amirah. 1975. *The White Women's Protection Ordinance: Sexual anxiety and politics in Papua.* London: Sussex University Press.

Jaurequiberry. 1924. *Les Blancs en Pays Chauds.* Paris: Maloine.

Jordan, Winthrop. 1968. *White over black: American attitudes toward the Negro, 1550–1812.* Chapel Hill: University of North Carolina Press.

Joyeux, Ch., and A. Sice. 1937. Affections exotiques du système nerveux. *Précis de Médecine Coloniale.* Paris: Masson.

Kantoor van Arbeid. 1935. *Werkloosheid in Nederlandsch-Indie.* Batavia: Landsdrukkerij.

Kennedy, Dane. 1987. *Islands of white: Settler society and culture in Kenya and Southern Rhodesia, 1890–1939.* Durham: Duke University Press.

Kennedy, Raymond. 1947. *The ageless Indies.* New York: John Day.

Kevles, Daniel. 1985. *In the name of eugenics.* Berkeley, Los Angeles, London: University of California Press.

King, Anthony. 1976. *Colonial urban development: culture, social power and environment.* London: Routledge & Kegan Paul.

Kirkwood, Deborah. 1984. Settler wives in Southern Rhodesia: A case study. In *The Incorporated Wife.* H. Callan and S. Ardener, eds. London: Croom Helm.

Knibiehler, Yvonne, and Regine Goutalier. 1985. *La femme au temps des colonies.* Paris: Stock.

———. 1987. *"Femmes et Colonisation": Rapport Terminal au Ministère des Relations Extérieures et de la Cooperation.* Aix-en-Provence: Institut d'Histoire des Pays d'Outre-Mer.

Kohlbrugge, J.F.H. 1910. *Prostitie in Nederlandsch-Indie.* Indisch Genootschap of 19 February 1901: 2–36.

Koks, Dr. J. Th. 1931. *De Indo.* Amsterdam: H. J. Paris.

Kroniek 1917. Oostkust van Sumatra-Instituut. Amsterdam: J. H. de Bussy.

Kroniek 1933. Oostkust van Sumatra-Instituut. Amsterdam: J. H. de Bussy.

Kuklick, Henrika. 1979. *The imperial bureaucrat: The colonial administrative service in the Gold Coast, 1920–1939.* Stanford: Hoover Institution Press.

La Femme dan les Sociétés Coloniales. 1982. Table Ronde CHEE, CRHSE, IHPOM. Institut d'Historie des Pays d'Outre-Mer, Université de Provence.

Laffey, John. 1977. Racism in Tonkin before 1914. *French Colonial Studies* 8: 65–81.

Lanessan, J.-L. 1889. *Indochine Française.* Paris: Felix Alcan.

Le Bras, Hervé. 1981. Histoire secrète de la fécondité. *Le Débat* 8: 76–100.

Leonard, Jacques. 1985. Les origines et les conséquences de l'eugenique en France. *Annales de Demographie Historique*: 203–214.

Lerner, Gerda. 1972. *Black women in white America.* New York: Pantheon.

Le Roux. 1898. *Je Deviens Colon.* Paris.

Loutfi, Martine Astier. 1971. *Littérature et Colonialisme.* Paris: Mouton.

Lucas, Nicole. 1986. Trouwerbod, inlandse huishousdsters en Europese vrouwen: Het concubinaat in de planterswereld aan Sumatra's Oostkust 1860–1940. In *Vrouwen in de Nederlandse Kolonien.* J. Reijs, et al. Nijmegen: SUN. Pp. 78–97.

Mackinnon, Murdoch. 1920. European Children in the Tropical Highlands. *Lancet* 199: 944–945.

Malleret, Louis. 1934. *L'Exotisme Indochinois dans la Littérature Française depuis 1860.* Paris: Larose.

Mannoni, Octavio. 1956. *Prospero and Caliban: The psychology of colonization.* New York: Praeger.

Mansvelt, W. 1932. De Positie der Indo-Europeanen. *Kolonial Studien* 16: 290–311.

Marks, Schula, ed. 1987. *Not either an experimental doll: The separate worlds of three South African women.* Bloomington: Indiana University Press.

Marle, A. van. 1952. De group der Europeanen in Nederlands-Indie. *Indonesie* 5 (2): 77–121; 5 (3): 314–341; 5 (5): 481–507.

Martinez-Alier, Verena. 1974. *Marriage, class and colour in nineteenth century Cuba.* Cambridge: Cambridge University Press.

Mason, Philip. 1958. *The birth of a dilemma.* New York: Oxford University Press.

Maunier, M. René. 1932. *Sociologie Coloniale.* Paris: Domat-Montchrestien.

Mazet, Jacques. 1932. *La Condition Juridique des Métis.* Paris: Domat-Montchrestien.

McClure, John A. 1981. *Kipling and Conrad: The colonial fiction.* Cambridge: Harvard University Press.

Mercier, Paul. 1965. The European community of Dakar. In *Africa: Social Problems of Change and Conflict.* Pierre van den Berghe, ed., 284–304. San Francisco: Chandler.

Metcalf, Thomas. 1964. *The aftermath of revolt: India, 1857–1870.* Princeton: Princton University Press.

Middendorp, W. 1924. *De Poenale Sanctie.* Haarlem: Tjeenk Willink.

Ming, Hanneke. 1983. Barracks-concubinage in the Indies, 1887–1920. *Indonesia* 35 (April): 65–93.

Moore-Gilbert, B. J. 1986. *Kipling and "orientalism."* New York: St. Martin's.

Moses, Claire Goldberg. 1984. *French feminism in the nineteenth century.* Albany: SUNY Press.

Mosse, George. 1978. *Toward the Final Solution.* New York: Fertig.

———. 1985. *Nationalism and sexuality.* Madison: University of Wisconsin Press.

Nandy, Ashis. 1983. *The intimate enemy: Loss and recovery of self under colonialism.* Delhi: Oxford University Press.

Nash, J. 1980. Aztec women: The transition from status to class in empire and colony. In *Women and Colonization: Anthropological Perspectives.* M. Etienne and E. Leacock, eds., 134–148. New York: Praeger.

Nieuwenhuys, Roger. 1959. *Tussen Twee Vaderlanden.* Amsterdam: Van Oorschot.

Nora, Pierre. 1961. *Les Français d'Algerie.* Paris: Julliard.

O'Brien, Rita Cruise. 1972. *White society in Black Africa: The French in Senegal.* London: Faber & Faber.

Onselen, Charles van. 1982. Prostitutes and proletarians, 1886–1914. In *Studies in the social and economic history of the Witwatersrand 1886–1914,* vol. 1. New York: Longman. Pp. 103–162.

Ons Nageslacht: Orgaan Van de Eugenetische vereeniging in Ned-Indie. Batavia.

Painter, N. I. 1988. "Social equality": Miscegenation, labor and power. In *The Evolution of Southern Culture*. N. Bartley, ed. Athens: University of Georgia Press.

Pollmann, Tessel. 1986. Bruidstraantjes: De Koloniale roman, de njai en de apartheid. In *Vrouwen in de Nederlandse Kolonien*. Jeske Reijs, et al., 98–125. Nijmegen: SUN.

Pourvourville, Albert de. 1926. Le Métis. In *Le Mal d'Argent*. Paris: Monde Moderne. Pp. 97–114.

Price, Grenfell A. 1939. *White settlers in the Tropics*. New York: American Geographical Society.

Prochaska, David. 1989. *Making Algeria French: Colonialism in Bone, 1870–1920*. Cambridge: Cambridge University Press.

Pujarniscle, E. 1931. *Philoxène ou de la littérature coloniale*. Paris.

Ralston, Caroline. 1977. *Grass huts and warehouses: Pacific beach communities of the nineteenth century*. Canberra: ANU Press.

Ramuschack, Barbara. N.d. Cultural missionaries, maternal imperialist, feminist allies: British women activists in India, 1865–1945. In *Women Studies International* (forthcoming).

Raptchinsky, B. 1941. *Kolonisatie van blanken in de tropen*. Den Haag: Bibliotheek van Weten en Denken.

Reijs, J., E. Kloek, U. Jansz, A. de Wildt, S. van Norden, and M. de Bat. 1986. *Vrouwen in de Nederlandse Kolonien*. Nijmegen. SUN.

Rich, P. 1984. The long Victorian sunset: Anthropology, eugenics and race in Britain, c. 1900–48. *Patterns of Prejudice* 18 (3): 3–17.

Ridley, Hugh. 1981. *Images of imperial rule*. New York: Croom & Helm.

Ritter, W. L. 1856. *De Europeaan in Nederlandsch Indie*. Leyden: Sythoff.

Robertson, Claire, and Martin Klein, eds. 1983. *Women and Slavery in Africa*. Madison: University of Wisconsin Press.

Robertson, Claire. 1987. Developing economic awareness: Changing perspectives in studies of African Women, 1976–85. *Feminist Studies* 13: 1, 97–135.

Rodenwaldt, Ernest. 1928. Eugenetische Problemen in Nederlandsch-Indie. In *Ons Nageslacht*. Orgaan van de Eugenetische Vereeniging in Nederland-Indie (1928): 1–8.

Ross, Ellen, and Rayna, Rapp. 1980. Sex and society: A research note from social history and anthropology. *Comparative Studies in Society and History* 22: 1, 51–72.

Said, Edward W. 1978. *Orientalism*. New York: Vintage.

Sambuc. 1931. Les Métis Franco-Annamites en Indochine. *Revue du Pacifique*, 256–272.

Schneider, William. 1982. Toward the improvement of the human race. The history of eugenics in France. *Journal of Modern History* 54: 269–291.

Schoevers, T. 1913. Het leven en werken van den assistent bij de Tabakscultuur in Deli. *Jaarboek der Vereeniging "Studiebelangen."* Wageningen: Zomer. Pp. 3–43.

Schmidt, Elizabeth. 1987. Ideology, economics, and the role of Shona women in Southern Rhodesia, 1850–1939. Ph.D. dissertation, University of Wisconsin.

———. N.d. "Race, sex and domestic labour: The question of African female servants in Southern Rhodesia, 1900–1939." MS.

Showalter, Elaine. 1987. *The female malady*. New York: Penguin.

Silverblatt, Irene. 1987. *Moon, sun, and witches: Gender ideologies and class in Inca and colonial Peru.* Princeton: Princeton University Press.

Simon, Pierre-Jean. 1977. Portraits Coloniaux des Vietnamiens (1858–1914). *Pluriel* 10: 29–54.

———. 1981. *Rapatriés d'Indochine: Un village franco-indochinois en Bourbonnais.* Paris: Harmattan.

Sivan, Emmanuel. 1983. *Interpretations of Isalm, past and present.* Princeton: Darwin Press.

Smith-Rosenberg, C., and C. Rosenberg. 1973. The female animal: Medical and biological views of woman and her role in nineteenth-century America. *Journal of American History* 60: 2, 332–356.

Spear, Percival. 1963. *The nabobs.* London: Oxford University Press.

Spencer, J. E., and W. L. Thomas, 1948. The hill stations and summer resorts of the orient. *Geographical Review* 38: 4, 637–651.

Stepan, Nancy. 1982. *The idea of race in science: Great Britain, 1880–1960.* London: Macmillan.

Stocking, George. 1982 (1968). *Race, culture, and evolution.* Chicago: University of Chicago Press.

Stoler, Ann. 1985a. *Capitalism and confrontation in Sumatra's plantation belt, 1870–1979.* New Haven: Yale University Press.

———. 1985b. Perceptions of protest: Defining the dangerous in colonial Sumatra. *American Ethnologist* 12: 4, 642–658.

———. 1989a. Rethinking colonial categories: European communities and the boundaries of rule. *Comparative Studies in Society and History* 13 (1): 134–161.

———. 1989b. Making empire respectable: The politics of race and sexual morality in 20th century colonial cultures. *American Ethnologist* 16 (4): 634–660.

Strobel, Margaret. 1987. Gender and race in the nineteenth- and twentieth-century British empire. In *Becoming visible: Women in European history.* Boston: Houghton Mifflin.

Stuurman, Siep. 1985. *Verzuiling, Kapitalisme en Patriarchaat.* Nijmegen: SUN.

Sumatra Post. Medan, Sumatra.

Sutherland, Heather. 1982. Ethnicity and access in colonial Macassar. In *Papers of the Dutch-Indonesian historical conference.* Dutch and Indonesian Steering Committees of the Indonesian Studies Programme. Leiden: Bureau of Indonesian Studies. Pp. 250–277.

Takaki, Ronald. 1977. *Iron Cages.* Berkeley, Los Angeles, London: University of California Press.

Taylor, Jean. 1977. The world of women in the colonial Dutch novel. *Kabar Seberang* 2: 26–41.

———. 1983. *The social world of Batavia.* Madison: University of Wisconsin Press.

Tiffany, Sharon, and Kathleen Adams. 1985. *The wild woman: An inquiry into the anthropology of an idea.* Cambridge, Mass: Schenkman.

Tirefort, A. 1979. "Le Bon Temps": La Communauté Française en Basse Cote d'Ivoire pendant l'Entre-Deux Guerres, 1920–1940. Troisième Cycle, Centre d'Etudes Africaines.

Travaux du Groupe d'Etudes Coloniales. 1910. *La Femme Blanche au Congo.* Brussels: Misch and Thron.

Treille, G. 1888. *De L'Acclimatation des Europeens dan les Pays Chaud.* Paris: Octave Doin.

Union Géographique International. 1938. *Comptes Rendus du Congres International de Géographie, Amsterdam 1938.* Leiden: Brill.

Van-Helten, Jean J., and K. Williams. 1983. "The crying need of South Africa": The emigration of single British women to the Transvaal, 1901–1910. *Journal of South African Studies* 10: 1, 11–38.

Van Heyningen, Elizabeth B. 1984. The social evil in the Cape Colony 1868–1902: Prostitution and the Contagious Disease Act. *Journal of Southern African Studies* 10 (2): 170–197.

Veerde, A. G. 1931. Onderzoek naar den omvang der werkloosheid op Java (November 1930–June 1931). *Koloniale Studien* 16: 242–273, 503–533.

Vellut, Jean-Luc. 1982. Materiaux pour une image du Blanc dan la société coloniale du Congo Belge. In *Stérotypes Nationaux et Préjugés Raciaux aux XIXe et XXe Siècles.* Jean Pirotte, ed. Leuven: Editions Nauwelaerts.

Vere Allen, J. de. 1970. Malayan civil service, 1874–1941: Colonial bureaucracy/ Malayan elite. *Comparative Studies in Society and History* 12: 149–178.

Wanderken, P. 1943. Zoo leven onze kinderen. In *Zoo Leven Wij in Indonesia.* Deventer: Van Hoever. Pp. 172–187.

Wertheim, Willem. 1959. *Indonesian society in transition.* The Hague: Van Hoeve.

White, Luise. 1988. Book review. *Signs* 13 (2): 360–364.

———. 1990. The Comforts of Home: Prostitution in Colonial Nairobi. Chicago: University of Chicago Press.

Winckel, C. W. F. 1938. The feasibility of white settlements in the tropics: A medical point of view. In *Comptes Rendus du Congrès International de Géographie, Amsterdam,* vol. 2, sect. IIIc. Leiden: Brill. Pp. 345–356.

Woodcock, George. 1969. *The British in the Far East.* New York: Atheneum.

TWO

Original Narratives
The Political Economy of Gender in Archaeology

Margaret W. Conkey
with the collaboration of Sarah H. Williams

Archaeology has come late to the feminist arena. Although significant work on gender in sociocultural anthropology and many sister disciplines began to appear in the early 1970s, the first major review article for archaeology was published in 1984 (Conkey and Spector 1984). In the short period since, however, work on gender in prehistory and archaeology has begun to develop rapidly (e.g. Arnold et al. 1988; Bumstead 1987; Deagan 1983; all the papers in Gero and Conkey 1990; Gibb 1987; Marshall 1985; Pohl and Feldman 1982; Russell 1987; Stig-Sørenson 1987; Welbourn 1984; Zagarell 1986).

In what follows I will review the short history of gender inquiry and feminist research in archaeology (especially Anglo-American anthropological archaeology) and then focus on a critique of a particular domain of archaeological inquiry—"origins research." I will show how "origins research" seduces archaeology—and popular culture, which relies on archaeology for notions of human beginnings—into an untenable position. Origins research has inherited key constructions of the meaning of gender that it perpetuates through its authorial weight. That is, archaeological narratives embedding notions of gender in prehistory actually reflect notions of gender in the recent past, while heavily influencing our constructions of gender in the present.

Knowledge about our reconstructions or interpretations involving gender in the past is, of course, linked to and derived from the sociopolitics of archaeological practice (e.g. Conkey 1978; Gero 1983, 1985; Yellen 1983). To discuss the concepts and uses of gender in archaeology is just as much an inquiry into the question of gender in archaeological practice, although I will not deal with such practice directly. Rather, there is more than enough to say here about what the implications are for the anthropology of gender given how our objects of knowledge—what it is we want to know about the past, especially about "origins"—have been conceptualized, institutionalized and, thus, have structured both our research and our received views of human prehistory.

A LITTLE BIT OF HISTORY BY WAY OF INTRODUCTION[1]

In 1977, the American Anthropological Association's Committee on the Status of Women in Anthropology sponsored a symposium at the association's annual meetings on the impact of feminist research in the different anthropological subfields. As the spokesperson from the committee for archaeology, I found my task not too difficult (Conkey 1977). There were no edited volumes in archaeology to parallel even the earliest ones in sociocultural anthropology (e.g. Rosaldo and Lamphere 1974); there were no papers or books entitled "Gender Arrangements and Early Food Production," "Gender Structures and Culture Change," or even "Men and Women in Prehistory"! Yet this does not mean that little had been said or implied about men and women in the past, about gender relations, differences, and activities; what had been said can be seen from two perspectives.

On the one hand, notions about males/females, men/women, and about gender relations have always been—and still are—injected into representations and reconstructions of the past by numberless researchers and writers who have not, however, been practicing archaeologists (e.g. Diner 1973; Eisler 1987). In particular, of course, many have enunciated visions of early stages or forms of human (and prehuman) social life (e.g. Cucchiari 1981; Davis 1971; Engels 1972; Foley and Lee 1989; Lovejoy 1981; Morgan 1972; Parker 1987; Reed 1975). These reconstructions have often been used as part of hypothesized scenarios (some of them feminist) for human evolution that do not draw on actual archaeological fieldwork and analysis, if only because very little has been done that has been explicitly directed toward the attribution or interpretation of gender. Included here would be the recent scholarly works inspired by the development of feminist theories in the 1970s (e.g. Tanner 1981; Tanner and Zihlman 1976; Zihlman 1978, 1981), which simultaneously have been limited by the lack of archaeological research on gender that could be used to support alternative evolutionary scenarios.

On the other hand, archaeologists themselves have contributed to and perpetuated certain limited and ethnocentric (i.e. sexist) views on women and gender relations. Archaeology and prehistory, in a sense, have always been gendered—gendered "androcentric." This practice derives from many sources: from a *lack* of explicit social theory so that scholars implicitly employ present-ist notions about gender; from the differential use of language in discussing the activities and behaviors of males and females in past societies; from the particular way in which systems theory has been used in archaeology of the past decades; and from not having developed the questions or the methods with which to inquire into gender, although other equally "elusive" social phenemona, such as status, seem to have received great theoretical and methodological attention (e.g. Renfrew and Shennan 1982).[2]

ORIGINS RESEARCH AS CULTURAL LEGITIMATION

There is no doubt that there has been great public interest in the spectacular *results* achieved by archaeological research in extending the record of the human past, but this has been at the expense of understanding the *processes* by which the results have been achieved (Rowe 1956). To understand these processes, one must turn just as much to an analysis of the practice of archaeology, as an historically, culturally, and politically contingent enterprise, as to an analysis of the new techniques (e.g. radiometric dating techniques) and innovations in theory and method. Among the most favored research problems are those that implicitly or explicitly address "origins": from the origins of hominids to the origins of the state; the origins of agriculture, of ranking, trade, status, fire, art, toolmaking, hunting, the family, gender asymmetry, language, consciousness, symbolism, pottery, and so forth.[3] From the primacy of origins research comes its power to structure the inquiry of the discipline, to influence the career success of archaeologists, to reach the public, and to serve as a vehicle for political messages. In this section, I will discuss some features of origins research in general; in the next, I will consider some of the implications of origins research for archaeology and the study of gender.

Narratives and Categories

We do not even need to invoke the recent emphasis on anthropology-as-narrative, as-production-of-text (e.g. Clifford and Marcus 1986; Scholte 1986), to realize that origins research derives from and constitutes a methodology of narration. Like ethnographic texts, archaeological texts are "allegories of quest, allegories of comparison, allegories of origin" (Marcus and Clifford 1985: 26). Narratives, such as those that "tell the story of human evolution," must have a beginning, and those who write the scenarios are—like all writers—subject to their preferred narrative devices.

One prevalent device in evolutionary narratives is the use of/dependence upon gaps; we produce gaps as we fill them. With each "find" that may fill in some sort of a gap (in a regional sequence, for example), another gap is simultaneously created; a gap that is expected to be filled in some day by some equally heroic discovery. There are gaps in the sequence, in the record of fossils and of materials; gaps between the academic fields that write evolution; gaps between tool use and intelligence, between "man" and ape, between man and woman, between self and consciousness. The representation of the human career is

conditional upon gaps...that must be continually and simultaneously re-
solved and maintained. The "missing link" must be (and has been) repeatedly
found, *and* can never be found. (Williams 1986: 17)

Those who simultaneously fill and create gaps play a central role in the perpetuation and control of archaeological narratives.

Another narrative device derived from primacy-of-origins research is the
guarantee of continuity. We use the same analytical categories for phenomena that are millions of years and maybe six biological species apart: there
are flakes, cores, stone tools, sites, social groups, aggression, territories, division of labor and, for some, there are monogamous family units (e.g. Lovejoy
1981); pairbonds (monogamy) (e.g. Parker 1987); or "polygynous male
family groups" (Foley and Lee 1989: 905).

Archaeological narratives of origins tell only what we "know" but are
framed in differential contexts where the variables—humanness, language,
symbolism, the state, the family, division of labor—have multiple referents
and are embedded in contested and ever-changing agendas (e.g. Trigger
1984). They are culturally constructed variables—not inherent essential
qualities—and the narratives that are created are "archaeo-logical" and
"make sense" not only for the available and perceived archaeological data
but also for the historically contingent cultural contexts within which they
are situated. (See, for example, the discussion of the debate over the Mound-
builders of the prehistoric U.S. southeast, Willey and Sabloff 1980: 19–25.)
Our narratives—in structure (Landau 1984) and in content—"make sense"
and are archaeo-logical for us as actors in our specific historical contexts.

An anecdote brings to mind the way in which archaeological and evolutionary writers work. A Cree hunter came to Montreal to testify in court
concerning the fate of his hunting lands in the new James Bay hydroelectric
scheme. He was to describe his way of life, but (as Clifford tells the story,
1986: 8), when he was administered the oath, he hesitated: "I'm not sure I
can tell the truth...I can only tell what I know." This witness, Clifford
points out, "spoke artfully in a determining context of power" (1986: 8).

It has been argued that classification is ethnography's means of construction, and we know that it is archaeology's means of reconstruction. There is a
standard list of "institutions" in ethnographic research, and much inquiry is
about what forms they take and how they came into existence. This list provides the table of contents for the "full" description: societal or cultural
wholes are made from this list and exist (only) in texts (Marcus and Clifford
1985). The "institutions" are comprised of many ahistorical empirical categories designated by eighteenth-century (and later) European contexts in
which anthropology developed. They are more than familiar to us; they are
the givens of our discourse and the object of our inquiry: class, race, household, state, social structure, ranking, trade, status, man.

We have inherited these categories (and others); we continue to treat them as genera, of which each ethnographic or historic context produced variants or species. We think of each as having a given original form that changes under the effect of such reified phenomena as population growth, environmental change, or hypercoherence. Our attempts to study the ethnographic or histori-cal variations of these categories is overshadowed by *an implicit assumption of continuity* that makes the origins of these "things" the crucial issue. (McGuire 1985: 2)

We come to our subject with the implicit "table of contents," and when we assume that the "units" are universal characteristics or at least inherent "pulls" in the development of human societies, then we implicitly or explicitly rely on a search for origins—of domestication, of inequality, of the state.

Furthermore, as McGuire (1985) has argued, the origin of the state (or civilization) is seen as "the great divide in human history, which separates us from our egalitarian kin-centered past." We see this division not as a series of separate histories but as an evolutionary break. The primitive peoples of the world have been cast in a timeless ethnographic present (Fabian 1983) on the other side of this divide: "the cradles of civilization . . . lay on the brink of the great chasm linked in an ahistorical past" (McGuire 1985: 3).

This "great divide," historically, differentiated anthropologists and anthropological archaeologists from others in the social sciences:

> In the 19th century intellectual subdivision of the world, the primitive fell to the anthropologist, and prehistory (the time before civilization introduced writ-ing) fell to the anthropological (or prehistoric) archaeologist. The great divide—marked by the origin of the state—defined a unique subject for a unique investigator. In so doing, it legitimated and perpetuated an atomistic, evolutionary view of the world. (McGuire 1985: 3–4)

It also legitimated the intellectual position of the archaeologist within anthropology. Archaeology was originally framed within anthropology be-cause it could be the way in which origins were sought and the evolutionary forms could unfold. "Prehistory could prove evolution" (Lowie 1937: 22; cited by Miller 1983: 5).

Thus, origins research makes archaeology relevant: we take the attributes of the present and of "us"—ranking, trade, the state, gender asymmetry; or, we take the attributes or characteristics we think differentiate us from other classes of beings—toolmaking, food-sharing, language, symbolism, female orgasm—and we seek the origins of these: how, where, who, when? That some early hominids "colonized" the more northernly latitudes or Australia gives some contemporary human practices—for example, colonization— great temporal depth and, by extension, legitimacy. (By making Native Americans and Australian aborigines the original colonizers, the atrocities of subsequent colonialisms are diffused.) Thus, origins inquiry not only links us to the human and prehuman past but also legitimates those in power, justifying research funding. Origins research legitimates us as practitioners; our origins inquiry is legitimated by the theoretical superstructure of our own making.

Self-Consciousness in Archaeology

Such claims about the practice of archaeology are not particularly original, although the elaboration of a critical self-consciousness of the sociopolitics of archaeology is relatively recent (e.g. Gero et al. 1983; Gero 1985; Leone 1982; Leone et al. 1987; Patterson 1986; Shanks and Tilley 1987a, 1987b; Shennan 1986; Trigger 1980, 1984; Wylie 1985). Leone (n.d.) has argued that there are key domains in which a critical analysis (of archaeological practice) can help us better understand the past and our relationship to it. One such domain is in the large public archaeological issues, such as all sorts of human origins questions in which archaeological data (and their interpretations) play a central role in verifying positions that have important public and political implications.

The archaeological topics that are regularly reported on in the *New York Times* (especially the Science section), that comprise the few archaeology cover stories on weekly news magazines (Richard Leakey and human origins in *Time*; an early Cro-Magnon and the origins of art in *Newsweek*), and that dominate the archaeology reporting in *National Geographic* (Gero and Root 1989) all support the observation that the questions about origins—of social inequality, warfare, territoriality, "the" state, "the" family, art, symbolism, religion, or of specific groups (early "man" in the New World, or the first anatomically modern humans)—are specifically related to gender, race, class and foreign-policy politics in American life. Trigger, for example, shows the effects of the positivism of the "new archaeology" of the 1960s and 1970s:

> Viewing the (American) Indians' past as a convenient laboratory for testing general hypotheses about sociocultural development and human behavior may be simply a more intellectualized manifestation of the lack of sympathetic concern for native peoples that in the past has permitted archaeologists to disparage their cultural achievements, excavate their cemeteries, and display Indian skeletons in museums without taking thought for the feelings of native peoples. (Trigger 1980: 671)

That is, not only are the particular topics that are chosen for study socially constructed, but also a particular epistemology (positivism) is related to/endorsed by the same social contexts.

We have set origins apart, analytically, from the forms that phenomena may take; that is, we have isolated the study of the origins of "art," of "the family," or of "the state" apart from their historical contexts and historical formations. It is only recently that we have come to discuss, for example, that there is no such unified phenomenon as "the state" (e.g. Gailey 1985, 1987; McGuire 1985; Silverblatt 1988, and this volume). There are only states, set in particular historical instances. But "origins" have been constru(ct)ed as knowable entities amenable to positivist inquiries; entities that cannot only be located spatiotemporally but also manipulated, as discussed below, to fit the archaeo-logic.

This construction of origins as knowable entities, as objects of knowledge, follows directly from the practice of archaeology that sets "the past" aside from the present, at least at one analytical level. This allows us to conceive of "it" as a separate "know-able" entity or object of our inquiry. This tends to inhibit our confronting the ways in which aspects of the past—if not the very subject matters of the past—are defined and redefined in relation to the present.

Anachronisms and the Research Cone

Although archaeology, too, has its "table of contents," its list of institutions and cultural phenomena to seek the origins of and to use as the themes and tropes for writing the past, not all phenomena are thought to be equally knowable or "recoverable" archaeologically. There has long prevailed a "ladder of inference" (in the sense of the nineteenth-century French sociologist, A. Comte) and a hierarchy of knowables (e.g. Hawkes 1954), in the sense that aspects of technology, economy, and the "immediately material" are thought to be more readily inferred and "known" by archaeological research, whereas the more social, symbolic, religious, and spiritual are thought to be increasingly inaccessible. Although the recent influence of a structuralist method has allowed more work on the more cognitive, symbolic, and social (e.g. Deetz 1977; Hodder 1982a, b, c; Leone 1982), what is particularly relevant here is not the debate over ontological issues and knowledge claims but what has happened to certain of these more-or-less knowable aspects of the past *in relationship to the present*.

Within the past twenty-five years, a new field has emerged within anthropology—paleoanthropology—that has come to be defined explicitly as the study of human origins (Wolpuff 1980: v).[4] In conjunction with this field, this same time period has witnessed the investigation of many aspects of human origins, particularly relating to the earliest millenia of hominids and their development toward anatomically modern humans. We maintain a sequential narrative of human evolution, but it is always changing, at least in terms of where certain variables are first found along the trajectory of our evolutionary path.

But all categories of evidence—"read" primary and essential features of humanity—are not equally malleable in their positioning along the trajectory. Aspects of biology and technology have been pushed back in time, given, therefore, greater antiquity, and become more "natural" and "given."

Just compare with those of the 1960s the currently accepted dates for the first true hominids and bipedalism (1.6 million years ago vs. 3–4 million years ago); for the earliest stone tools (1.5 million years ago vs. perhaps 3 million years ago); and even brain reorganization, leading to our heralded cerebral dominance (1.8 million years ago vs. more than 3 million years ago). There are also arguments for the deliberate hominid mastery of fire at more than 1 million years ago, pushing it back from the previously claimed .4 to .6 million years ago (Toth and Schick 1986).

Yet those categories of evidence (and those cultural phenomena) that are "less-knowable"—and yet also more securely modern and fully human— have not (despite attempts) been succesfully pushed back in time: the first "art"; language-as-we-know-it, and, by extension, fully symbolic behaviors; ethnic or at least "identity-conscious social groups"; social aggregations; regional alliance networks, and so forth have all been kept quite close to "us" and to the emergence and spread of anatomically modern humans, *Homo sapiens sapiens*.

This differential emphasis on certain variables and the subsequent differences in which variables are more likely or more easily "pushed back" can be seen in the same terms that the historian DeLivre (1974) has used to analyze oral histories of the sequential kings among the Malagasy, who establish their positions as they come into office by employing what DeLivre calls ascending and descending anachronisms (see Kus 1986 for the introduction of DeLivre's work into the archaeological literature). With each new king, events from the past tend to be rearranged as to when they happened in relation to the king's having come into office; that is, as in archaeological histories, aspects of the past are redefined in relation to the present.

Ascending anachronisms are those events that are pushed back and thus "naturalized"—given continuity and tenacity. Descending anachronisms are events that are pushed ahead in a chronological sequence; such events are "drawn in" closer to the present where they may become a part of—if not a definer of—our own "cultural prowess" (Kus 1986).

If one overlays (fig. 1) the set of events in the human career over the "ladder of inference" that Hawkes (1954) has suggested for archaeology— with the decreasing reliability of knowledge as one moves from left (techniques of manufacture) to right (spiritual life)—there is a certain congruence between those phenemona and those "origins" that can be pushed back and those that can be most reliably "known." Drawing on the epistemological preferences of archaeology thàt hold not only that techno-environmental processes are more causal (certainly more causal than social or symbolic processes) in understanding prehistoric culture change (e.g. Gould and Watson 1982; c.f. Binford 1980 vs. Wiessner 1982), but also that they are more knowable, has enabled the privileging of origins research into such technoecological phenomena that, in turn, provides an "archaeo-logical" account and an

Hawkes' (1954) "Ladder of Inference"

MORE KNOWABLE	------------SECURITY OF KNOWLEDGE--------		LESS KNOWABLE
techniques of manufacture	subsistence economies	social organization	religious institutions and spiritual life

---

ASCENDING ANACHRONISMS?	DESCENDING ANACHRONISMS?
techno-environmental control	social and symbolic forms

```
-------------- fire                              "art"------------------
-------------- stone tools                              symbolism-----------
-------------- hominids as a biological form     ------ language-as-we-know-it---

   antiquity          --------------------TIME---------------------          most  recent
```

Fig. 1. This figure attempts to compare two aspects of archaeological knowledge. The top portion of the figure illustrates the classic "ladder of inference" specified by Hawkes (1954), which argues that some aspects of prehistoric life are more knowable than others. For example, subsistence and economics are "fairly easy" to know, whereas social organization and religious and spiritual life are close to impossible to know. This ladder of inference is compared here with the classes of archaeological data that are most often considered in evolutionary research, from fire to language. Some of these classes are regularly being "pushed back" in their antiquity, perhaps comparable to DeLivre's (1974) "ascending anachronisms"; others are generally guarded to remain "close" to our own biological species, much like DeLivre's "descending anachronisms" (see also Kus 1986). The point of interest here is that there is a correspondence between those data that are thought to be more easily known, those that are more easily acceptable as "ascending anachronisms," and those that are most directly related to technoenvironmental control.

antiquity for such deeper cultural premises ("ideo-logics") as "man shall have dominion over the earth." Once the techno-environmental (and, symbolically male) domain has been lent privilege, the very consideration of an archaeology of gender loses salience.

Of additional interest are those phenomena or "origins events" over which there is controversy, such as the current debate over when hunting (by males, it is assumed) became a primary mode of human subsistence and, therefore (it is assumed), a primary structuring principle of human social life. That this particular phenomenon—hunting—has now been brought into our more *recent* evolutionary history (as a descending anachronism) (see Binford 1981; but cf. Bunn and Kroll 1986, 1988) is due more to epistemological concerns than to raised consciousnesses about the androcentrism of "hunting prowess" models (e.g. Laughlin 1968; Washburn and Lancaster 1968) or about the problematic of the assumed correlate of hunting—a gender/sex-based division of labor—or about the existence of *social* relations of production.

In fact, these central issues of anthropological content—divisions of labor, social relations, gender roles, or if there even *was* gender—are never really addressed. Although Slocum's (1975) critique of the man-the-hunter bias and the important remedial work of Tanner and Zihlman (e.g. 1976; Tanner 1981; see also Dahlberg 1981) drew attention to woman-the-gatherer, this has not been what has challenged the antiquity and importance of hunting in early hominid life. Rather, the archaeologists' challenge to the antiquity and primacy of hunting has been for reasons of "evidence" (e.g. Binford 1981). One effect of these challenges, in concert with the woman-the-gatherer models (which *do* raise the importance of gathering and other-than-meat resources), has been to limit discussion of the primacy of women's roles in human evolution to more recent periods, when hunting *did* go on and must have been complemented by gathering. This has the further effect that the primacy of women's roles is denied antiquity. The discussion on early hominid scavenging—now thought to have led to many of the bone accumulations previously taken as evidence for hunting—is not explicitly gendered.

The debate over hunting versus scavenging is not really discussed in terms of human activities or relations but primarily in epistemological terms: how we securely establish evidence for hunting (Binford 1981). It has been taken up as simultaneously a methodological and an epistemological issue, framed in terms of what is "knowable." Those who have engaged in the debate are not arguing about substantive (social or cultural) models about the past, but more about methods and epistemologies. In fact, the concern for the (social) content of the human evolutionary narrative, which is what is raised by the woman-the-gatherer challenge to the man-the-hunter scenario, is deflected by the focus on the so-called broader and more fundamental issues of method and "evidence."

The debate over the "origins" of hunting has, of course, provided dozens of archaeologists—and several in particular—with dozens of publications and an "issue" for public and political exploitation. First, as Wobst and Keene (1983) have so insightfully noted, there is a blatant political economy of origins research. They picture archaeological research as a cone resting on its point (fig. 2). This cone, they suggest, can be viewed as the archaeological research process in two senses: first, one is in the very best research position if one begins with a very complete archaeological "present" and then works backward through time, by means of formal analogues, to the "point" of origins, using increasingly decontextualized "slices" from the developmental process to reach that "point."

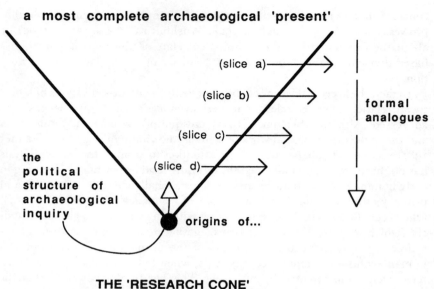

THE 'RESEARCH CONE'
(after Wobst and Keene, 1983)

Fig. 2. As argued by Wobst and Keene (1983), this research "cone" provides a model for the most efficacious (political) way to practice archaeology: (1) to begin with a most complete archaeological "present" and work backward in time (and in evolutionary development) by means of formal analogues, taking time-slices out of the sequence; and (2) to focus on and therefore claim intellectual control over an origin, as a point through which other research and researchers must pass.

Second, there is the structure of our practice: in order to consider phenomena, events, or processes which come *after* the "origins" (such as the study of early agricultural systems), one must first pass through the point of the cone (such as the study of the "first" domesticates). Those who control the point control that which comes after: they control knowledge, and anyone writing about subsequents must pass through—or at least reference—this point. One could depict the human career as a series of cones, with practitioner-gatekeepers at each point. Origins research, then, is a very effective and productive publishing strategy. Thus, as Williams (1986) has written in her critique of paleoanthropology:

> [T]he establishment of points, like the desire to create narratives about origins, produces essential features, whole identities, the sovereignty of the human subject, and a universal human psyche. Not only do these activities facilitate the commodification of knowledge and sustain the most prestigious measure of scholarly success—publications, but they explicitly structure thought: they

perpetuate an ideology in which human perception is itself static. (Williams
1986: 21)

It is not surprising that those subjects that are at the points—early
"man," tools, fire, agriculture, the family, the state—are fertile grounds for
territorial and competitive practice. We could have predicted that there
would be continuing debate (e.g. Johansen vs. Leakey; cf. Lewin 1987*a*) over
which evolutionary tree is the right one; that someone (e.g. Binford 1973)
would engage someone (e.g. Bordes and de Sonneville-Bordes 1970) over the
behavioral nature of those (Mousterian toolmaking Neanderthals) who immediately preceded modern humans of late Pleistocene Europe (see also the
debates in Mellars and Stringer 1989); and that the controversy continues
over the origins of early "man" in the New World (see Shutler 1983). The
successful competitor in the territoriality of origins research can have widespread impact upon the public and can be attributed with superhuman
powers. Richard Leakey, for example, has been featured in ads for Rolex
watches, where he has been imputed to control time and "redefine history." As Williams describes this ad, which promotes both Rolex watches
and Leakey himself:

> The focus on origins is crucial to the epistemology underlying both this ad and
> paleoanthropology: the search for "man's" origins can be understood as a
> search for man's re-presentation of time, the identification and re-ordering of
> space and time, as well as of human behavior within this representation of time
> and space. (Williams 1986: 25–26)

Origins research has selected for its routine, for its methodology, the empiri-
cal/analytical mode, which is a methodology for the acquisition of knowledge
to predict and control. This is in contrast to the historical/hermeneutical
mode, which (after Habermas 1971) is a routine to establish social and
mutual understanding.

Origins research is essentialism, promoting the definition of phenomena
in terms of their putative essential features: what *are* the essential features of
the earliest hominids, of the pristine states, of the division of labor? If, however, one holds that there are only state*s*, in particular historical settings, or
that gender relations and the division of labor are socially and culturally
constructed and highly variable (e.g. Moore 1988), then there is nothing
essential to be located at a point of origin; there is nothing essential about
gender nor about women's experience.

But the origins of the state and early human origins invoke a great deal
about gender and essentialisms. In the former, there has been much discussion over the idea that the supposed universal shift from kin-based to class-
based societies is the point at which female subordination really became
elaborated (cf. Gailey 1985, 1987; Rapp 1977; Reiter 1978; Silverblatt 1988;
and Silverblatt, this volume). And almost any discussion in early human

evolutionary studies that explicitly seems to be about gender has been framed in terms of man-the-hunter/woman-the-gatherer. But what are these human evolutionary discussions about? What *are* the implications of the primacy and forms of origins research for archaeologies of gender?

ORIGINS RESEARCH, WOMEN, AND GENDER

Because origins research takes as its very categories for analysis the phenomena that exist in the present (agriculture, monogamy, capitalism, female subordination) or that appear to have existed, given what the present has come to look like (e.g. earliest anatomically modern humans, or even an earlier species of *Homo*), it is obvious how "presentist"[5] and limited origins research is. The categories that we are to look for (the origins of. . .) have already been defined; our abilities to imagine the multiple pasts of many humans—and our abilities to imagine other gender relations—are truncated; origins narratives are aptly "narratives of closure" (Elshtain 1986). We have little to learn from what we already "know." We are almost bound to teleological accounts in which we invoke the present in the origins of a phenomenon and then use the origin to explain the present (Barrett 1980; Delphy 1984; Solomon 1989: 14).

To seek the origins, for example, of gender asymmetry is first to assume that such a normalized phenomenon exists, which can be analytically detached from the particular social and historical contexts within which it was/ has been situated, and which then reinforces the notion that this is an inevitable phenomenon that has some antiquity and therefore a certain "natural" character.[6] Origins research tends to make decontextualized phenomena seem inevitable. We may admit that certain phenomena exist/have existed in the "ethnographic present," but we should be under no obligation to find them in the past.

Handsman (1988) has argued that our very dependence on "culture" as our primary analytical framework is a "discursive power that homogenizes and constructs a unified whole." Thus, with

> a gaze that homogenizes, social *relations* are rendered invisible. The human past is dehumanized and real people are substituted for by statistical patterns. (Handsman 1988: 14).

A homogenizing gaze dissolves such things as gender categories, relations, separations, and, therefore, "culture is made sexless and it is women who become invisible through it" (Handsman 1988: 15).

How, then, are women and/or gender relations made visible, especially— for our purposes here—in origins accounts and through origins research? Women and gender categories have been made visible in origins texts in many domains, two of which we will discuss here: in the grand narratives of human origins ("early man" studies) and in the narratives surrounding the origins of "art" with the earliest anatomically modern humans in the Eurocentric world. We should not be surprised to find that in human origins accounts, women are neither active agents—despite their primary role as reproducers—nor the "result" of our evolution. And in the narratives surrounding the "earliest" spectacular "art," women are again not the active agents but the objects and commodities of visual culture.

Human Origins: A Not Her Story

The insights about women in human origins research developed here are primarily from the ongoing work of Sarah Williams (1986; 1990), although her critique of origins research in paleoanthropology is not limited to gender. Some of the other topics—control over time, the uses of the social technology of travel, the representation of racism in the practice of origins research—unfortunately cannot be discussed here.

As noted above, paleoanthropology takes human origins as its object of knowledge (Wolpuff 1980: v). The relatively short (roughly thirty years) "history" of this focused inquiry has produced a cornucopia of scholarly and academic work, and it exemplifies, more than any other topic of origins research, the competitiveness (Wobst and Keene 1983), territoriality (e.g. Lewin 1987a), and predominance of male researchers. The "journey through time" that this inquiry into "the human adventure" claims to provide is itself provided by the (predominantly male) ability to travel (Clark and Howell 1966: v), particularly to Africa and other "cradles" of human origins.

By the 1960s and into the 1970s, American archaeologists, long concerned with the past of North and South America, began to break from their own "colonies" to an imperializing (Trigger 1984) concern with "origins"—of humans, agriculture, the state—and to practice this research at a global scale, supported by the developing and expanding funding of both the National Science Foundation and Wenner-Gren Foundation for Anthropological Research. The search for cross-cultural laws (as advocated by the New Archaeology; c.f. Watson, Redman, and LeBlanc 1971), and the renewed search for "origins"—of humans, of agriculture, of the state (or, for the "big questions," as Binford [1983: 26–30] calls them)—transcend nationalistic and/or colonial archaeologies. The concomitant development of primate studies (cf. Haraway 1978, 1983), the "discovery" of new dating techniques (e.g. potassium/argon), which have shown the unanticipated antiquity of humanity, and the resurgence of interest in hunter-gatherers (e.g. Lee and DeVore 1968), who were taken (and often still are seen) as the representatives of the life-styles of our prehistoric ancestors (see Howell's critique, 1988), contributed further to imperialist paleoanthropology and archaeologies.

The principal objects of paleoanthropology are fossil bones and other "durable residues" of hominids. That the very objects of inquiry—stone tools, fossils, "sites"—are the same throughout the supposed four-million-year course of hominid evolution insures a continuity through time and space (see Toth and Schick 1986 for a recent review of early hominid research). The goal of paleoanthropology, as Williams describes it, is "the reconstruction through time and space of [what inevitably turns out to be] male Caucasian bodies and behaviors from these bones" and from these residues (just look at the "results" of human evolution in any introductory textbook).

> [B]y using and naming fossils and collections of stone tools, as representations of an original reality—an original world—[the paleoanthropologist] has been able to produce and reproduce our world by representation. (Williams 1986: 12)

Elsewhere (Conkey 1990), I have discussed the striking appropriateness of Baudrillard's (1983) term *simulacrum* for most of our reconstructions of human origins; a "simulacrum" is "the identical copy for which no original has ever existed" (Jameson 1984: 68).

Our origins have been represented to us both visually and in writing; textbooks, the *National Geographic*, and professional publications have all, in fact, "propagated our origins in specific [and similar] ways" (Williams 1986: 6). The most common form is simultaneously linear and chronological. The image of "running men" (fig. 3) as the visual metaphor for human evolution is widespread, whether in texts, popular journals in the United States and in Europe, or as logos for research foundations. But there are persistent characteristics of these lineages: they are always males, and the attributes of the earliest representatives of humanity are apelike, followed by negroids, and finally Caucasians. But,

> Just as we see female anthropologists only rarely, and then only as wife or mother of a paleoanthropologist, as anonymous workers, or as primatologists (Haraway 1983) *fossil women, when seen, are not on a phylogenetic line.* (Williams 1986: 6; emphasis added)

Women are not *in* the lineage, although they gave birth to it (fig. 4). They are carrying or nursing children.

As anthropology students, we are told that there are people (of color) in places like Africa (e.g. the !Kung Bushmen) whose behaviors can help us reconstruct the behavior of our ancestors in early times (cf. Lee 1976).[7] Thus:

> The original men of color, our ancestors and descendants of apes, were born, we are repeatedly shown, in Africa—their cradle and the cradle of humankind. However, narratively speaking, what *results* from our "human" origin in the cradle of Africa excludes anything African, anything female, anything other. Rather, reconstructions of our supposed human origin represent another story: a human story of caucasian man that is not her story. (Williams 1986: 6)

Fig. 3. Although popular and scholarly texts are replete with various and very familiar versions of this image—"running" or "striding" men—which is the prevalent
construction of the human evolutionary lineage, this particular rendition is the
trademark of the L.S.B. Leakey Foundation. The Foundation has kindly allowed us
to use their logo, although, in so doing, they wish to recognize explicitly that not only
did women evolve as well but also that there are questions that can be raised about
the linearity and/or gradualism of evolution implied by such a rendering. Most other
renditions are more detailed, and with those details, the depiction often turns into
"striding men" who begin with the swarthy and "dark" australopithecines through
the increasingly hairless and "light" early *Homo* to modern "man."

The narrative of human origins is explicitly chronological. Landau (e.g.
1984) has shown how in the different interpretations of various scholars the
variables (e.g. bipedalism, brain-size increase) of that narrative have been
rearranged but that—despite the rearrangement of the variables—the structure of the myth has remained intact. It is a structure that conforms to that of
the Northern European heroic folktale. In the narrative of human evolution,

> an authorial subject and subjectivity are constructed: man evolves from nature
> (i.e., plants, animals, Africa, men of color, woman) to become sovereign, the
> hallmark of which is a large brain, capable of self-awareness. (Williams 1986:
> 12)

Objects of Culture, Not Objects of Knowledge

The way in which the "narrative of progressive monoculture" has been written leads to the (now questionable) Eurocentric position at the "end" of a
unified human history that has been "gathering up, memorializing the
world's local historicities" (Clifford 1988: 14–15). The Eurocentric "end" has
traditionally "begun" with the appearance and simultaneous cultural suc-

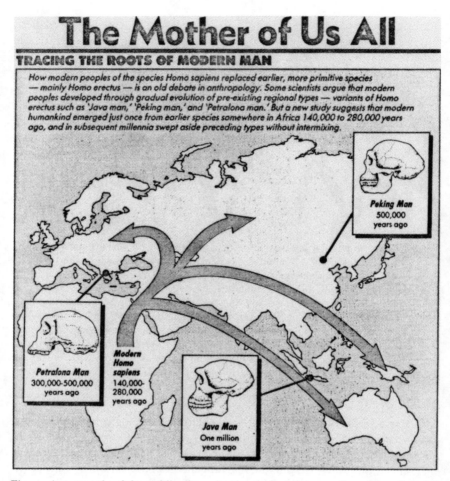

The Mother of Us All

TRACING THE ROOTS OF MODERN MAN

How modern peoples of the species Homo sapiens replaced earlier, more primitive species — mainly Homo erectus — is an old debate in anthropology. Some scientists argue that modern peoples developed through gradual evolution of pre-existing regional types — variants of Homo erectus such as 'Java man,' 'Peking man,' and 'Petralona man.' But a new study suggests that modern humankind emerged just once from earlier species somewhere in Africa 140,000 to 280,000 years ago, and in subsequent millennia swept aside preceding types without intermixing.

Peking Man
500,000
years ago

Petralona Man
300,000-500,000
years ago

Modern Homo sapiens
140,000-280,000
years ago

Java Man
One million
years ago

Fig. 4. An example of the public dissemination (*sic*) of the narrative of "our" evolution, which "shows" us how, in tracing the roots of modern man, the Mother of Us All gave rise to Java, Petralona, and Peking Man: the "result" of our evolution is a not-her-story. © *San Francisco Chronicle*. Reprinted by permission.

cesses of anatomically modern humans, *Homo sapiens sapiens*, somewhere around 35,000 to 40,000 years ago. Although recent discoveries and much earlier dates on fossils of modern humans and/or their presumed cultural materials have recast Europe into a "late" niche for these modern humans (Lewin 1987*b*; Dibble and Montet-White 1988), the cultural record of dense archaeological sites, abundant and diverse material culture, and the presence of "art" and imagery in many media and forms from Spain across into the central Russian plain have always (and continue to) provide for the modern humans of this time and place a most privileged position in the narrative of human cultural accomplishments.

This is not the place to question why only the Upper Paleolithic imagery of Europe and Russia should be taken as *the* origins of "art" (Conkey 1983). There is much imagery elswhere on the globe in Ice Age times (cf. Bahn and Vertut 1988); and we should not, in any event, label this imagery as "art" or even attempt to account for 25,000 years of widespread imagery in many media and forms within an inclusive (if not monolithic) interpretation (e.g., Breuil 1952; Leroi-Gourhan 1965; Marshack 1977; see Conkey 1987, n.d., for reviews).

Among the more popular and frequently reproduced Paleolithic images are the female statuettes, often called "Venus figurines" (see Ucko 1968: 409–414, for a discussion on the history of the label, "Mother Goddess" for such figures). And, as Bahn (1986) has pointed out, these statuettes and the earlier so-called vulva-imagery have "contributed much toward a belief in the importance of fertility and sexual symbolism in Paleolithic iconography" (Bahn 1986: 99; and see, for some extremes to which this belief can go, Guthrie 1984; Collins and Onians 1978).

Now it *is* the case that among the earliest (c. 32,000 years ago) preserved imagery are some ovaloid, trianguloid shaped engravings on stone slabs, which have derived from a few sites in a localized valley in southwestern France (see Delluc and Delluc 1978 for a detailed description). Bahn (1986: 99–101) tells the story of how the energetic Paleolithic art scholar, the French priest Henri Breuil, came to "identify" these shapes as female vulvas.[8] "One subjective interpretation of certain shapes," writes Bahn (1986: 99), "has become an *idée fixe* and one of the most durable myths of prehistory." This is not just an idle and titillating example among many subjective interpretations. This depiction of (supposedly) female genitalia from the beginning of Upper Paleolithic image-making, and the very early (in 1911) "identification" of the imagery as female genitalia, have contributed in significant ways to particular (though often implicit) representations of women and of gender relations in the origins story that reveals for us how "we" became fully symbolic modern *Homo sapiens sapiens* in "our" Eurocentric homeland. (See fig. 5, the cover of the November 10, 1986, *Newsweek*, which—with a white, Rembrandt-looking male—proclaims the cover story to be about "The Way *We* Were"; this certainly invites the colloquial reply: "What do you mean by *we*?.")

The late Andre Leroi-Gourhan (e.g. 1965, 1968, 1978) argued that Paleolithic imagery is the product of an underlying generative "mythogram" based on principles of male and female complementarity and opposition. This has been the most inclusive and anthropologically provocative of the recent interpretations of Paleolithic cave art. Leroi-Gourhan himself noted

Newsweek

November 10, 1986 : $2.00

The Way We Were

Our Ice Age
Heritage:
Language,
Art, Fashion
and the
Family

Fig. 5. The cover of *Newsweek* suggests that our modern origins lie in the European Ice Age, where Upper Paleolithic peoples are attributed with the very categories of life that feature so prominently in contemporary upper-/middle-class white America: "language, art, fashion, and the family"—regular features of such media as the *Sunday New York Times Magazine*. One might also note the implied whiteness and maleness of these ancestors in the artist's drawing of this progenitor; his resemblance to such prominent Western artists as Rembrandt is also problematic. Reprinted by permission from *Newsweek*.

that the entire basis for his mythogram rests on the assertion that some of the signs are explicit representations of *le sexe feminin* (Leroi-Gourhan 1973: 91). However, there is a larger point to be made than that one important interpretation of cave art is directly derived from assertions about representations of femaleness. We have been operating with the long-standing implicit assumption that even in the Upper Paleolithic, women—or parts of them— were not only suitable but desirable as objects of depiction, as cultural commodities.

When we come to study Paleolithic visual images as "art," we draw heavily on "strong covert influences of powerful modern ideologies" (Davis 1985: 9) as to what constitutes some of the fundamental categories with which we work (Preziosi 1982). We have yet to work through what it is that constitutes "an image." With the "identification" of the vulvae, it was easy for "scholars" to suggest the development of an artistic tradition of depicting females with particular attention to their reproductive parts, and to assume that these depictions indicate reverence for female fertility. This, in turn, allows the further unspoken assumption that it was the Paleolithic *men* (males) who were the artists. In nearly every text, popular magazine, or other source that I have found *only* males are depicted in the act of image-making, from cave-wall art to female figurines.[9]

The statistics, however, do not support the idea that females dominate the human images; there *is* Paleolithic male imagery and much that is "neuter" (i.e., not clearly attributable to the male or female sex) (Delporte 1979; Ucko and Rosenfeld 1972). And insofar as there *is* imagery of females, it does not necessarily follow that it is (all) made by males and for males. In particular, there is no evidence that these depictions acted as commodified imagery—as both pornographic and "high art" representations of sexualized women have in Western history. The priest, Breuil, however, was not troubled by the need to avoid such anachronistic inferences. He assumed that the Paleolithic low-relief engraving of "reclining" women at Le Magdeleine (Penne, Tarn [France]) was placed there "to give Paleolithic man pleasure during his meals" (Breuil 1954; cited by Ucko and Rosenfeld 1967: 119).

The presentist gender paradigm has infused most reconstructions of Upper Paleolithic "artistic" life. We can now read about how the "fertile" female statuettes (made by males) can be taken as evidence for the male appropriation of female labor (Faris 1983), or about how Paleolithic art is all "about" male hunting and sexual prowess (Guthrie 1984), including female imagery as "trophy" (see also Eaton 1978). We are told how images can be visual and tactile substitutes for delayed male sexual gratifications (Collins and Onians 1978). Thus, sexist twentieth-century notions of gender and sexuality are read into the cultural traces of "our ancestors." The authority residing in "origins" then further legitimizes and naturalizes these (currently contested) notions.

ARE THERE ANY CONCLUSIONS?

The major implication, to date, then, of origins research for women and for inferences about gender in the human past is that there is no substantive place for women in the "human career" on earth.[10] Rather than producing narratives that assume the social dynamics of males and females in simultaneous conflict and cooperation, as equal historical agents, and as situationally engaged in diverse relationships, evolutionary and archaeological narrators have written a not-her-version of our past.

Origins research, I have suggested, has simultaneously generated "narratives of closure" (Elshtain 1986)—in which our imaginative powers about the many ways in which people could have lived are suppressed—and privileged the techno-environmental domain, particularly for the longest and most formative (they say) stretch of human life, from hominid origins through the rise of agriculture to the appearance of states. Recall that most of so-called "hallmarks" of human evolution are linked to techno-environmental control: tools, fire, hunting, food-storage, composite tools, language, agriculture, metallurgy, and so forth. The "Ages of Man" have always been defined in technological terms: Paleolithic, Neolithic, Bronze Age, Iron Age. And this privileging of technological innovation and control is clearly sociohistorically contingent:

> Technological innovation has in our time the certainty—and the moral, intellectual and social significance—that theological speculation had in the medieval period. (Harding and O'Barr 1987: 47, in an editorial note on McGaw 1987)

This privileging of the techno-environmental comes in a package of reinforcing assumptions that leaves very little space for feminist thinking. First, *ontologically*, the techno-environmental domain has been considered to be more causal in culture change. Second, *epistemologically*, technological phenomena and even aspects of economy are considered to be more "knowable." Third, the phenomena through which techno-environmental control can be effected, and which constitute the *preferred data* (bones, stone tools), are more likely to be treated as ascending anachronisms and are readily "pushed back," so that greater antiquity and a more "natural" state to such hallmarks are assured. Thus, human techno-environmental effectiveness is naturalized. Fourth, because there is the tacit association of these activities, objects, and the very *acts* of innovation with males, other characteristics are naturalized as well: male instrumentalism, as in man-the-toolmaker (but cf. Gero 1990 for a critique); male-as-provider; male-as-innovator; man/active-woman/passive. Even the labels for many archaeological sites are in techno-environmental terms: hunting stands, lithic production site, quarrying sites, base camps. Whoever heard of rephrasing such site types into terms having to do with hypothesized social relations, such as a hunting stand being called instead a male-bonding site (Chris Hoffman: pers. comm.)?

Watson and Kennedy (1990) have shown how the anthropological "givens" of male/active/hunter and female/passive/plants, which are deeply embedded in origins accounts, have led to the most ingenious and problematic (unlikely) scenarios for the cultural innovation (i.e. origins) of plant domestication in the U.S. northeastern woodlands. They reveal how researchers—in order to avoid a disruption of the sacred associational chain of female/passive/plants that would suggest female/*active*/plants (and therefore, women as innovators of plant domestication/agriculture)—have invoked as causal *either* a shaman (male, of course), whose ceremonial use of gourd rattles led him to domesticate cucurbits, *or* the idea of "co-evolution"—that the domesticability and increasing production of certain plant species gradually happened on its own in the disturbed areas of living sites; that is, that the plants domesticated themselves!

Many of the questions and discussions on gender, as now phrased, become irrelevant if we reject "origins research," as it has come to be conceptualized and practiced—a sociopolitical strategy of intellectual territoriality in the service of a never-ending refinement on the narrative of "progressive monoculture." We need not deny the existence of and the inquiry into pervasive or even "global processes unevenly at work" (Clifford 1988: 17) in order to write other narratives. But we do need to problematize the categories and the objects of knowledge.

Origins research has encouraged ahistorical and decontextualized analysis and interpretation. The study of Paleolithic "art" imagery is not relevant because it is the origins of anything; it is anthropologically interesting and relevant because we have a rich archaeological record deriving from the production and reproduction of symbolic repertoires in a variety of historical and social contexts over many millenia and thousands of kilometers.

The debate over man-the-hunter/woman-the-gatherer is really a debate over when two very nineteenth-century social science institutions came into being: the nuclear family and a gender-based division of labor. This debate should be transformed into a series of inquiries into the social relations of production, into particular food-getting strategies in varying sociohistorical contexts in which gender relations are not "givens" but historical forces.

Previously neglected areas of inquiry, such as women as spinners and weavers in the Aztec state, become domains in which we can not only "see" women in the past, but in which their activities—as Brumfiel argues (1990; see also McCafferty and McCafferty 1988, n.d.)—should be understood in the context of, as part of, and a contributor to (if not the very basis for) the economy of the Aztec state, which experiences its own historical trajectory. It is not enough to make women visible by elucidating "women's roles" in some normalizing way; this merely frames in, encloses, and positions women (and men) in expectable, normativized, homogenized ways (Handsman 1988, 1990).

Even if women—as a particular social group—do apparently lose social ground, such as with the Spanish takeover of the Inca, what is anthropologically interesting, as Silverblatt has shown (1987, 1988, this volume) is how the particular social formations of the Inca are transformed into those of the Spanish. To seek the origins of female subordination is to accept this as natural and legitimate, rather than as a particular historical process of variable forms and with its own histories.

We have tried to show here just some of the ways in which certain conceptualizations of gender are embedded in and structure origins research so that origins research—as presently practiced—then structures and perpetuates certain perspectives on gender and gender relations, both in the past and in archaeological practice. Women are taken to be reproducers, passive, outside the privileged techno-environmental domain, and as mere cultural objects, never cultural agents. The uncritical and unquestioned explanation of origins (or of "the past") presumes a relationship between the past and present that often reproduces intact and unchallenged modern concepts of time, causality, consciousness,[11] and social relations.

WHAT ARE SOME QUESTIONS NOW?

Given the rich tradition of feminist research in related fields, the rapid evolution of feminist theories, and the increasing concern with gender studies and/or feminist research in the literature of archaeology itself (e.g. Conkey and Spector 1984; Hodder 1986: 159–161), we can identify at least three important general domains for inquiry that should have surfaced some time ago.

First, we are just coming to know more—and from explicit "case studies"—about women in prehistory, about women as producers of labor, and/or about women as producers of meaning. The literature of the next decade will be particularly rich in this regard for a number of reasons. We have already seen (e.g. the papers in Gero and Conkey 1990) that the *ways* in which archaeologists can do research about women in the past are so varied and different that there need not be *a* programmatic way to use archaeological data. Furthermore, we anticipate that we need not repeat the problematic aspects of "merely remedial" research, which just "add women and stir" (Boxer 1982; Lerner 1986; Scott 1986; for archaeology, see Conkey and Gero 1988; Wylie 1990). And there are, already, researchers explicitly concerned with the "archaeology of gender" who would not consider themselves to be feminists (e.g. Thomas 1989), yet whose work informs on women and men in prehistory and who, in any event, are contributing to the teaching and doing of archaeology in a different way (for more on curricula, see Spector and Whelan 1989).[12]

Second, as Wylie has suggested (1990), a "space" seems to have been opened in the epistemological and theoretical domains of archaeology for research not just about women-as-subjects but into the cultural construction of gender, in general, in prehistoric life; research into how gender roles and relations may have been defined, enacted, manipulated, enabled, or negotiated in varying sociohistorical contexts in the past and/or in relation to various other social processes. This will necessarily involve the development and expansion of the *social* theory from which archaeologists draw, particularly since the dominant theoretical frameworks of most archaeologists (e.g. cultural ecology, cultural evolutionism) have relatively little to say about *social* life (Shanks and Tilley 1987*a*, 1987*b*; Shennan 1986).

The contributions then, to pursuing this domain of inquiry, will necessarily come from some aspects of what has been labeled "post-processual" archaeologies[13] (Hodder 1985; Leone 1986; Shanks and Tilley 1987*a*, 1987*b*) because of their attempts to develop and apply social and symbolic theory in archaeological research. Other contributions have already come from ethnoarchaeological studies (e.g. Braithwaite 1982; and especially Moore 1986). The published attempts to investigate actual prehistoric contexts from this particular perspective—the cultural construction of gender and gender relations—have, as yet, been few and decidedly "initial" (e.g. Hodder 1984).

Third, these two sets of research—about women (and men) in prehistory, and about the cultural constructions of gender—should impact on the practice of anthropological archaeology so that the traditional archaeological "paradigms" will be radically questioned by a large number—not just a few—archaeologists (recall, for example, the Watson and Kennedy [1990] study of the "origins" of horticulture, cited above, as an excellent example of a paradigm-challenging study). It is interesting to note—but outside the immediate scope of this chapter to discuss—that many of the calls for post-processual archaeologies refer to feminist approaches as a welcome "outcome" of their mission (e.g. Hodder 1986: 159; Shanks and Tilley 1987*b*: 191), yet I would argue that it may not be possible to effect the very "paradigm shifts" (for lack of a better phrase) that they call for *without* a well-developed feminist archaeology that takes, as its central concern, the study of gender and its cultural construction (Conkey and Gero 1988). That is, one could turn Wylie's argument (1990)—that the post-processualists and the challenge to Binfordian archaeology have opened up a space for an archaeology of gender—"on its head" and argue that the former (post-processualism) may not be sustainable *without* a feminist archaeology.

Furthermore, the impact of the emergent research in archaeology on women and on gender should also lead to a radical alteration in the very set of notions about prehistoric humans and human evolution that underlie *all* of anthropology. In fact, archaeology has a much larger role to play than we realize in restructuring the inquiry of anthropology. Despite decades of disclaimers, there remains an underlying pervasiveness of evolutionism—and evolutionism of a progressive sort (Dunnell 1980)—in anthropology as a whole.[14] The intellectual heritage of anthropology has been to provide the narrative of "progressive monoculture" (Clifford 1988: 15); a narrative that must be told in such a way as to end up with Western civilization.

Given this, the findings of archaeology all too easily set certain definitional parameters for the categories and institutions that have been unquestioned anthropological givens. If archaeology "shows," for example, the antiquity of the nuclear family, pair-bonding, and the home-base (read domestic unit) (see e.g. Lovejoy 1981; Isaac 1978), these all too easily become legitimate analytical units, as natural, unquestioned elements of human social life (but see Collier and Yanagisako 1987; Yanagisako 1979). Without developing this position further here, I merely suggest that the restructuring of anthropological interpretation *cannot* happen without an archaeological restructuring.

ON PARADIGM CHANGES

The latter aspects of paradigm change, within both archaeology *and* anthropology as a whole, are perhaps the more unruly of the changes implicated by a feminist archaeology. Even as presented here, such paradigm changes *appear* to be the last to happen sequentially, as it always is with an empiricist/positivist style of inquiry (a style that has certainly characterized Anglo-American archaeology for many decades). The assumption is that the paradigm changes will fall into place once the data are in, once the case studies have *accumulated*, once knowledge has "grown." But this chapter is intended to suggest otherwise: in order to carry out even the most basic search for women in the past—even if you just want to "add women and stir"—means that we must challenge the structuring values of the discipline itself, and in at least two ways.

First (and only briefly considered here), the challenges must come at the level of anthropological practice. Archaeological and, more widely, anthropological studies of gender must refuse to be marginalized within the accepted definition of the discipline *and* simultaneously must refuse to be accommodated and to peacefully coexist as an alternative specialization, a more-or-less tolerated sideline. How many of us have just added "gender studies" to the list of research specialities after our name in the *Guide* to Anthropologists? Given that women have already been marginalized by their "preferred" subject matters within archaeology (Gero 1985), what is the likely future of a feminist archaeology or the archaeology of gender if it is primarily taken up by women archaeologists (as certainly appears to be the case so far)?

Further, there will not be a single methodological solution for all of our challenges in the study of (engendered) social life; there will be no one privileged critique to adopt that will itself grow into a coherent practice, subsuming other diversifications. This is amply illustrated by the widespread debate among feminist scholars today about assumptions, categories of analysis, theory, and methodologies (e.g. Benhabib and Cornell 1987; Hooks 1984; Keller 1989; Moraga and Anzaldua 1981). Within archaeology, it is clear that the so-called New Archaeology (e.g. Binford and Binford 1968; Binford 1972; cf. Dunnell 1986) has not been able to sustain its position as the privileged critique (Courbin 1988; Hodder 1985; Leone 1982). The paradigm challenge is more difficult than methodological solutions and privileged critiques.

Second, then, as the foregoing critique of origins research has shown, the issues to be challenged are what we can call our objects-of-knowledge. It is particularly relevant to archaeology to point out that, being a very object-oriented field, these objects of knowledge are not the same thing as the objects we study. As has been discussed before (Conkey and Spector 1984; Conkey and Gero 1988), we can see this confusion in archaeology in many remedial gender studies. For example, there has long been the claim (e.g. Isaac 1978) that if we could only find pollen in early hominid sites to counteract the overwhelming visibility of the more durable residues left by scavenging (formerly hunting) males, *then* we would have women in the Pleistocene; we would have women in "early man" studies. But this is not the point at all: adding pollen studies to document the role of women is a methodological diversion away from the more fundamental and unquestioned assumption—and object—of knowledge—that there is a gender-based division of labor (man-the-hunter/woman-the-gatherer) in early hominid life (some 2 million years ago!), a specific division of labor that is then taken as an *essential* feature of human social life.

As long as we operate with and defend a given definition of our objects of knowledge—and we do defend, passively, by not questioning the taken-for-granteds—while, at the same time, we (if only, again, by not questioning, just doing) the permissible methods for constructing and establishing such knowledge, then we—as archaeologists, as anthropologists—reproduce a dominant paradigm and the fundamental values on which it rests. The paradigm always appears as given, but it is, in fact, *produced* (Williams 1981).

The introduction of new methods (and by this, I don't only mean methods such as palynology and the study of fossil pollen, but even interpretive frameworks-as-methods, such as semiotics, feminism, Marxism) in itself will not be a clear measure of whether any radical paradigm shift is taking place. As Raymond Williams has argued, we must discriminate between those tendencies, even if unusual and provoking, that have been compatible and even congruent with the orthodox paradigm, and others that "necessarily include the paradigm itself as a matter of analysis rather than as a governing definition of the object(s) of knowledge" (Williams 1981: 65).

This observation is equally applicable to archaeological research. We have here considered one of our cherished objects of knowledge—origins research—cherished in archaeology, in anthropology, *and* by the public.

Such an object of knowledge—"origins"—has become the primary means through which archaeology interfaces with the public. I have tried to show the ways in which this object of knowledge is presently conceptualized, institutionalized, and operationalized, and how it embodies the structuring values of the discipline itself. These values, however, are not particularly comfortable because they are imperialist, sexist, and racist, which is the last thing anthropology would want to say about itself.

Even the simplest cultural accounts are intentional creations; interpreters constantly construct themselves through the others they study. Archaeological accounts, like the oral histories of the Malgasay kings, make use of a structured political philosophy that uses "origins" as a key element in its "ideologic" (Kus 1986). But what difference does critical knowledge make?

Once we have uncovered the reflection of certain aspects of the present in the past, we may decide to do something with that knowledge. The delayed but increasing and rich developments in archaeological studies of gender and in feminist archaeologies promise not merely more details about the social lives of prehistoric peoples but a suite of important challenges to original narratives and to the structure of archaeological practice.

NOTES

1. An original version of this paper was presented at the 1986 annual meetings of the Society for American Archaeology, as a compilation of ideas drawn primarily from Williams (1986) and McGuire (1985). Subsequent elaboration was added for the 1987 presentation in the Yale lecture series, organized by the editor of this volume, and some of these additional ideas were presented at McMaster University (January 1987), when I had the privilege of being the Redman Lecturer. I wish to thank many for their comments, inspiration, and bibliographic suggestions, especially Russell Handsman, Catherine Lutz, Irene Silverblatt, Ruth Tringham, Sarah Williams, Alison Wylie, and the students in various classes at SUNY-Binghamton and U.C.-Berkeley who, without choice, had to sit through various readings of the paper.

In fact, Sarah Williams's 1986 seminar paper plays such a central role around which the rest of the paper could take shape (and without which it probably couldn't have come together), that she is a full collaborator and inspiration. She would like to acknowledge the collaborative culture of her own paper by thanking faculty and student participants in History of Consciousness seminars, and Feminist Studies FRA at the University of California, Santa Cruz.

Avis Worthington did a wonderful job on the bibliography, and Les Rowntree provided continual support. I also thank the reviewers of this book for their insightful and enthusiastic comments on this chapter, and, in particular, I thank Micaela di Leonardo for her infinite patience, gentleness, and yet firm and clarifying editorial hand.

2. As one reviewer of this chapter points out, it is interesting—if not ironic—that in sociocultural anthropology "certain foci on 'status' have been intimately bound up with attention to and conceptualizations of gender," yet in archaeology, where indeed

status has been so prevalent a concern (when social phenomena *are* entertained explicitly), there has still not been the development of theory or method necessary to illuminate issues of gender!

3. In 1986, the *American Journal of Physical Anthropology* reported on National Science Foundation funding percentages (proportion funded out of submissions) by topic: Human Origins research (62% of the proposals funded) and the related field of Primate Evolution (72%) are the most successful domains. (Only 31% of the Human Biology applicants were, however, awarded research funds). (*AJPA* 69: (1986) 517–526; with thanks to Catherine Lutz for drawing this information to my attention).

4. Cartmill et al. (1986) claim a "century" for this field, but this is a way of writing the history of a field so as to extend its lineage. This kind of historical claim is a perfect example of what DeLivre (1974) has written about—an ascending anachronism—and which is discussed in the text (p. 72).

5. "Presentism" (as used by Stocking 1968, as taken from Butterfield 1963) refers to the use or the study of the past for the sake of the present; "to produce a story which is the ratification, if not the glorification, of the present" (Butterfield 1963: v). Stocking contrasts presentism with historicism, which he views as "the commitment to the understanding of the past for its own sake" (Stocking 1968: 4).

The resultant attributes of a presentist interpretation include a judgmental mode (rather than an understanding one), a focus on agents or agencies that direct change (rather than a concern with the complex processes by which change emerges), and a decontextualization of phenomena (from their contemporary context) in order to view them in abstracted relation to analogs in the present (Stocking 1968: 3–4).

6. Even those radical feminist views that see gender as primarily a political division, as inseparable from the relations of domination, with questionable relationship to biological/anatomical sex, or as necessarily a hierarchical social division (e.g., Delphy 1984), in fact, see the hierarchical nature (favoring male domination) as inevitable. Even when denouncing origins (of gender asymmetry) research as teleological, the very inevitability of gender hierarchy and political division is assumed rather than problematized.

7. Unfortunately, much of what we "learn" about these "people of color" who are potential analogues for prehistoric hunter-gatherers—even from an archaeologist—is problematical. We have elsewhere (Conkey and Spector 1984: 13) detailed some of the biases in Yellen's (1977) ethnoarchaeological studies of the !Kung, but it is relevant here to point out that !Kung women are never named (except in relation to others) and the phrases used to describe their "activities" are strikingly different from those applied to the males. As Kennedy (1979: 14–15) has reported: "If we are constantly presented with a picture of men who move about with nameless, faceless families in tow, we will use that picture when we evaluate the archaeological record." (See also Silberbauer [1981] for similar problematic representations of Kalahari hunter-gatherers.)

8. Bahn (1986) reports that Breuil was presented with the first discovered "vulvae" imagery by Didon in 1911 and he, it is reported, "recognized vulvas without hesitation" (Stoliar 1977/1978: 42, as cited by Bahn 1986: 99). Bahn notes "tongue in cheek . . . that a man of Breuil's profession (the priesthood) should not be considered an expert on this particular motif," but he also notes that Breuil did invoke similar-

ities to Egyptian cunieform and zoological classification symbols. Both of these, Bahn demonstrates, are completely inappropriate analogues, and he concludes that "Breuil was talking through his beret" (1986: 100).

9. One exception to this is the reconstruction that I commissioned to accompany my contribution on cave art to the 1988 *World Book: Science Year*, which does not have the same potential for exposure as do TIME-LIFE books or archaeology texts.

10. The human career (cf. Klein 1989) is the term used at the University of Chicago in the mid-1960s (begun in the heydays of paleoanthropology there and elsewhere) and since for a sequence of courses that cover human evolution and its archaeology. Catherine Lutz (personal communication) points out how this could be read as the projection of the academic's positioned concerns into the past.

11. Of course, we have our own particular cultural construction of what "consciousness" is, and how, therefore, it might be "identified" archaeologically. This construction is very much an instrumentalist one, which "entails the notions of rationality, objectivity, control of attentional processes in the solving of technical problems, non-emotionality, and linear thought, among others" (Lutz, in press). Archaeologists, not surprisingly, have used such evidence as "tool manufacturing sequences" and the existence of "art" to document the "origins" of symbolic behavior and fully modern consciousness (e.g., Chase and Dibble 1987).

12. The debate or discussion on the relation between feminist theory and archaeologies of gender are not yet widespread (but cf. Conkey n.d.; and Wylie n.d.). The interesting question to ask about nonfeminist gender research is to what extent does this work "inform" about gender or merely construct another narrative that is still problematic (see also Conkey and Gero 1990).

13. There is now a well-recognized debate between the so-called processual archaeology that has prevailed since the mid-1960s guided by the programmatics of Binford (e.g., 1965, 1972, 1981) and the assortment of alternative theoretical and methodological approaches, referred to as "postprocessual" archaeologies (see, e.g., Hodder 1985). These latter have in common primarily—if not only—their challenge to the Binfordian paradigm that advocates the inquiry into culture process by means of a concept of culture as an adaptive system and its associated positivist methodologies. The postprocessualists include those who take structuralist, poststructuralist, Marxist, feminist, and other stances (see, e.g., Leone 1986 on the symbolic, cognitive, and critical archaeologies).

14. Fabian (1983) provides a history of the "temporalizing rhetoric" of anthropology and how Judaeo-Christian time was secularized, which culminated in the nineteenth-century evolutionary time frame that, he suggests, spatialized time. As a result, the (spatial) relationships between parts of the world came to be understood as *temporal* relations: the dispersal or distributions of peoples in space directly reflect the temporal sequences and—by implication—progressive evolutionary sequences. As a result of spatialisation, (anthropological) subjects were naturalized and denied meaning in a historical sense.

BIBLIOGRAPHY

Arnold, Karen, Roberta Gilchrist, Pam Graves, and Sarah Taylor, eds. 1988. Archaeological review from Cambridge. *Women and Archaeology* 7 (1) (Spring).

Bahn, Paul G. 1986. No sex, please, we're Aurignacians. *Rock Art Research* 3 (2): 99–120.

Bahn, Paul, and Jean Vertut. 1988. *Images of the ice age.* London: Bellew Publishing Co., Ltd.

Barrett, M. 1980. *Women's oppression today: Problems in Marxist analysis.* London: Verso. (5th impression, 1986.)

Baudrillard, Jean. 1983. The precession of simulcra. *Art and Text* 11: 3–47.

Benhabib, Seyla, and Drucilla Cornell, eds. 1987. *Feminism as Critique.* Minneapolis: University of Minnesota Press.

Binford, Lewis R. 1965. Archaeological systematics and the study of culture process. *American Antiquity* 31 (2): 203–210.

———. 1972. *An Archaeological Perspective.* New York: Seminar Press.

———. 1973. Interassemblage variability—The Mousterian and the "functional" argument. In *The Explanation of Culture Change.* Colin Renfrew, ed., 227–254. London: Duxbury.

———. 1980. Willow-smoke and dog's tails: Hunter-gatherer settlement systems and archaeological site formation. *American Antiquity* 45: 1–17.

———. 1981. *Bones: Ancient Men and Modern Myths.* New York: Academic Press.

——— 1983. *In Pursuit of the Past: Decoding the Archaeological Record.* London: Thames and Hudson.

Binford, S. R., and L. R. Binford, eds. 1968. *New Perspectives in Archaeology.* Chicago: Aldine.

Bordes, François, and Denise de Sonneville-Bordes. 1970. The significance of variability in Paleolithic assemblages. *World Archaeology* 2 (1): 61–73.

Boxer, Marilyn. 1982. For and about women: The theory and practice of women's studies in the United States. In *Feminist theory: A critique of ideology.* N. Keohane, M. Rosaldo, and B. Gelpi, eds., 237–371. Chicago: University of Chicago Press.

Braithwaite, Mary. 1982. Decoration as ritual symbol: A theoretical proposal and an ethnographic study in Southern Sudan. In *Symbolic and structural archaeology.* Ian Hodder, ed., 80–88. Cambridge: Cambridge University Press.

Breuil, Henri. 1952. *Four hundred centuries of cave art.* Paris: Sapho Press.

———. 1954. Bas reliefs feminins de la Magdeleine (Penne, Tarn près Montauban [Tarn-et-Garonne]). *Quaternaria* 1.

Brumfiel, Elizabeth. 1990. Weaving and cooking: Women's production in Aztec Mexico. In *Engendering archaeology: women and prehistory.* Joan Gero and Margaret Conkey, eds. Oxford: Basil Blackwell.

Bumstead, Pamela. 1987. Recognizing women in the archaeological record. Paper presented at Annual Meetings, American Anthropological Association. Chicago, Illinois.

Bunn, Henry, and Ellen Kroll. 1986. Systematic butchery by Plio/Pleistocene hominids at Olduvai Gorge, Tanzania. *Current Anthropology* 27: 431–452.

———. 1988. Fact and fiction about the FLK *Zinjanthropus* floor. *Current Anthropology* 29: 135–149.

Butterfield, H. 1963. *The Whig Interpretation of History.* New York: Norton.

Cartmill, Matt, David Pillbeam, and Glynn Isaac. 1986. One hundred years of paleoanthropology. *American Scientist* 74: 410–420.

Chase, P., and H. Dibble. 1987. Middle Paleolithic symbolism: A review of current evidence and interpretations. *Journal of Anthropological Archaeology* 6: 263–296.

Clark, J. Desmond, and F. Clark Howell. 1966. Preface, special issue on paleoanthropology. *American Anthropologist* 68 (2): v–vii.

Clifford, James. 1986. Introduction: Partial truths. In *Writing culture: The poetics and politics of ethnography.* James Clifford and George Marcus, eds., 1–26. Berkeley, Los Angeles, London: University of California Press.

———. 1988. *The predicament of culture: Twentieth-century ethnography, literature, and art.* Cambridge: Harvard University Press.

Clifford, James, and George Marcus, eds. 1986. *Writing culture: The poetics and politics of ethnography.* Berkeley, Los Angeles, London: University of California Press.

Collier, Jane, and Sylvia Yanagisako, eds. 1987. *Gender and kinship: Essays toward a unified analysis.* Stanford: Stanford University Press.

Collins, D., and J. Onians. 1978. The origin of art. *Art History* 1 (1) (March): 1–25.

Conkey, Margaret. 1977. By chance: The role of archaeology in contributing to a reinterpretation of human culture. Paper presented at Annual Meetings, American Anthropological Association, Houston, Texas.

———. 1978. Getting grants: Participation of women in the research process. Paper presented at Annual Meetings, American Anthropological Association, Los Angeles, California.

———. 1983. On the origins of paleolithic art: A review and some critical thoughts. In *The Mousterian legacy: Human biocultural change in the upper Pleistocene.* E. Trinkhaus, ed., 201–227. Oxford, England: British Archaeological Reports, International Series no. 164.

———. 1987. New approaches in the search for meaning? A review of research in Paleolithic "art." *Journal of Field Archaeology* 14: 413–430.

———. 1989. Structural studies of Paleolithic art. In *Archaeological thought in America.* C. C. Lamberg-Karlovsky, ed., 135–154. Cambridge: Cambridge University Press.

———. 1990. Contexts of action, contexts for power: Material culture and gender in Magdalenian times. In *Engendering archaeology: Women and prehistory.* Joan Gero and Margaret Conkey, eds. Oxford: Basil Blackwell.

———. n.d.*a.* Magic, mythogram, and metaphors for modernity: The interpretation of Paleolithic art. In *Handbook of human symbolic evolution.* Andrew Lock and Charles Peters, eds. Oxford: Oxford University Press.

———. n.d.*b.* Must we be feminists to do archaeologies of gender? Paper presented at Plenary Session, Archaeology of Gender, Chacmool Conference. Calgary: University of Calgary (November 1989).

Conkey, Margaret, and Joan Gero. 1988. Towards building a feminist archaeology. Paper presented at Fifty-third Annual Meeting, Society for American Archaeology. Phoenix, Arizona.

———. 1990. Tensions, pluralities, and engendering archaeology: An introduction to *Women and prehistory.* In *Engendering archaeology: Women and prehistory.* Joan M. Gero and Margaret W. Conkey, eds. Oxford: Basil Blackwell.

Conkey, Margaret, and Janet Spector. 1984. Archaeology and the study of gender. In *Advances in archaeological method and theory,* 7: 1–38. M. Schiffer, ed. New York: Academic Press.

Courbin, P. 1988. *What is archaeology? An essay on the nature of archaeological research.* Trans. Paul Bahn. Chicago: University of Chicago Press.

Cucchiari, Salvatore. 1981. The gender revolution and the transition from bisexual horde to patrilocal band: The origins of gender hierarchy. In *Sexual meanings*. S. Ortner and H. Whitehead, eds., 31–79. Cambridge: Cambridge University Press.

Dahlberg, Frances, ed. 1981. *Woman the gatherer*. New Haven: Yale University Press.

Davis, Elizabeth Gould. 1971. *The first sex*. New York: Putnam.

Davis, Whitney. 1985. Present and future directions in the study of rock art. *South African Archaeological Bulletin* 40: 5–10.

Deagan, Kathleen. 1983. *Spanish St. Augustine: The archaeology of a colonial creole community*. New York: Academic Press.

Deetz, James F. 1977. *In small things forgotten: The archaeology of early American life*. Garden City, N.Y.: Anchor Press-Doubleday.

DeLivre, A. 1977. *L'histoire des Rois Merina: Interpretation d'une Tradition Orale*. Klincksieck: Paris.

Delluc, B., and G. Delluc. 1978. Les manifestations graphiques Aurignaciennes sur support rocheux des environs des Eyzies (Dordogne). *Gallia Préhistoire* 21 (1–2): 213–438.

Delphy, C. 1984. *Close to home: A materialist analysis of women's oppression*. D. Leonard, ed. London: Hutchinson (in association with the Explorations in Feminism Collective).

Delporte, Henri. 1979. *L'image de la Femme dans l'Art Préhistorique*. Paris: Picard.

Dibble, Harold, and Anta Montet-White, eds. 1988. *The Upper Pleistocene of Western Eurasia*. University Museum Symposium Series, vol. 7. Philadelphia: University of Pennsylvania Museum.

Diner, Helen. 1973. *Mothers and Amazons: The first feminine history of culture*. New York: Doubleday Anchor. (Orig. 1965.)

Dunnell, Robert. 1980. Evolutionary theory and archaeology. *Advances in archaeological method and theory*. M. B. Schiffer, ed., 3: 35–99. New York: Academic Press.

———. 1986. Five decades of American archaeology. In *American archaeology past and future*. D. J. Meltzer, D. D. Fowler, and J. A. Sabloff, eds., 23–49. Washington and London: Smithsonian Institution Press.

Eaton, R. 1978. The evolution of trophy hunting. *Carnivore* 1 (1): 110–121.

Eisler, Riane. 1987. *The chalice and the blade: Our history, our future*. San Francisco: Harper & Row.

Elshtain, Jean B. 1986. The new feminist scholarship. *Salamagundi* 70–71: 3–26.

Engels, Frederic. 1972. *The origin of the family, private property and the state*. Eleanor B. Leacock, ed. New York: International Publishers.

Fabian, Johannes. 1983. *Time and the other: How anthropology makes its object*. New York: Columbia University Press.

Faris, James. 1983. From form to content in the structural study of aesthetic systems. In *Structure and cognition in art*. Dorothy Washburn, ed. Cambridge: Cambridge University Press, 90–112.

Foley, R. A., and P. C. Lee. 1989. Finite social space, evolutionary pathways, and reconstructing hominid behavior. *Science* 243 (Feb. 17, 1989): 901–906.

Gailey, Christine. 1985. The state of the state in anthropology. *Dialectical Anthropology* 9 (1–4): 65–91.

———. 1987. *From kinship to kingship: Gender hierarchy and state formation in the Tongan Islands*. Austin: University of Texas Press.

Gero, Joan. 1983. Gender bias in archaeology: A cross cultural perspective. In *The socio-politics of archaeology*. J. M. Gero, D. Lacy, and M. L. Blakey, eds., 51–57. Amherst: Research Report Number 23, Department of Anthropology, University of Massachusetts.

———. 1985. Socio-politics of archaeology and the woman-at-home ideology. *American Antiquity* 50: 342–350.

———. 1990. Genderlithics: Women's roles in stone tool production. In *Engendering archaeology: Women and prehistory*. Joan Gero and Margaret Conkey, ed. Oxford: Basil Blackwell.

Gero, Joan, and Margaret Conkey, eds. 1990. *Engendering archaeology: Women and prehistory*. Oxford: Basil Blackwell.

Gero, Joan, David Lacey, and Michael Blakely, eds. 1983. *The sociopolitics of archaeology*. Amherst: Research Report 23, Department of Anthropology, University of Massachusetts.

Gero, Joan, and Dolores Root. 1989. Public presentations are private concerns: Archaeology in the pages of *National Geographic*. In *Politics of the past*. P. Gathercole and D. Lowenthal, eds. London: Unwin.

Gibb, Liv. 1987. Identifying gender representation in the archaeological record: A contextual study. In *The archaeology of contextual meanings*. Ian Hodder, ed., 79–89. Cambridge: Cambridge University Press.

Gould, Richard, and Patty Jo Watson. 1982. A dialogue on the meaning and use of analogy in ethnoarchaeological reasoning. *Journal of Anthropological Archaeology* 1: 363–381.

Guthrie, R. Dale. 1984. Ethological observations from Paleolithic art. In *La Contribution de la Zoologie et de l'Ethologie à l'interpretation de l'Art des Peuples Chasseurs Préhistoriques*. H.-G. Bandi, W. Huber, M.-R. Sauter, and B. Sitter, eds., 35–74. Fribourg, Switzerland: Editions Universitaires.

Habermas, Jürgens. 1971. *Knowledge and human interest*. Boston: Beacon Press.

Handsman, Russell. 1988. Whose art was made at Lepenski Vir? Paper presented at Women and Production in Prehistory, a conference. The Wedge, South Carolina (April).

———. 1990. Whose art was made at Lepenski Vir? Gender relations and power in archaeology. In *Engendering archaeology: Women and prehistory*. Joan M. Gero and Margaret W. Conkey, eds. Oxford: Basil Blackwell.

Haraway, Donna. 1978. Animal sociology and a natural economy of the body politic, part II: The past is the contested zone: Human nature and theories of production and reproduction in primate behavior studies. *Signs* 4: 37–60.

———. 1983. The contest for primate nature: Daughters of man-the-hunter in the field, 1960–1980. In *The future of American democracy*. M. Kahn, ed., 175–207. Philadelphia: Temple University Press.

Hawkes, C. 1954. Archaeological theory and method: Some suggestions from the Old World. *American Anthropologist* (n.s.) 56: 155–168.

Hodder, Ian. 1982a. *Symbols in action*. Cambridge: Cambridge University Press.

———. 1982b. *Symbolic and structural archaeology*. Cambridge: Cambridge University Press.

———. 1982c. Theoretical archaeology: A reactionary view. In *Symbolic and structural archaeology*. I. Hodder, ed., 1–16. Cambridge: Cambridge University Press.

————. 1984. Burials, houses, women and men in the European Neolithic. In *Ideology, power and prehistory*. Daniel Miller and Christopher Tilley, eds. Cambridge: Cambridge University Press.

————. 1985. Post-processual archaeology. In *Advances in archaeological method and theory*, M. B. Schiffer, ed., 8: 1–26.

————. 1986. *Reading the past*. Cambridge: Cambridge University Press.

————. 1990. *The domestication of Europe*. Oxford: Basil Blackwell.

Hooks, Bell. 1984. *Feminist theory: From margin to center*. Boston: South End Press.

Howell, Nancy. 1988. The Tasaday and the !Kung: Reassessing isolated hunter-gatherers. Paper presented at the Fifty-third Annual Meeting, Society for American Archaeology, Phoenix, Arizona.

Isaac, Glynn L. 1978. The food-sharing behavior of protohuman hominids. *Scientific American* 238 (4): 90–108.

Jameson, Frederic. 1984. Post-modernism or the cultural logic of late capitalism. *New Left Review* 146: 85–106.

Keller, Evelyn Fox. 1989. Holding the center in feminist theory. *Women's Studies International Forum* 12 (3): 313–318.

Klein, Richard. 1989. *The human career: Human biological and cultural origins*. Chicago: University of Chicago Press.

Kennedy, Mary C. 1979. Status, role, and gender: Preconceptions in archaeology. Manuscript, Department of Anthropology, University of Minnesota.

Kus, Susan. 1986. The power of origins. Paper presented at the Fifty-first Annual Meeting, Society for American Archaeology, New Orleans, Louisiana.

Landau, Misia. 1984. Human evolution as narrative. *American Scientist* 72: 262–268.

Laughlin, William. 1968. Hunting: An integrating biobehavior system and its evolutionary implications. In *Man the hunter*. Richard B. Lee and Irven DeVore, eds., 304–320. Chicago: Aldine.

Lee, Richard B. 1976. Introduction, *Kalahari hunter-gatherers*. Richard B. Lee and I. DeVore, eds., 3–24. Cambridge: Harvard University Press.

Lee, Richard B., and I. DeVore, eds. 1968. *Man the hunter*. Chicago: Aldine.

Leone, Mark P. 1982. Some opinions about recovering mind. *American Antiquity* 47 (4): 742–760.

————. 1986. Symbolic, structural and critical archaeology. In *American archaeology past and future*. D. J. Meltzer, D. D. Fowler, and J. A. Sabloff, eds., 415–438. Washington and London: Smithsonian Institution Press.

————. n.d. Critical theory in archaeology. Paper presented at SUNY-Binghamton Regional Archaeological Theory Symposium, March 1984.

Leone, Mark, Parker Potter, Jr., and Paul A. Shackel. 1987. Toward a critical archaeology. *Current Anthropology* 28 (3): 283–302.

Lerner, Gerda. 1986. *Creation of patriarchy*. Oxford: Oxford University Press.

Leroi-Gourhan, André. 1965. *Treasures of Paleolithic art*. New York: Abrams.

————. 1968. The evolution of Paleolithic art. *Scientific American* (February): 58–74.

————. 1973. *Préhistoire de l'art occidental*. 3d ed. Mazenod: Paris.

————. 1978. The mysterious markings in the Paleolithic art of France and Spain. *CNRS Research* 8: 26–32.

Lewin, Roger. 1987a. *Bones of contention: Controversies in the search for human origins*. New York: Simon and Schuster.

————. 1987*b*. Africa: Cradle of modern humans. *Science* 237 (September 11, 1987): 1292–1295.

Lovejoy, C. Owen. 1981. The origin of man. *Science* 211 (4480): 341–350.

Lowie, Robert. 1937. *The history of ethnological theory*. New York: Rinehart.

Lutz, Catherine. In press. Culture and consciousness: A problem in anthropological knowledge. In *Self and consciousness*. P. Cole, D. Johnson, and F. Kessel, eds. Hillsdale, N.J.: Erlbaum.

Marcus, George, and James Clifford. 1985. The making of ethnographic texts: A preliminary report. *Current Anthropology* 26 (2): 267–271.

Marshack, Alexander. 1977. The meander as a system: The analysis and recognition of iconographic units in upper Paleolithic compositions. In *Form in indigenous art*. Peter Ucko, ed., 285–317. Canberra: Institute of Aboriginal Studies.

Marshall, Yvonne. 1985. Who made the Lapita pots? *Journal of the Polynesian Society* 94: 205–233.

McCafferty, G., and S. McCafferty. 1988. Powerful women and the myth of male dominance in Aztec society. *Archaeological Review from Cambridge* 7: 45–59.

————. n.d. Mexican spinning and weaving as female gender identity. In *Cloth and clothing in Mesoamerica and the Andes*. M. Schevill, J. C. Berlo, and N. Dwyer, eds.

McGaw, Judith. 1987. Women and the history of American technology. In *Sex and scientific inquiry*. Sandra Harding and Jean F. O'Barr, eds., 47–78. Chicago: University of Chicago Press.

McGuire, Randall. 1985. Conceptualizing the state in a post-processual archaeology. Paper presented at Annual Meetings, American Anthropological Association, Washington, D.C.

Mellars, Paul, and Chris Stringer, eds. 1989. *The human revolution: Behavioural and biological perspectives on the origins of modern humans*. Edinburgh and Princeton: The University Presses.

Miller, Daniel. 1983. THINGS ain't what they used to be. *Rain* (Royal Anthropological Institute News) 59: 5–7.

Moore, Henrietta. 1986. *Space, text and gender: An anthropological study of the Marakwet of Kenya*. Cambridge: Cambridge University Press.

————. 1988. *Feminism and anthropology*. London: Polity Press.

Moraga, Cherrie, and Gloria Anzaldua, eds. 1981. *This bridge called my back: Writings of radical women of color*. Watertown, Mass.: Persephone Press.

Morgan, Elaine. 1972. *The descent of woman*. New York: Stein and Day.

Parker, Sue T. 1987. A sexual selection model for hominid evolution. *Human Evolution* 2 (3): 235–253.

Patterson, Thomas. 1986. The last sixty years: Towards a social history of Americanist archaeology in the United States. *American Anthropologist* 88 (1): 7–26.

Pohl, Mary, and Lawrence Feldman. 1982. The traditional role of women and animals in lowland Maya economy. In *Maya subsistence*. Kent Flannery, ed., 295–311. New York: Academic Press.

Preziosi, Donald. 1982. Constru(ct)ing the origins of art. *Art Journal* (Winter): 320–325.

Rapp, Rayna. 1977. Gender and class: Archaeology of knowledge concerning the origin of the state. *Dialectical Anthropology* 2 (4) (November): 309–316.

Reed, Evelyn. 1975. *Women's evolution: From matriarchal clan to patriarchal family.* New York: Pathfinder Press.

Reiter, Rayna Rapp. 1978. The search for origins: Unraveling the threads of gender hierarchy. *Critique of Anthropology* 3 (9–10): 5–24.

Renfrew, Colin, and Stephen Shennan, eds. 1982. *Ranking, resources and exchange.* Cambridge: Cambridge University Press.

Rosaldo, Michelle Z., and Louise Lamphere, eds. 1974. *Woman, culture, and society.* Stanford, Calif.: Stanford University Press.

Rowe, John. 1956. Problems in the history of archaeology. Unpublished manuscript, Department of Anthropology, University of California, Berkeley.

Russell, Pamela M. 1987. Women in upper Paleolithic Europe. Master of arts thesis, Department of Anthropology, University of Auckland, N.Z.

Scholte, B. 1986. The charmed circle of Geertz's hermeneutics: A neo-Marxist critique. *Critique of Anthropology* 6 (1): 5–15.

Scott, Joan W. 1986. Gender: A useful category of historical analysis. *American Historical Review* 91: 1053–1075.

Shanks, M., and C. Tilley. 1987a. *Re-constructing archaeology.* Cambridge: Cambridge University Press.

———. 1987b. *Social theory and archaeology.* Albuquerque: University of New Mexico.

Shennan, Stephen. 1986. Towards a critical archaeology? *Proceedings of the Prehistoric Society* 52: 327–356.

Shutler, Richard, ed. 1983. *Early man in the new world.* Beverly Hills, Calif.: Sage Publications.

Silberbauer, G. 1981. *Hunter and habitat in the central Kalahari Desert.* Cambridge: Cambridge University Press.

Silverblatt, Irene. 1987. *Moon, sun and witches: Gender ideologies and class in Inca and colonial Peru.* Princeton: Princeton University Press.

———. 1988. Women in states. *Annual Review of Anthropology* 17: 427–460.

Slocum, Sally. 1975. Woman the gatherer: Male bias in anthropology. In *Toward an anthropology of women.* R. R. Reiter, ed., 36–50. New York: Monthly Review Press.

Solomon, Anne Catherine. 1989. Division of the earth: Gender symbolism and the archaeology of the southern San. Master of arts thesis, Department of Archaeology, University of Cape Town, South Africa.

Spector, Janet D., and Mary K. Whelan. 1989. Incorporating gender into archaeology courses. A curriculum guide for introductory human evolution and archaeology classes. Washington, D.C.: American Anthropological Association.

Stig-Sørenson, Marie-Louise. 1987. Material order and cultural classification: The role of bronze objects in the transition from Bronze Age to Iron Age in Scandinavia. In *The archaeology of contextual meanings.* Ian Hodder, ed., 90–101. Cambridge: Cambridge University Press.

Stocking, G. 1968. On the limits of "presentism" and "historicism." In *Race, evolution and culture.* George Stocking, ed. Chicago: University of Chicago Press.

Stoliar, A. D. 1977/1978. On the sociohistorical decoding of upper Paleolithic female signs. *Soviet Anthropology and Archaeology* 16: 36–77.

Tanner, Nancy. 1981. *On becoming human.* Cambridge: Cambridge University Press.

Tanner, Nancy, and Adrienne Zihlman. 1976. Women in evolution, part I: Innovation and selection in human origins. In *Signs: Journal of Women in Culture and Society* 1 (3): 104–119.

Thomas, D. H. 1989. *Archaeology*. 2d ed. New York: Holt, Rinehart and Winston.

Toth, N., and K. Schick. 1986. The first million years: The archaeology of proto-human culture. *Advances in archaeological method and theory*. M. B. Schiffer, ed., 9: 1–96. New York: Academic Press.

Trigger, Bruce. 1980. Archaeology and the image of the American Indian. *American Antiquity* 45 (4): 622–676.

———. 1984. Alternative archaeologies: Colonialist, nationalist, imperialist. *Man* (n.s.) 19: 355–370.

Ucko, Peter. 1968. *Anthropomorphic figures of pre-dynastic Egypt and Neolithic Crete*. Royal Anthropological Institute, Occasional Paper 24. London.

Ucko, P., and A. Rosenfeld. 1967. *Paleolithic cave art*. New York: McGraw-Hill.

———. 1972. Anthropomorphic representations in Paleolithic art. In *Santander symposium*, 149–211. Santander: Actas del Symposium Internacional de Art Prehistorico.

Washburn, Sherwood, and Chester S. Lancaster. 1968. The evolution of hunting. In *Man the hunter*. Richard B. Lee and Irven DeVore, eds., 293–303. Chicago: Aldine.

Watson, Patty Jo, Charles L. Redman, and Steven LeBlanc. 1971. *Explanation in archaeology*. New York: Columbia University Press.

Watson, Patty Jo, and Mary Kennedy. 1990. The development of horticulture in the eastern woodlands of North America: Women's role. In *Engendering archaeology: Women and prehistory*. Joan Gero and Margaret Conkey, eds. Oxford: Basil Blackwell.

Welbourn, Alice. 1984. Endo ceramics and power strategies. In *Ideology, power and prehistory*. D. Miller and C. Tilley, eds. Cambridge: Cambridge University Press.

Wiessner, Polly. 1982. Beyond willow-smoke and dog's tails: A comment on Binford's analysis of hunter-gatherer settlement systems. *American Antiquity* 47 (1): 171–178.

Willey, Gordon, and Jeremy Sabloff. 1980. *A history of American archaeology*. 2d ed. San Francisco: W. H. Freeman & Co.

Williams, Raymond. 1981. Marxism, structuralism and literary analyses. *New Left Review* (Sept.–Oct.): 65.

Williams, Sarah. 1986. Paleoanthropology and the construction of mankind: An outline. Paper on file with the author, History of Consciousness Program, University of California, Santa Cruz.

———. 1990. Woman writing, man's science: Supplementary differences. Ph.D. qualifying exam paper, History of Consciousness, University of California, Santa Cruz.

Wobst, H. Martin, and Arthur Keene. 1983. Archaeological explanations as political economy. In *Sociopolitics of archaeology*. J. Gero, D. Lacy, and M. Blakey, eds., 59–65. Amherst: University of Massachusetts Department of Anthropology Research Reports No. 23.

Wolpuff, Milford. 1980. *Paleoanthropology*. New York: A. Knopf.

Wylie, M. Alison. 1985. Putting Shakertown back together: Critical theory in archaeology. *Journal of Anthropological Archaeology* 4: 133–147.

———. 1990. Gender theory and the archaeological record: Why is there no archaeology of gender? In *Engendering archaeology: Women and prehistory.* Joan Gero and Margaret Conkey, eds. Oxford: Basil Blackwell.

———. n.d. Beyond objectivism and relativism: Feminist critiques and archaeological challenges. Paper presented at Plenary Session, Archaeology of Gender, Chacmool Conference. Calgary: University of Calgary (November).

Yanagisako, Sylvia. 1979. Family and household: The analysis of domestic groups. *Annual Review of Anthropology* 8: 161–205.

Yellen, John. 1977. *Archaeological approaches to the present.* New York: Academic Press.

———. 1983. Women, archaeology and the National Science Foundation. In *The sociopolitics of archaeology.* J. M. Gero, D. Lacy, and M. L. Blakey, eds., 59–65. Amherst: University of Massachusetts Department of Anthropology Research Report No. 23.

Zagarell, Alan. 1986. Trade, women, class, and society in ancient western Asia. *Current Anthropology* 27 (5): 415–420.

Zihlman, Adrienne. 1978. Women in evolution, part II: Subsistence and social organization in early hominids. *Signs: Journal of Women in Culture and Society* 4 (1): 4–20.

———. 1981. Women as shapers of the human adaptation. In *Women the gatherer.* Frances Dahlberg, ed., 75–102. New Haven: Yale University Press.

THREE

Interpreting Women in States
New Feminist Ethnohistories

Irene Silverblatt

*Viewed apart from real history, these abstractions have in themselves no value whatso-
ever. They can only serve to facilitate the arrangement of historical material. . . . But
they by no means afford a recipe or schema . . . for neatly trimming the epochs of history.
On the contrary, our difficulties begin only when we set about the observation and the
arrangement—the real depiction—of historical material, whether of a past epoch or of
the present. The removal of these difficulties is governed by premises which it is quite
impossible to state here, but which only the study of the actual life-process and the
activity of the individuals of each epoch will make evident.*
    —Karl Marx and Fredrich Engels, 1983 [1845–1846]

*It is now almost impossible . . . to remember a time when people were not talking about a
crisis in representation.*
    —Edward Said, 1989

*When the problem of connecting isolated phenomena has become a problem of categories,
by the same dialectical process every problem of categories becomes transformed into a
historical problem.*
    —Georg Lukacs, 1971

*. . . throughout our continent [South America] there are many "schools" whose profes-
sors use the lessons of torture and humiliation to teach us to lose the memories of
ourselves. Beware: in little schools the boundaries between story and history are so subtle
that even I can hardly find them.*
    —Alicia Partnoy, 1986

INTRODUCTION: A CRISIS OF CATEGORIES

Ethnohistory—the use of documents, archaeological findings, oral histories,
and ethnographies to construct the histories of non-Western peoples—came
early to the feminist table.[1] Because of both academic and popular concern

140

over the "origins" (i.e. cause) of women's oppression in the 1970s, feminist ethnohistorians found their formerly marginalized work—on, for example, transformations in Native American gender relations with the French colonization of Canada—catapulted to the center of feminist attention. The hope was that histories of non-Western peoples could reveal something fundamental about the relationship between society, culture, and the position of women. Would analysis uncover broad variations and similarities in women's lives worldwide and across time? Might it disclose the existence of regularities—laws, perhaps—that could account for women's status in terms of specific features of society?

Here entered the "women and the state" debate, one of the principal threads of this first wave of anthropological theorizing. Simply put, one group of scholars, following Marx and Engels, associated the "world historical defeat of the female sex" (Engels 1972: 218) with the evolutionary rise of the state—the centralizing and institutionalizing of power in the context of extreme economic and social stratification. Opposing groups claimed that women's oppression was universal and linked to structural conditions that cross-cut state and nonstate societies (Silverblatt 1988b: 428–429; and see di Leonardo, this volume).

Over the course of the last decade this debate—with its particular way of framing analyses of women and gender—has seemed increasingly barren. Such concerns about our categories and theories come from a gnawing recognition that the common sense of anthropology—whether evolutionary, functionalist, or structuralist—has systematically denied its subjects' place in the history of world politics. Anthropologists are beginning to recast (ethno)histories; and we are beginning to reexamine our own. Anthropology's crisis of history, however, is part of a more generalized crisis of confidence in the categories structuring Western intellectual practice. Some movements of academic self-doubt, characteristic of these "postmodern" times and crucial to reappraisals in anthropology and feminism, have turned to "texts" and "discourse" as key to the analysis of cultural experience and human activity.

To assert that the pivot of feminist debate in anthropology has shifted, that the "women and the state" frame no longer seems adequate, is only the beginning of our task. In what follows I review and reinterpret this recent chronicle—a critical account that is autobiographical in spirit. My purpose is to engage current movements of intellectual skepticism and to sketch some implications of anthropology's turn to history and postmodernism's turn to "discourse" for a critical feminist ethnohistory.

Feminist ethnohistorians can no longer offer an unambiguously clear evolutionary narrative of women's degradation with the rise of the state. But we can offer historical narratives of the varying activities of women and men, and their contentions over gender imageries and practices, in the making and unmaking of states. And though our accounts are partial and contingent tales, limited by sources and perspectives, at the very least they deny neither historical experience nor its significance in the public record. Anthropology's crises have again propelled ethnohistory to feminist attention.

Finally, to follow Lukacs's lead, I note that crises in categories through which history and society are apprehended demand a history of those categories along with a profound examination into the nature of knowledge and its production. Frustration with anthropology's received wisdom on "women and the state" is then a historical question, one that points to the complex conditions shaping the construction of anthropological knowledge. It is, of course, a political question as well.

ANTHROPOLOGY'S HISTORIES

The expansion of Europe in the sixteenth century merged the destinies of the Earth's peoples. Western trade and conquest, colonial and later imperial designs, intertwined our futures. Yet the West's official experts on newly "encountered" "primitives" by and large ignored the very processes of intervention through which "primitives" were "discovered," named, and classified. Anthropology maintained historical and political links to the procedures of colonization—both direct (as part of foreign missions) and indirect (as intellectuals living with, defining, and publicizing those "primitives" within the Western ken). Yet anthropology's theories about itself—about the conditions in which it produced knowledge about its "objects" of study— camouflaged its political and historical antecedents. Disregarding or ignorant of the ways in which their destinies joined those of their "objects" of study, and of the hierarchy of power that lay behind academic musings, ethnographers produced, in Wolf's phrasing, "people without history" (1982).[2]

The academic traditions that denied colonial peoples their histories also refused women theirs. With roots in centuries-old Western traditions of common sense and practice, and enshrined first by religious and then by secular intellectuals, mainstream social science has systematically excluded "others" from active, defining roles in official social theory and practice. Over the last twenty or so years, these "others" of the West—women, colonized peoples, ethnic minorities, blacks, laboring people—have disputed their displacement by the intellectual mainstream, effecting profound changes in the disciplines of history and social life.[3]

The 1980s have witnessed a growing and sharpened attack on mainstream epistemologies with significant implications for our understandings of gender and colonized "others." These attacks come from two trends in the study of culture—postmodernism and Marxist cultural studies—that are intertwined, embattled, yet at times mutually enriching. The characteristic themes of our so-called "postmodern" age include an emphasis on the partiality and fallibility of knowledge, a preoccupation with form and the human construction of modes of expression in art and the intellect, and a recognition of the way power insinuates itself into and propagates itself through the seemingly objective institutions of knowledge. These concerns are not new to the West; they echo one of the most important oppositional trends in modernist thinking to emerge in the interwar years, Western Marxism. Critical of beliefs in automatic social progress and absolute objectivity, horrified by the social concomitants of those beliefs which dominated the scholarly and popular moods of the time, the work of these committed intellectuals—including Lukacs (1971), Benjamin (1969), and Gramsci (1971)—resonates with today's concerns (Taussig 1984; Huyssen 1986; Anderson 1984; Lunn 1982).[4]

Feminist criticism has played a significant and eloquent role in furthering postmodern visions.[5] Concerned with the ways in which some of the supposedly "innocent" vehicles of communication are biased as cultural constructions, feminist scholars have focused on language itself as a complicit carrier of political and cultural bias. This focus has led to damning critiques of enlightenment and bourgeois discourse for cloaking the bias of a white male elite in claims of an objective and universal subject of history. In its most extreme versions, however, these postmodernists rest their study of power in language itself. Their subsequent fascination with the rhetoric of texts deflects attention from the unequal social conditions in which knowledge is produced. Moreover, when theories portray human beings narrowly as either constructed by linguistic means or as the vehicles through which discourses gain expression, they neglect the dialectical ability of human beings to engage language, let alone their world. Consequently, some attempts to expose Western androcentrism seem to celebrate, almost frenziedly, the discursive (as opposed to historical) construction of "others" and "difference"—and the hopelessness of any political solution.[6]

Marxist anthropology early on recognized the discipline's complicity in both Western expansion and the political history of constructing "others." Over the past two decades, nevertheless, Marxist anthropologists have been forced to revalue some of their (our) glaring deficiencies. As the 1970s chastised economic reductionism, and as postmodern thinking put discourse in the forefront, Marxist anthropologists began to reexamine their understandings of culture. Some turned to the critical Marxist writers of the 1920s and 1930s. Feminist anthropology also contributed in important ways to this reevaluation of the Marxist tradition. As we will see, scholars like Eleanor Leacock and Karen Sacks pointed to the significance of cultural forms in social process by studying how transformations in gender were inherent in the development of social classes and the state. Yet their own analyses, indebted to Engels's vision, reinscribed many of the assumptions about social process and social theory characteristic of the century past.

ENGELS AND ORIGIN QUESTS[7]

Many feminist anthropologists turned to Marx and Engels, censors of the bourgeois society in which they lived, for help in shaping the mounting critique of its late-twentieth-century legacy. They particularly scrutinized Engels, as the author of a treatise (*The Origin of the Family, Private Property, and the State* [1884]) on the entwining of family forms and emerging political and economic inequality—in which the position of women played a pivotal role.

The nineteenth-century intellectual debates that oriented Engels's thinking on women centered on the character of the family. What was the patriarchal family's historical status? As fundament of state and society, universalists argued that it had to be intrinsic to all human experience; opposing views, buttressed by conflicting information compiled by travelers, government officials, and burgeoning anthropologists, no longer supported such universalist claims. Rather than an entailment of human nature, the patriarchal family, or an idealized middle-class variant, was perceived to be the culmination of a lawful evolutionary process away from the "natural" living conditions of savagery.[8]

Living in the age of Darwin, Engels, like other social theorists of his time, understood human society, like the animal world, to be propelled by developmental laws. Assuming, then, the developmental character of family forms, Engels's arguments against universality took on an evolutionary cast. Historical reasoning was blurred by evolutionary considerations; and this merger of two apparently similar but profoundly contrary methods of analysis would prove to be significant for debates surfacing a century later.

Unlike other Victorian social thinkers, Engels challenged a cherished commonplace of his time—the belief that the Victorian family represented the culmination of evolutionary progress. Engels, elaborating Morgan's argument in *Ancient Society* (1964 [1877]), passionately held the view that primitive culture, organized communally, offered women their most democratic experiences. Society's evolutionary march to the state rendered women's downfall; and only the resurrection of primitive communalism in the next stage of human development would signal a return to gender equality.

Engels envisioned the advance of mankind in terms of transformations in its fundamental material relations: technological improvements, an increasingly complex division of labor, the growth of exchange, and the elaboration of private property—economic processes that culminated in the rise of the state. The "world historic defeat of the female sex" emerged as a byproduct of these developments. Pressures tied to demands of inheritance urged the "overthrow of mother right by father right" (1972: 120). To ensure that private wealth would be retained by the male kinsmen who produced it, previously matrilineal extended family arrangements gave way to a tightly circumscribed, patrilineal nuclear family. Transformations in inheritance signaled transformations in relations between the sexes. Women's activities, which under conditions of primitive egalitarianism still contributed to community welfare, were converted into a private service for husbands. Although Engels's general theory of women's degradation was modeled on perceived changes in the Western world (ancient Mediterranean, classical Greece, and modern European), it was also dependent on another assumption that contemporary anthropologists and feminists would find highly questionable: the notion that biology determines the activities of women and men.

Like others of his century, Engels supposed that the allocation of tasks by sex represented an extension of the inherent natures of men and women. So even in the early matriarchies of primitive society, he has "the woman look-[ing] after the house and the preparation of food and clothing," while "the man fights in the wars, goes hunting and fishing, procures the raw materials of food and the tools necessary for doing so" (1972: 218). Engels's reconstructions of gender relations have been severely challenged by contemporary anthropological and feminist research (Coward 1983; Sayers et al. 1987; Vogel 1987; Krader 1973; Lee and DeVore 1968).

If beliefs in the naturalness of the division of labor by sex were intrinsic to nineteenth-century notions of how society and history worked, so were classifications of society into developmental categories. Indeed one mission of the nineteenth century's emerging field of ethnology was to categorize the growing variety of human populations in the Western ken.[9] The social-type abstractions developed at that time were to become the common sense of the field—the division of the world's peoples into bands (lower savages, primitives), tribes (upper savages, lower barbarians), chiefdoms (upper barbarians), and states (civilization). Scientists assumed that this particular way of slicing up the globe would form the basis for meaningful comparisons within and between societal types. The comparative method—with its tendency to divorce cultures from their temporal matrix—implied that neither history nor context were necessary to the task of creating explanations of any social scientific significance (Cohn 1980, 1981).[10]

1970s DILEMMAS: THE ORIGIN OF WOMEN'S DOWNFALL

As we have noted, the problem of women's status framed the pivotal debate of 1970s feminist anthropology. On one side were aligned anthropologists who declared gender relations always to have been asymmetrical, and who pointed to a universal domestic/public orientation of society to account for women's denigration (Rosaldo 1974; Ortner 1974; Whitehead 1976). Other anthropologists, who would not accept a transcultural explanation for women's lower status, found an ally in Engels and were inspired by his insistence on exploitation's historical character. In tune with the debate's guidelines, the nature of women's lives in "egalitarian" societies—a precondition for evaluating the impact of the "state"—became a hotly contested topic. Regardless of persuasion, however, scholars considered it appropriate to couch their inquiries in terms of a dispute over origins. "Women and the state" formed one branch of an acceptable ethnohistorical and ethnographic controversy.

This 1970s debate clearly owes much to the past century's bequests. For wasn't the universal-vs.-state foundation of women's lowered status shaped by an "origin question"—that paradigmatic concern of the nineteenth century? (Rosaldo 1980; Conkey, this volume.) And didn't that origin question presuppose not only the uniformity of status but the uniformity of social types—the existence of a model egalitarian (hunting and gathering, "primitive," communal) society that was easily contrasted to its opposite (stratified state) on an evolutionary scale of social complexity? Thus feminist ethnohistorical pundits jointly reproduced two elements of Victorian anthropological wisdom: that the social spectrum could be meaningfully and judiciously divided into societal types, of which "the state" was one; and that a basically uniform "standing" of women would follow these categories.

Eleanor Leacock pioneered a resurgence of interest in Engels's scholarship with the publication of a highly influential 1972 edition of the *Origin of the Family, Private Property and the State*. In the introduction, and then elaborated in subsequent publications, Leacock presented a theory of the origin of gender hierarchy clearly inspired by a critical interpretation of Engels (Leacock 1972). Her theory also, however, incorporated some of Engels's most striking contradictions (striking, that is, from the perspective of 1980s concerns). Like Engels, Leacock insisted on the historical foundations of women's oppression; like Engels, she blurred historical analysis with evolutionary projections and fell into the trap of abstracting a pattern from Western experience and generalizing it to account for the changing fortunes of women in all the world's states.

Leacock was critical of Engels's unilineal evolutionism, yet she never abandoned evolutionary theory in her own work. Following developmental presumptions, she saw particular societal variations as examples of large-scale evolutionary tendencies, including a necessary correspondence between the formation of the state and the degradation of women's status. Her explanation of the shared origin of gender hierarchy, class inequality, and the state was jarringly reminiscent of Engels's. The development of productive forces, economic specialization, and the growth of exchange dictated the emergence of a circumscribed nuclear family as the state's principal property-holding and transmitting unit—processes, which, in turn, led to the diminution of women's activities to private services owed husbands and male kin, and consequently to women's debasement (Leacock 1972, 1978, 1983).

The model for Leacock's evolutionary trajectory, moreover, was rooted in Engels's: gender relations were transformed from egalitarian relations, typified by the Iroquois; to the institutionalization of sexual antagonism found in ranking societies, like Melanesia; to full-blown patriarchy and the complete privatization of women's work as represented by the classical Middle East and Mediterranean states (Leacock 1978: 268–270). Thus, as for Engels, processes discerned in the West became the model for the rest. Leacock, then, is subject to the same charges of Western bias she leveled against Engels. Ironically, she specifically recognized the possibility of divergent patterns of development in the Old and New Worlds and was responsible for encouraging research—including my own (1987)—into the dynamic of gender systems and state building in societies outside the bounds of Western influence.

How do some of Leacock's predictions hold up under historical scrutiny? She claimed that women's activities became a private service for men in state systems. Yet if we examine the dynamics of gender relations and political hierarchy in the Andes, we find little to corroborate her projections. Although the demands made by the Inca empire radically transformed the lives of noble and elite women (and men), during the Incas' reign women of neither class performed the kind of dependent, "wifely" duties that seem to mark Old World states. Moreover, Andean structures of gender parallelism ensured that women, independently from men and through a line of women, inherited access to their society's wealth, as well as access to political and religious office. Rather than privileging patrilineality, as Leacock would suppose, Inca empire-building actually reinforced parallel descent (Silverblatt 1987: 20–66).

Leacock's enduring contributions to studies of gender are rooted in a steadfast insistence on historical process, despite her contrary adherence to evolutionary principles. Placing anthropology's objects in history, she challenged anthropologists to stop ascribing stasis to egalitarian societies. Such attributions, Leacock warned, had led and would lead to serious misconstruals of gender relations by deflecting awareness from changes induced by colonization and the market economy. Leacock turned to the historical record and used ethnohistory, in her reassessment of Native American Montaignais bands, to document gender change with Western contact and thus to dispute some of anthropology's most sacred propositions.

Other evolutionary theorists, pursuing Engels's and Leacock's suggestions, furthered ethnohistorical investigations into the origins of women's oppression. Karen Sacks attempted to explain variations in women's status in several African societies. Arranging these societies along a continuum based on level of political organization and development of productive forces, Sacks discerned the deterioration of women's status with the development of economic and political complexity. Although heeding Engels's general framework, Sacks disputed his emphasis on the destructive influence of private property. In her first approximations Sacks turned to the role of women in social production as an indicator/cause of their status (1974); later, in a highly influential book, she sought causality in women's relative access to productive means within the context of the power of kin corporations (1982).

Sacks brought a degree of complexity to the analysis of women's position by pointing out the dual statuses simultaneously held by women in African societies. Although women were dependent as "wives," as "sisters" they attained economic autonomy by means of access to resources guaranteed them as members in a kin group of corporate owners. The state undermined women's status by eroding the economic and political integrity of kin groups; the process of state-making, Sacks argued, thus tended to favor women's role as wives, to the detriment of their personal autonomy.

Like Leacock, Sacks was also sensitive to historical cases that did not fit her evolutionary frame. For example, she noted the status differences experienced by women living in two of Africa's states: Buganda and Dahomey. Yet Sacks's paradigm highlighted Buganda—the state where the dismantling of kin corporations was most severe, and where women's possibilities seemed most restricted—as the culmination of evolutionary progression. Evolutionary compulsions appeared to demand selection of a prototypical "state," and Sacks chose Buganda.

Women's standings in Dahomey did not mesh with the Buganda mold. Even though they lived in weakened kin groups, Dahomey's peasant women maintained control over much of their productive activities through their marketing associations. And traditions of doubled offices among the elite— which Sacks tended to play down—guaranteed women important decision-making powers at the state level.

Sacks's evolutionary assumptions ran counter to the complexities of women's standing and the variations in state structures which her African research suggested. *Sisters and Wives* invoked an inevitable societal destiny, as gender configurations functioned in tandem with evolutionary ends. As Buganda represented the state, so did the lot of Buganda women foretell the fate of women in the state: domination by an uncontradicted male elite.

Christine Gailey, indebted to and refining Sacks and Leacock, constructed the most powerful contemporary evolutionary argument to account for the subordination of women with the rise of the state (1987a, 1987b). Eschewing some of the westernized aspects of state formation proffered by Engels, she continued in his tradition by locating the solution to the "women and the state problem" in the turmoil of class formation. Gailey contended that tributary state-making's unavoidable erosion of kin-group autonomy and the politicization of kinship generated processes compelling the devaluation of women.

To be free from producing their own subsistence, ruling groups in tributary states had to gain access to the labor, or product, of what were autonomous kin communities. This process, Gailey argued, fragmented both the local division of labor as well as the cohesion of kin-group identity. The public/tribute sphere, which was wrenched from the kin group, was able to sever dimensions of gender and age from the community's cohesive social persona. While the emergence of a civil sphere created the conditions requisite for people to be able to be defined in terms of their sex—as abstract "man" and "woman" versus the mother/sister/father/brother, etc., classifications of kin group (1987a: 56), the dominance of the state ensured that the latter's definition of gender would gain prominence. Gailey then argued that by delineating tributary labor in terms of abstract qualities, the state promoted a kind of biological reductionism, which, in turn, advanced sex, class, and racial stereotypes rooted in notions of innate difference.

Reduced to their biological attributes by the state, women were then stereotyped as childbearers. As a result, kinswomen more than kinsmen, Gailey contended, were likely to become associated with the ability of a community to direct its reproduction independently of state intervention. Moreover, as the bearers of laborers, women, more than men, would be subject to state control. These dual female attributes, allied with tributary state formation's needs to capitalize on women's reproductive potential and to undermine the autonomy of local reproduction, encouraged the kind of "extreme ideological debasement" (1987a: 57) suffered by women in state society.

Like Leacock, Sacks, and others, Gailey appealed to history to substantiate her arguments; and thus she invited us to reexamine histories to assess the strength of her interpretations. Would such a reassessment allow us to conclude, with her, that there was a tendency for state formation (all states?) to impose a comprehensive and universal gender ideology on women—and that all women, peasant and elite, ended up accepting state dictates? Or that state gender ideologies, later mirrored by conquered groups, necessarily restricted women to a reproductive role, reified them as childbearers, and then disparaged them because of an "obvious metaphor" (1987b: 22–23), linking their sex to kin-group reproduction and autonomy?

Although Gailey pointed to uncanny parallels in gender imageries in a variety of states, her assumptions seem, on closer scrutiny, to belie the complexities of gender ideologies in states as they were forged in history. Let us first consider some of these historical parallels in greater detail. As Gailey indicated, both Dahomey and the Inca empire developed institutions in which elite representatives systematically alienated girls from their natal communities and placed them in full-time service for the state; both states defined this claim in terms of sexual rights and marriage—these women were called "wives of the king," or "wives of the Inca/Sun," and their chastity was vigilantly guarded (Gailey 1987a: 56–58). Should we concur, then, that these are paradigmatic examples of developing states' drive to degrade the kin sphere and women, to capitalize on women's reproductive potential, and to intervene in local reproduction? If we carefully examine Dahomean and Inca gender ideologies we find an intricacy that prohibits any unilateral interpretation of their significance; we also uncover the inadequacy of interpretations that do not take seriously the specific histories in which gender configurations were produced.

First, the issue of ideological uniformity. Gailey did call attention to the king's wives ambiguous standing as demeaned representatives of conquered groups and as exalted wives of the Crown. Yet this complex of norms regarding the king's wives was not the sole constituent of gendered structures and imageries in Dahomean life. They were in dialogue with others, like those of sexual dualism, which governed Dahomean forms of economic and political organization. Structures of sexual dualism directed women into a panoply of state offices, including positions of national importance. Many women took advantage of these opportunities to amass wealth, others to attain privileges for their lineages of birth (Bay 1985; Sanday 1981: 86–88, 90, 176). Moreover, marketing associations that, as Sacks had pointed out, were very important in the lives of Dahomey's non-noble women, allowed them to govern their economic affairs directly and provided them with some political clout.

Like Dahomey, Inca gender ideologies were complex, even contradictory. Along with the ambiguous evaluations attributed to the wives of the Inca kings, the Andean world was permeated by norms of gender parallelism, as I have noted above. Prior to the Inca conquest and after their incorporation into the empire as nobility and peasantry, Andean women inherited rights to material resources from their mothers; and these rights underwrote parallel female and male political and religious organizations. Following Inca victories, these norms were at the heart of imperial organizations that governed the authority of elite women over their subaltern gender-mates. Traditions of gender parallelism were, then, of tremendous consequence for women and men, elite and peasant, brought together by the Inca conquest.

There was no one "structure" of gender in either Dahomey or the Andes. And even more to the point, why should we assume that gendered institutions or metaphors were uniformly understood, interpreted, or complied with? In her rendition of the demeaning of women in state formation, Gailey argued that the state's gender norms became those of the society as a whole. Even peoples resisting state penetration adopted an analogue of state norms: Gailey provided the example of West African communities, who, defending themselves from state encroachment, mirrored their strict policies controlling women's sexuality and reproductive potential (Gailey 1987a: 58–60; 1987b: 21–23).[11]

But the Inca record is not so neat, not if we look carefully at our documentary sources with an eye to the contentions over meanings and institutions inherent in and spawned by state-making practices. We find that

Inca attempts at transformed definitions, possibilities, and restrictions of gender could be differentially disputed, challenged, and/or complied with by varying Andean polities. In spite of the aura of holiness that surrounded the select "wives of the Inca" or "wives of the Sun," many saw the Inca designation of young women as a form of tribute and an institution enforcing subordination to Cusco's imperial designs. Examples abound of communities willfully submitting women to Cusco's charge, and of women in such communion with Inca designs that they joyfully celebrated their physical sacrifice to the empire's deity of conquest. But the steadfast refusal of some polities to consent to the Inca's claimed rights over women, along with reports of holy women defying the imperial strictures of chastity, suggest that Inca gender norms were not so easily imposed; indeed, they were actively resisted (Silverblatt 1987: 81–108; Silverblatt 1988*a*). And if particular ruling factions manipulated gender ambiguities, harnessing them to designs of political control, then could not contentions over gender ideologies be a site of state-subverting measures as well?

Moreover, why should we assume that elite women and men share valuations of gender? Carroll Smith-Rosenberg has argued that as the American North was being transformed from a region of farmers into a center of industrial and commercial capitalism, women and men experienced and interpreted ensuing changes in social relations and family forms in different ways. Conflicting male and female expectations regarding gender wrought a fault line in the emerging American middle class that was not substantially overcome until the middle of the nineteenth century (Smith-Rosenberg 1986). Although evidences of such gendered disputes internal to class might be difficult to uncover in noncapitalist states, Smith-Rosenberg points our ethnohistorical researches in fruitful directions. How did women of the Buganda elite, for example, experience and explain the diminution of their sisterly prerogatives? How did Inca women grapple with the changes in gender relations arising out of institutions of imperial politics like the "wives of the Sun"? Was the massive show of defiance on the part of Inca noblewomen to changes in burial practices initiated by Pachacuti Inca—something I have not been able to explain—an expression of an elite skirmish over imperial morality, spurred by contentions over gender?

Second, a question of interpretation. In spite of the apparent similarities between structures of "sexual dualism" and state categories like "wives of the King," gender configurations differed significantly in the Andean and West African states. Dahomey kinship was patrilineal, as opposed to the parallel descent forms of the Andes. Inca female political offices were not "doubled" as in Dahomey; rather, women, attaining posts through succession from their mothers, other female kin, or by achievement, sponsored their own religious and political structures, dominated—at least in state theory— by the queen. Moreover, the Inca institution specifying the "chosen women/

wives of the king" was a particular elaboration of a common pre-Inca political structure that specified the ranked order of kin groups composing an Andean political community. Did (could) such a structure exist in Dahomey or ancient Sumer? and would not it be of consequence in interpreting the interplay of political hierarchy and gender in Inca—as opposed to Dahomean and Sumerian—processes of state-making? Although the abstraction of similarities from these states—existing in different centuries and continents—can prove enticing, how are their characteristics to be explained? Gender systems, at least in the states under review here, were not as consistent or uniform as we had been led to expect; rather, an intricate dynamic of contending gender configurations encrusted in broad crises of social relations and power (suggested by Gailey) formed each state's specific legacy. Inca gender norms are comprehended by placing them in the context of Andean history.

If cases were marshaled by Engels's followers to support the contention that the origin of gender hierarchy rested in the state, those on the opposing side of the divide could refute them by arguing that the state or social hierarchy was responsible for elevating women's status. Sherry Ortner (1981), turning Engels on his head, provocatively argued just that.

In "Gender and Sexuality in Hierarchical Societies" (1981), Ortner's aim was to establish the existence of a coherent set of "sex/gender patterns" characteristic of socially stratified societies. Focusing on Polynesian material, she then compared her findings with Goody's and Tambiah's accounts of Southeast Asia. Detecting important differences between the two culture areas, Ortner determined that kinship/marriage systems played an important part in mediating the relationship between gender patterns and social hierarchy. Nevertheless she also discerned broad similarities in the gender systems of both regions, similarities that were tied to their embeddedness in hierarchical societies. One of these resemblances was the apparently universal esteem in which chastity was held.

Ortner did not expect to find such accord; and to explain it, she argued that virginity's high prestige was linked to general features exhibited by hierarchical systems. She suggested controversially that this preoccupation with chastity reflected an overall higher estimation of women. "Clearly virginity downplays the uniquely feminine capacity to be penetrated and give birth to children. A virgin is still a genetic kinsperson: a non-virgin is downgraded to mere womanhood" (1981: 401). Ortner thus reversed the conclusions of Gailey and the Engels school, which saw the control over female sexuality as a sign of women's debasement by the state. She maintained, on the contrary, that since virginity signified high status and personhood—as opposed to the low-status, reproductive role with which simpler societies saddled women—all women stood to benefit by the ascent of the state.

Ironically, Ortner's explanatory design shared much with the one she had set out to refute. Even though explicitly confronting the Engels school, Ortner was using a methodology and harboring assumptions about the nature of gender relations, status, social process, and social analysis that were surprisingly similar to theirs. Ortner concluded with generalizations resembling (although they were inversions of) those of her chief adversaries because she looked for explanations, as they did, outside of specific cultural histories.

So the problematic "women in the state," with roots in the larger problematic defining women's status as a question of origins, echoed dominant concerns of nineteenth-century thinkers. In spite of major antievolutionary periods in anthropology's history, "social type" and evolutionary assumptions have proved tenacious. It is precisely those assumptions of the nineteenth century which current concerns, many inspired by a critical Marxism, are bringing into focus.

EVOLUTIONISM, SOCIAL TYPES, AND THE CHALLENGE OF HISTORIES

We are rediscovering how much the past century's intellectual heritage and social vision have shaded prevailing anthropological convention. New studies in "culture and political economy" question the implications of evolutionary laws and functionalist explanations, along with the utility of global typologies of humankind. Not only is the validity of categories like "state" (Jessop 1982) and "status" (Quinn 1977) up for review, not only do we question "origins" frameworks that have subtly, or not so subtly, shaped anthropological investigations into gender, but we are querying the nature, limitations, and possibilities of theorizing itself, of understanding and explaining social process.

Although colored, in different ways, by origin questions and societal types, the works of Leacock, Sacks, Gailey, Ortner, and others (including myself: cf. Silverblatt 1978, 1987: 3–40) share assumptions about anthropological explanation and the role of historical record. Following their explanatory models, history functions as a laboratory for social science—a showcase of examples to substantiate predictive hypotheses that are, ironically, ahistorical. For as the source of cases demonstrating regularities between gender and the state (or political hierarchy), history is turned into the "proof" of explanatory relationships that are abstracted from cultural contexts and the constraints of time.

As we place historical explanation in historical process, we can better perceive analytical problems tied to origin quests. As many contemporary debunkers have pointed out, origin-oriented research ends up distorting historical process by envisioning history as the unfolding of prepackaged essences (Rosaldo 1980; Connell 1988; Conkey 1987, and this volume). The equation of change with the "origin's" unfolding takes for granted a kind of global homogenization of historical experience. Whatever is essentialized (in our case, the "subordination of women") is rendered an assumed fact of life. Its basic, fundamental form—associated with its "origin" in simpler social arrangements (the tributary as opposed to bourgeois industrial state)—is presumed to underlie its manifestations in more complex configurations. Consequently, what should be accounted for is instead "naturalized," removed from historical investigation. As an "essential" thing, the "origin," much like the social type, is conceptualized apart from its historical form and experienced context.[12]

Such abstractions from historical process beg the question of precisely how gender imageries and relations are constituted, experienced, and struggled over in the historical processes that both form and subvert states. Ultimately, like all evolutionary and functionalist rationales, they are bound to a logic of adaptation: gender ideologies and institutions are accounted for by their consequences for societal (ruling group, hierarchical system, or male elite) reproduction. But, neither evolutionary trends nor functional outcomes explain the emergence of ideologies or of institutions. These are the progeny of human encounters, of women and men who engage, as they occasion, the potentialities and limits of their circumstances of living—including impassioned notions of male and female etiquette and possibilities. Although the powers of elites to realize—through force or persuasion—their structures, sentiments, and visions cannot be underestimated, we cannot jumble gender imageries of ruling groups and state policy with those of society as a whole. By doing so we would ignore both how women and men become accomplices to specific state policies, as well as how they have confounded them. More acutely, we could not envision how women and men living in and embodying varying dimensions of their state-fractured worlds simultaneously reconstitute state structures—even as they might struggle to subvert them.[13]

When we demand that history not be reduced to an evolutionary outcome, we also insist that history not be added, like an ingredient, to the unfolding of "systems."[14] To grasp history as part of societal process and not outside of it requires a conceptualization of social dialectics: of the human construction of society shaping, in turn, society's construction of human possibilities. Social forms do not, as in neo-evolutionary jargon, reproduce themselves; they are remade and unmade by the human beings who live them—in a course tempered by historically construed dynamics of expectations, interests, alliances, conflicts, and accommodations. Placing history in the thicket of social process means placing human beings—gendered (and "classed" in states, among other things)—in that thicket as well.

With human beings at centerstage, evolutionary and functionalist scales fall from our eyes. We can better grasp how the comparative method's abstraction of societal types and diminution of temporal contexts produced phantoms: categories alive with forces all their own, "the state" as an active subject of history. Further, these categories, under evolutionary spells, appear to wield compelling reins of change. We talk about the exigencies of modernization, mechanization, industrialization, capitalist penetration, as if they possessed powers distinct from, outside of—and therefore capable of dominating—human beings. Historical explanation, Natalie Z. Davis, reminds us, should never be conflated with such basically evolutionary and functionalist presumptions (Davis 1981; see also Taussig 1980, 1984). "State-making" is not a power, although powerful human beings shape the course of states and specific state institutions contour the way power is articulated (Jessop 1982). "State formation" cannot, then, account for the subordination of women.

"Women in the state" categories seem defective because they do not do justice to the entangled and contradictory variety of women's experiences in tributary states; they offend by denying that human beings play a role—no matter how constrained—in the constitution of their destinies. Human activity is belittled when converted into "trends" of the state, just as historical experience is trivialized when converted into proof of ahistorical abstractions. Moreover, assuming universal compliance with "tendencies" that benefit (and culminate in) state power, making "state formation" into a living force, risks celebrating it.

WOMEN IN HISTORIES

Like history, "women" cannot be added to social process, since they are the stuff of social process. Like the "state," "women" is not a self-evident category to be presumed by social theory; rather, the construal of gender relations and of women must be in accord with specific histories and contexts. And finally, like all products of the social imagination, such conceptualizations carry ideological shadings: the images of women and society we bring to bear in social analysis have their history, too, one that is also enmeshed in the social swings of power.

Chandra Mohanty's critique of the representation of third world women in Western feminist discourse strikes a blow against those studies that would deny women—and conceptions of women—their historical due (Mohanty 1988). In a systematic assessment of a British Marxist press series on third world women, she suggests how hierarchies of dominance between the first and third world permeate Western feminist imageries. Homogenizing the experiences of third world women into a stereotype of victimization, these authors, in Mohanty's words, "colonize" the historical complexities and contradictory social relations that constitute their lives. Simple oppositions that contrast victim (third world have-nots) to victimizer (first world haves)—sharpened by the addition of "women"—turn into an implicit commemoration of first world women's superiority. For the process renders them the active subjects of history as textually compared with their have-not, bottom-of-the-barrel sisters.

How are such celebrations of power inscribed in social science texts? Mohanty points to the dislodging of third world (and, I might add, first world) women from the specific interplays of social bonds and histories through which they fashion their lives. Images that bestow women with full-blown identities and dispositions before they enter into social relations turn them into presocial, ahistorical objects, and elide differences between women and within them. Further, by ignoring that women (and men) constitute social relations, women are easily made into the victims/objects not only of men but of those very social relations; they become pawns of man-made social institutions: the family, colonial structures, development projects—the state.

Not surprisingly, the "impact of the state" on women living in more egal-itarian societies was one of the heated issues to emerge from the "origin of women's status" debate. It was the question that drove my own dissertation research on women in the Inca empire. Hindsight of the late 1980s helped me see ways in which this problematic divorces women (and subaltern groups) from history by overlooking that those who are supposedly "impacted" by the state are integral to and indissoluble from state-making itself (Stacey 1983).[15]

No longer envisioning women (or gender configurations) as "affected by," and thus apart from, state-making procedures, challenges representations that have sapped women of their historical souls. And this, in turn, encour-ages us to rethink the categories we use to grasp historical process. For couldn't the "impact of the state on women" be yet another resurrection of Western conceptual dualisms, of categorical splits of social living into self-contained realms of economy versus ideas, power versus culture, state versus gender?

The "impact of the state" frame implies not only the atomization of social relations but a lineality of cause: (uncultured) economic and political prac-tice determines cultural constructs, like gender. It thus blinds us to the hu-man creation of economic and political forms, to the indelible cultural and historical imprints they must bear. As embodiments of social engagement, of the activities of women and men in history, relations of power and economy are cultural construals—and so molded by conventions of gender. Instead of opposing economy to culture, we might better envision their dynamic: cul-tured political and economic forces (or materialized cultural forces) con-struct a terrain limiting and enabling future generations and societal possi-bilities.

Aware of the distortions of economic reductionism, our new understand-ings also reject its contemporary inversion: trends that want to cut culture loose from its moorings in social practice. Anthropology's traditional "cultural realm"—ideologies and symbols, values and expectations, feelings and understandings—now seen through the lens of "culture and political economy," fashions the material from which women and men make sense of, experience, and engage their universe. As part of, even motivating, that engagement they actively forge the material relations (materialized cultural forces) empowering and constraining the possibilities of women and men living in states' class-fractured worlds. Placing women in states' histories entails recognizing the dialectics inscribed here; failure to do so hazards recreating abstractions, whether by denying the historical construction of material relations or by denying the enabling constrictions they impose.

We risk further distortions by taking gendered imageries and representations out of the swirl of human activity. Chandra Mohanty again instructs us here. Mohanty was able to pinpoint misconceptions conveyed by the discursive representations of third world women because she recognized their play in contests of power beyond the text at hand. Her insights force us to take our image-making seriously.

Our formal analyses of gender configurations in other states are tinged with directives—often not so carefully parsed—regarding the dynamics of gender, social relations, economy, and power. And although formal and informal visions are cut from the same cloth, their kinship often goes unrecognized. Feminist ethnohistorians must be vigilantly aware of the ideologies transmitted—deliberately or not—through our portrayals of history, social process, and gender configurations. We hope to sharpen our conscience through critical dialogues with past representations of women in states; and whatever understandings ensue should be honestly applied to our own intellectual practices. The images of women in history that we are currently striving to muster aim to transcend our heritage's determinisms—whether in the guise of victimization, economic reductionism, or cultural idealism—as well as encourage awareness of their political entailments. Recognizing our gender imageries' ideological shadings and historical contingencies, we strive to comprehend the elaborate dialectics of which they are born.

TO GO ON THEORIZING

The 1980s rejection of distortions inscribed in nineteenth-century theory—spawning a return to context, dialectics, agency, and historical specifics—provokes new inquiry into the nature of social analysis. Stuart Hall, inspired by critical theory, the richest strain in Marxist thought about culture, has written several pieces that help focus our thinking about questions of theory, history, gender, and the state (1977, 1986a, b, c). Stimulated by the Italian Marxist Antonio Gramsci, who was a student of the cultural dimensions of power, Hall eloquently spoke for the undogmatic in Marxist tradition and against the way Marxist methodological suggestions have been vulgarly diverted into rigid orthodoxy. Censuring economic reductionism, he also condemned its corollary, that societal change follows lawful patterns.

Gramsci's contributions, and Hall's, pivot around what is called "conjunctural analysis"—the analysis of what can only be grasped as it is produced in history (Hall 1986a: 7–8). Hall argued that all questions involving political struggles, the nature of state regimens, cultural forms, and ideological issues—determined as they are by specific historical circumstance—converge at this level. I would add that analyses of gender, women, states, and their interplay must join them.

Hall's distrust of nineteenth-century grand theories made him particularly sensitive to the abuse of abstraction, to social science's bad habit of confounding broad generalizations with the specifics of historical process. Categories like the state, he would argue, which describe in most general terms what all states hold in common, are of little use in helping us grasp the formation of any particular historical state. Furthermore, by jumping back and forth between common properties and specific histories, academic calisthenics expose deeply embedded empiricist notions of the transparent, self-evident character of research designs and categories of understanding. In line with the contrary thrust of feminist and postmodern critiques, Hall proposed a method—rooted in Marx's most explicit statement on social science procedure—that is contingent upon the conscious reckoning of "thoughtful" intervention (1977).

When Marx explained how we grasp in thought the world of human experience, he made explicit that our understanding is never a direct, immediate, reflection of concrete reality. In opposition to positivist and empiricist traditions, Marx argued that all analyses of society and history work through socially constructed ideologies and categories of thinking. Thus aware of any method's inherent, human limitations, Marx suggested a procedure to help specify concepts that, with increasing precision, would be able to illuminate the many significant relations contouring social reality (Marx 1973).

In Marx's terms, abstractions, distillations of commonalities—the hallmark of bourgeois social science—constituted only the most meager of beginnings (Marx 1983: 170–171). To apprehend reality requires creative thinking, conceptual images that penetrate the generalities of social appearance to discern the multiple, paradoxical, and tangled relations that constitute social process. Marx's historical method is not a question of adding historical detail; it is a question of complexly thinking the many "levels of determination" that do analytic justice to the intricacies of reality (Hall 1977, 1986a).[16]

This analytical process stands intimately linked to what it is intended to interpret; the analyses' creative and "complexifying" concepts, to use Hall's phrase (1986a: 7) are born out of dialogue with specific histories themselves.

The particulars of social process that mark conjunctural analysis—the "level" in which we find ideologies of gender and the politics of states—are bound by precisions of time and place; so, then, are their "many determinations" (Hall 1986a: 7).

Thus although a Marxist concept like the "tributary mode of production"[17]—an abstraction based on the logic of economic categories characteristic of many noncapitalist states—is instructive, it says little about the political dynamics that contoured Inca empire-building. The latter, we discover, is considerably enriched by untangling its distinctive gender ideologies and politics. For examples, let us look briefly at the institution of the "Inca's wives" and Cusco's administration of gender parallelism. To begin with, our endeavor demands sensitivity to the empire's contradictions: how Inca state-making enshrined ethnic identities as an instrument of political control, identities that, paradoxically, refreshed social memories of autonomous living outside of Inca dominion. Inca attempts to undermine ethnic autonomy involved reconstruing local ancestral histories by, among other things, sanctifying women of conquered communities as "wives of the Inca/Sun." Furthermore, according to the rationale of Cusco's gift-giving politics, the highly esteemed awards of wives of the Inca/Sun to subordinates played a special role in binding political hierarchy. Yet for many Andean peoples, their loss of sovereignty, the heaviest burden, lay in the Inca's claims to authority over the marriages of community women. And, as already noted, many refused to accept Inca appraisals of sexuality, chastity and, most crucially, their pretense to jurisdiction over women.

These composite relations stand counterpoised to structures of gender parallelism, institutions that afforded all women the experience of being part of female chains of kinship and inheritance. In spite of commonalities, however, that experience was hardly shared, as lines of political and economic privilege shattered any uniformity of sense and practice. Inca noblewomen seized what was familiar and projected themselves rulers of a female chain of authority extending from Cusco to the provinces. Inca noblewomen, with independent access to their society's resources, could engage in the gift-giving so crucial to imperial politics. Yet as the empire expanded, noblewomen found their material possibilities were increasingly diminished relative to noblemen. The politics of Inca empire-building were genderized—in terms specific to the Andes.

Although empire-building, in most general terms, is about tribute garnering and political dominion, Gramscian insights suggest that states be envisioned as terrains of struggle—always historically constituted—that are curbed by, but not reducible to, a broad political-economic rationale. So concerns over the nature of alliance building, the structures articulating power and its perceived legitimacy, the means allowing ruling groups to make liens on the product and labor of others, the constitution of hegemonic visions in which notions of justice, personhood, kinship, and history become contested domains—and, of course, sensitivity to the gendered character of social relations and ideologies—should guide us in selecting "determinations." Nevertheless, the "complexifying concepts" that reconstruct Inca history in our thought are born from our encounter with Inca history.

Neither Marx nor Hall, then, provide any sure-fire list of conceptual hangers upon which to structure social analysis. That is because their method denies the propriety or possibility of doing so. If there is no necessary or specific relationship between gender/women and states, then attempts at formulating a universal theory of women and the state are misplaced.[18]

The inappropriateness of a general theory does not imply that state-making proceeds without regard to gender, or that gender concerns do not function in the interior of state-building; on the contrary, the study of historical states teaches us just how crucial—indissolubly linked—gender relations can be to the dynamics of power. Such comparative reflections, not the comparative method, can help us think creatively about the particular histories—and explanations—we are reconstructing. Obsession with chastity and marriage arrangements in medieval India might stimulate us to look into possible relations between ideologies of women's sexuality and political control in Dahomey; the first, however, does not reflect a general theory that should then account for the second. If they no longer serve to generate abstractions, sensitively drawn comparisons improve analysis by recommending new lines of investigation as well as by suggesting the strengths and limits of particular interpretations. Inca gender relations, for example, with their structures of sexual parallelism, check generalizations about patriarchal forms necessarily accompanying state power. An (implicit) comparative frame, then, enriches and sharpens analysis.[19]

But even if universal theories are not our goal, we can, to use Hall's phrase, "go on theorizing" (1986c: 60). We can work hard at discerning those "complexifying" concepts: concepts that, following the concerns of our day, are alive to process and paradox, to contradiction and context, to human agency and its limits;[20] concepts that open our eyes to significant relations, including those of gender, produced in the history of state-making. Taking Marx's method seriously, however, with its insights into the grounding of thought in the swirl of social relations, means recognizing thought's unavoidable partialities. The starting point of theorizing can be no other than our position in this world[21]—with all its possibilities, blinding limits, and potentials for critical transcendence.

PARTIALITIES

Critical feminist ethnohistories must appreciate these dilemmas. Our analyses employ "dualities" and replicate "essentialisms," even as we repudiate them. Our histories create "closure," even as we look for ways to express the incompleteness of social process. Yet, at least some of our histories now recognize gender as a "level of determination" (Fox-Genovese 1982, 1988; Scott 1986); and many are freshly attuned to the politics of historical production (Hobsbawm 1984; Fox-Genovese and Genovese 1976).

For some, the impossibility of attaining absolutes in knowledge signals despair. Extreme "postmodernists," praising the collapse of "genres," and reveling in the fiction (or cultural construction) of all social analyses, have even denied the possibility of doing history (see Smith-Rosenberg 1986: 31–32). But countering trends, of which a critical ethnohistory plays a vital part, teach a different lesson, one of critical caution (see Roseberry 1988; di Leonardo 1989; Smith-Rosenberg 1986; Gordon 1986).

Aware of thinking's limitations, new ethnohistories promote a critical stance toward all intellectual practice. Wary of the dogmatic reductionisms that have plagued Marxist tradition, they encourage a posture of openness. Yet the acceptance of these limits is not a repudiation of determinacy in social process. The very conception of knowledge and its practices as being contoured by the relations that engage it—the insistence that social theorizing can never step outside of its historical conditions of production—suggests otherwise.

NEW RESEARCH TACTICS

Awareness of the mutual implications of society, power, and the construction of knowledge has made feminist ethnohistorians acutely aware of the limits of our sources. The old view of history as a straightforward account of the past based on the accumulation of "facts" is increasingly suspect. Distrust of the "self-evident" status of facts, a linchpin of bourgeois ideology, has led (ethno)historians to reexamine documents—their sacred texts and sources of "facts."

Our traditional sources—chronicles, wills, judicial hearings, notarial records, missionary accounts—were written with a purpose and sometimes with a vengeance. Recognizing the biases in documents requires us to treat them most suspiciously; we must ask about their authorship and to what ends they were written. However, the most forbidding discernment involves distortions that run deeper than authorial intent. The unconscious prejudices of culture and class, of society and gender, permeate documents just as they permeate our analytical apparatus. Archives, caches of records, are all cultural inventions (see Cohn 1980); and the documents of ethnohistory, as likely as not products of the colonial encounter, bear that process in their marrow.

There are deep historiographical implications to the truism that colonials understood the peoples they dominated through their own cultures' categories and perceptions. They concern more than the more obvious justifications of colonial rule or Christian evangelism. Basic assumptions of how society functions, the nature of humanity, along with profound notions of accountability, political hierarchy, morality, and history are inscribed in colonial documents.[22] And furthermore, as feminist theory has so well instructed, neither colonials nor colonized spoke in one voice; these internal divisions have also left their mark on sources.

The same intellectual tradition that refused colonial peoples a place in history denied women theirs. This denial is esconced in historical theory where women were stereotyped as history's passive objects, as well as in the historical practice of archive-building. The gatekeepers to colonial history, as writers and fact-makers, have tended to ignore women or muffle their achievements. Native women often appear as variations of Western stereotypes, no doubt fulfilling Western expectations. Sometimes they scarcely appear at all—possibly as much a reflection of European prejudice as an indication of their presence or activity.

However, before laying all the blame on European shoulders, we should remember that gender relations could structure the communication of knowledge before Europeans began to make native worlds known. A priest sent out to recently colonized Andean communities at the turn of the sixteenth century was astonished by the depth of gender divisions in Inca ritual life. Committed to uncovering "idolatrous" practices, Hernandez Principe bemoaned that even the Incas did not keep good records of what women were doing, since women's religious organizations were considered women's business (Hernandez Principe 1923). Furthermore, women could benefit by their exclusion from public scrutiny. As some Andean women discovered, Spanish tendencies to deny them access to public life—resulting in their absence from much public record—actually furnished them with means to thwart the burdens of colonial rule.

Now that "others" are in our view, scholars are asking how they could have been "disappeared" so long from historical record. The French historian Marc Bloch, who resurrected the lives of the common people of the feudal ages, was plagued by their nonexistence in the accepted, conventional documentation of his day. In his manual of history-writing (1953), Bloch encouraged us both to look for new sources and to ask new questions in our attempts to restore the lives of those not so easily discovered in archives. He implored us not to underestimate the variety of ways in which human beings leave "tracks"—or intimations—of their activities in the world. Historical reconstruction is not limited to the written word, and, as I was fortunate to discover in Peru, it can be expanded by paintings and the slope of plowed fields, by the style of dress, and by the cut of an irrigation canal. Bloch also reminded historians that, although the present is understood by the past, so is the past understood by the present. The "vibrance of human life," hard to reproduce in old texts, "is in the present" (1953: 44); and that vibrance of human life, as Trigger noted (1986: 258), can stand as a good check to some of the blatant prejudices of historical account or archival report, as well as provide a context to help make sense of the stacatto of evidence left by documents.

However problematic our sources might be, as ethnohistorians we are bound to them. Incomplete and biased, they still constitute the basic materials with which we must work. As such they too impose limits on what we can write. Intellectual and political integrity demand that we take these sources and their limitations seriously and, to quote the feminist historian Linda Gordon, no matter what we might want to find, we are not at ethical liberty to pick and choose (1986: 22; also see Hawkesworth 1989).

The very dilemmas of historical reconstruction—the cultural partialities of all perspectives, coupled with the uncertainties of the ethnohistorical record (or lack of record), demonstrate the impossibility of historical absolutes. But awareness of the delusion of absolute truths in social life is not license to abandon the entire enterprise. Critical reflections point to lines of judgment and self-conscious responsibility: following Hall, we can evaluate histories in terms of their "complexifying" potentials; we can talk about the limits and distortions of simplifying accounts, and the enabling possibilities of involved, multi-dimensional, and critical reconstructions—spurs to imagine beyond the boundaries of our received categorizations. Some of what we write (in good faith) might end up being historically inaccurate. That still does not grant us the arrogance to deny historical experience. We owe more to our pasts, including the ones still to be written.

CRITICAL FEMINIST ETHNOHISTORIES

In the context of politicized social relations, history tends to be "made" by those who dominate—by Inca noblemen, provincial chiefs, kings, colonial bureaucrats, presidents, official scribes, university professors (Diamond 1974: 1–48). The privileges enjoyed by dominant groups facilitate both the accomplishment of their designs and the commemoration of their heroes in official, authoritative accounts of the past. But they never have the entire word. Radical intellectual practices—including feminist ones—have demonstrated that sanctioned histories often belie counter-versions not so advantaged in record or in power. And these counter-histories, subversive and oppositional, strain and shape the official stories that deny them.

The danger of forgetting this lesson is serious; and as Alicia Partnoy was aware, ruling groups' hostility toward revisionist histories, or their own often blatant forays into historical reconstructions, makes history-writing more than an "academic" exercise (Partnoy 1986; see also Williams 1977: 116). To overlook the political antagonisms that permeate historical ideologies leaves us colluding with "heroes" and canonizing their partisan vision. It also dulls us to the public nature of historical practice: the ways in which versions of the past, with their exigent role in the building of hegemonies, actively construe political orders (Hobsbawm 1984; Thompson 1977).

Critical feminist ethnohistorians, then, have to take account of our own field—its ideas and procedures, its institutionalizations and practices—by assessing its place in the thicket of social, ideological, and political relations. As part of anthropology, ethnohistory must not shirk the politics at its core: namely that the object of anthropological research emerged out of colonial encounters (Friedman 1987; Asad 1973; Said 1989). Although anthropology is not simply the child of imperialism, as Kathleen Gough (1967) characterized the field a generation ago, it is inextricably entangled with it.

But even while a part of and contributor to imperial relations, ethnohistory, at its most integral, has challenged dominant versions of "others," the politics creating "others," as well as its own complicity in propagating Western stereotypes. Feminism, as well, has mounted a significant intellectual opposition to dominant disciplinary trends; while within that broad space of feminism very important challenges have been made to a kind of Western feminist imperialism, of which Chandra Mohanty has spoken. These questions have shown again the ambiguities of challenge from within the belly of the beast, and admonish Western feminists trying to assess critically the history of "others." For like Western ideology, Western feminism is surrounded by the aura, the powerful advantages, attained by any Western intellectual practice. Writing critical feminist ethnohistory entails responsibility for ascertaining, as best as possible, the consequences and implications of academic activities.

Some Western feminist studies have tried to do justice to the complexities of gender configurations in colonial contexts (see Stoler and Guyer, this volume). These studies recognize the interplay—and paradoxes—of gender and power in colonial and class-splintered worlds. They are sensitive to the multiple horizons spawned by the intersections of gender, class, and colony, and to other complexifying relations that human beings in history and in society have produced. The challenge lies in capturing the historical construction and consequences of the overlapping and opposing social relations constituting women and men in states, the intricacies of women's potentialities in states at particular times and places, and in heeding the contradictory positions with which cross-cutting political and economic forces imbue them. It entails an awareness of the trickiness of power relations in their play with gender (after all, the paramount aim of most state-building, to paraphrase Fox-Genovese [1982], was not to subjugate women), and of the diverse, albeit constrained forms that that play has taken in the world's states.

As critical ethnohistorians we are responsible for our image-making and our ethnohistories: we can no longer pretend innocence of their political shadings. Nor can we pretend innocence of our humanity: as a human endeavor, the knowledge of our categories' social construction, like our knowledge of the past, is condemned to incompleteness. Yet no matter how faulty and tentative, these (ethno)historical reconstructions form the basis of our inquiries and our debates; they are indispensable to our self-awareness and conscience. And as part of history's public record, they can contribute to the consciousness of others in ways still unimagined.

As we censure Enlightenment delusions, we should be careful not to forget Enlightenment hopes. Although its ideology of universals bred the distortions rebuked by today's critics, it also charged emancipating ambitions. Proclamations of liberty and equality were taken seriously by those to whom they were denied in experience, and Western feminism grew out of such encounters between social practice and social ideals. These emancipating visions were tied to a committed social science; and although nineteenth-century illuminaries exaggerated human rationality, they never doubted that the "human sciences"—indispensable to politics and morality—were more than an academic enterprise.

As Enlightenment antagonists and inheritors, today's feminists have contributed to a reexamination of our humanness: to the cultural and political boundedness of our knowledge claims, and to the ethical and political imperatives of our intellectual activities. Although feminists do not speak in one voice, they share a hope and a commitment to a world free of dominations. This commitment has roots in understandings of humanity's presents and pasts; and if the twinned anchors of absolutes in knowledge and certainties in social process have been cut adrift, enlightening enterprises, like feminist ethnohistories, at the very least, contribute those precious materials in which debates about gender hierarchy and exploitation can be grounded.

The feminist ethnohistories that this paper advocates come from a long-standing anthropological (intellectual and political) tradition, a tradition that sees history as an indispensable component of social analysis (even as its historical practice has been found wanting); that recognizes the social construction of categories and knowledges (even as it has been lured by certainties of economic reductionism); that has encouraged intellectual self-reflection and doubt (even as it has countenanced dogmatism); and that has unswervingly demanded that intellectual practice be bonded with humane ideals (even as it has "colonized" the experience of third world women). The spirit of Marxism's critical legacy, honed, in part, by contemporary encounters with postmodern critiques and anthropology's crisis of history, has thrust these paradoxes into our intellectual consciousness and conscience.

Most important, however, is the tenor of openness, the vitality of debate, that this meeting of Marxism, feminisms, anthropology, and ethnohistory promises. Removing the burden of certainties opens dialogues between presents and pasts that offer rich contentions over histories' trajectories, opportunities missed and seized, feasible strategies, and future visions. Aware that the past is more than an accumulation of outcomes but encompasses the imaginable etched within, a critical feminist ethnohistory suggests, then, not the inevitability of history but the potentials of histories. And by restoring possibilities to our foremothers and fathers, as Lukacs reminds us, we also restore possibilities to ourselves (Lukacs 1971; see also Westkott 1979).

NOTES

1. This paper owes much to many good friends and able critics. Special thanks to Nan Woodruff, Elizabeth Fox-Genovese, Rayna Rapp, Michael Taussig, and Micaela di Leonardo. Micaela has been the kind of editor that all contributors hope for: patient, exacting, knowing when to turn the screws, encouraging, and a first-rate critic.

2. The Marxist tradition in anthropology has been sensitive to the colonial position of those studied, if not always so sensitive to gender. In addition to Wolf, see Diamond (1974), Asad (1973), and Hymes (1969).

3. These challenges, marking and precipitating changes in the intellectual climate, have had profound effects in both history and anthropology. Where history used to be devoted to histories of the predominantly male rich and famous—the so-called makers of history—it began to recognize the contributions of the not-so-privileged (see Fox-Genovese and Genovese 1976). Anthropology also became aware of its own limiting assumptions that distorted its task of writing the lives of the colonized.

4. Anthropology's growing awareness of the inadequacies of Marxist theories with respect to culture must also be understood in the context of wider intellectual trends in the Marxist tradition. The work of British cultural historians and literary critics spurred an interest in the study of the cultural dimensions of political economy. See Thompson (1978) and Williams (1977) among others.

5. Feminist critiques spurring on and spurred by postmodernist trends are significant in cultural/literary studies see De Lauretis 1986; Spivak 1987; and Moi 1985 among others).

6. See Friedman (1987) in particular for a trenchant analysis of this trend, which he calls the spectacularization of the other.

7. The following two sections draw, in part, from Silverblatt (1988b). See that article for a more detailed demonstration of some of the arguments presented here.

8. The principal theorist of patriarchal universalism was Sir Henry Maine, who wrote *Ancient Law* (1963) in 1861. Other feminist scholars who have commented on these nineteenth-century debates include Coward (1983), Fee (1973), Fox-Genovese (1977), Nicholson (1986), and Vogel (1987).

9. See Cohn's two witty discussions of the history of history and anthropology (1980, 1981). Cohn points out that according to Western popular belief, history—or the chronological sequencing of facts—is in itself explanation.

10. Ironically, although specific historical circumstances were played down in anthropological explanation, the primary goal of the comparative method itself was to recreate a global chronology. It became a tool for constructing a history, The History of Mankind (*sic*), which could overcome the lack of adequate "real" evidence. Social types, in this early formulation, represented different stages of a universal history,

with "primitives" beginning and the "state" or "civilization" ending an evolutionary sequence.

11. Although an elaborate control over women might be explained as a defensive strategy of kin groups struggling to resist state incursion, I should point out that it was hardly universal. Our chroniclers offer no evidence of Andean polities assuming similar defensive postures. On the contrary, premarital sexual experimentation was encouraged in peasant communities. And outside of the "wives of the Inca/Sun," there were limited checks on women's sexual activities—including, as far as I can tell on the practices of noblewomen (Silverblatt 1987: 81–108).

12. Rosaldo, who was a spokeswoman for the universal gender asymmetry camp, wrote an eloquent denunciation of origin-guided research (1980). Yet she still insisted that gender asymmetry had to be universal; and thus seemed unable to break out of the "origin" mold in spite of her extensive criticisms.

13. See Genovese (1974, 1981) for an elaboration of this Gramscian notion.

14. Could the notion of systemic reproduction be a current reincarnation of the unfolding of "origin"? The following section owes much to the current discussions of structure and agency, whose principal contemporary theorist is Anthony Giddens (1987). Connell (1988) elaborates on structuration theory, while sensitively incorporating gender issues. He is highly critical of the concept of reproduction for its functionalist implications.

15. Moreover, this paradigm encourages the polarization of societies into egalitarian/kinship-versus-state categories—an echo of Engels—which I feel contributed to my unduly romantic portrayal of pre-Inca peoples in *Moon, Sun, and Witches* (Silverblatt 1987).

16. We can thus envision the movement of history and theory as proceeding in opposite directions. What appears to be a "result" in history, figures, in theory, as that which must be produced (Hall 1977: 150).

17. The tributary mode of production, to cite Eric Wolf's succinct definition, is characteristic of states "in which the primary producer, whether cultivator or herdsman, is allowed access to the means of production, while tribute is extracted from him by political or military means" (1982: 79–80).

18. Even some very recent work in feminist anthropology fails to take in these conclusions. Henrietta Moore (1988), in a very interesting chapter on women and the state, stresses the importance of historical context. Nevertheless, she argues that "anthropology must develop such a theory [feminist theory of the state] as a matter of urgency" (1988: 185). Although I heartily agree with her first emphasis, I disagree with her second.

19. Eugene Genovese (1964, 1984), for some of the reasons spelled out above, argues for the importance of a comparative focus when trying to make sense of the diverse patterns of race found in the New World. It seems important to stress the need for continued comparative work in light of current scholarly trends that center on the particular. These particularizing trends, of course, are responding to the improper generalizations of mainstream history and social science.

20. Thanks here to Fitz John Porter Poole.

21. See Jehlen (1983), writing from a feminist perspective, on the illusory enticements of the Archimedian point.

22. B. Trigger (1986) suggests that ethnohistory often tells us more about the prejudices of ethnohistorians than about the lives of native peoples.

BIBLIOGRAPHY

Anderson, Perry. 1984. *In the tracks of historical materialism*. London: Verso.

Asad, Talal, ed. 1973. *Anthropology and the colonial encounter*. London: Ithaca Press.

Bay, E. G. 1985. Women in the palace of Dahomey: A case study in West African political systems. In *For alma mater: Theory and practice in feminist scholarship*. P. Treichler, C. Kramarae, and B. Stafford, eds., 238–253. Urbana: University of Illinois Press.

Benjamin, Walter. 1969. *Illuminations*. Hannah Arendt, ed. New York: Schocken Books.

Bloch, Marc. 1953. *The historian's craft*. New York: Vintage.

Cohn, Bernard S. 1980. History and anthropology: The state of play. *Comparative studies in society and history*, pp. 198–221.

———. 1981. Anthropology and history in 1980s: Toward a rapprochement. *Journal of Interdisciplinary History* 12 (2): 227–252.

Conkey, M. 1987. Gender origins and origins research in archaeology. Paper presented at Women in Society Seminar, Yale University. Manuscript Chap. of this vol.

Connell, R. W. 1988. *Gender and power: Society, the person, and sexual politics*. Stanford: Stanford University Press.

Coward, R. 1983. *Patriarchal precedents: Sexuality and social relations*. London: Routledge & Kegan Paul.

Davis, Natalie Z. 1981. Anthropology and history in the 1980s: The possibilities of the past. *Journal of Interdisciplinary History* 12 (2): 267–275.

Diamond, Stanley. 1974. *In search of the primitive: A critique of civilization*. New Brunswick: E. P. Dutton-Transaction.

De Lauretis, Teresa. 1986. *Feminist studies/critical studies*. Bloomington: Indiana University Press.

di Leonardo, Micaela. 1989. Malinowski's nephews: Review of *Predicament of culture* and *works and lives*. *Nation* (March 3): 350–352.

Engels, F. 1972. *Origin of the family, private property, and the state* [1884], ed. E. Leacock. New York: International Publishers.

Fee, Elizabeth. 1973. The sexual politics of Victorian social anthropology. *Feminist Studies* 1 (3–4): 23–39.

Flax, J. 1987. Postmodernism and gender relations in feminist theory. *Signs* 12(4): 621–643.

Fox-Genovese, Elizabeth. 1977. Property and patriarchy in classical bourgeois political theory. *Radical History Review* 4: 36–59.

———. 1982. Placing women's history in history. *New Left Review* 133: 5–29.

———. 1983. The ideological bases of domestic economy: The representation of women and the family in the age of expansion. In *Fruits of merchant capital*. E. Fox-Genovese and E. D. Genovese, eds., 299–336. Oxford: Oxford University Press.

———. 1986. Women's rights, affirmative action, and the myth of individualism. *The George Washington Law Review* 54: 338–374.

———. 1988. *Within the plantation household*. Chapel Hill: University of North Carolina Press.

Fox-Genovese, Elizabeth, and Eugene D. Genovese. 1976. The political crisis of social history: A Marxian perspective. *Journal of Social History* 10: 205–220.

Friedman, Jonathan. 1987. Beyond otherness or the spectacularization of anthropology. *Telos* 71: 161–170.

Gailey, C. W. 1987a. Evolutionary perspectives on gender hierarchy. In *Analyzing gender*. B. Hess and M. Ferree, eds. 32–67. Beverly Hills: Sage.

———. 1987b. *From kinship to kingship: Gender hierarchy and state formation in the Tongan Islands*. Austin: University of Texas Press.

Genovese, Eugene D. 1964. *The world the slaveholders made*. New York: Vintage.

———. 1974. *Roll Jordan roll*. New York: Pantheon.

———. 1981. *From rebellion to revolution*. New York: Vintage.

———. 1984. The comparative focus in Latin American history. In *In red and black*. E. D. Genovese, ed. Knoxville: University of Tennessee Press. Pp. 375–390.

Giddens, Anthony. 1987. *Social theory and modern sociology*. Stanford: Stanford University Press.

Gordon, Linda. 1986. What's new in women's history. In *Feminist studies/critical studies*. Teresa de Lauretis, ed. Bloomington: University of Indiana Press. Pp. 20–30.

Gough, Kathleen. 1967. A social consciousness for anthropology. Pacifica Tape Library.

Gramsci, A. 1971. *Selections from the prison notebooks of Antonio Gramsci*. ed. and trans. Q. Hoare and G. N. Smith, ed. and trans. New York: International Publishers.

Hall, Stuart. 1977. Marx's notes on method: A "Reading" of the "1857 Introduction." *Working Papers in Cultural Studies* 6: 132–170.

———. 1986a. Gramsci's relevance for the study of race and ethnicity. *Journal of Communication Inquiry* 10 (2): 5–27.

———. 1986b. The problem of ideology—Marxism without guarantees. *Journal of Communication Inquiry* 10 (2): 29–43.

———. 1986c. On postmodernism and articulation: An interview with Stuart Hall. L. Grossberg, ed. *Journal of Communication Inquiry* 10 (2): 45–60.

Hawkesworth, Mary E. 1989. Knowers, knowing, known: Feminist theory and claims of truth. *Signs* 14 (3): 533–557.

Hernandez Principe, Rodrige. 1923. Mitologia andina [1621]. *Inca* 1: 24–68.

Hobsbawm, Eric. 1984. Introduction: Inventing traditions. In *The invention of tradition*. E. Hobsbawm and T. Ranger, eds. Cambridge: Cambridge University Press.

Huyssen, Andreas. 1986. *After the great divide*. Bloomington: Indiana University Press.

Hymes, Dell. ed. 1969. *Reinventing anthropology*. New York: Pantheon.

Jehlen, Myra. 1983. Archimedes and the paradox of feminist criticism. In *The signs reader: Women, gender, and scholarship*. E. Abel, ed., 69–96. Chicago: University of Chicago Press.

Jessop, Bob. 1982. *The capitalist state*. New York: New York University Press.

Koonz, C. 1986. *Mothers in the fatherland*. New York: St. Martin's Press.

Krader, L. 1973. The works of Marx and Engels in ethnology compared. *International Review of Social History*. 18: 223–275.

Leacock, E. 1972. Introduction. In *Origin of the family, private property and the state* by F. Engels. New York: International Publishers. Pp. 7–67.

———. 1978. Women's status in egalitarian society: Implications for social evolution. *Current Anthropology* 19 (2): 247–275.

————. 1983. Interpreting the origins of gender inequality: Conceptual and historical problems. *Dialectical Anthropology* 7: 263–283.

Lee, Richard, and Irven DeVore, eds. 1968. *Man the hunter*. Chicago: Aldine.

Lukacs, Georg. 1971. *History and class consciousness*. Trans. R. Livingstone. London: Merlin Press.

Lunn, Eugene. 1982. *Marxism and modernism*. Berkeley, Los Angeles, London: University of California Press.

Marx, Karl. 1973. Introduction to a contribution to the Critique of Political Economy [1857], in *Grundrisse*. M. Nicolaus, ed. Hamondsworth: Penguin.

Marx, Karl, and Fredrich Engels. 1983. The German ideology. In *The portable Karl Marx*. E. Kamenka, ed. New York: Penguin.

Maine, Henry. 1963. *Ancient law*. Boston: Beacon.

Mohanty, Chandra. 1988. Under Western eyes: Feminist scholarship and colonial discourses. *Feminist Review* 30: 61–88.

Moi, Toril. 1985. *Sexual/textual politics: Feminist literary theory*. New York: Metheun.

Moore, Henrietta L. 1988. *Feminism and Anthropology*. Minneapolis: University of Minnesota Press.

Morgan, Lewis Henry. 1964. *Ancient society* [1877]. Cambridge: Harvard University Press.

Nicholson, L. 1986. *Gender and history*. New York: Columbia University Press.

Ortner, S. 1974. Is female to male as nature is to culture? In *Women, culture and society*. M. Rosaldo and L. Lamphere, eds., 67–88. Stanford: Stanford University Press.

————. 1981. Gender and sexuality in hierarchical societies. In *Sexual meanings: The cultural construction of gender and sexuality*. S. Ortner and H. Whitehead, eds., 359–409. Cambridge: Cambridge University Press.

Partnoy, Alicia. 1986. *The little school: Tales of disappearance and survival in Argentina*. Pittsburgh and San Francisco: Cleis Press.

Polier, Nicole, and William Roseberry. N.d. Tristes Tropes. *Economy and Society*. Forthcoming.

Quinn, N. 1977. Anthropological studies on women's status. *Annual Review of Anthropology* 6: 181–222.

Rosaldo, Michelle Z. 1974. Woman, culture, and society: A theoretical overview. In *Women, culture, and society*. M. Rosaldo and L. Lamphere, eds., 17–42. Stanford: Stanford University Press.

————. 1980. The use and abuse of anthropology: Reflections on feminism and cross-cultural understanding. *Signs* 5 (3): 389–417.

Roseberry, William. 1988. Political economy. *Annual Review of Anthropology* 17: 161–185.

Sacks, K. 1974. Engels revisited: Women, the organization of production, and private property. In *Woman, Cutlure, and society*. M. Z. Rosaldo and L. Lamphere, eds., 207–222. Stanford: Stanford University Press.

————. 1982. *Sisters and wives: The past and future of sexual equality*. Urbana: University of Illinois Press.

Said, Edward. 1989. Representing the colonized: Anthropology's interlocutors. *Critical Inquiry* 15: 205–225.

Sanday, P. R. 1981. *Female power and male dominance: On the origins of sexual inequality*. Cambridge: Cambridge University Press.

Sayers, J., M. Evans, and N. Redclift, eds. 1987. *Engels revisited*. London: Tavistock.

Scott, J. W. 1986. Gender: A useful category of historical analysis. *American Historical Review* 91 (5): 1053–1075.

Silverblatt, I. 1978. Andean women in the Inca society. *Feminist Studies* 4: 37–61.

———. 1987. *Moon, sun, and witches: Gender ideologies and class in Inca and colonial Peru*. Princeton: Princeton University Press.

———. 1988a. Imperial dilemmas, the politics of kinship, and Inca reconstructions of history. *Comparative Studies in Society and History* 30 (1): 83–102.

———. 1988b. Women in states. *Annual Review in Anthropology* 17: 427–460.

Smith-Rosenberg, Carroll. 1986. Writing history: Language, class, and gender. In *Feminist studies/critical studies*. Teresa de Lauretis ed., 31–54. Bloomington: Indiana University Press.

Spivak, Gayatri. 1987. *In other worlds: Essays in cultural politics*. New York: Metheun.

Stacey, J. 1983. *Patriarchy and socialist revolution in China*. Berkeley, Los Angeles, London: University of California Press.

Taussig, Michael. 1980. *The devil and commodity fetishism in South America*. Chapel Hill: University of North Carolina Press.

———. 1984. History as sorcery. *Representations* 7: 87–109.

———. 1987. *Shamanism and the wildman*. Chicago: University of Chicago Press.

Thompson, E. P. 1977. Folklore, anthropology, and social history. *The Indian Historical Review* 3: 247–266.

———. 1978. *The poverty of theory and other essays*. New York: Monthly Review Press.

Trigger, Bruce. 1986. Ethnohistory: The unfinished edifice. *Ethnohistory* 33 (3): 253–267.

Vogel, L. 1987. *Marxism and the oppression of women*. New Brunswick, N.J.: Rutgers University Press.

Westkott, M. 1979. Feminist criticism of the social sciences. *Harvard Education Review* 49: 422–430.

Whitehead, Harriet. 1976. Review, *Women's Evolution* by E. Reed. *Signs* 1 (3): 746–748.

Williams, Raymond. 1977. Marxism and literature. Oxford: Oxford University Press.

Wolf, Eric. 1982. *Europe and the people without history*. Berkeley, Los Angeles, London: University of California Press.

PART TWO

Gender as Cultural Politics

FOUR

Between Speech and Silence
The Problematics of Research on Language and Gender[1]

Susan Gal

INTRODUCTION

The historic silence of women in public life, and women's attempts to gain a voice in politics and literature, have been major themes of recent feminist scholarship. It has become clear that gender relations are created not only by a sexual division of labor and a set of symbolic images, but also through contrasting possibilities of expression for men and women. Feminists have explicitly written about scholarship's responsibility to "hear women's words" and have rightly argued the theoretical importance of "rediscover-[ing] women's voices" (Smith-Rosenberg 1985: 11, 26).

In these writings, silence is generally deplored, because it is taken to be a result and a symbol of passivity and powerlessness: those who are denied speech cannot make their experience known and thus cannot influence the course of their lives or of history.[2] In a telling contrast, other scholars have emphasized the paradoxical power of silence, especially in certain institutional settings. In religious confession, modern psychotherapy, bureaucratic interviews, and in police interrogation, the relations of coercion are reversed: where self-exposure is required, it is the silent listener who judges, and who thereby exerts power over the one who speaks (Foucault 1978: 61–62). Similarly, silence in American households is often a weapon of masculine power (Sattel 1983). But silence can also be a strategic defense against the powerful, as when Western Apache men use it to baffle, disconcert, and exclude white outsiders (Basso 1979). And this does not exhaust the meanings of silence. For the English Quakers of the seventeenth century, both men and women, the refusal to speak when others expected them to marked an ideological commitment. It was the opposite of passivity, indeed a form of political protest (Bauman 1983).[3]

The juxtaposition of these different constructions of silence highlights the three issues I would like to raise in this chapter. First, and most generally, the example of silence suggests a close link between gender, the use of speech (or silence), and the exercise of power. But it also shows that the link is not direct. On the contrary, it appears that silence, like any linguistic form, gains different meanings and has different material effects within specific institutional and cultural contexts. Silence and inarticulateness are not, in themselves, necessarily signs of powerlessness. Indeed, my first goal is to draw on a cultural analysis to show how the links between linguistic practices, power, and gender are themselves culturally constructed.

Yet these cultural constructions are not always stable, nor passively accepted and reproduced by speakers. The examples of silence as subversive defense and even political protest suggest that linguistic forms, even the most apparently quiescent, are strategic actions, created as responses to cultural and institutional contexts (Gumperz 1982). Although sociolinguistic studies have long noted differences between men's and women's everyday linguistic forms, much early research considered talk to be simply an index of identity: merely one of the many behaviors learned through socialization which formed part of men's and women's different social roles. Recent reconceptualizations of gender reject this implicit role theory and promise a deeper understanding of the genesis and persistence of gender differences in speech. They argue that gender is better seen as a system of culturally constructed relations of power, produced and reproduced in interaction between and among men and women.[4] I draw on sociolinguistic studies of everyday talk to provide evidence that it is in part through verbal practices in social interaction that the structural relations of gender and dominance are perpetuated and sometimes subverted: in social institutions such as schools, courts, and political assemblies, talk is often used to judge, define, and legitimate speakers. Thus, small interactional skirmishes have striking material consequences. My second goal is to show how verbal interaction, whatever else it accomplishes, is often the site of struggle about gender definitions and power; it concerns who can speak where about what.

Finally, such struggles about gaining a voice, and my earlier example of women's silence in public life, draw attention to a currently widespread and influential metaphor in both feminist and nonfeminist social science. Terms such as "women's language," "voice," or "words" are routinely used not only to designate everyday talk but also, much more broadly, to denote the public expression of a particular perspective on self and social life, the effort to represent one's own experience, rather than accepting the representations of more powerful others. And similarly, "silence" and "mutedness" (E. Ardener 1975) are used not only in their ordinary senses of an inability or reluctance to create utterances in conversational exchange, but as references as well to the failure to produce one's own separate, socially significant discourse. It is in this broader sense that feminist historians have rediscovered women's words. Here, "word" becomes a synecdoche for "consciousness."

Yet, despite this metaphorical link, everyday talk and the broader notion of a gendered consciousness have only rarely been investigated together, or by the same scholars. Studies of gender differences in everyday talk have tended to focus on the formal properties of speech—intonational, phonological, syntactic, and pragmatic differences between men and women, and the institutional and interactional contexts in which they occur. In contrast, studies of "women's voice" have focused more on values and beliefs: whether or not women have cultural conceptions or symbolic systems concerning self, morality, or social reality, different from those of the dominant discourse.[5] That the two are inextricably linked becomes evident when we view both kinds of research as studies of symbolic domination.

As my discussion of the culturally defined links between speech and power will show, some linguistic strategies and genres are more highly valued and carry more authority than others. In a classic case of symbolic domination, even those who do not control these authoritative forms consider them more credible or persuasive (Bourdieu 1977*b*). Archetypal examples include standard languages and ritual speech. But these respected linguistic practices are not simply forms; they deliver characteristic cultural definitions of social life that, embodied in divisions of labor and the structure of institutions, serve the interests of some groups better than others. Indeed, it is in part through such linguistic practices that speakers within institutions impose on others their group's definition of events, people, and actions. This ability to make others accept and enact one's representation of the world is another aspect of symbolic domination. But such cultural power rarely goes uncontested. Resistance to a dominant cultural order occurs when devalued linguistic strategies and genres are practiced and celebrated despite widespread denigration; it occurs as well when these devalued practices propose or embody alternate models of the social world.

Several influential social theories that differ importantly in other respects have in one way or another articulated this insight. Whether we use Gramsci's term "cultural hegemony," or symbolic domination (Bourdieu 1977*a*); oppositional, emergent, and residual cultures (Williams 1973); or subjugated knowledges (Foucault 1980), the central notion remains: the control of discourse or of representations of reality occurs in social interaction, located in institutions, and is a source of social power; it may be, therefore, the occasion for coercion, conflict, or complicity.[6] Missing from these theories is a concept of gender as a structure of social relations (separate from class or ethnicity), reproduced but also challenged in everyday practice. These theories neither notice nor explain the subtlety, subversion, and opposition to dominant definitions which feminists have discovered in many women's genres, and sometimes embedded in women's everyday talk. Indeed, even the authority of some (male) linguistic forms and their dominance of social institutions such as medicine or the political process remain mysterious without a theory of gender.

This interaction of gender and discourse has been explored by recent feminist analyses in literature and anthropology; some have suggested that women's "voices" often differ significantly in form as well as content from dominant discourse.[7] The importance of integrating the study of everyday talk with the study of "women's voice" becomes apparent: the attention to the details of linguistic form and context typical of research into everyday talk is indispensable in order to gain access to women's often veiled genres and muted "words." And both kinds of studies must attend not only to words but to the interactional practices and the broader political and economic context of communication in order to understand the process by which women's voices—in both senses—are routinely suppressed or manage to emerge. My final aim is to show that, if we understand women's everyday talk and linguistic genres as forms of resistance, we hear, in any culture, not so much a clear and heretofore neglected "woman's voice," or separate culture, but rather linguistic practices that are more ambiguous, often contradictory, differing among women of different classes and ethnic groups and ranging from accommodation to opposition, subversion, rejection, or autonomous reconstruction of reigning cultural definitions.

Thus, my theme is the link between gender, speech, and power, and the ways this can be conceptualized on the basis of recent empirical research. I will first explore what counts, cross-culturally, as powerful speech; then show the differential power of men's and women's linguistic strategies in social institutions; and finally reinterpret women's strategies and linguistic genres as forms of resistance to symbolic domination.

CULTURAL CONSTRUCTIONS

Many cultures posit a close connection between the use of language and the emergence of the self. This is well illustrated by the Laymi Indians of Highland Bolivia, a group of settled peasants engaged in subsistence agriculture. They represent a newborn individual's progression to a fully socialized human in terms of the child's relation to language: a baby becomes a child when it starts to say words; the passage from childhood to young adulthood is said to occur when the individual can speak and understand fully (Harris 1980: 72). Some cultural conceptions that link person and language appear not to be focused on gender at all. For instance, the metalinguistic discourse of the Kaluli in New Guinea classifies speakers largely on the basis of clan or village origin (Schieffelin 1987). Similarly, in Samoa rank seems much more important in ideas about speech than gender (Ochs 1987). Nevertheless, there are many cases in which not just personhood, but gender as well are conceptualized in terms of language. Such conceptualizations define the symbolic significance of men's and women's speech features: what is powerful and weak, beautiful or execrable, masculine and feminine, in the realm of talk. Men's and women's linguistic practices are profoundly shaped by such cultural images.[8]

Perhaps the best example is Keenan's (1974) study of the Malagasy of Madagascar, who explicitly associate different styles of talk with men and women. According to the Malagasy, men characteristically use an indirect, ornate and respectful style that avoids confrontation and disagreement with others; women use a direct style of speaking associated with excitableness and anger, that is seen as a source of conflict and threat in interpersonal relations. Women are excluded from the major formal genre of oratory that is required for participation in political events. And men avoid a series of speech activities that women engage in, such as accusations, market haggling and gossip. Importantly, these differences are linked to notions about power. First, both men and women consider men's speech far superior. Second, it is women's directness, defined as inept, that is said to bar them from political authority and from speaking at political meetings where the egalitarian social system requires that the existence of conflict be skillfully hidden.

Yet, cross-cultural evidence indicates that indirectness is not always associated with masculinity, nor confrontation with women. The case of American gender stereotypes provides an informative contrast. The cultural evaluation of American middle-class speech is revealed in studies of Midwestern teenagers who think of men's speech as "aggressive," "forceful," "blunt," and "authoritarian," whereas women's speech is considered "gentle," "trivial," "correct," and "polite." Only careful empirical research can document the subtle differences that actually exist between American men's and women's speech, but these stereotypes provide the expectations and ideals against which speakers are routinely judged (Kramarae 1980). Indeed, there is an entire literature of advice books, etiquette manuals, and philological and linguistic tracts published in the United States and Western Europe which have for several centuries constructed, without benefit of evidence, images of male and female "natures" linked to their supposed speech patterns (Kramarae 1980: 91).[9] From the example of the Malagasy and American stereotypes it might appear that, whether blunt or indirect, verbal skills of some kind are associated with authority and power. A contrast to both is provided by Irvine's (1979) description of the Wolof of Senegal, who are organized into a stratified caste system. High caste nobles derive their power from an inherited quality manifested as a sense of reserve in all activities. Diffidence and inarticulateness are so much a part of noble demeanor that elite men often hire low-status professional orators to speak for them in order to avoid showing verbal fluency in public. Thus, cultural conceptions demand that ordinary men and women be more articulate than men with high status.

Although inarticulateness is a trait that is a sign of a Wolof man's elite identity, it is exactly inarticulateness that is represented as women's defining and debilitating condition in rural Greece. The image of women is not unitary in Greece: they are seen as both garrulous and silent. But in both modes women are conceptualized as incapable of controlling themselves and therefore of achieving the articulate and swaggering self-display that constitutes the culturally constructed image of powerful men (Herzfeld 1985).

These examples from disparate groups provide a useful demonstration that the links between gender, power, and linguistic practices are not "natural" and can be constructed in quite different ways. But these examples are static and seem to imply that speakers passively follow abstact cultural dictates. A historical case is helpful then, because it charts *changes* in conceptualizations and shows how ideals come to restrict women's possibilities of expression. Outram (1987) considers the dilemma of elite women during the French Revolution. The discourse of the French Revolution, glorifying male *vertu*, identified the influence of women with the system of patronage, sexual favors, and corruption of power under the Old Regime, in which elite women had actively participated. The discourse of the Revolution, in deliberate contrast, was committed to an antifeminine logic: political revolution could only take place if women and their corrupting influence were excluded from public speaking and from the exercise of power. Outram argues that, in part as a result of this new conceptualization, the famous and powerful political participation of upper-class women in the Old Regime was replaced, in the era of the Revolution, with vigorous attacks on female political activists. By the new logic, elite women's public speech and activities brought their sexual virtue into question. For a woman, to be political was to be corrupt; the revolutionary discourse of universal equality applied only to men. Women who wanted to be both respectable and political had very few choices: one of the best-known figures of the Revolution, who was later imprisoned for her participation, provides a telling example. Mme. Jeanne Roland's political activity included providing a forum in which men debated the issues of the day. Her memoirs and letters reveal that it demanded a painful compromise: this well-informed woman retained respect by listening to the men's political discussions but remained herself utterly silent.

The historical dimension in Outram's study allows us not only to chart the effect of changing discourse but to specify the social source of the cultural constructions in a way not possible in the more static descriptions of non-Western cases. These particular cultural definitions were not simply the product of some age-old and monolithic male dominance but emerged articulately in the ideas of revolutionary theorists and Enlightenment philosophers. Perhaps other patterns of ideas about gender differences in speech could be traced to similarly specific times and social contexts. For example, it is a recurrent and unexplained finding of recent sociolinguistic surveys that in North American, British, and some other industrialized cities, middle- and working-class women more frequently use phonological forms associated with the highest ranking socioeconomic classes than do men of their class. Middle- and working-class men more frequently use pronunciations charac- teristic of the working class than do their female counterparts. And all men evaluate working-class features more positively than do women (e.g. Labov 1974; Trudgill 1983). Clearly the phonological symbolizations of gender and of social class are inextricably linked. The universalizing explanations offered so far credit women in general with greater sensitivity to language and pres- tige. But these theories founder on counter-examples from other societies. Instead, I suggest these findings gain meaning within a broader cultural pat- tern. The linguistic evidence links manliness with "tough" working-class cul- ture and femaleness with "respectability," "gentility," and "high culture" as part of a general symbolic structure that, many analyses suggest, emerged on both sides of the Atlantic in the nineteenth century and continues to be one component of current gender images.[10]

In short, the culturally constructed link between types of verbal skill, gen- der identity, and power not only is variable but is dependent on an entire web of related conceptions and, as the final examples hint, on historical and political economic processes as well.

POWER IN EVERYDAY TALK

Jeanne Roland's silence was neither natural nor an automatic acquiescence to Revolutionary cultural conceptions. Instead, her letters and memoirs allow us to understand the forums she created and her public silence as strategic responses to a cultural double-bind that offered her either speech or respect, but not both. Neither wholly determined by cultural images and changing social structures, nor entirely a matter of her own agency, Mme. Roland's speech and interaction are excellent examples of *practices* that reproduce gen- der images and relations or, as later examples will show, sometimes tacitly criticize and resist them.

Interactional sociolinguistics provides the tools for analyzing speech strategies as practices actively constructed by speakers in response to cultur- al and structural constraints. If speech enacts a discourse strategy and is not simply a reflex or signal of social identity, then attention must be paid not only to the gender identity of the speaker but also to the gender of the audi- ence and the varying cultural salience of gender in different social contexts. Male-female differences in speech have been found in every society studied; but the nature of the contrasts is staggeringly diverse, occurring in varying parts of the linguistic system: phonology, pragmatics, syntax, morphology, and lexicon (see Philips 1987). Here I will pay special attention to co-occurring features of speech that form patterns, called styles, genres, or ways of speaking, which are linked, in some way, to gender.[11]

Unlike the earliest studies that noted only obligatory linguistic differences between men and women, current research distinguishes cases where a speech form is normatively *required* for men or women from cases where it is a favored strategy for one gender because it enacts, consciously or not, men's and women's contrasting values or interactional goals (McConnell-Ginet 1988). Such differences in values and goals emerge with force when the division of labor creates largely separate worlds for men and women, so that "members of each sex learn to be proficient in different linguistic skills and to do different things with words" (Borker 1980: 31). Indeed, considerable ethnographic evidence suggests that differences in verbal genres between men and women are widespread, especially where men's and women's activities are distinctly defined (Sherzer 1987).

For example, among the Kuna Indians of Lowland Panama, speech genres emerge from the division of labor. Genres associated with public political meetings and ritualized attempts to cure illness are largely restricted to men, whereas the more privately performed genres of lullabies and tuneful mourning are restricted to women (Sherzer 1987). Similarly, among the Kaluli, living in the Southern Highlands of Papua New Guinea, it is the men who tell several types of stories, recite magical formulae for hunting, and perform songs and dances in major political and ceremonial contexts. Women compose more limited ceremonial songs and engage in expressive public weeping on occasions of profound loss (Schieffelin 1987). Among the Laymi Indians of Bolivia, women control and create genres of publicly performed song and music that are essential to courting and to the ritual cycle; men control speaking in the local political assembly and speaking directed to the spirits in curing rituals (Harris 1980).

These studies underline the fact that in many societies women actively create and perform major expressive activities, often in public, a point also emphasized by feminist folklorists (Jordan and deCaro 1986). Such evidence effectively counters the persistent but erroneous image of women as universally silent in public or restricted to domestic activities. It highlights as well one function of speech in a gender system: genre differences create the kind of pervasive behavioral contrast that transforms gradients of human difference into culturally salient dichotomies of masculinity and femininity. But, a simple catalogue of "his-and-hers" genres obscures the important insight that women's special verbal skills are often strategic *responses*—more or less successful—to positions of relative powerlessness.

For example, in a Hungarian-German bilingual town in Austria, women use German more than men do. Women's use of German corresponds to their general rejection of the peasant way of life associated with the Hungarian language and their acceptance of the wage labor symbolized by speaking German. It is, in part, women's relative powerlessness in the peasant social order that makes the escape to worker status so attractive for them and, thus, explains the verbal strategies they use (Gal 1978).[12]

Strategies are not always directed toward change. In a Tenejapan village of southern Mexico, women are more polite than men in two ways. They use many more linguistic particles that emphasize solidarity with their interactional partner and also use more of a contrasting set of particles that avoid imposition and stress the listener's separateness and autonomy. Indeed, women's intent to impose by requesting, commanding, or criticizing is often couched in irony. Because irony requires the listener to infer the speaker's intent, irony allows the speaker to disclaim the intent if it results in challenge or threat. Men use less irony and fewer particles of either kind, showing considerably less sensitivity to the details of social relationships and context. Women's usage is an interactional strategy, an accommodation arising from their social and even physical vulnerability to men, and the consequent necessity to show deference to men, on the one hand, and maintain strong networks of solidarity with women, on the other hand. This suggests that levels and types of politeness strategies used by women to men and to other women may well be a sensitive measure of women's structural power in many societies (Brown 1980).

But women's responses to powerlessness, although they may also be attempts to subvert male authority, may only end by reproducing it. A striking example is Harding's (1975) analysis of a peasant village in Spain. Women and men characteristically occupy different physical spaces (the house and shops versus the plaza and the fields); have different work and concerns (family and neighbors versus land, politics, economics); and different speech genres. Whereas men argue in public, as a form of verbal play requiring an appreciative audience; women talk in small, closed groups of kin, often practicing "gossip"—the gathering and evaluating of information about people—as their only means of social control. Harding argues that it is women's subordinate position to men, and not simply separation, that leads women to develop special "manipulative" verbal skills such as teasing out information, carefully watching others so as to anticipate their needs, and using irony or self-effacing methods of persuasion. Gossip itself is women's most powerful verbal tool, but it is two-edged. It tends to subvert male authority, by judging people in terms of values the male-dominant system rejects. But partly as a result of this subversion it is condemned and decried by the dominant culture. Moreover, it is seen by all as a negative form of power that makes or breaks reputations, causes conflict, and disrupts relationships. It is negative in another sense too. As Harding reveals, women develop this genre for lack of other forms of power, but they are trapped by it themselves:

"Th[e] sense, if not fact, of being under constant verbal surveillance restricts the behavior of women and helps keep them in their place" (1975: 103).

Although there is no parallel separation of the sexes in the United States, American men and women also seem to use somewhat different verbal strategies in conversation. In a provocative synthesis of recent research findings, Maltz and Borker (1982) argue that sex-segregated children's play groups, common in American society, create gender-specific verbal cultures whose practices speakers retain into adulthood. But the gender differences are so subtle people are aware only of their result: frequent miscommunication between men and women who otherwise claim to be friends and status equals. Maltz and Borker rely in part on Goodwin's careful studies of children's play groups in an urban black neighborhood, but information on white children and adults of various classes and ethnic groups also seems to support their generalizations about men's and women's strategies.

For instance, boys and men organize into relatively large hierarchical groups, using direct commands and vying with one another for leadership positions by holding forth in competitive verbal display. Side comments and challenges are the proper responses by those who do not have the floor. Girls, by contrast, play in smaller groups, forming exclusive coalitions. There is plenty of conflict in all-girl groups, but their verbal interactions implicitly deny conflict and hierarchy, phrasing commands as proposals for future activity (Goodwin 1980). Girls and women carefully link their utterances to the previous speaker's contribution and develop one another's topics, asking questions for conversational maintenance rather than for information or challenge. But these differences are not as innocent as Maltz and Borker's image of parallel, mutually miscomprehending gender-cultures would suggest.

One way of interpreting the female strategies is as a set of practices that, whatever the actual power relations within the girls' or women's group, nevertheless enact values of support and solidarity that directly oppose and implicitly criticize the boys' and men's practices of heroic individuality, competition, and the celebration of hierarchy. In this sense the two "cultures" are not separate at all, but define each other, enacting in speech forms several familiar cultural oppositions in American discourse about gender.

They are also not equal in power. Goodwin and Goodwin's most recent reports (1987) indicate that when boys and girls argue together, the boys' strategy is employed by all. This suggests that the boys' strategy is dominant in two senses: the girls but not the boys must learn both, and the boys seem to be able to impose theirs on the girls in cross-sex interaction. This kind of dominance is also suggested by a series of studies on patterns of interruption in cross-sex interactions among status equals. Between pairs of speakers who knew each other well, as well as between those who were strangers, men interrupted women more than either sex interrupted in same-sex interactions. Moreover, the assumption that interruption is a gesture of dominance is supported by the finding that adults interrupt children more than the reverse (West and Zimmerman 1983).[13] A study of naturally occurring conversation by young American married couples in their homes is also suggestive in this regard. Although the women raised almost twice as many topics of conversation as the men, the topics raised by men were the ones that were accepted and elaborated in the conversation by both men and women. Yet it was the women who provided most of the interactional "work," the questions and minimal responses ("uh-huh") that kept the conversation going (Fishman 1978). More systematic evidence is needed, especially about the effects of social context on the details of such everday talk. And we need replications across classes and ethnic groups of studies relying on very small samples of white middle-class speakers. Nevertheless, in cross-gender talk, as in the cross-ethnic miscommunication on which Maltz and Borker model their analysis (Gumperz 1982), it seems clear that the differences in strategies provide an opportunity for the more powerful group to enact and reinforce its dominance through the microprocesses of verbal interaction.

But a major flaw in many of the studies of linguistic strategy I have discussed so far is their assumption that speech and gender are best investigated in informal conversations, often in one-to-one or small-group relationships in the family or neighborhood. This creates the illusion that gendered talk is mainly a personal characteristic or limited to the institution of the family. Yet, as much feminist research has demonstrated, gender as a structural principle also organizes other social institutions: workplaces, schools, courts, political assemblies, and the state show characteristic patterns in the recruitment, allocation, treatment, and mobility of men as opposed to women. These are inscribed in the organization of the institution. Patterns of talk and interaction play an important role in maintaining, legitimating, and often hiding the gendered aspect of these institutional arrangements. The role of men's and women's linguistic strategies within institutions deserves considerably more attention than it has so far received. I will discuss only a few suggestive examples from schools and bureaucracies in the United States, and from political assemblies in several small-scale societies.

Within institutions, such settings as interviews, meetings, and other characteristic verbal encounters are often crucial for decision making. On the basis of talk some individuals are hired, chosen to participate, receive resources or promotions and authority, while others are denied. In complex, capitalist societies the class and ethnic background of speakers is crucial in such gate-keeping encounters (Erickson and Schultz 1982). And gender routinely interacts with class and ethnicity. For instance, in a study of speech in American courts, the testimony of witnesses using the linguistic forms characteristic of women with no courtroom experience and of low-status men was judged by experimental subjects to be less credible, less convincing, and less trustworthy than testimony delivered in a style characteristic of speakers with high status (O'Barr and Atkins 1980). It appears that courts reinforce the authority of forms associated with high-status speakers, who tend to be men.

The "meeting" is a speech event ubiquitous in American bureaucratic, corporate, and academic life. In a study of faculty meetings, Edelsky (1981) approached the university as a workplace and not as an educational institution. In meetings with equal numbers of male and female participants of equal occupation status, she asked whether women were as successful as men in "getting the floor," that is, in winning the opportunity to talk and thereby contribute to the decisions. But a direct comparison of men's and women's participation was not possible. Who spoke and how often depended on the implicit rules by which speakers participated. And there were at least two sets of rules, two kinds of "floors." In episodes characterized by the first kind of "floor," speakers took longer and fewer turns, fewer speakers participated overall, they did not overlap much, there were many false starts and hesitations, and speakers used their turns for reporting and voicing opinions. The other kind of "floor" occurred at the same meetings but during different episodes. It was characterized by much overlap and simultaneous talk but little hesitation in speaking, and by more general participation by many speakers who collaboratively constructed a group picture of "what's-going-on." Several speakers performed the same communicative functions such as suggesting an idea, arguing, or agreeing; joking, teasing, and wisecracking were more frequent.

It is evident that the interactional strategies of American men and women, as outlined by Maltz and Borker, are differently suited to the two kinds of "floor." It was men who monopolized the first kind of floor, by taking *longer* turns, holding forth and dominating the construction of the floor through the time they took talking. In the second kind of floor, where everyone took shorter turns, men and women took turns of about equal length, and all speakers participated as equals in the communicative functions performed (1981: 416). Importantly, the first, more formal kind of floor, in which women participated less, occurred vastly *more* frequently, at least in this institutional setting. Explicit and tacit struggles between speakers about how meetings are to be conducted are conflicts about the control of institutional power. Even among status equals and in mixed-sex groups, the interactional constraints of institutional events such as meetings are not gender neutral but weighted in favor of male interactional strategies. Although organization of the meeting *masks* the fact that speakers are excluded on the basis of gender, it simultaneously *accomplishes* that very exclusion.

Perhaps more pervasively than any other institution, schools judge, define, and categorize their charges on the basis of linguistic performance. The different strategies of boys and girls can also affect their access to linguistic resources, such as literacy, that schooling offers. A single example will suffice to suggest how ethnic differences interact with gender in this process. In her fine comparison of language acquisition and training for literacy in three Southern communities in the United States, Heath (1983) carefully describes the complex and artful linguistic practices of a black working-class community. Children must master "analogy" questions posed by their elders, in which they are encouraged to see the parallels and connections among disparate events and tell about them cleverly, without spelling out explicitly what the links are. Such descriptions differ from school requirements that match middle-class patterns. And what is expected of black girls at home differs considerably from the more extensive verbal skills demanded of boys. Working-class black girls, in contrast to boys of their own group, are neither expected nor encouraged to practice a wide range of story-telling tactics in competitive "onstage" public arenas where community adults as well as children watch and judge (1983: 95–98, 105–112).

The results of these differences emerge in a parallel study of teacher-student interaction in a first-grade classroom with both black and white students (Michaels 1981). When the white teachers—all women—instituted a "sharing time" ("show and tell") activity, they had the explicit goal of bridging the gap between the oral discourse the children already knew and the literate discourse strategies they would eventually have to use in written communication. They asked the children to tell about a specific object or give a narrative account about some important past event. For the white boys and girls this worked quite well. They told topic-focused stories that the teachers understood; and the teachers' questions and comments helped the students make their stories more explicit and develop the more complex structures of standard literacy. The working-class black girls, however, organized their stories to resemble children's responses to "analogy" questions. They noted abstract parallels between disparate situations and events and relied on the listener to infer the implicit links. Although the white teachers were of the same gender as the black girls and had excellent intentions, they failed to understand this principle and thus were unable to collaborate with the black girls in producing more elaborate, structurally complex stories. The black girls felt frustrated; their stories were rarely even completed before the teachers cut them off. As a result, they could not benefit from the steps toward literate, standard discourse that the classroom activity apparently accomplished for the white children. The teachers were also frustrated. To them it appeared that the girls could not "stick to the point" nor discern what was "important." On the basis of many such interactions the black girls would be judged intellectually inadequate.

This ability of social institutions to create gendered definitions of speakers through talk is equally illustrated by political assemblies in small-scale societies where adult men consider each other equals. In many such societies, as among the Malagasy and the Laymi Indians described above, only men talk at public, political meetings. Ethnographers have repeatedly described men's talk in this context as allusive and indirect, making use of images, parables, and metaphors to hide, veil, or render ambiguous the referential message, thereby denying conflict (Brenneis and Myers 1984). Women are excluded on the grounds that they lack the necessary verbal subtlety. This seems to suggest that speech differences are powerful indeed, since they seem to directly limit women's access to the political process. However, ethnographers also report that the meetings are not the main site of decision making, and indirect speech is not primarily a means of persuasion or coercion. Usually decisions are made and consensus reached before and after the meeting in informal discussions that employ a more direct style and in which women participate actively, thereby having considerable effect on decisions (Harris 1980: 73; Keenan 1974; Lederman 1984). What, then, is the meaning and effect of women's exclusion from speaking at meetings?

The linguistic form of political meetings defines not how decision making actually occurs, but rather what can be shown "onstage"; what can be focused on as the legitimate reality. Comparative evidence suggests that meetings at which orders are given or announced by leaders ratify an ideology of hierarchy, regardless of the way decisions were originally reached. Meetings in which indirectness creates a lack of coercion and hierarchy between participants ratify an ideology of egalitarian relations, at least in societies where there are few other institutionalized political structures (Irvine 1979). If men's indirect oratory constructs the social reality of an egalitarian male polity, then the exclusion of women creates the reality and legitimates the ideology of women's subordination to that polity. As Lederman (1984) points out about the Mendi of New Guinea, for the women listening in silence at such a meeting, this reality is all the harder to challenge since it is formally acted out but never explicitly articulated.

In sum, societal institutions are not neutral contexts for talk. They are organized to define, demonstrate, and enforce the legitimacy and authority of linguistic strategies used by one gender—or men of one class or ethnic group—while denying the power of others.[14] Forms that diverge are devalued by the dominant ideologies. "Floors" with many participants, black girls' stories, women's gossip in Spain, Mendi women's directness, all attempt to contest the hegemony of the dominant forms. But it is not the "floor" that is judged inauspicious, rather women are seen as timid or unable to express themselves; it is not that the black girls have different story-telling experiences than white children and less training than black boys, but that they cannot think properly. Despite the resistance demonstrated in women's linguistic practices, Bourdieu's (1977*b*) remark about the effects of this kind of linguistic domination applies: by authorizing some linguistic practices and not others, the institution appears to demonstrate the inferiority of those who use unauthorized forms and often inculcates in them feelings of worthlessness.

But notice that the Mendi meeting, the forums of Mme. Roland, and single-speaker "floors" also illustrate another sort of symbolic power I mentioned at the start of this chapter: they are interactional and linguistic forms, but they also attempt to impose and legitimate certain definitions of women, men, and society. I now turn to a fuller discussion of this second aspect of symbolic domination and the way women's voices are sometimes raised against it.

GENRES OF RESISTANCE

Despite the long-standing Western emphasis on language as primarily a means of representing an already existing reality, anthropologists have long been aware of the ways in which the metaphors, literary genres, and interactional arrangements readily available in a community actively shape the way speakers define the social world. In short, conventional language and its conventional usage are not neutral media for describing social life. Some formulations about social life, when inscribed in a division of labor or other organizational form, serve one group's interests better than that of others. A hegemonic discourse, in this broad sense, is a form of power, and it is sometimes resisted or contested.

This important and quite general notion of a dynamic between dominant and subordinate discourses or practices has been discussed, in many forms and with many terminologies, by a variety of social theorists. However, feminist scholars have been strongly influenced by a limited version of this insight, explicitly applied to women. E. Ardener (1975) and S. Ardener (1975) argue that women, due to their structural positions, have models of reality that differ from the male-dominated societal model. The form of women's models is often nonverbal, inarticulate, or veiled, while the discourse of men is more verbal and explicit, and thereby more congruent with the usual discourse of Western social science. Being unable to express their structurally generated views in the dominant and masculine discourse, women are neither understood nor heeded, and become inarticulate, "muted," or even silent. In such cases women may talk a lot, but they do not express their own, different social reality.[15]

The "muted-group" thesis usefully draws attention to the importance of the symbolic language, the form, of dominant and subordinate discourse. However, as I will demonstrate with a series of examples, the Ardeners' formulation is flawed in several respects. First, it assumes that "mutedness" is a static reflex of women's structural position. In contrast, when viewed in terms of broader theories of gender and symbolic domination, "mutedness" becomes only one of many theoretically possible outcomes of gender relations. A much wider array of women's verbal strategies and genres become visible, some considerably more articulate and more actively oppositional to dominant models than the "mutedness" thesis allows. Second, if domination and resistance are matters of interactional practice as well as structure, as I have been arguing, then we must focus not on "mutedness" as a structural product but on the processes by which women are rendered "mute" or manage to construct dissenting genres and resisting discourses. Finally, as Warren and Bourque suggest: ". . . understanding dominance and muting [as processes] requires a broader analysis of the political, economic and institutional contexts in which reality is negotiated" (1985: 261).

Ethnography itself is such a context, for ethnographic reports are deeply implicated in the process of representing self and others, creating images of social reality through language. Keenly aware of this, feminist critics of anthropology have charged that women in the societies studied were ignored or perceived as inert because androcentric ethnographers dismissed women and their concerns, making them appear passive and silent. Feminists challenged the authority and credibility of these male-biased accounts. But the Ardeners' thesis suggests that the problem is more complex. It claims that women rarely "speak" in social anthropological reports because social science investigators of both sexes demand the kind of articulate models provided by men, not by muted women. And indeed, some women anthropologists have also complained of the inarticulateness of women informants in some contexts. It seems there is a need to reexamine how ethnographies are created. Currently, just such a reexamination is also the project of anthropologists who are similarly challenging the authority of ethnographic writing, but on different grounds. Following postmodernist trends in philosophy, they assert that traditional ethnographies mask the actual practice of fieldwork and writing (Clifford and Marcus 1986). By claiming to accurately represent the facts about an exotic culture, the naive realist conventions of ethnographic writing implicitly deny that ethnographic facts are selected, indeed constructed, in the encounter between the anthropologist and the "other" who is her/his subject. In order to reflect the process of ethnographic knowledge, these critics suggest experimentation with literary forms so that writing may be a "polyvocal" and dialogic production in which the ethnographer lets the people speak and ethnographic facts are shown to be jointly produced by ethnographer and informant.

What has received too little attention in all these critiques is the unavoidably power-charged verbal encounter in which anthropologists and native speakers, with different interests, goals, and deeply unequal positions, meet and attempt to talk. Keesing (1985) provides a fine example of the ethnographic interview as a linguistic practice. In order to record women's versions of native life (kastom) among the Kwaio, a tenaciously traditional group living in the Solomon Islands of the South Pacific, Keesing had to analyze what he calls the "micropolitics" of talk. In response to Keesing's requests, the men created and told life histories eagerly and artfully, even though the Kwaio lack such a genre as well as a tradition of self-revelation and self-explanation on which the Western literary form of the autobiography is based. In contrast, Keesing recounts that he could not elicit autobiographical narratives from women, not even those who were old, knowledgeable, and influential. They spoke to him in a fragmented, inarticulate and joking way, especially in front of elder men who urged them to cooperate. They appeared distressed with what was requested of them: "mute." A subsequent fieldtrip, eight years later, this time with a woman ethnographer, brought quite different results. In sessions with *both* ethnographers, Kwaio women took control of the encounters, even bringing female friends as audience to the recording sessions. But, unlike the men, who had provided societal rules and personal life narratives, the women rejected the ethnographers' personal questions and instead created moral texts about the virtues of womanhood, inserting personal experiences only to illustrate women's possible paths through life. Through their texts, Kwaio women were reformulating and embellishing a long-standing strategy of Kwaio men: to enlist the (at first) unknowing anthropologist in their efforts to codify and authorize Kwaio custom. By legitimating their own customs in an anthropologized form the Kwaio men were able to use it to resist the demands of state regulations, thereby attempting, through vigorous neo-traditionalism, to maintain their political autonomy in the face of colonial and neo-colonial incursions.

A deeper understanding of Kwaio women's talk requires revisions of all three critiques of anthropological fieldwork. Clearly Kwaio women were not so much structurally mute and inarticulate as responsive to the immediate interactional context, especially relations of gender inequality within their own society and in the ethnographic interview. Pragmatic analyses of the interview as a speech event suggest it is the ethnographer's task to discover the conditions under which informants can talk. Similarly, it is not enough to insist, as the postmodernist critics do, that the ethnographic encounter and the genres that emerge from it are jointly produced. Although important and accurate, this observation by itself ignores the importance of gender and other forms of inequality. It omits the several levels of unequal power and privilege that characterize the ethnographic encounter and which also determine who is able to talk and what it is possible or strategic to say. The women's inarticulateness and subsequent "voice," as much as the men's systematization of their culture, were responses to wider fields of force that assure that some texts or genres are more powerful than others, making a simple coproduction of ethnographic texts impossible (Asad 1986; Polier and Roseberry 1988: 15). Finally, feminists would have confidently predicted the changes produced by the presence of a woman anthropologist and would have understood that the genre of autobiography is problematic, not only because it is culturally specific to the West, but also because it has been shaped by Western gender ideology that assumes a male subject.[16] Yet the case of Kwaio women suggests revisions and expansions for gender theories as well: a female ethnographer may be only part of the answer. In this case, the presence of the male anthropologist was also important, for the women were attuned to his established role as mediator between the Kwaio and the outside world. Thus, attention must be paid to relations of power that connect Kwaio society to a world system in which, as the Kwaio are aware, anthropologists, as wielders of Western discourse, have authority that Kwaio women, perhaps differently than men, can try to channel to their own ends through the ethnographic interview.

Ethnography is only one of the many contexts in which we can observe the processes that make women seem "mute." Another example is provided by an elite intellectual study group, the Men's and Women's Club of 1880s London, and their discussions of sexuality (Walkowitz 1986). Club rules asserted men's and women's equality, but rule number seventeen, which was accepted by all, stipulated that discussion must stay within a Darwinian, scientific framework. This proviso both assured and hid men's dominance. For women members respected, but lacked, such scientific knowledge. This is at once an instance of linguistic domination and an attempt at imposition of a social reality: women's private letters reveal that many found the terms of such a science inadequate to express "complex thought and feeling" about the difficulties of their sexual lives. Minutes of the meetings suggest that face-to-face with men, women were often silenced by this dilemma. But other data show various attempts to formulate opposition: transforming or adapting men's scientific arguments in papers written for the club, writing private letters of complaint to one another, and even attempting to create a different idiom for talking about sexuality by drawing on public events of the time.

If women are not always silent or inarticulate, then the task of anthropology is to seek out and understand the genres and discourses women produce. Especially revealing are genres created by speakers themselves, to reflect on their own experience, that are not primarily a product of the ethnographic interview. As I have already shown, students of everyday talk have identified men's and women's often different verbal genres; students of oral literature have catalogued their forms and the rules for their performance (e.g. Sherzer 1987). But these are not simply "ways of speaking"; the differences in content or perspective that they often construct deserve equal attention. Indeed, it is in the conjunction of form, content, and context of performance that women's consciousness emerges. First, my examples will demonstrate the great range of articulateness evident in women's genres. Second, although women's genres often diverge from men's, and are sometimes autonomous constructions, the evidence does not support a thesis of separate women's cultures. On the contrary, women's genres can best be read as commentary that shows a range of response—acceptance, resistance, subversion, and opposition—to dominant, often male discourse.

Women sometimes produce a cultural commentary of gesture and ritual that may be called inarticulate because it rejects words altogether. An important instance occurred in the Nigerian Women's War of 1929. During the massive protests against proposed taxation of women's property by the colonial government, women reformulated on a large scale a locally practiced custom of obscene dancing, called "sitting on a man," that traditionally occurred at the houses of men who had overstepped social mores upheld by women. Contemporary witnesses of the Women's War report that women's protests included marching nude, lying on the ground kicking their legs in the air, and making obscene gestures. As Ifeka-Moller (1975) explains, these gestures were mysterious and alarming to European observers but, for the women and men involved, they constituted an eloquent protest against the male political control and government taxation that women saw as a violation of their rights.

A similarly gestural but much more contradictory and acquiescent practice is American women's consumption of popular romantic novels. If we analyze only the texts themselves, romance readers appear as passive consumers of a hegemonic popular culture that demeans them by presenting images of women as illogical and magnetized by male brutality. But Radway (1984) examines not just the content but the social event of reading. She shows that for many romance readers, reading itself, often done in stolen moments of privacy, is a combative act, contesting the usual self-abnegation of their lives. Yet, although revealing a real tension in dominant gender ideology, this is a limited and self-defeating protest: reading allows temporary escape from limited lives, but the texts make those limited lives seem more desirable.

A more verbally explicit and subversive, yet veiled and ambiguous genre, is the oral lyric poetry (ghinnawas) performed among intimates by the Bedouin of Egypt's Western Desert. In describing these delicate, brief, and artfully improvised performances, Abu-Lughod (1986) stresses that the dominant ideology, the "public language" of the Bedouin, is one of honor, autonomy, self-mastery, personal strength, and sexual modesty. The poems directly violate this code of honor and implicitly criticize it by expressing the feelings of dependency, emotional vulnerability, and romantic longing condemned by the official view. The poetry constitutes what Abu-Lughod calls a "dissident or subversive discourse . . . most closely associated with youths and women, the disadvantaged dependents who least embody the ideals of Bedouin society and have least to gain in the system as structured. . . . Poetry is the discourse of opposition to the system and of defiance of those who represent it" (1986: 251). But the poetry is anything but a spontaneous outpouring of feeling. Indeed, its formal properties and context of performance enhance its ability to subtly carry messages counter to official ideals. It is formulaic, thereby disguising the identities of poet, addressee, and subject. It is fleeting and ambiguous, performed by women and youths among trusted intimates who can decipher it exactly because they already know the reciter well. Yet, this poetry of subversion and defiance is not only tolerated; it is culturally elaborated and admired because of the paradoxical intertwining of official and dissident discourse. The oral poetry reveals a fundamental tension of Bedouin social and political life which, while valuing and demanding autonomy and equality between lineages, demands inequality between the genders and generations within lineages and families. "A discourse of defiance by those slighted in the system, [poetry] is exalted because a refusal to be dominated is key to Bedouin political life, and it is avoided by [male] elders because it threatens to expose the illegitimacy of their authority" (Abu-Lughod 1986: 254). Thus, the verbal genre of women and youths reveals the contradictions of the ruling ideology.

My final example is a poetic genre more verbally explicit, more directly critical of social and political relations, and much less accepted by official ideologies. Though limited to a much smaller segment of the female population, it is equally revealing of contradictions in dominant discourses. Migrant laborers, moving between the mines of South Africa and their native Lesotho, compose a genre of poetic songs called *lifela*, performed competitively by "men of eloquence," often for a fee, usually at social gatherings in border towns. They sing of poverty and forced migration; their songs reinforce a rootedness in the rural village, despite migration, and a longing for traditional gerontocratic and patriarchal social relations. However, there are also some women who sing lifela. But their circumstances, as well as the content of their poetry, are significantly different.

In the current migrant system, women's position is in many ways even worse than men's. Women are forbidden to migrate by the legal system, but left alone in the village they must make decisions without being granted the autonomy to do so. "The South African government, the Lesotho government and male Basotho attitudes have openly conspired to prevent female migration, which threatens the divided-family system on which both the migratory labor system and male domestic power are based" (Coplan 1987: 424). Female poets are among those who have managed to escape these constraints and have migrated illegally. Although for men South Africa is unequivocally a land of wage slavery, for these migrant women it represents relative choice, opportunity and autonomy. Women have borrowed the men's genre but have transformed it, providing a considerably more radical social critique. Rather than identifying with rural life, the women's poetry sharply and explicitly criticizes men, proclaims traditional marriage unworkable, but recognizes as well the physical dangers and insecurity of life as an illegal migrant. The women's opposition is palpable not only in the content of the poetry, but also during the performance of the poems/songs in the tavern: "Male . . . patrons, stung by the critical barbs of female performers routinely rise to sing spontaneous retorts . . . [but] are shouted down or even pushed aside by [female poets] determined to hold the floor" (Coplan 1987: 429).

Such attempts to silence the protest songs of migrant women in Lesotho return us to the *process* by which women are either rendered "mute" or are able to construct an alternate discourse, resisting attempts to suppress it. I have attempted one approach to this question, examining women's genres as practices, analyzing ethnographic interviews or Bedouin poetry very much as I did earlier examples of "ways of speaking" such as collaborative "floors" and gossip: focusing on the immediate interactional context of the genre— the participant structure of the interview, the intimacy of Bedouin confidantes, the liminality of border taverns—for clues to the forces that allow it to be performed. More broadly, however, the issue of when and how women's subversion or opposition to hegemonic culture emerges is as much a question about the structure of gender systems and political economy as about linguistic practices, genres, and counter-discourses. Comparative work, such as Warren and Bourque's (1985) study of women's public speaking in two quite differently organized Peruvian communities, or study of the social identities of women who sing lifela, can start to illuminate this issue, as can historical research into changing images of sex and gender (Steedman et al. 1985; Walkowitz 1986). Another research tactic is to compare women of different classes and ethnic groups, using linguistic practices to raise the classic issue of the relationship between consciousness and social position.

A study of this kind is Martin's investigation of American women's discourse about their own reproductive processes, as compared to the dominant discourse on this subject, which is medical science. Martin (1987) used the same linguistic metric to compare medical textbooks and women's folk models: the system of metaphors through which reality is made comprehensible and meaningful in each. She demonstrates that medical texts construct the body as a model of industrial society, with cells as factories having systems of management and control. The physical events of menstruation are constructed by science as failed production and an alarming breakdown of authority in the body.

Comparing this system of metaphors to women's ways of talking about menstruation in interviews, Martin found that middle-class women acquiesce to the medical model. They explain menstruation in medical terms, dwelling on internal organs and processes, worrying about the "correct" color of the blood. But working-class women, both black and white, shared "an absolute reluctance to give the medical view of menstruation" (1987: 109), in spite of exposure to it at school and the interviewers' many efforts to elicit it. Instead, working-class women described menstruation in phenomenological terms untouched by the medical model: what it feels like, looks like, smells like in immediate experience. Martin concludes that "middle class women appear much more 'mystified' by the general cultural models than working class women. They have bought the . . . medical accounts" (1987: 111). Perhaps this is due to their favorable opportunities for satisfying employment and thus positive attitudes toward both the image of production and schooling as a source of information. Once again, gender and class are intertwined. This is certainly a start toward understanding the processes by which some women but not others develop divergent and resistant consciousness; or why subordinate men sometimes share women's practices.[17]

These diverse examples of women's genres, drawn from many parts of the world and many kinds of sociopolitical formations, were chosen in part to highlight the observation that women's resistance or criticism is sometimes couched in implicit forms such as ambiguity and irony but is, in other cases, much more directly expressed. Indeed, the examples illustrate a range of linguistic explicitness (gestural; brief and ambiguous; extended and explicit); diverse social contexts (public demonstration, closed meeting, intimate conversation, paid performance); and several levels of subversion or opposition to dominant discourses (from self-defeating complicity, to resistance, to open criticism). Interestingly, it seems that these three parameters do not correlate in any simple way. Strong protest can appear in silent gestures, as in the women's war; or in the explicit public performances of critical poetry. Resistance may be knowing yet silent, as in American working-class women's refusal of some medical metaphors, verbal yet veiled as in Bedouin poetry, verbal but privately expressed, as in the Men's and Women's Club, or explicit and public, as in bilingual Austrian women's use of German. But in each case, women's linguistic practices made visible a crack, a fault line in the dominant male discourse of gender and power, revealing it to be not monolithic but contradictory and thus vulnerable.

CONCLUSIONS

I have argued that gender relations are constructed, in part, through different possibilities of expression for men and women. Tools from several scholarly traditions are needed in order to unravel how linguistic practices, gender, and power are intertwined. The research and analyses from several traditions, which I have brought together here to clarify and inform one another, deserve to be conceptually integrated. The notions of symbolic domination through patterns of language use and of gender as both structure and practice are essential to that endeavor.

Cultural constructions of language, gender, and power shape men's and women's ideas and ideals about their own linguistic practices. Students of everyday talk have often neglected this symbolic side of interaction. For instance, even such seemingly small details as the systematic differences between American boys' and girls' turn-taking in single-sex play groups fit and reinforce the broad cultural logic of gender symbolism in the United States. However, women's acquiescence to such cultural expectations is neither passive nor automatic. Indeed, as students of everyday talk have shown, women actively construct linguistic strategies in response to these cultural conceptions and to the relations of gender inequality they encode. Although women's practices sometimes bring change in established structures, often, as in the case of Spanish women's gossip, the strategy may aim to resist male dominance but ends by reproducing and legitimating it. This is in part because men and women interact not as individuals but in institutions such as workplaces, families, schools, and political forums, where much decision making about resources and social selection for mobility occurs through talk. And institutions are far from neutral arenas: they are structured along gender lines, to lend authority not only to reigning classes and ethnic groups but specifically to men's linguistic practices.

But power is more than an authoritative voice in decision making; its strongest form may well be the ability to define social reality, to impose visions of the world. Such visions are inscribed in language and enacted in interaction. Although women's everyday talk and women's "voice" or consciousness as evidenced in expressive genres have been studied quite separately, I have argued that both can be understood as strategic responses, often of resistance, to dominant, hegemonic cultural forms. Thus, attention to linguistic detail, context of performance, and the nature of the dominant forms is essential to both endeavors. The precise form of questions and turn-taking is crucial in understanding the construction of different "floors" in American meetings (everyday talk); the exact, formal conventions of intimate Bedouin poetry (expressive genre) is indispensable to understanding how it is suited to the expression of vulnerability and dependence. Although the linguistic materials are quite different, both collaborative "floors" and intimate poetry locate a contradiction in dominant discourse and subvert it through rival practices. One undermines the hierarchical form and ideology of meetings that favor men's expertise in competitive talk; the other is seen as the opposite of ordinary talk and undermines the cultural rule of honor, threatening to reveal the illegitimacy of elder men's authority. This returns us to the cultural constructions we started with, now revealed not only as ideas that differentiate the genders but as discourses that are sources of power, which are enacted, and sometimes contested, in talk.

NOTES

1. I would like to thank Micaela di Leonardo, Judith Gerson, Suzanne Lebsock, Michael Moffatt, Kit Woolard, and Viviana Zelizer for careful readings and en-

couragement, and Bambi Schieffelin for her bibliographic suggestions. This paper is dedicated to the memory of Ruth Borker.

2. The question of "silence" in feminist scholarship is twofold. On the one hand, the titles of some recent books suffice to illustrate a concern with obstacles to women's self-expression: *Silences* (Olsen), *On lies, secrets and silence* (Rich), *Stealing the language* (Ostriker), *Man made language* (Spender). On the other hand, the fact that social science has neglected women makes women of the past and other cultures *seem* silent, when in fact the silence is that of current western scholarship. I return to this issue in sec. 4. Even everyday usage, such as the generic "he" for persons of unspecified sex, has the effect of making women appear silent.

3. There is a growing literature on the meanings of silence, which is usefully reviewed in D. Tannen and M. Saville-Troike (1984). The relationship of silence to women's speech is mentioned in Thorne, Kramarae, and Henley (1983; 16–17). S. Smith (1987: 49) highlights the irony of Foucault's assertions, when applied to women's writing; Moi (1985) discusses femininity and silence from the perspective of literary criticism.

4. Some of the influential works that have developed and argued for this conception are: Rubin 1975, Kelly-Gadol 1976, Gerson and Peiss 1985, Connell 1987.

5. Among such works, perhaps the best-known evocation of "women's voice" is Gilligan (1982) and the literature inspired by it. Also relevant here are historians' discussions of women's culture which stress the content of beliefs and values (e.g., Smith-Rosenberg 1985; see debate in Feminist Studies 1980).

6. Lears (1985) provides an excellent discussion of Gramsci's contribution and the analytical uses of "cultural hegemony"; see also Lukes (1974). I have pointed to a very general and fundamental concern that these theorists share, ignoring for my purposes their many differences, e.g. the relative importance of history and human agency as opposed to structure, or how to conceptualize the relationship between material and ideational forces.

7. Feminist literary critics have provided diverse analyses of this relationship; see Furman (1980) and Moi's (1985) critical review. Recent western feminist practice itself provides a handy example in consciousness raising, which is a new *form* of linguistic practice as well as a challenge to dominant definitions about gender. Sec. 4 discusses the anthropological evidence.

8. Borker (1980) makes this point and provides many examples, some of which are also cited here. Hymes (e.g. 1974) has long argued for the analysis of speakers' ideas about speaking and its relation to social categories. Silverstein (1985) provides a detailed discussion of the way such conceptions, along with culturally constructed notions about how language works, that is, linguistic ideology, mediate between social change and changes in the internal workings of language, e.g. phonology, address systems, morphology.

9. For a fine example of linguistic advice to eighteenth-century American women, see Lebsock (1987: 42). Linguistic theory itself has been more deeply involved with definitions of gender than is generally recognized. Cameron (1985) provides a useful discussion of the way notions of gender originally drawn from definitions of men and women were used to define grammatical gender, then later recycled from language to social life and used to justify gender arrangements.

10. Such a gender/class link is suggested, in passing, in a number of works. For

example, the relationship between working-class culture and masculinity is described for British adolescents by Willis (1977) and extended to adults by Connell (1987: 109). The connection between images of femininity and middle-class gentility in nineteenth-century America is suggested by Halttunen (1982) and Douglas (1977). Smith-Rosenberg (1985) discusses Davy Crockett as the poor, tough, "uncultured" archetype of American masculinity, along with other, contrasting images of gender in the nineteenth century.

11. I will not be discussing a range of important, related issues that are critically reviewed by McConnell-Ginet (1988), e.g., the process by which speech strategies become part of *language* as a form of cognitive competence, and the semantic coding of gender inequality in the lexicon, among others. An early and influential essay that offered hypotheses about men's and women's styles in middle-class America was Lakoff (1975).

12. Such strategic language choices, associated with the differential life circumstances of men and women in bilingual communities, have been reported by several researchers. The choices of women vary according to the specific historical and political economic circumstances of the community, so that women are sometimes conservers of ethnic languages and sometimes leaders in the shift away from them.

13. The generality of these patterns of interruption has been questioned by some researchers and deserves more study. Other studies of parent-child interaction provide interesting and contrasting evidence of power asymmetry in speech and how it supports American cultural conceptions about gender. Ochs (in press) compared Samoan and middle-class American patterns of childrearing and found that American mothers accommodate much more to children, both verbally and nonverbally; indeed, the middle-class image of the "good mother" requires this. For instance, American mothers routinely reinterpret speech and action that are joint activities of mother and child as the praiseworthy accomplishment of the child alone. This has important consequences for children's view of women. It not only constructs the child as more competent than he or she really is but also serves to deny or veil the contribution and greater knowledge of the female caregiver. For both male and female children, American devaluations of women are reproduced through such interaction.

14. Interactions in many other institutions deserve more attention in these terms. For a recent attempt to understand interactions between women patients and doctors in American clinics see Fisher (1988). For a discussion of educational reform based on similar ideas, see Treichler and Kramarae (1983), and the very different approach of Walkerdine (1985).

15. The Ardeners' thesis is more complex, but the parts I have summarized have had strong influence not only on the Ardener's own circle (see articles in Ardener 1975) but also on other feminist writers such as Showalter, Kramarae, Spender, and Warren and Bourque (1985).

16. Many scholars argue that the Western genre of autobiography arose in the late Middle Ages, in the midst of profoundly reformulated notions of individualism and its relation to the movement of history (Olney 1980; Stanton 1984). Because these notions of the new "Man" assumed a male subject, women's autobiographies in the West have often been perceived as illegitimate and suspect (Smith 1987: 43). Kwaio women's refusal to recite the personal narratives and societal rules characteristic of men's responses to similar ethnographic questions, their insistence instead on moral

justifications of womanhood, evoke a parallel strategy in Western women's autobiographies, in which a recurring figure of divided consciousness can be read as the authors' awareness that they are being read as *women* and thus judged differently in their self-constructions (Smith 1987).

17. The evidence about class is more ambiguous when birth metaphors are also considered. Women of all classes (as well as some doctors) have invented new metaphors for birth that reject the analogy between the production of goods and the production of babies. Such new metaphors, essential for *re*-organizing experience, have been embodied in the varied new institutions of birth clinics, at-home births and other women's health movements in the United States and Europe. As Martin (1987) argues, linguistic practices are not only reflexes of existing structural categories of speakers, but are also newly created, forming the conditions necessary to build new institutional structures.

BIBLIOGRAPHY

Abu-Lughod, L. 1986. *Veiled sentiments.* Berkeley, Los Angeles, London: University of California Press.

Ardener, E. 1975. Belief and the problem of women. In *Perceiving women.* S. Ardener, ed. London: Malaby.

Ardener, S. 1975. Introduction. In *Perceiving women.* S. Ardener, ed. London: Malaby.

Asad, T. 1986. The concept of cultural translation in British social anthropology. In *Writing culture.* J. Clifford and G. Marcus, eds. Berkeley, Los Angeles, London: University of California Press.

Basso, K. 1979. *Portraits of the whiteman.* New York: Cambridge University Press.

Bauman, R. 1983. *Let your words be few.* New York: Cambridge University Press.

Borker, R. 1980. Anthropology. In *Language and women in literature and society.* S. McConnell-Ginet, R. Borker, and N. Furman, eds. New York: Praeger.

Bourdieu, P. 1977a. *Outline of a theory of practice.* New York: Cambridge University Press.

———. 1977b. The economics of linguistic exchanges. *Social Science Information* 16 (6): 645–668.

Brenneis, D. L., and F. Myers. 1984. *Dangerous words.* New York: New York University Press.

Brown, P. 1980. How and why are women more polite: Some evidence from a Mayan community. In *Women and language in literature and society.* S. McConnell-Ginet, R. Borker, and N. Furman, eds. New York: Praeger.

Cameron, D. 1985. *Feminism and linguistic theory.* New York: St. Martin's Press.

Clifford, J. and G. Marcus, eds. 1986. *Writing culture.* Berkeley, Los Angeles, London: University of California Press.

Connell, R. W. 1987. *Gender and power.* Stanford: Stanford University Press.

Coplan, D. B. 1987. Eloquent knowledge: Lesotho migrants' songs and the anthropology of experience. *American Ethnologist* 14 (3): 413–433.

Douglas, Ann. 1977. *The feminization of American culture.* New York: Alfred A. Knopf.

Edelsky, C. 1981. Whose got the floor? *Language in Society* 10 (3): 383–422.

Erickson, F., and J. Schultz. 1982. *The counselor as gatekeeper*. New York: Academic Press.

Fisher, S. 1988. *In the patient's best interest*. New Brunswick, N.J.: Rutgers University Press.

Fishman, P. 1978. Interaction: The work women do. *Social Problems* 25 (4): 397–406.

Foucault, M. 1978. *The history of sexuality*. Vol. 1. New York: Pantheon.

———. 1980. *Power/knowledge: Selected interviews and other writings*. Colin Gordon, ed. New York: Pantheon.

Furman, N. 1980. Textual feminism. In *Women and language in literature and society*. S. McConnell-Ginet, R. Borker, and N. Furman, eds. New York: Praeger.

Gal, S. 1978. Peasant men can't get wives: Language and sex roles in a bilingual community. *Language in Society* 7 (1): 1–17.

Gerson, J., and K. Peiss. 1985. Boundaries, negotiation, consciousness: Reconceptualizing gender relations. *Social Problems* 32 (4): 317–331.

Gilligan, C. 1982. *In a different voice*. Cambridge, Mass.: Harvard University Press.

Goodwin, M. 1980. Directive-response speech sequences in girls' and boys' task activities. In *Women and language in literature and society*. S. McConnell-Ginet, R. Borker, and N. Furman, eds. New York: Praeger.

Goodwin, M., and C. Goodwin. 1987. Children's arguing. In *Language, gender and sex in comparative perspective*. S. Philips, S. Steele, and C. Tanz, eds. New York: Cambridge University Press.

Gumperz, J. 1982. *Discourse strategies*. New York: Cambridge University Press.

Harding, S. 1975. Women and words in a Spanish village. In *Toward an anthropology of women*. R. Reiter, ed. New York: Monthly Review.

Harris, O. 1980. The power of signs: Gender, culture and the wild in the Bolivian Andes. In *Nature, culture and gender*. C. MacCormack and M. Strathern, eds. New York: Cambridge University Press.

Haltunnen, K. 1982. *Confidence men and painted women*. New Haven: Yale University Press.

Heath, S. 1983. *Ways with words*. New York: Cambridge University Press.

Herzfeld, M. 1985. *The poetics of manhood*. Princeton: Princeton University Press.

Hymes, D. 1974. *Foundations in sociolinguistics*. Philadelphia: University of Pennsylvania Press.

Ifeka-Moller, C. 1975. Female militancy and colonial revolt: The Women's War of 1929, eastern Nigeria. In *Perceiving women*. S. Ardener, ed. London: Malaby.

Irvine, J. 1979. Formality and informality in communicative events. *American Anthropologist* 81: 779–790.

Jordan, R. A., and F. A. DeCaro. 1986. Women and the study of folklore. *Signs* 11 (3): 500–518.

Keenan, E. 1974. Norm-makers and norm-breakers: Uses of speech by men and women in a Malagasy community. In *Explorations in the ethnography of speaking*. R. Bauman and J. Sherzer, eds. New York: Cambridge University Press.

Keesing, R. 1985. Kwaio women speak: The micropolitics of autobiography in a Solomon Island society. *American Anthropologist* 87 (1): 27–39.

Kelly-Gadol, J. 1976. The social relation of the sexes: Methodological implications of women's history. *Signs* 1: 809–824.

Kramarae, C. 1980. Gender: How she speaks. In *Attitudes towards language variation*. E. B. Ryan and H. Giles, eds. London: Edward Arnold.

Labov, W. 1974. *Sociolinguistic patterns*. Philadelphia: University of Pennsylvania Press.

Lakoff, R. 1975. *Language and women's place*. New York.

Lears, J. 1985. The concept of cultural hegemony: Problems and possibilities. *American Historical Review* 90: 567–593.

Lebsock, S. 1987. "*A share of honor*": *Virginia women 1600–1945*. Richmond: Virginia State Library.

Lederman, R. 1984. Who speaks here: Formality and the politics of gender in Mendi, Highland Papua New Guinea. In *Dangerous words*. D. Brenneis and F. Myers, eds. New York: NYU Press.

Lukes, S. 1974. *Power: A radical view*. London: Macmillan.

Maltz, D., and R. Borker. 1982. A cultural approach to male-female miscommunication. In *Language and social identity*, J. Gumperz, ed. New York: Cambridge University Press.

Martin, E. 1987. *The woman in the body*. Boston: Beacon.

McConnell-Ginet, S. 1988. Language and gender. In *Linguistics: The Cambridge survey*. F. Newmeyer, ed. New York: Cambridge University Press.

Michaels, S. 1981. "Sharing time": Children's narrative styles and differential access to literacy. *Language in Society* 10 (3): 423–442.

Moi, T. 1985. *Sexual/textual politics*. London: Methuen.

O'Barr, W. M., and B. K. Atkins. 1980. "Women's language" or "powerless language"? In *Women and language in literature and society*. S. McConnell-Ginet et al., eds. New York: Praeger.

Ochs, E. 1987. The impact of stratification and socialization on men's and women's speech in Western Samoa. In *Language, gender and sex in comparative perspective*. S. Philips et al., eds. New York: Cambridge University Press.

———. In press. Indexing gender. In *Gender hierarchies*. Barbara Miller, ed.

Olney, J. 1980. Autobiography and the cultural moment. In *Autobiography: Essays theoretical and critical*. J. Olney, ed. Princeton: Princeton University Press.

Outram, D. 1987. Le langage male de la vertu: Women and the discourse of the French Revolution. In *The social history of language*. P. Burke and R. Porter, eds. New York: Cambridge University Press.

Philips, S. 1987. Introduction. In *Language, gender and sex in comparative perspective*. S. Philips et al., eds. New York: Cambridge University Press.

Polier, N., and W. Roseberry. 1988. Tristes tropes. MS. New York: New School for Social Research.

Radway, J. 1984. *Reading the romance*. Chapel Hill: University of North Carolina Press.

Rubin, G. 1975. The traffic in women: Notes on the "political economy" of sex. In *Toward an anthropology of women*. R. Reiter, ed. New York: Monthly Review.

Sattel, J. W. 1983. Men, inexpressiveness and power. In *Language, gender and society*. B. Thorne, C. Kramarae, and N. Henley, eds. Rowley, Mass.: Newbury House.

Schieffelin, B. 1987. Do different worlds mean different words?: An example from Papua New Guinea. In *Language, gender and sex in comparative perspective*. S. Philips et al., eds. New York: Cambridge University Press.

Sherzer, J. 1987. A diversity of voices: Men's and women's speech in ethnographic perspective. In *Language, gender and sex in comparative perspective*. S. Philips et al., eds. New York: Cambridge University Press.

Silverstein, M. 1985. Language and the culture of gender: At the intersection of structure, usage and ideology. In *Signs in society*. E. Mertz and R. Permentier, eds. New York: Academic.

Smith, S. 1987. *A poetics of women's autobiography*. Bloomington: University of Indiana Press.

Smith-Rosenberg, C. 1985. *Disorderly conduct: Visions of gender in Victorian America*. New York: Oxford.

Stanton, D. 1984. Autogynography: Is the subject different? In *The female autograph*. D. Stanton, ed. Chicago: University of Chicago Press.

Steedman, C., C. Unwin, and V. Walkerdine, eds. 1985. *Language, gender and childhood*. London: Routledge & Kegan Paul.

Tannen, D., and M. Saville-Troike, eds. 1984. *Perspectives on silence*. Washington, D.C.: Georgetown University Press.

Thorne, B., C. Kramarae, and N. Henley. 1983. Language, gender and society: Opening a second decade of research. In *Language, gender and society*. B. Thorne et al., eds. Rowley, Mass.: Newbury House.

Treichler, P. A., and C. Kramarae. 1983. Women's talk in the ivory tower. *Communication Quarterly* 31 (2): 118–132.

Trudgill, P. 1983. Sex and covert prestige: Linguistic change in an urban dialect of Norwich. In *Language in use*. J. Baugh and J. Sherzer, eds. Englewood Cliffs, N.J.: Prentice-Hall.

Walkerdine, V. 1985. On the regulation of speaking and silence. In Carolyn Steedman, Cathy Urwin and Valerie Walkerdine, eds. *Language, gender and childhood* London: Routledge and Kegan Paul.

Walkowitz, J. 1986. Science, feminism and romance: The Men's and Women's Club 1885–1889. *History Workshop Journal* (Spring): 37–59.

Warren, K, and S. Bourque. 1985. Gender, power and communication: Responses to political muting in the Andes. In *Women living change*. S. Bourque and D. R. Divine, eds. Philadelphia: Temple University Press.

West, C. and D. Zimmerman. 1983. Small insults: A study of interruptions in cross-sex conversations between unacquainted persons. In *Language, gender and society*. B. Thorne et al., eds. Rowley, Mass.: Newbury House.

Williams, R. 1973. Base and superstructure in Marxist cultural theory. *New Left Review* 82: 3–16.

Willis, P. 1977. *Learning to labor*. Westmead, England: Saxon House.

FIVE

Baboons with Briefcases vs. Langurs in Lipstick

Feminism and Functionalism in Primate Studies[1]

Susan Sperling

Studies of monkeys and apes have never been just about monkeys and apes. Historically, humans have wondered about the status of nonhuman primates, about the ways in which they are like and unlike us. With the rise of evolutionary thought in nineteenth-century Europe, our visions of the nonhuman primates became firmly tied to understandings of our own development over evolutionary time. In the Western imagination, primates are now central to the iconography of the human past, including the meanings of sexual divisions in human societies.

Modern primate studies arose largely through "natural" field studies in decolonized Africa in the period following World War II.[2] Soon thereafter, anthropological primatologists and their advocates in other disciplines began to fit data about monkeys and apes into models of human evolution.[3] Field and laboratory observations of primates have produced a large body of data on the behavior of diverse species. The integration of these facts into models for human evolution has consumed over two decades of scholarship. Gender differences in hominids (humans and proto-humans) have been a major focus of these models, which have often proposed changing reproductive behavior as the central factor in the hominid transition.[4]

Women—from "media stars" such as Jane Goodall and Dian Fossey to well-known academics such as Jeanne Altmann, Alison Richard, and Thelma Rowell—have always been a visible element in the demographics of modern primate research. This fact alone has sometimes produced a vague sense that feminist "correctives" to male models of primate behavior exist, but such an impression can be deceptive. The history of accounts of gendered behaviors among primates cannot be encompassed by a simple evolutionary story of the triumph of good feminist women over bad sexist men. In order to assess the feminist tree in primatology, it is necessary to view it as part of an entire forest of modern intellectual devolopments.

Theories about the evolution of human behavior incorporating primatological data have most often been guided by functionalist agendas. Functionalists assume that all behaviors can be explained in terms of their adaptiveness to a larger social system or, in more recent theories, to the reproductive goals of individuals. Functionalists tend to ignore both proximate causes of behaviors and the development of specific behaviors over time.

For over two decades, an obsession with gender role dimorphism (sexually differing behaviors) as an adaptative mechanism has impeded our understanding of the origins and maintenance of such sexually distinct behaviors in primates—behaviors that, after all, vary greatly both within and across species. Functionalist interpretations of primate behavior view sexually dimorphic traits as end-points of natural selection and attempt to explain the selective pressures that might have been responsible for bringing these traits into being, while failing to explain their mechanisms of development and great variety of expressions. These approaches propose a kind of Panglossian philosophy that all behavior is adaptive, although there is much accumulating evidence that this is by no means the case.

The uses of nonhuman primate behavior for understanding human evolution raise important epistemological questions about how we know things in evolutionary science; these questions are beginning to be addressed by feminist scholars and others in the evolutionary sciences. As Stephen Jay Gould (1986) and others have argued, many aspects of morphology and behavior cannot be explained only as direct results of natural selection. Researchers must begin to examine the multiply contingent pathways along which biological systems develop and the complex ways in which extra-organismic factors interact with organisms at every stage of development. Emphasis on contingency in the development of biological and behavioral systems leads inevitably away from the biological essentialism (the belief that gendered behaviors are genetically determined) so pervasive in functionalist evolutionary models in primatology.

But such epistemological critiques of functionalism are rarely raised outside the scholarly enclaves in which evolutionary biologists meet. Such discourse almost never reaches social scientists, among whom the debate has been disastrously constructed as *one between reductionists in the biological and evolutionary sciences who contend that genetic mechanisms selected over phylogenetic history control important human behaviors, and feminists and other cultural constructionists who deny that biology has any important role in human experience.* In both scholarly and popular discussions, writers disseminate the currently privileged functionalist model in journals, at conferences, and in the popular press.[5] Although a number of primatologists have argued for years against the obsession with ultimate causality that has come to dominate the field, their ideas have not been widely conveyed outside the discipline.[6]

Two theories of ultimate causality have dominated primatological models for the origins of monkey, ape, and human gendered behavior: structural-functionalism and sociobiology. The structural-functionalist model, British social anthropology's key contribution to twentieth-century social science, explains the structural pattern of social institutions in terms of how they function as integrated systems to fulfill individual and societal human needs. Anthropologists studying nonhuman primates in the period following World War II translated this theory to their observations of nonhuman primates; they viewed savannah baboon behaviors as adaptations that "functioned" to promote both individual survival and to maintain stable troop life. As we shall see, this perspective structured much theory about the evolution of human gendered behaviors as extrapolated from studies of baboons and other monkeys and apes. Male dominance was viewed as functioning to organize and control the troop in a simple analogy to the functions of political leadership in human cultures. There are many problems with this assumption.

In the mid-1970s, sociobiology replaced structural-functionalism as the preeminent explanatory model. According to the sociobiologists, behaviors always evolve that maximize the reproductive fitness of individuals (the relative percentage of genes passed on to future generations). Although differing in some significant ways, both models explain the existence of gender dimorphic behaviors as functioning to increase evolutionary fitness and as controlled in unspecified ways by genes. Both kinds of functionalist arguments for the origin of sexually dimorphic behaviors among humans explain these behaviors as adaptations to past selective pressures in primate or hominid phylogeny. In the past, many of these reconstructions have been overtly sexist; some more recent functionalist hypotheses have attempted to redress former androcentric biases. For instance, some sociobiologists have recently asserted that female primates harass each other in an effort to increase their own genetic advantages (such an interpretation has been applied to attacks on pregnant monkey and ape mothers by other females—assumed to be efforts to maximize the number of offspring of the attacking female at the expense of the victim). Superficially, such models may seem at times to tell a "good" feminist primate story—for example, by positing that female primates are aggressive strategists in pursuit of their own reproductive advantages rather than passive objects over which males compete. But these new narratives, although more palatable for some feminists, rest on poor empirical foundations. We do not fully understand the biological, social, and ecological roots of nonhuman primate aggression. But in order to understand feminist sociobiology and its deficiencies we need a better sense of the unfolding story of primate studies and structural-functionalist and sociobiological models.

STRUCTURAL-FUNCTIONALIST MODELS OF PRIMATE
GENDERED BEHAVIOR

When I began my tenure as a graduate student in physical anthropology at Berkeley in the 1970s, primate studies had emerged from a period in which a relatively small number of researchers collected natural histories of a variety of primate species in the field and had entered an era of widespread structural-functionalist model building. The first period, the natural-history stage of primate studies, occurred roughly between 1950–1965. In the second stage (from the mid-1960s to late 1970s) data from a variety of field studies, particularly those of savannah baboons and the chimpanzees of the Gombe Reserve in Tanzania, were incorporated into structural-functionalist models for human evolution centering on the sexual division of labor, the origins of the family, and the origins of human gendered behavior. The third phase came in the late 1970s with the hegemony of sociobiology as the functionalist model *par excellence* for understanding behavioral evolution.[7]

Between the two world wars, the primatological enterprise declined, to reemerge in the 1950s. Physical anthropologist Sherwood Washburn has pointed out the relationship between changes in transportation and the development of antibiotics as enabling graduate students from the West to undertake research ventures in the third world (Haraway 1989).

The first wave of anthropological primatology included a number of long-term studies that laid the foundations of the discipline (Haraway 1989). Jeanne and Stuart Altmann (Altmann and Altmann 1970) studied baboon ecology and behavior at Amboseli National Park, Kenya; Stuart Altmann (Altmann 1962) initiated research on rhesus monkeys on the Carribbean Island of Cayo Santiago, followed by Donald Sade and his student Elizabeth Missakian (Sade 1965, 1967) and others, and several researchers worked on the Smithsonian project with howler monkeys at Barro Colorado (Collias and Southwick 1952). Research accelerated in the 1960s: Goodall (1963) began her observations at the Gombe Stream Reserve in Tanzania (Japanese workers had studied chimpanzees in Tanzania since 1965 [Nishida 1972]); Struhsaker and others studied several species of monkeys in the Kibale Forest of Uganda (Struhsaker 1971); DeVore and Washburn (Washburn and DeVore 1961) studied savannah baboons in the Serengeti National Park, Kenya; Fossey intiated observations of mountain gorillas in 1967 in Rwanda's Parc des Volcans (Fossey 1970); and Phyllis Dolhinow (1972) researched Indian langur monkeys at several sites in India. Most of these studies (and this is only a partial list) were descriptive natural histories with few explicit links made to human evolution. [8]

During the second stage of modern primatology, which began in the mid-1960s, structural-functionalist analysis became central to the problem-oriented studies that replaced the earlier emphasis on natural history.[9] Primatology was then, as it is today, a heterogenous field that included research on proximate causal factors affecting social behavior and on the complex interaction between social structure, behavior, and ecology (socioecology).[10] But it is the structural-functionalist grand theory builders, those who have focused exclusively on ultimate causality, who have been the progenitors of the most influential and popular visions of primate behavior.

In the functionalist models of the 1960s and 1970s, all aspects of behavior within a primate troop were explained as adaptive mechanisms. Thus, the roles of females and males in different species were interpreted as selected during the phylogenetic history of the species because they "functioned" to promote survival. An article by psychologists Carol McGuinness and Karl Pribram illustrates a pervasive phenomenon of the second wave of primatology, the insertion of primatological data into structural-functionalist models for the evolution of gendered human behavior:

> In all primate societies the division of labor by gender creates a highly stable social system, the dominant males controlling territorial boundaries and maintaining order among lesser males by containing and preventing their aggression, the females tending the young and forming alliances with other females. Human primates follow this same pattern so remarkably that it is not difficult to argue for biological bases for the type of social order that channels aggression to guard the territory which in turn maintains an equable environment for the young. (Quoted in Goldman 1978: 56)

McGuinness and Pribram's interpretation appeared in *Psychology Today*, one of many popular journals publishing articles on human nature and its biological roots. Although the template here is the savannah baboon troop as described by Washburn and DeVore—and contested early in this period by Rowell and others with data from baboon groups calling into question all of the fundamental assumptions of the savannah model (Rowell found that older females in her sample determined the route of daily foraging)—"all primate species" collapsed the diversity and specificity of data on primates into a single category, "primate societies." Here, and in a plethora of popular books and articles published during this period, monkeys and apes were used explicitly as exemplars of earlier stages of human evolution. The ubiquitous primate ancestral group now occupied a position like that of "tribal societies" in the evolutionary schemas of nineteenth-century anthropologists. The diffusion of cultural relativism into all branches of modern social science had made it embarrassing and untenable to fit tribal groups into this slot. If "primitives" were our equals and had complex and meaningful cultures, they could not also represent the proto-human past. But monkeys and apes provided the new early ancestral group from which human institutions could be seen to have evolved.

This replacement of human "primitives" by nonhuman primates also relates to global political events of the postwar period: "With the progressive disappearance of human 'primitives' as legitimate objects of knowledge and colonial rule, and with the discrediting of pre-war eugenics, Western anthropologists had to rethink the meaning and processes of the formation of 'man'" (Haraway 1989: 7). The substitution of primates for "primitives" thus neatly retained an important Western cosmological category for use in the era of decolonization and the construction of the third world.

One consequence of this key insertion of the nonhuman primate in the Western symbolic niche for "primitive progenitor" was an implied obliteration of the border between human and nonhuman. The passage by McGuinness and Pribram is a mass of terminological ambiguities. What is meant by terms such as "the divison of labor" when referring to nonhuman primates, and does this term mean the same thing when applied to human groups? Monkeys and apes do not have a division of labor along gender lines as do human cultures; each animal performs subsistence tasks in approximately the same way, consuming what is individually foraged on the spot. Human divisions of labor by sex are complex historical and socioeconomic phenomena embroidered with symbolic meanings unavailable to animals. But when DeVore and Hall wrote, "The baboon troop is organized around the dominance hierarchy of adult males" (1965: 54), they meant it both literally and figuratively. They perceived dominant males as "culturally" binding together a loose, potentially chaotic aggregate of females, subadult males, and young. In the same work, they offered a spatial schematization of primate societies: a series of concentric circles with the most dominant animals in the center. DeVore and Hall visualized male dominance as, literally, the cement of primate social organization.

Robin Fox, the social anthropologist, among many others, recognized the utility of the baboon data for evolutionary model building and wrote of it in the *New York Times Magazine* as "the area where evolutionary studies, primatology, and social anthropology meet in earnest." About the baboon model, he wrote:

> If this kind of social system was, in fact, typical of man's [*sic*] ancestors, then it provides some powerful clues concerning the evolution of the brain. Clearly it was those animals with the best brains who were going to do the breeding and each generation would see a ruthless selection of the best-brained males, with the dumbest and weakest going to the wall. (1968: 87)

This view of baboon society was highly anthropomorphic: it scandalously ignored the whole question of the lack of close phylogenetic relationship between human and baboon (baboons, like other monkeys, are biologically much more unlike humans than are apes such as chimpanzees and gorillas). The baboons were pictured as politically organized in a very human, albeit totalitarian, fashion (the baboon troop is, according to Fox, "anything but democratic" [p. 82]), centered around their leaders who had many of the idealized attributes of human male leadership in Western culture. This use of the baboon troop as model for ancestral human populations was very influential in forming both sexist and anthropomorphic views of monkeys in popular culture.

The baboon model was compatible with, and tended to bolster, a Hobbesian view of human society, while the use of chimpanzee behavior originally tended to reflect a more benign view, stressing the mother-infant pair and a more flexible, less hierarchical social structure. But many of the assumptions underlying the early use of ape and baboon behavioral data in models for hominid evolution were equivalent: ape and monkey behaviors were microcosms of human social behavior and political life.

Linda Fedigan (1986) has reviewed many of the evolutionary reconstructions of this period. She points out that the "baboonization" of early human life in such models rested on a savannah ecological analogy: since protohominids evolved on the African Savannah, presumably they would have shared certain selective pressures with modern baboon troops, particularly for predator-protection by large males.[11] Fedigan argues that the other primary model for protohominid evolution—that of the chimpanzees studied by Goodall at the Gombe Reserve in Tanzania—was far more preferable. Here the analogy rested on a phylogenetic relationship, between chimp and human, which is immensely closer. This model emphasized the mother-offspring bond, sharing within the matrifocal family, the immigration of young females to new groups, birth-spacing, and temporary sex-bonding. It is to this chimpanzee behavioral model that the first wave of feminist authors, in particular the constructors of the "woman the gatherer" model (Tanner and Zihlman 1976) would turn for primatological evidence of the social centrality of females in early hominid evolution.

Fedigan points out that the "baboonization" of protohominids became so common that by the early to mid-1970s not a single introductory text in human evolution omitted reference to it. As Rowell (1974) and other critics of this model stressed, many of the generalizations and assumptions about function made by Washburn and DeVore were unsubstantiated by data from other research sites. For instance, Rowell's studies of troop movement among forest baboons indicated that the direction of daily foraging routes was determined by a core of mature females, rather than by the dominant males. As feminist scholars such as Sandra Harding (1986) and Donna Haraway (1989) note, women primatologists have often had a different vision of group structure and behavior because they attended to female actors in a way that male primatologists did not. Thus, the focus on female behavior in baboons and a variety of other species became fuel for the critical deconstructions of the baboon model during the 1970s. In addition, a number of studies questioned the assumption that male dominance conferred a reproductive advantage on particular males, thus contributing to selection for male aggression (Fedigan 1983).

Nonhuman primates became the missing link in the evolutionary models of the late 1960s and 1970s. But nonhuman primates are as unwieldy a link as were the "primitives" of the early evolutionists. All living species of organisms have undergone separate histories combining both evolutionary and chance events. There is immense variation in behavior among primate species, and cross-phylum generalizations are hard to make. For instance, sexual behavior among monkeys and apes exhibits a wide variety of patterns that defy neat phylogenetic analysis. Monkeys display a variety of mating patterns (Rowell 1972), but the most telling data in this regard are from the apes (Nadler 1975). There are significant differences between the sexual behavior of chimpanzee, gorilla, and orangutan which in no way relate to their phylogenetic closeness to humans. For instance, hormonal and behavioral states appear closely correlated in gorilla reproductive behavior, somewhat less so in chimps, and least of all in orangutans. But chimpanzees are much more closely related to humans than are orangutans. Thus, all three of the great apes display different mating patterns that in no way relate to their phylogenetic closeness to humans. This contradicts the linear evolutionist's view that the more advanced the phylogenetic relationship to humans, the less hormonal control of sexual behavior and greater resemblance to human reproductive behavior will be found in a species of animal.

Social anthropologist and popularizer Robin Fox is typical of the many writers who ignored all these scientific arguments in their headlong quest for evolutionary legitimations of male dominance among humans. In *Biosocial Anthropology* (1975) Fox was quite explicit about his use of nonhuman primates as replacements for human "primitives":

> Older theorists speculated on the "earliest conditions of man," and as we know debates raged between proponents of "primitive promiscuity" and "primitive monogamy." The former were usually seen as a prelude to "matriarchy" (now popular again) and the latter to "patriarchy." This has all been dismissed as ridiculous for well-known reasons. But I think we can now go back to the question in a different way. We know a great deal about primates which can tell us what is behaviorally available to our order in general and, therefore, what must have been available by way of a behavioral repertoire to our ancestors . . . "early man" then, in this sense, was less like modern man gone wild than like a primate tamed. *And even if we cannot deduce accurately the kinship systems of early man* [sic] *from those of the most primitive humans, we can do something better—we can distill the essence of kinship systems on the basis of comparative knowledge and find the elements of such systems that are logically, and hence in all probability chronologically, the "elementary forms of kinship."* (11; my emphasis)

The differences between Fox's assumptions and the Victorian evolutionists' are negligible. Fox traced the evolution of human kinship through the primates, borrowing, as he admits, "somewhat recklessly from the jargon of social anthropology, descent and alliance" (11). According to his analysis, these two elements are present in nonhuman primate social systems but are only combined in human groups. He divides primate social systems into two types, single-male and multi-male groups, which all have in common

> a threefold division of the larger group into: a) adult males; b) females and young; c) peripheral males. We can look at any primate social system, including our own, in terms of the "accommodations" made between these three blocks. (1975: 13)

According to Fox, in single-male groups (gorillas and hamadryas baboons) the basic unit is the "polygenous family," while in the multi-male group (common baboons, chimpanzees) "if the sexual relationship is brief and un-enduring, the consanguineal relationship is long lasting and of central importance" (1975: 15). The phylogenetic histories of different primates are thus collapsed into several categories with a certain internal consistency but little relationship to actual data.[12] Once Fox raises the question of the relationship of complex human behaviors to nonhuman primate behavioral variation, his evidence becomes a confusing array of randomly chosen bits and pieces of behavior from species with varying phylogenetic relationships to one another and to humans. Although nodding briefly at the issue of variation, Fox goes on to the heart of his argument about nonhuman primates and human culture:

> [T]he real question is do the rules represent more than a "labelling" procedure for behavior that would occur anyway? . . .
>   If group A and B were called "Eaglehawk" and "Crow," and the various lineages "snake," "beaver," "bear," "antelope," etc., then a picture emerges of a proto-society on a clan moiety basis . . .

An important consequence of this approach is that it obscures many of the culturally unique aspects of human kinship that make it fundamentally different from social relations among nonhumans; the widespread existence of putative kin among human cultures is but one example.

Examples of this missing link approach to the use of nonhuman primate behavior abound in the literature of this period, often focusing on gendered behavior and its presumed "functions." Many popularizations of this approach have had a wide audience (Morris 1967; Reynolds 1981). In one such account, the sexologist and gerontologist Alex Comfort explained the presumed continual receptivity of human females:

> At some point in primate evolution, the female became receptive all year round and even throughout pregnancy. This apparently trifling change in behavior

was probably the trigger, or one of the triggers, which set off the evolution of man [*sic*]. Between baboons and higher apes we find the effects of this change. Baboons behave very like other pack-living animals. Higher apes, with sexual activity continuing all the year round, and unrelated to heat, develop a hetero-sexual social life which is not confined to the coital encounter. (1966: 13)

Comfort's order of ascent is baboon, ape, and human, and the character "continual sexual receptivity" is traced along this ladder in much the same way that the Victorians associated "primitive promiscuity" with savages, group marriage with barbarians, and monogamy with civilized humans.

In a parallel argument for neuroanatomy Hodos (1970) has criticized the persistence of this *scala naturae* or "Great Chain" concept in the neurosci-ences, citing the confusion between a phylogenetic scale or ladder and a phy-logenetic tree. In neuroanatomical texts the brains of codfish, frog, alligator, goose, cat, and human are frequently compared as if they are in evolutionary order. But one living form is not ancestral to another. Such comparisons often imply that a particular species represents the essence of its type (for instance, the concept of the brain of "the reptile" or "the mammal"). Hodos's critique may be applied equally well to functionalist evolutionary models that have attempted to trace the evolution of a behavioral character-istic down the ladder from human to baboon, as Fox does with human kinship (1975*a*) or Comfort with reproduction. As we move up and down the phylogenetic scale, monkeys and apes are anthropomorphized, and behaviors of diverse species are used as simple analogues of human characteristics. Much of the "second wave" scholarly and popular evolutionary writing that uses nonhuman primate models reproduces this logical failing. Selected ex-amples of group structure, kinship, and dominance behavior in nonhuman primates are viewed as precursors of human social structure and behavior. The influence of these models on popular perceptions of the relationship of humans to animals and the meanings of gender divisions has been profound.

SOCIOBIOLOGY AND THE EVOLUTION OF GENDERED BEHAVIOR IN PRIMATES

The 1975 publication of *Sociobiology: The New Synthesis* by Harvard entomol-ogist E. O. Wilson was a signal event for students of animal behavior in numerous disciplines. Wilson makes two major assertions in *Sociobiology*: that all important social behaviors are genetically controlled, and that natural selection of the genome is caused by a set of specific adaptive mechanisms (kin selection), which produce behaviors maximizing an organism's ability to contribute the greatest number of genes to the next generation. The historical roots of sociobiology lie in nineteenth- and early twentieth-century argu-ments about the level at which natural selection operates—that of the group or the individual. Evolutionists like Darwin, Haldane, Wright, and Wynne-

Edwards contended that traits may be selected because they are advantageous for populations. In the 1960s, William Hamilton and Robert Trivers proposed that traits can only be selected at the individual level, and that all social behaviors are tightly genetically controlled.

Hamilton's theory of kin selection is based upon the concept that the "fitness" of an organism has two components: (1) "fitness" gained through the replication of its own genetic material through reproduction, and (2) "inclusive fitness" gained from the replication of copies of its own genes carried in others as a result of its actions (Hamilton 1964). According to this theory, when an organism behaves altruistically toward related individuals, fitness benefits to kin also benefit the organism, but the actor's benefits are devalued by the coefficient of relatedness between actor and relatives. Thus, genes are viewed as being selected because they contribute to their own perpetuation, regardless of the organism of which they are a part. Trivers (1972) defined reciprocal altruism as behavior that appears to be altruistic but, given mutual dependence in a group, may be selected if it confers indirect benefits on the altruist.[13]

Wilson took the concept of kin selection and applied it to all animal and human behavior from the social insects to humans, suggesting that the social sciences and biological sciences be subsumed by sociobiology. Not surprisingly, many scientists viewed the idea of their disciplines' cannibalistic incorporation into the body of sociobiology as an unsavory prospect. Some objected on political grounds to its explicit reductionism and potential for racist and sexist interpretations. The Boston-based collective "Science for the People" issued a critical attack on sociobiology, calling it another form of biological determinism like nineteenth-century eugenics and Social Darwinism (1976). At the same time, sociobiology began to establish a foothold in American and European departments of anthropology, zoology, and psychology. The American Anthropological Association held a two-day symposium on sociobiology at its 1976 yearly meeting, and departments in the biological and social sciences began to offer seminars and classes on the topic. By the late 1980s it had become the dominant paradigm among anthropological primatologists, replacing the structural-functionalist models of the second period of modern primatology.

I cannot here discuss the many reasons—from national political trends to individual departmental politics—for the ascendence of sociobiology over structural-functionalism in primate studies. Researchers studying proximate mechanisms, many of them socioecologists, continued to work at various sites with little interest or involvement in postulations of ultimate causality. But, as had structural-functionalism, sociobiology became the grand theory conveyed to social scientists interested in human evolution and widely popularized through newspaper and magazine articles and popular books.[14] By the mid-1980s a number of important empirical critiques appeared deconstructing the logic of sociobiological arguments. These have yet to be widely circulated outside classes and seminars in evolutionary theory.

Early sociobiological views of the evolution of human gendered behaviors incorporated primatological data and viewed males and females as having differential reproductive strategies. Because of the presumably greater "investment" of female primates in infant-rearing, female behaviors were viewed as selected because they advanced a female's chances of gaining male protection during vulnerable periods for herself and her offspring (offspring are seen as fleshy packets of shared genes). Females were frequently pictured as conservative, coy, and passive. By contrast, it behooves males to inseminate as many females as possible, thus forwarding their attempted genetic monopoly of the future. E. O. Wilson wrote: "It pays males to be aggressive, hasty, fickle and undiscriminating. In theory it is more profitable for females to be coy, to hold back until they can identify the male with the best genes. . . . Human beings obey this biological principle faithfully" (1978). Irven DeVore and other sociobiologists have maintained that the sexual and romantic interest of middle-aged men in younger women, and their presumed uninterest in their female-age cohort, stems from selective pressures on male primates to inseminate as many fertile females as possible.[15]

Wilson applied sociobiological arguments to the meaning of the middle-class nuclear family in American culture:

> The building block of nearly all human societies is the nuclear family. . . . The populace of an American industrial city, no less than a band of hunter-gatherers in the Australian desert, is organized around this unit. In both cases the family moves between regional communities, maintaining complex ties with primary kin by means of visits (or telephone calls and letters) and the exchange of gifts. During the day the women and children remain in the residential area while the men forage for game or its symbolic equivalent in the form of money. The males cooperate in bands or deal with neighboring groups. (Wilson 1975: 553)

It is no coincidence that sociobiology and the second wave of Western feminism were simultaneous occurrences. Early sociobiologists clearly envisioned their new model as "disproving" feminism. The sociobiologist van den Berghe wrote: "Neither the National Organization for Women nor the Equal Rights Amendment will change the biological bedrock of asymmetrical parental investment" (van den Berghe 1979: 2, quoted in Kitcher: 5) Kitcher (1985) has commented on the sexism of many sociobiological arguments:

> Sometimes the expression is tinged with regretful sympathy for ideals of social justice (Wilson) at other times with a zeal to *epater les feministes* (van den Berghe). . . . [I]t is far from clear that sociobiologists appreciate the political implications of the views they promulgate. These implications become clear

when a *New York Times* series on equal rights for women concludes with a serious discussion of the limits that biology might set to women's aspirations and
when the new right in Britain and France announces its enthusiasm for the
project of human sociobiology. (Kitcher: 6)

More recently, a feminist discourse in sociobiology has shifted attention to
the presumed gender-specific reproductive strategies of female primates. By
stressing female variance, feminist sociobiologists assert that selection acts on
females as well as males to encode genetic programs for enhanced fitness.
The primatologist Sarah Hrdy (Hrdy and Williams 1983), an important contributor to this literature, has lauded the emphasis in sociobiology on
variance in reproductive success for contributing a bracing dose of feminism
to primatology. Thus, these researchers see female mate choice, female elic-
itation of male support, and protection in rearing young, as integral to the
competitive strategies of females vis-à-vis other females. They describe "prolonged female receptivity" in some nonhuman primates and human females
as an evolved mechanism to manipulate male behavior. Variation in mothering styles and skills, and the degree of selfishness of caretakers are said to
reflect variance in reproductive interests that are sometimes at odds with
those of offspring. They also describe (as kin-selection strategies) competition
between females whenever fertility and the rearing of young are limited by
access to resources, and the competition of dominant females on behalf of
their offspring by eliminating competitors or forestalling reproduction in the
mothers of potential competitors:

> Female primates have evolved to be fierce competitors and they are obsessed
> with signs of status differences or disrespect only when it pays off in terms of
> access to energy resources. . . . Female primates may compete sexually . . . they
> may harass other females, especially low-status ones, to such an extent that
> they are unable to conceive effectively, maintain gestation or adequately lac-
> tate. There are also scattered reports that females may kill and cannibalize the
> infants of low-status females, or seize them and "aunt" them to death. (Lancas-
> ter quoted in Small 1984)

This new view of females among academic sociobiologists is mirrored in
popular journalism about primate infanticide and infant abuse, and inter-
female aggression and competition. Here, human females are portrayed as
bearers of behavioral homologue from their nonhuman primate ancestors
and early hominid past, predisposing them toward certain modes of inter-
individual competition, rather than as the passive and nurturant weaklings
of some former functionalist models. In these newer accounts, female competition has taken center stage. It is tempting to blame journalists and
science writers for these lurid images and their extension to human females,
but that would be a mistake: the academic sociobiological model is clearly

meant to apply across the primate order to humans. DeVore, for example, interprets soap operas to reflect his vision of female reproductive strategies:

> Soap operas have a huge following among college students, and the female-female competition is blatant. The women on these shows use every single feminine wile. On the internationally popular soap Dynasty, for example, a divorcee sees her ex-husband's new wife riding a horse nearby. She knows the woman to be newly pregnant—so she shoots off a gun, which spooks the horse, which throws the young wife, and makes her miscarry. The divorcee's own children are living with their father and this woman; the divorcee doesn't want this new young thing to bring rival heirs into the world to compete with her children . . .
>
> Whole industries turning out everything from lipstick to perfume to designer jeans are based on the existence of female competition. The business of courting and mating is after all, a negotiation process, in which each member of the pair is negotiating with those of the opposite sex to get the best deal possible, and to beat out the competition from one's own sex. . . . I get women in my class saying I'm stereotyping women, and I say sure—I'm stereotyping the ones who make lipstick a multibillion dollar industry. It's quite a few women. Basically, I appeal to students to look inside themselves: what are life's little dilemmas? When your roommate brings home a guy to whom you're extremely attracted—does it set up any sort of conflict in your mind? (Anderson 1986: 47)

Many sociobiologists disclaim the reductionism of their popular interpreters; Wilson (1978) and Hrdy (1981) have both published statements about the importance of human cultural transmission and the possibility of change in human social relations caused by cultural factors. This is disingenuous; it has now become fashionable for both biological and environmental reductionists to claim interactionism as the only reasonable view, and then to revert immediately to the reductionist theories that belie their assertions. In fact, academic sociobiologists draw the same conclusions as their journalistic interpreters.[16]

Haraway (1986) has applauded recent "feminist sociobiology" as telling a better story for feminists than earlier functionalist models, but she notes its failure to suggest a fully alternative theory about gender differences and human origins:

> Feminist contests for authoritative accounts of evolution and behavioral biology are not simply alternatives, but equally as biased as the masculinist stories so prominent in the early decades of the field. To count as better stories, they have to better account for what it means to be *human* and *animal*. They have to offer a fuller, more coherent vision, one that allows the monkeys and apes to be seen more accurately. . . .
>
> But what will count as more accurate, fuller, more coherent? Rarely will feminist contests for scientific meaning work by replacing one paradigm with

another, by proposing and successfully establishing fully alternative accounts and theories. Rather, as a form of narrative practice or story-telling, feminist practice in primatology has worked more by altering a "field" of stories or possible explanatory accounts, by raising the cost of defending some accounts, by destabilizing the plausibility of some strategies or explanations. (80–81)

"Fully alternative accounts" of the development of gendered behaviors in primates can, and must, be developed. Feminist sociobiology does not represent progress for feminist evolutionary science because it suggests a biological essentialism at the heart of human behavior. In following its path, we abandon those research strategies that might lead us to insights about gendered aspects of human aggression, among other things.

Feminist sociobiologists have retold the story of evolution, giving females an active role, but in using the old narrative structures they tell us little about the development of complex behaviors and their context-dependent expressions. The new female primate is dressed for success and lives in a troop that resembles the modern corporation: now everyone gets to eat power lunches on the savannah. But is it advantageous merely to change one narrative element, as feminist sociobiology has done, so that the category female, like male, is constructed as active, dominant, and looking out for genetic advantages? I think not, and I want to argue instead for a deconstruction of all functionalist models, including sociobiological ones, of sex-linked primate behaviors. I think we can hope for more accurate, fuller, more coherent approaches to the study of primate gender differences (some of which may help us to understand aspects of human behavior) than those proposed by functionalists of the last two decades.

WHAT WE KNOW ABOUT GENDERED PRIMATE BEHAVIOR

Scientists now criticize many former assertions about reliably differentiating behavioral dimorphisms across primate phyla as based on incomplete data (Smuts 1987; Fedigan 1983; Bernstein 1987). The more we know about nonhuman primate behavior, the more examples of intra- and interspecific variety emerge. Several common functionalist assertions about gender differences now appear to be unsubstantiated. For instance, male monkeys and apes of a variety of different species have been described as more aggressive than conspecific females. Smuts (1987), however, finds no consistent sex difference in frequencies of aggression in numerous primate species. She focuses on the contextual factors influencing agonistic behaviors in both males and females, including how males and females influence each other, rather than positing inherent, genetically controlled behavioral dimorphisms.

Another widely proposed functionalist theory about nonhuman primates is that social dominance is highly correlated with reproductive success and that dominance behaviors have beeen selected over the phylogenetic histories of species. Bernstein (1987), in reviewing data from numerous primate studies, suggests that there is little association between dominance rank and reproductive success. Fedigan (1983) summarizes the whole era of reports on male copulations, mating success, consortship, and male dominance and concludes that none of the measures provides a convincing picture of dominant males monopolizing estrous females. High levels of male aggression and wounding during the breeding season may have more to do with male mobility, "xenophobia," and rank instability among males during the breeding season than with fighting over females (Bernstein 1987).

In many species, sexual dimorphism has seemed a significant factor in male domination of smaller females. Smuts (1987), however, notes a number of primate species in which adult females may sometimes dominate larger males. Aggression, reproductive access, and dominance are emerging as more complex, variable, and context dependent, and as less subject to generalizations easily applied cross-phyla. Nor do all, or possibly even many, primate species show a pattern of male protection from predators for females and young (their own or those of other males). Harding and Olson (1986) report that the vivid displays of male patas (a type of African monkey), long assumed to distract predators from females and young, who remained frozen in the grass, now appear to be associated with intermale competition during the breeding season. To complicate the picture further, these large African cercopithecines were thought to live in exclusively single-male groups. In fact, it is now clear that patas females mate with a variety of males.

How can we generalize with any certainty about gendered behavior in nonhuman primates? We know that female primates conceive, gestate, and lactate and that in most species it is the female who primarily nurtures the young (although nonhuman primate "nurturance" should not be confused with the cultural traditions with which this word is associated in human groups). Males inseminate females. There is little or no sexual division in subsistence labor among nonhuman primates, one fact among many others which makes them strikingly different from human beings. All nonhuman primates forage for themselves and there is little sharing of food. (A few exceptions to this generalization exist, such as the occasional opportunistic hunting by some male chimps and baboons.) In many, but not all, species of monkeys and apes, males are larger than females, more muscular, and have larger canines. Size dimorphism seems to be important in a number of species in giving priority of access to environmental incentives (such as desired grooming partners or preferred foods), but larger males by no means always dominate smaller females. Aggressive and affiliative behaviors of male and female primates vary depending on species, social context, and individual. In fact, we are confronted with an enormous range of variation in intraspecific and interspecific behavior which defies neat classificatory schemas. Rather than study the ontogeny of behaviors across the life span of individual animals—a daunting task, but one likely to yield some important clues about the development and maintenance of behaviors—many primatogists have most often continued to posit tidy *ex post facto* explanations about function.

CRITIQUES OF FUNCTIONALISM

A recent and more refined discourse in evolutionary studies has suggested that important influences on the development of organisms cannot be explained by reductionist-adaptationist models (Bateson 1981; Fausto-Sterling 1985; Gould and Vrba 1982; Kitcher 1985; Oyama 1985). Bernstein (1987) has noted the concentration on function, rather than mechanism, in the literature and points out that, although functional consequences may influence genetic change in a population's future, they do not always reflect evolutionary history. The concept that evolution always produces ideal solutions ignores many other factors that may have had varying degrees of importance in a species history: random processes, phylogenetic inertia, environmental change, and the random nature of mutation. As the zoologist Kummer noted: "Discussions of adaptiveness sometimes leave us with the impression that every trait observed in a species must by definition be ideally adaptive, whereas all we can say with certainty is that it must be tolerable, since it did not lead to extinction" (Bernstein 1987: 101).

Whether they propose masculinist or feminist arguments, both structural-functionalism and sociobiology commit the fallacy of affirming the consequent. In 1951 the ethologist Tinbergen posed a set of questions for understanding the reason for the existence of a biological structure:

1. What were the immediate preceding events leading to changes producing the structure or behavior?
2. What are the consequences of the structure (its functions)?
3. What processes from conception to the present have influenced the attributes of the structure?
4. What were the evolutionary selective pressures that influenced the genetic contributions to the structure?

It is important to note that Questions 2 and 4 are separate questions: function is a future consequence; it is not the same as evolutionary history because environments are not constant (Bernstein 1987: 101). Tinbergen's first and third questions deal with proximal and developmental factors that bring about behaviors, levels of analysis often completely ignored by functionalists but likely to yield the most interesting developmental data on gendered behavior. Tinbergen's classic construction throws into relief the error of trying to answer all questions at the level of function alone, as so many of the grand theory-builders in modern primatology have done without explicating proximal cause and mechanism.[17]

For two decades, functionalist-reductionism in primatology has seemed almost immune to sophisticated arguments about evolutionary epistemology in other disciplines, and primatologists who have addressed this problem have sometimes found themselves tarred with the brush of "anti-Darwinianism" and "antievolutionism." Gould (1987) has written of the frustrations involved in critiquing adaptationism: "A former student of mine recently completed a study proving that color patterns of certain clam shells did not have the adaptive significance usually claimed. A leading journal rejected her paper with the comment: "Why would you want to publish such nonresults?" (50–51). As Gould points out, the study of gender differences suffers from the same bias, a problem in what is privileged as publishable. Measured gender differences are reported and attract attention from the press. What we don't know is how often such differences are not found, and the results not published.[18]

Other things shape behavior beside genes, and shape it in important ways for the organisms in question. In rodents, for instance, there are a number of maternal behavioral responses resulting from developmental sensitivity to normally invariant environmental conditions. In many species, only females show parental care behaviors, whereas males are always aggressive or indifferent toward infants. But this difference is not determined solely by genetics or hormones. It is a developmental behavioral response in females, who are always present at the time of birth. Males develop some of the same caretaking patterns, for example, posturing for nursing, when exposed to newborn young. From an evolutionary point of view, such new behaviors may develop and persist in a population either because of changes in the average genotype by natural selection *or* by enduring changes in the environment in which the average genotype develops. As biologist Susan Oyama (1985) points out, an ant larva may become a worker or a queen depending on nutrition, temperature, and other variables, just as a male rodent may exhibit nurturant behaviors when exposed to certain stimuli. Control does not flow only from the gene outward. To understand the vastly more complex developmental sequences involved in the acquisition of gendered primate behavior, it is necessary to study it developmentally rather than to attempt to reduce discourse to arguments about ultimate genetic fitness. There is much more to understanding the development of behavior than retrospectively hypothesizing its adaptive function.[19] Considering the presently confounding array of data on gender-role dimorphism in different primate species, it seems likely that (1) emphasis on both context and development of behavior, (2) a rejection of essentialism and gender dualism, and (3) focus on the interaction between organisms and their environments of development are likely to provide both better questions and answers about behavioral dimorphism (Smuts 1987). This does not mandate the complete abandonment of functionalist models, but their integration with other levels of causality.

TOWARD AN EPIGENETIC PERSPECTIVE ON GENDERED
PRIMATE BEHAVIOR

Although linear functionalist agendas have prevailed in reconstructions of the evolution of human gendered behavior, views of what female and male monkeys and apes are doing, and why they are doing it, have changed considerably.[20] The new assertions of "feminist sociobiology" can be analyzed in the light of recent epistemological discourse in feminist theory. Haraway and others have contextualized primatology both historically and culturally: some compelling feminist deconstructions have viewed primatology as a mythic science of "good stories" and "bad stories." Primates are icons for us. They seem to live at the boundary of nature and culture, and the ways they appear in current Western symbolism reflect the political and socioeconomic discourses of the historical periods during which primate studies has developed as a discipline. But postmodern feminist deconstructions of primatology have tended to avoid the issue of good science versus bad science in relationship to feminist goals.[21]

Harding's recent treatment of the "science question in feminism" provides a useful way to frame the epistemological issues raised when primatologists study the evolution of gendered behavior. Harding discusses three feminist epistemologies, which she calls "feminist empiricism," "the feminist standpoint," and "feminist postmodernism." Feminist empiricism assumes that more women in science will create a less patriarchal agenda and that the selection of appropriate problems for inquiry will change as women become practitioners. Critics of the early androcentric foci of male primatological researchers have pointed out that their models were masculinist and have suggested correcting this by removing their biases and thus "fixing" the bad science involved in their construction.

As we have seen, many primatologists in the early 1970s showed the centrality of female agency. Early feminist critics exposed the androcentric bias of much former research, which focused on male agonistic behavior to the exclusion of other axes of social life in the baboon troop. A number of women primatologists sought to redress the masculinist models of the past by describing female roles and behaviors within the baboon troop and by privileging female behaviors as integral to troop structure.[22] The work of women primatologists on a multitude of species has given us a more balanced description of behavior by focusing on female animals and their interactions, showing that female primates are active and important to troop life.

As important as these feminist correctives to male biases in primatology are, an emphasis on female primates and female personnel does not challenge the functionalism that underlies much primatology of this period. Once these new data on female behavior were linked to functionalist models, they often suffered from the same empirical inadequacies as did the male-centered models, using adaptationist hypotheses in a way that seems to tell a better story for feminists but that nevertheless ultimately defeats scientific goals.

Harding calls her second epistemology "the feminist standpoint." Here, men's dominating role in science is seen as resulting in "partial and perverse" understandings, the subjugated position of women allowing for the possibility of a more complete vision. Primatology has had a disproportionately high number of successful women compared to any other area of evolutionary studies. But the social experience of women varies enormously according to class, race, and culture. Bourgeois women who become primatologists will not necessarily reflect a less perverse view of primate social behavior, partaking of a position of social and economic privilege that may itself produce perverse understandings. This is not a minor issue: professional male and female primatologists in the United States have come, almost without exception, from the white upper-middle or upper classes. Feminist primatologists from the economically privileged classes of the West have focused much energy on identifying and describing status roles of female primates. We do not know the primatological issues that might emerge from scholars who are the products of radically different social experiences. For example, were the class background of many primatologists different we might have less emphasis on social dominance and more on the mutually supportive interactions of non-"alpha" monkeys and apes.[23]

Many primatologists have been slow to realize that the primates they studied were part of changing third-world ecologies; that opportunities must be created for human communities if nonhuman primates are to survive in the context of rapidly changing political economies. For example, the role of the poacher as entrepreneur and the need for viable alternatives for those humans who depend economically on this activity are rarely considered in primatological accounts. The naive conservationism of many primatologists and their supporters is evident in the *National Geographic* vision of the African apes: innocent hairy primates and the lone white women who study them and defend them against Africans (Haraway 1989).

Third, Harding discusses feminist postmodernism, which challenges many of the assumptions on which the first two espistemologies are based. Like structuralism, semiotics, deconstruction, and psychoanalysis, feminist postmodernism "requires seeking a solidarity in our oppositions to the dangerous fiction of the naturalized, essentialized, uniquely 'human' (read 'manly') and to the distortion and exploitation perpetrated on behalf of this fiction" (1986: 28). Some of the most interesting critiques of evolutionary models have come from postmodernist deconstructionists who read primatology as text in order to reveal its cultural meanings.

Like the recent "ethnography as text" deconstruction of cultural anthropology, a growing number of historians and sociologists of science have viewed the evolutionary models of primatologists as a series of myths, one replacing another, and contextualized them in relation to wider social and political issues. Donna Haraway is an important exemplar of this school. She writes in "Primatology Is Politics by Other Means" (1986): "But *values* seems an anemic word to convey the multiple strands of meaning woven into the bodies of monkeys and apes. So I prefer to say that the life and social sciences in general, and primatology in particular, are story-laden; these sciences are composed through complex, historically specific storytelling practices. Facts are theory-laden; theories are value-laden; values are story-laden. Therefore, facts are meaningful within stories" (79). Postmodernists have tended to see less sexist and more female-centered origin myths as good for feminism. Such perspectives have led firmly away from considerations of the role of biology in human behavior in favor of analysis of the textual content of evolutionary stories. But there are problems with this approach, for it is one thing to say that science is socially constructed, but another to deny, as postmodernists have often done, that biology has a role in human evolution and behavior. This view leaves untouched the question of the relative worth of epistemologies in evolutionary science, because postmodernists tend to view all epistemologies as equally mythic social constructions.

Harding discusses the tensions inherent in each of these approaches and endorses a radical enterprise that considers not the "woman question" in science but rather the "science question" in feminism: she sees the elimination of masculine bias in science as requiring a "fundamental transformation of concepts, methods and interpretations; an examination of the very logic of scientific inquiry" (108). The movement away from linear functionalist models in primatology toward a more robust epigenetic vision of evolutionary biology fits squarely within this last enterprise. The resistence to this change is strong: the linear reductionism of the past is clean and orderly, whereas for many, the ambiguity of the kind of approach I am suggesting is often unbearably dirty. Such approaches are also time-consuming; primates are long-lived species, and the research strategies necessary for a full explication of gendered behavior requires life-history studies—a difficult prospect within the current structure of academic science (in which most primatological data are acquired during one or two field seasons for doctoral dissertations).

Can there be a feminist evolutionary biology that does more than retell functionalist stories in a less sexist format? Although feminist functionalism has "told new stories" about male and female primates, the narrative logic of functionalist models of primate behavior is ultimately antithetical to feminist goals. It proposes a reductionist science of genetic essences of maleness and femaleness which does not explain the diversity observed in nature. An epigenetic approach, one that looks at genetic and extragenetic factors in the origin, diversity, and persistence of gender dimorphic behaviors, is more useful, although more complicated and problematic, than reductionist-functionalist models.[24] Life-history studies of primates, which view development in the perspective of both proximate and ultimate causality, are necessary to our future understanding of all aspects of behavior, including gender roles.

Feminists in the social sciences have often turned away from a consideration of evolutionary biology because of their awareness of the dangers of its frequently reductionist paradigms. But a more robust and sophisticated primate ethology may have something to offer us all in terms of elucidating developmental mechanisms that apply across primate phyla, and of defining the important differences between human and nonhuman primates. Human gendered behavior involves uniquely human cultural, cognitive, and linguistic characteristics that appear to be recent developments in hominid evolution and which are not shared by other primates. Biological anthropologists can only contribute to an understanding of human gendered behavior by first attending to its historical, economic, and cultural causes. Without a sophisticated grasp of human social behavior they have little to offer the social sciences by way of theorizing about biological "roots" of complex human behaviors.

Feminist theory is dependent on the larger intellectual ecology. Recent discourse in the social and biological sciences points out problems with normative studies that assume that behaviors are fixed dimorphisms to be measured in adulthood. Recent critiques in evolutionary theory challenge reductionist-adaptionist models that collapse variation into theories of male and female reproductive strategies. Primatologists must attend to these arguments as well as acknowledging that the human world has never existed before and that its conditions are constantly changing (Oyama 1985). This fact sets important limitations on what we can know about human evolution from studies of monkeys and apes.

Ultimately, baboons with briefcases are not an improvement over langurs in lipstick: we must return them all to their natural environments. This mandates changes in research style involving description and coherent explanation of what actually happens during life-cycle development. With more sophisticated methodologies, and more robust theoretical models, primatology may yet have something valuable to offer those of us interested in gendered human behavior.

NOTES

1. I want to acknowledge Abraham Sperling for pointing out the importance of critical deconstruction early in my development. Some of the ideas in this paper are the result of a long, ongoing dialogue with Micaela di Leonardo about anthropology, feminism, and the relationship between social theory and evolutionary science. I

gratefully acknowledge her help in the articulation of these topics as presented here. Donna Haraway's perspectives on modern primate studies have played an important role in my approach to various functionalist agendas in primatology.

2. For a full acount of these developments, see Donna Haraway's *Primate Visions* (1989). This paper focuses on Western primatology, but Japan has also been a major center for primatological research. It should also be made clear that following the early postwar studies at African sites, primatologists worked in Asia, South America, and the Caribbean as well.

3. Primatologists work in a variety of disciplines such as zoology and comparative psychology. Although a concern with human evolution has never been universal among primatologists, it is ubiquitous among anthropologists who study prosimians, monkeys, and apes.

4. For opposing views on this issue, see Zihlman (1978) and Lovejoy (1981).

5. For instance, the epistemological failures of sociobiology have been critiqued since the early 1980s by "Science for the People" and other groups who find them politically unpalatable, as well as evolutionists who find them scientifically flawed. The latter have had little voice in the popular diffusion of ideas about evolution and animal behavior. Gould's antisociobiological volleys in the *NYRB* article, "Cardboard Darwinism," are a rare exception. For a strong and exhaustive critique of sociobiology see Kitcher's (1985) *Vaulting Ambition*.

6. A recent expression of this minority opinion is primatologist Bernstein's (1987) statement on functionalism in primatology: "Proof by assertion, plausible argument and consensual validation are no substitute for evidence. The scientific method consists of developing hypotheses from available observation or theory and then testing to see if the null hypothesis, that there is no relationship between the phenomenon under study and the hypothesized independent variable, can be rejected at some predetermined level of confidence. Many sociobiologists seem satisfied only to have proposed an hypothesis, and expect others to do the world of providing the evidence. . . . Ideas are cheap. Evidence from rigorous scientific tests is hard to produce" (p. 111).

7. Primate studies began early in the century with the world of Robert Yerkes and Clarence Carpenter. For discussion of the origins of twentieth-century primate studies and the social agendas informing the early work see Haraway's *Primate Visions* (1989).

8. A number of important organizational events served to consolidate modern primatology as a science. Important among these was the 1962–1963 "Primate Year" organized by Washburn and Hamburg at the Stanford Institute for Advanced Study in the Behavioral Sciences. Three major international conferences took place in 1962 producing edited volumes. See Haraway's *Primate Visions* (1989) for a list of these events.

9. See Fedigan (1982) and Haraway (1989) for discussion of the periodization of primatology.

10. A number of primatologists have seen primate studies as part of socioecology, viewing primates as mammals rather than human surrogates. For this approach, see Alison Richard's *Primates in Nature* (1985).

11. For a thorough review of this model and its many offshoots, see Fedigan's *Primate Paradigms* (1989).

12. Ibid.

13. The roots of these arguments can be traced to three important papers: Wynne-Edwards (1963), Hamilton (1964), and Trivers (1972). Altruism was defined as any behavior that benefits another organism, not closely related, while being apparently detrimental to the organism performing the behavior; benefit and detriment being defined in terms of contributions to inclusive fitness. Examples of such altruistic behaviors might be food-sharing with nonrelatives and helping nonrelatives in times of danger.

14. See Haraway's *Primate Visions* (1989) for a history of the actors involved in the demise of structural-functionalism and the ascendance of sociobiology.

15. DeVore is an actor in the primatological drama who has made a smooth transition from the functionalist agendas of the 1960s to those of the 1980s. He was an important proponent of the use of the baboon troop as a functionalist's microcosm of human society and later became a strong advocate of sociobiology.

16. Oyama (1985) discusses the many ways that biological reductionists hedge their bets by making sociobiological assertions about the different reproductive interests of the sexes, but adding that cultural factors are "important for humans." As she points out, this is an additive model of human culture pinned onto the "primate biogram" (p. 83).

17. I am following Bernstein's (1987) use of Tinbergen's construction of causality in behavior.

18. An excellent investigation of these null-hypotheses may be found in Fausto-Sterling's (1985) *Myths of Gender*.

19. Within the functionalist framework, development is usually viewed backward from the adult form, taking as the starting point sex differences in adult behavior. Birke (1986) has made this point and critiques the hormone and behavior literature of the 1950s and 1960s (i.e. Money and Erhardt) from this perspective in which genes rather than hormones are reified as causal factors.

20. The ascendance of functionalist models in primate studies mirrors the debate over hierarchical versus nonhierarchical models in interactionist theories in biology throughout the twentieth century. In many cases the proponents of hierarchy have won out. For a discussion of this point see Keller (1983).

21. Keller (1985) has made this point: "The intellectual danger resides in viewing science as pure social product; science then dissolves into ideology and objectivity loses all intrinsic meaning. In the resulting cultural relativism, any emancipatory function of modern science is negated, and the arbitration of truth recedes into the political domain. Against this background, the temptation arises for feminists to abandon their claim for representation in scientific culture and, in its place, to invite a return to a purely 'female' subjectivity, leaving rationality and objectivity in the male domain, dismissed as products of a purely male consciousness" (p. 113).

22. For examples of this emphasis, see the 1984 anthology *Female Primates: Studies by Women Primatologists*, ed. Meredith Small.

23. I don't mean to imply that a simple relationship exists between social position and ideology. But in aggregate the ideas of working-class and minority members have been little represented in primatology, whose practitioners tend to come from an elite homogeneous class background, and to be white.

24. Keller (1983) uses geneticist McClintock's radical interactionism as an example of this approach: "In lieu of the linear hierarchy described by the central dogma of

molecular biology, in which the DNA encodes and transmits all instructions for the unfolding of a living cell, her research yielded a view of the DNA in delicate interaction with the cellular environment—an organismic view. Far more important than the genome as such (i.e the DNA) is the "overall organism." As she sees it, the genome functions "only in respect to the environment in which it is found." In this work, the program encoded by the DNA is itself subject to change (p. 121).

BIBLIOGRAPHY

Altmann, Jeanne. 1974. Observational study of behavior: Sampling methods. *Behaviour* 49: 227–267.

———. 1980. *Baboon mothers and infants*. Cambridge, Mass.: Harvard University Press.

Altmann, Stuart A., ed. 1962. A field study of the sociobiology of rhesus monkeys, *Macaca mulatta*. *Annals of the New York Academy of Sciences* 102 (2): 338–435.

———, ed. 1967. *Social communication among primates*. Chicago: University of Chicago Press.

Altmann, Stuart A., and Jeanne Altmann. 1970. *Baboon ecology: African field research*. Chicago: University of Chicago Press.

Anderson, Duncan M. 1986. The delicate sex: How females threaten, starve, and abuse one another. *Science* 86 (April): 43–48.

Ardrey, Robert. 1961. *African genesis*. London: Collins.

———. 1966. *The territorial imperative*. New York: Atheneum.

———. 1970. *The social contract*. New York: Atheneum.

———. 1976. *The hunting hypothesis*. New York: Atheneum.

Bateson, Patrick. 1981. Ontogeny of behaviour. *British Medical Bulletin* 37 (2): 159–164.

Bernstein, Irwin S. 1968. Primate status hierarchies. *American Zoologist* 8: 741 (abstract).

———. 1976. Dominance, aggression, and reproduction in primate societies. *Journal of Theoretical Biology* 60: 459–472.

———. 1981. Dominance: The baby and the bathwater. *Behavioral and Brain Science* 4: 419–458.

———. 1987. The evolution of nonhuman primate social behavior. *Genetica* 73: 99–116.

Birke, Linda. 1986. *Women, feminism and biology: The feminist challenge*. New York: Methuen.

Blier, Ruth, ed. 1984. *Science and gender: A critique of biology and its theories on women*. New York: Pergamon.

———, ed. 1986. *Feminist approaches to science*. New York: Pergamon.

Bogess, Jane. 1979. Troop male membership changes and infant killing in langurs (*Presbytis entellus*). *Folia Primatologica* 32: 65–107.

Bourne, Geoffrey. 1971. *The ape people*. New York: Signet.

Buettner-Janusch, John, ed. 1962. The relative of man: Modern studies of the relation of evolution of nonhuman primates to human evolution. *Annals of the New York Academy of Science* 102 (2): 181–514.

Burton, Frances D. 1977. Ethology and the Development of Sex and Gender Identity in Nonhuman Primates. *Acta Biotheoretica* 26: 1–18.

Bygott, J. D. 1979. Agonistic behavior, dominance, and social structure in wild chimpanzees of the Gombe National Park. In David A. Hamburg and Elizabeth McCown, eds. 1979. *The Great Apes*. Menlo Park, Calif.: Benjamin/Cummings: 405–428.

Campbell, Bernard, ed. 1972. *Sexual selection and the descent of man, 1871–1971*. Chicago: Aldine.

Carpenter, Clarence Ray. 1964. *Naturalistic behavior of nonhuman primates*. University Park: Pennsylvania State University Press.

Cheney, Dorothy L. 1977. Social development of immature male and female baboons. Ph.D. Thesis. University of Cambridge.

Cheney, Dorothy L., Robert M. Seyfarth, and Barbara Smuts. 1986. Social relationships and social cognition in nonhuman primates. *Science* 234 (12 Dec. 1986): 1361–1366.

Cheney, Dorothy L., Robert M. Seyfarth, Barbara Smuts, and Richard W. Wrangham. 1987. Future of primate research. In Barbara B. Smuts, Dorothy L. Cheney, Robert M. Seyfarth, Richard W. Wrangham, and Thomas T. Struhsaker, eds. 1987. *Primate Societies*. Chicago: University of Chicago Press: 491–498.

Chevalier-Skolnikoff, Suzanne. 1971. The ontogeny of communication in *Macaca speciosa*. Ph.D. thesis. University of California, Berkeley.

———. 1971. The female sexual response in stumptail monkeys (*Macaca speciosa*), and its broad implications for female mammalian sexuality. Paper presented at the American Anthropological Association Meeting, New York City.

Clutton-Brock, Timothy H. 1983. Behavioural ecology and the female. *Nature* 306: 716.

Collias, Nicholas E., and Charles H. Southwick. 1952. A field study of population density and social organization in Howling Monkeys. *Proceedings of the American Philosophical Society* 96: 143–156.

Comfort, Alex. 1966. The nature of human nature. New York: Harper and Row.

Crook, John Hurrell, and Stephen Gartlan. 1966. On the evolution of primate societies. *Nature* 210: 1200–1203.

Dahlberg, Francis, ed. 1981. *Woman the gatherer*. New Haven: Yale University Press.

Daly, Martin, and Margo Wilson. 1978. *Sex, evolution, and behavior*. North Scituate, Mass.: Duxbury Press.

Dawkins, Richard. 1976. *The selfish gene*. London: Oxford University Press.

DeVore, Irven. 1962. "The social behavior and organization of baboon troops." Ph.D. thesis. University of Chicago.

———, ed. 1965a. *Primate behavior: Field studies of monkeys and apes*. New York: Holt, Rinehart and Winston.

———. 1965b. Male dominance and mating behavior in baboons. In *Sex and behavior*. F. A. Beach ed. New York: Krieger. (1965): 266–289.

DeVore, Irven, and K. R. L. Hall. 1965. Baboon social behavior. In *Primate behavior: Field studies of monkeys and apes*. I. DeVore, ed. New York: Holt, Rinehart, and Winston.

Dolhinow, Phyllis, ed. 1972. *Primate patterns*. New York: Holt, Rinehart and Winston.

Dolhinow, Phyllis, and Naomi Bishop. 1972. The development of motorskills and social relationships among primates through play. In Phyllis Dolhinow, ed. 1972. *Primate Patterns.* New York: Holt, Rinehart and Winston: 312–337.

Eimerl, Sarel, and Irven DeVore. 1965. *The Primates.* Life Nature Library. New York: Time, Inc.

Fausto-Sterling, Anne. 1985. *Myths of gender. Biological theories about women and men.* New York: Basic Books.

Fedigan, Linda Marie. 1982. *Primate paradigms. Sex roles and social bonds.* Montreal: Eden Press.

———. 1983. Dominance and reproductive success in primates. *Yearbook of Physical Anthropology* 26: 91–129.

———. 1986. The changing role of women in models of human evolution. *Annual Review of Anthropology* 15: 25–66.

Fedigan, Linda Marie, and Laurence Fedigan. n.d. Gender and the study of primates. American Anthropological Association: Project on Gender Curriculum. In manuscript.

Fisher, Helen. 1982. *The sex contract: The evolution of human behavior.* New York: Morrow.

Fossey, Dian. 1970. Making friends with mountain gorillas. *National Geographic Magazine* 137: 48–68.

———. 1983. *Gorillas in the mist.* Boston: Houghton-Mifflin.

Fox, Robin. 1968. The evolution of human sexual behavior. *New York Times Magazine,* March 24: 32 ff.

———, ed. 1975a. *Biosocial anthropology.* New York: John Wiley and Sons.

———. 1975b. Primate kin and human kinship. In *Biosocial anthropology.* New York: John Wiley and Sons.

Jamieson, Ian G. 1986. The functional approach to behavior: Is it useful? *American Naturalist* 127: 195–208.

Galdikas, Birute. 1980. Living with orangutans. *National Geographic Magazine* 157 (6): 880–853.

Gartlan, John S. 1964. Dominance in East African monkeys. *Proceedings of the East African Academy* 2: 75–79.

Gilmore, Hugh. 1981. From Radcliffe-Brown to Sociobiology: Some aspects of the rise of primatology within physical anthropology. *Journal of Physical Anthropology* 56 (4): 387–392.

Goldman, D. 1978. Special abilities of the sexes: Do they begin in the brain? *Psychology Today* 12 (6): 48 ff.

Goodall, Jane. 1963. My life among the wild chimpanzees. *National Geographic Magazine* 124 (2): 272–308.

———. 1967. Mother-offspring relationships in chimpanzees. In Morris, ed. *Primate ethology.* London: Weidenfeld and Nicolson: 287–346.

———. 1971. *In the shadow of man.* Boston: Houghton-Mifflin.

———. 1986. *The chimpanzees of Gombe. Patterns of behavior.* Cambridge: Harvard University Press.

Gould, Stephen Jay. 1986. Cardboard Darwinism. *New York Review of Books* (September 25): 47–54.

Gould, Stephen J., and E. Vrba. 1982. Exaptation—A missing term in the science of form. *Paleobiology* 8: 4–15.

Hall, K. R. L., and Irven DeVore. 1965. Baboon social behavior. In *Primate Behavior: Field studies of monkeys and apes*. Irven DeVore, ed. New York: Holt, Rinehart and Winston: 53–110.

Hamburg, David A. 1963. Emotions in the perspective of human evolution. In Knapp, ed., *Expressions of emotions in man*. New York: International Universities Press. (1963): 300–317.

Hamburg, David A., and Elizabeth McCown, eds. 1979. *The great apes*. Menlo Park, Calif.: Benjamin/Cummings.

Hamilton, W. D. 1963. The evolution of altruistic behavior. *American Naturalist* 97: 354–356.

———. 1964. The genetical evolution of social behavior, I and II. *Journal of Theoretical Biology* 7: 1–52.

Haraway, Donna J. 1978a. Animal sociology and a natural economy of the body politic, part I: A political physiology of dominance. *Signs* 4: 21–36.

———. 1978b. Animal sociology and a natural economy of the body politic, part II. The past is the contested zone: Human nature and theories of production and reproduction in primate behavior studies. *Signs* 4: 37–60.

———. The biological enterprise: Sex, mind, and profit from human engineering to sociobiology. *Radical History Review*, no. 20: 206–237.

———. 1983. The contest for primate nature: Daughters of man the hunter in the field, 1960–80. In *The future of American democracy: View from the left*. M. Kann, ed. Philadelphia: Temple University Press. (1983): 175–207.

———. 1986. Primatology is politics by other means: Women's place is in the jungle. In *Feminist approaches to science*. Ruth Blier, ed. New York: Pergamon: 77–118.

———. 1988. Situated knowledges: The science question in feminism as a site of discourse on the privilege of partial perspective. *Feminist Studies* 14 (3): 575–600.

———. 1989. *Primate visions: Gender, race, and nature in the world of modern science*. New York: Routledge.

Harding, R., and D. Olson. 1986. Patterns of mating among male Patas monkeys in Kenya. *American Journal of Primatology* 11: 343–358.

Harding, Sandra. 1986. The science question in feminism. Ithaca: Cornell University Press.

Hausfater, Glenn. 1975. Dominance and reproduction in baboons: a quantitative analysis. *Contributions to primatology*. 7. Basel: Karger.

Hausfater, Glenn, and Sarah Blaffer Hrdy, eds. 1984. *Infanticide: Comparative and evolutionary perspectives*. New York: Aldine.

Hinde, Robert, ed. 1983. *Primate social relationships. An integrated approach*. Sunderland, Mass.: Sinauer.

Hodos, W. 1970. Evolutionary interpretation of neural and behavioral studies of living vertebrates. *The Neurosciences* 2.

Hrdy, Sarah Blaffer. 1977. *Langurs of Abu*. Cambridge: Harvard University Press.

———. 1981. *The woman that never evolved*. Cambridge: Harvard University Press.

———. 1986. Empathy, polyandry, and the myth of the coy female. In *Feminist approaches to science*. Ruth Blier, ed. New York: Pergamon: 119–146.

Hrdy, Sarah Blaffer, and George C. Williams. 1983. Behavioral biology and the double standard. In *Female Vertebrates*. Samuel K. Wasser, ed. New York: Academic Press (1983): 3–17.

Hubbard, Ruth. 1982. Have only men evolved? In *Biological Woman: The Convenient Myth*. Ruth Hubbard, M. S. Henifin, and B. Fried, eds. Cambridge: Schenkman: 17–46.

Jay, Phyllis, ed. 1968. *Primates: Studies in adaptation and variability*. New York: Holt, Rinehart, and Winston.

Jolly, Alison. 1966. *Lemur behavior*. Chicago: Chicago University Press.

Jones, Clara B. 1981. The evolution and socioecology of dominance in primate groups: Theoretical formulation, classification, and assessment. *Primates* 22: 70–83.

Jordanova, Ludmilla J. 1980. Natural facts: A historical perspective on science and sexuality. In Carol Mac Cormack and Marilyn Strathern, eds. 1980. *Nature, culture, gender*. Cambridge: Cambridge University Press: 42–69.

Kaye, Howard L. 1986. *The social meaning of modern biology. From social Darwinism to sociobiology*. New Haven: Yale University Press.

Keller, Evelyn Fox. 1983. *A feeling for the organism*. New York: Freeman.

———. 1985. *Reflections on gender and science*. New Haven: Yale University Press.

———. 1987. Reproduction and the central project of evolutionary theory. *Biology and Philosophy* 2: 73–86.

Kevles, Bettyann. 1976. *Watching the wild apes*. New York: Dutton.

Kinzey, Warren G., ed. 1987. *The evolution of human behavior. Primate models*. Albany: SUNY Press.

Kitcher, Philip. 1985. *Vaulting ambition. Sociobiology and the quest for human nature*. Cambridge: MIT Press.

Kummer, Hans. 1971. *Primate societies. Group techniques of ecological adaptation*. Chicago: Aldine.

Lancaster, Jane B. 1973. In praise of the achieving female monkey. *Psychology Today* 7 (4): 30–36, 99.

———. 1984. Introduction. In Small (1984): 1–12.

Leavitt, R. R. 1975. *Peaceable primates and gentle people*. New York: Harper and Row.

Lee, Richard, and Irven DeVore, eds. 1968. *Man the hunter*. Chicago: Aldine.

Leibowitz, L. 1978. *Females, males, families: A biosocial approach*. Belmont, Calif.: Duxbury.

Lewontin, R. C., Steven Rose, and Leon J. Kamin. 1984. *Not in our genes: Biology, ideology, and human nature*. New York: Pantheon.

Lovejoy, O. 1981. The origin of man. *Science* 211 (4,480): 341–350.

MacCormack, Carol, and Marilyn Strathern, eds. 1980. *Nature, culture, gender*. Cambridge: Cambridge University Press.

Martin, M. Kay, and Barbara Voorhies. 1975. *Female of the species*. New York: Columbia University Press.

Maynard-Smith, J. 1964. Group selection and kin selection. *Nature* 201: 1145–1147.

Morris, Desmond. 1967. *The naked ape*. New York: McGraw-Hill.

———, ed. *Primate ethology*. London: Weiden and Nicolson.

Nadler, Ronald. 1975. Laboratory research on sexual behavior of the great apes. In *Reproductive biology of the great apes*. C. E. Graham, ed. New York: Academic Press.

Napier, John R., and N. A. Barnicot, eds. 1963. *The primates: Symposium of the London Zoological Society*, no. 10.

Napier, John R., and P. H. Napier. 1967. *A handbook of living primates.* New York: Academic Press.

Nishida, Toshisada. 1972. Preliminary information on the pygmy chimpanzees *(Pan paniscus)* of the Congo Basin. *Primates* 13: 41–425.

Oyama, Susan. 1985. *The ontogeny of information. Developmental systems and evolution.* Cambridge: Cambridge University Press.

Patterson, Francine. 1978. Conversations with a gorilla. *National Geographic* 154: 438–465.

Poirier, Frank, ed. 1972. *Primate socialization.* New York: Random House.

Radcliffe-Brown, A. R. 1952. *Structure and function in primitive society.* New York: Free Press.

Reite, Martin, and Nancy Caine, eds. 1983. *Child abuse: The nonhuman primate data.* New York: Alan Liss.

Reiter, Rayna Rapp, ed. 1975. *Toward an anthropology of women.* New York: Monthly Review Press.

Reynolds, P. 1981. *On the evolution of human behavior. The argument from animals to man.* Berkeley, Los Angeles, London: University of California Press.

Richard, Alison F. 1981. Changing assumptions in primate ecology. *American Anthropology* 83: 517–533.

———. 1985. *Primates in nature.* New York: Freeman.

Rosaldo, Michelle Z., and Louise Lamphere, eds. 1974. *Woman, culture, and society.* Palo Alto: Stanford University Press.

Rowell, Thelma. 1966. Forest living baboons in Uganda. *Journal of Zoology* 149: 344–364.

———. 1972. *The social behavior of monkeys.* Middlesex, England: Penguin Books.

———. 1974. The concept of dominance. *Behavioral Biology* 11: 131–154.

Sade, Donald S. 1965. Some aspects of parent-offspring and sibling relations in a group of rhesus monkeys, with a discussion of grooming. *American Journal of Physical Anthropology* 23 (1): 1–17.

———. 1967. Determinants of dominance in a group of free-ranging Rhesus monkeys. In S. A. Altmann (1967): 99–114.

Science for the People (Sociobiology Study Group), 1976. Sociobiology—another biological determinism. *Bioscience* 26 (3): 182–86.

Small, Meredith, ed. 1984. *Female primates. Studies by women primatologists.* New York: Alan Liss.

Smuts, Barbara B. 1985. *Sex and friendship in baboons.* Chicago: Aldine.

Smuts, Barbara B., Dorothy L. Cheney, Robert M. Seyfarth, Richard W. Wrangham, and Thomas T. Struhsaker, eds. 1987. *Primate societies.* Chicago: University of Chicago Press.

Southwick, Charles, ed. 1963. Primate social behavior. Princeton: Van Nostrand.

Sperling, Susan. 1988. *Animal liberators: Research and morality.* Berkeley, Los Angeles, London: University of California Press.

Struhsaker, Thomas. 1971. Social behaviour of mother and infant vervet monkeys *(Cercopithecus aethiops).* *Animal Behaviour* 19: 233–250.

Strum, Shirley. 1982. Agonistic dominance in male baboons: An alternate view. *International Journal of Primatology* 3: 175–202.

Sussman, Randall L., ed. 1979. *Primate ecology: Problem oriented field studies.* New York: Wiley.

Symons, Donald. 1979. *The evolution of human sexuality.* New York: Oxford University Press.

Tanner, Nancy. 1981. *On becoming human.* Cambridge: Cambridge University Press.

Tanner, Nancy, and Adrienne Zihlman. 1976. Women in evolution, part I: Innovation and selection in human origins. *Signs* 1: 585–608.

Tiger, Lionel, and Robin Fox. 1971. *The imperial animal.* New York: Holt, Rinehart, and Winston.

Trivers, Robert. 1972. Parental investment and sexual selection. In Bernard Campbell, ed. 1972. *Sexual selection and the descent of man, 1871–1971.* Chicago: Aldine: 136–179.

van den Berghe, Pierre. 1979. *Human Family Systems.* New York: Simon and Schuster.

de Waal, Frans. 1982. *Chimpanzee politics. Power and sex among apes.* New York: Harper and Row.

Washburn, Sherwood L. 1961. *The social life of early man.* Viking Fund Publication in Anthropology, no. 31. New York: Wenner-Gren Foundation for Anthropological Research. Chicago: Aldine.

Washburn, Sherwood L., and Irven DeVore. 1961. Social behavior of baboons and early man. In Washburn (1961): 91–105.

Washburn, Sherwood L., and Phyllis J., eds. 1972. *Perspectives in human evolution,* vol. 2. New York: Holt, Rinehart and Winston.

Williams, George C. 1966. *Adaptation and natural selection.* Princeton: Princeton University Press.

Wilson, Edward O. 1975. *Sociobiology: The new synthesis.* Cambridge: Harvard University Press.

———. 1978. *On human nature.* Cambridge: Harvard University Press.

Wynne-Edwards, V. C. 1962. *Animal dispersion in relation to social behaviour.* New York: Hafner.

Zihlman, Adrienne. 1978. Women and evolution, part 2: Subsistence and social organization among early hominids. *Signs* 4: 4–20.

———. 1985. Gathering stories for hunting human nature. *Feminist Studies* 11: 364–377.

SIX

Organizing Women
Rhetoric, Economy, and Politics in Process among Australian Aborigines

Elizabeth A. Povinelli

During a hot, humid June day at the Twofella Creek Outstation,[1] I was collecting turtle eggs and mudcrabs with three senior women—Margarie Bilbil, her sister Gracie Binbin, and their aunt Maggie Timber. Tired, we decided to boil a billy[2] and eat. I rounded up some wood. Margarie washed some yams we had brought and then began to make a flour damper (commonly known as "lour"). As the billy boiled and the yams and lour cooked, Maggie Timber, coughing over a cigarette, began to speak of the "bush" and "bedagut" (whiteman) shops.

> We didn't eat that before tjamela, when I been young. We didn't sabi makim. None of this either. We got one bush, dishan now gamen bla tjimoke, but nothing strong one wipella. Nothing di, tjugar. These things now im been make wipella lazy. Been make us need that shop longa Belyuen. We got two shops, true, that shop and bush. We get tired one, we go that nother one. That bedagut, im got only one. . . . These things now though, im been make us bunch up le shop, sit down longa one place.
>
> [We didn't eat that (lour) before, granddaughter, when I was young. We didn't know how to make it. We didn't know how to use these cigarettes. We have one bush that is like tobacco, but we don't have any plants as strong as tobacco. We didn't have tea or sugar. These foods have made us lazy. They made us need the Belyuen shop. Really we have two shops, the Belyuen shop and the bush. The whiteman only has one. . . . These foods though have made us gather around stores and settle down in one place.]

Later Margarie added:

> You watch those people [at Belyuen]. They go Shop, book up [charge for goods], then Center, book up. They got no money, they go bush.

The shop, bush, and center Margarie and Maggie speak of are the three main places[3] Belyuen families get foods and goods: a community store,[4] the land and coastal area surrounding Belyuen, and a women's market center managed by the adult education assistant, the same Margarie Bilbil. Located in an old school building, the "Center" includes a childcare facility, a food cooperative, and a crafts center . Belyuen women use the Center to plan food-gathering trips and women's rituals, to play cards, and to gossip about community events.[5]

In 1985, a new adult educator came to Belyuen and decided to locate his office at the Center. Belyuen women "asked" him to use the main school building since the Center was a "woman' s place."[6] When the adult educator declined to do so, Belyuen women threatened to boycott any classes held at the Center; the Community Council wrote a letter to the Education Department in Darwin; and the adult educator assistant threatened to quit her job. Needless to say, the new adult educator decided to relocate his office.

The successful "defense" of the Center, as the Belyuen women phrased it, created a stir among a bevy of social and educational officials in Darwin who sought to duplicate the Center on other aboriginal communities. They wondered how Belyuen women were able to maintain control over a small, working market in an aboriginal community they perceived as beset by alcohol and unemployment problems. In such a setting, they expected to see a deterioration of aboriginal values and of the social control of senior women and men over juniors. Such would be consistent with the effect colonialism has had on other small indigenous communities (cf. Burbank 1988; Leacock and Safa 1982; Etienne and Leacock 1980; Nash and Fernandez-Kelly 1983).

The questions these Darwin officials were trying to answer were similar to those of my ethnographic inquiry: how has women's food gathering affected and been affected by colonialism, how has capital penetration altered the economic and social relations between junior and senior women, and what effect have these new economic conditions had on Belyuen women's agency?

Many studies have looked at the effect of world capitalist growth and shifts in female status, production, and reproduction. Colonialism and the money economy have in general produced many cultural, political, and economic problems on aboriginal communities: substance abuse (alcoholism and petrol sniffing), sedentarism (resulting in the weakening of the traditional political authority of elders), and increased dependency on the dominant economy.

Here I invert this vantage point, asking instead how women living at Belyuen use a blend of indigenous and colonial ideologies to organize, manipulate, and reconstitute European market structures. I will neither concentrate on the social ills listed above nor, as is often the counter-strategy, idealistically portray aboriginal social life as still reverberating with traditional practices. Whether or not the particular behavior they describe as "traditional" actually represents precontact aboriginal activities is less important to my analysis than how what looks and can be described as traditional senior women's authority is now constructed from an array of aboriginal and non-aboriginal economic and rhetorical practices.

In order to dismantle the traditionality of women's authority and replace it with a more complex model of female agency in a postcolonial context, I will look at the material conditions at Belyuen, how colonialism and capital penetration have wrought new political and economic constraints on activity in the community and how Belyuen women perceive and manipulate these new conditions to their benefit. In particular, I look at senior Belyuen women in relation to their food collecting, childcare, and card-playing practices to show how economic relations between senior and junior Belyuen women are established in the emergent market system. I highlight the roles of speech acts and rhetorical frames in this economic and social activity.

THE POLITICS OF FOOD

Organizing the Understanding of Food Gathering

Belyuen is a small aboriginal community located on the Cox Peninsula in the Northern Territory of Australia. Belyuen was first established as Delissaville, named for a Michael Delissa who attempted to establish a sugarcane plantation there in the late 1900s.[7] Although the Larrakia are the traditional owners of this land, presently there are seven major language groups represented among Belyuen families (cf. Tryon 1974; Stanner 1932–1933, 1933–1934; Coombs, Brandl, and Snowdon 1981). In 1979, the Northern Territory Government turned over control of the settlement to the Delissaville aborigines. The new Community Council renamed the settlement "Belyuen" after a dreaming site located at its center.[8] In 1979 Belyuen and some Larrakia families presented a claim for traditional land to the Lands Commissioner (Brandl, Haritos, and Walsh 1979). In the ten years that have followed, various groups have been put forward as the "traditional owners" of the Cox Peninsula, but in 1989, Belyuen and Larrakia families were once again united in their petition for the land (cf. Walsh 1989).

The Belyuen community's prolonged involvement with the land-claim process—a process of uneasy articulation between an aboriginal practice of "land tenure" and an Anglo-Australian legal system for aboriginal land-grants in the Northern Territory—has repositioned women's role and status. During land-claim presentations and hearings, senior women have emerged as the knowledge holders and practitioners of culture who can provide the forensic evidence of traditional ownership, spiritual responsibility, and strength of attachment to a particular stretch of land. Senior Belyuen women are relied upon to display their extensive knowledge of place names and sacred stories before lawyers and anthropologists, and their importance to

the survival of the community is reiterated in formal community meetings
and informal conversations. Belyuen aborigines also maintain that the display of stereotypical aboriginal practices such as hunting-gathering and
ritual (now largely the women's concern) is a crucial element to their winning the land claim (cf. Myers 1988; Clifford 1988; Maddock 1980; Scheffler
1984).

Berndt and Berndt's *End of an Era* describes the effects settlement life in
the early half of the twentieth century had on Northern Territory aborigines,
many of whom resettled at Belyuen. Internment in holding camps brought
stringent work and living restrictions. The jobs held by aboriginal women
and men reflected Anglo-Australian ideas of the division of labor according
to gender: women held domestic jobs and worked in laundries and cafeterias;
men were trained in mechanical and supervisory positions and engaged in
heavy labor. This division of labor according to gender had little to do with
aboriginal notions of female and male productive spheres.[9]

Social life at internment camps during World War II and later at Delissaville was marked by movement restrictions for women, poor diet, and high
death rates. European technologies were introduced and became an essential
part of aboriginal economic life. Rifles, shotguns, and cars increased the tem-
po and range of men's hunting. Canned foods, well-water, and flour became
common at aboriginal camps and reduced the necessity for women to gather
foods. Nevertheless, ritual activities, food gathering, and aboriginal culture
continue[10], seemingly alongside new economic and social conditions.

In order to understand how cultural and social patterns are constituted
and maintained in such settings over time, historical analysis must go
beyond the simple recollection of events that led to the formation of extant
communities such as Belyuen. Historical analysis in anthropology must cut
closer to *histoire*, a weaving together of event and narrative, what happens
over time, what the actors themselves construe as meaningful, and how they
construct that meaning.[11] We must pay attention to how those we study
frame activities as meaningful, and how these frames work to constitute
socioeconomic patterns.

The political history Belyuen women narrate is usually tied to their food
collection practices. In my experience, such histories take several forms.
Belyuen women present stories that are elicited, retold, and can be read as
stable texts:[12]

> Mitjemore he would never let us go hunting, young girls. He would say, "you
> gonna gu make love in the bush, gamon bla hunt." We were little girls, no
> titties anything yet! So we would sneak out, gu for crab, yam, tjugarbag. Come
> back now, finished. He would growl le we. "Where that boyfriend bla you?"
> Make a lot a trouble for us that wulman. Wulman kill a lot of youngpella cuz of
> that kind. That how it was with that Mitjemore. . . . He could eat that Mitje-
> more, no more little bit. We make lour, regular kind. "No, no, bigger," im le.

So we make biggest one. He could eat the whole thing by imself. All the young kids belly out watchim.

[Mister Michaelmore would never let us go hunting when we were young girls. He would say, "You're going to go make love in the bushes. You're just pretending to go hunting." We were little girls. We didn't even have breasts yet! So we would sneak out of camp and collect crab, yam, sugarbag. Finished, we would return. He would yell at us. "Where is your boyfriend?" The older aboriginal men poisoned (with bush poison and magic) many young men because of remarks like this. It was always like that with Michaelmore. . . . And could he eat! Not just a little. We would make a regular size lour, "No make it bigger," he would say. So we would make an enormous damper. He could eat the whole thing by himself. All the little hungry kids would stand around and watch him.]

Belyuen women's stories also typically relate historic events to the land-claim case and to the dreaming. So, for example, when in 1985 a fighter-jet on strafing drills disappeared just off the coast of the Cox Peninsula, and the local newspapers wrote a few articles about the "Bermuda Triangle" there, Belyuen senior women began telling the following story.

We told them last time. Those two wulmen been testify. In World War Two a big boat disappeared there too. Same place. That cuz of that Lizard Dreaming, sabbi that frill lizard. Im been open that fan place and swallow im. Maybe that government try and blame us, but we been tellim before, that place now you caan bomb. That why we need to get this land back see?

[We told them the last time this happened. Those two old men testified. During World War Two a big boat (battleship) disappeared there too. They disappear because of the Lizard Dreaming, you know, that frill lizard. The lizard opens its neck frills then closes them, swallowing them (ship and plane). Maybe the government will try to blame us, but we warned them before, you cannot bomb those islands. This is why we need to get this land back, do you see?]

The above stories are characteristic of histories Belyuen women tell. They constitute social boundaries by caricature (Anglo-Australians are excessive, stingy, quick to blame others; cf. Povinelli MS.), and they demonstrate the power that Belyuen families claim to manage. In the last example, women state that they cannot be held responsible for the actions of the Lizard Dreaming if they are not given control of the Cox Peninsula. At the same time they underline the tremendous power available to them if they were.

The themes set forth in these rich historical texts are reinforced in everyday conversation. After women gather foods, or rest on a porch, conversation often turns to issues of land use and women's economic activities. The following transcript of a conversation between two senior women and me while we were collecting body paints for a tourist corroboree is a good example of how political and economic issues are discussed in casual conservation. The brackets indicate where the conversation overlaps.

A: auntie, tell im alawa 1. [dishun auntie threepella lettim onepella, threepella auntie]

A: Auntie tell her about the beach, this beach. They only let three people, or one person go there, auntie.

M: 1. [mmm now they caan use this part,] but they go down this way.

M: mmm
They cannot use this part now. They go down this way now.

B: uh ya

B: uh yes

M: ask im and they gu down la beach 2. [way]

M: You can ask them (officials at Charles Lighthouse) and get permission to go down the beach.

A: 2. [they] gu la beach

A: They go down the beach.

M: They work de le lighthouse.

M: They work at the lighthouse.

B: yeh? there road there or what?

B: Yeh? Is there a road there?

M: mmm
hassle

M: mmm
It is a hassle.

A: djiben, datun, let you gu two hours auntie.

A: Those men let you go hunting for two hours auntie.

B: two HOURS

B: Two hours!

M: 3. [mmm]

M: mmm

A: 3. [if gu in] morning gotta get out bout two o'clock.

A: If you go in the morning you have to leave around two o'clock.

B: ah yeh . . .
two o'clock.

B: ah yes . . .
two o'clock.

A: too silly
you can't have im full day walk around
you got to get around at three in morning now.

A: It's ridiculous.
You can't have a full day hunting. You have to start at three in the morning these days.

B: at night huh?

B: At night huh?

A: law down there walk around maybe (. . .) lay down there walk around.

A: The Law (dreaming) walks around over there. Maybe (. . .) it lays down there and walks around.

In this conversation, M and A explain to B (the author) the restrictions on gathering foods and paints along Lighthouse Beach. The beach is not closed, but time restrictions imposed on aborigines make food collection there "too silly," even though the mangroves, reefs, and shoreline are rich crab, sting-ray, and yam sites. Once again we note that caricature and reference to the Dreaming ("law down there walk around") are used to set social and economic boundaries between Belyuen aborigines and Anglo-Australians.

Finally, elder women compare their own activities to those of Belyuen men, saying they do more to feed and clothe Belyuen families and to support the land claim.

We keep our side up. Them Land people come, bedagut, im see women only. Men should do more.

[We (women) keep our side (women's ritual and economic activities). The Land Claim lawyers come, they are whitemen, and only see women. Men should do more.]

Indeed, Belyuen men echo these thoughts. At community meetings, the male president often chastised Belyuen men for not helping the women "keep the culture going" by hunting and camping in the surrounding bush.[13]

The above stories do more than register the weapons the weak use to protest their oppression (cf. Scott 1986). Stories work (get jobs done): they provide political frames for the food contributions of Belyuen women, reconstitute the social boundaries of women's economic work in a "traditional" pattern, and pass on cultural material to listeners . Through women's conversations, the land becomes a visible sign system[14] that is constantly cueing issues of power, group inclusion and exclusion, and economic and political agendas for Belyuen families.[15] Stories that frame activity in the environment create group consciousness and orient people to action, in this case to fight for the land-claim case.[16] Stories also work (are successful) because they are backed up by the important dietary and nutritional contribution women make to the Belyuen community.

The nutritional and dietary importance of aboriginal women's food contributions have been well-documented (Altman 1986; Meehan 1983). Women collect a variety of fish, shellfish, roots, palms, fruits, honeys, and small game. In the main, they concentrate on seafish (stingray, *Urolophus testaceus*, barramundi, *Scleropages lelchhardi*, red snapper [*Lutianus argentimaculatus*], mudcrabs [*Sesarma smithi*], sea snails [long bum], *Telescopium telescopium*, periwinkles, *Nerita lineata*, clams, *Mactra obesa*), the long yam (*Dioscorea transversa*), goanna (*Varanus* species), and sugarbag (indigenous wild honey). In addition to these foods, Belyuen women are involved in men's hunting. They often provide the petrol, shot, and guns that men use to hunt. The women expect and receive part of the hunted game and fowl in return.

The dietary importance of bush foods to the nutrition of Belyuen children is recognized both on and off the community (Brandl and Tilley 1981) and is supported by a number of studies that analyze the nutritional content of bush foods (Brand et. al. 1983). Belyuen families' awareness of these findings helps to reinforce the perceived importance of senior women's contributions and knowledge inside the community.[17] In the summer of 1984, for example, the Health Care Unit at Belyuen listed eight children as seriously undernourished. A senior woman took two of these children to an outstation to "fatten im up on bush food." When the children returned healthier, the Health Care nurses met with other Belyuen mothers and urged them to do the same. Now, Belyuen women regularly take underweight and sick children to the shore for fresh sea products and yams.[18]

Bush foods are used not only for their dietary and nutritional content but also to influence socioeconomic patterns in the community. Short-term monetary crises provide the clearest example of this use. Belyuen families have been involved in a cash economy since the early 1940s. Yet patterns of money accumulation and spending still reflect stereotypical aboriginal economic strategies: few families save money, cash is immediately spent, and resources are spread along a kin-based distribution network (cf. Turner 1974; Ball 1985). Because of these economic practices, families often experience large fluctuations of available cash, making produce from the community store unavailable unless the manager extends credit. Often managers will not do so, either because they believe a person or family is overextended or because managers are trying to "teach" Belyuen families "sound money practices."

As stated above, mudcrabs and long yams continue to provide a significant source of calories to the community diet. A large mudcrab can serve as two people's meat intake for a day, while yams provide a high-quality carbohydrate to the otherwise nutritionally poor flour damper.[19] Combined with their influence over the distribution of game and fowl, women's bush food contributions give them control over a significant amount of food on the Belyuen community. They use the distribution of food, especially when other sources are unavailable, to manipulate household composition, to move younger children from hearth to hearth, and to influence marriages.

Thus far, I have looked at some rather recent stories, anecdotes, and conversations of senior Belyuen women, how these stories are concerned with relating older food-collection and land-use practices to newer issues of power and landownership, and the way food-gathering reinforces the validity of these speech acts. Belyuen women say that storytelling itself is not new. They remember that after a long day of food gathering, a fire would be made, foods cooked, and women would gossip and recount old and new stories as other women rested. These days, the setting is quite similar, but the stories pass on cultural information in new political frames. The economic importance of food gathering enforces the message of the stories, and the stories frame the importance of continuing to collect foods. Yet bush foods are no longer the only economic resource on the Belyuen community. Senior women must constitute and maintain their authority within a fluctuating cash economy, the rules of which change over time, and the conceit of which lies in other cultures than their own.

WHO'S ZOOMIN' WHO?

The Organization and Distribution of Welfare Benefits

Belyuen families have three major sources of money: government benefits, community labor (community and school jobs), and small craft sales. Government benefits, in particular, reflect European-based notions of household structure. Widow, child-support, and unemployment benefits are designed to provide for senior women deprived of their major income earner, single mothers without extensive kin-based support, and the unemployed who are deprived access to any means of production. Such conditions rarely occur in rural aboriginal groups. Senior women are viewed as the main food providers, single women and widows are incorporated into other households through extended kinship, and the "unemployed" petition relatives for foods or the use of land to obtain foods. This is not to say that benefits are not needed at Belyuen (for in the current money economy they are arguably more needed since land is increasingly restricted, jobs scarce, and single mothers and widows are expected to provide for upward of fifteen people on their benefits). Rather, benefits, once in the community, function quite differently than might be expected in Anglo-Australian communities. Government benefits concentrate a significant amount of money into older women's hands, and senior Belyuen women use rhetoric that tacks between aboriginal and Anglo-Australian notions of child-minding to obtain other welfare benefits.

Jobs provided by the Community Council tend to reflect stereotypical Western notions of the gender division of labor. Women staff the secretarial jobs, men the mechanical and carpenter jobs. The majority of school jobs are held by women, and Council positions are split between women and men.

Most of the funds from outside the community go to senior women in the form of widow and child-support benefits. When households are broken down according to their support by gender, one finds that 41.5 percent are supported by unmarried women (widows, divorced women, or unwed mothers); 17.9 percent by married women, the man providing little if any support; 21.1 percent by the husband with little or no support from the wife; and 19.5 percent are supported equally by the wife and the husband.

Research on the effects of colonialism on indigenous women's lives suggests three broad characteristics: the denigration of women's traditional labor, gender-based differential access to new technology, and a repatterning of household structure and gendered activities after those of the dominant group (Bourque and Warren 1987; Caplan and Bujra 1982). At Belyuen, therefore, one would expect to see a rise in nuclear households, in households in which men earn the money and women raise the children, and to see a loosening of the traditional authority of elder women. I have already shown that this is frequently not the case. Women provide the major source of income to two-thirds of Belyuen households. Though Belyuen men hold the stereotypical "male jobs" of mechanic and carpenter, women have comparable positions in the school and on the Community Council. Further, as the Center incident suggests, senior Belyuen women retain power and authority in community affairs.

Such economic figures at best only approximate the socioeconomic pattern at Belyuen. They necessitate freezing benefits in time and the aboriginal family into a "household" rather than presenting its fluid, extended, kin-based structure. Such an analysis also does not explain how such "households" are achieved or maintained over time.

The composition of a Belyuen household depends on a number of factors. Belyuen elders still emphasize the importance of children's recognizing classificatory mothers and fathers, aunts and uncles, brothers and sisters as an integral part of the family unit. Children are sent, or go themselves, to these relatives. This practice helps maintain the connection between the households.

> Use to be, young girl or boy im been go stay with im other father, mother, help im, learn. We think them kids should shift some. Not give that mother a problem alla time.

> [It used to be that young girls and boys would go stay with their other fathers and mothers. The children would help and learn from them. We think those kids should change residence every so often. They shouldn't always be giving their (biological) mother trouble.]

Older Belyuen women raise their grandchildren if their own children have died, are unemployed, or otherwise unable to care for them. Finally, households swell when relatives from other communities visit—visits that can last for days or years, or become permanent. The result of such social patterns is that the support structure of the aboriginal household is composed of extended and multiple links. For example, two women might exchange gathered foods, if their son and daughter are married to each other, and each of the mothers may exchange childcare with their child for welfare benefits or store goods. The senior woman may also be giving another son-in-law shot (provided by the first son-in-law) in exchange for some of the game killed on the hunt. Each transaction between mother-in-law and son-in-law would need to go through a third person since each has profound "shame" for the other and must avoid him or her. Such economic relations are contingent on recognized kin or marriage relations that, at various periods of stress, are more or less salient. Counting a given community member as a member of the family group is therefore a dynamic process. Belyuen women must work to achieve and maintain households that give them significant agency in the community. Two social activities predominate in this work—child-minding and card-playing. Each activity constitutes social and economic boundaries between generational groups to the advantage of senior women, and senior women constitute each by tacking between aboriginal and Anglo-Australian notions of family and childcare systems.

Senior women at Belyuen emphasize that child-rearing is a learned activity. They do not regard biological mothers as child-minders by nature. Such phrases as "someone should teach that woman," and "no one taught that young one, only that old woman sabis [knows how to] mindimbet kid," remark on the learned dimension of childcare and on the special place senior women have in the system. This is not to say that these women deny "motherhood." Rather, the manner in which they conceive of childcare allows several members of the extended family to provide adequate care for the child. Sometimes young women are "growled at" for leaving their children with their grandparents without providing monetary or dietary support, but such women are never labeled as "naturally" unfit if they leave the care of their child to another.

Many welfare officials who work at Belyuen see young women as unnatural mothers who abandon their children. They are profoundly disturbed that young women do not seem to worry about where their children wander or who feeds them. What is surprising is that senior Belyuen women seem to support such an outlook. They tell such officials that younger women have "dropped that kid" on them. This is surprising, for outside the earshot of such officials, senior women are just as likely to refer to overprotective mothers as "baby-faced" and to narrate the following anecdotes:

> When I was young gibbim them kids to wulgamen and go bush for hunting. Old, tjamela, mindimbet im, pikininies. Young women go hunt for crab, yam, when im come back wulgamen got lour, tea ready. Like trade, see. Now, this time, young girls caan let go them kids. You mob should let go, go hunting.

> [When I was young I left my kids with old women and went hunting in the bush. Old grandmother would mind the young children. Young women would go hunting for crabs, yams; when they came back the old women had lour and tea ready. It was like a trade, see. These days, young girls cannot leave their children. You young girls should leave them and go hunting.]

What junior and senior aboriginal women see as beyond the natural pale of child-rearing is the relationship *mitjtjitj* (white women) have with their children. They say, "them mitjtjitj can only stay in one place," "mindimbet kid all day, washimbet sock, sock, sock," and "only got one mother them white kids."

There seems to be a large difference between what Belyuen women consider proper extended childcare and what they consider "mitjtjitj" childcare, yet they do or do not articulate this difference depending on who is listening. On the one hand, these women stress that a child can be raised by a variety of people and that senior women are the most experienced of child-minders. On the other hand, in the company of welfare officials, they remark on how irresponsible young women are, emphasizing that children should be raised by the "real" mother or mother's mother. What are the results of such contradictions between rhetorics of childcare?

Two substantial benefits accrue through maintaining this contradictory rhetoric. First, if they mind their children's children and can convince welfare workers, senior women can receive the child-support benefits for their grandchildren. Second, even if senior women only mind their grandchildren part-time, they have rhetorically framed such care as part of a reciprocal economic arrangement with their daughters. Whereas in the precolonial period (and now, when large fresh-meat supplies enter the community) senior women received food in return for child-minding, currently they receive part of the child-support benefits. In either case, we see a traditional-looking economic pattern of exchange between senior and junior women emerging out of the current money economy. Combining the benefits gotten from childcare with their other welfare benefits and their food-gathering contributions, senior Belyuen women end up with considerable economic and political authority in the community. This economic connection between generational levels is also seen in other money activities of the community, especially during card games.

GAMBLING AND THE MARKET

Foraging for Cards

Cardplaying is a rankling ambiguity for anyone who has spent much time on an aboriginal settlement. Gambling is big bucks, high drama, and the center of much social activity. Games go on for days or weeks, are played with ten-cent pieces or hundred-dollar notes, and are the cause of endless teeth-grinding by social workers. Seeing the great piles of money resting in the center of a dirt plaza is enough to stop any observer. Two weeks' pay or more is often lost on a turn of a card. Anglo-Australians who work at Belyuen interpret women's gambling as evidence of the deterioration of traditional aboriginal values. Yet women often tell humorous stories about playing cards when they were young.

> We would play, play, play. All day tjamela. Back then we played for clothes, tjibeka, dea. Sometimes, finished, no more clothes bla we. Mipella's yingis hang out now. So we tellim, that wulman who used to run this place, "Give us little bit more." He would. If not we run around nakedfella.
>
> [We would play, play, play, all day granddaughter. Back then we played for clothes, tobacco, and tea. Sometimes at the end (of the game) we wouldn't have any more clothes. Our breasts would hang out. So we would tell that old man who used to run Belyuen, "Give us a few more clothes." He would. If he hadn't we would have run around naked.]

Whatever else is going on, card-playing is a carnival of high tension and old stories as people win and lose hands. Nearby, small children play with grass spears and plastic machine guns, and older men sing or tell stories.

What casual observers and judgmental social workers do not acknowledge is that gambling is also a serious economic activity that redistributes cash among family groups (cf. Altman 1986). Yet even Belyuen women speak equivocally about the effects gambling has on the social structure of the community. On the one hand, women and men talk disparagingly about the games, especially if critical ears are nearby.

> Alla women on this community card-faced.
> [All the women on this community care about is cards.]
>
> All im thinkabet is boota, boota, boota.
> [All they think about is winning, winning, winning.]

On the other hand, one constantly hears gambling compared to food collection.

> Really im like hunting. Sometime you lucky with those cards. Findim, sabi, like crabs, there, there, there. Get that money share it around.
>
> [Really card-playing is like hunting. Sometimes you are lucky with the cards. Find the right numbers, you know, like you find crabs wherever you look. You get the money and then you share it with others.]

Terms associated with hunting and gathering are also incorporated into gambling slang (e.g. *kamanggamang*, "I have no money"; *mongmarratj*, "big yam"), and normative rules and regulations governing food collecting are also exended to card-playing: families should help one another to find the right cards (play together to better the odds of the family winning the hand) and share the results of the "hunt." If a woman has a run of bad luck, other family members should lend her *mong* (money, substance, rock) until she begins to win again, just as family members should share gathered foods if a woman has had a bad day hunting. If an unlucky streak continues, players should stop playing for a while until they can "see the mong more properly again," as a woman will stop digging yams for a few days or a week if she has been finding only very small yams or yams with very long necks (these are difficult to dig and do not give a good return for the effort). Unusual luck with the cards is also recontextualized into the aboriginal cultural concept of the clever man or woman.

> That wulman, cleverwan bla wulgaman, Daphne, im been sabi that time im come. He went played cards all day. Boota, boota, boota. He couldn't lose. He went to everyone, gibbim money—wife, sister, brother. Too much im been win that day. Next thing, I heard that wailing start. Too clever that wulman. He knew you see. Lots of time im like that. You watch.
>
> [That old man, a clever man who was Daphne's mother's husband, knew his time had come. He went and played cards all day. Won, won, won. He couldn't lose. (Afterward) he went and gave everyone money, his wife, sister, brother. He won a great deal that day. That old man was very clever. You see he knew. It is often like that. You watch.]

There are two periods during which gambling redistributes cash along a kin-based network. The first is immediately after people receive their paychecks. Women who do not receive government benefits or have community jobs will ask for playing money from closely related kinswomen. Usually, younger women ask their older female kin. This exchange is explained as a traditional obligation of kin to share resources and is often predicated on the need to provide foods and goods for the family. A second phase of distribution occurs during the game. Close kin will work together to win large bills from other women with high-paying jobs. Women slip playing money to sisters, daughters, or mothers, so that they can stack the deck in a particularly rich hand. (The more family members that play, the better odds your group has to win.) Although senior women are subject to the same laws of chance as are the other players, they usually start with more money and so can loan their family and kin cash to stack these hands. As I mentioned above, these two phases are homologous to redistribution phases in food collecting. Prior to a food-gathering trip, if a woman has no food, or cannot go food gathering, she will ask kinswomen for a portion of their hunt. If a woman or man constantly asks for food, never pulling her or his weight, they will be "growled at" but seldom refused. During a food-gathering trip, close kinswomen will share the task of digging a large yam or cover a section of the mangrove to increase the number of crabs their family will collect.

The result of such social cooperation and competition is that most senior women leave food-collecting trips and cardgames with a sufficient amount of food or money to buy foods and goods, and senior women usually leave with the most money earned. Senior women also have created the widest network of shared money due to loans made before and during the games. But as luck and probability works, although women play to "boota, boota, boota," usually hands even out to small gains and losses. Those women who have amassed small fortunes distribute cash among the women who have helped them play and among other family members. Big winners are approached for a "loan" by other Belyuen members who know they have won.[20] Why then do Belyuen women say they play to win when most of the time they are actually distributing cash throughout the community?

A partial answer comes when we note that although winning big has its draw, so does the social information that circulates during card games. Economic and social interests converge at the card grounds: to miss a card game is to lose an opportunity to increase your weekly paycheck as well as to participate in an important portion of the social activity of the community. During the cardgame, in the exchange of social information or in the midst of social conflict (fights regularly occur during cardgames), senior women emerge as sources of information and mediation. In short, card-playing constitutes monetary and social relations in which senior women are the constant reference.

Ethnographers have only recently begun to study in depth the role of gambling on aboriginal communities, but in one sense aboriginal women have been involved with gambling long before the colonial period—whether to enter a particular mangrove on a particular day, whether to dig for yams or search for wild honey, whether to redistribute foods to one's sister or mother. Yet what is interesting is how Belyuen women have incorporated card-playing (gambling with cards), its meaning and productivity, into their "traditional" economic and social system.

CONCLUSION

I have "hovered" close over the ethnographic material in this piece, but I believe my analysis has broader implications for the study of gender and colonialism. By and large, the study of gender within a political-economic framework and the study of political rhetoric and speech acts have remained separate concerns in anthropology. There have been several attempts to bridge the gap between the vantages of political economy and rhetoric (Brenneis and Myers 1984; Bloch 1975; Liberman 1985; Moerman 1989), but it remains generally the case that those who study the effects of capitalism on women's production, reproduction, and agency overlook the way speech frames economic activity, orienting people to action and providing the pathway through which such activity must run. By contrast, those who study speech acts have concentrated on social organization to the exclusion of the political and economic content of speech by genders (for an exception, see Susan Gal, this volume).

As a consequence, our understanding of the way women's traditional political and economic activities are changed by capital penetration remains mechanistic. We are apt to speak of the "natural" breakdown of women's traditional production on a matrix of superimposed orders of male to female, culture to nature (Rosaldo and Lamphere 1974), or of the "natural" effects of capitalism on women's production and reproduction (Young, Wolkowitz, and McCullah 1981). Instead, in the play between speech and economy, power and agency take some unexpected twists and turns. Senior Belyuen women wring economic authority from a situation that should lessen it. It is in the middle ground between activity and understanding that Belyuen women use speech to gain authority in their lives, and it is to this middle ground that we should focus our attention if we are to understand how women work to maintain or to change their social conditions.

ACKNOWLEDGMENTS

The patience and understanding of members of the Belyuen Community made this paper possible, but I would also like to thank the Thomas J. Watson Foundation, Sigma Xi, the Scientific Research Council, the National Science Foundation, and the Department of Anthropology at Yale for funds supporting this research. I also want to thank Micaela di Leonardo, Hal Scheffler, Keith Basso, Sylvia Forman, Grey Gundaker, Tom Bishop, and Susan Edmunds for helpful comments made during the course of writing this paper, Liz Waldner for countless thoughts on feminism and writing, but especially thanks to Ada Fall wherever you are.

NOTES

1. Twofella Creek is located on the northern shore of the Cox Peninsula in the Northern Territory of Australia some twenty kilometers from Belyuen. The Outstation was set up to stem a growing influx of nonaboriginal tourists who, unwittingly and unconcernedly, bothered many sacred sites around the area.

2. "Billy": a tin used for heating food and water. At Belyuen the tin is usually a discarded powdered-milk container.

3. In the latter part of 1989 another grocery store opened. It is located within a small nonaboriginal residential development on the Cox Peninsula's northeastern shore and is run by two nonaboriginals. This store, in order to compete with the Belyuen shop, began extending credit to Belyuen residents. Although budgeting paychecks and balancing bills between the two grocery stores has become very difficult for Belyuen residents, basic strategies I outline in this paper have not changed.

4. The community store was started with a loan from an Australian corporation that specializes in remote groceries. The council manages the store, and some of the profits go back into the community. Sometimes a portion of this profit is allocated to "the women mob."

5. Haviland (1977) has written a fine text on the social function of gossip and rumor.

6. Bell's *Daughters of the Dreaming* describes how the *jilimi* and separate gender spheres function in the ritual practice of Walpiri women. Although ritual is sporadic at Belyuen, women and men there still mark the importance of separate gendered space and activity ("that a man place," "thatim woman place thatun"). Such spaces and activities can include ritual performances, recreation, and economic practices.

7. Elder Belyuen aborigines tell many stories concerning life on Delissa's plantation. Most are uncomplimentary. Government documents and newspaper articles from this time, however, laud Delissa for his attempt to establish a profitmaking farm, a difficult—and ultimately for Delissa a failed—task in the wet-dry climate of the Northern Territory.

8. Dreaming: Stanner has written, "A central meaning of the Dreaming is that of a sacred, heroic time long long ago when man and nature came to be as they are, but neither 'time' nor 'histories' as we understand them is involved in this meaning . . . we shall not understand The Dreaming fully except as a complex of meanings. A blackfella [*sic*] may call his totem, or the place from which his spirit came, his Dreaming. He may also explain the existence of a custom or law of life as causally due to his dreaming" (Rothenburg and Rothenburg 1983: 201). Others have spoken of the Dreaming as an "energy," "power," or "life-force" that resides in the land (Strehlow

1971; Sansom 1980). I think all these give an idea of the personal and sacred relations Belyuen people have with dreaming sites and the land.

9. Gale's *Women's Role in Aboriginal Society* is a classic text that reoriented the way in which we view the productive, reproductive, and ceremonial importance of Australian aboriginal women. Bell (1983), Hamilton (1981), and Goodale (1980) have also written informative works on this subject.

10. The issue of what "traditional culture" refers to has been problematized by Marcus and Fisher (1986), Hobsbawm and Ranger (1983), and Clifford (1988).

11. Natalie Zemon Davis's *The Return of Martin Guerre* and her collection of essays *Society and Culture in Early Modern France* represent an attempt to develop this notion of histoire as part chronicle and part narrative. Close analysis of conversations concerning historical events will also help us understand how meaning is delineated and then set forth as a historical or metahistorical record.

12. Tedlock (1983), Basso (1984), and Moerman (1988) have discussed methods for presenting oral texts that retain their social function and oral characteristics. The use of creole and the interactional style of creole use on aboriginal communities is a topic that merits more attention (cf. Liberman 1985; Sansom 1980; and Povinelli MS.).

13. Although the president of the Belyuen Community has been male over the last six years I have been going to Belyuen, before this there was a female president. The permanent town secretary is female.

14. Vygotsky (*Mind in Society* 1978) and Wertsche (*The Concept of Activity in Soviet Psychology* 1980), to my understanding, present the best attempts to describe the process by which external signs are organized and act on internal mental activities and, reciprocally, how internal mental functions affect the organization of the exterior world.

15. Thompson (1968), Whisnant (1983), and Skocpol (1984) have demonstrated some ways cultural behavior can lead to the development of class consciousness. At Belyuen there are at least two levels to the creation of group consciousness. First, identification as a member of the "Belyuen mob" has to be forged from membership in one of the seven language groups whose families have lived in the Belyuen area for the last hundred years or so. Second, the broader identification of oneself as an "aborigine" must be established from membership across a diverse set of aboriginal social and cultural practices (cf. Trigger 1987).

16. Belyuen people constantly scan the environment for signs from the Dreaming. In particular they watch a cheeky yam Dreaming that moves off the western shore of the Cox Peninsula and the Wariyn Dreaming located on the northwestern coast. Activity from these two sites provokes long discussions concerning the need to get the land back in order to supervise and properly protect these sites, and is used to explain why outstations are and should be built along the western coast of the peninsula.

17. Giddens writes, "The relation between technical vocabularies of social scientists and lay concepts, however, is a shifting one: just as social scientists adopt everyday terms—'meaning,' 'motive,' 'power,' etc.—and use them in specialized senses, so lay actors tend to take over the concepts and theories of the social sciences and embody them as constitutive elements in the rationalization of their own conduct" (1976: 159). In a later work, he continues, "There are no universal laws in the social sciences . . . due to the changing knowledge actors have about their social condition"

(1984: xxxii). Belyuen aborigines seem to demonstrate some of Giddens's points by adopting the studies of social workers and anthropologists to support their own native agendas.

18. The women collect *Telescopium telescopium* for flus and colds, crabs and sugarbag for weight loss and lethargy.

19. As stated above, Belyuen women and men are aware of the nutritional advantage of their bush foods. Yams in particular are known to be high in fiber and good for those with diabetes, a growing problem in aboriginal communities (as in Native American communities) where refined sugar and flour comprise a large portion of people's diet. Yams are said to make one feel light, active, and clean.

20. Loans are rarely paid back as such. Instead the loanee becomes loaner when he or she has the money. Asking for a loan is so common that people will often, after buying their week's groceries, give away all their money so that they will not be "pestered."

BIBLIOGRAPHY

Altman, J. 1986. *Hunter-gatherers today*. Canberra: Australian Institute of Aboriginal Studies.

Ball, R. 1985. The economic situation of aboriginals in New Castle. *Journal of Australian Aboriginal Studies* (Spring).

Basso, K. 1984. "Stalking with stories": Names, places, and moral narrative among the Western Apache. In *Text, play, and story: The construction and reconstruction of self and society*. E. Bruner, ed., 19–55. Washington, D.C.: American Ethnological Society.

Bell, D. 1983. *Daughters of the dreaming*. London: Routledge & Kegan Paul.

Berndt, C. 1954. *Women's changing ceremonies in Northern Australia*. Paris: L'Homme Libraire Scientifique Hermannet Cie.

Bloch, M. 1975. *Political language and oratory in traditional society*. New York: Academic Press.

Bourque, S., and K. Warren. 1987. Technology, gender, and development. *Daedalus* (Journal of American Academy of Arts and Science) 116 (4) (Fall): 173–197.

Brand, J., C. Rae, V. Cherikoff, and A. Truswell. 1983. The nutritional composition of Australian aboriginal bushfoods. *Food and technology in Australia*, 35 (6): 293–98.

Brandl, M., A. Haritos, and M. Walsh. 1979. *Kenbi land claim to vacant crown land in the Cox Peninsula, Bynoe Harbour and Port Patterson areas of the Northern Territory of Australia*. Darwin: Northern Land Council.

Brandl, M., and E. Tilley. 1981. Marching to a different drum, the uses of anthropology in the Belyuen Health Care Center, NT of Australia. CRES Working Paper. Canberra: Australian National University.

Brenneis, D., and F. Myers, eds. 1984. *Dangerous words: Language and politics in the Pacific*. New York: University of New York Press.

Burbank, V. 1988. *Aboriginal adolescence: Maidenhood in an Australian community*. New Brunswick and London: Rutgers University Press.

Caplan, P., and J. Bujra, eds. 1982. *Women united, women divided*. Bloomington: Indiana University Press. Midland Book Edition.

Clifford, J. 1988. *The predicament of culture: twentieth century ethnography, literature and art.* Esp. "Identity in Mashpee," 277–346. Cambridge: Harvard University Press.

Coombs, H., M. Brandl, and W. Snowdon. 1983. *A certain heritage.* CRES Monograph 9. Canberra: Australian National University Press.

Crawford, I. 1985. *Traditional aboriginal plant resources in the Kulumuru area.* Supplement No. 15. Perth: Recordings of the Western Australian Museum.

Davis, N. 1975. *Society and culture in early modern France.* Stanford: Stanford University Press.

———. 1983. *The return of Martin Guerre.* Cambridge: Harvard University Press.

Etienne, M. and E. Leacock, eds. 1980. *Women and colonization.* New York: Praeger.

Gale, F. 1983. *We are the bosses ourselves.* Canberra: Australian Institute of Aboriginal Studies.

———, ed. 1974. *Women's role in aboriginal society.* Canberra: Australian Institute of Aboriginal Studies.

Giddens, A. 1976. *New rules of sociological method: A positive critique of interpretative sociologies.* New York: Basic Books.

———. 1984. *The constitution of society.* Berkeley: University of California Press.

Goodale, J. 1980. *Tiwi wives: A study of the women of Melville Island.* Seattle: University of Washington Press.

Hamilton, A. 1981. *Nature and nurture: Aboriginal child-rearing in North-Central Arnhemland.* Canberra: Australian Institute of Aboriginal Studies.

Haviland, J. 1977. *Gossip, reputation and knowledge in Zinacatan.* Chicago: University of Chicago Press.

Hobsbawm, E., and T. Ranger. 1983/1987. *The invention of tradition.* Cambridge: University of Cambridge Press.

Leacock, E., and H. Safa. 1982. *Women's work: Development and the division of labor by gender.* South Hadley, Mass.: Bergin and Garvey.

Levitt, D. 1981. *Plants and people: Aboriginal uses of the plants of Groote Eylandt.* Canberra: Australian Institute of Aboriginal Studies.

Liberman, K. 1985. *Understanding interaction in central Australia.* Bloomington: University of Indiana Press.

Maddock, K. 1980. *Anthropology, law, and the definition of Australian aboriginal rights to land.* Nijmegan: Publikates over Volksrecht.

Marcus, G., and M. Fisher. 1986. *Anthropology as cultural critique.* Chicago: University of Chicago Press.

Meehan, B. 1983. *Shell bed to shell midden.* Canberra: Australian Institute of Aboriginal Studies.

Moerman, M. 1989. *Talking culture: Ethnography and conversational analysis.* Philadelphia: University of Pennsylvania Press. Second Edition.

Myers, F. 1988. From ethnography to metaphor: Recent films from David and Judith MacDougall. *Cultural Anthropology* 3 (2) (May): 205–220.

Nash, J., and M. Fernandez-Kelly, eds. 1983. *Women, men, and the international division of labor.* New York: SUNY Press.

Povinelli, E. (MS.) The practice of parody and the production of folly on an Australian aboriginal community."

Rosaldo, M., and L. Lamphere, eds. 1974. *Women, culture and society.* Stanford: Stanford University Press.

Rothenburg, J., and D. Rothenburg. 1983. *Symposium of the whole: A range of discourse toward an ethnopoetics of the whole*. Berkeley, Los Angeles, London: University of California Press.

Sansom, B. 1980. *The camp at Wallaby Cross*. Canberra: Australian Institute of Aboriginal Studies.

Scheffler, H. 1984. Rites and rights. *Journal of the Australian Institute of Aboriginal Studies* (Canberra).

Scott, J. 1986. *Weapons of the weak: Everyday forms of resistance*. New Haven: Yale University Press.

Skocpol, T. ed. 1984. *Vision and method in historical sociology*. Cambridge: Cambridge University Press.

Stanner, W. 1932–1933. The Daly River Tribes: A report of fieldwork in Northern Australia. *Oceania* 3: 377–405.

———. 1933–1934. The Daly River Tribes: A report of fieldwork in Northern Australia. *Oceania* 4: 10–29.

Strehlow, T. 1971. Geography and totemic landscape in central Australia. In *Australian aboriginal anthropology*. R. Berndt, ed. Nedlands: University of Western Australia Press.

Tedlock, D. 1983. *The spoken word and the work of interpretation*. Philadelphia: University of Pennsylvania Press.

Thompson, E. P. 1968. *The making of the English working class*. Harmondsworth: Penguin Books.

Trigger, D. 1987. Languages, linguistic groups and status relations at Doomadgee: An aboriginal settlement in North West Queensland, Australia. *Oceania* 57 (3): 217–238.

Turner, D. 1974. Tradition and transformation. *Australian Institute of Aboriginal Studies Journal*, no. 53.

Tryon, D. 1974. *Daly River family languages, Australia*. Pacific Linguistic Series C, No. 32. Canberra: Australian National University Press.

Vygotsky, L. 1978. *Mind in society: The development of higher psychological processes*. Cambridge: Harvard University Press.

Walsh, M. 1989. *Ten years on: A supplement to the 1979 Kenbi land claim*. Darwin: Northern Land Council.

Wertsche, J. 1980. *The concept of activity in Soviet psychology*. Armonk, N.Y.: M. E. Sharpe.

Whisnant, D. 1983. *All that is native and fine: The politics of culture in an American region*. Chapel Hill: University of North Carolina Press.

Young, K., C. Wolkowitz, and R. McCullah, eds. 1981. *Of marriage and the market*. London: CSE Books.

PART THREE

Representing Gendered Labor

SEVEN

Female Farming in Anthropology and African History

Jane I. Guyer

The intellectual space to cultivate gender studies within anthropology was created by a series of bold and sweeping attacks on the undergrowth of naturalistic assumptions, reporting biases, and sheer neglect of the topic. In the 1970s a generation of feminist scholars repositioned earlier trail-blazing studies—such as Margaret Mead's comparison of sex and temperament in three New Guinea societies (1935) and Phyllis Kaberry's ethnography of women of the Cameroon Grassfields (1952)—at the center of a newly recognized tradition of scholarship. They reread the ethnographic corpus for insights hardly given theoretical attention thus far. And they opened up the whole issue of gender to an interdisciplinary approach emanating from feminist thinking, drawing on concepts from nonanthropological classics: "domination" and private property as used by Engels, autonomy and patriarchy as applied by Simone de Beauvoir. This stage is best exemplified by the two collections, *Women, Culture and Society* (Rosaldo and Lamphere 1974), and *Toward an Anthropology of Women* (Reiter 1975). Empirical synthesis, conceptual experimentation, and polemic statement were the agendas of the day.

To the next generation of scholars falls the task and the opportunity to explore the space created and decide how to use it. The present work labors in the clearing created by Ester Boserup's (1970) brief but highly effective synthesis of the ethnography and colonial history of African female farming. She drew dramatic attention to the importance of women's productive roles in Africa. "Africa is the region of female farming par excellence," where men fell the trees "but to women fall all the subsequent operations" (1970: 16, 17). Against the backdrop of her earlier influential work on the evolution of agricultural intensification with rising population densities (1966), she argued plausibly that persistently low population densities in Africa provide no incentive for the development of plow agriculture, private property in land, and increased male labor input into farming. In the twentieth century, colonial export-crop and labor policies have withdrawn male labor thereby reinforcing a feminized subsistence food economy. She deals only briefly with the basis for positing a preexisting connection between African farming techniques and female labor, citing prominently Baumann's classic work that suggests that an association of forest ecology, dominance of root crops over cereals, minimal cultivation of the soil, and female farming have persisted "in the African primeval forest. . . from time immemorial" (1928: 294).[1]

For the 1970s feminists, Africa's female farmers seemed living proof— analogous to woman-the-gatherer—of women's original and massive contribution to the productive economy, of the possibility of integrating childcare with independent work, and of the historically late and derivative nature of women's relegation to the "domestic domain." The whole image fit beautifully with Engels's revived classic, which argued that women's status had declined with the rise of private property and the state and, thereby, with the feminist mission of liberation, which in industrial societies included reasserting the right to work. It also fit with current critiques of colonial economic policy which, it was argued, had developed Africa's export potential at the expense of stagnation in other sectors. The fact of African female farming therefore threw light on a range of other feminist concerns: the historical bases of "patriarchy," women's work and social status, the effects of state policies, and the implications for women of the dynamics of "the world system." Boserup's vision was clear, consonant with others, and intellectually and politically revitalizing across the spectrum of social sicence disciplines.[2]

The clarity and simplicity of this vision starts blurring, however, when inspected consistently and carefully through Africanist rather than comparative and theoretical lenses. For understanding the variety of divisions of labor and their change over time *within Africa*, the model of female farming is not only—like all generalizations—necessarily blunt in its discriminations, but also misleadingly focused. Patterns of production *have* been deeply gendered in Africa and Boserup's work reopens that field of enquiry. But the times and places are limited for which the terms "female" and "farming" can be linked so tightly together and given such prominence in the interpretation of production. The empirical sources no longer support Baumann's assertion of a primordial division of labor, but rather lend credence to a view that the features of "female farming" are relatively recent innovations associated with the spread of the New World staples of cassava and maize from the sixteenth century onward. I briefly review the evidence for this assertion below.

But the issues embedded in the concept of "female farming" are more far-reaching than those of empirical veracity alone. The fundamental problem is precisely what made the vision attractive and plausible in the first place, namely the assumption Baumann expressed so un-self-consciously and graphically, that African farming in the twentieth century can be taken to represent an early stage of human social evolution. If "female farming" is taken as the fixed starting point of agricultural evolution, rather than a variable product of society and history, then interpretations of African dynamics themselves become trapped within a framework of evolutionary directionalities. They can either realize or deviate from, the path of intensification achieved elsewhere, either crossing or failing to cross the evolutionary Rubicons of household organization of production, intensive agricultural techniques with fertilization, irrigation and the plow, and private ownership of resources. Other configurations of technical change and social dynamics, organization of work, and cultural constructions of gender then tend to be assessed in terms of their relationship to world evolution; the specific dilemmas and directions of current change can hardly be "seen" through this optic. One needs to shift the perspective, to see African farming not as a living exemplar of a primitive stage but as a system of knowledge and practice with its own history, innovations, and prospects, some—but not all—of which may bear usefully provocative resemblance to others, past and present.

Comparison then shifts to new ground as well. The relevant descriptive methods are those applicable to *all* work, regardless of whether it is agricultural or industrial, in one continent or another, in the "domestic" or "public" domains. In this framework for considering work and gender, studies of Africa may offer intellectual resources to a wider debate, rather than merely provide a model of the foundation from which other systems evolved. In the second part of this chapter I analyze the changing division of labor in the Beti region of Southern Cameroon, drawing on a concept that appears in the literatures of anthropology, sociology, and social history, namely the idea of rhythmic structures, and highlighting its potentials for a dynamic understanding of the gendered division of labor.

PART 1: THE LIMITS OF EVOLUTION[3]

Baumann constructed his female farming model on the following assumptions: that forest farming is the primary form of African agriculture, that root crops can be grown by rudimentary techniques, that women are suited to such techniques, and that productive work in such economies is socially individuated and culturally unelaborated. When cereal cultivation enters the cultural repertoire Baumann suggests that all this shifts: to the savannah, to more intensive techniques, to greater male input, and to elaborated social forms to deal with peak harvest labor demand and the managerial demands of storage.

Logical and plausible as it seems, this picture is now radically at variance with historical knowledge, mainly because the root/cereal distinction fails to discriminate between the ancient African cultigens—yams within the root category and sorghum, millet, and rice within the cereal category—and the recently imported cultigens of cassava (a root) and maize (a cereal). The social organization and gendered division of labor for cultivation of the ancient staple crops taken together, and for the imported cultigens taken together, have their own striking uniformities, cutting completely across the roots/cereal distinction.

Cultivation of the ancient staples is characterized by *interdigitation* of male and female, group and individual tasks, supported by an *activity*-specific cultural definition of the division of labor, often literally choreographed and set to music, and infused with ritual symbolism. Yams—a root crop— provide one example. As Forde (1964) described cultivation by the Yakö of southwestern Nigeria, ownership of seed yams is individual and heritable. Men clear the new farms, working in groups of twelve or more. The women then make the mounds in which the yams are planted by both men and women working together. Weeding is female; staking and training the vines is male. Harvesting is a joint activity; washing and carrying are female. Storage barns are built by men, but ownership of the harvested yams is individual according to ownership of the seed-yams. Distribution is further structured by social ties between the owner and his/her network, and the harvest is marked by collective ceremonial.

Audrey Richards's (1939) classic work on the Bemba productive economy provides a comparable example for the indigenous cereal, millet. Tree-pollarding was carried out by groups of young men following the chief's ritual declaration of the opening of a new fertility cycle. Women stacked the branches, men put fire to the fields, and then men planted with their wives following behind to cover up the seed. Men fenced the fields against wild animals, while women did whatever tending was required and were exclusively responsible for reaping. The collective and individual choreographies are particularly intricate for indigenous rice production in West Africa (Linares 1981; Johnny et al. 1981), which remains ritualized even where it has ceased in recent times to be a major staple (Brydon 1981).

The contrast with the common mode of cultivation of *both* of the New World staples is striking. The division of labor for cassava and maize is based less on activities in sequences than on *products* or *field-types* in repertoires. Throughout Africa cassava is generally grown on individuals' fields, with little collective labor and—as far as I have found—no ritualization at all. In many regions it is predominantly a female crop. Richards's description of maize among the Bemba fits the same pattern as cassava: hoeing mounds in individual plots for crops other than millet "was considered hard and unromantic work by the Bemba, quite unlike millet cultivation" (1939: 304).

To add a further piece of circumstantial evidence to the emerging picture of close consonance among the old staples, there seems to be no basis for any evolutionary assumption that root-crop cultivation in the forest preceded cereal cultivation in the savannah. In fact, archaeological work on the oldest African farming system studied in detail, the Kintampo culture in Ghana of well over two thousand years ago, suggests a savannah-border ecology and a combination of root and cereal production (Flight 1976: 219). Extrapolating from the ethnography, one can speculate that both types of crop may have been grown under the interdigitated, activity-specific, sacralized regime characteristic of current cultivation methods for the old staples. None of the old staples was monopolized by female labor. Since by contrast the individuated, secular, product—or field-specific—female farming seems so particular to cassava and maize, one can suggest that it has been produced historically by a recombination of elements in the old system, and by both technical and social innovations.[4] By the time Baumann synthesized the ethnography in the 1920s, this process was already deeply entrenched enough to seem "traditional" and, as Boserup suggested, was probably reinforced by colonial policies that directly or indirectly favored maize and cassava cultivation.

The shift in labor organization from the old to new staples is likely to have entailed important consequences for distribution of the product. Under the old regime, specific productive activities often implied specific claims on the product. Rubrics for distribution were enacted through the significance given to generative interventions in the agricultural cycle, whether prayer and consecration by chiefs, tree-cutting by men, seed acquisition by individuals of both sexes, or observation of routine religious and pragmatic nurturing rituals by women. Crop cycles, labor cycles, the cultural emphases given to certain phases of cycles, and rights in resources and products were all mutually implicated. The individuation of entire crops or field-types brought shifts not only in labor synchrony itself—group/individual, male/female, senior/junior—but thereby also in the jural and cultural legitimation of claims on the product. If precolonial agricultural practices were progressively incorporating New World crops, then gender configurations had already changed and were probably still changing by the time that colonial civil servants, missionaries, and early anthropologists made the "baseline" descriptions that Baumann relied on.

The approach to gender and agricultural change through crop and labor cycles is consonant with new work in African history and with both old and new ethnography of African production systems. It also fits with a broader literature on the apparent generality of rhythm and synchrony as aspects of labor control. Within anthropology, Douglas and Isherwood (1979) have pointed to the gender and status concomitants of the frequency of obligatory tasks; female and low-status workers tend to engage in the higher-frequency tasks carried out within narrow spatial confines, a pattern that male and high-status workers try to avoid. The profound status implications of changing work routines can turn the timing of work into a subject for bitter antagonism, subterfuge, and sabotage. E. P. Thompson's (1967) famous article on the subordination of the new industrial labor force to factory discipline and Sabean's (1978) work on gender-specific intensification patterns in European agricultural history are peaks in a large corpus of work in several disciplines on the power and meaning of work rhythms and the implications of trying to change them.[5]

But before simply applying these ideas to the modern history of an African "female farming system," it is necessary to backtrack, to reassess the available methodologies for describing the gendered division of labor, including those on which the evolutionary position has rested. Besides referring issues upward to the abstract level of guiding paradigms—either universal evolutionary paths or African historical dynamics—one has to dig down into the tools and concepts of description and analysis through which theory and data are linked. Since change is an entirely relative concept, the terms of description and the choice of historical time frame more or less create the degree and kind of change one can perceive. The terms of description contain guiding theoretical assumptions and determine analytical possibilities, even though they can often seem to be independent and self-evidently "right" for the topic. It is worth asking, therefore, about the nature of the working concepts and methods which generated the relatively unchanging—"stagnant"—vision of women's agricultural work in Africa. They may have been too blunt and undifferentiated to capture subtle shifts. By implicitly working with the major stages of evolutionary change as criteria of significance, only a very few African innovations in the smallholder sector, such as the plow and animal traction in parts of Central and Southern Africa, could possibly qualify as significant change. Thereby, relevant data may have been altogether omitted.

The longest anthropological tradition of sustained concern with the gender division of labor is in cross-cultural studies. Here, researchers have relied on *task specificity* by gender as the basic data for comparison, and for two legitimate reasons: such descriptions are simpler and less ambiguous than any alternatives, rendering highly diverse ethnographic sources amenable to comparison; and they can be reduced to a standard list, allowing scholars to make inferences about universals, correlations, and contingencies—concepts central to the theoretical thrust of cross-cultural studies.[6]

Task lists, however, are too crude a mesh to capture the nuances of change in labor patterns as African agriculture has altered over this century. The criteria of definition become too concrete. If a male farmer uses hired labor and his wife cooks for them, is this "cooking" or something else? If women stretch the old rubric of harvesting crops for family provisioning to cover wage work on cash crops on local peasant farms or seasonal labor for agribusiness, is this still "harvesting" and in what sense? If women are doing the same tasks on the farm as at the beginning of the century, but doing them on larger areas and with greater control of the product, how does this figure as change? It is easy but deceptive to see any task over time as "the same thing" regardless of context. Cooking looks like cooking, whether done by a whole village collectively once a week in a clay oven or by an individual three times a day with a battery of implements and props for stage-managing the meal.[7] But such a definition automatically generates static images, with major, even revolutionary, changes of technique and social relations automatically relegated to secondary and contingent importance.

Imprecise and conservatively biased at best, a task-structure approach has the added limitation of providing no way of addressing the comparative *value* of men's and women's work, nor any shifts in *labor time* or *claims* on resources and products. Since male/female differentials of time and value are revealing—as task structures are not—of gender inequality, feminist scholarship has homed in on methods that measure these dimensions of the gendered division of labor.[8] No interpretation of change can do without attention to value and time allocation. My own concern is not whether they are important at all, but whether they can figure prominently in *initial* descriptions of change in the labor process, and for two reasons. First of all and most pragmatically, they are very difficult to reconstruct with precision for the past. Second, as quantitative scales they depend on prior definitions of what is to be measured: "work" as a category of activity, modalities of value (price, returns to labor or cultural construction), and units of labor (time spent or effort expended). All are problematic, and the easiest solution to each may lead straight back to tasks as the single least ambiguous and most empirically identifiable descriptive term. Better—it seems to me—would be to try to illuminate aspects of the path of change first so as to apply any of the conceptually difficult methods for addressing relative value only to those particular cultural themes, historical turning points, or social loci which one has already identified to be crucial. These are the pivots of change: the tasks, routines, or cultural conceptions which constrain possibilities and set the terms in which alternatives can be envisaged. It is at this later stage in the iterative process of conceptualization, data-generation, interpretation, and further, more focused data-generation that other approaches—including evolutionary approaches where appropriate—can be brought back in as experimental explanatory models.

A focus on the timing of work meets the criteria for such an initial description. It throws into relief changes in agricultural practice, however limited they may seem by comparison with great evolutionary watersheds; it highlights the social and cultural links between activity and claim which seem so central to African material life but are poorly captured by standard descriptions of task structures; and it allows us to perceive the power of gender in shaping—rather than simply submitting to—forces for change. At the same time it opens up, rather than closing out, the possibility of drawing on other available methods for dealing with specific aspects of the course of change.

In what follows I present Beti agricultural history as such an exploration, recapitulate the interpretive and methodological problems presented above for an empirical case, and apply the alternative method of focusing on the rhythmic structures of work.

PART 2: GENDER AND MODERN AGRICULTURAL CHANGE IN BETI SOCIAL HISTORY

The Beti-speaking peoples have historically inhabited a vast territory extending from what is now Southern Cameroon into Gabon and Equatorial Guinea. They moved around in migratory patterns that seemed to have no particular direction until the nineteenth century, when the presence of trade in European goods at the coastal ports attracted village headmen to move deeper into the forest, toward the coast and away from the savannah-border environment that seems to have been their home for centuries (see Laburthe-Tolra 1981). Language and certain common cultural principles are the only manifestations of Beti unity. Precolonial Beti society was segmentary in structure, constituted by independent villages linked to one another by ties of kinship, affinity, and the exchange relationships of their headmen.

German and French colonizers, and then independent government after 1960, enacted measures and pursued policies which effectively halted Beti migration, abridged village autonomy, transformed religion, and brought production into the service of regional and national interests. Beti villages were forcibly sedentarized as the road network was built during the first part of this century. A chieftaincy hierarchy was instituted, replaced after 1945 by a civil service hierarchy for local government. During the interwar years most of the Beti population around the Cameroon capital city of Yaoundé converted to orthodox Roman Catholicism. Three great forces for change have reshaped production: export-crop production of rubber and palm kernels initially enforced through cash taxation and direct requisition up to the mid-1930s, the rapid development of cocoa cultivation around this time and particularly after 1945, and the rapid expansion of the urban food market for Yaoundé, after national independence.

"Female farming" of food crops can seem stagnant by comparison with the radical nature of other social, cultural, and economic change in Beti life. Women still carry out the same tasks they did in the precolonial period, with a similiar repertoire of crops, tools, and field types. They are still responsible for the daily diet with some of the same valued components at its core, still work longer hours than men, still have little direct control over wealth and heritable resources. Various theoretical orientations could be used to address and interpret this situation. Boserup could certainly see her classic combination of low population density and colonial extraction of male labor. Neo-Marxists posit articulated modes of production with patriarchal control of junior and female labor as a structural feature ensuring conservatism in familial relationships and activities (Meillassoux 1981: Rey 1979). Cultural theorists could well see the persistence of fundamental gender conceptions, not only in sanctioned modes of labor control but in the symbolism of male work as vertical in movement, dealing with wood and creating erectness or height (tree cultivation, yam-staking and harvesting, tomato cultivation with long-handled hoes) and female work as dealing with mud and foliage, bending, circular or pliant in motion (over the short-handled hoe, the cooked fire, the grinding stone, the mud for house-building, the groundnut harvest spread out to dry in the sun). An economic rationalist could look at conditions in the food market and suggest that no household could afford to specialize out of self-provisioning without sacrificing the quality of the diet. And undoubtedly an ecologist could gloss "stagnation" in more positive terms as "stability," pointing out the fine-tuning of the cropping system to the social and natural context.

Each of these explanations of stability/stagnation is plausible for the Beti case even though they would seem to be theoretically opposed to one another. But each is also quite partial. Colonial export-crop policy may help to explain patterns in the feminization of food-farming practices during the palm kernel and cocoa eras, but state policy is not as helpful in addressing the very limited response to policies promoting male participation in food farming in response to the urban market after 1960. "Patriarchal control" is likewise quite variable over time. Its social forms in the nineteenth century were quite different from those of the late twentieth century due to the decline in large-scale polygyny, a rising age of marriage for women, the legal requirement—in principle—of a woman's consent to her own marriage and the legal recognition of her capacity to consent to her daughters' marriages, the disappearance of widow inheritance, and a general increase in formal legal rights for women. Similarly cultural constructions of gender have surely shifted in some respects in response to the replacement of quite powerful female cults by Christian doctrine (Fernandez 1982). Economic rationality as a sole explanation of conservatism in female farming begs the question of why rural food markets were so slow to develop in this area, leaving self-provisioning as the only viable mode of acquiring a regular food supply. And the "indigenous knowledge" argument must incorporate not only the cautious experiments in food cultivation but also the quite rapid and bold innovations made by smallholders in cocoa cultivation and market gardening of fresh vegetables, and by large-scale agricultural entrepreneurs in a variety of undertakings (Guyer 1984*b*). Each one of these explanations adds a dimension of understanding; each relies on—and therefore promotes the collection of—a different set of data.

Rather than elevate the interpretive problem to an abstract theoretical level where one could try to reconcile these various positions with one another, we need, as I have argued, to return to the descriptive level. At the level of ethnography, one asks whether the descriptive categories have tended to discriminate too little or, conversely, discriminated too much or too soon by assuming that the criteria for defining the key elements or processes were unproblematic. If one starts over, puts the whole picture back together, then there is a simple initial question to ask about the remarkable sense of continuity that all observers, of all theoretical persuasions, have seen in systems such as this: is there any particular aspect of the position of women and the nature of their agricultural practice which creates the impression of stability over time or which they themselves identify as central to their productive lives?

Through participating in women's daily routine and reconstructing farming patterns for the past, my own vision became centered on a particular field-type, the *afub owondo*, groundnut field. Alone among the differing fields in the Beti repertoire, the groundnut field has general and persistent importance, grown by all women farmers, apparently continuously over at least the past hundred years. It is central to women's work routine. Its crops are a source of pride in farming skill, provide essential ingredients to their cooking, and represent their contribution to wealth and welfare. Thus, the groundnut field gives the impression of an anchor or pivot to women's position and to the agricultural economy and ecology. Agricultural improvisations and innovations over the years, by both men and women, have integrated with it rather than invading or replacing it.

It is not an exaggeration to suggest that the characteristics of this field represent in a lived routine many of the pragmatic, social, and cultural aspects of gender relations more generally. It is cultivated with the female tool, the short-handled hoe. For reasons having to do with the type of land, the cropping pattern, and the sequence of activities, the groundnut field has always been amenable to cultivation by a woman working alone. This entails both pragmatic advantages, due to women's unpredictable access to male or group labor, and the personal prestige advantage of demonstrating individual skill. Groundnuts are the only crop that can represent this skill in the public context since they alone of the crops that women control have a single harvest season and need to be dried in the open courtyard in front of her kitchen. When older women try to convey the changes in their groundnut harvest over their lifetimes, they indicate the area of their courtyard covered by the drying nuts rather than the area of farm cultivated or even the number of baskets stocked away. By virtue of their storability, groundnuts in the past constituted the only agricultural crop through which a woman contributed personally and uniquely to her husband's wealth. Each wife gave a certain proportion of her harvest to her husband to be kept for his own or other collective purposes. Besides being a regular ingredient in the daily diet of starch and vegetable-based stews, groundnuts can also be prepared as roasts and cakes for the festive, favored, and transportable diet associated with the male activities of travel, exchange, and entertainment. For all these reasons a woman can express a pride in her groundnut harvest which goes beyond the routine satisfaction of fulfilling a mundane duty.

By focusing on this field, with its deep associations with female life and labor, one can ask, not what has happened to "female farming" but, how has *this field*, with all its symbolic gender load and pragmatic gender implications, changed in both its internal organization and its external links to the entire field system, and to the wider productive economy? The changing rhythms of work and control of the production, taken as a whole, become the central subjects to describe. Subjects such as the "position of women" or "female farming" are then removed from the center of direct attention, to be replaced by a descriptive method that is intrinsically imbued with gender conceptions. The varying and shifting ways in which gender conceptions and practices have worked over time can then be treated as an empirical question, in a word, discovered, rather than derived from theoretical premises.

In the late nineteenth century the woman's groundnut field constituted one phase in the farming cycle. The culturally dominant cycle lasted over twenty years, extending from the clearing of new land—often virgin forest—through a year of predominantly male cultivation (esep), followed by a short fallow (bindi), two to three years of female cultivation (afub owondo: the groundnut field), and a long fallow (ekodog) back to primary forest. The long temporal reach of the full cycle was matched by its distant spatial reach into the lands surrounding the village, eventually establishing plots far enough away to facilitate the removal of the village itself. The female cycle appears as a subcycle: following the esep field, the cultivation-fallow cycle was shorter and the plot was considerably smaller than esep, so it could be repeated within a single long cycle of forest to forest. A further set of field types operated on a yet more restricted time-space cycle; single-season fields were often cultivated by individuals opportunistically and devoted to monocrops or dry-season vegetable gardens on wetland.

The long cycle demanded the most male labor and evoked the greatest social and symbolic resonances: the warrior symbolism of treecutting and cultivation in the esep field of the prestige crop of melon-seed (ngon) used in exchange and feasting. To clear the land was to establish a general claim on the fertility thus activated. A man, "he clears, he eats": *a li, a di*. In its most literal meaning this refers to the two points at which an important man—*mfan mot*, a real man—participates in the food economy: at the beginning and at the end. Culturally, the act of clearing set powers of creativity in motion analogous to marriage and impregnation, establishing claims that reached forward into the indefinite future. A wife's claims were derived and encompassed, just as the field itself was spatially and temporally contained within the longer cycle. She did have claims: on the crops needed for cooking, including the intercrops and second-season harvest in the esep field and all the crops in the groundnut field. But these claims were themselves culturally validated by prior generative acts.

The two smaller cycles—a repetitive groundnut-ekodog cycle for women and the single-season plots for women and dependent men—were associated with low status. Widows, clients, and junior men regularly cultivated on restricted cycles because the ideal cycle embodied a scale of collective activity and a division of labor that could only be mobilized by a man of importance with wives, clients, and sons who could be mobilized to fulfill each of the stages.

The pre-cocoa system consisted of a set of variations on these themes, tailored to regional ecological conditions, embroidered by particularities of local politics, or improvised by individual headmen exercising the essential freedom of leaders to go a step beyond customary knowledge and social organization. During the early colonial period from the end of the nineteeth century to the 1930s several new crops, activities, and kinds of labor organization were grafted onto the indigenous pattern. Palm kernel production hardly affected cultivation because the palms grew wild and labor for cracking the kernels was not demanding enough, except possibly during the Great Depression, to result in any dramatic reworking of the field system to accommodate it. Obligatory contributions to requisitions for urban food supply, village rice fields to feed construction crews, and free labor on the administrative chiefs' large and experimental plantations have all come and gone. New crops were introduced, but they were retained very selectively after government pressures were lifted. Cocoa was by far the most important of the introduced cultivars, but its expansion among ordinary farmers dates from the mid-1930s and particularly from 1945. Innovations in farming techniques, labor organization, and distribution during the early colonial period all depended on administrative pressure of one sort or another, which ultimately limited their long-term direct effect.

Important indirect effects of colonial rule on farming practice stem from measures other than those specifically aimed at production. Forced sedentarization of settlements implied restrictions on the long esep cycle and encouraged repetition of the embedded shorter cultivation cycles. During the same period, people began to experience the contradictory effects of colonial and church policies on marriage and the position of women. They abandoned large-scale polygyny and thus eroded the conditions under which men could mobilize enough clients and sons to clear large new esep plots and enough wives to divide up a large esep fallow (bindi) into the smaller groundnut plots. By the time cocoa became a major crop there were already reasons why esep cultivation might have slipped in frequency of cultivation if not in cultural importance.

To a considerable degree, cocoa took over the esep (or *ekpak* in Eton dialect) type of field. Asked what happened to ekpak, one man told me, "Our cocoa fields are our bikpak [pl.]." Cocoa was planted in the shade of the food crops and grew up to occupy permanent forest plots. The annual work rhythm—the timing of the cocoa harvest, and the tasks themselves of cutting the pods, decorticating, and drying the beans—resembles very closely the timing and organization of tasks for the melon-seed harvest. The smoothness of fit is remarkable. This quality, along with the opportunity that cocoa afforded for the small producer to make a significant cash income for the first time, accounts, I believe, for the apparent lack of dispute over labor issues. Women had always tended the secondary esep crops and helped with the melon-seed harvest, and they continued the same functions when the main esep crop was cocoa.

Rubrics for male-female shares in cocoa income seem also to have followed very closely the principles of distribution for the melon-seed crop. Wives and dependent female kin get a small lump sum or proportion of the crop in kind, and female harvesters get a share of the beans. The cash income realized from cocoa is treated like the headman's own share of melon-seed, associated with feasting, exchange, and social investment rather than routine needs.

After about seven years, however, when the trees are fully bearing, the divergence between cocoa and esep becomes more apparent. When cocoa trees grow beyond a certain height there can be no intercrops and the land does not go through the full cycle back to fallow. There are two results: the grand cycle and its dependent short cycles are severed from one another into two separate land-use cycles, and women lose—through their literal disappearance—the staple food crops from the male stages of the old cycle. Not only the esep intercrops but also the other predominantly male staple crop, yams, went into decline because of seasonal pressures on male labor.

The disappearance of the material embodiment of what were contingent and derivative claims was a serious loss for Beti women. Replacement of a crop, task, or technique by another with similar characteristics—such as happened with melon-seed and cocoa—provides a basis for extrapolation from the old rubrics for distribution without the need to invoke abstract principles. By contrast, when an element is dropped from the task or crop repertoire altogether, renegotiation of claims entails abstracting from their material representation and dealing with them in a conceptually explicit way, for example, as outright dispute. For the 1940s and 1950s, the sources give little sense that Beti women could validly bring issues into the public arena for debate. One of the most often quoted proverbs with respect to women is, "The hen does not crow in front of the cock" (Tsala 1975: 275). Women did complain, but as Binet (1956: 60) suggests for the 1950s, by opting out rather than engaging in the claim system: "They cannot help but envy the men and look for ways of equalling them, by planting their own crops or by escaping to the cities."

Women adjusted to the loss by extending those farming activities that depended least on male participation: by planting two groundnut fields a year instead of the single large one that had in the past been grown only in the technically optimal of the two growing seasons. This gave not only more groundnuts, compensating for the decline in melon-seed, but a greater and more seasonally constant supply of the major female-produced staple, cassava, making up for the partial loss of male-produced yams. A colonial agricultural report suggests that crop density was also increased at about the same period, around the late 1940s.

To gain access to men's newly augmented incomes women took an indirect route, through developing a whole series of seasonal occupations such as liquor distilling, cooked-food selling, and trade in imported beer which diverted men's incomes through the market, rather than demanding it through the claim system. Such responses by women to income loss must be seen as an expression of political weakness, of their lack of access to a public platform from which they might renegotiate directly, in terms of general principle rather than traditionally accepted material embodiments, their claims to goods produced outside their own restricted cycle. The entire response creates an agro-ecological and economic dynamic that is critically marked by cultural constructions of gender and the social constraints on resource mobilization by women.

The expansion of food for Yaoundé as a result of post-Independence urban growth set up dynamics that flowed into the ongoing processes of domestic and technical adjustment to the cocoa conditions described above. In the early 1960s returns to labor were still low in the food sector, so men were not lured back en masse into food farming in the initial expansion period. Moreover, it was now difficult for men to requisition female labor back into a jointly defined agricultural operation, a household endeavor. Women had already expanded the restricted cycle of the field system to cover both growing seasons. The groundnut field was already managed on an individual, day-in/day-out work rhythm, and its staple crops of cassava, groundnuts, and leaf-vegetables had become the dependable core of the diet.

The three main strategies available to women for expanding production, given an already intensified cultivation system were: (1) to expand and intensify the groundnut field itself to include more marketable crops; (2) to revive (in some areas and by some women who could still get access to male labor for heavy clearing) a smaller version of the esep field, feminized in its products and labor patterns not to conflict with the insistent demands of the groundnut field; and (3) to extend the most restricted cycle of specialized one-crop, one-season plots requiring neither male labor nor multi-year occupation of the land.

Again, patterns of labor have adjusted without major dispute, because they have built on the already advanced separation of the two cycles. It is income rather than labor that has become the issue of male-female dispute.

And since it is men's claims to women's income which are now at issue, not vice versa, there has been a public and general aspect to the debate. The "a li, a di" (he clears, he eats) formula loses conviction when the cycles of production are disconnected, when there is very little clearing of virgin forest any more, and when women clear their short-fallow plots for themselves. Even longer cycles of claims have always existed, however, behind the one embedded in production itself, and both of them publicly articulated: resources are inherited from one generation to the next in the male line, and bridewealth payment entitles a husband, in principle, to the wealth his wife produces.

The three cycles linking act and claim—the intergenerational, the marital, and the productive—provide layers of justification. None is intrinsically more important than the other because they coexisted without obvious contradiction in the past. In the twentieth century, their relative priority as a principle for male-female spheres of control has been thoroughly confused by modern customary and legal interventions that have tried to institutionalize inconsistent bits and pieces of "tradition." Legislation and the court system have strengthened inheritance in the male line, tried to undermine bridewealth payment, and given quite strong legal backing to rights based on *mise en valeur*, actual development (cultivation) of the land. The first strengthens the long male cycle of intergenerational claims, the second undermines a man's claims over his wife, and the third provides women with a positive weapon against male control.

As Sally Moore (1986) has pointed out for customary law, the rules are always open to interpretation, and one of the most ambiguous aspects may be which strand, within a system containing multiple links between act and claim, should predominate as conditions shift and be elevated to an abstract principle as Western legal concepts based on status are brought in. Even in situations where people are not in outright dispute about the general nature and validity of the claims themselves, this issue of priority among several relevant bases for claims may render the whole situation ambiguous. And these are issues affecting key interests since there may be profoundly different implications for control and distribution depending on which "rhythmic tension," with which temporal reach, is invoked.

Beti men have an interest in maintaining a long, encompassing concept of productive cycles. The interpretation of "a li, a di" most favorable to a man is: *because* he clears—no matter how long ago, or even if it was his father or father's father who organized the actual work—he eats. The claim is affirmed, even though its material justification in the act of clearing has receded into the distant past. The strongest basis for all male claims would be to fix the key generative act so far back in personal and family time that it is no longer contingent on any production cycle, of whatever length. Ownership of the land would then be claimed by virtue of inheritance.

Beti women, in contrast, have an interest in a narrow and literal interpretation, at least with respect to control of their cash income: *if* he clears—recently, himself—he eats. Otherwise, since a woman can clear the secondary bush for herself, her husband has tenuous grounds to claim his share of her income. Using the same act, clearing, and by extrapolating from virgin forest to secondary bush, a woman can elevate what used to be a derivative claim to a primary claim.

The twentieth-century legal and social process of abstracting general principles about resource claims involves extrication from the material embodiments—the crop, the technique, the task, the generative intervention—which were their outward and visible expression in the past. This is not a simple translation, as the example explored here indicates. The levels can become dissonant with one another, for material, cultural, or jural reasons. And since it is only under certain circumstances that principles are openly disputed as such, one has to look for other means besides confrontation by which control is avoided, attenuated, or gradually won over. In some cases the dissonances may be unintended consequences of changes elsewhere in the system. But the possibility that they are strategically and deliberately engineered must not be ruled out. Ideally the difference between unintended consequences and the production of confusion for particular long-term purposes could be supported with evidence. Often such evidence is almost impossible to come by except for the policies of functionaries in the public sector. For a particular council of chiefs, or a particular colonial regime, and in relation to particular measures taken, one might plausibly differentiate between contradictions in the outcomes of an inadvertently incoherent policy, and the formation of a coherent policy to create contradictions. But the difficulty of generating historical evidence for negotiations of the ordinary population should not dissuade us from considering the possibility that similar processes were at work in local arenas.

The issue is not so much to categorize responses—opportunism, innovation, passive resistance, or concerted conscious struggle—but to develop ways of recognizing dissonance so that some sense of the parameters of agency is preserved—even where the documentation is lacking, even where there is no clear agreement on the criteria for defining elusive processes such as "struggle." At least the space can be created in which an understanding of the terms and implications of "struggle," negotiation, and the processes of change in the gendered division of labor can be nurtured.

This method may also help to illuminate the interaction of local systems with the wider political and economic context. Prices, legal policies, and a host of other interventions affect the conditions under which the members of local groups deal with one another; and working outward from the rhythms of work and income to the forces that account for them may help to incorporate such supralocal forces into analysis. The influence can work in the other direction also, from local to supralocal. At certain moments, issues that have smoldered within local communities may blaze across the regional or national horizon. In Southern Cameroon, dispute over control of women's incomes made waves at the national level in 1983, in a way that cannot be understood in terms of the history of stagnant food-farming techniques or female subordination alone.

Through the 1960s and 1970s most of women's cash incomes were not only too low but earned on too much of a routine, penny-penny basis to be devoted to any expenditures beyond direct analogues of their past in-kind responsibilities for food, plus a few personal needs. In the early 1980s, a change in the national government provided a somewhat more liberal atmosphere for local organizations, and women's incomes had risen enough to support a mushrooming growth in rotating credit associations. In 1983 a furor developed within the national political party about the apparent loss of control by the women's branch of the party of these women's associations in the Beti area, the Centre-South Province. The concern at the national level was that spontaneous organizations were growing far too fast to be incorporated into the structures of a one-party state. Party dismay, however, was expressed in gender terms; the women's branch was brought under scrutiny for its inability to control the female population. In the public debate, criticism of the association meetings invoked the symbolism of male claims: in sexual terms (what were women really doing at their credit association meetings?) and in terms of the grounding of women's life rhythms in insistent domestic demands (were they neglecting their cooking and childcare duties to take off on Sunday afternoons?).

The ambiguous state of gendered income claims is at the heart of the issue. Credit associations give women something they can hardly produce from their pattern of cultivation, namely intermittent peaks in their cash income. Never before have women produced a rhythm of income with marked peaks and troughs, except through their groundnut harvest, which is hardly commercialized at all. Their pattern of agricultural intensification over the twentieth century has reinforced a smooth seasonal income profile. Women's open participation in a means for producing lump-sum income peaks tacitly demonstrated the relative freedom of their own cycle of activity and claim on income from the male cycle that had enclosed it.[9]

CONCLUSION

The Beti example is organized as a series of interrelated cycles. In attempting to understand the course of change, one is then not working with dubiously measurable processes such as intensification, subordination, and increased work, but with changed elements, changed synchronies, and specific dissonances under particular historical conditions. This method has the added advantage of not separating material, cultural, and political descriptions from each other, nor making an analytical distinction between "macro" and "micro." A single basic description of time-space rhythms and their meaning obviates the awkward stage at which such standard analytical distinctions have to be superseded in order to splice the various dimensions of social processes back together. Having made a time-space description, one can then expand the analysis in a number of analytically different directions—symbolic, organizational, ecological, and drawing where necessary on the older intellectual resources of structural and evolutionary analysis—without losing all potential for coming back to an analysis based on their unity in social practice.

Such an approach does several things at once. It allows us to see significant changes in production and distribution in African family systems that have been left hidden by past descriptive techniques. It preserves agency without giving up the inspiration provided by structural theory. It builds gender into the method of studying production, rather than making the position of women the central focus. And finally, it allows the specifically African course of agricultural change in the past century to be reconstructed, to stand alongside the evolutionary hypotheses about intensification derived from other places and other eras of history.

The image of African female farming is a kind of origin myth. In shifting the methods of description, one brings African farming into the same moment of world history as we also inhabit, and opens it to the same debates about the intellectual tools necessary for understanding the gendered division of labor.

ACKNOWLEDGMENTS

This chapter is based on field research carried out in Cameroon, financed by the National Institute of Mental Health (1975–1976) and the Joint Committee on African Studies of the Social Science Research Council and American Council of Learned Societies (1979). I was a research associate at the National Advanced School of Agriculture in Yaoundé. The chapter synthesizes arguments made at greater length elsewhere (Guyer 1984a and b, 1988). Part 2 recapitulates data reported in my article in *Current Anthropology* (1988) and does so with the permission of the journal. I have benefited from many comments on this piece, particularly from the Gender Studies group and Micaela di Leonardo at Yale University, where it was first presented in this form.

NOTES

1. Boserup herself steps deftly around an explicit commitment to Baumann's timeless view of precolonial agricultural history, insisting that "It is widely but mis-

takenly assumed that such 'traditional' systems are necessarily passed on from one generation to the next without ever undergoing changes . . ." (1970: 17). With her central focus on the era of "development," however, she offers no alternative to Baumann's vision of the precolonial past and hence implies the evolutionary primordiality of female farming.

2. Critiques of this logic appeared quite early (see Huntington 1975), rediscovering Baumann's initial poor opinion of the status implications of women farming; to him it was poor and primitive agriculture they were practicing.

3. This section of the chapter is abstracted from Guyer 1984*a*.

4. It lies beyond the arguments of the present chapter to reconstruct what these might have been for the precolonial era. Insofar as the same kind of shift in the division of labor seems to hold when one old staple is replaced by another, as Haswell describes for the Gambia (1975), it seems not explicable either in purely technical terms or in terms of the cultural foreignness of the crop. Possibly the economics and politics of slavery, increasing military ambition, religious conversion, and expanded horizons of trade both drew men out of local contexts and undermined the collective ritual basis for old agricultural styles.

5. Concepts and methods are more fully elaborated in Guyer (1988).

6. The most salient papers here are Murdock and Provost (1973), Burton, Brudner, and White (1977), Ember (1983), and Burton and White (1984). The authors of this series of papers have begun to critique their own methods. They note that certain categories need to be broken down: animal husbandry varies according to the type of animal. But the problem is broader than subdividing old categories. In history, evolutionary sequences go backward: stratification within societies may decline as well as rise. Some correlations cannot possibly be read as sequential entailments: under most preindustrial conditions cereal production with peak labor needs cannot evolve out of processes of intensification in tropical forest root-crop zones. What were thought to be derivative developments appear to have their own dynamic: the effect of craft specialization on agricultural intensification seems, on further examination, to be stronger than the reciprocal (Dow 1985). All these conclusions suggest that for more fine-grained analysis task structures need to be redefined and variables that capture relative values and time allocation need to be added.

7. See Guyer (1981).

8. It is worth noting that the concern with gender inequality in feminist scholarship cuts across quite radically different theoretical positions. Strathern insists on *culture-specific* approaches to value, personhood, and transactability (1984, 1985), whereas the thrust of both neo-Marxist value studies and comparative time-allocation studies has been to work toward a *single scale*, usable for direct comparisons.

9. The information on this episode is taken from a confidential report commissioned by the government. It is not published and therefore cannot be cited. The report itself showed considerable wisdom, pointing out that these associations are a major economic and development asset and should not be destroyed—even if that were possible. I do not know how the report was acted upon, although certainly the relationship between the central party and the women's branch was addressed. It may be some years before the real effect of such momentary eruptions—among all the others that affect political dynamics—can be assessed.

BIBLIOGRAPHY

Baumann, H. 1928. The division of work according to sex in African hoe culture. *Africa* 1: 289–319.

Binet, Jacques. 1956. *Budgets familiaux des planteurs de cacao au Cameroun*. Paris: Orstom.

Boserup, Ester. 1966. *The conditions of agricultural growth*. Chicago: Aldine.

———. 1970. *Woman's role in economic development*. London: St. Martin's Press.

Brydon, Lynne. 1981. Rice, yams and chiefs in Avatime: Speculations on the development of a social order. *Africa* 51 (2): 659–677.

Burton, Michael L., L. A. Brudner, and D. R. White. 1977. A model of the sexual division of labor. *American Ethnologist* 4: 227–251.

Burton, Michael L., and D. R. White. 1984. Sexual division of labor in agriculture. *American Anthropologist* 86: 568–583.

Douglas, Mary T., and Baron Isherwood. 1979. *The world of goods*. New York: Basic Books.

Dow, Malcolm M. 1985. Agricultural intensification and craft specialization: A non-recursive model. *Ethnology* 24 (2): 137–152.

Ember, Carol R. 1983. The relative decline in women's contribution to agriculture with intensification. *American Anthropologist* 85: 285–305.

Fernandez, James W. 1982. *Bwiti: An ethnography of the religious imagination in Africa*. Princeton: Princeton University Press.

Flight, C. 1976. The Kintampo culture and its place in the economic prehistory of West Africa. In *Origins of African plant domestication*. J. R. Harlan, J. DeWet, and A. Stemler, eds. The Hague: Mouton.

Forde, Daryll. 1964. *Yako studies*. London: Oxford University Press.

Guyer, Jane I. 1981. The raw, the cooked and the half-baked: Observations on the division of labor by sex. Boston University African Studies Center Working Paper No. 48.

———. 1984a. Naturalism in Models of African Production. *Man* (n.s.) 19: 371–388.

———. 1984b. *Family and farm in Southern Cameroon*. Boston University African Research Series No. 15.

———. 1988. The multiplication of labor: Historical methods in the study of gender and agricultural change in modern Africa. *Current Anthropology* 29 (2): 247–272.

Haswell, Margaret. 1975. *The nature of poverty*. London: Macmillan.

Huntington, Suellen. 1975. Issues in woman's role in economic development: Critique and alternatives. *Journal of Marriage and the Family* (1975): 1001–1012.

Johnny, M., J. Karimu, and P. Richards. 1981. Upland and swamp rice farming systems in Sierra Leone: The social context of technological change. *Africa* 51: 596–620.

Kaberry, Phyllis. 1952. *Women of the grassfields: A study of the economic position of women in Bamenda, British Cameroons*. London: Her Majesty's Stationery Office.

Laburthe-Tolra, Philippe. 1981. *Les Seigneurs de la Foret. Essai sur le passe historique, l'organisation sociale et les normes ethiques des anciens Beti du Cameroun*. Paris: Publications de la Sorbonne.

Linares, Olga. 1981. From tidal swamp to inland valley: On the social organization of wet rice cultivation among the Diola of Senegal. *Africa* 51: 557–595.

Mead, Margaret. 1935. *Sex and temperament in three primitive societies*. New York: W. Morrow.

Meillassoux, Claude. 1981. *Maidens, meal and money: Capitalism and the domestic community*. London: Cambridge University Press.

Moore, Sally Falk. 1986. *Social facts and fabrications: "Customary" law on Kilimanjaro, 1880–1980*. London: Cambridge University Press.

Murdock, G. P., and C. Provost. 1973. Factors in the division of labor by sex: A cross-cultural analysis. *Ethnology* 12: 203–225.

Reiter, Rayna, ed. 1975. *Toward an anthropology of women*. New York: Monthly Review Press.

Rey, Pierre-Philippe. 1979. Class contradiction in lineage societies. *Critique of anthropology* 4: 41–60.

Richards, Audrey. 1939. *Land, labour and diet on Northern Rhodesia: An economic study of the Bemba tribe*. London: Oxford University Press.

Rosaldo, Michelle, and Louise Lamphere, eds. 1974. *Women, culture and society*. Stanford: Stanford University Press.

Sabean, David. 1978. Small peasant agriculture in Germany at the beginning of the nineteenth century: Changing work patterns. *Peasant Studies* 7 (4): 218–224.

Strathern, Marilyn. 1984. Subject or object? Women and the circulation of valuables in Highlands New Guinea. In *Women and property—women as property*. Renee Hirschon, ed., 158–575. London: Croom Helm.

———. 1985. Kinship and economy: Constitutive orders of a provisional kind. *American Ethnologist* 12 (2): 191–209.

Thompson, E. P. 1967. Time, work discipline and industrial capitalism. *Past and Present* 38: 56–97.

Tsala, Theodore. 1975. *Minkana Beti*. Douala: College Libermann.

EIGHT

Women, Technology, and International Development Ideologies
Analyzing Feminist Voices[1]

Kay B. Warren and Susan C. Bourque

INTRODUCTION

Although anthropology has seen the study of social change as central to its mission, the field has been strikingly ambivalent about "international development." On the one hand, anthropologists with a commitment to applied research on Third World poverty have long been involved in international development agencies and projects. And researchers in academia have urged the field to turn its attention to the global economy, the state and national policy, and grassroots movements for social change. On the other hand, anthropologists have been skeptical about development because this conceptualization of change tends not to be self-reflexive; that is, it fails to see the cultures and political economies of developed countries as being just as problematic as those of so-called underdeveloped countries. These anthropologists find it necessary to critique the ethnocentrism in unilinear narratives of change that advocate and link "development," "westernization," and "progress." In what follows, we attempt to put a new generation of development ideologies, which focus on women and gender issues, in tension with anthropological studies of gender, culture, and change. In the process we examine the ways in which gender is being incorporated as a category of analysis in the study of social and technological change; how formulations of change such as "development" and "technology transfer" both color our understandings of the Third World and reflexively reveal Western cultural and political preoccupations; and how feminist anthropologists are responding with ethnographic studies of gender, culture, and political economy.

The explosive growth of research on gender since the beginning of the United Nations Decade for women in 1975 has resulted in new empirical work and a range of conflicting perspectives formulated by researchers studying "the integration of women into development." Anthropologists and feminist scholars have urged researchers to internationalize the study of work, family, and policy. In this chapter, we evaluate the *conceptual* contributions that recent research has made to formulating and answering questions about the consequences of changing technologies for women and women's responses to the changing circumstances of their lives. This task is important because the models and languages of analysis that inform current research influence the direction and scope of future studies and strategies for change. As one would expect from an anthropological approach, the issue of "technology" quickly dissolves into wider discussions of the cultural and political situations that determine the significance of particular technologies.[2] That much of the international development community and many social scientists are able to identify technological concerns as primarily technical and to "factor out" or "bracket" cultural context, political economy, and history is something we need to treat in our research and writing (cf. Warren and Bourque 1987).

Researchers and critics have identified ironies in the call to "integrate women into development." In reality women have always been integrated into development in the sense of being caught in the currents of change, forging their own understandings of change, and responding as people with multiple identities, affiliations, and concerns. Another irony involves the use of the word *development* to capture the directionality of change in the Third World. Development is an example of a transition narrative that evokes a range of problematic associations, from evolutionary (i.e. the transformation of "primitive" to "developed"), to psychobiological (i.e. the individual's growth from "infancy" to "adulthood"), to Western-focused definitions of "progress" (i.e. the movement from "traditional" to "modern"), and finally to the uncritical tendency to blame the victims of political and economic marginalization for their poverty.

For some social scientists, "development" simply refers to the actual patterns of change that nations have experienced with industrialization, mechanization, and the expansion of capitalist markets in the nineteenth and twentieth centuries. For others, the concept involves state intervention and planning to achieve a higher "Gross Domestic Product" (GDP) or other macro-level changes measurable with aggregate statistics that are understood to reflect changes in standards of living.[3] For many scholars, the issue is both standards of living and grassroots participation in agendas for change. In this case, development is not fully measured by conventional statistical indicators, but rather by structural changes to promote equity, to widen women's and other "minorities'" economic and political participation, to recognize women as agents rather than as passive "targets" or "end users" of change, and to empower local groups to engage in development focusing on their own perceived needs. A concern with equity versus growth lies at the center of a new generation of "non-governmental organization" (NGO) development activists who are promoting decentralized development projects. As our analysis of alternative perspectives on women and technological change shows, however, "decentralization" means very different things in different models of change.

In this chapter, we first examine four major approaches to the study of gender and technology: the integrationist, appropriate technology, feminization of technology, and global economy perspectives. Then we move on to current anthropological literature and its interpretation of women in multinational, high-technology production, examining the significance of contrasting portrayals of women's experience in multinational corporations in Hong Kong and Mexico.[4] Finally, we examine the ways in which feminist scholars participate in an explicit Western debate about the "sameness" or "difference" of women and men and in an implicit debate about the "sameness" or "difference" of societies undergoing change.

Doubts about the impact of technology transfer on the Third World began in the 1960s with the reassessment of international development programs and their implications for women. Feminist critics[5] of such programs observed first that women were absent from the calculations of most development planners. As a result women's economic contributions were dismissed or underestimated, and the destructive effects of imposed change on women's lives were ignored (Boserup 1970; Rogers 1980; Chaney and Schmink 1976).

Critics argued that contemporary patterns were reflections of a long history in which Western technology, particularly agricultural technology for the production of commercial and export crops, was differentially available to men and women in rural communities. European colonial administrators, applying their own notions of appropriate gender relations, made men the preferred recipients of training by Western technicians even in areas where women were the primary agriculturalists. As a result of the differential access of each gender to novel technologies—to plows, high-yield seed varieties, fertilizers, training to grow commercial crops, mechanized equipment, or motor-driven transportation—women's powers in community affairs were eroded. Moreover, local cultural values stemming from male dominance in community politics, rather than female centrality in productive activities, were often reinforced in the organization of work around newly introduced tools and crops (Boserup 1970: 53–54; Etienne and Leacock 1980). Of course this process did not occur in a vacuum: changing modes of production, the introduction of commercial plantations, and the consolidation of new national elites who bought up land resources, often meant that rural men were forced into cyclic migration in search of income-generating employment while women became specialists in the production of food crops for family consumption. As internationally oriented commercial agriculture displaced small-scale agriculturalists, creating land-poor populations in an increasingly monetized economy, gendered cleavages in access to resources were also established.

To the extent that feminists and development critics defined *access* as the crucial issue, the logical solution was to equalize it. Poor women needed the ability to use tools and machines, as well as literacy and education.[6] The message was explicitly protechnology: women had lost ground because of restricted access. The solution to inequities was to open the restricted channels of education and training.[7]

Early analyses of development and modernization often assumed that the process was progressive and unproblematic. Like wider access, national development might be difficult to achieve in the twentieth century given the legacies of colonialism, but it was clearly the goal. Development, however, was to come under closer scrutiny. In the late 1960s and early 1970s, critics pointed out that industrialization and modernization policies were not producing the expected social and economic improvements in Third World countries. Conditions in the Third World were deteriorating due to the dependence of these economies on the capital, credits, technology, training, and markets of the developed nations . This troubled dependency led many scholars to conclude that the wide-ranging adoption of Western models and technologies might not be the appropriate solution for developing nations.

Women and development, as a field of inquiry, and the dissemination of technologies to developing societies, as a strategy for change, have been criticized for reflecting Western ethnocentrism. Many Third World scholars argue that the concept of "technological development" is an invention of the industrialized states to serve their own economic interests as marketers of capital-intensive and consumer-oriented technologies. Similarly, they argue that Western feminism as a political movement and a scholarly tradition has paid too little attention to imperialism, colonialism, racism, and differences among women. Moreover, they contend that Western priorities are very different from those appropriate to the Third World (D'Onofrio-Flores 1982; Tadesse 1982; Srinivasan 1982). Specifically they find that Western development strategies have been insensitive to cultural differences in the significance of the family and kinship groups, the value of children, the devastating inequities born of class differences, and the economic realities of impoverished dependent economies.

ALTERNATIVE PERSPECTIVES ON TECHNOLOGY AND WORK

Scholars have elaborated distinctive lines of argument to conceptualize the impact of international development on women. Some approaches see technology as a potential liberator for women, who must commonly spend hours every day in labor-intensive food processing on top of other heavy family and agrarian duties. Other approaches see technology as an integral aspect of changing national and global political economies with complex, differential consequences for women and men given culturally specific sexual divisions of labor. Our recent review of the literature suggests that these diverse approaches have coalesced into several distinctive viewpoints (cf. Bourque and Warren 1987). Each approach elaborates a political critique and strategies to enhance women's position in the face of technological change.

THE INTEGRATIONIST STRATEGY

The integrationist framework is a liberal, reformist analysis largely focused on the professional and technical classes. Its faith resides neither in a socialist challenge to the inequities of capitalism nor in a radical feminist revolution to humanize technology. In arguing for the integration of women into formal decision-making positions in government, business, and the professions, it is the flip-side of the appropriate technology model that focuses on involving poor women in grassroots programs. Its adherents are concerned about the limited number of women trained as scientists and engineers and the absence of women from positions of scientific leadership. They share a belief in the possible benefits of technology and a desire to see women participate in its development. This perspective argues that the "integration" of women will result in the transformation of basic institutions because comprehensive female participation would challenge existing sexual divisions of labor and authority, as well as differential male-female earnings. Although this view does not conclude that wider female participation would result in a trans-formative feminization of technology and industry, it does hold that women would introduce a distinctive range of values and concerns to the work world (Jahan 1985).

The integrationist perspective seeks to account for women's low representation in fields directly related to technology, to identify obstacles to women's educational and employment achievements, and to devise programs to reverse gender asymmetries (Briscoe and Pfafflin 1979; Hall 1979; Anderson 1985). Researchers holding this position have focused attention on the ideologies that surround the acquisition of technical competence and the structural arrangements that reinforce stereotypes marking scientific fields and expertise as masculine in the West and in the Third World. Not surprisingly, they see the key to change in the political culture of education and the workplace (A. Sen 1984; Namboze 1985).

In order to erode gender stereotypes and widen opportunities, they argue, we must understand the processes that reproduce existing patterns. This implies that we must understand gender differences and hierarchies as a product of culturally created social ideologies and the material conditions of women's and men's lives. Explanations that justify gendered divisions of learning and work as necessary and natural because they are biological or functional or because they are the vestiges of early human evolution are instances of science as social ideology in the service of existing hierarchies. The school and the workplace also need to be examined as cultural and political environments where expectations are reinforced by practices that promote female exclusion, segregation, and avoidance. Fundamental to this perspective is an understanding of how institutions shape meaning and value, as well as how individuals can both internalize and challenge social norms (Bourque and Warren 1981a; Keller 1984) . These analyses can be extended to fields in which women are underrepresentated, exploring ways to increase women's enrollment in science and engineering, and developing strategies for dealing with math anxiety and stereotypes that place women in the category of nonscientist (Briscoe and Pfafflin 1979).

At their best proponents of this viewpoint do not make the classical liberal mistake of assuming that individuals are autonomous decision-makers who freely decide to participate or not in technological development. Nor do they consider education to be a "variable" that mechanically accounts for higher rates of technology usage. Rather, these analysts see education as a process of structural and ideological tracking. As a result, they have had to readdress the question of wider *access* as a solution to gender-inequality and to take on institutional change as necessary for transforming structures that constrain choice and equity.

The challenge for the integrationist perspective is that the arenas that need to be transformed have been remarkably resistant to change. Reforms in education or the workplace require the intervention of political forces that must be convinced of reason and reward for pursuing substantial change (cf. Buvinić 1983). Moreover, change must take place at a variety of levels: in the institutional arenas of national governments as well as in household politics. Since many of the changes sought can be affected by governmental or bureaucratic action, it is possible to imagine a political plan of action to influence policymakers in education and labor. Yet for the types of change envisioned it is often individuals, mothers, fathers, teachers, co-workers, and employers who will be the primary instruments for change. Policies and programs must grapple with both levels.

Amartya Sen's (1984) insightful analysis of the intrahousehold power dimensions of gender relations makes an important contribution to this perspective. He notes the generalized reluctance to face the powerful conflicts of interest that exist within households and, for the Indian case, identifies a pattern of "adapted perception" which involves "systematic failures to see intrafamily inequalities and perceiving extraordinary asymmetries as normal and legitimate." Sen notes that

> problems of conflict within the family tend to get hidden by adapted perceptions both of "mutuality" of interests (going well beyond the actual elements of

congruence that do, of course, importantly exist) and of "legitimacy" of inequalities of treatment. As a result no policy analysis in this area can be complete without taking up the question of political education and understanding. . . . This is an area in which social illusions nestle closely to reality, and terrible inequities are cloaked firmly in perceived legitimacy. (1984: 3)

In addition to family social ideologies and political issues, there are difficulties at the national level for the reforms proposed by the integrationist perspective. On the one hand, this top-down strategy bets on the educationally privileged in environments where national debt burdens severely limit social programs for the poor. On the other hand, although most leaders must publicly declare themselves in favor of greater educational opportunity, privately they may fear that expanded education will create political problems, especially when they are unable to meet the demand for jobs from those already educated (Jahan 1985). It should not be surprising, therefore, that women in many countries have reacted to the limited scope of top-down programs by creating their own coalitions of poor and educated women to pursue experiments in nonformal education.

APPROPRIATE TECHNOLOGY

The advocates of appropriate technology hope to attack Third World poverty and underdevelopment by increasing local productivity without reinforcing patterns of dependence on industrial nations. This viewpoint has roots in those sectors of the international, but-basically-Western development community that philosophically favor decentralized, small-scale approaches to development. This is a direct offshoot of the "small is beautiful" philosophy of the 1960s and 1970s involving a critique of centralization and the capital-intensive economic strategies that had dominated development planners' solutions to poverty. In practice this approach advocates scientific rationality and technical efficiency as ways to increase productivity. The strategy is to move away from capital-intensive solutions toward less expensive intermediate technologies emphasizing local resources.

Appropriate technology is envisioned as increasing women's productivity and giving them more time for other obligations and community development efforts. For example, in rural societies where women spend hours every day gathering fuel for their kitchen fires, development planners have worked on new designs for low-tech mud-brick stoves that would significantly cut fuel consumption. In the very common cases where rodents, insects, or rot destroy more than a third of family harvests during the early months of storage, design projects concentrate on low-cost storage practices that would increase available food. Hand-operated grinding machines for corn, wheat, and millet, as well as rice hullers and palm-oil presses, are promoted to free women from hours of daily drudgery without displacing workers. Solar energy, wind power, and biogas are thought of as forms of energy that would cut dependence on expensive commercial fuels (Tinker 1981; Carr 1981, 1984).

Most appropriate-technology development projects see cultural variability as an impediment to the adoption of more efficient technology. The technological focus of this approach has meant that local communities in the Third World are not generally consulted when it is decided which local problems need to be addressed. Rather, a combination of international technical experts and state development agents work to assess which technologies to develop locally. Communities are generally consulted in the dissemination stage of the development process. As is evident from the failures of this approach, its well-meaning paternalism—reflecting a common development ideology—has undermined many of its projects.

Although in conception, appropriate technology seems eminently reasonable, in practice it has brought additional dilemmas. Foremost is the fear of increased unemployment with new technologies. For women the cost of innovation is often high, especially when they find themselves caught in a double-bind. Limited financial resources generally restrict women's use of technologies that might increase their productivity and give them wider access to credit, education, and land (Ahmed 1985). Women's economically marginal position makes it very difficult for them to experiment with their family's welfare. For novel technologies to break through women's realistic skepticism, they must substantially increase women's productivity in order to pay for the equipment and compensate women for the time lost from other work while experimenting with new techniques (Tinker 1981: 58).

Leading exponents of appropriate technology have come to criticize top-down decision making in the development of technologies, noting that although they may appear clearly so to engineers and development workers, the people who expect to use the new techniques may not find them appropriate at all (Carr 1981: 193). Certainly, African women, who experimented with solar cookers, found serious drawbacks in an allegedly fuel-saving technology when they had to cook during the heat of the day, move the stove continually to collect the sun's rays, and were unable to fit their family-sized pots on the delicate stoves (Carr 1981).

Even if full consultation with the "end users," as they are called, takes place and designs are consistent with local needs and use patterns, the concept of "appropriate" technology to lighten women's work may have fundamental pitfalls. A sexual division of technology may be created in which women gain appropriate technology for domestic work while men become the focus of wider technology training that generates employment opportunities (Leet 1981). The issue is of particular significance in societies in which women are expected to be the financers of the traditional domestic economy with their own earnings as well as in cases where social change has multiplied the number of women-headed households.

Critical advocates of appropriate technology call for women to be involved in high-tech policy planning in order to influence the use of technology, the agenda of research priorities, the choice of government subsidies, and the discussion of needs (Leet 1981). They conclude it is not the form of technology that determines which gender uses it, but rather who controls its development, dissemination, and products (Overholt et al. 1985). Yet the practice of appropriate technology as a development strategy continues to be top-down.

THE FEMINIZATION OF TECHNOLOGY

The feminization of technology represents a radical feminist social critique and strategy for social change and has adherents in the United States, Europe, and India, among other countries. The language of this approach has also been incorporated in many ecological, peace, and grassroots political movements. As technological innovation is now organized, according to this school of thought, distinctive "masculinist" values determine its development and applications. The result is the continued dominance of values emphasizing hierarchy, competition, immediate measurable results, material accumulation, depersonalization, and economic and political expansionism. It is not that bearers of masculinist views are ignorant of other values; rather, they have been coerced by the economic order to suppress their "needs for subjectivity, feelings, intimacy, and humanity" and instead to "project them onto the private life and women" (Bergom-Larsson 1982: 35).

The feminization-of-technology position holds that technology must be redirected to serve new values, including human growth (rather than economic profit), conservation, decentralization, self-reliance, self-sufficiency, and caring. This view postulates a distinctive women's culture and sees it as a critical tool for transforming the social order toward a more humanistic, egalitarian one, concerned with relationships and welfare rather than individual success and profit. The primary source of this utopian vision is women's involvement in the family, where (this perspective idealistically holds) hierarchy is deemphasized, nonviolent persuasion is stressed, and investment is directed toward the nurturance of future generations. Women learn a wider lesson from their familial vantagepoint: hierarchy, whatever its form, inevitably subordinates the weaker (Boulding 1981; Bergom-Larsson 1982).

Unfortunately, according to these authors, women's values are currently imprisoned by the separation of spheres of home and work. Effective change requires an expansion of the women's sphere and a new political procedure for evaluating technology, one that involves women in policy-making roles and questions the impact of new technologies on women and women's culture. If female values were successfully to inform the public world, then distinctions between the value of "productive, paid" work and "nonproductive, unpaid" work would be challenged; women and men would share a personal commitment to respond to the needs of their communities, and unnecessary divisions of labor would be rejected (H. Scott 1984; Bergom-Larsson 1982).

This perspective argues that women should not necessarily pursue integration into Western-directed development efforts. If they do, they are likely to lose the decentralized, relatively egalitarian social order of "traditional" society which Western women ill-advisedly gave up long ago. For those free to experiment outside Western patriarchies, the best strategy would be to strengthen women's networks and expand the women's sphere as a source of new economic and political organizations (Boulding 1981).[8] Western women must cope with more pervasive patriarchy, the sharp division of public and private life, and an economic system devoted to masculinist values.

Feminization-of-technology is best regarded as a utopian political model rather than an accurate analysis of international development problems or realities. Its roots and values are reflections of a radical feminist critique of Western "patriarchy." This perspective evokes the psychoanalytic imagery of feminist psychologists and anthropologists who have been influenced by American readings of Freudian object-relations theory (cf. Ortner 1974; Chodorow 1978; and Gilligan 1982).[9] This language pictures women as being more nurturant and other-directed than men because they give birth and take responsibility for infant care. A psychology of caring roots women in the domestic sphere, whereas men gain their identity and dominant independence by transcending the authority of their mothers and creating the public sphere in the form of a world of politics, abstract thought, and cultural achievements.

The elaboration of this language of contrasts and oppositions for women's and men's natures is naive and insufficient for cross-cultural research. This perspective dangerously romanticizes women's values, the family, the separation of "domestic" and "public" spheres, and the nature of Third World societies. One has only to look at the complex and various constructions of gender in contemporary societies, the negotiations of gender identities as they are realized in practice, and the interplay of family dynamics and legal systems to challenge these images of male and female.[10]

Instead of embracing psychoanalytic representations, we need to contextualize "motherhood"; that is, to analyze the ways in which various images of motherhood are constructed, imposed, subverted, manipulated, enshrined, and doubted in the everyday life and ideologies of other societies and our own. This reformulation calls for culturally sensitive research on the multiple meanings of motherhood (and, obviously, of other gendered identities): when and how constructions of gender are used to exclude women from the workplace, when they are used by women to mobilize politically, when they are evoked to identify failures in the sexuality of young women, and how constructions and practices vary by class, race, and age within particular social systems.

The final limitation of the feminization-of-technology approach is political: by distancing men from the "natural" concerns of women, this perspective limits, by definition, those with whom women might ally themselves, those whose vested interests are to question current arrangements, to articulate options, and to promote change to more humanistic and egalitarian social orders.

THE GLOBAL ECONOMY

The global-economy perspective questions "technology" in the narrow sense as the focus of "development," arguing that, in an interpenetrating world system, the primary issue is the capacity of expansionist capitalist classes to channel economic accumulation through the exploitation of other classes. This critique uses neo-Marxist language to define important historical forces that shape international divisions of labor, national economies, and developing countries' capacities to compete in international markets. Of central concern is the way that market economies have shaped an international order in which developing countries are sources of cheap labor and raw materials for technologically sophisticated countries where capital is accumulated. These scholars agree that one should not consider technology without studying the issues of its production and consumption in the contexts of global economics, the transformation of agrarian and industrial class relations in different regions and countries, and national policies that favor certain sectors at the expense of others. Feminist anthropologists have contributed a gendered dimension to these analyses by studying the impacts of economic change on class formation, sexual divisions of labor, and the reproduction of the labor force in the household (Stolcke 1981).

This perspective has been very influential among international women's and development circles. For many, it provides a crucial linkage between, critiques of capitalism, imperialism, and gender stratification (cf. Reiter 1975b; Etienne and Leacock 1980; Young et al. 1981; Nash and Fernández-Kelly 1983; Nash and Safa 1985; Leacock and Safa 1986; Nash 1989). As Benería and Sen conclude:

> The problem for women is not only the lack of participation in this process [of development] with men; it is a system [of international capital accumulation] that generates and intensifies inequalities, making use of existing gender hierarchies to place women in subordinate positions at each different level of interaction between class and gender. This is not to deny the possibility that capitalist development might break down certain social rigidities oppressive to women. But these liberating tendencies are accompanied by new forms of subordination. (1986: 150)

Representing another current of this perspective, Stolcke describes the function of women's domestic subordination in perpetuating wider inequalities:

[T]he perpetuation of class relations and domination—mediated directly by the institutions of marriage, the family and inheritance . . . determines both women's primary assignment to domestic labour and the undervaluation of this function. In class society, in other words, the sexual division of labour— women's domestication—is ultimately the product of man's control over women's reproductive capacity in the interests of perpetuating unequal access to the means of production. (1981: 34)

Both nationalists who reject Western influence in their politics and economics and socialists who seek redistributive alternatives to free market economies find these perspectives useful. Although liberal researchers do not share the utopian socialist vision, it is clear that materialist analyses have influenced their thinking about the importance of an international perspective that sees various forms of inequality as interactive and central to explanations of current patterns of development.

The insights from the perspective of global economy also allow us to focus on a neglected element in many feminist analyses of technology: the interplay of national governments and international markets in shaping national planning, policy development, and the allocation of resources (Afshar 1987). Of particular concern is the state's creation of labor force policy in areas such as employment, migration, education, housing, agriculture, and industrial development. How do states formulate priorities for national development? For the agrarian sector, how do they balance the need to produce food crops for domestic consumption with the need to encourage the production of commodities for export? What alternatives do they see for increasing domestic production, for dealing with shifts in subsistence agriculture and wage labor, and for regulating dependency on the international market for basic food supplies?

From our point of view, the global-economy perspective gives the issue of decentralized, small-scale work a much more complex shape than does the feminization-of-technology analysis. The latter's proponents see decentralization as a positive and absolute contrast to hierarchical, centralized systems. The global-economy perspective, however, reveals that decentralization is not inherently positive or negative, nor is it always an exclusive alternative to centralized modes of production. As in the case of multinational assembly plants, contemporary industrialization can foster decentralized modes, such as subcontracting to domestic outworkers, to produce at a lower cost (Benería and Roldán 1987). The issue is how these work patterns influence households, whether women are able to gain greater control of work processes in the smaller units, and whether companies exploit a fragmented labor force by raising production quotas for constant wages.

The global-economy perspective questions the common tendency to treat women as individuals without other competing identities, and to see women as a category with uniform interests and concerns. To overcome the conceptual simplification of other feminist frameworks, this view argues that, rather than studying individual women, we should instead examine household units by their class position in mixed subsistence, cash-crop, and urban economies. Women's domestic responsibilities vary by class and involve intricate balances of monetized and nonmonetized activities, rapidly responding to changing market conditions (Ahmed 1985; Agarwal 1985; Bryceson 1985; Bourque and Warren 1981a, 1981b). However socially valued or devalued, women's privatized household roles are critical for the physical and social reproduction of the labor force. The central analytic project is to study women's reproductive and productive roles as they are mediated by their class positions in the wider economy (cf. Lamphere 1987). Thus, another important contribution of this perspective is to help restore concrete social contexts to women's work and perceptions.

There can be unfortunate consequences, however, when analysts focus their concerns about women on the household and the family. Men are seldom viewed as members of households unless it is to see them as "heads" or as "breadwinners." The focus on women's domestic and reproductive roles has sometimes limited concerns to those roles. Of course, the family and household are central elements in both men's and women's lives, and reproduction and childcare responsibilities affect women's participation in the labor force and politics. However, the history in this area of political movements as well as policy and development programs has shown that if concern is directed at reproduction and domestic roles, those issues are likely to set limits on national policy directed to women (cf. Jaquette and Staudt 1985; Benería and Sen 1982; Buvinić 1983, 1984; Evans 1985). As a result, women become the targets of population programs and welfare projects, or they are integrated into the lowest levels of production as part-time workers. Little thought is given to providing women access to the full range of skills that would allow them to control and direct development activities (see Buvinić 1984; Sen 1985). As long as women are primarily conceived of as members of households, there may be a tendency to leave unquestioned their absence from society's significant political, social, and economic institutions.

MULTINATIONALS: A TECHNOLOGICAL CASE STUDY

In analyzing the impact of global patterns of change on women's roles a number of issues must be considered. First is the impact of technology on agricultural production. As subsistence farming has given way to mechanized commercial agriculture for national and international markets, women's earlier work in agriculture has been transformed in a variety of ways. As wage labor and migration have come to dominate many rural economies, some women have specialized in the production of subsistence crops while others have been pushed into the growing urban labor force in search of service sector employment (Bunster and Chaney 1985; Babb 1989). Because many women in developing countries still live in rural settlements and are engaged in agricultural work, food processing, and regional commerce, these issues will remain an essential focus for research (cf. Ahmed 1985; Benería 1982; Bourque and Warren 1981a; Creevey 1986; Deere and León de Leal 1987; Dixon 1978; Ehlers 1990; Kader 1986; Leacock and Safa 1986; Moock 1986; Stoler 1985). In this essay, however, we have chosen to examine an urban issue: women's employment in multinational factories. Multinational employment reveals the paradoxical effects of new options in the labor force, increased education, family expectations, and young women's agency in patriarchal families. In the past decade, anthropologists have produced a number of impressive studies of multinational employment; ethnographically rich while making important comparative contributions, they carry on central debates about the impact of contemporary patterns of industrialization on women (cf. Benería and Roldán 1987; Daud 1985; Fernández-Kelly 1983; Jann n.d.; Ong 1987; Nash 1989; Nash and Fernández-Kelly 1983; Salaff 1981, 1988).

In the last fifteen years industrial production in the third world has proliferated as multinational companies have searched for cheap labor to assemble high-technology products, to manufacture clothing, and to grow and process food. Recent relocations of manufacturing to Third World countries have been spurred by Japanese successes in capturing Western markets for consumer goods and the transforming of national firms into multinationals in Hong Kong, South Korea, and Singapore. Faced with new competition, European and U.S. companies have looked to the Third World to cut their labor costs and retain international competitiveness. In the case of the United States, this process was encouraged by new tariff regulations in the 1960s and 1970s which allowed goods sent to other countries for further processing to be reimported, with duty to be paid only on the value added as a result of labor (Lim 1983: 71–72; Nash 1983: 10). For their part, national governments have often competed to attract multinational investments in order to deal with high unemployment and lack of capital.

These developments build on a long history of transnational involvement in the developing world—with a new twist, for women are now being recruited in large numbers for bench-assembly production work. "Heavy" multinational industries such as mining, petrochemicals, iron and steel, and shipbuilding continue to employ many more men than women,[11] whereas "light" industries like clothing manufacture, food processing, pharmaceuticals, and electronics tend to be mixed-labor forces where women may predominate on the assembly line. In 1980, over 4 million people in developing countries worked in multinational enterprises: 63 percent in Latin America, 31 percent in Asia, and 6 percent in Africa. Of this total it is estimated that over 1 million women were directly employed and an additional half-million worked in national firms that subcontracted work for multinationals (Lim 1985: 7–9, 28).

Multinational companies involved in microelectronic assembly, clothing manufacture, and food processing have built production plants dispersed at great distances from corporate headquarters in the United States, Europe, or Japan (cf. Chapkis and Enloe 1983; Arizpe and Aranda 1981). Generally, new products are developed in the industrial countries and sent along with the appropriate production machinery to factories in the developing world. Local labor, labeled "semi-skilled" or "unskilled," is recruited for production, and a plant's output is sold in external markets, such as the United States and Europe. Manual assembly is preferred in rapidly changing industries when it successfully competes with the higher cost of continually retooling automated systems to keep pace with technological, stylistic, and market-driven changes.

The current literature contrasts two views on the consequences of multinational expansion for women. One view argues that multinationals offer women important new employment opportunities in the face of rural-urban migration, urban underemployment, and cultural systems that reinforce male domination. The other argues that multinationals lock women into new patterns of inequality, destabilize existing family forms, and socialize young women into westernized competitive consumerism at the cost of other cultural values.

Authors such as Lim (1981, 1983, 1985) and Salaff (1981) argue that the new industrial employment provides young women with important options and financial resources seen as successfully coexisting with Asian family structures and expectations for daughters. Although multinationals pay low wages by industrial countries' standards, Lim points out that multinational wages are generally higher and working conditions better and safer than national companies, which tend to be smaller and, thus, subject to greater economic pressure. The contrast is starker for women who face the exploitative and marginally paying alternatives of work as farm laborers, domestic servants, and market vendors, all typical alternatives to assembly work. The reason for the disparity between multinationals and national firms is due not to better intentions on one side but rather to the multinationals' larger size, greater productivity, and profitability. Furthermore, multinationals tend to conform to national standards in their sexual divisions of labor (Lim 1985: 24–25, 60–61).

Lim argues that without multinationals women would have fewer employment opportunities, would be forced to work for more exploitative national enterprises, and have less say in the face of local culture that establishes male dominance as the natural state of affairs:

> [A]lthough the multinational does take advantage of national and sexual wage differentials and sometimes reinforces them, it is not responsible for creating

them and cannot by its own actions eliminate them. National wage differentials are the result of differences in the development of capitalist relations of production between nations, whereas sex wage differentials originate in indigenous patriarchy. (1983: 85)

Many of the problems women face result from the generalized cultural expectation, reproduced in families and workplaces, that they are temporary workers who will later turn their attention and time to marriage and children. As a result, more young unmarried women are available for work, and employers elaborate justifications for paying women less than men. Young unmarried women are seen to have other advantages: they are able to work various shifts, have higher rates of education than older women, are mobile, and at least in theory will not need pregnancy benefits. For Lim, cultural expectations about women's marriage and job commitments, as well as family investment patterns that favor sons over daughters for education, explain most of the earning and promotion differentials between women and men. Additionally, women's chances for promotion from the assembly line are low because of the structure of the workplace. (But Lim observes that this would be true for plants in the West as well.) She concludes that these factors are more important than employers' gender biases in explaining female/male earning differentials in any particular country (Lim 1985: 59).

Lim questions the finding that multinationals are footloose and use threats of relocation to avoid unionization. She finds that in countries like Indonesia, the Philippines, and Thailand, where multinationals have been in place for long periods of time, their rates of unionization are higher than those of domestic industries. In these cases women may benefit from being brought together in large groups for the first time and having the opportunity to organize politically. For their part, multinationals may not fight unionization if it gives them a structure through which to negotiate efficiently with workers. Factories are more interested in political stability than they are fearful of unions; their departures are more commonly caused by business reverses, takeovers, and reorganizations. Lim argues that multinational factories have a life cycle; thus, countries with longer histories of multinational operations are more likely to have assembly plants with unions, higher wages, greater job security and worker longevity, and higher investment in capital-intensive production. They are also likely to have exported unskilled production work to countries like Bangladesh or Sri Lanka which have still lower wages. The tendency is for multinationals to upgrade their work environments over time, especially if national governments urge these developments and the labor market is tight. The spinoffs from mature multinational operations may support the growth of national industries and an entrepreneurial middle class (Lim 1983: 75–76, 83; 1985: 64–68).

In her study of Hong Kong, Salaff agrees with many of Lim's findings while adding an important cultural dimension to the analysis of women's industrial work (1981). Since 1949 Hong Kong has been a center of textile and assembly work promoted by local Chinese capitalists who tapped a growing international market. Their political and economic situation is unique; Hong Kong is a British colony facing an uncertain future when it becomes part of China after the British mandate expires in 1997. State policy is explicitly controlled by a profit-driven multinational commercial sector. Lacking sufficient land for large-scale agriculture while experiencing waves of migration from the mainland, the colony has both the economic policies and the labor force for multinational industrial production. The state offers very few social services beyond subsidized housing and education; there are few welfare provisions, no unemployment insurance or social security. Individuals must depend on their families for subsistence and welfare. Basic household expenses are so high in Hong Kong that multiple wage earners are necessary in every family.

Young women have played an important role in the success of multinationals in Hong Kong, and by the early 1970s they had become more than one-half the factory labor force. Typically young women from poorer families began working at the age of twelve to fourteen, though the entry age was increased to sixteen in the early 1980s. Until marriage, they enjoy a three-sphered life: commitment to their natal families, industrial work, and a peer culture of friends. Their earnings are most often used to pay for a higher standard of living and for the education of sons in the family, something that Salaff argues the young women do not resent because these contributions represent a valued contribution to family welfare as a whole.

This situation is compatible with the Chinese value placed on the family as a joint endeavor for social survival and continuity. Chinese culture stresses a religious commitment to a male-centered conception of family ancestors. Sons are particularly valued; daughters less so since marriage will inevitably take them to their husbands' families. In the past family inheritance was equally divided among the sons; now working families invest in the future by educating their sons for higher-paying skilled jobs. In this social world view, members of the family subordinate personal goals to their family's needs. Daughters do this by remitting three-quarters of their wages to their parents "to repay the cost of their upbringing." In return daughters gain the right to more personal freedom: reduced demands for household work, leisure time spent free from parental control with girlfriends from work, an allowance for their own purchases, the right to choose their own husbands, and higher levels of education than in past generations. Salaff argues that the frame of reference for these women workers is their mothers and grandmothers, rather than their brothers. As a result, although they would like more education for themselves, they do not resent their families' greater investment in sons. Women see themselves as gaining social freedom while maintaining strong family ties.

A second line of analysis is much more critical of multinationals and the opportunities they have offered women. This view, articulated by researchers like June Nash and María Patricia Fernández-Kelly (1983), emphasizes the failure of industrial work in the Third World to provide women with new options or long-term employment possibilities. Multinationals have not introduced changes that make a real difference because the recruitment of women into high-tech assembly work has not challenged the idea of a sexually segregated work force or the tacit understanding that women can be paid lower wages than men. Their analyses describe a situation in which multinationals take advantage of and reinforce gender, ethnic, and class inequities in industrialized and developing societies. In this respect they concur with Lim and Salaff. As Nash concludes:

> [S]ectors of the labor force based on gender, ethnicity, age, and education within both industrial core and peripheral nations are differentially rewarded and these differences, along with wage differences between nations, determine the long-run movement of capital. (1983: 3)

Where the two schools of thought differ, however, is that Nash and Fernández-Kelly find that the labor practices of multinationals challenge rather than complement cultural practices in ways that leave women particularly disadvantaged and with less social support than they had in the past.

Studies of high-tech assembly plants in Mexico, Hong Kong, Taiwan, Indonesia, Malaysia, Thailand, the Philippines, Brazil, and the Caribbean illustrate the widely accepted policies of recruiting young single women, maintaining paternalistic modes of plant organization, encouraging turnover after several years of employment, and providing virtually no opportunities for advancement or job security if the market sags (Fernández-Kelly 1983*a*, 1983*b*; Nash and Fernández-Kelly 1983; Fuentes and Ehrenreich 1983; Lim 1981; Ong 1987). Employers promote the idea that assembly work draws on presumed womanly skills—such as manual dexterity, attentiveness, docility, and the capacity to do repetitive work—and, thus, is an extension of women's conventional roles. Srinivasan notes the high cost to women of this sex-role stereotyping:

> [T]he reasons for employing [women] in modern high technology companies are the same reasons for which they are *excluded* from training, technical responsibilities, and high-paying jobs. (1982: 139; our emphasis)

By defining high-tech assembly as young women's work, plants are able to maintain low wages, favorably competing with U.S. labor despite the cost of transporting goods internationally for assembly.

These authors argue that within the plants employers further reinforce, manipulate, and distort cultural values by bringing their own cultures to bear on workers in order to foster control. For instance, in Japanese-managed firms, managers stress family commitments and self-discipline, while in U.S.-managed firms, they encourage Western aspirations through factory beauty contests, cooking classes, and make-up instruction, which emphasize the importance of cash incomes for competitive, consumer success and modern marriage (Grossman 1978/79; Elson and Pearson 1981; Ong 1987).

María Patricia Fernández-Kelly's ethnography of Mexican border industries in Ciudad Juárez (1983*a*, 1983*b*, 1983*c*) argues for this critical analysis. Like Hong Kong, Mexico has witnessed a growth in women's employment in multinational assembly plants. In contrast, however, Mexico's severe unemployment problems, growing population, stagnation of its agrarian base, dependence on an uncertain international petroleum market, and different cultural system mean that new work has very different implications for women, men, and their families.

Industrialization along the Mexican border has been directed by the overshadowing presence of the U.S. economy. Assembly plants (called *maquiladoras*) are the result of the Border Industrialization Program (BIP) that was jointly developed by Mexico and the United States in 1965.[12] The program was designed in part to generate local employment to counterbalance the effects of the U.S. termination of the Bracero Program, which left over 200,000 migratory agricultural workers, many of whom settled along the border, out of work. At the time, Mexico had a rapidly growing labor force, unemployment and underemployment of about 20 percent in key border cities, high birth rates and internal migration to the region, and a populace willing to work for one-sixth of U.S. wages. The BIP employed classical stategies learned from the Asian experience to foster multinational investment. Firms were allowed to import machinery, equipment, and raw materials free of duty into Mexico, providing that all production was exported. Multinational subsidiaries were permitted to be totally foreign-owned in contrast to the limitation of 49 percent foreign ownership for domestic firms. For its part, the U.S. tariff policy taxed only the value added for reimported goods including clothing and electronics. A final selling point was that U.S. managers would be able to commute to these plants from their homes across the border.

The growth of assembly plants along the border has been impressive: in 1965 there were 12 assembly plants employing 3,087 workers; by 1979 there were 531 plants employing 156,000 persons; by 1987 there were 1,259 plants employing 322,743 persons. Between 75 and 90 percent of the workers in these plants are women. These factories have been the third largest foreign exchange contributor to Mexico, just behind tourism and petroleum. One-third of the multinationals' expenditures went for workers' salaries; the rest entered the Mexican economy through rents, taxes, materials, and miscellaneous costs (Fernández-Kelly 1983*b*: 21, 34–35). With the devaluation of the peso and the decline in the world price of petroleum, Mexico's economy has experienced serious reverses, with increasing unemployment and great pressure on workers to seek employment in the United States (see Ruiz and Tiano 1987). Although the Mexican government sees multinational assembly plants as a fundamental development stategy, it is clear that these factories will not seriously alleviate national unemployment and underemployment.

Because the factories recruit many more women than men, Fernández-Kelly concludes that they have helped foster contradictory pressures on women and men in a situation where 80 percent of the border unemployment and underemployment is male. The companies prefer women because of women's putative greater docility, manual dexterity, and the fact that they are viewed as temporary workers who will accept the lowest possible wages. This is important because these labor-intensive industries are intensely competitive, quick to lay off workers if demand for their products weakens, and subject to collapse during U.S. recessions. One-half of the assembly plants in Ciudad Juárez closed during the 1974–1975 recession in the United States. Fernández-Kelly argues, from a male-centric point of view, that factories have not reduced unemployment rates but rather have introduced formerly "unemployable" women into the labor force. What is clear from her evidence is that women see assembly work as a step up from work as maids across the border, and they especially value the access to state medical care that they receive as a job benefit. Other women, who have worked as local secretaries, receptionists, and clerks, move to multinational jobs because the pay is higher than office positions. By contrast, high male unemployment forces men across the border, dividing families, resulting in abandonments, and creating pressures for wives to join husbands. The fact that much of this migration has been historically illegal in the United States clearly subjects the participants to great anxieties.

Most female assembly line workers are between the ages of seventeen and twenty-five. Electronics plants recruit younger single, childless women with an average of eight years of education. Companies test women for pregnancy when they are recruited because they do not want to pay for the eighty-two-day leave women are legally entitled to with the birth of a new child. Electronics workers most often live with one or both of their parents; their income is pooled with their fathers' who are often marginally employed in fields like construction. Generally the women give about half their wages to the family, money used for domestic expenses or education of a younger brother. Mothers in these households are less often members of the paid labor force, concentrating instead on household work. By comparison, older women, women with children, and less educated women who must enter the work force, find work in apparel factories where wages are lower and working conditions less desirable. One-third of the women working in clothing assembly are single mothers who have been forced into the labor market to support their families after the death or desertion of their husbands.

Women's job tenure averages three years as they experience pressures to leave positions from companies trying to avoid payments required under the Mexican labor law for vacations, yearly bonuses, and indemnity in the event of layoffs. Factories also note a drop in women's productivity over time as they become bored with highly monotonous work. For their part, women leave positions to marry, take care of their children, rest and change jobs, regain their health, and avoid tensions with factory personnel. Women do not see themselves as permanent workers and describe pressures from men to leave paid work to take on full-time domestic duties. Later, economic necessities may force them back into the paid labor force and into less desirable positions or illegal migration.

As a result of multinational employment, older women see a shift in the value of educating daughters, noting that in their generation fathers dismissed female education as a waste of time for women who would devote their lives to their children and domestic work.[13] Now mothers seek to persuade fathers to educate daughters to meet the minimum educational requirements for electronic assembly employment. Yet they worry that fathers will take advantage of daughters, reducing their own financial contributions to their families.

Fernández-Kelly feels very strongly that multinational industrialization has not solved existing problems, particularly male unemployment after the end of the Bracero Program, nor has it created realistic options for women. Rather, border industries have reinforced the magnetic attraction of the Mexican-U.S. frontier resulting in continuing migration from other regions of the country and growing unemployment. Women are caught in complex countercurrents: they are actively recruited for work, yet thought of as supplementary and temporary by companies and by themselves; they are major wage earners in families fighting for subsistence, yet pressured to retire from the labor force by husbands who seek submissive wives; they are often abandoned by men discouraged by poverty and unemployment on the Mexican side of the border. Young women have been recruited as a vulnerable and docile labor force. They have been stereotyped as supplementary and temporary workers at plants and as inevitably submissive wives and mothers at home. Although neither stereotype is accurate (cf. Jann n.d.), these constructions are utilized by institutions and individuals to constrain women's lives in important ways.

Comparing two societies as different as Hong Kong and Mexico is a very tricky matter; their histories, cultures, state politics, rates of unemployment, international contexts, and development problems could not be more different. Yet, both societies have been touched in important ways by the new wave of multinational expansion that has recruited young women as a first generation of female industrial workers in their families. Lim would account for the differences between the countries' multinational experiences in part by noting that multinationals have a more mature profile in Hong Kong, where women workers find the experience a more positive one economically and personally, families have adapted old cultural patterns to new modes of economic participation, and wages are higher and working conditions better. Fernández-Kelly would respond with an argument that the issues are structural, and that the basic asymmetry of the U.S. and Mexican economies has been intensified through the Border Industrialization Program. As a result, cultural patterns have been distorted, populations relocated, development priorities skewed, and families put under unbearable pressures that have intensified male-female tensions. Both would agree that the chronically high rates of unemployment in Mexico and the full employment in Hong Kong create different options for individuals, for families, and for the multinationals that are expanding production in these countries.

In Hong Kong the strong cultural consensus about family economic strategies channels the extra earnings of daughters to finance the education and upward mobility of sons. This appears to be a successful reconciliation of Chinese values and the sexual divisions of labor in multinationals. It allows poor families to amass funds and bet on one or two individuals, who with better schooling and high test scores might gain entrance into the university and eventually gain professional work. From an analyst's point of view, of course, these cultural values direct the choice of the individual by gender, not by scholarly potential. That these decisions have not provoked tensions between daughters and sons at this point is attributed to the fact that the daughters' frame of reference is still their mothers. Significantly, it is not clear that this family strategy for mobility actually bears fruit for the working class, given an educational system that tracks upper-middle-class children rather than working-class children toward the very few available university positions.

Along the Mexican border, there are crosscurrents and multiple-family strategies which reflect the mixture of cues families receive from the economy. On the one hand, Mexican values call for a greater educational investment in sons. Some families report saving daughters' assembly earnings to do this, although it is unclear how this might translate into upward mobility since most men cannot find local employment and must concentrate on crossing the border for higher earnings as manual laborers in the United States. On the other hand, the economy is demanding that daughters receive higher educational investments than in the past in order to qualify for what is considered high-status, well-paying work. This situation appears to translate into some intergenerational tensions, but more importantly into increased tension between young spouses when husbands put traditional patriarchical pressures on wives to leave work, to join them in the United States in very uncertain circumstances, or to face abandonment. It is not clear whether or not these tensions are greater on the border than in other areas of Mexico where internal migration for work is common but multinationals do not dominate local economies.

Frames of reference influence women's consciousness in Hong Kong and Mexico; they are also an issue for the analyst. What is clear from our comparison of Lim and Salaff with Nash and Fernández-Kelly is that these analysts are operating with distinctive economic models in very different contexts. Both lines of analysis acknowledge structural inequalities and envision the actions of individuals as constrained by wider economics and politics. Each finds areas of creative choice and resistance. They find gender to be an important dimension of international economics as well as the local cultures of developing societies. What distinguishes these analyses is one side's view that national labor markets operate with a certain level of independence and that integration into the world order will benefit women and workers, even as it brings new problems and inequities. The other side of this debate finds that capitalism has a long history of determining local and international markets and economic opportunities. This point of view seriously questions the benefits of increased economic involvements for developing societies because they have different needs and dilemmas from those of the industrialized countries. This contrast parallels the tendency of researchers who focus their work on the domestic domain to stress "traditional" patriarchy as shaping women's subordination, whereas those who examine the public domain more commonly emphasize capitalist economics as the primary determinant of gender inequality (cf. Leacock and Safa 1986: x). The irony here is that current feminist research on multinationals and on families makes it abundantly clear that "domestic" life and local culture are not separate or independent from the wider "public" and international worlds (cf. Nash 1989; Safa 1983; Bolles 1983; Jann n.d.; and Bourque and Warren 1981a). The challenge for the next stage of feminist anthropology is to conceptualize and research the interplay of transnational and local cultures as gender ideologies are negotiated, refined, and contested by multinational owners, managers, workers, their families, governments, religious groups, and social movements.[14]

CONCLUSIONS

Recent scholarship has helped us understand that many of the institutions and forces that are thought of as autonomous and neutral—like technology—are neither. Clearly a comprehensive consideration of "technology" must include an examination of the changing social relations and ideologies involved in its production, distribution, and use. As has become clear in this overview, gender—that is, the cultural representation and the practice of being "female" and "male" in the family, the workplace, the state, and international business—is a very important dimension in the study of technological change. These gendered social realities are, in turn, shaped by wider economic and historical transformations, often having cultural and political consequences distinct from the narrow implications of particular technologies. In the "development" field, for instance, we have found that "technology transfers" are cultural and political actions which often reinforce international and local inequities.

Our review of four approaches to the study of women, technology, and development demonstrates that adding gender as a category of analysis to current social science involves more than just recovering women's experience. Rather, the character of gender differences calls for the explanation of male and female inequalities, much as the cultural elaboration of racial differences calls for the explanation of racial inequalities. Consequently, it should not be surprising that approaches to the study of gender, technology, and development involve social critiques. Alternative feminist phrasings of the problem of gender and modernity are important to understand because they draw attention to unexamined ideologies that inform the actions of groups involved in development projects, social movements, academics, and policymaking, both in the West and in the Third World.

On another level these new development ideologies resonate with familiar Western cultural preoccupations: the "sameness" or "difference" of peoples' natures, capacities, and experiences . Clearly, the study of gender and technology is another arena in which "Western" cultural concepts and values are being used to define the nature of human diversity. In this case the issue is the sameness or difference of the West and Third World as an interesting subscript to the explicit question of the sameness or difference of female and male. The contemporary West has been obsessed with the idea of control, with technology's potential to control nature and harness nature's powers for human ends. This language tends to polarize the contrast of Western and third world societies, to argue for a radical difference in experience and potential, because so-called underdeveloped societies are thought of as closer to nature (even a part of nature) while the West's stature as transcending nature can be measured by its technological advances.[15] In this construction, variations of Western experience and the striking diversity of Third World societies are ignored.

For feminist scholars the issue of technological development involves the problematizing of who controls technology and the terms of debate about its development as well as of who benefits in the process of change. These questions have been pursued for both the production and the use of technologies. As a result, we are forced to confront the contradictions between the exploitation of women in the production of technology, through policies of low wages and minimal job security, and the benefits for women of new consumer and "labor-saving" technologies.[16] The conflict is not over technology in the narrow sense, so much as over values, gendered social ideologies, the organization of work, the distribution of profits, and control.

Yet, even as feminist writers have joined the effort to ask new questions, we are still heirs to conflicting models of Third World societies. The message of research coming from the study of the international division of labor is that working-class women in some Western and Third World settings share structurally similar work environments as a result of recent patterns of change. The global economy's dependence on low-paid female-dominated, centralized/decentralized work is common in industrialized as well as in developing countries.[17] The emerging global pattern is clear: women are becoming deskilled workers in the modern office, in high-tech assembly plants, in the mechanization of the harvest, and in the distribution of appropriate technology. These structurally similar patterns in very different settings may challenge the old discourse of the vast differences between the West and the Third World.

Nevertheless, the idea of categorical differences between developed and underdeveloped countries is perpetuated in at least some of the appropriate-technology literature. This discussion of similarity and difference does not for a moment deny significant cultural variations throughout the world. The problem is the use of stereotyped and categorical we/they discourses of contrast, opposition, and hierarchy which pervade discussions of "Western" versus "non-Western" societies. This language of difference portrays other societies as victims (as passive "targets" of programs or "receptors" of technology), rather than as constructors of their own cultural understandings of change and technology (see also Silverblatt, this volume). In these cases, the West is assumed to be technologically in control, whereas Third World countries are pictured as out of control, as the victims of harsh natural environments, archaic traditions, and authoritarian regimes that are not interested in (or economically not able to be concerned with) the welfare of peasants and the urban poor. The poor are seen as a homogeneous group of subsistence-oriented victims, with physical survival their most demanding issue. The paternalism of some of the classical appropriate-technology literature is a result of this construction.[18]

To do a greater justice to the real diversity of cultures, we need a reciprocal view at the onset, one that is sensitive to the importance of power differentials, inherited inequities, and cultural dynamics. One suspects that if we could undermine the positional superiority of Western analysts and see the poor as collaborators and active interpreters of their social worlds,[19] then development would take on a longer-term participatory quality rather than a one-way technical transfer. Moreover, the complexity of the undertaking could be acknowledged, instead of the current tendency to see project failure as a disheartening lack of responsiveness of the poor (cf. Warren and Bourque 1987). Under these circumstances, resistance might be seen as active and meaningful subversion rather than as passive ignorance (cf. Ong 1987), and discussions of appropriate technology would be seen as just as important for the West as for the developing world.

The Western duality of constructions of sameness and difference also appears when one looks at assumptions about gender. On the one hand, much of the literature on global factories assumes a basic sameness of men and women. These researchers are not arguing that high-tech production should be feminized, but rather that women workers must organize to improve working conditions (Ruiz and Tiano 1987). Women, in particular, are portrayed as needing to break through sex-segregated labor markets and the deskilling of the workplace to gain transferable skills and a future in the labor force. To do so they will have to confront social ideologies, focusing on women's distinctive feminine qualities and responsibilities, that have been promoted by employers to encourage a passive and submissive work force in the face of the pace and demands of assembly work. Multinational research demonstrates that we do not have to posit polar psychologies for men and women in order to understand that women bear the added economic responsibility for their children in unstable economic circumstances. Nor do we have to posit distinctive psychologies to research women's psychosocial negotiations with the workplace, their families, or the men in their lives.

In contrast, advocates of the feminization of technology rest their case on the polarized psychological differences of male and female. This literature assumes a universal set of positive female values and sensitivities, resulting from women's roles as mothers and nurturers. Femininity, in this view, is not an array of internalized abilities, liabilities, and attitudes manufactured to control women but rather a set of idealized virtues standing in opposition to capitalism, competition, and hierarchy. Thus, one approach sees the feminine as externally imposed, the other as universally inherent.

The internationalization of research and the cultural concerns of anthropologists have provided important moments in the development of feminist scholarship. These contributions have spurred the reassessment of earlier understandings of change as "westernization," caused a wider range of analysts to be self-conscious about the projection of Western stereotypes of gender onto other societies, and encouraged formulations of change that incorporate the global interplay of cultures as well as economies. In addition to calling into question assumptions about universal male and female characteristics, recent research demonstrates the problematic ways in which contrasts like developed/underdeveloped, Western/Third World, public/private, domestic/political, nature/culture, and similarity/difference have influenced and distorted models for change in development studies.[20] We are left with a radical skepticism about the capacity of categorical oppositions to capture reality. We are also left with a sense of the importance of decoding the ideologies and power relations of those explanations that still depend on these categories. One final irony: to show how "gender" is constructed in our multinational world, feminist research has demonstrated that we also need to deconstruct the concept; that is, to show how identities and experiences are simultaneously structured by class, culture, race, nationality, religion, age, sexuality, individual experience, as well as by gender.

As anthropologists, we approach the study of development ideologies as contested cultural constructions with important political implications for all parties involved. Development ideologies, of course, are not the full story of cultural transformation. In addition anthropologists seek to understand the ethnographic particularities of cultural diversity and patterns of change which are so often overlooked or ignored by development specialists. Our goal is a more subtle, comprehensive understanding of change, one that does not exclusively rely on economic indicators and Western pragmatism as yardsticks with which to measure transformations, and one that continuously questions the language of analysis.

NOTES

1. Our thanks to Micaela di Leonardo, Sandra Morgen, Fitz John Porter Poole, Ralph Faulkingham, Natalie Davis, Joan Scott, Jim Scott, Lourdes Benería, our colleagues at the 1985 Bellagio seminar on "Gender and Technology," and at the 1986 Brown conference on women and development for inspiring discussions of the issues and readings of earlier versions of this analysis. Our analysis of the frameworks initially appeared in Bourque and Warren (1987). We thank the American Anthropological Association for permission to reprint portions of our article from the Morgen anthology (1989).

2. For anthropologists this means a concern with the related processes of colonialism, the concentration of land resources and growing landlessness in rural areas, state intervention in rural affairs, population growth, rural-urban migration, the importance of marginal service-sector employment for underemployed urban populations, and national policies that define development priorities in economic planning, agrarian reform, education, labor, housing, social services, and political participation. Women play significiant roles in these processes and are disproportionately affected by many of them, as is clear by differential rates of female/male subsistence-crop cultivation, access to cash incomes, involvement in agrarian reforms, migration to urban centers, literacy, marginal service-sector employment, and responsibility for the economic support of urban families. For historically and culturally sensitive treatments of these issues, see, for example, Bourque and Warren (1981a), Stoler (1985), Nash and Fernández-Kelly (1983), Nash and Safa (1985), Ong (1987), Benería (1982), and Deere and León (1987).

3. The problem with aggregate statistics is that their averages often hide the differential impact of change on individuals within populations and, thus, important variations in the quality of life.

4. In an essay of this scope we are very aware of the limits of our cultural comparisons. Our goal here is obviously not a comprehensive description of either situation, but rather a comparison of distinctive analytic approaches and their consequences.

5. Our notion of feminist research includes scholarship by women and men who have taken gender as a central category of analysis and are interested in understanding the diversities of experience both within and between genders. Internationally, this research tends to examine not just the cultural construction of "female" and "male," but rather the interplay of gender, sexual, class, ethnic, religious, and national stratifications and identities.

6. Of course this is only one stream of the history of development strategies. Another important focus of international concern has been population control, which has defined women's fertility as a major cause of third world poverty. Here women have often been conceptualized as "targets" of new technologies. This language veils the politics of development and creates a passive role for women while justifying the external intervention and control of reproductive decision making (Warren and Bourque 1987).

7. Boserup's pioneering work has sparked insightful critiques by Benería and Sen (1986).

8. It is interesting that Bergom-Larsson draws upon Margaret Mead's *Cultural Patterns and Technical Change* (1955) for her analysis. She argues that women and women's culture should be viewed with a sensitivity similar to the way that Mead advocates we treat people in other cultures. Both are understood as exhibiting collective distinctiveness, having the right to autonomy, and suffering special vulnerability to external forces that would degrade them.

9. See di Leonardo (introduction, this volume) for a reading of this intellectual history which traces important anthropological connections to French structuralism.

10. See Ortner and Whitehead (1981), MacCormack and Strathern (1980), Reiter (1975), and Caplan and Bujra (1979) for cultural examples.

11. Accounts like Barrios de Chungara's make it clear, however, what a vital, though unpaid, role women play in reproducing and sustaining this labor force (1978).

12. Fernández-Kelly notes that this development was part of a longer historical trend of Mexican industrialization through free-trade privileges begun in the 1930s in response to the depression and the end of prohibition, which hurt Mexican liquor production along the border (1983b: 25).

13. Educational levels, which may vary dramatically from country to country for the same work, are used as a screening device for multinationals, just as gender, ethnicity, and class are used to regulate labor pools in segmented labor forces. Multinationals often require educational levels that have very little to do with the work required in "skilled" or "unskilled" positions. In Mexico the average educational level for all workers is 3.8 years, while the average for young women in electronics firms is 8 years (Fernández-Kelly 1983b, 1983c). Because education is really being used to regulate numbers of applicants in the labor force, when demand for products is down and there are fewer positions available, educational requirements may well be increased. Moreover, Lim observes that education is regarded by multinationals as "a proxy for other desired workforce characteristics such as hard work, perseverance, ability to perform repetitive tasks, tolerance of authority and discipline" (1985: 34–35). Education is felt by multinationals to preadapt workers to the regimentation of industrial settings.

14. Clearly the culture of assembly plants is a complex, situation-specific amalgam of local culture and transnational labor practices. What anthropology is begin-

ning to reveal is that the transnational corporate influence is *itself* an amalgam of transplanted local cultures (from Japanese codes of family responsibility in Malaysia to American codes of consumer success in Mexico). To what extent do particular multinational corporate cultures retain some consistency across national contexts? To what extent do they, both in conforming to and challenging cultural expectations, create a special kind of "disjunction"? Does this disjunction now give women with multinational work experiences more in common culturally, over and above the fact of their structurally similar working conditions? What implications do these changes have for feminist movements and feminist political consciousness? Our thanks to Fitz John Porter Poole for these issues.

15. See MacCormack and Strathern (1980) for examples of the distinctive ways notions of "culture" and "nature" have been constructed in other societies as well as in our own history. These distinctions are internalized and subverted in a variety of ways (cf. Srinivasan 1982: v).

16. H. Scott (1984) hopes for a different kind of society made possible because of the displacement, in Western societies, of jobs by high-tech economics. This, she argues, will force people to think of alternative ways to use their time and to place a greater emphasis on expanding the informal sector to take on what governments cannot afford to fund in human services. Apparently Scott does not consider the cost or contradictions of present forms of high-tech production; that is, the very different effects of high-tech industrial production on workers and producers wherever they may be.

17. Japan and Mexico are good examples of countries where multinationals depend on high levels of decentralized subcontractors for national production.

18. This can be the case both in centralized and in decentralized, mixed-technology options for development. By paternalism, we mean that external experts determine another society's needs, without consulting the participants for their understandings of change. If there appears to be a conflict in priorities, experts assume that they know what is best because of their professional training and sense of responsibility.

19. The goal of this formulation is to treat people equivalently in order to escape the hierarchical power relations inherent in virtually all formulations of development. The problem for Western analysis is that equity is so often confused with mathematical identity; that is, to gain equality one must give up cultural distinctiveness.

20. For critiques of these polarities and separate-spheres approaches to gender politics see Reiter (1975a), Strathern (1980), MacCormack (1980), and Warren and Bourque (1981a).

BIBLIOGRAPHY

Afshar, Haleh. 1987. *Women, state and ideology: Studies from Africa and Asia.* Albany: State University of New York Press.

Agarwal, Bina. 1985. Women and technological change in agriculture: The Asian and African experience. In *Technology and rural women: Conceptual and empirical issues.* Iftikhar Ahmed, ed., 67–114. London: George Allen and Unwin.

Ahmed, Iftikhar, ed. 1985. *Technology and rural women: Conceptual and empirical issues.* London: George Allen and Unwin.

Anderson, Mary B. 1985. Technology transfer: Implications for women. In *Gender roles in development projects*. Catherine Overholt et al., eds., 57–58. West Hartford, Conn.: KuMarían Press.

Arizpe, Lourdes, and Josefina Aranda. 1981. The "comparative advantages" of women's disadvantages: Women workers in the strawberry export agribusiness in Mexico. *Signs* 7: 453–473.

Babb, Florence. 1989. *Between the field and the cooking pot: The political economy of market-women in Peru.* Austin: University of Texas Press.

Barrios de Chungara, Domitila, with Moema Viezzer, ed. 1978. *Let me speak! Testimony of Domitila, a woman of the Bolivian mines.* New York: Monthly Review Press.

Benería, Lourdes, ed. 1982. *Women and development: The sexual division of labor in rural societies.* New York: Praeger.

Benería, Lourdes, and Gita Sen. 1982. Class and gender inequalities and women's role in economic development—Theoretical and practical implications. *Feminist Studies* 8 :1.

———. 1986. Accumulation, reproduction, and women's role in economic development: Boserup revisited. In *Women's work: Development and the division of labor by gender.* Eleanor Leacock and Helen I. Safa, eds., 141–157. South Hadley, Mass.: Bergin and Garvey.

Benería, Lourdes, and Martha Roldán. 1987. *The crossroads of class and gender: Industrial homework, subcontracting, and household dynamics in Mexico City.* Chicago: University of Chicago Press.

Bergom-Larsson, María. 1982. Women and technology in the industrialized countries. In *Scientific technological change and the role of women in development.* Pamela M. D'Onofrio-Flores and Sheila M. Pfafflin, eds., 29–75. Boulder: Westview Press.

Bolles, Lynn. 1983. Kitchens hit by priorities: Employed working-class Jamaican women control the IMF. In *Women, men, and the international division of labor.* June Nash and María Patricia Fernández-Kelly, eds., 138–160. Albany: SUNY Press.

Boserup, Ester. 1970. *Woman's role in economic development.* New York: St Martin's Press.

Boulding, Elise. 1981. Integration into what? Reflections on development planning for women. In *Women and technological change in developing countries.* Roslyn Dauber and Melinda L. Cain, eds., 9–30. AAAS Selected Symposium 53. Boulder: Westview Press.

Bourque, Susan C., and Kay B. Warren. 1981a. *Women of the Andes: Patriarchy and social change in rural Peru.* Ann Arbor: University of Michigan Press.

———. 1981b. Rural women and development planning in Peru. In *Women and world change: Equity issues in development.* N. Black and A. Cottrell, eds., 183–197. Beverly Hills: Sage.

———. 1987. Gender, technology and development. *Daedalus* 116: 173–197.

Briscoe, Anne, and Sheila Pfafflin, eds. 1979. *Expanding the role of women in the sciences. Annals of the New York Academy of Sciences* 323.

Bryceson, Deborah A. 1985. *Women and technology in developing countries: Technological change and women's capabilities and bargaining positions.* Santo Domingo: UN/INSTRAW.

Bunster, Ximena, and Elsa Chaney. 1985. *Sellers and servants: Working women in Lima, Peru.* New York: Praeger.

Buvinić, Mayra. 1983. Women's issues in third world poverty: A policy analysis. In *Women and poverty and in the third world.* M. Buvinić et al., eds., 14–31. Baltimore:

Johns Hopkins University Press.

————. 1984. *Projects for women in the third world: Explaining their misbehavior.* Washington, D.C.: ICRW.

Caplan, Patricia, and Janet M. Bujra, eds. 1979. *Women united, women divided: Comparative studies of ten contemporary cultures.* Bloomington: Indiana University Press.

Carr, Marilyn. 1981. Technologies appropriate for women: Theory, practice and policy. In *Women and technological change in developing countries.* Roslyn Dauber and Melinda L. Cain, eds., 193–203. AAAS Selected Symposium 53. Boulder: Westview Press.

————. 1984. *Blacksmith, baker, roofing-sheetmaker.* London: Intermediate Technology Publications.

Chaney, Elsa M., and Maríanne Schmink. 1976. Women and modernization: Access to tools. In *Sex and class in Latin America,* June C. Nash and Helen Safa, eds., pp. 160–182. New York: Praeger.

Chapkis, Wendy, and Cynthia Enloe. 1983. *Of common cloth: Women in the global textile industry.* Washington, D.C.: Transnational Institute.

Charlton, Sue Ellen. 1984. *Women in third world development.* Boulder: Westview Press.

Chodorow, Nancy. 1978. *The reproduction of mothering: Psychoanalysis and the sociology of gender.* Berkeley, Los Angeles, London: University of California Press.

Creevey, Lucy, ed. 1986. *Women farmers in Africa: Rural development in Mali and the Sahel.* Syracuse: Syracuse University Press.

Daud, Fatimah. 1985. *"Minah Karan": The truth about Malaysian factory girls.* Kuala Lumpur, Malaysia: Berita Publishing.

Deere, Carmen Diana, and Magdalena León de Leal. 1982. *Women in Andean agriculture.* Geneva: ILO.

————. 1987. *Rural women and state policy: Feminist perspectives on Latin American agricultural development.* Boulder: Westview Press.

Dixon, Ruth. 1978. *Rural women at work: Strategies for development in South Asia.* Baltimore: Johns Hopkins University Press.

D'Onofrio-Flores, Pamela. 1982. Technology, economic development, and the division of labor by sex. In *Scientific-technological change and the role of women in development.* Pamela M. D'Onofrio-Flores and Sheila M. Pfafflin, eds., 13–28. Boulder: Westview Press.

Ehlers, Tracy Bachrach. 1990. *Silent looms: Women and production in a Guatemalan town.* Bolder: Westview Press.

Elson, Diane, and Ruth Pierson. 1981. The subordination of women and the internationalisation of factory production. In *Of marriage and the market: Women's subordination in international perspective.* Kate Young et al., eds., 144–166. London: CSE Books.

Etienne, Mona, and Eleanor Leacock, eds. 1980. *Women and colonialization.* New York: Praeger.

Evans, Judith. 1985. Improving program actions to meet the intersecting needs of women and children in developing countries: A policy and program review. With Robert G. Myers. The Consultative Group on Early Childhood Care and Development. High/Scope Educational Research Foundation.

Fernández-Kelly, María Patricia. 1983a. Gender and industry on Mexico's new frontier. In *The technological woman: Interfacing with tomorrow.* Jan Zimmerman, ed., 18–

29. New York: Praeger.

———. 1983*b*. *For we are sold, I and my people: Women and industry in Mexico's frontier.* Albany: SUNY Press.

———. 1983*c*. Mexican border industrialization, female labor force participation, and migration. In *Women, men, and the international division of labor.* June Nash and María Patricia Fernández-Kelly, eds., 205–223. Albany: SUNY Press.

Fuentes, Annette, and Barbara Ehrenreich. 1983. *Women in the global factory.* Boston: South End Press.

Gilligan, Carol. 1982. *In a different voice: Psychological theory and women's development.* Cambridge: Harvard University Press.

Grossman, Rachael. 1978/1979. Women's place in the integrated circuit. In *Changing Role of S. E. Asian women.* Joint issue of *Southeast Asia Chronicle,* no. 66, and *Pacific Research* 9 (5–6): 2–16.

Hall, Diana Long, 1974. Academics, bluestockings, and biologists: women at the University of Chicago: 1982–1932. In *Expanding the role of women in the sciences.* Anne Briscoe and Sheila Pfafflin, eds. New York: New York Academy of Sciences, volume 323: 300–320.

Huntington, Sue Ellen. 1975. Issues in woman's role in economic development: Critique and alternatives. *Journal of Marriage and the Family* 37 (4): 1001–1012.

Jahan, Rounaq. 1985. Participation of women scientists and engineers in endogenous research and development. In *Science, technology and women: A world perspective.* Shirley Malcom, et al. Washington, D.C.: AAAS and Centre for Science and Technology for Development, United Nations.

Jaquette, Jane, and Kathleen Staudt. 1985. Women "at risk" reproducers: Biology, science, and population in U.S. foreign policy. In *Women, biology and public policy.* Virginia Sapiro, ed. Beverly Hills: Sage.

Jann, Lisa Gayle. n.d. *Creative resistance: The Maquila women and social change on the Mexican border.* Unpublished senior thesis. Princeton: Princeton University.

Kader, Soha Abdel, et al. 1986. *Women and rural development in Africa.* Dakar, Senegal: Association of African Women for Research and Development/Association des Femmes Africaines pour la Recherche et le Developpement (AAWORD/AFARD).

Keller, Evelyn Fox. 1985. *Reflections on gender and science.* New Haven: Yale University Press.

Lamphere, Louise. 1987. *From working daughters to working mothers: Immigrant women in a northeastern industrial community.* Ithaca: Cornell University Press.

Leacock, Eleanor and Helen I. Safa, eds. 1986. *Women's Work: Development and the division of labor by gender.* South Hadley, Mass.: Bergin and Garvey.

Leet, Mildred Robbins. 1981. Roles of women: UNCSTD background discussion paper. In *Women and technological change in developing countries.* Roslyn Dauber and Melinda L. Cain, eds., 229–236. AAAS Selected Symposium 53. Boulder: Westview Press.

Lim, Linda Y. C. 1981. Women's work in multinational electronics factories. In *Women and technology change in developing countries.* Roslyn Dauber and Melinda L. Cain, eds., 181–192. AAAS Selected Symposium 53. Boulder: Westview Press.

———. 1983. Capitalism, imperialism, and patriarchy: The dilemma of third-world women workers in multinational factories. In *Women, men, and the international division of labor.* June Nash and María Patricia Fernández-Kelly, eds., 70–91. Albany:

SUNY Press.

———. 1985. *Women workers in multinational enterprises in developing countries.* Geneva: ILO.

MacCormack, Carol. 1980. Nature, culture and gender: A critique. In *Nature, culture and gender*, Carol MacCormack and Marilyn Strathern, eds., 1–24. Cambridge: Cambridge University Press.

MacCormack, Carol, and Marilyn, Strathern, eds. 1980. *Nature, culture and gender.* Cambridge: Cambridge University Press.

Mead, Margaret. 1955. *Cultural patterns and technical change.* New York: Mentor.

Moock, Joyce, ed. 1986. *Understanding Africa's rural households and farming systems.* Boulder: Westview Press.

Morgen, Sandra, ed. 1989. *Gender and anthropology: Resources for research and teaching.* Washington, D.C.: AAA.

Namboze, Josephine. 1985. Participation of women in education and communications in the fields of science and technology: A national perspective. In *Science, technology and women: A world perspective.* Shirley Malcom et al., eds., Washington, D.C.: AAAS and Centre for Science and Technology for Development, United Nations.

Nash, June. 1983. The impact of the changing international division of labor on different sectors of the labor force. In *Women, men, and the international division of labor.* June Nash and María Patricia Fernández-Kelly, eds., 3–38. Albany: SUNY Press.

———. 1989. *From tank town to high tech: The clash of community and industrial cycles.* Albany: SUNY Press.

Nash, June, and María Patricia Fernández-Kelly, eds. 1983. *Women, men, and the international division of labor.* Albany: SUNY Press.

Nash, June and Helen Safa, eds. 1985. *Women and change in Latin America.* South Hadley, Mass.: Bergin and Garvey.

Ong, Aihwa. 1987. *Spirits of resistance and capitalist discipline: Factory women in Malaysia.* Albany: SUNY Press.

Ortner, Sherry B. 1974. Is female to male as nature is to culture? In *Woman, culture and society.* Michelle Zimbalist Rosaldo and Louise Lamphere, eds., 67–88. Palo Alto: Stanford University Press.

Ortner, Sherry B., and Harriet Whitehead, eds. 1981. *Sexual meanings: The cultural construction of gender and sexuality.* Cambridge: Cambridge University Press.

Overholt, Catherine, et al. 1985. *Gender roles in development projects.* West Hartford, Conn.: Kumarian Press.

Reiter, Rayna. 1975a. Men and women in the south of France: Public and private domains. In *Toward an anthropology of women.* Rayna Reiter, ed., 252–282. New York: Monthly Review Press.

———, ed. 1975b. *Toward an anthropology of women.* New York: Monthly Review Press.

Rogers, Barbara. 1980. *The domestication of women: Discrimination in developing societies.* New York: St. Martin's Press.

Ruiz, Vicki, and Susan Tiano, eds. 1987. *Women on the U.S.-Mexico border: Responses to change.* Boston: Allen and Unwin.

Safa, Helen. 1983. Women, production, and reproduction in industrial capitalism: A comparison of Brazilian and U.S. factory workers. In *Women, men, and the international division of labor.* June Nash and María Patricia Fernández-Kelly, eds., 95–116. Albany: SUNY Press.

Salaff, Janet. 1981. *Working daughters of Hong Kong: Filial piety or power in the family?* New York: Cambridge Univeristy Press.

————. 1988. *State and family in Singapore: Restructuring an industrial society.* Ithaca: Cornell University Press.

Scott, Hilda. 1984. *Working your way to the bottom: The feminization of poverty.* Boston: Pandora Press.

Sen, Amartya. 1984. *Women, technology and sexual divisions.* Santo Domingo: UN/INSTRAW.

Sen, Gita, with Caren Grown. 1985. *Development, crisis, and alternative visions: Third world women's perspectives.* DAWN (Development Alternatives for Women for a New Era). Norway: A.s Verbum.

Srinivasan, Mangalam. 1982. The impact of science and technology and the role of women in science in Mexico. In *Scientific-technological change and the role of women in development.* Pamela M. D'Onofrio-Flores and Sheila M. Pfafflin, eds., 113–148. Boulder: Westview Press.

Stewart, Frances. 1977. *Technology and underdevelopment.* New York: Macmillan.

Stolcke, Verena. 1981. Women's labours: The naturalisation of social inequality and women's subordination. In *Of marriage and the market: Women's subordination in international perspective.* Kate Young et al., eds., 30–48. London: CSE Books.

Stoler, Ann. 1985. *Capitalism and confrontation in Sumatra's plantation belt, 1870–1979.* New Haven: Yale University Press.

Strathern, Marilyn. 1980. No nature, no culture. In *Nature, culture and gender.* Carol MacCormack and Marilyn Strathern, eds., 174–222. Cambridge: Cambridge University Press.

Tadesse, Zenebeworke. 1982. Women and technology in peripheral countries: An overview. In *Scientific-technological change and the role of women in development.* Pamela M. D'Onofrio-Flores and Sheila M. Pfafflin, eds., 77–111. Boulder: Westview Press.

Tinker, Irene. 1981. New technologies for food-related activities: An equity strategy. In *Women and technological change in developing countries.* Roslyn Dauber and Melinda L. Cain, eds., 51–88. AAAS Selected Symposium 53. Boulder: Westview Press.

Warren, Kay B., and Susan C. Bourque. 1985. Gender, power, and communication: Women's responses to political muting in the Andes. In *Women living change.* Susan C. Bourque and Donna Robinson Divine, eds., 355–386. Philadelphia: Temple University Press.

————. 1987. Gatekeepers and resources: Gender and change in Latin American countries. Report for the Gender, Technology, and International Development Project, cosponsored by the Rockefeller Foundation and the International Development Research Centre.

————. 1989. Gender, technology, and development ideologies: Frameworks and findings. In *Gender and anthropology: Critical reviews for research and teaching.* Sandra Morgen, ed. Washington, D.C.: American Anthropological Association.

Whitehead, A. 1985. Effects of technological change on rural women: A review of analysis and concepts. In *Technology and rural women: Conceptual and empirical issues.* Iftikhar Ahmed, ed., 27–64. London: George Allen and Unwin.

Young, K. C. Wolkowitz, and R. McCullagh, eds. 1981. *Of marriage and the market: Women's subordination in international perspective.* London: CSE Books.

NINE

Mujeres in Factories

Race and Class Perspectives on Women, Work, and Family

Patricia Zavella

INTRODUCTION

Anthropology has been considered on the forefront of feminist thinking in part because cultural anthropology's historic mission—to enunciate human similarities and differences through cross-cultural perspectives—was also on the agenda of second-wave feminist scholars in the 1970s. Feminist anthropology contributed much to feminist scholarship through spotlighting previously unseen areas of women's lives in different cultures (Moore 1988: 192). The complex notion of difference among women—whether based on nationality, race, ethnicity, class, age, status, or sexual preference—has been a major concern of feminist theorists, who now realize that not all women have common interests or subscribe to particular feminist viewpoints. Yet although feminist social scientists now note the importance of integrating the concept of racial or ethnic difference among women, particularly in North America, we have been more successful in offering single studies of particular groups of women than in providing systematic comparisons of different women in the same society.

Feminists are now debating how to create a body of scholarship and conduct research in ways that no longer "privilege" white women's concerns and strive for full integration of women of color (Aptheker 1982; Hooks 1984; Hurtado 1989). Women-of-color theorists have argued that race, class, and gender are experienced concurrently, and any attempt to disaggregate this lived experience into separate analytic categories seems reductionist, even impossible (Davis 1981; Joseph 1981; Hooks 1984; Swerdlow and Lessinger 1983). Although these critical reflections on feminist theory have left us with an understanding of the great complexity of all women's experiences, and variation among women within particular racial or ethnic groups, there is nevertheless still a need for structural perspectives that clarify the larger picture.

One key issue needing clarity is the choice of analytic focus. Many feminist theorists see women's common biologically based experiences as the central point of departure for the construction of theory. Highly influenced by French feminist literary criticism, this viewpoint has produced something of a quandary. On the one hand, proponents wish to recognize women's "many voices," that women from diverse class, ethnic, or racial groups have very different perspectives on so-called universal feminine experiences. On the other hand, simply recognizing the richness of diversity leads to an atheoretical pluralism. We need to research women's and men's lives in ways that identify the sources of diversity without resorting to the mechanistic conclusion that class, race, or gender alone gives rise to difference. Karen Sacks suggests that feminist studies should be based on a class analysis, but one which shows how class is socially constructed and "becomes both a gendered and racially specific concept, one that has no race-neutral or gender-neutral 'essence'" (Sacks 1989: 534). I suggest we must begin our analysis with the historically specific structural conditions constraining women's experiences. We can then link these conditions to the varieties of ways in which women respond to and construct cultural representations of their experiences. This suggestion helps us to avoid the problematic assumption of much recent feminist scholarship: beginning with historical material conditions rather than with "experience" embeds "women's diversity" as a theoretical a priori and frees us from the artificial task of deriving diversity from prior commonality.

On the economic front, feminist theory has made an important contribution to our understanding of the relationship between the historical expansion of capitalist production and women's privatized labors within and outside households. Many argue that this is a historically contingent relationship: women strategically consider participation in the labor market or in domestic activities in concert with capital's changing demand for wage labor (Eisenstein 1979; Hartmann 1981*a,b*; Lamphere 1987). Thus analyses of women's labor must be historical, showing how industries or labor markets expand, contract, or become dominated by workers of either gender. Further, feminists have argued that evolving family ideologies—including the presumed opposition of work and family—provide an important context for understanding how women view their situation as working mothers (Collier et al. 1982). Our nineteenth-century heritage of "women's place" constructions casts women as secondary workers who only supplement family income and masks women's segregation in labor markets, since they perform "women's work" on the job. At the same time, women's household labor is devalued as not being real "work" but the enactment of a role, and thus women's double day is discounted.[1] Moving from "women's roles" to "women's labor" was a major feminist scholarly accomplishment of the 1970s. My own original proposed research, under advisory duress, focused on Chicana working wives' experiences of "role strain." Breaking the "role" model and moving into feminist labor studies liberated my research.

Feminist scholarship on U.S. women of color has altered our understanding of the relationship between women's productive and reproductive labor by disentangling the ways that women (and men) of specified racial or ethnic groups have participated in particular labor markets; and by noting that women of color experience class—particularly through waged labor—differently than do white women, while often maintaining some resistance and sense of self based on racial/ethnic solidarity. Evelyn Nakano Glenn's (1986) analysis of three generations of California Japanese domestic workers, for example, or Mary Romero's (1987) discussion of Southwestern-born Chicana domestics show how these women asserted some autonomy over the labor process. Judith Rollins (1985) presents a nuanced commentary on Northern black women domestics and their strategies for dealing with white female employers, and Karen Sacks's (1988) ethnographically based analysis shows how Southern black women hospital clerical workers use social networks in a union organizing drive. This work suggests that the intersection of gender and race/ethnic segregation in the labor market has profound implications for social relations and domestic life, although most of the analyses focus on the public sphere of work. From this research we get a sense of the varying ways in which contemporary American working-class women of color experience the relationship between work and family life differently from white women workers.

Yet as valuable as these works are, they do not provide comparative analyses of women from the same racial or ethnic groups in differing contexts, nor of women from different racial or ethnic groups within the same context.(2) Our understanding of difference among women will only be enhanced through close attention to women's *social location* based on class, race, gender, and ethnicity within the same and differing structural contexts.(3)

Recent work on "ethnographies as texts" reminds us that "social location" in the research process applies to the researcher as well as the researched (see di Leonardo, this volume). There are two important domains that I wish to highlight: the race, class, ethnic, and gender dynamics *between* researcher and researched; and the "social locations" of intellectuals themselves, their places in the historical stream of the contending forces of knowledge production. These factors are as much "data" as are labor force participation rates, and they of course shape the very research questions we ask and the ways in which we go about seeking to answer them.

In what follows, I illustrate this approach through weaving together the intellectual traditions of Marxist Chicano Studies and feminist anthropological and other scholarship on North American working women. I first describe the social contexts of the rise of Chicano Studies, the internal challenge by Chicanas, and the importance of feminist theory with its focus on women's work and family within political economies. These are intellectual transformations in which I participated, first as a student, then as a scholar. Second, I interpret the divergent experiences of two working mothers who at first glance appear to be very similar—they are both working-class Chicana factory workers. The cases are drawn from historical and ethnographic research in two regions in different historical periods: the declining canning industry in northern California in the late 1970s, and the expanding electronics and apparel industries in Albuquerque, New Mexico, in the early 1980s. Using vignettes from the work and family lives of these women and their husbands, I show how a concern with social location gives us clearer insights into changing work and family relations in the United States and reorients the commonality/diversity problematic.

THE SOCIAL CONTEXT OF CHICANO ANTHROPOLOGY

Although anthropology was vitally influenced by the first and third world movements of the late 1960s (Hymes 1972; Weaver 1973), Chicano Studies was literally forged in their crucible. The very term "Chicano," previously denoting a lower-class or "rough" Mexican-American, was taken up by young, largely working-class-origin activists during this era and used as a politically conscious label expressing ethnic pride (Limón 1981). The Chicano Movement—which gained impetus through the anti-Vietnam war protests (a war in which Chicanos were heavily overrepresented in injuries and deaths), the United Farm Workers organizing drives, and student walk-outs in East Los Angeles high schools—eventually became a broad social movement, although activism took place primarily in the Southwest.[4] The nationalism of Chicano Movement ideology (that is, its focus on documenting and providing new interpretations of Chicano history and culture) greatly influenced Chicano scholarship, whose florescence began in the late 1960s as well. Centered at universities, where students had formed an important core of activists (Munoz and Barrera 1982), virtually all of the movement analyses, position papers, or proposals presented to university administrators included a demand for Chicano Studies programs and the legitimation of Chicano Studies as an interdisciplinary field of inquiry (Valdez 1969; Galarza and Samora 1970).

Many Chicano scholars of this, the first real generation, began their academic work as student activists who delved into Chicano history and social science approaches to Chicano populations (Garza 1984). Chicanos had been studied as if they were "traditional" Mexican peasants, and whether they would assimilate into American life or retain their alien, backward culture was the question usually raised by white researchers. This Chicago School approach was as faulty in application to Chicanos as it had been for southeastern Europeans and blacks, its other objects. The focus was ahistorical and antieconomic, and thus automatically denied the variations within migrant populations, differing times of arrival to the United States, varying American regional economies, and the macro shifts in the global economy that conditioned migration in the first place. (Of course, many Chicanos never migrated to the United States; after the U.S.–Mexico war, borders changed and incorporated them as citizens.) Movement-influenced Chicano scholars began creating a revisionist scholarship by formulating critiques of dominant structural-functionalist paradigms and by developing alternative explanations or interpretations of Chicano social reality. Like many scholars before them, the new Chicano researchers turned to Marxist theory for its attention to economy, history, and power—although Marxism was faulted for its inadequate concern with the material basis of racism (Almaguer 1975). Neo-Marxist approaches such as internal colonialism or race-and-class segmentation became the dominant theoretical frameworks in the field (Almaguer 1975; Barrera 1979).

During this early phase of Chicano studies, Chicana scholars protested that women were usually mentioned only in relation to their family roles and that Chicano families were often viewed on the basis of a functionalist "*machismo* model" in which patriarchal values and norms were said to govern women and men's behavior.[5] Even the new Chicano revisionist work, with its Marxist-inspired concern with labor and labor organizing, often portrayed men as public historical agents ("the Chicano worker" was usually male) and relegated women to the passive interstices of *la familia* as nurturers and bearers of culture. Nevertheless, we drew theoretical support from Chicano Studies for critiquing misogynist perspectives on women and for clarifying the racial dimension of the Chicana experience. For many of us, this meant developing a perspective that included the political economy of Chicana history.

The second wave of feminism of the late 1960s and early 1970s also influenced activist Chicanas, although many of us could not accept every feminist notion. In particular, we had problems with the separatist politics (automatically uncooperative with men) in some early women's organizations, and with the white, middle-class focus of American feminism, a focus implicitly and sometimes explicitly racist (Cortera 1980; Gonzales 1977; Zavella 1989). As young Chicana activists had also largely grown up in working-class families, both the lack of race *and class* consciousness in much 1970s feminist political and scholarly work came in for severe criticism. Thus Chicana feminist scholarship was founded, as was Chicano Studies, with scholarly protest and political activism as its "parents."

CHICANO DUAL-WORKER FAMILIES

The rise of Chicana scholarship was paralleled by (and spurred by) the historic rise in labor force participation by Chicanas. Historically lower than other women's labor force participation rates, between 1960 and 1970 Chicanas increased their labor force participation rate at twice the rate of white women; by 1980 Chicanas had very similar labor force participation rates to white and black women. Responding to the distortions generated by the machismo model, Chicana scholars focused on intrafamilial power dynamics in burgeoning dual-worker Chicano families. Lea Ybarra (1982a, 1982b) and Maxine Baca Zinn (1980) suggested that women gained power and autonomy when they became employed. They argued that when wives worked, Chicano couples were more likely to have "egalitarian" values regarding the household division of labor and to carry them out in practice, and that Chicana working wives had more influence in family decision making than homemakers. This revisionist work on Chicano families paralleled work on white Americans and was very important in setting a research trajectory and helping us to understand how women's employment generates economic resources that then affect the organization of Chicano family life, particularly positive new domestic arrangements. Although concerned with women's roles, however, this work did not incorporate larger feminist theory (Zinn 1982), relying on prefeminist resource-mobilization theory within sociology (Blood and Wolfe 1960; Hoffman and Nye 1974).

More recent feminist analyses of how dual worker couples divide up domestic work focuses on individuals' coping strategies. In *The Second Shift* (1989), Arlie Hochschild studied "a transitional phase in American life" (1989: 7), arguing that there is a "stalled revolution" between the changes experienced by American women as they combine full-time employment with marriage and motherhood and the absence of change "in much else" (1989: 12). For most of the couples she studied, this means that wives devote more time to housework and proportionately less time to childcare, while husbands "do more of what they'd rather do." The consequence is tension between husbands and wives, and emotionally drained women coping by performing the "second shift" while abandoning hope that their situations will change. Hochschild's analysis links individuals' strategies to gender identity and gender ideology, noting how women and men are socialized to expect different things in marriage, and how women, forming the "peasantry" of the labor force, bear the brunt for forging strategies. Hochschild's analysis is very helpful in understanding the national aggregate statistics, which indicate little change in the household division of labor yet may have limited application for some sectors of the American working class—especially for people of color. Although she interviewed working-class and minority couples, middle-class couples—the sectors usually studied in family studies—are the center of her research and the focus of her analysis. Although recognizing that Chicano households may well experience the processes that Hochschild delineates, my approach nevertheless focuses on how individuals strategize over cross-cutting constraints and opportunities which may keep couples in "traditional" household arrangements or push them toward more sharing of household chores. Further, I focus on how household arrangements originate in the "traditions" or transitions of larger societal forces and suggest that working-class households in general are more subject to adapting to changes in the political economy. As we will see below, class, race, and region (local economy) are major factors in determining how women and men understand and act on those understandings of the household division of labor.

As in other fields within Chicano Studies, Chicano anthropologists developed extensive critiques of major prior work on their population. Anthropology was probably the most vilified among the social sciences because of its focus on a reified Chicano "culture." White anthropologists were found to have provided ahistorical interpretations of the Chicano experience, misinterpretations of Chicano norms and folklore—sometimes based on lack of familiarity with the Spanish language or literal translations of figurative speech—and implicitly blamed Chicanos for their own social oppression, a familiar story in American social scientific work on ethnic and racial minorities.[6] Chicano anthropologists called for a revisionist view of Chicano culture that was embedded in a sociohistorical context, constructed by actors who took into consideration both given norms and the audience of particular cultural "performances" (Paredes 1977). Chicano anthropologists have further argued that Chicano culture is expressed in contexts in which differential power relations between Chicanos and Anglos are paramount, so that there is a "certain autonomy in people's patterned lifeways, suggesting that culture can both shape and reflect the larger political economy" (Rosaldo 1985: 410). The new Chicano anthropology, then, called for close attention to Chicano cultural expressions within the larger political and economic changes that were occurring in the dominant society, although few of these anthropologists were explicitly concerned with gender or with women's lives in particular.

More recently, Chicano anthropology has taken on new, exciting perspectives. Renato Rosaldo suggests that ethnographers should not assume themselves to be "blank slates" but inevitably are "positioned subjects," contributing a perspective on different cultures that itself is highly cultural. He reminds us that "the objects of social analysis are also analyzing subjects whose perceptions must be taken nearly as seriously as 'we' take our own" (1989: 206). Rosaldo's "remaking of social analysis" would mean "crossing borders" and would be explicitly self-reflective:

Although most metropolitan typifications continue to suppress border zones, human cultures are neither necessarily coherent nor always homogeneous. More often than we usually care to think, our everyday lives are crisscrossed by border zones, pockets, and eruptions of all kinds. Social borders frequently become salient around such lines as sexual orientation, gender, class, race, ethnicity, nationality, age, politics, dress, food, or taste. Along with "our" supposedly transparent cultural selves, such borderlands should be regarded not as analytically empty transitional zones but as sites of creative cultural production that require investigation. (1989: 207–208)

Speaking of Mexican-Americans, José Limón (1989) reflects on the marginality that would include women of color as well: "There at the margins, not fully dangerous or exotic; socially and politically lesser but not enough to make them a real problem or a real attraction for the imagination" (1989: 483). He sees the task of Chicano anthropology as a Foucaultian "archaeology of subjugated knowledges and practices" of a people seen in the dominant American popular, political, and anthropological discourse as marginal.[7] Limón agrees with Rosaldo that we should be reflexive and critically self-aware of our status as ethnographers.

CHICANA FEMINIST ANTHROPOLOGY

My focus on Chicanas' work and family lives thus "follows the field"— attends to important shifts in the population itself. Specifying women's social locations, both structurally and culturally, in relation to other women and to men, means, for Chicanas,[8] taking into consideration various attributes in addition to class and race or ethnicity that create "borders": whether they were born in the United States—and if so, what generation—or in Mexico; if immigrants, whether they were socialized in the United States, rural Mexican villages, or urban centers. Language use is critical and closely related to nativity. If Chicanas are born in the United States, they are more likely to be English-dominant and to speak without a Spanish accent, whereas Mexican-born Chicanas are likely to be bilingual or predominantly Spanish speakers. Cultural regional variation is important: whether one was reared in the Chicano population centers of South Texas, Northern New Mexico or Southern California, or grew up isolated from other Chicanos, has great implications for cultural knowledge. Whether women have fair or dark skin, Indian or European phenotype, or some combination thereof is important for how Chicanas are treated and how they reflect on their racial/ethnic status. Sexuality is clearly a significant demarcation of social location—whether women establish lesbian, heterosexual, or bisexual relationships is central to their identity and experience. The various combinations of these attributes create great variety in Chicanas' experience. Even within "borders," Chicanas are in positions or situations in relation to other women and men that allow greater or lesser autonomy, and women's consciousness and cultural expressions, although not determined by these factors, reflect them. Our analytic lenses should focus on the myriad locations within borders, specifying the relationships that sustain them.

CHICANAS IN THE CANNING INDUSTRY[9]

The Santa Clara Valley of northern California, now well-known as Silicon Valley, was formerly a major agricultural area. Agribusiness drove the California economy until recent decades, despite growing aerospace competition after World War II, and canneries were significant productive components of agribusiness until the late 1950s.

The labor force in northern California canneries has long been segregated by race, ethnicity, and gender, and more recently even by age. The perishable nature of the raw produce and the need for human judgment in handling it provided constraints in organizing production within canneries. These constraints created a divided cannery labor market, with mechanization of certain processes, such as cooking, occurring in the late nineteenth century while some labor processes, such as sorting produce, remain hand labor even today. Further, most canning production is seasonal and takes place during the summer months after the agricultural harvest. Besides mechanization, management and union practices—after unionization by the International Brotherhood of Teamsters—contributed to the development of a bifurcated labor force (Ruiz 1987). Some of these segmentations included the labeling of certain labor processes, such as truck driving, as "men's work" while others, such as the cutting of produce, was considered "women's work." Men usually held the skilled higher-paying, year-round jobs within canneries, whereas women could get only unskilled, low-waged jobs, usually only during the summer months. A system of dual seniority lists and other informal practices made it virtually impossible for women to be promoted into "men's jobs." Cross-cutting this pattern of gender segregation was a form of racial and ethnic stratification. Between the turn of the century and World War II a whole series of European immigrants—Italians, Portuguese, Spaniards, and Yugoslavs were the major groups—settled in the Santa Clara Valley. Thus it was white ethnic women who held most of the "women's jobs."

Chicanos began settling in the area in numbers after World War II, when the canning industry was expanding. Cannery employment in the Santa Clara Valley began declining beginning in the late 1950s, however, so that only workers with high seniority could survive the layoffs. When I did field research in the late 1970s, the cannery labor force was segregated by race and gender: the majority of seasonal workers were female, and over 60 percent were Mexican-American. Among the seasonal labor force, there were predominantly middle-aged women with high seniority who had survived the layoffs, with white ethnic women holding the higher-paying seasonal jobs. Thus cannery work for my Chicana informants was largely seasonal, poorly paid, low status, and with little job mobility.

Cannery workers had filed suit in 1973 alleging race and sex discrimination on the part of California Processors, Inc., a canning industry association (Zavella 1988). In 1976, the plaintiffs were awarded a 5-million-dollar settlement, which was then the largest employment discrimination case ever awarded by the San Francisco Federal District Court. A key victory was the removal of separate seniority lists for seasonal and full-time workers. I began fieldwork among cannery workers in the late 1970s, when implementation of the Affirmative Action Program was beginning. Yet paradoxically, the canning industry was undergoing decline, with the start of plant closures and relocation to rural areas of the state.

My first interview with Gloria Gonzales, a second-generation self-described "Mexican-American," forty-four years of age, who was fully bilingual but spoke mainly in English, reflected both this political-economic surround and the need for "social location" analysis. Gloria agreed to be interviewed only as a favor to an activist friend. Her work situation had changed as a result of the Affirmative Action program, and I was interested in documenting both her work and home life. I got more than I had bargained for.

Gloria Gonzales, who appeared fair-skinned with brown hair, invited me to sit in the living room with her husband and some neighbors who were drinking beer. I suggested that we go someplace else or meet at a different time, but she insisted that we begin at once. Despite my misgivings, I began explaining my interest in women workers. Gloria's husband, Frank (who worked in construction), interrupted by announcing, "Oh she doesn't work, she just sits around the house all day." I explained that I had been told Gloria was a cannery worker. "Oh she is," he said. I asked Gloria how long she had worked. "Twenty-four years this season," she responded.

Gloria and I began an informal conversation about her job while Frank continued to drink and joke with the neighbors. Throughout our conversation the other people present interjected their own commentary, teasing and arguing with one another. It became clear by their verbal jabs that Frank and Gloria had been quarreling. In the middle of our talk, Frank announced that Gloria was going to quit so she could take care of their seven-year-old son. (No child care was available: all Gloria's and Frank's female relatives were living outside the area.) Gloria had the option to "freeze" her seniority and retire early, and planned to do this after the next season. Gloria was pleased with this prospect: "It's better not to work, get unemployment and you get by." But then later, when I asked her general views about whether women should work, she had different thoughts: "Women *should* work outside the home, see what they can do for themselves. It brings you satisfaction to earn your own money when you're old and your husband is gone." With a glance to Frank, she laughed and said: "When I quit I'm going to start a housewives' union."

This proved the end of Frank's patience and he became verbally abusive. He accused Gloria of being lazy—providing a list of domestic chores, including making his dinner—that she had not completed. He informed me he was dissatisfied with her negligence and that they now slept apart. He then questioned my motivations and integrity, demanding to know what I was going to do with the interview information. He shouted, "You could be anybody, from the union—who knows. Gloria could get fired." When I tried to explain that I was doing independent research, he launched into a harangue about people who help "those Mexican People." He obviously did not identify himself as a "Mexican" (the term I had used un-self-consciously) and felt threatened by my questions. His anger was intense.

Clearly our meeting could not continue and, as she walked me to the car, Gloria apologized: "I know he's awful, but he's better than nothing."

During my second interview with Gloria, it became apparent that her nuclear household depended on her wages and unemployment benefits to get through the winter months when her husband was laid off from his construction job. Her income enabled them as well to construct a small second house on their property which they rented out for additional income. From his response to my questions, it was clear that Frank worried about the possibility of Gloria losing her job. Yet Gloria and Frank believed that men should support families. When asked why she had entered the labor force, Gloria indicated that their economic situation had forced the issue: "It was for my kids' benefit that I got a job, and not for anything else." She emphasized: "My family comes *first*." Her husband had opposed her seeking employment, and, along with the lack of available child care, this prevented her from seeking a full-time job. Frank retained the middle-class aspiration of having a wife who was a full-time homemaker and who kept house the way he wanted it. Because Gloria worked, even if on a seasonal basis, Frank was periodically reminded of his inability to support his family as he wanted. Her income and, more telling, her independence were threatening to him.

Gloria's tenure at the cannery had not been easy. She was proud that she had been promoted to work in the "lab," where cans were checked for quality control, a job much easier than working on the line as a sorter. Yet this promotion had come only after special goals for promoting women and minorities had been established. Prior to this program, Gloria had been passed over for promotions for many years. Her experience had been similar to those of her fellow Chicana and *Mexicana* workers, although recent immigrant Mexican women had an even harder time getting promoted. Gloria's experience was different from those of men—both Chicano and white—who had been promoted to high-paying, permanent jobs, and it contrasted with those of white women who had been promoted to the few high-paying seasonal jobs available to women. Indeed, a key point in the race/sex discrimination suit had been that Mexican-American women had been denied access to information and training that would have enabled them to qualify for better jobs. Chicanas' lack of information had been the product of their exclusion from social networks in which insiders had been apprised of impending job opportunities. White women, in this case white ethnic women of Italian, Portuguese, or other European heritage, had been promoted over Chicanas for the few better "women's jobs."

When I asked how having a seasonal job affected the domestic division of labor, Gloria denied that there was any effect at all: "There's none. It doesn't affect us, [because] I'm home in the evenings." Gloria admitted that she hated housework because "it's boring." Her husband occasionally helped with housework, but "not every day." Gloria found it more convenient to ignore her tedious home chores during the work season since, "It's hard to work and clean." She did not openly contest her husband's attempts to coerce more housework on her part. She asserted, "It's not that bad." Yet as she continued talking, a defensive edge came into her voice: "I feel I'm a good mother—although too soft, too lenient. But I try." With a defiant toss of her head she reiterated: "My family comes first." I sensed that she felt that my questions implied that she might be neglecting her family when she worked. Her husband's criticisms no doubt added to her unease in discussing this issue.

Gloria admitted that her employment created domestic problems: "It's not really good. I miss staying home with the children in the summer. They understand that if I don't work they don't get the extras. But it's hard for a person to work all the time. You have no time when you can relax once in a while." Gloria's strategy was to continue working for another season despite her husband's objections. With the rental income, her small pension, and her husband's wages—who after all was "better than nothing"—Gloria would be allowed the rest she desired upon retirement.

Thus Gloria faced a dilemma: she endured the double day if she worked at the cannery, putting in long days of wage work and housework; yet working only on a seasonal basis limited her annual income and the leverage she had over Frank's behavior. I'm not sure that Gloria was ready to leave her spouse, although other informants of mine did so, and for the same reasons. Clearly, though, she had thought about the prospect. She might have come to a different conclusion if she had been able to work full-time. Implicit in Gloria's statements were the contradictory views of women who believed that men should be breadwinners, yet were themselves driven to work to support their families. By evoking "traditional" family ideology—"my family comes first"—she could rationalize what to her seemed the nontraditional act of continuing to work, and she could minimize her own independence. Yet she did not necessarily see herself as being oppressed and cast a cynical eye on my efforts to document the situation of Chicana cannery workers.

The case of Gloria and Frank Gonzales illustrates both the constraints of social location and women's (and of course men's) varying strategic responses to the constaints they experience. At the point of the ethnographic present (1977–1978), as a result of organizing by Chicanos and Chicanas, cannery work had improved in status, pay, and job mobility potential—just as food corporations were beginning to "cash out" and the Santa Clara Valley's economy was switching over to computer research and the development of microchip production. Gloria, quite rationally, was also attempting to take advantage of her recently improved situation—and then "cash out" herself, with shifts in the political economy and Frank's attitude, and her perceptions of her children's needs as material constraints on her possible strategies. Both Gloria and Frank made strategic but divergent uses of notions of "traditional" family values—and note that Frank explicitly distanced himself from "Mexicans," recent migrants. And the yet race-segregated California job markets of both Gloria's and Frank's young adulthood had constituted the greatest constraints on their economic lives, channeling them into a handful of possible occupations that by middle-age were constraining.

HISPANA FACTORY WORKERS IN ALBUQUERQUE

I want to move now into a discussion of different industrial sectors, those of electronics and apparel, which have expanded and relocated around the globe during the past decades, including into the North American "sun belt," where Albuquerque, New Mexico, has become a major industrial site. Managers have established innovative, "participative management" styles in some of these new, American sun-belt factories, which may be changing the experience of industrial work for women. In contrast to plant relocation to the Third World, where availability of cheap female labor seemed to be the major criterion, these managers sought out "quality labor"—workers with at least a high school education and preferably some vocational training. Thus our sample reflects the predominantly Mexican-American rather than Mexican-immigrant character of Albuquerque's female manufacturing work force.[10] We conducted in-depth interviews with firm managers and Hispanic and Anglo dual-worker couples and single parents who had children under the age of six. Our informants were on the average fairly young (in their late twenties), at least third-generation born in the United States, and were the children of working-class families who had migrated from rural areas, although they themselves were reared predominantly in urban areas.

Ethnically, our Mexican-American informants were *Hispanos*: Virtually everyone preferred to identify themselves as "Spanish," "Spanish-

American," or "Hispanic" (the English equivalent of *Hispano*), terms they used interchangeably. Yet they did not discuss their ethnic identification with explicit pride, and many people indicated that this was a sensitive discussion. When asked to clarify the meaning of "Spanish," there was ambiguity and variation: to some informants "Spanish" meant ancestry from the original Spanish settlers; others pointed out the distinctive phenotype of European features and fair skin and hair; while others indicated "Spanish" meant a social category of people distinct from Indians or whites who were Spanish-speakers, but different from Mexicans from Mexico. Most of our informants did not use the term "Chicano," and about half suggested they were opposed to the term because it was slang or represented a tough lifestyle (Metzgar 1974; Limon 1981).

The term "Spanish" has been used to identify Mexican-Americans in northern New Mexico since the nineteenth century, and its usage became popularized in the changing political, economic, and social context of New Mexican politics during the early twentieth century. This was a time when the New Mexican economy was expanding in response to the construction of the railroads and the encroachment of an Anglo business class. It was also a time when native-born Mexican-Americans saw their portion of the population, which had been more than two-thirds, start to dwindle; when various political movements were active—including Mexican syndicalists and the populist *Gorras Blancas* (white caps) movement to retrieve Mexican-owned land; when there was an attempt to insure that the New Mexico statehood debate (in 1912) and the resulting decisions about apportionment included full participation by native New Mexicans. New Mexico Hispanics sought out a term that distinguished them from the racist disapprobations made against Mexicans, yet facilitated the structural integration of an ethnically distinct group (González 1969; Gonzales 1986). The term "Spanish" became hegemonic among Mexican-Americans in the northern part of the state.

New Mexico began industrializing in the late 1960s, fueled by the growth of the apparel and electronics industries, which increased employment by nearly 400 percent. Albuquerque's economy was heretofore based on "guns and butter"—military bases, government employment, and retail sales—by 1980 manufacturing was its third largest sector (Zavella 1984; Lamphere et al., forthcoming). Changes in industrial employment affected women and men differently, with women comprising 80 percent of the new apparel labor force and the majority of unskilled electronics workers. In both industries women were concentrated in low-waged jobs as sewing operators and electronic assemblers and operators, and Mexican-American women made up the majority of the new female factory workers. According to our informants' work histories, most of them had worked in low-waged jobs—such as waitress, motel maid, or fast-food clerk—in the secondary labor market prior to getting employed in apparel or electronics factories. Thus becoming employed in these new industries meant a step up within the working class: sun-belt jobs offered relatively higher wages for "women's work," and there was some job stability and excellent job benefits such as maternity and sick leaves and medical insurance. The increase in women's employment in Albuquerque occurred during a period when other industries that predominantly employed men—such as mining and other manufacturing—were declining. Chicanas' and Chicanos' participation in the Albuquerque labor market, then, was distinct, with women concentrated in the newly expanding, relatively stable industries while the men were often employed in declining or marginal ones or subject to high unemployment.

DUAL-WORKER FAMILIES

Among the Hispanos we interviewed, there were four major economic roles that women assumed in their households. Those who were single parents were the sole providers for their children, since none of these women received child support from their children's fathers. Secondary providers earned less than their spouses, whereas coproviders contributed an equal income with their spouses, and mainstay providers contributed more income than their spouses. The greater a woman's economic contribution to the household, the more likely was her husband to take part in household labor.[11] How did these Hispanos deal with, and talk about, their working lives and household division of labor? Beyond the just-mentioned economic considerations, the household divisions of labor were complex and revolved around three other sets of factors: husbands' and wives' work shifts, who cared for the children during working hours, and family ideology—the couple's commitment to "traditional" norms regarding who should be the breadwinner and who should take responsibility for housework (Hood 1983).

The Senas of Albuquerque provide an interesting comparison with the Gonzaleses of the Santa Clara Valley. Although younger than the Gonzaleses, the Senas had to deal with Leo Sena's extended bouts of unemployment, and to rely on Toni's wages to support their nuclear family. Leo worked as an unskilled sheet-metal worker. They had two girls, ages ten months and two years, and Leo's mother cared for her granddaughters at no charge. Like the Gonzaleses, the Senas had a relatively low income (about $19,500 the previous year). Yet the meaning of employment was different for the Sena family, in part because of slightly different material circumstances and in part because of their differing construction of family ideology. This couple had a relatively egalitarian division of labor.

The Senas were interviewed twice each, within a period of about two weeks, and one of the ethnographers, Felipe Gonzales, was from Albuquerque. Further, our ethnographic team was of similar age and family circumstances themselves—with a preschool-age child, living in the same area of town—the predominantly Hispano, rural South Valley. Perhaps due to these similarities in situations, neither Leo nor Toni seemed nervous about being interviewed, and each talked openly about work and family. Having previously attended college herself, Toni Sena was curious about our research, and from her expansive, often funny stories, seemed to enjoy being interviewed.

Toni Sena worked as a sewing operator on the day shift at an apparel factory, from 7:30 A.M. to 3:30 P.M., sewing hip pockets onto jeans. She was paid by piece rate—that is, her hourly wage was calculated based on a formula in which the speed and amount she produced were taken into consideration. On a good, full work day she sewed about 840 pockets onto pairs of jeans, which worked out to an hourly wage of about five dollars an hour. This was almost the same as her spouse's hourly wages. But at the time of the interview Toni had been working "short weeks" because of the recession of 1982–1983, so she made lower *weekly* wages than her husband. Toni was under pressure to sew even faster to raise her weekly wages.

Toni worked at Leslie Pants, where most of the workers were "Spanish," but she did not see the race issue as being significant. Although she identified herself as "Spanish," she had a hard time clarifying its meaning—"Um, I don't know, from the Spanish origin, I guess"—and did identify, but only vaguely, as one of the group of Spanish workers at Leslie Pants. The labor process was fragmented at Leslie Pants, with each woman working on one part of the product. It was possible, in theory, to get better-paying jobs by moving to more difficult labor processes or by becoming a supervisor, who were predominantly Spanish as well. But in practice there was very little job mobility, with the supervisory positions available only when women quit. Thus Toni's experience was similar to the other Spanish, white, and Indian women working at Leslie Pants with its relatively flat job ladder. Toni felt ambivalent about her job: she said, "I don't really like my job that much," then noted, "but it's a pretty good job, considering." She liked best the friendships with other women workers, her supervisor, and that her job did not interfere with her family responsibilities.

Within the household division of labor, Toni took responsibility for more housework than her husband, cooking breakfast (usually eaten only on weekends) and dinner, setting the table, making beds, washing the floor, cleaning the bathroom, purchasing food, and washing and ironing the clothes. She also took charge of the money and usually paid the monthly bills. Leo usually took responsibility for the "men's" chores—taking out the garbage, taking care of their car, doing general repairs around the house, including plumbing and electrical repairs, as well as yard work—and he usually made the bag lunches for himself and his wife, washed dishes, and vacuumed. Together they decided on large purchases, such as installing solar panels to their home.

The Senas shared the majority of the childcare tasks—they both would awaken the girls, dress them, feed them, bathe them (although Toni would do this more often), put them to bed, take them to activities, change diapers, and discipline them. Toni would usually take the girls to doctor or dentist appointments, and stay home with them if they were too ill for the mother-in-law to handle them.

On a typical work day, Toni would usually prepare the girls' diaper bags while her husband would dress and diaper them in the mornings before work. Toni usually drove them to her mother-in-law's house. (Leo's retirement-aged mother had never worked outside the home.) After work, she would pick up the girls and stay a few hours talking with her in-laws. Leo would come home and do housework:

> Then [after work] I'll clean the yard or do something around the yard; I'm putting a fence up now, doing little things like that. Or wash the dishes, or clean the house, vacuum, make the bed, and I'll just clean up until she comes with the babies. . . . Then, soon as she gets here, either she'll start cooking dinner or I'll have dinner cooked already. (OK, most of the time, who will do the dinner?) She will, sometimes I will. . . . If the house is dirty, we have dishes or something, which we mostly have, so we clean up first, both of us clean up; and then we'll play with the babies a little while and she'll start [dinner].

In the evenings, they would play with the girls, bathe them, and put them to bed, and "just talk, or go over what bills we have to pay." One of the daughters had the habit of going to sleep really late, and Leo took responsibility for staying up with the child until she fell asleep. Toni greatly appreciated this: "I don't know how he does it. I can't, I have to be asleep or *I won't be good the next day* [emphasis mine]. . . . I could never do that. But sometimes he'll stay up with them, watching TV, 'til 2:00 A.M. . . . He's real good about it; he gets up with the girls. I don't. . . . If they need to be changed or something, he gets up." Regarding the sum of childcare tasks, then, Leo may have done fewer than his wife, but in her mind he made up for this by taking on the particularly difficult and time-consuming chore of staying up with their daughter.

The Senas had not discussed how they would divide up household work. Leo said: "We just rely on instinct, on what has to be done"; while Toni noted: "It kind of just happened. We were both working and . . . he's always *helped*" [emphasis mine]. Yet Leo's "instincts" included a sensitivity to his wife's feelings of fatigue. Sometimes Toni came home feeling extra tired, so her husband would do more housework on those days. He said, "If she feels tired or something, then I'll just do it [the housework]," and estimated that this occurred about once a week. Both were generally satisfied with the household division of labor. When asked how she felt about the way chores were divided, Toni said:

> Real good. (Have you and your husband talked about doing things differently?) No, I think we both like the way it is right now. (When you first got married, did you talk about how you were going to divide up the chores?) I don't remember; I don't think so. I just think it kind of happened. We were both working, and I think it just . . . he's real good about that. He's always helped.

Toni admitted that she sometimes felt it was unfair that she had to work and spend so much time taking care of the home and children, but she qualified her response: "But that's only when I'm feeling bad. But most of the time, it's not bad, I don't complain." Leo said, "It's been working out pretty good. . . . I just watch more on how she feels and stuff, and *if she can't do it* [emphasis mine], I'll just go ahead and do it."

There were several factors that contributed to the Sena's relatively egalitarian practice. They had economic difficulties in the early years of their marriage. When they first married, Leo was working as a miner, making about ten dollars an hour, while Toni was attending college. Toni quit school to earn money to finance their wedding and make a down payment toward the purchase of their modest home. But then the Senas had a string of bad luck. Leo lost his job soon after they found out that Toni was pregnant. Because her husband was unemployed, Toni's primary motivation to return to her job was economic, although she liked the opportunity of "getting out of the house" and did not want to become a full-time homemaker. Toni got pregnant a second time while her husband was employed at a low-paying job, but he was laid off again, this time for an extended period. For about a year and a half Toni supported the family while Leo took care of their two babies. He eventually found his current job at half his former mining wages. Thus Toni's wages were crucial during those periods when her husband was unemployed and, after he started working, they relied on her wages—which were nearly equal to those of Leo's—to keep up their house payments. Clearly, Toni was an economic coprovider, and her family depended on her wages and job benefits.

The Senas contrasted strongly with the Gonzaleses in their relatively egalitarian construction of household sexual division of labor. Toni firmly believed that responsibility for economic maintenance should be shared between husband and wife. She also agreed strongly that women need to work to help their families and disagreed with the notion that men should get the higher-paying jobs, saying: "women have to support families sometimes too." She disagreed with the view that it is better for a marriage if a husband earns more money than his wife. She said: "We've had it both ways, and it doesn't seem to matter." Toni was not strongly committed to the notion of a woman being a full-time housewife and mother: "'Cause you don't always want to stay home. It's nice to stay home with them [children], but not, you know . . . it's good to go out and work too, to meet other people." Although she agreed that "working mothers miss the best years of their children's lives," she qualified this by saying, "But sometimes you have to work and you don't have any choice. I'd like to stay home with them, but not every day. I could stay with them, like maybe a couple days a week; it'd be nice." She found work to be an important part of her life that would be hard to give up: "I could give it up for awhile, but not for always."

Leo had more "traditional" views on family roles. He agreed that men should get most of the higher-paying jobs and that women should stay home with their families. He said: "Well, if they have small kids—I'm not saying they should—I mean, if they want, they should be with the kids. Like my wife, I know she would enjoy the kids lots more if she could stay home. But she can't, we can't afford to." He agreed strongly that women need to work because of the high cost of living. Leo hesitated in response to the notion that its better for a marriage if the man earns higher wages:

> That depends [chuckles]. I'm not sure. . . . (Would it be better for your marriage?) Well, for my marriage, I would prefer I would get more money, then she'll be able to go to school. From my point of view, if I was getting enough money, she wouldn't have to go to work. (OK, what if she goes to school and graduates and gets a good job and she's making more money than you, then how would you feel about that?) I would be happy for her. (It wouldn't bother you?) It wouldn't bother me.

The Sena's household division of labor was clearly related to the local economy. "Women's jobs," such as factory sewing operator, were still available in Albuquerque despite a recession (although with shorter hours), whereas mining jobs were part of a declining industry. Further, the actual organization of production within the factories where wife and husband worked affected family life in important ways. Leo's work schedule enabled him to come home early, and he chose to do housework while he waited for his wife. Finally, Toni was a coprovider for the family, and the more intensely she worked the higher were her wages. It was in both their interests for Toni to get plenty of sleep and, beyond his sensitivity to her feelings, this influenced Leo to do more housework and childcare. If she had her choice, she would quit her job, but she couldn't afford to. Implicit in both the Sena's statements about who did housework was the notion that he *helped* her with household chores, rather than that they were to be shared equally. Thus we can see how the Sena's circumstances, within the context of the contemporary, gendered Albuquerque labor market, and their strategic interpretations of "traditional family ideology," created a configuration of work and family experiences very different from that of the Gonzales'.

CONCLUSION

I've emphasized here a framework that links women's domestic and wage work, showing how economic circumstances and family ideology provide a backdrop for individual family members to negotiate a division of household labor. The Gonzales couple continued to accept the notion that husbands should support families and that wives' income was secondary, despite the fact that they relied on Gloria's wages to support their household. Frank Gonzales's anger over their precarious economic circumstances and the necessity that his independent wife continue to work generated much interpersonal conflict. The Senas, by contrast, were in a situation in which they both worked full-time, contributing equally to a "family wage," and had little conjugal conflict. Yet they were a young couple with hopes that Toni would eventually leave her factory job—but for a better-paying, more rewarding job, not for full-time motherhood. In both cases, family ideology as a cultural expression both shaped the couples' experiences in the labor market and reflected the larger political economy in which women's wage work has become crucial. In addition to family ideology, however, these two couples made household arrangements that responded to the specific circumstances of their employment.

In reflecting on the women's cases and my role as a feminist ethnographer, I should point out that these two women were interviewed under different circumstances, and I was perceived as a "positioned subject" in different ways. In my early feminist zeal to correct the record and study the lives of Chicana workers, I did not interview their spouses about the household division of labor. Thus Frank Gonzales never had the explicit opportunity to provide his side of the story, perhaps one reason for his outburst while his wife gave hers. Further, I was perceived as the young college student working on her paper, and middle-aged Gloria (as did other cannery-worker informants) often displayed friendly, maternal condescension and perhaps defensiveness about my questions regarding household division of labor. I interviewed Gloria twice, in the span of a few weeks, and during the second interview she felt compelled to assert that she remained on her job and with her husband for the sake of her youngest child. Gloria also felt defensive about the race/sex discrimination suit that had won her her new, better job, noting that "troublemakers" were involved and stating outright that things were not as bad as the activists had indicated. Thus Gloria's sense of ethnic identity was conditioned by what labor and Chicano activists would call accommodationist politics.

The Senas, by contrast, lived in a very different context. Toni Sena's vagueness about the meaning of "Spanish" reflected her social location in which both work and social networks were exclusively Spanish and there were no ethnically based political struggles at the factory. So there were few interethnic boundaries that would push her to clarify what was unique about "Spanish" people. Her vagueness is more interesting when we consider that a small minority of sewing operators at Leslie Pants were Spanish-speaking, Mexican-immigrant women, so presumably she had considered whether she was different from them or not. Further, Leo's honest admission to really wanting his wife to quit her job and return to college, and Toni's openness about how she and Leo had evolved into a sharing arrangement, may have been influenced by their sense that they had sympathetic interviewers in similar situations.

These two examples illustrate how specifying women's social location, in relation to other women and to men, clarifies structural and cultural similarities and differences among women of the same race and class. These two Chicana factory workers, although entering labor markets segregated by race and class, experienced factory work in very different ways because they entered at different points in the industries' histories and worked in economies where factory employment took on meaning relative to other "women's jobs." Further, these women were interviewed at different points in their life cycles, with the middle-aged couple becoming aware of the lack of options and change, while the younger couple hoped for better things. In addition, they lived in regions where constructions of ethnic identity were based on varied terms, with ethnic identity not as salient in the New Mexico workplace but forming the basis of worker-management conflict in northern California canneries. Finally, detailing these Chicanas' social locations—and their strategic responses to them—enables us better to enter into a "women, work, and family" analysis that does not take white, middle-class women as its normative subject.

NOTES

I'd like to thank Louise Lamphere and Felipe Gonzales for the discussions that stimulated the views developed here. I'm indebted to Deborah Woo for the term "social location." Micaela di Leonardo gave me many helpful, critical comments and was an extraordinarily patient editor.

  1. Feminist scholars have contributed to our understanding of activities that were not usually recognized as work, often because it was done by women. Thus we now have concepts of "consumption work," indicating the labor involved in provisioning households (Weinbaum and Bridges 1979), the "interaction work" that eases social relations and social interaction (Fishman 1978), and "kinship work" that links households with one another (di Leonardo 1987)—all of which is generally done by women.

  2. Some notable exceptions include research by feminist historians and historical anthropologists. See Dolores Janiewski's (1981, 1983) work on white and black

women tobacco workers, and Louise Lamphere's (1987) analysis of Colombian and Portuguese women textile and jewelry workers in Rhode Island.

3. For a very interesting discussion that attempts such a comparative analysis, see Nakano Glenn's suggestive overview of women of color (1985). Deborah Woo (1985) illustrates the importance of the social location of different groups of Asian American women, while Segura (1984) and Hurtado (1989) compare particular aspects of differences in social location between Chicanas and white women. My distinction between race and ethnicity recognizes each as being socially constructed but sees ethnicity as indicating cultural, linguistic, or regional variation within the same racial group.

4. The other major movements included Reyes Tijerina's Alianza for Social Justice, which sought justice for descendants of Mexican landholders displaced by the U.S.-Mexican War, Corky Gonzales's Crusade for Justice—which created an alternative Chicano-controlled school system in Denver—and the Crystal City, Texas, election takeover by the Raza Unida political party, lead by José Angel Gutiérrez. See Acuña (1981), Hammerback et al. (1985), García (1989), Munoz (1989).

5. For a full discussion and critique of the machismo model and Chicano families, see Ybarra (1982a, 1982b), Zavella (1987), and Zinn (1980).

6. The works of Octavio Romano (1968, 1970, 1971) and Nick Vaca (1970) were probably the most influential in criticizing the lack of historical perspectives on the Chicano experience, pointing out the flaws within the dominant theoretical models. Also see Paredes (1977) and Rosaldo (1985, 1986, 1989).

7. Limón also calls for a Bakhtinian "ethnography of the carnivalesque," which "can lead not only to ideological content but also an ideology of critical form," a project clearly beyond my parameters here.

8. I use the term *Chicanas* to refer to all women of Mexican heritage, distinct from *Latinas* who are from Latin American heritage. Although widely used, *Hispanic* is a term imposed by the U.S. Census Bureau, and many Chicanos and Latinos dislike it.

9. The following section is excerpted from Zavella (1987). Following ethnographic convention, all names are pseudonyms.

10. Louise Lamphere and Peter B. Evans were Principal Investigators of a National Science Foundation-funded project investigating the impact of sun-belt industrialization on working-class Hispanic and Anglo families, interviewed during 1982–1983. The following analysis on the household division of labor was developed in Lamphere et al. (forthcoming).

11. See Hartmann (1981b) for a discussion of this relationship between women's economic roles and men's contribution to household labor. My discussion here focuses on how Hispanos talk about the household division of labor, since we did not do participant observation.

BIBLIOGRAPHY

Acuña, Rodolfo. 1981. *Occupied America: A history of Chicanos*, 2d ed. New York: Harper & Row.

Almaguer, Tomas. 1975. Class, race, and Chicano oppression. *Socialist Revolution* 25: 71–99.

Aptheker, Bettina. 1982. *Women's legacy: Essays in race, sex and class in American history.* Amherst: University of Massachusetts Press.

Barrera, Mario. 1979. *Race and class in the Southwest: A theory of racial inequality.* Notre Dame: University of Notre Dame Press.

Blood, Robert, and Donald Wolfe. 1960. *Husbands and wives.* New York: Free Press.

Collier, Jane, Michelle Z. Rosaldo, and Sylvia Yanagisako. 1982. Is there a family? New anthropological views. In *Rethinking the family: Some feminist questions.* Barrie Thorne and Marilyn Yalom, eds., 25–39. New York: Longman.

Cortera, Marta. 1980. Feminism: The Chicana and the Anglo versions: A historical analysis. In *Twice a minority: Mexican American women.* Margarita B. Melville, ed., 217–234. St. Louis: C. V. Mosby.

Davis, Angela. 1981. *Women, race and class.* New York: Random House.

di Leonardo, Micaela. 1987. The female world of cards and holidays: Women, families and the work of kinship. *Signs* 12 (3): 440–453.

Eisenstein, Zillah. 1979. Developing a theory of capitalist patriarchy and socialist feminism. In *Capitalist patriarchy and the case for socialist feminism.* Zillah R. Eisenstein, ed. New York: Monthly Review Press.

Fishman, Pamela. 1978. Interaction: The work women do. *Social Problems* 25 (4): 397–406.

García, Ignacio M. 1989. *United we win: The rise and fall of La Raza Unida Party.* Tucson: University of Arizona Press.

Galarza, Ernesto, and Julian Samora. 1970. Chicano studies: Research and scholarly activity. *Civil Rights Digest* 3 (4): 40–42.

Garza, Hisauro. 1984. Nationalism, consciousness, and social change: Chicano intellectuals in the United States. Ph.D. Dissertation, Sociology Department, University of California, Berkeley.

Glenn, Evelyn Nakano. 1985. Racial ethnic women's labor: The intersection of race, gender and class oppression. *Review of Radical Political Economics* 17 (3): 86–108.

———. 1986. *Issei, nisei, war bride: Three generations of Japanese American women in domestic service.* Philadelphia: Temple University Press.

Gonzales, Phillip B. 1986. Spanish heritage and ethnic protest in New Mexico: The Anti-Fraternity Bill of 1933. *New Mexico Historical Review* 61 (4): 281–300.

Gonzales, Sylvia. 1977. The white feminist movement: The Chicana perspective. *The Social Science Journal* 14: 68–76.

González, Nancie L. 1969. *The Spanish-Americans of New Mexico: A heritage of pride.* Albuquerque: University of New Mexico Press.

Hammerback, John C., Richard J. Jensen, and Jose Angel Gutiérrez. 1985. *A war of words: Chicano protest in the 1960s and 1970s.* Westport, Conn.: Greenwood Press.

Hartmann, Heidi I. 1981a. The unhappy marriage of Marxism and feminism: Towards a more progressive union. In *Women and revolution.* Lydia Sargent, ed., 2–41. Boston: South End Press.

———. 1981b. The Family as the locus of gender, class and political struggle: The example of housework. *Signs* 6 (31): 366–394.

Hochschild, Arlie, with Anne Machung. 1989. *The second shift: Working parents and the revolution at home.* New York: Viking.

Hoffman, Lois, and F. Ivan Nye, eds. 1974. *Working mothers.* San Francisco: Jossey-Bass.

Hood, Jane C. 1983. *Becoming a two-job family*. New York: Praeger.

Hooks, Bell. 1984. *Feminist theory from margin to center*. Boston: South End Press.

Hurtado, Aida. 1989. Relating to privilege: Seduction and rejection in the subordination of white women and women of color. *Signs* 14 (4): 833–855.

Hymes, Dell, ed. 1972. *Reinventing anthropology*. New York: Vintage Books.

Janiewski, Dolores E. 1981. From field to factory: Race, class, sex and the woman worker in Durham, 1880–1940. Ann Arbor: University Microfilms International.

———. 1983. Sisters under their skins: Southern working women, 1880–1950. In *Sex, race and the role of women in the South*. Joanne V. Hawks and Sheila L. Skemp, eds. Jackson: University of Mississippi Press.

Joseph, Gloria. 1981. The incomplete menage a trois: Marxism, feminism, and racism. In *Women and revolution: A discussion of the unhappy marriage of Marxism and feminism*. Lydia Sargent, ed., 109–143. Boston: South End Press.

Lamphere, Louise. 1987. *From working daughters to working mothers: Immigrant women in a New England industrial community*. Ithaca: Cornell University Press.

Lamphere, Louise, Felipe Gonzales, Patricia Zavella, and Peter B. Evans. *Working mothers and "Sun Belt industrialization": New patterns of work and family*. Manuscript, forthcoming

Limón, Jose E. 1981. The folk performance of "*Chicano*" and the cultural limits of political ideology. In "*And other neighborly names*": *Social process and cultural image in Texas folklore*. Richard Bauman and Roger D. Abrahams, eds., 197–225. Austin: University of Texas Press.

———. 1989. *Carne, carnales*, and the carnivalesque: Bakhtinian *batos*, disorder, and narrative discourses. *American Ethnologist* 16 (3): 471–486.

Metzgar, Joseph V. 1974. The ethnic sensitivity of Spanish New Mexicans: A survey and analysis. *New Mexico Historical Review* 49 (1): 49–73.

Moore, Henrietta L. 1988. Feminism and anthropology. Minneapolis: University of Minnesota Press.

Munoz, Carlos. 1989. *Youth, identity, power: The Chicano movement*. New York: Routledge, Chapman and Hall.

Munoz, Carlos, Jr., and Mario Barrera. 1982. La Raza Unida Party and the Chicano student movement in California. *The Social Science Journal* 19 (2): 101–119.

Paredes, Americo. 1977. On ethnographic work among minority groups: A folklorist's perspective. *New Scholar* 6 (1/2): 1–32.

Rollins, Judith. 1985. *Between women: Domestics and their employers*. Philadelphia: Temple University Press.

Romano, Octavio Ignacio V. 1968. The anthropology and sociology of the Mexican-Americans. *El grito: A journal of contemporary Mexican-American thought* 2 (1): 13–26.

———. 1970. Social science, objectivity, and the Chicanos. *El grito: A journal of contemporary Mexican-American thought* 4 (1): 4–16.

———. 1971. The anthropology and sociology of the Mexican-Americans: The distortion of Mexican-American history. *El grito: A journal of contemporary Mexican-American thought* 1 (1): 13–26.

Romero, Mary. 1987. Domestic service in the transition from rural to urban life: The case of La Chicana. *Women's Studies* 13 (3): 199–222.

Rosaldo, Renato Jr. 1985. Chicano studies, 1970–1984. *Annual Review of Anthropology* 14: 405–427.

————. 1986. When natives talk back: Chicano anthropology since the late sixties. *Renato Rosaldo Lecture Series Monograph* 2 Spring.

————. 1989. *Culture and truth: The remaking of social analysis.* Boston: Beacon Press.

Ruiz, Vicki L. 1987. *Cannery women, Cannery lives: Mexican women, unionization and the California food processing industry, 1930–1950.* Albuquerque: University of New Mexico Press.

Sacks, Karen Brodkin. 1989. Toward a unified theory of class, race and gender. *American Ethnologist* 16 (3): 534–550.

Sacks, Karen Brodkin. 1988. *Caring by the hour: women, work and organizing at Duke Medical Center.* Urbana: University of Illinois Press.

Segura, Denise. 1984. Labor market stratification: The Chicana experience. *Berkeley Journal of Sociology* 29: 57–91.

Swerdlow, Amy, and Hanna Lessinger, eds. 1983. *Class, race, and sex: The dynamics of control.* Boston: G. K. Hall.

Vaca, Nick C. 1970. The Mexican-American in the social sciences 1912–1970, part II: 1936–1970. *El grito: A journal of contemporary Mexican-American thought* 4 (2): 17–51.

Valdez, Armando, ed. 1969. *El plan de Santa Barbara: A Chicano plan for higher education.* Oakland: La Causa Publications.

Weaver, Thomas, ed. 1973. *To see ourselves: Anthropology and modern social issues.* Glenview, Ill.: Scott, Foresman and Company.

Weinbaum, Batya, and Amy Bridges. 1979. The other side of the paycheck: Monopoly capital and the structure of consumption. In *Capitalist patriarchy and the case for socialist feminism.* Zillah R. Eisenstein, ed., 190–205. New York: Monthly Review Press.

Woo, Deborah. 1985. The socioeconomic status of Asian American women in the labor force: An alternative view. *Sociological perspectives* 28 (3): 307–338.

Ybarra, Leonarda. 1982*a*. Marital decision-making and the role of machismo in the Chicano family. *De colores: journal of Chicano expression and thought* (1 & 2): 32–47.

————. 1982*b*. When wives work: The impact on the Chicano family. *Journal of Marriage and the Family* 44 (1): 169–178.

Zavella, Patricia. 1984. The impact of "sun belt industrialization" on Chicanas. *Frontiers* 8 (1): 21–27.

————. 1987. *Women's work and chicano families: Cannery workers of the Santa Clara Valley.* Ithaca: Cornell University Press.

————. 1988. The politics of race and gender: Organizing Chicana cannery workers in Northern California. In *Women and the politics of empowerment.* Ann Bookman and Sandra Morgen, eds. Philadelphia: Temple University Press.

————. 1989. The problematic relationship of feminism and Chicana studies. *Women's Studies* 17 (1–2): 25–36.

Zinn, Maxine Baca. 1980. Employment and education of Mexican-American women: The interplay of modernity and ethnicity in eight families. *Harvard Educational Review* 50 (1): 47–62.

————. 1982. Mexican-American women in the social sciences: Review essay. *Signs* 8: 259–272.

PART FOUR

Contentious Kinship: Rethinking Gender and Reproduction

TEN

Rethinking the Sexual Division of Labor
Reproduction and Women's Work among the Efe

Nadine R. Peacock

Akodi is awakened by the whimpering and squirming of her infant daughter who has spent the night nestled in her mother's arms inside the family's igloo-shaped leaf hut. Akodi nudges her four-year-old daughter Mapiembi, urging her to rise, and mother followed by daughter exit the hut through the small, arched doorway. "You are awake, Nedina?" she calls to me in the traditional morning greeting, and I respond, "Yes, and you?" Mapiembi shivers in the damp morning air of the forest and complains of the cold. Akodi assures her that she will be warm in a moment and instructs her to sit down and hold the baby. The girl reaches into the hut for some dry leaf bedding, places it on a small damp log, sits, and unenthusiastically allows her mother to place the now bellowing infant in her arms. Akodi ducks back into the hut and emerges a few seconds later carrying the smoldering sticks that are the remains of the fire that warmed the family during the night. She uses the embers and the last of yesterday's firewood to build a new fire just outside the hut. Mapiembi inches closer, clearly enjoying the warmth and dryness generated by the leaping flames. Akodi heats a small amount of bathing water for her husband Mbula and then takes the infant from Mapiembi and begins to nurse her. Shortly Mbula emerges from the hut and, after sitting a short while with his wife and daughter, takes the warm water behind his hut for his morning ablutions.

A similar scene is being enacted a few meters away, in front of the hut occupied by Mbula's younger brother Melimeli, his wife Deani, and their two-month-old daughter. Today, as Akodi informed me yesterday, she and Deani will leave their forest camp to help in the rice harvest of a villager family who live on the road; in return they will receive some of the rice, as well as some cassava and cassava leaves; if they are lucky and perhaps willing to do a little extra work, they may be able to get some palm oil and perhaps a little tobacco as well. Yesterday the two women did not work in the village but rather accompanied other women and children of the group on a foraging trip. They returned with an assortment of small fish and crabs, as well as some mushrooms and forest fruits. Any of these items could be exchanged in the village for agricultural food, and some of the women did so. Akodi and Deani, however, decided that they would prefer to keep their tasty forest products for their own families' consumption, since they hadn't really collected that much. At any rate, today it is the "muto" or village trading partner of Akodi's husband who will be harvesting rice, and so on this day in particular her own labor will net more than would a few treats from the forest.

Mapiembi is now complaining that she is hungry, and Akodi interrupts her infant's feeding for a moment to retrieve some tidy leaf packages from the roof of her hut. These contain leftovers from last night's meal—some mushrooms and the last of the cassava that she had received in the village the day before yesterday in exchange for a small amount of meat. She warms the parcels in the coals and then hands food to her husband and daughter, also taking a bit for herself. Mbula interrupts his arrow sharpening to eat, while continuing to engage in a lively banter with the other men around the camp about their plans for the day's group hunt and recalling the highlights of yesterday's.

Noticing that Deani has already begun mobilizing for the village trip, Akodi tells Mapiembi, "I'm going to the village now; go to your grandmother." Mapiembi, though clearly very attached to her mother, seems quite delighted to stay behind today. The village is far away, and when she does go she has trouble keeping up with the women and older children on the rough forest paths. There is not much for her to do in the villager's garden but sit in the hot sun and watch her little sister sleep, whereas there are endless diversions in the camp; her grandmother gives her plenty of food, seldom scolds her, and even allows her to suckle, which her mother no longer permits. (It doesn't seem to matter to Mapiembi that her grandmother has no milk for her.)

Akodi picks up the length of cloth that she uses as an infant sling, knots the ends together, and puts the sling across her shoulder. The cloth is quite tattered; it is nearly a year old, and the frequent washings she gives it have taken their toll. If her husband is able to collect enough honey this year, he will be able to trade it in the village for one, perhaps even two new pieces of cloth. Otherwise, she will have to make do with a more cumbersome sling made from bark, or hope that her husband is able to kill an animal on his own so that he can make a sling for her from its hide. Akodi settles her baby at her hip, slides her small knife into her twine belt, and finally picks up her basket, placing its tumpline on her head. She walks out of camp behind Deani, who is also carrying her infant and an empty basket. Neither woman visibly reacts with anything but a faint smile when I pick up my daypack and notebook and follow them out of camp.

When Akodi and Deani arrive in the village about two hours later, they find that the harvest has already begun. Both infants, who had been lulled to sleep while their mothers were walking, are now awakened by the noise and bright light and begin to fuss. Deani sits down in the tiny bit of shade afforded by a nearby cassava plant and begins nursing her baby. Akodi, standing, nurses her baby as well, and once the infant has quieted, she hands her to Deani, who continues to sit with an infant at each breast, while Akodi goes to where the other women are working and begins cutting stems of rice with her knife, tossing them over her shoulder into the basket on her back. After an hour or so, Akodi tires of standing in the strengthening sun and walks over to her sister-in-law and the two infants. The babies are now asleep on banana leaves, and Akodi sits down next to them while Deani rises and goes to work on the rice harvest.

After several hours, both women have filled their baskets with rice, and Akodi informs the village woman in whose garden they have been working that it is time to return to camp. Mbula and the village woman's husband have been designated as trading partners since childhood, and their respective fathers were trading partners as well. Since marrying Mbula and moving to his camp, Akodi has cultivated a friendly relationship with the wife of her husband's "muto" and, at least during times when agricultural food is plentiful, she expresses satisfaction with the amount that she gets in return for forest foods and for her labor. On this trip, in addition to a portion of the rice she has harvested, the woman allows her to take some squash, bananas, cassava roots, and cassava leaves from the garden, and also gives her a bowl of palm nuts from which she will extract cooking oil. Deani also is allowed to collect food from the garden, but the village woman requests that she, unlike Akodi, fetch some water for her before leaving.

Having completed my "official" two hours of observation on Akodi and Deani, I am free to sit in the shade with them and the village woman, chatting and chewing on palm-nut fiber. After a while, the Efe women rise, arrange their babies and secure their basket loads, and prepare to head back to camp. The village woman helps them lift their heavy baskets onto their backs and admonishes Akodi to bring some meat next time she comes to the village. Though the workday in the village is now over, and though there are still several hours to go before sundown, the women move quite quickly under their burdens. They still must chop and carry firewood, collect water, and bathe before they can begin preparing their families' evening meals. If the men have had a successful hunt, there will be meat to prepare as well.

INTRODUCTION

Akodi and Deani[1] are two of the twenty-seven women who were the focus of my nearly two-year study among a people who call themselves Efe (pronounced *eff'-ay*) and who inhabit the Ituri Forest of northeast Zaire. To the rest of the world the Efe are commonly known as pygmies, though they themselves consider this name an insult.[2] The Efe sometimes refer to themselves as Mbuti, especially when dealing with outsiders. Although "Mbuti" is technically the name of a large population of pygmies inhabiting another part of the Ituri Forest, it has come to be used in popular and scholarly works, as well as by the Zairian population themselves, as the generic term for all Ituri pygmies.

The Efe along with other pygmy populations of central Africa are classified among the last of the world's foraging populations. One of my motivations for conducting research among the Efe was an interest in examining the subsistence ecology and, in particular, the role of women in subsistence within such foraging societies. The Efe were a particularly appealing study population because of the paucity in the anthropological record of quantitative data on the subsistence ecology of African foragers other than the !Kung San of southern Africa, and specifically because of the need for data on forest-living foragers. Like many biological anthropologists, I am interested in the origins of contemporary human behavior and demographic patterns and wish to investigate the extent to which contemporary foragers can be used as models for inferring the way of life pursued by all humans prior to the inception of plant and animal domestication. Though most scholars now doing research on contemporary foragers are very careful in making analogies to the past, this approach has been abused and misinterpreted by some, who present these populations as "stone-age peoples" or "living fossils." This ahistoric and biologically incorrect perspective is untenable. Not only are contemporary foragers biologically fully modern humans, just as we are; they have also lived within the same stream of history and thus have had the same amount of time to undergo cultural change. It would be unjustified and certainly incorrect to assume that foragers of today are living exactly as did foragers of the Paleolithic. Furthermore, despite occasional sensational reports of "previously uncontacted hunter-gatherers," there is no convincing evidence that there is anywhere in the world a foraging population that has not had contact with and/or been affected by the activities of more technologically advanced neighbors. This is obviously the case for the Efe and other pygmy groups in central Africa, who have long-standing traditional relationships with their agricultural neighbors, and who rely to a great extent on foods acquired in exchange from these neighbors; but it is no less true of any of the handful of African, South American, and Asian groups who still pursue hunting and gathering as a primary mode of subsistence but who have periodic, even if infrequent, interactions with agriculturalists, pastoralists, merchants, missionaries, or anthropologists.

Given these caveats, it is still almost certainly the case that contemporary foragers, the Efe included, share some key features of demography, technology, and social organization with foragers of the past and that these shared features may provide a model, however imperfect, of a statistically unusual and rapidly disappearing means of livelihood. With appropriate caution, for example, we can use ethnographic information gathered from these societies to generate testable hypotheses for archaeologists investigating remains left by foragers of the past. Such a systematic approach is much preferable to the all too common "armchair reasoning" about what life may have been like for prehistoric peoples. We can also examine foraging societies in combination with societies at other levels of technological development in a search for generalized patterns that might be used to explain cultural features in all human societies. An example of this approach is the effort to understand the origin and function of the division of labor by sex across human societies, an effort that has a long history within the social sciences.

Nineteenth-century social theorists from Spencer and Morgan to Marx and Engels gave the subject of the sexual division of labor a central place in their efforts to understand the origins of the family and of society. The twentieth century saw even greater interest in the topic. Theorists such as Durkheim used the conjugal union, in his view necessarily accompanied by a sexual division of labor, as a "prototype" for the integration and solidarity seen in large social systems (Durkheim 1964). Later, Boas and his intellectual progeny, most notably Mead, focused on the variability in sex roles cross-culturally as evidence of an almost infinite flexibility in the expression of cultural traits.

In the last two decades, the division of labor by sex, as part of the larger issue of the statuses and roles of women, has been a central issue in feminist scholarship. This scholarship has been motivated by efforts to document the extent and to discern the origins of male domination in human societies, as well as by the desire to effect changes in male-female economic and social relations. Among feminist scholars, it is perhaps anthropologists who have found this issue most compelling. The 1970s saw a burgeoning of scholarly activity by anthropologists who were critically scrutinizing the very substance of their field and the history of its treatment of women (Reiter 1975; Rosaldo and Lamphere 1974). Many people had explained and in effect justified the inequality of the sexes by alluding to its supposed antiquity and universality in human societies. Feminist anthropologists therefore carefully scrutinized existing ethnographic reports and scholarly treatments for data on this subject and, in the process, searched for and found evidence of male bias or the systematic underreporting or undervaluing of women's work and status (Martin 1978; Milton 1979). These tactics were echoed by a new generation of primatologists who uncovered analogous biases in existing studies of our nonhuman relatives, which tended to put inordinate emphasis on the behavior of males (Lancaster 1976; Hrdy 1981; and see Sperling, this volume).

The early feminist scholarship on the sexual division of labor of necessity consisted largely of reworkings of old data in light of new theories formulated from feminist perspectives. Often these efforts were frustrated because of the lack of uniform reporting of relevant data. Thanks to persistent efforts, however, we have some clear ideas about how the sexual division of labor varies across societies; we are now in a position to use all the resources available to gather and analyze new data aimed specifically at on-the-ground testing of a variety of theoretical constructs, the focus of which is the detection of rules and regularities in cross-cultural data.

A variety of new methodologies, in addition to traditional ethnographic ones, have been brought to bear in tackling these problems. Time-allocation analysis is gaining wide use in studies of work patterns and household economics, and proves very well suited to the study of gendered behavior (Mulder and Caro 1985). Quantitative behavior observation methods, along with increasingly sophisticated survey and interview techniques, allow us to achieve a clearer picture of intra- as well as intercultural variation in gender-specific behaviors. They also permit us to analyze the relationship between informants' expressed norms about gender-specific behavior on the one hand, and their actual behaviors on the other. When these analytic tools are carefully standardized, they greatly facilitate cross-cultural comparisons, and thereby the testing of hypotheses using cross-cultural data.

In what follows, I review recent ways in which feminist and nonfeminist scholars have considered the causes and functions of the sexual division of labor. I then use information from my work with Efe pygmies to interrogate these models.

Most anthropological treatments of the sexual division of labor produced in the last two decades have been inspired to some extent by a "brief communication" published by Judith K. Brown (Brown 1970). In this short but seminal contribution, Brown attempts to explain two central findings of studies on the sexual division of labor. These are that (1) the division of labor by sex is universal, and (2) there is, compared to men, a relatively "narrow range of subsistence activities in which women make a substantial contribution." These activities are identified specifically as gathering, hoe agriculture, and trade.

Brown summarizes a variety of theories put forth up to that time to explain these two observations. Most of these explanations deal in some way with a difference in innate capacities—both physical and psychological—between men and women. Although not denying that innate differences between men and women exist, Brown asserts that such differences are not very important in determining sex-specific task assignment. Rather, she makes the assumption that because women bear and nurse children, they will always have primary responsibility for childcare, and she suggests that other tasks will be assigned to women only to the extent that they are compatible with the simultaneous performance of childcare. For any given society, she says, knowledge of the major subsistence activity and of its compatibility with childcare permits one to predict "with considerable accuracy" the degree to which women contribute to subsistence. The characteristics of childcare-compatible tasks cited by Brown are the following: "they do not require rapt concentration and are relatively dull and repetitive; they are easily interruptible and easily resumed once interrupted; they do not place the child in potential danger; and they do not require the participant to range very far from home" (Brown 1970). Brown then predicts that tasks assigned exclusively or primarily to women in any society *that does not rely heavily on alternate caretakers* will be characterized by these childcare-compatible features and that the extent of women's contribution to subsistence for a given society will be a direct function of the extent to which the major subsistence activity is characterized by these features.

The key value of Brown's contribution is that she presents for the first time an explanation for the division of labor by sex that constitutes an explicit hypothesis testable against ethnographic data. In a nutshell, this hypothesis states that the sexual division of labor is based on a set of logistic constraints having to do with childcare, rather than any physical or biological constraints. A number of investigators have taken up the challenge of testing this prediction, most frequently in so-called holocultural studies.[3]

Murdock and Provost (1973) published a holocultural study in which they concluded that most of the cross-cultural variability in sex-specific task assignment can be accounted for by composite factors that they call "masculine advantage" and "feminine advantage." They describe masculine advantages as involving the "greater physical strength" of men as well as their "superior capacity for mobilizing it in brief bursts of excessive energy," while feminine advantage is essentially defined by Brown's criteria for childcare-compatible tasks. They also state that tasks of the latter type tend to require almost daily attention and are therefore disadvantageous to men, who are more likely to be involved in activities such as warfare, hunting, and herding which may require prolonged absences from the household.

A second holocultural study supports Brown's assertions about the primacy of childcare compatibility as a criterion for female-specific work activities (White et al. 1977). These authors conclude that the two characteristics of work activities that are *most* incompatible with childcare are distant travel and exposure of the mother and/or infant to danger (which are not unrelated) and that the demands of nursing place greater constraints on women's work activities than do the demands of other types of childcare.

There are two notable issues that are not explicitly dealt with in the works cited above. One is the use of alternate caretakers, and the other is the possibility of energetic constraints as opposed to logistic constraints of childbearing and child-rearing on women's subsistence tasks.

Nerlove (1974) addresses the first issue, pointing out that in order to accommodate what may be "incompatible" subsistence activities, women frequently modify their childcare activities—for example by the early introduction of weaning foods, which permits the use of alternate caretakers. She points out that substitute care is considered essential in many societies where women's contribution to subsistence is high, and she demonstrates a positive correlation between women's contribution to subsistence and early introduction of weaning foods. She point out, however, that this strategy has associated risks, such as increased risk to infants of morbidity or mortality when substitutes for breastmilk are introduced, as well as the probability of shortening the interbirth interval and hence increasing fertility, which may be an undesired consequence of reduced suckling frequency (Konner and Worthman 1980; Howie et al. 1982).

Nerlove also points out that populations that do not follow the "high female contribution equals early weaning" pattern tend to be those in which subsistence is based primarily on foraging for wild plants and animals. The !Kung San (Bushmen) of the Kalahari Desert in Botswana and Namibia are the most often cited example of a contemporary foraging society. Let us look then at their subsistence and infant-care practices.

The contribution that !Kung women make to subsistence is quite high: nearly 70 percent of all calories consumed by a group. Despite this substantial subsistence effort, !Kung mothers tend to keep their infants and small children with them throughout their daily round of work activities, making very little use of alternate caretakers (Lee and DeVore 1976; Lee 1979). They nurse their infants frequently, including at night, and do not introduce weaning foods until very late; this situation is thought to be largely responsible for the observed interbirth interval of three to four years—extremely long for a noncontracepting society (Howell 1976, 1979; Konner and Worthman 1980).

Given the absence of alternate caretaking among the !Kung in the face of high female contribution to subsistence, we might be tempted to conclude that the subsistence tasks undertaken by foraging women, or at least !Kung women, must be particularly compatible with the demands of childcare. A look at the list of tasks undertaken by !Kung women, however, makes this interpretation seem unlikely. !Kung women typically travel very long distances during the food quest and return with quite heavy loads, which they must carry in addition to the weight of their small children (Lee 1979). It is difficult to imagine that these tasks are any more compatible with childcare than the tasks performed by women in agricultural societies.

It seems unlikely, then, that childcare compatibility alone sufficiently explains why women do the work they do in different societies. By what means, however, can we determine for certain whether this is the case? If it can be shown that women in some societies are routinely assigned tasks that are not compatible with childcare, then the explanation loses its universality, and we must seek other alternative or additional explanations. The question now becomes: What criteria should we use to judge whether a given task is indeed compatible with childcare or, more to the point, whether it is more compatible with childcare than the tasks assigned predominantly or exclusively to men in the same society?

Many criteria we might consider, such as "degree of concentration required," involve very subjective judgments. Others, such as "interruptibility of female versus male tasks" or "relative exposure to danger," require quantified data simply not available to us for most societies. A somewhat less direct but perhaps more practical way to look for childcare compatibility of women's work is to consider the relative frequency with which a given task is performed by women who are at different stages of their child-bearing careers. For example, we can compare the activities of three groups of women: those who have not yet born children, mothers of small children, and women whose children are grown, in order to see which types of tasks each group performs and how often. We can also look at the extent to which childcare and the task in question are performed simultaneously. In other words, if tasks assigned predominantly or exclusively to women are indeed those which are compatible with childcare, we might predict that an observer would frequently see them being performed in conjunction with childcare. If, by contrast, we only observe these tasks being performed by women without children, or only by mothers who have enlisted the help of alternate caretakers, we could take this as an indication that the task is in fact not compatible with childcare. One would then need to search for another explanation for the assignment of the task to women and then, ideally, see whether this new explanation had any cross-cultural validity.

As I have noted, energetic constraints have obvious relevance to the issue of limits on women's task assignments. On the surface, this may appear to be just another version of the "males are stronger" hypothesis for task assignment, but it is in fact more an issue of resource allocation than of innate capacity. Both pregnancy and lactation are extremely demanding in terms of energetic requirements (Worthington-Roberts et al. 1985), and one could hypothesize that, particularly when food is in less than abundant supply, women may have to "choose" between the performance of energetically demanding tasks and the successful production and feeding of an infant. Energetic demand then, as opposed to logistics, becomes another criterion for childcare compatibility. In a society where women do perform energetically demanding tasks, one could monitor activities of women to see whether those who are pregnant and/or lactating curtail the performance of those tasks more than they curtail performance of tasks that are similar in time requirements, level of exposure to danger, and so forth, but are less strenuous.

My study of Efe women was designed in part to consider whether or not pregnancy, lactation, and/or childcare impose constraints on the type and amount of subsistence work Efe women can do, and to determine the nature of these constraints (e.g. logistic, energetic, other). Finally, I wished to know whether, if such constraints exist, they serve as the basis for cultural definitions of particular tasks as "women's work" or "men's work."

EFE WOMEN'S WORK AND REPRODUCTIVE LIVES

My research among the Efe was part of large, ongoing (since 1980) interdisciplinary study of both Efe and their village-living horticulturalist trading partners, the Lese (pronounced *less-ay*) (Bailey and DeVore 1989). Although the Efe-Lese relationship is not purely one of economic exchange (for example Efe and Lese individuals are frequently bound by fictive kin ties, and each is involved in many aspects of the other's social, political, and ritual life), it can safely be said that for the Efe at least, the most salient feature of their relationship with the Lese is that of material exchange. At certain times of the year, Efe camps are located very close to the Lese villages, in fact sometimes right in the Lese gardens. At other times the Efe move deeper into the forest in order to better exploit forest food resources (Bailey and Peacock 1988).

Efe women gather forest vegetable foods, harvest small aquatic fauna, build huts, and fetch firewood and water, but their primary subsistence activities involve the acquisition of agricultural produce from their village-living neighbors. To acquire these foods, they exchange hunted and gathered items and, more commonly, provide agricultural labor for the villagers. Men's work activities are primarily hunting and honey collection and, although men have very close inherited ties with particular villagers, they do not engage in village-oriented work activities to the extent that women do. In addition to cultivated foods, Efe acquire other items from the villagers, including clothing, tobacco, hemp, metal and clay cooking pots, metal implements (such as knives, machetes, and axes), and pieces of metal for making arrows.

Though they rely to a great extent on resources acquired from agriculturalists, the Efe share several important features with other foraging societies. For example, a significant amount of their subsistence effort is devoted to foraging (this is particularly true for the men), and they maintain no domesticated food sources of their own. They live in small, temporary, fluid encampments of three to fifty individuals. They have no strict rules of residence, nor do they recognize any formal positions of authority. Mothers wean their infants quite late, and among fertile women interbirth intervals are between three and four years. Though there is a division of labor by sex, there is flexibility in the system, and on many occasions men are seen performing tasks that are thought of as "women's work" without the denigration that would be attached to such actions in many sedentary societies.

In investigating women's subsistence and childcare work among the Efe, I conducted 387 hours of behavior observations on twenty-seven Efe women, using standard quantitative ethological methods (Peacock 1985). I observed each woman during randomly scheduled sessions, each lasting one hour, and during each session I made on-the-minute records of the woman's activities, including whom she was with and the type of subsistence, childcare, or leisure activity she was engaged in at that moment. The coding scheme, with multiple columns for recording simultaneous activities, allowed me to note points where women cared for infants or children while also engaging in other work.

I selected all women past the age of menarche in each of three residence groups for observation. These women ranged in age from nineteen to nearly eighty, and included young unmarried women, reproductive-age married women with and without children, and elderly women who had no children or whose children were grown. Two of the three residence groups, with a total of fifteen women, were what I called "low fertility groups," meaning that few of their reproductive-age members were pregnant or had children. The third group, with twelve women, was a "high fertility group." The presence of low fertility is an important aspect of the design of this study and merits consideration.

Most discussions of fertility in African societies focus on the alarmingly high fertility rates in countries like Kenya. One rarely hears about infertility as a significant social and health problem in Africa. There is nonetheless a well-documented "infertility belt" spanning the continent, characterized by many "pockets" of infertility. Within these pockets are societies in which often one-third to one-half of women reach the end of their reproductive years having never given birth to a live infant (Belsey 1976; Frank 1983). Like their horticultural neighbors the Lese, the Efe have a high prevalence of infertility, which is unevenly distributed in the population (i.e. in some residence groups none or few of the women are infertile, and in others many are). I will not discuss here the possible causes of the infertility, which are currently under investigation. Regardless of the cause, however, one result of the existing fertility pattern is that within all age categories of adult women, there are both women with and without children whose work activities can be compared, a state of affairs difficult to find in "normally fertile" noncontracepting societies. I thus had the opportunity to examine differences in time allocation and work effort between women of different child-bearing status, when those differences were not confounded by age differences or by the conscious decision of couples to remain childless.

But is it suitable to use such a demographically peculiar population as a testing ground for hypotheses concerning cross-cultural universals in the division of labor by sex? I am frequently asked whether infertile Efe women are "accepted" by their society. Although this question cannot be answered simply, it is important to address it, since the validity of my analysis rests on an assumption that observed behavior differences are actually due to the variable I am examining, rather than to society's view of infertile women as particularly aberrant persons. I must say from the outset that almost all childless women with whom I spoke expressed strong desires for children and regretted that their lives had not been so blessed. The desire for children among men was strong as well, and a childless woman was sometimes faced with the difficult choice of accepting the undesired presence of a co-wife or of leaving her home and family. But women with children sometimes faced this choice as well. In any event, not all women were necessarily opposed to polygynous unions, although this option was much less favorably viewed by Efe women than by villager women.

In general, I saw no evidence that infertile Efe women are in any way peripheral to their society. In fact, I was surprised by the extent to which a number of these women seem to play extremely central roles within the group, displaying a style of assertiveness and self-possession that also characterized the older "grandmothers." These are obviously very subjective impressions, but it can safely be said that these women could in no way be considered "social outcasts," as might be the case in some other societies.[4]

Efe women as a whole spent more than half of daylight hours engaged in subsistence and maintenance tasks. With childcare included, average work time for Efe women rises only slightly, reflecting both the fact that many women did not have children and that those who did tended to perform childcare tasks simultaneously with other work activities. Hence the total time spent working was not much different with childcare included, but the amount and variety of work done at any one time was often greatly increased.

Average figures for amount of time spent working by all women combined do not give us a very clear picture of varying work lives among the women. Some women spent less than half of their daylight hours working, whereas others spent nearly all. Even if we consider women individually, there is the problem that not all tasks are equivalent in the amount of mobility and energy expenditure they require. Two women who each spend 40 percent of their time working do not necessarily have similar work loads, since one may be doing primarily sedentary tasks while the other may be performing tasks that are much more energetically demanding. I predicted that more mobile, energetic activities would be more sensitive to constraints of pregnancy, lactation, and childcare than would more sedentary tasks, and it was therefore important to obtain some measure of these features.

I did not collect measurements of actual caloric expenditure for various tasks, but the specificity of the behavior code used in the observation allows the division of work activities into those that are relatively "energy intensive" and "nonintensive" ones. Examples of energy-intensive tasks are carrying heavy loads and chopping firewood, whereas typical nonintensive tasks are cooking rice and making sleeping mats. Different Efe women spent anywhere from 10 to 40 percent of their total *work* time engaged in energy-intensive tasks. Since I am proposing that constraints on women's work activities are at least partially energetic in nature, I therefore chose the amount of intensive work performed as a reasonable variable to look at when comparing women with and without children. In addition to "energy intensive work," I used another measure, "backload," to characterize work effort of Efe women. This measure is borrowed from the "backload model" of Blurton-Jones and Sibly (1978), and in my analysis a backload is any load carried weighing over five kilograms and includes the weight of children as well as food and other products. A final measure of workload is the average distance traveled per day by each woman. This gives us an indication of the proportion of energy-intensive work that involves locomotion. Again, I chose these measures because energetically demanding tasks, including those involving carrying heavy loads and traveling long distances, make up a significant proportion of the work activities performed by Efe women.

I compared the three measures of work activity ("intensive work," "backload," and "distance traveled") for three groups of women: those pregnant at the time of observation, those who were nursing infants, and those who were neither pregnant nor nursing and were experiencing regular menstrual cycles. Some telling findings emerged from this analysis. The most striking one is that pregnant women performed fewer energy-intensive work activities, traveled shorter distances, and carried heavy loads significantly less often than did either cycling or lactating women. It is interesting that pregnant women did not seem less *capable* of carrying heavy loads: when they did carry loads, the weight was not significantly different than that carried by cycling women. They did, however, reduce the number of occasions on which loads were carried. Though lactating women were scored as carrying loads quite frequently, they were most often carrying only a child, so that these mothers in fact carried loads as part of *subsistence* activity less often than did either pregnant or cycling women.

These findings contradict newly emerged feminist conventional wisdom that in its extreme portrays the subsistence work of women in foraging and other traditional societies as being totally unaffected by pregnancy, the birth process, or childcare. One is indeed struck when observing Efe women by the feats of strength and endurance they are able to accomplish in late pregnancy. One of my most vivid memories of fieldwork is watching the pregnant Akodi walk calmly into camp carrying a load of firewood that easily totaled three-quarters of her body weight. She dropped the load to the ground in the usual fashion and ducked into her hut. It was only through a quiet message from her companion that I became aware that Akodi was in fact in labor. A few hours later, she gave birth to her second daughter. With such dramatic examples to recall, I might easily have concluded that the subsistence and household work of Efe women is not at all affected by changes in reproductive status. It was in fact through the careful analysis of quantitative behavior data that I was able to detect the reduction in work intensity during late pregnancy as well as when infants are being cared for.

These data in combination indicate that both pregnant and lactating women curtail the performance of strenuous work activities in comparison with cycling women, even though most of the cycling women were childless and might be expected to have lighter workloads than women with families. The fact that pregnant women (including those pregnant with their first child) as well as women with infants curtailed strenuous activities supports the hypothesis that constraints on women's work are at least partially energetic as opposed to logistic in nature.

A different picture emerges when one looks at data on multiple tasks. Women with dependent children were nearly three times as likely to perform at least two tasks at once as were women without dependent children. By far the most common situation was for a woman to combine childcare with a subsistence or maintenance task, rather than combining two subsistence or maintenance tasks. The fact that childcare was commonly performed simultaneously with other work activities can be seen as support for the assertion that subsistence and maintenance tasks are assigned to women because of their compatibility with childcare. A closer look at the data, however, reveals that only *some* of women's activities are commonly combined with childcare, whereas other combinations are quite rare. Tasks frequently combined with childcare include sedentary tasks, such as food preparation, and travel—either to villages or on gathering trips. Activities seen less often than would be predicted in combination with childcare include agricultural labor, wood and water collection, and hut building—all very common women's tasks.

How then do mothers manage to meet their families subsistence needs *and* look after their dependent children, if they are not able to do these things at the same time? The opening vignette illustrates some ways in which Efe women accomplish these tasks. The use of alternate caretakers is not nearly as striking among the Efe as among many agricultural societies, in that weaning takes place quite late and infants are rarely left for extended periods of time in the care of someone other than the mother. Once weaned, however, toddlers are often left in the care of others. Women with small infants are able to balance subsistence and childcare tasks in part because Efe women breastfeed one another's infants, as Deani nursed Akodi's infant in the village garden. These patterns are set very early in the infant's life. From minutes after birth, an infant is passed around among members of the group, and commonly the very first suckling an infant does is at the breast of someone other than her mother (Tronick et al. 1987). This sharing of childcare duties is reflected in women's activity budgets: although mothers spend nearly threefold the amount of time performing childcare duties as women without dependent children, the amount of time the latter devote to childcare is not insignificant—nearly 6 percent of their time is devoted to the care of children who are not their own.

In addition to receiving help from other adult women, Efe women also are assisted by their older daughters. Although the Efe make use of child labor much less often than has been recorded for agricultural and pastoral societies, I frequently observed juvenile and subadult daughters of Efe women assisting their mothers both in subsistence and childcare tasks. When asked a pregnant woman who had already borne two sons and one daughter what her preference would be for the sex of her next child, she responded that she wanted a daughter since a daughter, unlike a son, would help her with her work. In order to assess the extent to which having daughters reduced women's workloads, I divided the sample of women into three categories: nonmothers, mothers without helpers, and mothers with helpers—helpers being defined as daughters over the age of twelve. Mothers without helpers spent significantly more time working than did nonmothers, and they spent significantly more time in subsistence work than did both nonmothers and mothers with helpers. They spent more time doing energy-intensive work than did mothers with helpers, and much more time than either of the other groups in performing two or more simultaneous tasks. In contrast, mothers with helpers spent less time in subsistence activities and more time in leisure activities than either of the other groups, even though mothers with helpers had on average the highest number of dependent children.

Is it impossible, then, for an Efe mother to accomplish necessary childcare and subsistence tasks without the assistance of daughters or other women? My observations indicate that it is not impossible, but it is very, very difficult. I base this conclusion primarily on the observation of one particular woman named Akbundi, whom circumstances placed in a rather unusual predicament.

Several years ago Akbundi separated from the father of her oldest child (who at the time of my study was about seven years old) and returned to her natal group, where she conceived two more children in an incestuous relationship with a member of her lineage. (The man is in fact currently the husband of Deani, whom we met in the opening vignette.) The paternity of the two youngest children is considered a source of shame and is not openly acknowledged by any of the group members. Akbundi, however, seems anything but a shamed person and has a quite forceful personality, being at one moment solicitous and downright jolly, and at the next angry and accusatory if she doesn't get her way. Her responsibilities are considerable, since she not only has three small children to look after, but the youngest, who normally would be walking at his age, is developmentally delayed because of a slight foot deformity and still must be carried. Furthermore, since she has no husband, Akbundi has no meat or honey to trade in the village, other than that which she is occasionally able to beg from someone else. Consequently, she must rely almost exclusively on her own labor or gathered products to exchange in the village. Most villagers, however, seem to view her more as a liability than an asset as a trading partner, and she frequently resorts to scavenging in abandoned gardens or taking food without permission from current gardens.

Despite the gravity of her transgression, Akbundi is not so much ostracized as marginalized by group members, particularly other women. These other women are willing to engage in interactions with her when she initiates them but do not go out of their way to offer her assistance, probably because she is so seldom able or willing to reciprocate. The fact that Akbundi and her children are quite healthy is a testament to her perseverance, but her life is not an easy one. This fact is reflected in data on her behavior patterns. She was observed to spend 76 percent of her time engaged in subsistence activities, compared to an average of 61 percent for other women with nursing infants. The figures for amount of time spent in childcare and amount of time spent performing two or more simultaneous tasks were much more dramatic: 73 and 56 percent respectively for Akbundi, compared to 29 and 21 percent for the other nursing women. Though Akbundi's is a single case and an extremely unusual one at that, it tells us quite a lot about the plight of the woman who not only has no older daughter as a helper but who, for social and cultural reasons, is unable to elicit much help from other adult women. Perhaps the most telling statistic is on the amount of time spent at "leisure" when no work is being performed. This figure was 40 percent for all women combined, 20 percent for nursing mothers other than Akbundi, and only 4 percent for Akbundi! Obviously this woman is working close to the edge of her capabilities, and one can easily imagine that one more child or a sickness or injury would push her beyond that edge, with dire consequences for herself and her children.

REVISITING THE MODELS

How does quantified, "on-the-ground" evidence on Efe gendered work patterns help us to test and elaborate on models of the functioning of sexual divisions of labor in foraging societies? Most of these models would lead us to conclude that a high female contribution to subsistence must be accompanied either by early weaning combined with intensive use of alternative caretakers, which is common in many agricultural societies, or by women's work activities that are logistically compatible with the care of infants and small children, which is assumed in these models to be the case among foragers. The Efe data challenge these assumptions, since Efe women display both late weaning of infants *and* high contribution to subsistence. Furthermore, they engage in some subsistence activities that appear to be minimally compatible with childcare.

I would suggest that we need to take a much broader view of both the nature of constraints on women's work activities and of the range of strategies available to women for dealing with those constraints. Models derived from feminist perspectives, in an effort to negate earlier emphases on sex differences in physical strength as determinants of task assignment, have tended to ignore the very real energetic constraints imposed by pregnancy and lactation, which in a food-limited environment can be significant. We have also tended to have too narrow a view of alternate caretaking, assuming that it necessarily involves a situation where infants are left for extended periods of time and is therefore incompatible with prolonged and frequent breastfeeding. The Efe case demonstrates that an intricate and varied pattern of cooperative work and mutual caretaking among women permits combinations of subsistence work and childcare that would at first glance seem unworkable. This illustrates the importance of looking at behavior from a collectivist as well as individualist perspective; it also suggests an important lesson for scholars of human evolution, who all too often make the assumption that only cooperation between males was crucial for the structuring of early human societies.

We still need to consider how women's tasks compare to those of men. Even if the tasks assigned to women do not seem particularly compatible with childcare, this criterion could still be important if the tasks assigned to men are even less easily performed in conjunction with childcare. The most common subsistence activities engaged in by Efe men are hunting, honey collection, and the making and repairing of implements used in hunting and honey collection. Providing labor for villagers comes in a distant fourth (Bailey 1985). For women, the most common activities are village work, food processing, foraging, and collecting firewood and water. How do men's and women's activities compare in terms of the criteria for childcare-compatible tasks proposed in the models?

A minimal exposure to danger is one feature said to characterize women's work activities, and this seems to be the case for the Efe. During the hunt, Efe men face significant risk of injury, both from stray arrows and from injured animals. When women participate in hunts (occasionally among the Efe and routinely among net hunters), they always act as "beaters," so that they are behind rather than in front of fleeing animals and are not in the immediate vicinity of weapon use. Honey collection is also a dangerous activity. The most favored hives are very high in trees and are reached by either climbing the tree or cutting it down. Both activities have been sources of mortality among Efe men. Efe women occasionally participate in honey collection, but they never climb the trees and they usually are not present when trees are cut. The only honey that women occasionally collect on their own is that of several species of stingless bees that build their hives near the ground. Snake bites are a source of danger for both men and women, but a greater risk for men, since venomous snakes are most commonly found in abandoned gardens, where men sometimes hunt but where women seldom have a reason to go. In short, although Efe women frequently suffer relatively minor traumas, it is the men who are placed in potentially fatal situations during the course of their regular subsistence activities.

A second criterion which is said to characterize women's tasks is that the activities should not require distant travel. This does not appear to be a strong pattern among the Efe, since both men and women perform tasks that at least potentially require traveling long distances from home. The Efe are seminomadic and therefore can place their camps according to the location of desired resources. Often, the interests of men and women are at odds, the men preferring to be close to areas that promise rich hunting and/or honey collecting, and the women not wanting to be too far from the village or, in certain seasons, from forest resources such as fruiting trees. Moreover, women are always concerned about a suitable water source being quite close by. Depending then on who has the most influence at any given time over the location of a new camp, either men or women or both may travel considerable distances in meeting their subsistence needs. We *have* documented the fact that men travel greater distances on average than do women (Bailey 1985; Peacock 1985), which suggests that although theoretically women's tasks involve just as much travel as do men's, the placement of camps is most often such as to decrease the amount of traveling women are obliged to do. Therefore, although distance is an important factor, women are not assigned tasks that require less travel, but rather other conditions are modified so as to reduce the amount of travel that women have to do.

A characteristic of Efe subsistence tasks which may be important is the predictability of location of a resource, rather than its absolute distance from the home base. Women usually know in advance which stream they will fish, or where fruiting trees are located, and they of course always know where the village is. This knowledge both permits them to budget their time effectively and also greatly decreases the probability of become lost in the forest. Men also exploit resources in known locations or decide in advance where they will hunt, but their quarry often lead them to unpredictable locations. It is not uncommon for men to return to camp after dark (which they would definitely prefer not to do), whereas this is extremely rare for women.

Interruptibility of and degree of concentration required by a task have both been suggested as important features in discriminating between men's and women's work. These are both, of course, extremely difficult to characterize in operational terms. I would argue, however, that they do not have much discriminating power in the Efe case. For some subsistence activities there are negative consequences to having one's attention diverted from the task at hand, and for others the consequences are trivial. Both men and women engage in both types of task. Some men's tasks may seem less interruptible and more attention-demanding than the average women's task (for example, climbing a tree or chasing an animal), but these are also dangerous, and the latter is almost certainly a more important criterion.

Although the risk of death or injury provides a tenable explanation of why Efe men rather than women hunt and collect honey, it does little to explain why women are assigned tasks, particularly those involving carrying of heavy loads, that are not only difficult to perform in conjunction with childcare but, in fact, during pregnancy and lactation can impose significant health costs on both mothers and infants in terms of their energetic demands. One explanation suggested by Murdock and Provost (1973) is that when men are away from home for extended and unpredictable periods, tasks that require daily attention, such as collection of firewood and water, are best left to women. Another possible explanation is that of entailment theory (White et al. 1977), which predicts that adjacent tasks in a production sequence are likely to be performed by the same person. One could suggest, for example, that women are primarily responsible for cooking and, therefore, will collect the firewood needed for cooking. One could just as easily predict, however, that since men kill animals, they should be the ones to carry meat to the village for trade; however, this is most often done by women. In fact, the association of burden carrying with women's work is so strong that when men kill a very large animal, they will travel considerable distances back to camp in order to fetch women to carry the meat, rather than carrying it back themselves.

The pattern of women as burden-carriers is not only very marked among the Efe but is quite common cross-culturally, particularly in foraging and hoe-agriculture societies, and is also contrary to what one would predict from patterns of sexual dimorphism in size and muscle mass found in humans. I do not have an explanation for this pattern, nor do I believe that the literature on sexual division of labor has addressed it. One place, though certainly not the only place, to look for an explanation, is to the physiological effects of high activity levels on human reproduction. Virtually all of the data come from studies of women athletes in the West, rather than women who routinely have heavy workloads, but evidence is strong that high levels of energy expenditure have a suppressive effect on women's reproductive function, just as prolonged and frequent breastfeeding has such an effect (e.g. Shangold et al. 1979; Bullen et al. 1985; Ellison and Lager 1986). It has been pointed out by several authors that there is an advantage to fairly long interbirth intervals in some cultures, particularly foraging societies, and that breastfeeding patterns help bring this about (Konner and Worthman 1980; Blurton-Jones and Sibly 1978). Could it also be that heavy work activities by women serve the same function (see Bentley 1985)? Although this is admittedly speculative, it is certainly worthy of further investigation in a variety of societies.

The issues that have emerged in this critical analysis of models of the sexual division of labor illuminate some of the contributions that biological anthropology can make to feminist anthropology. The emphasis within the subfield on the rigorous quantitative observation of behavior can buffer us against some of the pitfalls of armchair reasoning about key elements that structure the lives of women now and that did so in the past. Feminist anthropologists have stressed for nearly twenty years the role of women as key social actors, yet we still at times have trouble seeing women as negotiating, cooperating, and competing with other women as well as with men. Careful research on variations in *individual* Efe women's lives helps us to see the importance of *collective* behavior in structuring gendered work behavior. The important findings concerning energy costs during pregnancy and lactation help to overturn some new feminist pieties about constraints or lack thereof on women's work effort. Refinement of models through quantitative research on one society has helped us to see possibly key roles of danger and uncertainty rather than childcare compatibility and physical strength in the sexual division of labor. Further careful research of this nature on women in small-scale as well as industrial societies helps us to dethrone much received wisdom and to bring to light new perspectives on the nature of female bodies, their capacities, and their limits as women live out their productive and reproductive lives.

ACKNOWLEDGMENT

Many thanks to Micaela di Leonardo for organizing the Anthropology of Gender colloquium series and for her superb editorial comments. The research and analysis on which this essay is based was supported by funds from the National Science Foundation, the Fulbright Commission and the LSB Leakey Foundation. I am grateful to Dr. Kabamba Nkamany and the staff of the Nutrition Planning Center (CEPLANUT) in Kinshasa under whose sponsorship my research was conducted. I also wish to thank Chief Endite Sukali and the people of Malembi for their support and cooperation. This essay is dedicated to the memory of Pudada and Sisilia.

NOTES

1. All names in the body of this essay are fictitious.

2. I felt a good deal of empathy for my "informants'" sensitivity about ethnic labeling, since I, being an African-American of light complexion, initially found it quite annoying to be referred to as *mzungu*, the key Swahili word for a "white person."

3. A holocultural study is a cross-cultural study based on data from a large number of societies. These analyses are usually performed using data from large ethnographic data banks, such as the Human Relations Area Files, or any of its derivatives, such as the Ethnographic Atlas (Murdock 1967) or the Standard Cross-Cultural Sample (Murdock and White 1969).

4. This is not to say that there are no negative social consequences to being childless. Grinker (1989) says of the Lese: "Mothers in general, and mothers of sons in particular, enjoy greater status than infertile widows, and are far less often accused of doing harm by supernatural means." The same is undoubtedly true of the Efe as well. The negative consequences of childlessness (i.e. risk of banishment and witchcraft accusations) are experienced primarily in older age upon widowhood. Furthermore, these risks extend to all women who have no surviving sons, and not just to infertile women.

BIBLIOGRAPHY

Bailey, R. C. 1985. The socioecology of Efe pygmy men in the Ituri Forest, Zaire. Doctoral dissertation, Department of Anthropology, Harvard University.

Bailey, R. C., and I. Devore. 1989. Research on the Efe and Lese populations of the Ituri Forest, Zaire. *American Journal of Physical Anthropology* 78: 459–471.

Bailey, R. C., and N. R. Peacock. 1988. Efe pygmies of northeast Zaire: Subsistence strategies in the Ituri Forest. In *Coping with uncertainty in food supply*. I. de Garine and G. A. Harrison, eds. Oxford: Oxford University Press.

Belsey, M. A. 1976. The epidemiology of infertility: A review with particular reference to sub-Saharan Africa. *Bulletin of the World Health Organization* 54: 319–341.

Bentley, G. 1985. Hunter-gatherer energetics and fertility: A reassessment of the !Kung San. *Human Ecology* 13 (1): 79–109.

Blurton-Jones, N., and R. M. Sibly. 1978. Testing adaptiveness of culturally determined behaviour: Do bushman women maximize their reproductive success by spacing births widely and foraging seldom? In *Human Behaviour and Adaptation*. N. Blurton-Jones and V. Reynolds, eds. London: Taylor and Francis.

Brown, J. K. 1970. A note on the division of labor by sex. *American Anthropologist* 72: 1073–1078.

Bullen, B. A., G. S. Skrinar, I. Z. Beitins, G. von Mering, B. A. Turnbull, and J. W. McArthur. 1985. Induction of menstrual disorders by strenuous exercise in untrained women. *New England Journal of Medicine* 312: 1349–1353.

Durkheim, E. 1964. *The division of labor in society*. New York: Free Press.

Ellison, P. T., and C. Lager. 1986. Moderate recreational running is associated with lowered salivary progesterone profiles in women. *American Journal of Obstetrics and Gynecology* 154: 1000–1003.

Frank, O. 1983. Infertility in sub-Saharan Africa: Estimates and implications. *Population and Development Review* 9: 137–144.

Grinker, R. R. 1989. Ambivalent exchanges: The Lese farmers of central Africa and their relations with the Efe pygmies. Doctoral dissertation, Department of Anthropology, Harvard University.

Howell, N. 1976. The population of the Dobe area !Kung. In *Kalahari hunter-gatherers*. R. B. Lee and I. DeVore, eds., 137–151. Cambridge: Harvard University Press.

———. 1979. *Demography of the Dobe !Kung*. New York: Academic Press.

Howie, P. W., A. S. McNeilly, M. J. Houston, A. Cook, and H. Boyle. 1982. Fertility after childbirth: Infant feeding patterns, basal PRL levels and post-partum ovulation. *Clinical Endocrinology* 17: 315–322.

Hrdy, S. B. 1981. *The woman that never evolved*. Cambridge: Harvard University Press.

Konner, M., and C. Worthman. 1980. Nursing frequency, gonadal function, and birth spacing among !Kung hunter-gatherers. *Science* 207: 788–791.

Lancaster, J. B. 1976. Sex roles in primate societies. In *Sex differences: Social and biological perspectives*. M. S. Teitelbaum, ed., 22–61. Garden City, N.Y.: Anchor Books.

Lee, R. B. 1979. *The !Kung San: Men, women, and work in a foraging society*. Cambridge: Cambridge University Press.

Lee, R. B. and I. DeVore, eds. 1976. *Kalahari hunter-gatherers*. Cambridge: Harvard University Press.

Martin, M. M. 1978. Women in the HRAF files: A consideration of ethnographer bias. *Behavior Science Research* 13: 303–314.

Milton, K. 1979. Male bias in anthropology. *Man* 14: 40–54.

Mulder, M. B., and T. M. Caro. 1985. The use of quantitative observation techniques in anthropology. *Current Anthropology* 22: 323–335.

Murdock, G. P. 1967. Ethnographic atlas: A summary. *Ethnology* 6: 108–236.

Murdock, G. P., and C. Provost. 1973. Factors in the division of labor by sex: A cross-cultural analysis. *Ethnology* 12: 202–225.

Murdock, G. P., and D. R. White. 1969. Standard cross-cultural sample. *Ethnology* 8: 329–369.

Nerlove, S. B. 1974. Women's workload and infant feeding practices: A relationship with demographic implications. *Ethnology*. 13: 207–214.

Peacock, N. R. 1985. Time allocation, work and fertility among Efe pygmy women in the Ituri Forest of northeast Zaire. Doctoral dissertation, Department of Anthropology, Harvard University.

Reiter, R. R. 1975. *Toward an anthropology of women*. New York: Monthly Review Press.

Rosaldo, M. Z., and L. Lamphere. 1974. *Woman, culture, and society*. Stanford: Stanford University Press.

Shangold, M., R. Freeman, B. Thysen, and M. Gatz. 1979. The relationship between long-distance running, plasma progesterone, and luteal phase length. *Fertility and Sterility* 31: 130–133.

Tronick, E. Z., G. A. Morelli and S. Winn. 1987. Multiple caretaking of Efe (Pygmy) infants. *American Anthropologist* 89: 96–106.

White, D. R., M. L. Burton, and L. A. Brudner. 1977. Entailment theory and method: A cross-cultural analysis of the sexual division of labor. *Behavior Science Research* 12: 1–24.

Worthingon-Roberts, B. S., J. Vermeersch, and S. R. Williams. 1985. *Nutrition in pregnancy and lactation*. St. Louis: Times Mirror/Mosby.

ELEVEN

Sexism and Naturalism in the Study of Kinship

Harold W. Scheffler

I

Empirical studies of and theory about kinship, marriage, and family are among the major foci of feminist criticism and reconstruction, not only in anthropology, but also in sociology, history, and other disciplines. That is because sexist notions are especially likely to find their way into discussions of such topics, and they are likely to be represented as immutable "facts of nature" with which each society must somehow come to terms. Such facts are commonly said to include pronounced differences in body size and in physical strength between men and women; the physical handicaps and vulnerabilities that women suffer when pregnant; the prolonged dependence of their infants on them; and, as a consequence, a strong tendency for adult males and females to form durable mating pairs in which the woman and her offspring are dependent on and, in general, subordinate to the man. All of that, it is commonly maintained, accounts not only for the near universality of the nuclear or elementary family, but also for the more general subordination of women and children to adult males.

Because these contentions would naturalize inequitable features of gender relations in our own social order and make them appear inevitable, feminists have contested them in various ways.[1] This essay is a commentary on one such response: the strange alliance of some feminists (anthropologists and others) with the antikinship school in symbolic anthropology—an alliance by means of which those feminists seek not only to denaturalize and deuniversalize but also to deconstruct or dismantle the categories[2] "kinship," "marriage," and "family" and, with them, the putative natural and universal subordination of women and children to men. Foremost in this school are Jane Collier and Sylvia Yanagisako, who take this stance in their introduction to the 1987 feminist anthropological anthology *Gender and Kinship*. The arguments and analyses of the kinship dismantlers are, I argue, an insecure basis on which to found a feminist resistance to the naturalization of male dominance.

II

In 1891 the British scholar Edward Westermark concluded his encyclopedic study *The History of Human Marriage* with this observation:

> The history of human marriage is the history of a relation in which women have been gradually triumphing over the passions, the prejudices, and the selfish interests of men. (559)

Westermark believed that the dominant tendency in that history had been "the extension of the wife's rights." He pointed out that in his own society the wife was "no longer the husband's property," and he characterized it as "the modern idea" that "marriage is, or should be, a contract on the footing of perfect equality between the sexes." Eighty years later, an American anthropologist, Ward Goodenough (1970a, 1970b), proposed to discuss marriage as though it had no history.[3] As a necessary preliminary, he argued, to construction of a definition of "kinship" for purposes of cross-cultural comparison, Goodenough defined "marriage" as a transaction and resulting contractual relation in which a person or set of persons establishes a continuing and exclusive right of sexual access to a woman and in which that woman is eligible to bear children (Goodenough 1970a: 6–17; Goodenough 1970b).

A few years later, Micaela di Leonardo (1979) objected that this definition is deeply sexist. It treats women only as objects of rights and ignores their rights as wives, which in many ethnographic instances (including a number cited by Goodenough) are no less extensive than the rights of men as husbands.[4] Goodenough might have replied that his definition does not preclude the possibility that the wife may herself be given an exclusive sexual right in relation to the husband, and he did note that typically each party acquires rights and duties of other kinds in relation to the other party. But, as he saw it, those other rights and duties are much too variable from one society to another to permit use of them in a generally applicable definition of marriage. In other words, Goodenough's definition of marriage is not so much reductionist as it is minimalist. But even so it *is* sexist. The claim that it is necessary to define "marriage" in Goodenough's asymmetrical fashion rests on the presumption that, if there is an asymmetry in the marital relation, it will favor the male party (or his surrogate). That presumption rests in turn on the conviction that there is in "human nature" (another timeless entity) a "universal tendency to a division of labor by sex and [a] universal tendency to male dominance of women and children" (Goodenough 1970a: 11–12, 18).

In proposing to define marriage in this asymmetrical fashion, and as a preliminary to formulation of a universally applicable definition of "kinship," Goodenough was indulging in a long-established anthropological practice.[5] At least since the founding of modern anthropology in the 1860s, most scholars have regarded it as self-evident that, for purposes of cross-cultural comparison, "kinship" cannot be defined independently of marriage. The principal difficulty has been the apparent necessity to define the key concepts "maternity" and "paternity" in somewhat different ways, with the latter based on the former and on the additional concept "marriage."

In our own culture, kinship consists in relationship by birth to a woman, or maternity, and relationship by birth to a man, or paternity, and it has seemed wholly obvious that "maternity," so defined, but not "paternity," will be found in each and every culture. The received ethnographic and epistemological wisdom has been that maternity is plainly observable (in the form of pregnancy and parturition) and is therefore a highly probable concept; it is also necessary because the prolonged physical dependency of the human infant makes it compelling for species survival that each infant be suckled and reared by its mother and that she should have the right and duty to do that. In contrast, paternity has not been regarded as a directly observable relation but as one that is only tenuously inferable. The consequence (or so it is reasoned) is that in those societies where "the relationship between sexual intercourse and pregnancy is unknown," no one is presumed to have a genitor or a direct male contributor to his or her being; and in many more societies although some concept of "genitor" is present, the notorious difficulty of knowing with certainty who is the genitor of any particular child has had the result that the identity of the genitor is largely if not wholly discounted for social purposes.

For all that, however, it has not been generally accepted that a society can get by without a concept of paternity or a functional analogue of it. As Bronislav Malinowski, one of the founding fathers of modern social anthropology, put it in his 1930 essay "Parenthood—The Basis of Social Structure," it is a

> most important moral and legal rule [he gave it the name "the principle of legitimacy"] . . . that no child should be brought into the world without a man—and one man at that—assuming the role of sociological father, that is, guardian and protector, the male link between the child and the rest of the community. (Malinowski 1930 [1963: 63])

Making ignorance of or uncertainty about paternity no excuse for not having at least a "social father," Malinowski and other anthropologists have argued that, in general, and not only where there is "ignorance of physical paternity," it is *not* being the begetter that makes a man socially the "father" of a child; it is instead the marriage of that man to the mother of that child. In the words of A. R. Radcliffe-Brown (1950: 4), "Social fatherhood is usually determined by marriage." Malinowski at least was not merely generalizing about human social practice; he was also hypothesizing a natural origin for his "principle of legitimacy" in the presumed natural debilitations of women and their offspring, both of whom therefore require adult male guardians and protectors.

In Goodenough's updated version of this theory, "derives from" replaces "determined by," and human beings are attributed a natural propensity for heterosexual pair bonding; jealous and possessive adult males compete for sexual access to females and for control over their labor and that of their offspring; and that competition is, as it must be, socially regulated (for some of the background to this argument see Sperling, this volume). The prototypical way of meeting this functional requisite of social order is said to be via the institution of marriage, and "marriage" itself is defined (for this theoretical purpose) as the attribution to an adult male of exclusive sexual rights in relation to a particular female, which rights typically underpin various other rights in relation to her and her offspring.[6] Goodenough argues that "marriage" must be defined in that way because "jural fatherhood" cannot be defined in a way that is broadly applicable except in terms of the rights that a man has in relation to the offspring of his wife, irrespective of their actual paternity (if known).

This version of "the nature of kinship" has always been resisted, and not only because it would naturalize the patriarchal nuclear family and the sexual double standard. One of the longest-standing objections is that it assumes ethnocentrically that "kinship," so defined, is and must be a ubiquitous component of human social orders, and it does so in the face of substantial evidence to the contrary. It has been argued repeatedly since the 1860s that the ethnographically so-called kinship concepts and institutions of many societies are *not* rooted in local theories of procreation and are *not* responses to what David Schneider (1972) has called "the problem of reproduction." The ethnographically so-called kinship terms of many if not most languages are not expressions of egocentric genealogical reference but are expressions of some other semantic kind or kinds; and, instead of being described as kinship terms, they ought to be described as "social category" or "jural category" or "relationship" terms. They only appear to be kinship terms because of certain superficial and purely formal similarities between the categories they designate and Western kinship concepts.[7]

Anthropologists who take this second position acknowledge that relationship by birth is a condition, even a sufficient condition, for inclusion in "relationship" categories, but they deny that it is *the* necessary and sufficient condition or, in some sense, the "most important" condition. Indeed, some have gone so far as to argue that even Western kinship concepts are not exclusively or even chiefly about relationship by birth, and neither are they designed to cope with or to adapt to "the problem of reproduction." According to Schneider (1972: 47), although our own (American) "symbols of kinship" are phrased in terms of consanguinity ("blood relationship"), they really "mean or stand for [relations of] diffuse, enduring solidarity," and their function is "to provide a meaningful social order."[8]

Although Collier and Yanagisako (1987: 30) contend that Schneider has "denaturalized kinship" and has shown that "the fundamental units of kinship" are not always, if ever, "genealogical relationships," what he and others have actually tried to do is to "decenter" relationship by birth, that is, to deprive it of the structural primacy attributed to it in numerous ethnographic accounts of other social and cultural orders. Indeed, Schneider himself once wrote that, try as he would, even he could not "make biology and sexual intercourse go away," because, he said, "All known kinship systems use biological relationship and/or sexual intercourse in the cultural specification of what kinship is" (1965: 97, 98). In other words, relationship by birth *is* a criterion (*even a sufficient condition*) for inclusion in the various categories ethnographically described as kin categories (otherwise, why describe them as *kin* categories to begin with?), but it is not anywhere the only criterion or even culturally the somehow "most important" criterion. But, even so, Schneider and others now claim that what they have shown is that "kinship," as commonly defined by anthropologists, simply does not exist; it is merely an anthropological fiction which they have dismantled. More accurately, the claim is that there are no such things as cultural categories that are wholly and solely genealogically constituted; genealogical relationship or relationship by birth is nowhere the necessary and sufficient condition but is a merely sufficient condition, for inclusion in any so-called kin class.

As already noted, this rather extreme relativistic—we would now say "social constructivist"—view is not all new. Something more or less like it has long enjoyed a degree of popularity among liberal social reformers, feminist and nonfeminist, who contend that the character of our social relations is not given in nature, that those relations are largely if not wholly conventional, and therefore that different systems of social relations are not indicative of differences in biological constitution. It has seemed necessary to establish that so as to establish also "the psychological unity of [hu]mankind," despite the patent diversity of cultures, and to establish the noninevitability of discriminatory gender relations and practices. Via that argument anthropology has been a major contributor to liberal humanism (Fee 1973; Stocking 1987). Kinship has figured prominently in those debates precisely because it has seemed self-evident to many people that it is, as John Barnes (1973: 64) once put it, that "aspect of culture with the closest links to the natural world." Therefore, if it could be shown not only that kinship practices vary from place to place and time to time but also that concepts of kinship are not universal, that there can be genuine human societies without them, it would (seem to) follow by implication that our social relations in general are not rooted in nature but are purely conventional. To suggest otherwise was and still is construable as undermining the (political) cause by undermining the claim that we have made ourselves what we are and we can, if we wish, make ourselves different and better than we are.

But the arguments of the kinship dismantlers do not really address the issue of naturalism and, therefore, they are largely silent on the issue of sexism as well. Because that criticism of kinship theory leaves its naturalistic and sexist elements standing where it found them, those elements may reappear, and they have in fact reappeared, in some feminist attempts to theorize kinship—albeit not as natural but as culturally constituted relations, and with a positive rather than a negative valuation. After expanding on these remarks, I discuss the possibility of formulating a more satisfactory conception of kinship for purposes of cross-cultural comparison.

III

Refutation of the naturalistic and sexist assumptions of the standard theory of kinship has never been on the agenda of the kinship dismantlers. From the outset, those theorists have called for a self-contained cultural-anthropological project that would render those assumptions largely if not wholly irrelevant. Building on a Parsonian distinction between social system and cultural system, and taking a radically relativistic methodological stance, they insist that the first and most essential ethnographic task is to understand and then to describe each culture, as the saying goes, "in its own terms." They are especially worried about the possibility that, if we suppose that "recognition of kinship" is a functional requisite for coping with or adapting to the natural facts of biparental reproduction and the physical dependency of infants, we will dispose ourselves to find kinship everywhere we look and even where it does not exist. As David Schneider (1972: 46) once put it, "No one can disagree that man [*sic*] must cope with the facts of life and the facts of nature, whether or not he knows what those facts are scientifically or has only erroneous beliefs." What we must disagree with, he says, is the presumption that it is necessary to have a kinship system with which to do that coping. He claims that careful, unbiased ethnographic research has shown that many societies do lack kinship concepts and institutions, and that many so-called kinship concepts and institutions are not designed to cope with or to adapt to "the problem of reproduction."[9]

Following Schneider, Collier and Yanagisako (1987: 42) go further in the social-constructionist direction. They assert:

> [h]aving recognized our [own Western folk] model of biological difference as a particular cultural mode of thinking about relations between people, we should be able to question the "biological facts" of sex themselves.

They expect that such a "questioning of the presumably biological core of gender" will lead, eventually, to "rejection of any dichotomy between sex and gender as biological and cultural facts." The question, "What, if not a kinship system, is the local means for coping with the natural facts of bisexual reproduction and the dependency of infants?" is thus left unanswered and even unasked. It is *set aside* in favor of getting on with the purely cultural and self-contained project of analyzing and describing each culture (and more specifically its construction of gender) "in its own terms."

That, however, is an impossible project. The difficulty is not only the most obvious one, that ethnographic analysis and description are theory-laden activities. It is also that ethnographic inquiry begins and ends as a theory-laden act of comparison. In the course of it we try to detect in the speech and actions of another people concepts and practices that are analogous to those we know from our own social experience or from other ethnographic studies. Our initial hypotheses about such analogies may well require modification as we go along, but they can be replaced only by other, if more complex and sophisticated, hypotheses of the same general kind. We can and should continually interrogate our own culture's constructions of gender, kinship, and reproduction through cross-cultural comparison; but there is no way to abandon such constructions altogether, for when reporting the results of our observations and analyses in some scholarly language, we must again, explicitly or implicitly, compare the concepts and practices of one people with those of our own and other societies.[10] Finally, a purely culturalogical approach divorces our considerations of our own and other societies' cultural constructions of gender and kinship from the corporeal realities of our ongoing inhabitation of the planet. As feminists we should seek to transform the study of human biology, not to turn our backs on it.

So, the contention that most if not all reports of the existence of kinship concepts and institutions are biased by ethnocentrism boils down to a complaint that the process of comparison has been foreshortened, that an initial hypothesis has been put insufficiently to the test. We are told that evidence for that claim is contained in certain facts that ethnographers often report but refrain from incorporating systematically into their analyses. By far the most common observation of that kind is that it is often reported of expressions described as kinship terms that they are used not only in reference to persons presumed to be related by birth but also in reference to persons *not* presumed to be related in that way. Therefore, it is argued, an expression such as Trobriand *tama* "cannot mean 'father'"; because its reference is not exclusively to one's presumed genitor, it must mean something else. If it is suggested that, like English *father*, *tama* is polysemous—that it has two or more related meanings or even kinds of meaning—the reply is that it is unwarranted to say that. What it is warranted to say, we are told, is that "the category *tama*" happens to include the person who is one's presumed genitor, but that that is not sufficient reason to gloss *tama* as "father" or to say it is a kinship term.[11]

That argument turns, however, on a theoretically naive conflation of terms and categories (words and meanings, signifiers and signifieds), as in phrases like "the category *tama*," incautious use of which commonly leads to the supposition that the task is to "define the term (or the category) *tama*," rather than to define the perhaps several categories that *tama* designates and to specify the logical-structural relations between them. In that way polysemy[12] is made virtually invisible, and the way is opened for freewheeling invention of "exotic" cultures and of reinventions of our own (as in Schneider 1968).

Consider, for example, how such a set of assumptions directs us to interpret practice in American English whereby a child may be taught to address or even to refer in the third person to a close male friend of a parent as *uncle* so-and-so. We would be constrained to argue that *uncle* is not, after all, a kinship term, or at least not only a kinship term; to believe that "the category 'uncle'" is not genealogically defined or constituted; and that it is not necessary, and perhaps not even sufficient, to be related by birth to someone in order to be classified as a kinsperson or relative of that person. We must take into account, however, that to address or otherwise refer to a parent's male friend as *uncle* so-and-so is not at all the same thing as classifying him as a relative or even as a particular kind of relative (in this case as an "uncle"). Also, although a person may assert of a parent's friend who is spoken of as *uncle* so-and-so that he is not in fact that person's uncle or relative or kinsman, the same may not properly be said of that person's parent's brother. That shows, of course, that we have to deal with two distinctly different uses and meanings of *uncle*, one of which *is* a kin-classifying usage, the other not. The same thing is shown by the fact that the use of *uncle* in reference to a parent's male friend is *not* complemented by the use of *nephew* or *niece* in reference to the children of one's close friends, although in the domain of kin classification it is a mere truism that a child of a sibling is a nephew or a niece. In short, there is no category "uncle" that is partly genealogically and partly "socially" defined. However we may wish to describe the other, asymmetrical use of *uncle*, it cannot fairly be used as evidence that egocentric, genealogically constituted categories simply do not exist, either in English or in any other language.

Although these points have been made repeatedly in other contexts,[13] many ethnographers continue to hold radical social-constructionist notions concerning kinship and gender. Most recently, in a collection of anthropological essays on gender (and not incidentally, kinship), J. Weiner (1987: 262) reports that among the Foi of the Southern Highlands of Papua-New Guinea, when men migrate into a community to "live together" and "eat together" with men born into it "they [all] consider themselves 'brothers' in the widest sense of the term." He adds: " 'relationship' or 'kinship' in this sense is an automatic consequence of long-term coresidence and the sharing it implies for the Foi." It is significant that Weiner does *not* report the Foi expression he glosses as "relationship" or "kinship," and neither does he show that the Foi themselves describe a "brother" by coresidence, as well as a "brother" by birth, as a "relative" or "kinsman." Once again, it seems, cultural categories have been violated ethnographically via methods widely proclaimed virtually to guarantee authenticity.

A slightly different argument against genealogically based kinship derives from the Victorian anthropological contention that expressions such as Trobriand or Fijian *tama* "cannot mean 'father' " because they are used not only in reference to one's presumed genitor but also in reference to his brothers and male cousins, and, indeed, in reference to all men of more or less his age who are comembers with him of some social group usually designated a clan, whether or not it is possible to demonstrate via a pedigree that they are related genealogically to one's father. Thus, *tama* is not a kinship term but is a "social category" term, one that signifies something like "man of my father's group and of more or less his age." There is, however, ample evidence not only for the metaphoric use of kinship terms (as in the uses of *uncle* discussed above) but also for polysemy within the domain of kin classification. As (for example) in the difference between English *father* and *stepfather*, so also in many other languages kinship terms often occur in unmarked/marked pairs, and that is a sure sign of polysemy. Fijian *tama* or "father" has the complementary marked forms *tama-levu* for father's elder brother and *tama-lailai* for father's younger brother. Those forms are definitive evidence that "father" is the structurally primary or logically most basic sense of *tama*.[14] It has to be noticed also that the definition usually proffered as the only or structurally basic one—that is, "man of my father's group. . . "—is logically based on and presupposes the category "father." That renders "father" the structurally most basic sense of the expression, and "man of my father's group . . . " a structurally derivative sense.

The semantic-theoretical foundations of the arguments of the antikinship school are not only simplistic and seriously misleading. They also routinely muddle up questions that must be kept quite distinct because the answers to them require at least partially different kinds of data. Questions about synchronic-structural relations get mixed up, confused with, and answered as though they were questions about historical or diachronic relations; and questions about logical relations get mixed up, confused with, and answered as though they were questions about the "mental states" of single social persons.[15]

Thus, when feminist and nonfeminist anthropologists take the anti- or no-kinship line, some of them in reaction to sociobiological attempts to naturalize our social relations as kin of one another and as males and females, they do nothing to refute them. For example: in their essay " 'Explanations' of Male Dominance," Stephanie Coontz and Peta Henderson (1986: 6) seek to discredit sociobiological accounts of gender, and to do so they cite Marshall Sahlins's *The Use and Abuse of Biology* (1976). He has shown, they say, that in societies "based on kinship as an organizing principle," it is "expediency rather than actual blood relationship" that dictates the form of interaction between individuals. Sahlins's point was, however, the rather different one, that kinship conduct—the social relations between persons who account themselves kin of one another—cannot be explained by appeal to some sort of universal reproductive and genetic rationality, any more than it can be by appeal to a crude, presocial notion of "expediency." He sought to turn the arguments of the sociobiologists on their heads, as it were, by showing that it is not even recognition of one another as kin, much less simply being genetically related, that governs how people interact; instead, it is often because they agree voluntarily to interact in a certain way that they then recognize one another as "kin." As he put it, "The relation between the recognition of kinship and an appropriate mode of action is often reciprocal" (Sahlins 1976: 26). Thus depriving a complex, multilayered cultural reality of most of its detail, the ethnographer or theorist is bound to end up arguing that what passes for kinship elsewhere is not at all the same kind of thing as what passes for kinship at home. But turning that line against the naturalizers of kinship *conduct* is bound to be futile when it is recognized, as it was by Sahlins, that relationship by birth is typically a sufficient, even if not also a necessary, condition for inclusion in a so-called kin class and for designation by a so-called kinship term. As my colleague Alison Richard has pointed out to me, sociobiological theory does not require that *all* persons treated socially as close kin should be also genetically close kin. It requires only that at least 51 percent are, and it is highly probable that in most societies that condition is more than fulfilled. Surely, also, the common use of kinship terms metaphorically to establish kinlike social relations between nonkin (which is what Sahlins was writing about) is testimony *for*, rather than against, the case of the sociobiologists.[16]

Wholly "culturalizing" kinship not only leaves us vulnerable to sociobiological arguments; it also opens the door to feminist essentialism. In the place of Universal Woman the Natural Reproducer and Nurturer, bound by her physical disabilities and by her helpless infant to her naturally dominant and legally superordinate mate, some feminist anthropologists have substituted Universal Woman the Culturally Constituted Reproducer not only of dependent infants, but also of social persons and even of whole systems of social relations (Yeatman 1983, 1984; A. Weiner 1976, 1978, 1979, 1980). In some accounts she appears as The Controller of Reproduction, almost to the exclusion of men. This theme is especially strong in the work of A. Weiner (1976, 1978, 1979, 1980), which shows a pronounced tendency to objectify as the essence of womanness the "biological *and* cultural regenerative powers that women possess" and that men are continually expending their power "in attempts to assume and incorporate" (Weiner 1976: 235–236; but cf. Strathern 1981, 1987). Expectably, when the question is raised, why Universal Woman should be culturally constituted in that way, the answer is likely to revert to the fact that it is women, and not men, who bear and rear infants. Thus, the difference between this account and the more standard masculinist-anthropological account becomes one of value. Woman's Body, instead of being a burden and a handicap that must be compensated for by "male dominance" over women and children, becomes in this construction a natural resource that she does, or certainly can, "control," and thus also a potential source of power in women's relations with men. But women's much touted "control over reproduction" appears to amount to nothing more than women's ability to bear offspring.[17] How can it be that in the absence of the necessary technology and the freedom legally to use it, having no choice but to bear children or to do without heterosexual intercourse constitutes having control over reproduction? And, in fact, Woman the Moral Mother has been and still is a potent symbol for both popular feminism and antifeminism in the West (see di Leonardo, this volume).

Janet Sayers (1982), Alice Echols (1984), Marilyn Strathern (1981), and others have already pointed out that reconstituting the essence of Woman culturally is bound to turn out to be just another way of constituting her naturally—this time in opposition, rather than in relation, to Man. It reproduces our own dominant cultural assumptions about women, albeit with a different valuation. At this juncture, the issue becomes not "Are we going to tolerate sexism in theory construction?" but "Must we flee sexism only to be landed with feminist essentialism?" The answer must and can be a definite "No!" because there is a more moderate, both naturalistic and social-constructionist, but also nonsexist alternative.

IV

I noted earlier that in trying to understand another culture we always begin by trying to detect in the speech and actions of a people concepts and practices that are similar to ones we know from our own native social experience or from other ethnographic studies. In the matter of "kinship," because it is so defined in their own cultures, anthropologists have looked for concepts of interpersonal relationship established via processes of reproduction; they have looked for some "recognition" that heterosexual intercourse is a necessary (though perhaps not also sufficient) part of that process; and, thus, for "recognition" that each person has both a male and a female contributor (via the process of reproduction as locally conceived) to his or her being. Ethnographers have never had any qualms about supposing that, because childbirth is a plainly observable event, relationship by birth to a woman is a "known fact" in any society, as it is in their own, and no one has ever reported the existence of a society from which a concept of maternity is absent. Even if the local conception and evaluation is that a woman merely carries and nurtures *in utero* a being that a man placed there via sexual intercourse with her, ethnographers have not been disposed to talk about "ignorance of maternity" (or even of physical, biological, or physiological maternity). But the positivist-empiricist epistemology that makes maternity seem obvious and a concept of maternity seem inevitable, also makes paternity seem just the opposite, and it has, as a consequence, seemed entirely plausible that there are (or were) many societies in which "ignorance of paternity" *is* the state of affairs; or, if a concept of paternity is present, that being the genitor of a child counts for little or nothing socially because of the notorious difficulty of knowing with certainty who the genitor of any particular child really is. It is not without significance for this discussion of sexism in the theory of kinship that anthropologists have usually attributed that difficulty to, as Westermark (1891: 113) put it, "adultery on the woman's side." All that has had the further rather curious consequence that the criteria for "having a concept of paternity" have been typically far more stringent than the criteria for "having a concept of maternity." That in turn has led to the conversion of a seemingly plausible state of affairs into an "actual" state of affairs.

One of the positive features of the social-constructionist orientation in contemporary anthropology is that it does at least try to dispense with that epistemology and to treat the concepts of other cultures as positive knowledge, and *not* as just so many more or less "erroneous beliefs" or manifestations of "savage nescience" of one thing or another (see Schneider 1965 for a useful discussion of some of these issues). It forces us to see that local concepts of "maternity" (female reproductive contribution) are no less *cultural* constructs than are local concepts of "paternity" (male reproductive contribution); and, as I have already shown in some detail in other contexts (Scheffler 1970; 1973: 748–756; 1978: 5–13), it enables us to see that concepts of the latter kind are no less common than are those of the former kind.[18] Moreover, it is simply not true that genitors not wed to the mothers of their offspring are typically devoid of rights and duties in relation to their offspring.[19] Appearances to the contrary have been ethnographically and theoretically created and sustained by ignoring moral and sentimentally sanctioned rights and duties in favor of legally sanctioned ones and by mistaking what counts as *legal* evidence for paternity with the nature of the relationship itself (see references in n. 19).

There is, then, no need for the concept of the purely "social father"; it is an anthropological red herring, and we will get by much better without it. That is just as well because it has been the apparent necessity to institute that concept that has led also to the ahistorical and sexist definition of marriage as rooted, like maternity, in presumed timeless, natural, biological facts, especially in a presumed tendency for men to "dominate" women and their offspring, and for their own good.

We can now define "kinship" for purposes of cross-cultural comparison as culturally postulated "relationship by birth to an ego or propositus," and we can generalize that, wherever we find it, it is "bilaterally" constituted. We can do that without presupposing that postulation (*not* "recognition") of kinship is a cultural universal and is a functional requisite of a recognizably human social order. Nevertheless, the ubiquity of that kind of cultural form does suggest that there has been, all along, some sociological wisdom in the suspicion that you won't have to look very hard to find culturally constituted kinship wherever you find human beings. After all, it does not follow from its being perhaps ethnocentric from the outset that a suspicion *is* wrong. Assuming, then, that kinship constructs are ubiquitous, it becomes an interesting question why they are.

As soon as we ask that question radical social-constructionism (at least of the "symbolic anthropology" kind) becomes useless, because it is not an explanatory but only a methodological paradigm. For the radical social-constructionist whose purpose is to understand and to describe each culture "in its own terms," that question is an irrelevant "social system question," one about "how roles are defined and articulated into a set of patterns for action which adapt *man* to the facts of his environment" (Schneider 1972: 47, emphasis added). Indeed, as N. Redclift (1987: 125) has noted, what is strikingly and most deliberately *absent* from this perspective is "any idea that sexuality or sexual divisions are a relevant, or problematic, aspect of kinship"; and that, as she goes on to remark, entails that many of the most contentious and difficult questions feminists need and want to raise about kinship and its relations with gender cannot even be asked.

Collier and Yanagisako's (1987: 7, 15, 29) claim to the contrary that the "domains" of "gender and kinship are mutually constituted" or are "one field," because both center on folk conceptions or theories about human reproduction, is not a tenable reply. On the one hand, it is contrary to Schneider's insistence that "kinship" does *not* center on, although it does include, concepts of bisexual reproduction; and were it not for that insistence there would be very little to differentiate his views, which Collier and Yanagisako wish to adopt, from those of most other anthropologists. On the other hand, it must be admitted that "gender" and "kinship" are related categories that are central to related fields or topics of study, and relations between social relations of gender and of kinship are urgently in need of further theorization and empirical research—as Collier and Yanagisako (1987) and Redclift (1987) strongly stress. But "mutual constitution" begs the question and prevents us from attending to this intellectual task.

In contrast to kinship deconstructionism, the standard theory of kinship is explanatory in intent. What is wrong with it is not its attempt to explain the ubiquity of kinship concepts and practices by positing certain, as Clyde Kluckhohn once put it, "invariant points of reference supplied by the biological [and] psychological . . . givens of human life" (cited in Goodenough 1970*a*: 2). It is, after all, one of those "givens" that humans *do* reproduce bisexually and *do* produce helpless offspring who *do* require physical and psychological nurturance for many years. The real defect in the standard theory is that it constructs some of those "givens" in a blatantly sexist fashion and then uses them to constitute the ethnographic facts to be explained.

To acknowledge that, because of our evolutionary history, we humans are disposed to form fairly durable heterosexual mating pairs, the members of which cooperate in, among other things, the rearing of their offspring, is not to say also that the only "natural" form of human sexuality is heterosexuality and that homoerotic attraction and interaction are perversely contrary to nature. R. W. Connell (1987: 72) and others have already pointed out that widely diverse social-sexual arrangements are consistent with the occurrence of more than enough heterosexual intercourse to reproduce species. To do that, it is hardly necessary for humans to be innately and exclusively heterosexual in erotic orientation. Also, primate studies have shown that playful homoerotic attraction and interaction are common in various species, are a powerful socializing force, and are among the ways in which adolescent animals learn sexual and other social behaviors (see e.g. Lancaster 1979; Hrdy and Whitten 1986; Smuts 1986*a*, 1986*b*).

V

The long-standing anthropological debate about the nature of kinship has been all along not only an intellectual but also a moral and political controversy. Early on it had no direct feminist voice, although as shown by the final sentence of Westermark's *The History of Human Marriage* (which I quoted at the outset), feminist voices were being heard and, to some extent, even attended to. Now that feminists are in a much better position to have a direct voice, we are well advised not to indulge in or to poach off the arguments of the kinship dismantlers, but to direct our critical attention, as many of us already have, to the naturalness of that vaguely defined syndrome "male dominance" and of a social division of labor that has infants dependent primarily on their mothers and their mothers on their mates or husbands.[20] It is all too easy, though, in the social contexts in which anthropology is practiced, to get seduced into thinking that, if we grant the radical social-constructionist premise that it is culture that constitutes what is "real" for any society (as per Yeatman 1983), we are relieved of the necessity to do that.

Anthropology is often represented as a liberal-humanitarian voice that speaks for the "other," and to the extent that we do that we have a strong interest in assimilating that "other" to ourselves and, in the process, to a common humanity equally entitled to the same human rights. In the past that effort took the form of a search for the elements of "the psychological unity of [hu]mankind" or for "the universal categories of culture," one of which was "kinship." Nowadays, the tendency is to define "Man" as "The Culture-Maker" whose creative capacities, including the possibility of self-definition, are virtually unbounded. Although this stance may appear to serve the feminist cause, it also makes us all the more susceptible to being pulled in the opposite direction. Barbara Lloyd (1976) has shown how the ideal, statistical-experimental, scientific method leads to a tendency to treat only findings of difference as "real results," with the consequence that findings of similarities between males and females are often treated as no findings at all. Although anthropology is not that kind of science, we have a similar problem.

Because our discipline operates in the context of late-capitalist, consumption-oriented society, we have a strong interest in maintaining, even producing, cross-cultural difference, that of *creating* the "other" as an esoteric and exotic object, not merely of disinterested knowledge, but of commodity exchange and consumption. Just as each year's Ford must be made to appear not only different from but also new, better, and improved in comparison with last year's if the Ford Motor Company is to survive in the marketplace, so also must culture *x* be made to appear different from other cultures in general if the ethnographer is to make his or her mark in anthropology *as a trade*. As a consequence, hardly a year goes by without the appearance of yet another New Theory of Culture that stresses its symbolic constitution and dissociates it from the taint of anything natural or even material; or of yet another New Theory of Women's Status that would conventionalize the whole thing; or, even more frequently, of yet another claim that culture *x* lacks that, sometimes alleged, most "basic" of all human social institutions, "kinship" itself. What all those enterprises have in common is that they would deprive us of any dimensions of human, cross-cultural similarity, other than our symbol-creating capacity, by reference to which cross-cultural differences may be ordered and understood. They would, thereby, open the way for virtually endless commodity differentiation unconstrained by even the most minimal standards of intellectual or social value.

Surely, though, all human social orders have it in common that they have come to terms culturally with the biological givens that women bear children and need the assistance of men to engender them; and it does seem to be a cross-cultural social reality that, however varying the patterns, both women and men contribute to the rearing of dependent children. Kathleen Gough (1975: 75), Janet Sayers (1982: 191), and many others have already pointed out that feminists need not fear to acknowledge these patterns and, indeed, must do so as a preliminary to showing also that historically it has not always entailed the subordination of women to men and, certainly, it need not do so in the future.

ACKNOWLEDGMENTS

I am grateful to Micaela di Leonardo, Jan Simpson, Sharon Hutchinson, and Fitz John Porter Poole for their careful readings of and constructive comments on earlier drafts of this essay.

NOTES

1. See e.g., the essays by Leibowitz, Slocum, and Gough, all in Reiter (1975); Dahlberg (1981), Harding (1987); also the essays by Peacock, Sperling, and Conkey in this volume.

2. For the purposes of this chapter, and in general, it is vitally important not to conflate words and the categories or concepts they designate. Accordingly, in references to a word that word is italicized (e.g., *marriage*), and in references to a category or concept the word is put in double quotes (e.g., "marriage").

3. For many feminists the classic treatment of the history of marriage, family, and kinship is F. Engels's (1884) *The Origin of the Family, Private Property, and the State*. Some feminist surveys and criticisms are Gough (1975), Collier, Rosaldo, and Yanagisako (1982), Sayers, Evans, and Radclift (1987).

4. Additional relevant ethnographic accounts include Nash (1974, 1978a, 1978b, 1981, 1987) and Bell (1980, 1983, 1987).

5. In addition to the one discussed below, we might question also the presumption, hardly unique to Goodenough, that it is either necessary or wise *for any purpose* to attempt to devise a universally applicable definition of "marriage." An alternative strategy, which cannot be elaborated on here, would be to settle for a category of marriagelike cultural categories and social institutions. Of course, the same goes for "kinship" and "family."

6. I have here simplified Goodenough's definition of marriage by omitting from it the possibility that the party who acquires the relevant rights in relation to a particular woman may be someone other than an adult male. Doing that is not critical for the argument being developed here.

7. For the details on the antikinship side, see Schneider (1972, 1984), Needham (1971), Barnard and Good (1984); on the other side see Scheffler (1972), Scheffler and Lounsbury (1971), where the argument presented is critically quite different from Schneider's (1984) representation of it.

8. For Schneider's full "cultural" analysis of American kinship see Schneider (1968). The "second edition" of 1983 differs only in the addition of brief replies to a few critics; they deal with *none* of the issues mentioned here or in Scheffler (1976).

9. Because of the severity and persistence of Schneider's condemnation of what he represents as rampant ethnocentrism in the study of kinship in the past, it is only fair to note that the general outlines and many of the details of his own reanalysis of "American kinship" (Schneider 1968) have been reproduced by two dozen or more of his students and other young anthropologists influenced by him and his students in their studies of cultures scattered all around the world, though mainly in South Asia and Oceania. Is it ethnocentrism or something else that has produced this remarkable series of results?

10. The same general points are made also in Barnes (1973) and Horton (1982: 203), and they are rapidly becoming commonplace in the burgeoning literature focusing on ethnographies as texts (e.g. Asad 1986).

11. For fuller representation of this view see Hocart (1935) and Leach (1958). The Hocart essay, despite some major logical flaws (see Scheffler 1972) is often cited as authoritative and conclusive by Louis Dumont and his followers. Westermark (1891: 88–89) also took this position, but he thought he had to in order to refute claims that relationship terminologies can be used to deduce archaic forms of social organization and, especially, of marriage.

12. Polysemy is the condition wherein an expression designates two or more related categories, one being derived (logically and usually, though not necessarily, temporally) from another. It contrasts most directly with homonymy, the condition wherein an expression designates two or more categories, but there is no relation of derivation between them (as in *bare* = uncovered, and *bear* = the animal, words having the same pronunciation but wholly unrelated meanings). See also Scheffler and Lounsbury (1972: 6–12).

13. Scheffler (1972, 1973, 1976), Scheffler and Lounsbury (1972).

14. The relevant Fijian data are in Sahlins (1962). For more general discussions of markedness relations in systems of kin classification see Scheffler (1984, 1987).

15. For an example of the first confusion see again Hocart (1935); and for an example of the second confusion see Hirschfeld (1986). Both kinds of confusion are dealt with in Scheffler and Lounsbury (1971, esp. chaps. 1 and 7), also Scheffler (1972).

16. It ought to be a matter for serious scholarly concern that the logical fallacies that underpin the arguments of the antikinship school in modern cultural anthropology are filtering into gender studies more generally, where they are sometimes made foundational to ambitious claims. Consider Kessler and McKenna's (1978: 38) claim that in some North American Indian societies "gender role" rather than genital anatomy determined "gender attribution" or classification as a male or a female. (They sometimes qualify the "determined" with "sometimes.") Their "ethnomethodological" argument is intended to liberate gender from any biological basis; to show that it is instead a "social accomplishment"; and to show that a system of two genders is by no means inevitable. They acknowledge, however, that "gender role" is definable only as conduct or behavior normative for a member of one or the other genital-sex class (in their terms, gender category) and that assignment to one or the other sex class is typically at birth and *not* dependent on any

conduct or behavior on the part of the person being classified. Because, logically, categories must be defined or constituted by criteria independent of the normative implications of inclusion in those categories, certain forms of conduct cannot be both criteria for and normative implications of inclusion in one and the same category. It must be that Kessler and McKenna are dealing with situations in which some men (less often women) are permitted to act, in some degree, as *though* they were women (or men), and may be spoken of as though they were women (or men), or as anomalous "he-she" or "she-he." Ethnographic data cited by Kessler and McKenna, and more recently summarized or revealed in Williams (1986), provide definitive evidence that such persons were not regarded as having somehow moved from one sex (or in Kessler and McKenna's terms, gender) category to the other, but were only metaphorically "women" (or "men"). It is only to be expected that Kessler and McKenna cannot in the end produce any linguistic data to demonstrate that the so-called *berdache* are treated in any language as a genuine third gender. In any event, a third gender would be just another gender straightjacket, hardly an open door leading out of Kessler and McKenna's prison house of gender.

17. A. Weiner frequently asserts that Trobriand women control reproduction of the *dala* or lineage. Of course, women do, with the cooperation of men, reproduce human beings, and it does deserve to be stressed, as Weiner does, that what is produced are not mere corporeal entities but are social persons. One of the features with which any Trobriander is born is an identity as a member of a dala (lineage), and he/she necessarily shares that identity with his/her mother. That is because the constitutive rule of the dala kind of group is that being an offspring of a female member is the necessary and sufficient condition for inclusion in her group. Such a rule gives neither the mother nor anyone else any powers of choice or decision in the matter of group affiliation and, thus, no "control" over either individual or lineage reproduction (or, we might more accurately say, perpetuation), except, again, in the instance of the woman who refrains from heterosexual intercourse and thus from getting pregnant. For a general discussion of such rules of group affiliation see Scheffler (1986).

18. In one of those contexts (Scheffler 1973: 749), and still too much under the influence of the epistemology of which I am here being critical, I wrote: "the foundation of any kinship system consists in a folk-cultural theory designed to account for the fact that women give birth to children, i.e., a theory of human reproduction." Collier and Yanagisako (1987: 32) misrepresent this as a claim that "kinship is everywhere about the same biological fact," although (following Schneider 1965) I had already cautioned against representing folk concepts which posit genealogical relationship or relationship by birth as "biological" concepts or knowledge. They object also to what they say is my assumption that "biological motherhood is everywhere the core of the social relationship of motherhood." I have done no more, however, than to argue that the very existence of "social relations of motherhood" is contingent on the prior existence of the category "mother" (i.e., female reproductive agent of . . .) and to point out the logical and technical-linguistic errors of the claim (insisted on by Schneider [1968] and by Collier and Yanagisako) that one and the same category named "mother" may have "alternate" genealogical and behavioral distinctive features.

19. Yet so entrenched is this view in academic anthropology that one historian (Trautmann 1981: 60) has asserted that "consanguinity and affinity are related as

chicken and egg," exactly as though it were an irrefutable ethnographic fact that relations of consanguinity (especially of paternity) created out of wedlock nowhere count as kinship and are everywhere wholly discounted for any and all social purposes. Modern ethnographic evidence is wholly to the contrary (see e.g. Evans-Pritchard 1945; Fortes 1949; Scheffler 1970; and for a summary Scheffler 1973: 751–756).

20. There are, of course, innumerable essays and books that attack that naturalization and that vagueness. Among them I have benefited from Rosaldo (1980), Sayers (1982), Leacock (1981), Coward (1983), Hartsock (1985), Tabet (1982), Harding (1987), and Connell (1987).

BIBLIOGRAPHY

Asad, T. 1986. The concept of cultural translation in British social anthropology. In *Writing culture: The poetics and politics of ethnography.* J. Clifford and G. Marcus, eds., 141–164. Berkeley, Los Angeles, London: University of California Press.

Barnard, A., and A. Good. 1984. *Research practices in the study of kinship.* London: Academic Press.

Barnes, J. A. 1973. Genetrix : genitor :: nature : culture? In *The character of kinship.* J. Goody, ed., 61–74. London: Cambridge University Press.

Bell, Dianne. 1980. Desert politics: Choices in the marriage market. In *Women and colonization.* M. Etienne and E. Leacock, eds., 239–269. New York: Praeger.

———. 1983. *Daughters of the dreaming.* Sydney: Allen and Unwin.

———. 1987. The politics of separation. In *Dealing with inequality: Analyzing gender relations in Melanesia and beyond.* M. Strathern, ed., 112–129. London: Cambridge University Press.

Collier, Jane, Michelle Rosaldo, and Sylvia Yanagisako. 1982. Is there a family? New anthropological views. In *Rethinking the family: Some feminist questions.* B. Thorne and M. Yalom, eds., 25–39. New York: Longman.

Collier, Jane, and Sylvia Yanagisako, eds. 1987. *Gender and kinship: Essays toward a unified analysis.* Stanford: Stanford University Press.

Connell, R. W. 1987. *Gender and power.* Stanford: Stanford University Press.

Coontz, S., and P. Henderson, eds. 1986. *Women's work, men's property: The origins of gender and class.* London: Verso.

Coward, R. 1983. *Patriarchal precedents.* London: Routledge.

Dahlberg, F., ed. 1981. *Woman the gatherer.* New Haven: Yale University Press.

di Leonardo, M. 1979. Methodology and the misinterpretation of women's status in kinship studies. *American Ethnologist* 6: 627–637.

Echols, A. 1984. The taming of the id: Feminist sexual politics. In *Pleasure and danger: Exploring female sexuality.* C. Vance, ed., 50–72. Boston: Routledge & Kegan Paul.

Engels, Frederick. 1972 (1884). *The origin of the family, private property and the state.* Edited by Eleanor Leacock. New York: International Publishers.

Evans-Pritchard, E. E. 1945. *Some aspects of marriage and the family among the Nuer.* Rhodes-Livingstone Papers, no. 11.

Fee, E. 1973. The sexual politics of Victorian social anthropology. *Feminist Studies* 1: 23–29.

Fortes, M. 1949. *The web of kinship among the Tallensi* London: Cambridge University Press.

Goodenough, W. 1970a. *Description and comparison in cultural anthropology*. Chicago: Aldine.

———. 1970b. Epilogue: Transactions in parenthood. In *Adoption in Eastern Oceania*. V. Carroll, ed., 391–410. Honolulu: University of Hawaii Press.

Gough, K. 1975. The origin of the family. In *Toward an anthropology of women*. R. R. Rapp, ed., 51–76. New York: Monthly Review Press.

Harding, S. 1987. The politics of the natural: The case of sex differences. In *Sexuality and medicine*. E. E. Shlep, ed., 1: 185–203. Dordrecht: D. Reidel.

Hartsock, N. 1985. *Money, sex, and power*. Boston: Northeastern University Press.

Hirschfeld, E. 1986. Kinship and cognition: Genealogy and the meaning of kinship terms. *Current Anthropology* 27: 217–242.

Hocart, Arthur M. 1935. Kinship systems. *Anthropos* 32: 545–551.

Horton, Robin. 1982. Tradition and modernity revisited. In *Rationality and relativism*. M. Hollis, ed., 201–260. Cambridge: MIT Press.

Hrdy, S., and P. Whitten. 1986. Patterning of sexual activity. In *Primate societies*. B. Smuts et al., eds., 370–384. Chicago: University of Chicago Press.

Kessler, S., and W. McKenna. 1978. *Gender: An ethnomethodological approach*. New York: Wiley.

Lancaster, J. 1979. Sex and gender in evolutionary perspective. In *Human sexuality*. H. A. Katchadourian, ed., 51–79. Berkeley, Los Angeles, London: University of California Press.

Leach, E. R. 1958. Concerning Trobriand clans and the kinship category *tabu*. In *The developmental cycle in domestic groups*. J. Goody, ed., 120–145. London: Cambridge University Press.

Leacock, E. 1981. *Myths of male dominance*. New York: Monthly Review Press.

Leibowitz, Lila. 1975. Perspectives on the evolution of sex differences. In *Toward an anthropology of women*. R. R. Rapp, ed., 20–35. New York: Monthly Review Press.

Lloyd, B. 1976. Social responsibility and research on sex differences. In *Exploring sex differences*. B. Lloyd and J. Archer, eds., 1–23. London: Academic Press.

Malinowski, Bronislav. 1930 (1963). Parenthood—The basis of social structure. In *Sex, culture and myth* (Collected essays of Bronislav Malinowski). Pp. 42–88. New York: Harcourt, Brace, and World.

Nash, J. 1974. *Matriliny and modernization: The Nagovisi of South Bougainville*. New Guinea Research Bulletin No. 55. Canberra: Australian National University Press.

———. 1978a. A note on groomprice. *American Anthropologist* 80: 106–108.

———. 1978b. Women and power in Nagovisi society. *Journal de la société des Océanistes* 58 (34): 119–126.

———. 1981. Sex, money, and the status of women in aboriginal South Bougainville. *American Ethnologist* 8: 107–126.

———. 1987. Gender attributes and equality: Men's strength and women's talk among the Nagovisi. In *Dealing with inequality: Analyzing gender relations in Melanesia and beyond*. M. Strathern, ed., 150–173. London: Cambridge University Press.

Needham, R. 1971. Remarks on the analysis of kinship and marriage. In *Rethinking kinship and marriage*. R. Needham, ed., 1–34. London: Tavistock.

Radcliffe-Brown, A. R. 1950. Introduction. In *African systems of kinship and marriage*.

A. R. Radcliffe-Brown, ed., 1–85. London: Oxford University Press.

Redclift, N. 1987. Rights in women: Kinship, culture, and materialism. In *Engels revisited: New feminist essays*. J. Sayers, M. Evans, and N. Redclift. eds., 111–143. London: Tavistock.

Reiter, R. R., ed. 1975. *Toward an anthropology of women*. New York: Monthly Review Press.

Rosaldo, M. 1980. The use and abuse of anthropology: Reflections on feminism and cross-cultural understanding. *Signs* 5: 389–417.

Sahlins, M. 1962. *Moala: Culture and nature on a Fijian island*. Ann Arbor: University of Michigan Press.

———. 1976. *The use and abuse of biology*. Ann Arbor: University of Michigan Press.

Sayers, J. 1982. *Biological politics: Feminist and anti-feminist perspectives*. London: Tavistock.

Sayers, J., M. Evans, and N. Redclift, eds. 1987. *Engels revisited: New feminist essays*. London: Tavistock.

Scheffler, H. W. 1970. Kinship and adoption in the northern New Hebrides. In *Adoption in Eastern Oceania*. V. Carroll, ed., 68–89. Honolulu: University of Hawaii Press.

———. 1972. Kinship semantics. *Annual Review of Anthropology* 1: 309–328.

———. 1973. Kinship, descent, and alliance. In *Handbook of social and cultural anthropology*. J. Honigmann, ed., 747–793. Chicago: Rand McNally.

———. 1976. Kinship in American culture: Another view. In *Meaning in Anthropology*. K. Basso and H. Selby, eds., 57–91. Albuquerque: University of New Mexico Press.

———. 1978. *Australian Kin Classification*. Cambridge: Cambridge University Press.

———. 1984. Markedness and extensions: The Tamil case. *Man* 19: 557–574.

———. 1986. The descent of rights and the descent of persons. *American Anthropologist* 88: 339–350.

———. 1987. Markedness in systems of kin classification. *Journal of Anthropological Research* 43: 203–221.

Scheffler, H. W., and F. G. Lounsbury. 1972. *A study in structural semantics: The Siriono kinship system*. Englewood Cliffs, N.J.: Prentice-Hall.

Schneider, D. M. 1965. Kinship and biology. In *Aspects of the analysis of family structure*. A. J. Coale, ed., 83–101. Princeton: Princeton University Press.

———. 1968. *American kinship: A cultural account*. Englewood Cliffs, N.J.: Prentice-Hall.

———. 1972. What is kinship all about? In *Kinship studies in the Morgan centennial year*. P. Reining, ed., 32–63. Washington, D.C.: Anthropological Society of Washington.

———. 1984. *A critique of the theory of kinship*. Ann Arbor: University of Michigan Press.

Slocum, S. 1975. Woman the gatherer: Male bias in anthropology. In *Toward an anthropology of women*. R. R. Rapp, ed., 36–50. New York.: Monthly Review Press.

Smuts, B. 1986a. Sexual competition and mate choice. In *Primate societies*. B. Smuts, et al., eds., 385–399. Chicago: University of Chicago Press.

———. 1986b. Gender, aggression and influence. In *Primate societies*. B. Smuts, et al., eds., 400–412. Chicago: University of Chicago Press.

Stocking, G. 1987. *Victorian anthropology*. New York: Free Press.

Strathern, M. 1981. Culture in a netbag: The manufacture of a subdiscipline in anthropology. *Man* 16: 665–688.

———. 1987. Conclusion. In *Dealing with inequality: Analyzing gender relations in Melanesia and beyond.* M. Strathern, ed., 278–302. Cambridge: Cambridge University Press.

Tabet, P. 1982. Hands, tools, and weapons. *Feminist Issues* 2: 3–62.

Trautmann, T. R. 1981. *Dravidian kinship.* London: Cambridge University Press.

Weiner, A. 1976. *Women of value: Men of renown.* Austin: University of Texas Press.

———. 1978. The reproductive model in Trobriand society. *Mankind* 11: 175–186.

———. 1979. Trobriand kinship from another view: The reproductive power of women and men. *Man* 14: 328–348.

———. 1980. Reproduction: A replacement for reciprocity. *American Ethnologist* 7: 71–85.

Weiner, J. F. 1987. Diseases of the soul: sickness, agency, and the men's cult among the Foi of New Guinea. In *Dealing with inequality: Analyzing gender relations in Melanesia and beyond.* Marilyn Strathern, ed., 255–277. Cambridge: Cambridge University Press.

Westermark, E. W. 1891. *The history of human marriage.* London: Macmillan.

Williams, W. L. 1986. *The spirit and the flesh: Sexual diversity in American Indian culture.* Boston: Beacon Press.

Yeatman, A. 1983. The procreative model: The social ontological bases of gender-kinship systems. *Social Analysis* 14: 3–30.

———. 1984. A rejoinder (to comments on Yeatman 1983). *Social Analysis* 16: 26–43.

TWELVE

Moral Pioneers

Women, Men, and Fetuses on a Frontier of
Reproductive Technology

Rayna Rapp

Each year, scores of thousands of American women choose to monitor their pregnancies for prenatal disabilities via amniocentesis, and the number is rapidly growing. Indeed, the exact number of amniocenteses performed each year is unknown: in the same year (1983) three different government sources suggested 40,000, 80,000, and 120,000. The lack of a "ballpark estimate" should alert us to the fact that we are observing a medical technology that is becoming widespread under conditions of a "free market economy," without much centralized monitoring. In 1950, there were only a handful of genetic centers in the United States; now, there are over five hundred where amniocentesis is performed. And although the technology was initially developed to monitor Down's Syndrome (a leading cause of mental retardation, worldwide), it can now detect about two hundred inherited conditions, most of them quite rare recessive diseases. Unless otherwise indicated by family health history, a standard amniocentesis is performed to look for chromosome defects and open neural tube defects, and not for more arcane conditions.

Those recommended for the test include: women whose families already have a member with a condition that can now be detected prenatally; people from ethnically specific populations in which the risk of certain recessively transmitted genetic diseases is elevated (Tay-Sacks among people of Ashkenazi Jewish descent; sickle cell anemia among those of African descent, for example); and "older" pregnant women. "Older" is, however, a social and not a simply biological construct: although the incidence of live-born babies with Down's Syndrome goes steadily up throughout a woman's child-bearing years, the cutoff age for the test has varied considerably. As amniocentesis becomes safer, the age at which it is offered has dropped from forty to thirty-eight to thirty-five, and it is now hovering in the lower thirties. There is no

automatically "correct" age at which the test is indicated: the current suggestion that women thirty-five years of age and older have the test while
pregnant springs not from any jump in the incidence of Down's Syndrome,
but from the intersection of two epidemiological statistics: at thirty-five, the
incidence of live-born babies with Down's Syndrome is about 1 in 360;
amniocentesis is considered a very safe test, but it does add an additional risk
of miscarriage to the pregnancies of women who undergo the procedure.
That added risk is one-third of 1 percent, or 1 in 330, a number which
approximates the risk of bearing a live-born child with Down's Syndrome for
thirty-five-year-old women. If the technology caused one less miscarriage per
thousand, the age at which it is recommended would drop considerably. And
as new technologies like the chorionic villus sampling technique and, eventually, maternal/fetal blood centrifuges become clinically available, the
population recommended to use prenatal diagnosis is likely to expand.[1] We
are thus witnessing the intersection of a routinizing technology with an
epidemiological pattern, and not just a biologically absolute threshold of
pregnancy risk.

Amniocentesis and its related technologies (like diagnostic ultrasound)
are part of the new reproductive technologies—*in vitro* and *in vivo* fertilization, embryo transfer, embryo replacement, donor insemination—which
have been much touted in the popular press as "playing god" with baby-
making. Are we replacing mothers with machines? fathers with doctors?
nature by mechanical culture? How are these technologies changing the
experiences of pregnancy, of becoming a parent, and or family life?

In studying amniocentesis as an anthropologist, I hope to restore a social
context, and probe the cultural meaning, of one new reproductive technology
as it is becoming routinized. Moreover, I am examining one aspect of biological science in American culture, and of medicine as the applied arena in
which most Americans routinely experience scientific language and technology. Genetics holds a privileged position in this medical discourse, for it has
fired the popular as well as the scientific imagination in ways that are deeply
consonant with some of our most cherished beliefs in American culture. In
thinking about the historical discourse on biometry, Mendelianism, eugenics,
sociobiology and, now, the new genetic-engineering technologies, we see that
genetics provides metaphors of human perfectability and definitions of the
individual as holding within itself its own potentialities. Medical attention to
the individual reflects deeply held cultural beliefs. Although legal and medical expert definitions of personhood increasingly prevail, they are based on
notions of individuality that fit well with the historical roots of American
culture.

The problems of prenatal diagnosis have been discussed by geneticists
(who assess the potentials and limits of their technologies); by health econ-

omists (who use cost-benefit analysis to tell us that it is cheaper to screen scores of thousands of pregnancies than to support the services required for each live-born baby with a genetic disability); and by bioethicists (who have raised important questions concerning informed consent, the eugenic potentials of amniocentesis, and parents' right to know and not know). But what is stunning when one enters the discourse on prenatal diagnosis as an anthropologist (and, in my case, I was then a pregnant woman) is that all the audible voices belong to experts. And the experts are predominantly male and white. Silent are the multicultural voices of the women and their families who use, or might use, the new technology. We have very little sense of what their experiences, choices, responses, and images of amniocentesis are all about. And what little research exists concerning users of amniocentesis is constrained by the assumptions of methodological individualism: the personalities of pregnant women have been assessed for anxiety and information retention, and to study how rationally they respond to risk factors. But no one has tried to situate their experiences in a larger social picture. Yet when we step back, it is apparent that reproductive "choices" are far more than individual, or psychological. Broad demographic, sexual, reproductive (and nonreproductive) patterns are ultimately *social* patterns, contextualized by the rationalities of class, race, ethnicity, sex, religious background, family, and reproductive history, and not simply by individual "risks and benefits." It is this larger context I seek to identify and interpret in my fieldwork as an anthropologist.

Although nationally, amniocentesis is becoming a ritual of pregnancy mainly for highly educated, urbanized sectors of the white middle classes, in New York City, the situation is somewhat different. I am presently conducting fieldwork through the Prenatal Diagnosis Laboratory (PDL) of the City of New York, which was set up, beginning in 1978, explicitly to offer amniocentesis to low-income (and thus, disproportionately Afro-American and Hispanic) women. The lab accepts Medicaid and has a sliding scale fee that begins at no-cost. It works through twenty-four city hospitals (both voluntary and municipal), and it initially made counseling available in several languages. The samples of amniotic fluid it collects come from women whose ethnic background is approximately one-third Afro-American, one-third Hispanic, and one-third white. About half are clinic (low-income) and about half are private patients. From an anthropological perspective, it is thus a "social laboratory" as well as a biological one.

My fieldwork focuses on seven contexts, or constituencies. In exploring multiple perspectives on the meaning of prenatal diagnosis, I hope to construct a social and political understanding of one new reproductive technology. One of my salient goals is to demedicalize the discourse on amniocentesis, helping to make its implications available for discussion by the people who use, or might use, it. Although this complex story must await a longer presentation, in this chapter I shall name the contexts in which my research occurs, indicating some of the social and cultural issues that each reveals.

1. *In the Laboratory:* With the support of PDL's chief geneticist, I was a participant-observer at the lab for two months, watching geneticists, genetic counselors, lab technicians, and support staff work in dense and daily interaction. In addition to conducting extensive interviews with both professional and support staff, I followed apprentice technicians through their training, so as to understand both the language and labor of genetics. Using an "ethnography of science" perspective, I observed the practices of ordinary science: scientific personnel making meaning, rehearsing rituals, negotiating significance, as well as "producing results" (Latour and Woolgar 1979; Knorr-Cetina and Mulkay 1982; Goodfield 1981).

Given the powerful place science in general, and genetics in particular, currently hold in late-twentieth-century American culture, I focus on the metaphors deployed in the translation of one cutting edge of research into clinical practice and public policy. Those metaphors are, of course, quite gender-laden in their descriptions of hierarchy and reciprocity within DNA and chromosomes, and throughout medicine itself (Hubbard 1982; Minden 1984).

At the sociological level, the labors involved in prenatal diagnosis are women's work. Not only are pregnant women the clients for this new reproductive service, but virtually all the workers in this "industry" are female, as well. Medical geneticists working in this field are disproportionately women. Although men predominate on the research frontier of genetic engineering, medical genetics is known to be hospitable to women. It provides nine-to-five working hours without late-night emergencies and is thus compatible with the domestic sexual division of labor. More than 98 percent of all genetic counselors are female. Although they are experts in a technical and rapidly changing science, counselors are situated in the medical hierarchy like social workers, and paid as such. Most lab technicians are women, as well. This work is often cited as appropriately "feminine" because it focuses on pregnancy and does not disrupt family responsibilities. A new field of employment at the cutting edge of genetics thus emerges with job descriptions, prestige, and pay scales that reproduce familiar gender hierarchies.

In the laboratory, genetic technicians peer through microscopes, constructing karyotypes, searching for atypical chromosomal patterns. They do so constrained by working relations that separate fetal cells from babies, blood samples from pregnant women, diagnoses from family trauma. It is important to examine both the benefits and the boundaries of the scientific division of labor as it constructs amniocentesis.

2. *Genetic Counselors:* Genetic counseling is a profession in formation (Roll-nick 1984; Reed 1974; Kevles 1985). In its scant fifteen-year history, the field has trained a new group of predominantly white, middle-class female health professionals to explain chromosomes and genetic disability to lay audiences. The initial wave of genetic counselors tended to be well-educated suburban housewives raising their children first and then returning to the job market. Many lived near Sarah Lawrence College, in Westchester County, New York, where the first training program opened its doors in 1971. Recently, a second wave of genetic counselors has begun to appear on the job market. Younger, a bit more ethnically and linguistically diverse, second-wave counselors tend to have postponed child-bearing in favor of careers. These background factors are important, as both waves of counselors are unlikely to have experienced the technology they now offer to other women. And their own experiences surrounding female work and family life necessarily inform their attitudes toward pregnant patients.

I have conducted interviews with thirty genetic counselors, at least one from every health facility in New York City where amniocentesis is offered. I have also worked closely with the PDL counseling team during a two-year period, observing their intake interviews at hospitals throughout New York City. Genetic counselors are quick to identify the ethical complexity of pro-viding prenatal information and health services, including abortion services, to women of diverse ethnic, racial, linguistic, and religious backgrounds. They are trained to be empathic as they convey statistics and to practice Rogerian therapy, a noninterventionist technique aimed at helping the pa-tient to make up her own mind. Yet genetic counselors all know how perilous the position of value-free counseling is. On the one hand, they are always making linguistic code-switches as they determine what sort and how much information a pregnant woman needs and can use. On the other hand, all the information a woman receives comes directly from the counselor, as she is unlikely to have a "folk model" of most of the diseases and risks associated with amniocentesis. Not so with other aspects of pregnancy, which are also discussed informally, among kin, neighbors, and friends, in a popular, as well as a medical voice.

So the genetic counselor really is the gatekeeper between science and so-cial experience, regulating the quantity and quality of the information on which decisions will be made. In their work, genetic counselors identify with and serve pregnant women, while representing the universal claims of sci-ence. At stake in their profession is the technological transformation of pregnancy and maternal "choice."

3. *During Counseling:* For two years, I have observed hundreds of intake interviews in three city hospitals where genetic counselors explain heredity

and amniocentesis to a polyglot, multicultural patient population. Here, genetic counselors elicit a great deal of information from their patients— ethnic background (to know if they are at risk for any ethnically specific diseases, like Thalassemia, Tay-Sacks, or sickle-cell anemia), occupation (to check for hazardous exposures), method of payment, as well as personal, reproductive, and family health histories. I observe code switching ("baby" versus "fetus"; "tummy" versus "womb" or "uterus"; "waters" versus "amniotic fluid") as counselors deal in dizzying succession with Gucci-briefcased husband-wife-law-teams, Dominican high school dropouts, and Seventh Day Adventists from Harlem. I observe not only what questions are asked, but what questions are unasked as well. Thus, a middle-class professional couple queries whether the husband's Aunt Hannah, who had a perfectly healthy baby at forty-five, is included in the counselor's health statistics. But a clinic patient waiting three hours to keep her appointment may respond to the query, "Do you have any questions to ask me?" with, "Where's the Medicaid office"? And a pregnant black teenager with sickle trait may confront the counselor with a folk explanation: as the last child, she has a touch of trait because all last children do. Or a recently migrated Haitian couple may reject amniocentesis because they've never heard of Down's Syndrome, or Mongolism, for which no word appears to exist in their native Creole.[2]

In a forty-five-minute session, conversations (and silences) are rich with possible communication, and miscommunication. Here, the local meaning of a pregnancy, a fetus, heredity, and technology are all under negotiation. And the language of science often confronts polyglot dialects of daily life.

4. *At Home:* The waiting period between amniocentesis and its results is a very long and stressful one. The test can't be administered before the sixteenth week of pregnancy, when enough fluid has accumulated for a successful and safe tap. The lab work includes a lengthy cell-growth period and tedious karyotyping, which take three to four weeks. And results must be known before the twenty-fourth week of pregnancy, the legal limit in the state of New York for termination of a pregnancy, should a woman discover she is bearing a disabled fetus and wants to abort. During this stressful waiting period, women and their families are often quite willing to speak with friendly outsiders about their experiences with amniocentesis.

In visiting at home with a selected sample of forty-five Afro-American, Hispanic, and white families (stratified by occupation and payment method to get a class-diverse picture), I have queried how women feel about the test, the health care professionals, and the information they are given. My data includes peoples' responses to knowing, or not knowing, fetal sex.[3] I also probe for images of pregnancy, disability, and dependency. Most people, for example, can articulate a description of Down's Syndrome. But fewer know about spina bifida (neural tube defects) for which the test is also done, and almost none know about other chromosome problems.

Pregnant women in ethnically specific populations confront not only the diseases, but also the health politics of the conditions for which they may be at risk in deciding to use amniocentesis. Tay-Sacks disease, for example, is most prevalent among Jews of Ashkenazi descent, and sickle-cell anemia is most prevalent among people of African descent. Both are transmitted recessively. But the health consequences of the diseases vary enormously. The first is inevitably fatal for children; the second produces a condition that can vary from extremely mild to painful and life-threatening. And the history of screening programs and community education is very different for the two diseases. Responses to being offered a prenatal screen and a subsequent abortion of an affected fetus are quite different. Although Jews of Ashkenazi descent are likely to go for screening, and to abort all affected fetuses, there is much less compliance with the test in black communities, and abortion rates following sickling detection are probably about 40 percent.

Above all, home interviews reveal how women think about pregnancy with the advent of this technology. My data centers on the connections, responsibilities, and maternal identities pregnant women express in the context of their social, rather than their medical, biographies. Attitudes about abortion and sick children are central to this section of my work.

Does amniocentesis offer women a "window of control," or an anxiety-provoking responsibility, or both? Is there a transition for those who use prenatal diagnosis between an image of mothers as all-nurturant, self-sacrificing madonnas, and mothers as agents of quality control on the reproductive production line? Neither is a simple image, for both are constructed by interests with which women may come into conflict. But the second reveals the limits of selflessness that mothers are alleged to have. It is perhaps part of a larger transformation of the meaning of motherhood in an age of high female labor-force participation rates; later marriages; high divorce rates; smaller families and later child-bearing (at least for some Americans); and an increased use of legal abortion. In this context, a decision to bear or not to bear a child with serious health problems in a society that provides meager services for disabled children and their families takes on new meanings.

5. *Positive Diagnosis:* Although 98 percent of the women who undergo amniocentesis will receive the good news that their fetuses are free of the conditions for which they have been tested, 2 percent will face the distressing news of fetal disability. Medical discourse here systematically inverts maternal experience: "positive" diagnoses have enormously negative impacts on the lives of women who receive them. Yet we know very little about the benefits and burdens of the information this reproductive technology reveals

from the perspective of the women who use it (Blumberg et al. 1975; Jones et al. 1984; Furlong and Black 1984). Twenty-nine retrospective interviews focus on the moral and cultural reasoning of women—and their support networks—who had to make a decision to continue or end a pregnancy science had revealed to be affected.

Although most women receiving positive diagnoses go on to abort, the solutions people choose are in part dependent on the specific diagnosis and their cultural background. Down's Syndrome, for example, carries an abortion rate of close to 100 percent, but the sex-chromosome anomalies are aborted at rates that are probably between 50 and 75 percent. And sickle-cell anemia is cause for abortion in about 40 percent of the women who receive it as a fetal diagnosis.[4] Interviews with women and their families who had to make a difficult decision to continue or end a pregnancy that technology revealed to be affected point to the cultural diversity of both problems and solutions. Similar decisions may illuminate very different cultural premises. For example, two couples who aborted after receiving a prenatal diagnosis of Klinefelter's Syndrome (XXY, a sex chromosome anomaly) gave these differing rationales: one said, "If he was gonna be slow, if he wasn't gonna have a shot at being president, that's not the baby we wanted." The other said, "With all the problems a child has to face, it isn't fair to add this burden." The first couple was middle-class and professional; the second, recent migrants and very poor.

Prior knowledge, medical networks, and support systems also enter into the decision to end or continue an affected pregnancy. And religious background is clearly significant here. Virtually all the Jews in my sample described technology in general and amniocentesis in particular as humane additions to their lives, despite the pain of ending a desired pregnancy. Other groups were more ambivalent. And attitudes toward abortion are connected to religious practices in complex, mediated ways. Many Hispanic women, for example, report multiple early abortions but consider *late* abortion to be a sin. Here, a finely honed set of female-centered distinctions is being developed as popular theology. The local meanings of pregnancy, maternity, parental love, and adult gender identity shape the decisions surrounding abortion or the birth of a disabled child.

Despite their diversity, retrospective interviews also reveal the common depths of isolation inherent in pursuing the consequences of this new reproductive technology. No one interviewed had ever met another woman who sustained this same experience of "positive" diagnosis. This is not true for other reproductive losses like abortion, miscarriage, stillbirth, all of which have social as well as medical aspects that can be located. Technology here creates a traumatic experience that is so deeply medicalized and privatized that its social shape has yet to be excavated, and a cultural language for its description is yet to be found.

6. *Paradoxes of Disability:* Some of the same conditions that can now be screened prenatally can also be better managed postnatally due to both medical and social advances. Paradoxically, children with Down's Syndrome and spina bifida have much better survival rates, and can lead much richer lives, than was possible twenty years ago. Down's Syndrome, for example, no longer leads to institutionalization. Most DS children now receive infant stimulation and are able to function as only mildly to moderately retarded. Many go to school, learning to read and write. Once, children with spina bifida didn't survive unless their condition was extremely mild ("passing" as normal), but now infant surgery and physical therapy have helped to create a generation of young adults who have grown up with this condition. We have yet to hear their voices very directly, but surely some are represented in the disability rights movement (Saxton 1984, Asch 1986; Asch and Fine 1984).

In order to understand the social, rather than medical, implications of giving birth to a child with a genetic disability, I have spent almost three years as a participant-observer in a support group for parents of children with Down's Syndrome. From scores of parent-activists I have learned about the "courtesy stigmas" involved in having a disabled child (Goffman 1963; Darling 1979; Featherstone 1980). Support-group members are disproportionately white and upper-middle class. Consequently, I have also interviewed fifteen Afro-American and Hispanic parents of genetically disabled children, located through an infant-stimulation program.

Families whose children have the same conditions that amniocentesis now diagnoses prenatally speak discourses counter to medical authority. Here, religion, ethnicity, class, and family history powerfully shape responses to having a child with a genetically stigmatized condition. Reflections on the meaning of maternity and paternity and the value of children are embedded in the stories parents of the disabled tell as they transform medical diagnoses into the social fabric of daily life. Strategies for coping and making cultural meaning through a life crisis and family transformation vary enormously. The benefits of a self-help learning network may work best for those who are most comfortable with medical labels as part of their self-definitions. These tend to be white, middle-class families. Many parents in the Down's Syndrome support group refer collectively to "our kids," for example. But a black mother of a child with the same condition said, "My kid's got a heart problem, my kid's gonna be slow. First let me deal with that, love him for that, then I'll check out this Down's Syndrome thing."

7. *Refusers:* About 50 percent of clinic patients and about 10 percent of private patients break their appointments for genetic counseling. Of the 1,000 women counseled by the PDL genetic counselors each year, about 750 go on to amniocentesis and 250 do not. Of those small numbers receiving a positive diagnosis, an even smaller number decides not to abort. It is impor-

tant to locate and listen to those who refuse to use a technology in the process of routinization, removing themselves, at any point along the line, from the conveyor belt of its assumptions and options. The reasons for refusing amniocentesis are many: religious beliefs, nonscientific constructions of pregnancy and motherhood, distrust of the medical system, fear of miscarriage. The commentary of refusers provides clues to the cultural contradictions involved in the technological transformation of pregnancy. Low-income Afro-American women, for example, often expressed a "homegrown" sense of statistics that varied radically from the sensibilities of middle-class couples. When a woman has birthed four other children, comes from a family of eight, and all her sisters and neighbors have had similar histories, she has seen scores of babies born without recognizable birth defects. It requires a leap of faith in abstract reasoning to contrast these experiences with a number produced by a lady in a white coat proclaiming that the risk of a baby with a birth defect is steadily rising with each pregnancy. Among middle-class professional families, however, child-bearing is likely to be delayed, and the counselor is discussing a first, or at most a second, pregnancy. Children are likely to be scarce throughout the social network of the professional couple. To them, "1 in 300" sounds like a large and present risk, whereas for the low-income mother of four, the same number may appear very distant and small. Moreover, chromosome defects seem a weak explanation for the problems that children may suffer. One Haitian father, firmly rejecting prenatal testing on his wife's behalf, said, "The counselor says the baby could be born retarded. They always say Haitian children are retarded. What is this retarded? Many Haitian children are said to be retarded in the public schools. If we send them to the Haitian Academy (a community-based private school) they learn just fine." In his experience, chromosomes don't loom large as an explanatory force when compared to ongoing prejudices and labels already present in the lives of the children of his community.

Science speaks a language of universal authority. Diverse women express their gender consciousness and the core meanings of reproduction in polyglot, multicultural voices. The analysis and interpretation of this tension illuminates one aspect of late-twentieth-century American culture, where science and technology make powerful claims on the transformation of pregnancy and personhood. At stake is the cultural negotiation of gender and parental practices in a world shaped by both social diversity and scientific hegemony. Until we locate and listen to the discourses of those women who encounter and interpret a new reproductive technology in their own lives, we cannot evaluate it beyond the medical model. Whether amniocentesis represents social control, or subversion of female subordination, or both, is a question to which only local and unstable responses may be given. It cannot be settled by recourse to a universal explanation, as if all women held similar interests in the problems of pregnancy, or of disabled children.

The perspectives of feminist scholarship, on the one hand, and the women's health movement, on the other, suggest that the lived experiences of reproduction reflect far more than medical progress and problems. When examined from these more cultural and political perspectives, we begin to see the shifting meaning of motherhood implied in our national struggles for reproductive rights, and in the cultural diversity of women's ability to control the conditions under which they do and don't mother children. We badly need an analysis from the perspective of women and their families in which reproductive rights will not be pitted against disability rights. Beyond the Reagan neonatal hotlines, and beyond the attempt to illegalize second-trimester abortion in part by using disabled fetuses as icons of maternal responsibility gone awry, lies a terrain we need to explore. In it, I hope to describe a political and cultural logic by which we can and must defend both access to high-quality medical care for pregnant women, including access to abortion when and if they choose it, while at the same time destigmatizing disability and defending the special needs and services for people who cannot "get ahead" in a society where autonomy and independence are so central to the ideological definitions of personhood.

ACKNOWLEDGMENT

The fieldwork on which this essay is based was funded by the National Science Foundation and the National Endowment for the Humanities. I am grateful to both. I also want to thank the many women and their families who took this inquiry to heart, sharing their amniocentesis stories with me. The health professionals who aided my work have all believed in the importance of understanding their patients' experiences. I'm grateful for their trust. Many audiences of feminists—scholars and activists—have sharpened my work through the questions they have posed. Without them, the context for this inquiry would be immeasurably impoverished.

A version of this article appeared in *Women and Health*. Permission to reprint is gratefully acknowledged.

NOTES

1. Chorionic villus sampling is a first-trimester prenatal diagnostic test. A sample of preplacental tissue containing fetal cells is removed through a transcervical procedure. It can be read directly, without lengthy laboratory culturing. Results are thus available by the tenth week of pregnancy. More widely used abroad, the test is still considered experimental in the United States, in part because it causes a higher rate of miscarriage than amniocentesis does. It is increasingly available under "study conditions" in major medical centers. Maternal/fetal blood centrifuges are not yet

clinically available but may become a potentially powerful diagnostic technique in the future. A useful blood centrifuge would have to discriminate between the maternal blood supply and the small number of fetal blood cells within it. In principle such a test could be done at the time of a first, positive pregnancy test, giving the woman information about her fetus's chromosomal status at the moment she discovered she was pregnant.

2. The incidence of Down's Syndrome appears to be invariant, worldwide (Hook 1981). In a country that suffers the worst health statistics in the Western hemisphere, where the infant mortality rate is close to 50 percent, and healthy as well as fragile babies may rapidly fall ill and die of unexplained causes, it is not surprising that the characteristic physical signs of Down's (tongue, eyes, hair, palm creases, muscle looseness, etc.) are not recognized as a "syndrome."

3. See Hanmer (1981) and Corea (1985) for important discussions of sex selection via prenatal diagnosis. Rothman (1985) has a thoughtful chapter on the implications of knowing fetal sex for parental attitudes.

4. These figures are compiled from the PDL "positive diagnosis" follow-up file.

BIBLIOGRAPHY

Asch, A. 1986. Real moral dilemmas. *Christianity and Crisis* 46: 237–240.

Asch, A., and M. Fine. 1984. Shared dreams: A left perspective on disability rights and reproductive rights. *Radical America* 18: 81–88.

Blumberg, B. D., et al. 1975. Psychological sequelae of abortion performed for a genetic indication. *American Journal of Obstetrics and Gynecology* 122: 799–808.

Corea, G. 1985. *The mother machine.* New York: Harper and Row.

Darling, R. 1979. *Families against society.* Beverly Hills, Calif.: Sage.

Featherstone, H. 1980. *A difference in the family.* New York: Basic Books.

Furlong, R., and R. B. Black. 1984. Pregnancy termination for genetic indications: The impact on families. *Social Work in Health Care* 10: 17–35.

Goffman, E. 1963. *Stigma: Notes on the management of spoiled identity.* Englewood Cliffs, N.J.: Prentice-Hall.

Goodfield, J. 1981. *An imagined world.* New York: Penguin.

Hanmer, J. 1981. Sex predetermination, artificial insemination, and the maintenance of male-dominated culture. In *Women, health and reproduction.* H. Roberts, ed. London: Routledge & Kegan Paul.

Hook, E. B. 1981. Rates of chromosome abnormalities at different maternal ages. *Obstetrics and Gynecology* 58: 282–285.

Hubbard, R. 1982. The theory and practice of genetic reductionism: From Mendel's law to genetic engineering. In *Towards a liberatory biology.* S. Rose, ed. London: Allison and Busby.

Jones, O. W., et al. 1984. Parental response to mid-trimester therapeutic abortion following amniocentesis. *Prenatal Diagnosis* 4: 249–256.

Kevles, D. 1985. *In the name of eugenics.* New York: Knopf.

Knorr-Cetina, K., and M. Mulkay, eds. 1982. *Science observed.* Beverly Hills, Calif.: Sage.

Latour, B., and S. Woolgar. 1979. *Laboratory life.* Beverly Hills, Calif.: Sage.

Minden, S. 1984. Designer genes: A view from the factory. In *Test-tube women*. R. Arditti, R. Duelli-Klein, and S. Minden, eds. Boston: Routledge & Kegan Paul.

Reed, S. 1974. A short history of genetic counseling. *Social Biology* 21: 332–339.

Rollnick, B. 1984. The national society of genetic counselors: An historical perspective. *Birth Defects* 20: 3–7.

Rothman, B. K. 1986. *The tentative pregnancy*. New York: Norton.

Saxton, M. 1984. Born and unborn: The implications of reproductive technologies for people with disabilities. In *Test-tube women*. R. Arditti, R. Duelli-Klein, and S. Minden, eds. Boston: Routledge & Kegan Paul.

NOTES ON CONTRIBUTORS

Susan Bourque is Professor of Government at Smith College. Her books include *Women of the Andes* (co-written with Kay Warren, University of Michigan Press). She recently co-edited *Learning about Women* (University of Michican Press) and *Women Living Change* (Temple University Press).

Margaret Conkey is Associate Professor of Anthropology at the University of California at Berkeley. She has recently co-edited (with Joan Gero) *Engendering Archeology: Women and Prehistory* (Basil Blackwell). She is beginning a research project on material culture and social life in the prehistory of the French Pyrenees.

Micaela di Leonardo is Associate Professor of Anthropology and Women's Studies and Fellow of the Urban Affairs Center at Northwestern University. She has written *The Varieties of Ethnic Experience: Kinship, Class and Gender among California Italian-Americans* (Cornell University Press). She is finishing a book on anthropology and American culture and is doing ethnographic research (with Adolph Reed) among working-class blacks and whites in New Haven, Connecticut.

Susan Gal is Associate Professor of Anthropology at Rutgers University. She has written *Language Shift: Social Determinants of Linguistic Change in Bilingual Austria*, and is working on a book on language, politics, and nationalism in Hungary.

Jane Guyer is Associate Professor of Anthropology at Boston University. She has edited *Feeding African Cities* (Indiana), and written numerous articles on gender and African economies.

Nadine Peacock is an assistant Professor of Anthropology at the University of California at Los Angeles. As a reproductive ecologist, she has published a number of articles on biology and gender in foraging societies and comparative mammalian reproductive responses to ecological stress.

Elizabeth Povinelli is a postdoctoral fellow in Anthropology at Emory University. Her dissertation examines local Australian aboriginal understandings of the relations among human bodies, language, and the land, and how these conflict with western models of the productive activities of "hunter-gatherers." She also works with aboriginal political organizations on land rights in northern Australia.

Rayna Rapp is Professor and Chair of Anthropology at the New School for Social Research. She edited the original *Toward an Anthropology of Women* (Monthly Review Press), and has co-edited *Promissory Notes* (Monthly Review Press). Her contribution in this volume is part of a larger study of amniocentesis in New York City.

Harold Scheffler is Professor of Anthropology at Yale University. He has written extensively on kinship and related topics and has done ethnographic research among North American Indians and in the Solomon Islands and Australia.

Irene Silverblatt teaches anthropology at the University of Connecticut. She has written *Moon, Sun, and Witches: Gender Ideologies and Class in Inca and Colonial Peru* (Princeton University Press), and is currently investigating constructions of the "Indian Problem" and the "Woman Problem" by Peruvian and American anthropologists, 1945–60.

Susan Sperling teaches anthropology at Chabot College in Hayward, California. She has written *Animal Liberators: Research and Morality* (University of California Press), and is currently doing medical anthropological research with Central American refugees in northern California.

Ann Stoler is Associate Professor of Anthropology, History and Women's Studies at the University of Michigan. She has written *Capitalism and Confrontation in Summatra's Plantation Belt, 1870–1979* (Yale University Press). Her piece in this volume is part of a larger project.

Kay Warren is Professor of Anthropology at Princeton University. She has written *Symbolism of Subordination: Indian Identity in a Guatemalan Town* (University of Texas Press) and co-written (with Susan Bourque) *Women of the*

Andes (University of Michigan Press). She recently edited *Confronting Violence: Anthropological and Political Analyses of National Conflicts* (forthcoming).

Sarah Williams is a student in the History of Consciousness Program at the University of California at Santa Cruz. She is completing her dissertation, "Professing Culture: Anthropology among Anthropologists," a feminist critique of anthropology based on fieldwork in Australia and Kenya. She will be teaching feminist theory at Evergreen College.

Patricia Zavella, an anthropologist, is Associate Professor of Community Studies at the University of California at Santa Cruz. She has written *Women's Work and Chicano Families: Cannery Workers of the Santa Clara Valley* (Cornell University Press), and co-authored *Working Mothers and "Sunbelt Industrialization": New Patterns of Work and Family* (forthcoming).

INDEX

Designer: U.C. Press Staff
Compositor: Asco Trade Typesetting Ltd.
Text: 10/12 Baskerville
Display: Baskerville
Printer: Edwards Bros., Inc.
Binder: Edwards Bros., Inc.